Studies in Southeastern Indian Languages

Studies in Southeastern Indian Languages

edited by James M. Crawford

The University of Georgia Press
Athens

Library of Congress Catalog Card Number: 73-90840
International Standard Book Number: 0-8203-0334-8
The University of Georgia Press, Athens 30602

Printed in the United States of America

Contents

Preface

The publication of a collection of papers on some of the Indian languages of the southeastern United States was suggested in 1970 following the annual meeting of the Southern Anthropological Society in Athens, Georgia. At this meeting a symposium was held on the Indian languages of the Southeast, probably the first symposium ever held which was devoted exclusively to the languages of the region. The University of Georgia Press expressed interest in publishing the proposed volume and asked me to be its editor and to proceed to obtain manuscripts from participants. By the time manuscripts were received from the participants who were willing to submit their papers, plans were well under way for another symposium on southeastern Indian languages to be held in conjunction with the 1971 meeting of the Southern Anthropological Society in Dallas, Texas. It was decided to solicit manuscripts of papers from participants of the Dallas symposium for inclusion in the proposed volume. Participation in the second symposium was double that of the year before, with twelve papers being presented in two sessions.

During the solicitation of papers for the Dallas symposium it became expedient to define "southeastern Indian language" as a category to be used in the selection of papers for presentation at a symposium on languages of the Southeast. As organizer of the symposium, I made the decision to accept papers for presentation if the language reported upon belonged to a family which had a representative in the geographical southeastern United States.

I justified the decision on the grounds that scholars doing work in a particular language would be interested in all its sister languages, no matter where they were spoken. The Southeast was defined geographically as the region south of the Potomac and Ohio rivers and westward across the Mississippi River to include Arkansas, Louisiana, and a strip of eastern Texas. It was thus possible to permit the inclusion of two papers on Wichita and Mandan, languages which belong to families represented in the Southeast, but which are spoken outside the Southeast as geographically defined.

Not all participants in the Dallas symposium provided manuscripts of the papers they read. Additional contributions were invited later from several people who did not attend either symposium but who had worked on southeastern languages. The papers by Willard Walker and by Frank T. Siebert, Jr., were received as a result of this invitation.

I wish to express my gratitude to Charles Hudson, who has not hesitated, when I called upon him, to offer advice and encouragement. I am especially indebted to him for the suggestion that a map be included to show the locations of the southeastern Indian languages. I am grateful to Charles Hudson and to Frank T. Siebert, Jr., for much needed criticism of an earlier draft of the introductory essay on the southeastern Indian languages. I appreciate the interest taken in the volume by Kenneth Cherry of the University of Georgia Press and the patience he has shown in seeing the manuscripts through the numerous stages to their final form. I also wish to express my gratitude to Mrs. Louise Brice who typed the manuscripts.

James M. Crawford
Athens, Georgia
May 1974

Studies in Southeastern Indian Languages

LOCATION OF INDIAN LANGUAGES
IN THE
SOUTHEASTERN UNITED STATES
ABOUT THE YEAR 1700

Southeastern Indian Languages

James M. Crawford

The Indian tribes which once inhabited the Southeast were sufficiently similar in culture that it is possible to speak of a southeastern cultural province, a geographical region more or less coterminous with the traditional and modern conception of the southeastern United States. This region extends southward from the Potomac and Ohio rivers to the Atlantic Ocean and Gulf of Mexico and westward beyond the Mississippi River for some two hundred miles or more. The central area of the southeastern cultural province was in Georgia, Alabama, and Mississippi. Cultural differences were greater among the tribes along the outer limits of the region, e. g. , the tidewater tribes of Virginia and North Carolina, the tribes of southern Florida, the Quapaw in Arkansas, and the Shawnee in Kentucky and Tennessee. Although these latter tribes were marginally southeastern in culture, they nevertheless shared numerous cultural features with the tribes of the central area.

Differences in culture in the Southeast were minimal in comparison with the differences in the languages spoken by the tribes of the region. John Lawson, who traveled in the Carolinas shortly after 1700, reported that Indian towns only a dozen miles apart spoke entirely different languages (Lawson 1709:225).[1] Robert Beverley (1705) wrote that tribes in Virginia only a moderate distance apart did not understand each other without recourse to a lingua franca (p. 24, Book 3). We can never know just how different the Indian languages were in colonial times, for hardly anyone who had dealings with the Indians bothered to write down words in their languages. The names of a large number of tribes have come down to us, but we can only speculate as to the languages spoken by many of these tribes. If the diversity of languages as reported by Lawson and Beverley was typical of the region, then it would appear that many dozens of individual languages have become extinct without leaving a trace as to their linguistic affinity. Indeed, it may be that some families of languages, of which we know nothing, have entirely disappeared.

To the colonists, from New England to Georgia, the Indians were considered a nuisance and a hindrance to a westward expansion of settlements. The settlers of the southeastern colonies lacked the missionary zeal of the New England colonists or of the Franciscans of Florida. Among the settlers of Virginia, Georgia, and the Carolinas there was no John Eliot or Francisco Pareja who learned the languages of the Indians and wrote catechisms and translated the Bible in their languages.[2] An interest in the native languages eventually did develop, but not before many tribes and languages had long since become extinct. There were a few individuals among the early colonists, e. g. , John White, Captain John Smith, and William Strachey, who were sufficiently curious about the native languages to write down words in them, although their collections of Indian words were incidental to their general descriptions of the newly settled lands and of the Indians dwelling upon them. During the eighteenth century occasional travelers and colonial or governmental agents, such as John Lawson, William Gerard de Brahm, and Benjamin Hawkins, recorded Indian vocabularies. A few of the traders, as James Adair did when living among the Chickasaw, learned to speak an Indian language. Hawkins, who was United States agent among the Creeks during the last few years of the eighteenth century, wrote, or had written for him, letters in the Creek language, which he addressed to certain members of the Creek tribe (Hawkins 1916:82, 84-85).

Toward the end of the eighteenth century there was interest among scholars in collecting vocabularies of exotic languages of the world, including the Indian languages, and in classifying the languages into stocks or families.

The classifications were made on the basis of superficial resemblances and surmises. Many of the surmises have turned out to be correct, although some, like Duponceau's "Floridian" stock containing most of the southeastern languages, were wrong.

Albert Gallatin's 1836 classification, revised and expanded in 1848, was the most accurate and the first comprehensive classification of North American languages. Gallatin obtained his vocabularies from many sources, both published and manuscript materials. Vocabularies were collected from visiting Indian chiefs in Washington, by military officers throughout the country, among whom the Secretary of War had distributed prepared schedules, and by Gallatin himself. Much material was obtained by Gallatin with the aid of missionaries, who by the early 1800's had begun to establish missions among the tribes of the interior. Gallatin's classification, as noted by Haas (1969a), "was a landmark in the history of the genealogical classification of North American languages and was not superseded until the work of Powell and his coworkers completed what Gallatin had begun" (p. 244).

During the middle decades of the nineteenth century numerous vocabularies were secured, largely from western tribes by engineering and other government exploring parties. Also during this period much material in the form of Bible translations, grammatical treatises, and dictionaries was produced by the missionaries who had followed or joined the Indians west of the Mississippi River after the removal. In 1879 Major J. W. Powell became head of the newly established Bureau of Ethnology. Powell had previously become interested in ethnology while conducting explorations for the Geological Survey of the Rocky Mountain region. With the help of several men of unusual linguistic ability Powell brought forth in 1891 his classification of Indian languages, which grouped all the languages north of Mexico into 58 families. According to Goddard (1914), Powell's classification "marks the end of the first period of scientific linguistic work in America" (p. 559). Two of Powell's assistants, James Owen Dorsey and Albert S. Gatschet, "inaugurated the second period of linguistic work stimulated by scientific interest rather than missionary zeal" (Goddard 1914:560).[3]

Dorsey and Gatschet, along with Boas, Mooney, Swanton, and numerous others, both inside and outside the Bureau, worked in several fields of ethnology and collected information from Indian tribes throughout the country.

According to Hoijer (1973), Franz Boas dominated this period of linguistic research "and in effect dominated both American anthropology and linguistics from about 1899 until his death in 1942" (p. 664). Boas worked with many Indian tribes in North America and on many Indian languages, as did his students. During the first four decades of this century a considerable number of texts, dictionaries, and grammars of Indian languages was published by Boas and by his students. Boas never worked in the Southeast, but sent, in the 1920's and 1930's, several young linguists to work on neglected southeastern languages, e. g. , Günter Wagner to the Yuchi, Morris Swadesh to the Chitimacha, and Mary R. Haas to the Tunica and Natchez (Haas 1971:47).

Partly because of the number and diversity of the languages found in California, attempts were made in the early 1900's, notably by Alfred L. Kroeber and Edward Sapir (former students of Boas), to reduce Powell's 58 linguistic families to a smaller number of stocks. Twenty-two of Powell's 58 families were represented in California alone. Sapir joined Kroeber and his California colleagues in classifying and grouping the California languages. In 1921 Sapir presented his idea for a grouping of all languages of North America into six great stocks and in 1925 made a slight rearrangement of one of the stocks (Hokan-Siouan). In 1929 Sapir presented again his notions of the classification of North American languages, with slight modification of previous classifications and with some discussion and explanation, but with no linguistic evidence.

During the past two decades there has been an examination of Sapir's classification, which was actually only a "proposed classification" (Sapir 1958:172), by several scholars, in particular by Mary R. Haas, who was a student of Sapir. This examination of relationships among American Indian languages is still in process by Haas, and by others, and suggests relationships considerably different, in some respects, from those proposed by Sapir.

We know that five families of languages were represented at one time in the Southeast: Algonquian, Caddoan, Iroquoian, Muskogean, and Siouan. One of these, Muskogean, had no representatives outside the Southeast. In addition, there were six languages which do not seem to have a close relationship to any other language, called "language isolates" by Haas (1969b:60-61). The language isolates are: Atakapa, Chitimacha, Natchez, Timucua, Tunica, and Yuchi. There is evidence that Atakapa, Chitimacha,

Natchez, and Tunica are distantly related to each other and to the Muskogean family. The four isolates and Muskogean have been called Gulf by Haas. The closest relative to Timucua may be in the Antilles or in South America. Yuchi may be distantly related to the Siouan languages. Algonquian may be related to Gulf, as well as to Tonkawa. Siouan, Iroquoian, and Caddoan show some evidence of a distant relationship to each other. It may be that practically all the languages east of the Rocky Mountains can eventually be shown to have derived from a common ancestral language.

In the following pages a history of the work on the languages of the southeastern region of the United States is described in some detail. The families are presented first, followed by the language isolates. For each of the five families a sketch of work done to demonstrate intrafamilial relationships is presented. Under each language heading a brief sketch of the history of the tribe speaking the language is given, followed by a more or less chronological history of the descriptive work done on the language, including a brief notice given to the "Taensa language" hoax of the 1880's. There is finally a description of efforts to demonstrate relationships beyond the family level, i. e., between families, between families and isolates, and between isolates.

The southeastern Indian languages are as follows:

ALGONQUIAN

- Pamlico
- Powhatan
- Shawnee

CADDOAN

- Caddo

IROQUOIAN

- Cherokee
- Nottoway
- Tuscarora

MUSKOGEAN

- Alabama
- Apalachee
- Chickasaw
- Choctaw

Creek
Hitchiti
Koasati
Mikasuki
Mobilian
Seminole

SIOUAN

Biloxi
Catawba
Ofo
Quapaw
Tutelo
Woccon

LANGUAGE ISOLATES

Atakapa
Chitimacha
Natchez
Timucua
Tunica
Yuchi

Languages are discussed in the order presented above. Notice of the Taensa hoax is given after Yuchi. Mobilian is a lingua franca based on one or more of the Choctaw-Chickasaw dialects and is discussed under Muskogean. A brief note on Wichita is given at the end of the section on Caddo.

ALGONQUIAN

The Algonquian languages had the most widespread distribution of any language family in North America. Algonquian languages were spoken from Labrador to North Carolina and in the northern United States and Canada westward into the plains. In Canada they extended as far as the Rocky Mountains. Impressions of the Indians by the early colonists were obtained almost wholly from the Algonquian tribes. There were about three dozen Algonquian languages, nearly half of which were spoken along the Atlantic seaboard. Early missionaries, particularly in New England and eastern Canada, produced dictionaries, grammars, and translations of the Bible in the Indian languages. Consequently, we have considerable information about many languages which became extinct before any except the missionaries gave thought to the study of Indian languages. Missionary activity further to the south was less than in the north, or nonexistent. Our knowledge of the Algonquian languages of Virginia and North Carolina, where missionary activity was absent, is restricted to a few poorly recorded vocabularies.

Except for the western languages (Blackfoot, Cheyenne, and the Arapaho dialects), the Algonquian languages are relatively close. It was early apparent to scholars that the Algonquian languages of eastern North America belonged to the same linguistic family. Michelson (1912) classified the Algonquian languages into four divisions: Blackfoot, Cheyenne, Arapaho, and Eastern-Central (pp. 229, 289-90). Michelson (1912) emphasized the intimate connection between the Eastern and the Central branches, as compared with Blackfoot, Cheyenne, and Arapaho (p. 237), but noted there are resemblances to Eastern Algonquian in Sauk, Fox, Kickapoo, and Shawnee (pp. 289-90), with Shawnee standing "nearest to Fox, and next to Eastern Algonquian; in fact it stands nearly halfway between the two" (p. 257).

Trumbull (1870a) published an article in which he attempted to analyze Powhatan words recorded by Captain John Smith and "a few others" and concluded that "the Powhatan and the Massachusetts did not differ more from each other than either from the Delaware" (p. 47).[4] In the early 1900's a minor controversy developed between W. R. Gerard (1904, 1905) and W. W. Tooker (1904, 1905) concerning the etymologies of Virginia Indian words. Also, Gerard tried to show that Powhatan was a Cree dialect; Tooker disagreed. Michelson had ignored Powhatan in his 1912 classification of Algonquian. Many years later Michelson (1933) considered the status of Powhatan in a one-page article, in which he took to task Gerard (1904), who claimed Powhatan was merely a dialect of Cree. Michelson (1933) wrote that the main result of the Gerard and Tooker controversy "was to show the incompetence of both", but that Gerard was on the right track, and summed up by saying that Powhatan clearly belongs with the Cree group, being closer to Cree than to any other member of the Cree group, but that "it cannot be classified as a mere Cree dialect" (p. 549).

Michelson (1935) made use of Blackfoot, Arapaho, and Cheyenne in Algonquian reconstructions. Leonard Bloomfield worked extensively on Algonquian and did field work on several Algonquian languages. Using Fox, Cree, Menomini, and Ojibwa of the Central group, Bloomfield (1946) made reconstructions which he believed will "fit all the languages and can accordingly be viewed as Proto-Algonquian" (p. 85).[5] Siebert (1941) dealt with three Proto-Algonquian consonant clusters, establishing the validity of a new cluster and, like Michelson, placed Cree and Powhatan in the same group (pp. 298, 302). Siebert now believes, however, that similar changes in Powhatan and Cree are due to "an independent parallel innovation perhaps contingent upon a similar phonetic drift" and places Powhatan in the Eastern Algonquian group.[6]

Bloomfield (1925:130) placed Shawnee in the Sauk group of Central Algonquian languages, along with Sauk, Fox, and Kickapoo. Later, Bloomfield (1946:85) separated Shawnee from the other three, placing it in a group by itself. Miller (1959) has shown the development of Shawnee from Proto-Central Algonquian and has placed "Shawnee in the Central Algonquian language group" (p. 16). According to Miller (1959), "Shawnee has more in common with the Sauk group than with any of the other groups treated by Bloomfield, and must be considered a member of that group" (p. 21).[7]

The Algonquian languages have received more attention than any other language family in North America. Both descriptive and comparative work is being conducted at present in the United States and Canada. In 1964 the Ethnology Division of the National Museum of Canada, Ottawa, sponsored a conference on Algonquian linguistics. This apparently was the first time a conference was devoted entirely to a single family of American Indian languages. Some dozen Algonquianists attended and presented papers, which were later published (Conference 1967)[8].

In a recent article Teeter (1973) has described the status of Algonquian research in North America.

Pamlico

The Pamlico were living on the lower Pamlico River and southward to the Neuse River in North Carolina when first encountered by the English in 1584-85.[9] They were nearly destroyed by smallpox in 1696. About seventy-five Pamlico survived and were living in a single village in 1710. The Pamlico fought the English on the side of the Tuscarora in 1711-13. At the end of the Tuscarora War, those Tuscarora who had sided with the English agreed to exterminate the Pamlico. The Pamlico who survived were probably incorporated as slaves with the Tuscarora.

Harriot (1972) published in 1590 a few animal, plant, and personal names, collected between 1585 and 1587 probably by John White. White's drawings, on which appear Indian names, were published in facsimile by Hulton and Quinn (1964). The language is Algonquian and may be Pamlico. The words recorded by White were the first taken down in any Algonquian language. Lawson (1709:225-227) recorded the only known vocabulary of Pamlico, which was reprinted by Pollard (1894:14).[10]

Powhatan

The Powhatan tribes lived in tidewater Virginia from the Potomac River south to the vicinity of the James River. Their lands extended west beyond the present-day cities of Fredericksburg, Richmond, and Petersburg. Powhatan tribes also occupied that part of Virginia east of Chesapeake Bay and perhaps a portion of southern Maryland. Verazzano in 1524 and Gomez in 1525, both of whom landed in the region of Chesapeake Bay, were the first Europeans to make contact with the Powhatan. Gomez took possession of the land for the king of Spain. Throughout part of the sixteenth century Spanish slave hunters raided the Virginia coast. In 1570 the Jesuit, Father Segura, established a mission which was destroyed by the natives after a brief existence. The Indians massacred the entire company of the mission except a boy, an action that was revenged by the Spanish not long afterward.

When the Jamestown colonists landed in 1607, the Indians already knew and hated the whites, although they were friendly to the colonists during the early period of settlement. Petty warfare soon broke out between the Indians and the colonists, with peace being brought about by the marriage of John Rolfe to Pocahontas, daughter of the chief, Powhatan. Powhatan died in 1618 and was succeeded by Opechancanough, who began preparations for a general uprising against the whites. In 1622 a simultaneous attack was made on the whole frontier. Every settlement except those around Jamestown was destroyed. When they recovered from this attack, the colonists began a war of extermination of the Indians. The war lasted for 14 years, until 1636, when peace was made, with both sides exhausted. New encroachments by the whites started the war again in 1641. Opechancanough led an attack himself and was captured and shot. With his death the confederation of tribes was broken up and the individual tribes, having made separate treaties with the whites, were placed on reservations. The reservations were constantly reduced in size by the whites either by confiscation or by sale.

In 1656 100 Indians of the Pamunkey tribe and their chief joined the whites in resisting an invasion of Cherokee who came down from the mountains. Almost all the Pamunkey were killed in a battle near Richmond. In 1675 some Conestoga came down from their country on the Susquehanna River and committed depredations on the whites. The Virginia Indians were accused of the act and several expeditions were led against them. The Indians suffered heavily from the attacks by the whites and gathered in a fort near Richmond for a final defense. The whites stormed the fort in 1678 and massacred men, women, and children. The scattered survivors asked for peace, which was granted on the condition of an annual tribute from each village.

From 1722 on, after the Iroquois, ancient enemies of the Powhatan, agreed to cease their attacks upon them, the history of the Powhatan tribes practically ceased. In 1831 the remnant on the eastern shore, as a result of intermarriage, were hardly distinguishable from the Negroes and were driven off by the whites during the excitement caused by the slave uprising under Nat Turner. When the Powhatan were first known, they had nearly 200 villages, over 160 of which are named by Captain John Smith (Smith 1969b: [facing] 364). Mooney (1910c) reported that they "now number altogether about 700 [persons], including the Nandsemond, Pamunkey, and Mattapony... with several smaller bands" (p. 301), having been reduced from an estimated population, at the time of John Smith, of about eight thousand (p. 302). The Pamunkey and Mattapony still retain tiny reservations east of Richmond, on, respectively, the Pamunkey and Mattaponi rivers, about ten miles apart. The deed for the Mattaponi reservation dates from 1658 (Speck 1928:249); that for the Pamunkey, from 1677 (Speck 1928:238).[11] Speck (1928) reported about one hundred and fifty "souls" on the Pamunkey reservation and about seventy-five "souls" on the Mattaponi reservation (p. 249), and a total of some two thousand as the descendants of all the Powhatan tribes in tidewater Virginia (p. 236).[12]

Our knowledge of the language of the Powhatan tribes comes almost entirely from two sources: a vocabulary collected by Captain John Smith between 1607 and 1609 and first published in 1612 in Smith's "A map of Virginia..." (Smith 1969b:331-34) and a longer vocabulary by William Strachey, first secretary to the colony, collected in 1610 or 1611. Strachey's vocabulary was appended to a manuscript written by Strachey entitled "Historie of Travaile into Virginia Britannia. . . ." There are three known copies of the manuscript, located in the Princeton library, the Bodleian library, and the British Museum. The Princeton copy lacks the vocabulary. The Bodleian copy is earlier than the copy in the British Museum. The British Museum copy of the "Historie", including the vocabulary, was published by the Hakluyt Society in 1849. The Princeton copy also was published by the Hakluyt Society (Wright and Freund 1953), to which was appended (pp. 174-207) vocabularies of both the Bodleian and British Museum copies. The vocabularies in Wright and Freund (1953) were deciphered by James B. Geary, who discussed the problems of decipherment and compared some of Strachey's forms with "Primitive Algonquian" and several of the Algonquian languages (Geary 1953). John P. Harrington (1955) published a facsimile reproduction of the vocabulary contained in the Bodleian manuscript, along with his version of the decipherment of Strachey's writing of Indian and English words.

In 1844 Rev. Mr. Dalrymple collected 17 Pamunkey words, which included the numerals one through eight and the numeral ten (Dalrymple 1858). These words, according to Harrington (1955), agree with either Delaware or "with the Virginia language elsewhere on record" (p. 195). There are other minor sources for words in the Virginia Indian language, two noted by Harrington (1955): the Indian names of 37 birds and fishes accompanying John White's watercolors, recorded about 1587 or 1590 (p. 194) and the Lord's Prayer in the Virginia Indian language published in Livonia in 1789 (p. 195). Swanton (1934) reported on about a dozen newly discovered Powhatan bird names recorded by an English clergyman, Edward Topsell, in Virginia shortly before 1614.

Barbour (1973) wrote an article in which he discussed the problems of interpreting and analyzing the transcriptions of the Virginia Indian languages. Barbour (1973) observed that "it is not yet time to apply analytical linguistics to the scattered remains of Carolina and Virginia Algonquian" (p. 5).[13] Frank T. Siebert, Jr., has worked at deciphering and analyzing Virginia Algonquian, especially as recorded by Strachey. Siebert's knowledge of the other Algonquian languages has enabled him to resolve many ambiguities of Strachey's handwriting and to arrive at the probable phonological shape of most of Strachey's forms. In other words, Siebert has attempted to reconstitute the phonology of Powhatan. The results of Siebert's efforts at reconstitution are reported in a paper in this volume, along with some of the grammatical features of Powhatan. In the lexicon Siebert has presented the historical development of Powhatan words from Proto-Algonquian and forms in other Algonquian languages cognate to the Powhatan words. At the end of the paper Siebert has given a detailed classification of the Eastern Algonquian languages.

Shawnee

Swanton (1922:317) placed the earliest known home of the Shawnee on the Cumberland River in north central Tennessee. There is evidence, according to Swanton (1946), that in very early historic times, the Shawnee "were on the Ohio River, which they had evidently reached from some point farther south" (p. 184). Swanton (1946:184) believed that their location on the Cumberland was due in part to the Spanish post at St. Augustine, Florida, which the Shawnee visited for the purposes of trade. The first mention of the Shawnee may have been in the Jesuit Relation of 1648, in connection with a tribe in Illinois (Mooney 1910d:534). There is another mention of the Shawnee in the Jesuit Relation of 1670. Frequent notices of the Shawnee by French writers in the early eighteenth century agree in placing the Shawnee on the Cumberland River, "which is called the River of the Shawnee on all the old maps down to about the year 1770" (Mooney 1910d:534).[14]

Royce (1880-81) called the Shawnee the "Bedouins" and "Ishmaelites" of the North American Indians: "As wanderers, they were without rivals among their race" (p. 177). There are references to the Shawnee in early documents which place them in widespread locations in the eastern states, from Georgia and South Carolina to Ohio and Pennsylvania. There were numerous bands of Shawnee (Swanton 1946:184) and they all seem to have been constantly on the move.[15] The Shawnee appeared first on the Savannah River in 1674, where by 1708 they had established three towns (Swanton 1922:317). Some of the Shawnee on the Savannah River may have moved to Pennsylvania soon after their arrival, in 1677 or 1678, according to Mooney (1910d:533), although Swanton (1922:317) expressed doubt as to the time of the move to the north. Johnston (1820), in a letter to Caleb Atwater in 1819, wrote that the Shawnee had been established in Ohio about sixty-five years, having come here "from West Florida, and the adjacent country. They formerly resided on Suwaney river, near the sea. —Black Hoof, who is eightyfive [sic] years of age, was born there, and remembers bathing in the salt water when a boy" (p. 273). There were several Shawnee settlements among the Upper Creeks near the Coosa River about 1752 (Swanton 1922:319). Hawkins (1848:34-35) described a Shawnee town near the Coosa River in 1798-99 and observed that some Yuchi had settled with the Shawnee. The Shawnee on the Coosa probably came from the north (Swanton 1922:319). About 1805-10 Tecumseh led the southern Shawnee north to Indiana Territory and the Shawnee separated from the Creek tribes. The Shawnee reservation in Indian Territory adjoined the Creek Nation, to the west of the Creeks. The two tribes have retained their old-time intimacy (Swanton 1922:320). There are now three main groups of Shawnee in Oklahoma: the Eastern Shawnee in Ottawa County; a group living among the Cherokee in Craig, Rogers, and other northern counties; and the Absentee Shawnee near Shawnee in Pottawatomie County and east of Norman in Cleveland County (Wright 1951:241).

The earliest recording in Shawnee listed by Pilling (1891) is the Lord's Prayer by Rev. Le Jau, published in 1715 (p. 307), although Trumbull wrote Pilling that this language (in the Lord's Prayer) is not Shawnee (p. 79). Numerals in several Indian languages, including Shawnee, were published in Gentleman's Magazine in London in 1756 (Pilling 1891:523). The earliest vocabulary of Shawnee may be that recorded by Major Ebenezer Denny in 1776 (Pilling 1891:112). Thomas Ridout, who was a prisoner of the Shawnee in 1788, learned some of the Shawnee language and recorded a vocabulary of 225 words and phrases (Pilling 1891:437). In 1788 General Richard Butler recorded a vocabulary of Shawnee (Pilling 1891:64). In 1793 Captain William Preston recorded vocabularies of several Indian languages, including Shawnee (Pilling 1891:408). John Johnston, agent for Indian affairs in Ohio, collected a Shawnee vocabulary about 1819 (Pilling 1891:264), which was published by Caleb Atwater (Johnston 1820:287-92).

Translations of the gospels and hymns into Shawnee were published in the 1830's and 1840's (Pilling 1891:320-22, 351-56). Between 1835 and 1842 a Shawnee newspaper was published, the first newspaper ever published exclusively in an Indian language (Pilling 1891:459). Rev. Johnston Lykins, the Baptist missionary to the Shawnee, prepared and published a primer of the Shawnee language (Pilling 1891:320).[16]

Richard W. Cummings, United States agent in Indian Territory, collected a Shawnee vocabulary that was published by Schoolcraft (1852:470-81). A Shawnee vocabulary of some 250 words was collected and published by Lieutenant A. W. Whipple (1855:56-60). About 1861 General Albert Pike collected a Shawnee vocabulary of some fifteen hundred words (Pilling 1891:403). George Gibbs in 1866 collected a vocabulary of over two hundred Shawnee words (Pilling 1891:206). In 1879 Albert S. Gatschet collected a Shawnee vocabulary at Vinita in Indian Territory; in 1880 Gatschet obtained Shawnee sentences and texts; and in 1885 at the Quapaw agency, near Seneca, Missouri, Gatschet collected additional Shawnee material (Pilling 1891:202). Gatschet's Shawnee materials remain unpublished in the archives of the Bureau of American Ethnology.

C. F. Voegelin worked on the three dialects of Shawnee, as spoken in Oklahoma in the 1930's (Voegelin 1935:23).[17] Voegelin published an article on Shawnee phonemes (1935) and an article on Shawnee paradigmatic affixes (1936b). In a series of five articles, Voegelin (1938-40) published a lexicon of Shawnee stems which are compared with Miami words. Whorf (1938-40), at Voegelin's suggestion, illustrated in the appendix to the fourth article of the series (pp. 391-406) "the application of a different aspect of linguistic method, which can be applied only after a formal grammatical analysis has been made" (p. 393) in analyzing stem composition in Shawnee. Voegelin used a Shawnee informant at the 1952 Linguistic Institute and recorded texts in Shawnee, which were subsequently analyzed and translated (Voegelin 1953, Voegelin, Robinett, and Hickerson 1953). Nancy P. Hickerson made an acoustic analysis of Shawnee sounds, which served as her Ph. D. dissertation in 1957 at Indiana University, and presented the results in a series of four articles (1958, 1959). Douglas R. Parks worked on Shawnee in 1966 and 1967 and has written on Shawnee noun inflection in a paper which appears in this volume.

According to Chafe (1962:168), there are three hundred to four hundred speakers of Shawnee, all over twenty years of age, living in Oklahoma.

CADDOAN

The Caddoan languages are Pawnee, Kitsai, Wichita, Caddo, and possibly Adai. Except for Caddo and Adai, the Caddoan languages were spoken by tribes outside the southeastern region of the United States. Adai was spoken in western Louisiana. Caddo was spoken in western Louisiana, southeastern Arkansas, and northern Texas. There were two Pawnee dialects in southern Nebraska and northern Kansas and a third dialect, Arikara, on the Missouri River in North Dakota. Kitsai and Wichita were spoken in northern Texas.

Pawnee, Kitsai, and Wichita are about equally divergent and form one subgroup, while Caddo, the most divergent, forms a second subgroup (Lesser and Weltfish 1932:1-2). Adai "must be Caddoan, but where it belongs is still unclear; perhaps it constitutes an independent branch" (Taylor 1963a: 131).

When Gallatin (1836) prepared his comparative vocabularies, he had word lists of Adai, Caddo, and Pawnee, but none for the other Caddoan languages. Gallatin published vocabularies from these three languages (1836:307-67, 1848:95-98) but did not suggest the languages might be related. All the Caddoan languages, except Adai, were grouped together by Brinton (1891: 95-97) as the "Pani stock", but by Powell (1891a:58-62) as "Caddoan". Swanton (1952) assumed a Caddoan affinity for Adai, but Lesser and Weltfish (1932) were less certain (see Taylor 1963a:57).

Taylor (1963a) has written an historical sketch of the work on the classification of the Caddoan languages and has assembled (1963b) "in print enough cognate sets to permit a preliminary reconstruction of the outlines of Proto-Caddoan phonology" (p. 114).[18]

Caddo

First white contact with the Caddo tribes, who lived in western Louisiana, eastern Texas, and southeastern Arkansas, may have been by Cabeza de Vaca when he and his companions crossed a portion of the Caddo country in 1535-36 (Fletcher 1907:179).[19] De Soto in 1540-41 encountered Caddo tribes. The Caddo did not become well known until La Salle entered their country in 1686, and again in 1687, from the Texas coast in his search for the Mississippi River. In 1690 Alonso de Leon traveled eastward through the Caddo country as far as the Adai.[20] The Spanish established missions in the western part of the Caddo country during the early years of the eighteenth century, but they were all withdrawn by 1772-73. Henry de Tonti visited the eastern Caddo in 1690. Iberville heard of the Caddo in 1699 and in the following year his brother Bienville traveled to the country of the Natchitoches from the Taensa villages. From about 1702 to 1714 the Natchitoches tribe lived on the Mississippi, near the Acolapissa. The Natchitoches were helpful to the French in 1731 in defeating a body of Natchez.

With the acquisition of Louisiana by the United States in 1803 the Caddo were pushed toward the west. In 1835 the Caddo ceded all their land to the United States government and agreed to move at their own expense beyond the boundaries of the United States. They moved to Texas to join their kindred and settled in 1855 near the Brazos River. Troubles between whites and Comanches, with the whites showing no discrimination among Indians in their retaliations for Comanche raids, caused great suffering for the Caddo. After a company of white settlers fixed a date for the massacre of all reservation Indians, the Caddo in 1859 made a forced march of 15 days in the heat of July to the banks of the Washita River in Indian Territory, where a reservation was set apart for them. During the Civil War they took refuge in Kansas, having sided against the Confederates, but returned to their reservation in 1867-68. The Caddo numbered 535 in 1904.

The Caddo live at the present time in Caddo county, Oklahoma, with their largest settlement in the vicinity of Binger (Wright 1951:48).[21]

Although none has survived, the first Caddo word lists, in Hasinai, a Caddo dialect, were taken by La Salle and by the Spanish Franciscan missionaries in the late seventeenth century (Taylor 1963a:51, fn. 5). The earliest vocabularies which have survived were taken by John Sibley (Taylor 1963a:52, 57). Sibley collected a vocabulary of Adai in 1802 and a vocabulary of Caddo in 1804. George Gray, Sibley's successor as Indian agent, also collected Caddo vocabularies (Taylor 1963a:52). Gray's vocabulary and a portion of Sibley's list were published by Gallatin (1836) in his comparative vocabularies (pp. 307-67). Shorter Caddo word lists were collected in the 1850's by Captain Randolph Marcy, published by Schoolcraft (1853: 709-12), and by Lieutenant A. W. Whipple (Whipple 1855:70). Sibley's full list of Caddo words was published by Otis T. Mason in 1879 in the American Naturalist, pp. 787-90 (Gatschet 1879-80:236). In late 1884 Gatschet was at Anadarko, Indian Territory, where he collected Caddo vocabularies, including the "hitherto unstudied dialects of Anadarko and Yatasi" (Powell 1888:xxxv). James Mooney (1896) collected and published a Caddo vocabulary (pp. 1102-3). Leslie Spier (1924) obtained Caddo and Wichita kinship terms in 1919. Caddo forms are given by Parsons (1941), collected either by Parsons or by Gladys Reichard (Taylor 1963a:52).

Recent work has been done on Caddo by Daniel Da Cruz and by Wallace L. Chafe (Taylor 1963a:52). Chafe's materials were collected between 1959 and 1962. Neither Chafe nor Da Cruz has published his results. Da Cruz wrote a paper in 1957 on the segmental phonemes of Caddo (Taylor 1963a:52). Troike (1964) wrote on the origin of the Caddo word for "water".

According to Chafe (1962:124), there are three hundred to four hundred speakers of Caddo, twenty years of age or over, living in Oklahoma.

Wichita. The Caddoan family is represented in this volume by a paper on Wichita, whose speakers in earlier times lived in northern Texas adjacent to the Caddo. The first Wichita word list was collected by Captain Marcy in 1852 and published by Schoolcraft (1853:709-12). Gatschet collected a Wichita vocabulary in 1884 (Powell 1888:xxxv). Spier (1924) published Wichita and Caddo kinship terms collected by him in 1919. Paul L. Garvin visited the Wichita in 1949 and wrote on Wichita phonemics (1950). The Wichita language has been studied recently by David S. Rood, who has contributed to the present volume a paper on the inflectional categories of the Wichita verb.[22]

According to Chafe (1962:169), there are one hundred to two hundred speakers of Wichita, over fifty years of age. The Wichita live north of the Washita River in Caddo County, Oklahoma, in the general vicinity of Gracemont (Wright 1951:256).

IROQUOIAN

Iroquoian tribes occupied at least three distinct regions when first encountered by explorers and settlers. Early French explorers found Iroquoian tribes in Canada along the St. Lawrence River and the northern shores of Lakes Erie and Ontario. Jacques Cartier in 1534 met an Iroquoian tribe as far east as the Bay of Gaspé. The account of Cartier's second voyage of 1535-36 in this region, published in 1545, contains the first vocabularies ever printed of a North American Indian language (Pilling 1888:26). The early home of the Iroquoian tribes may have been in the St. Lawrence region, from which they moved southwest along the shores of the Great Lakes (Powell 1891a:77). The northern Iroquois were bordered on all sides by Algonquian tribes. To the south, in Pennsylvania and Maryland, along the lower Susquehanna River were other Iroquoian tribes whose territory may have adjoined the Iroquoian tribes further north before the Algonquian Delaware began their westward movement (Powell 1891a:78). Further south, in coastal Virginia and North Carolina, were two, and probably several, Iroquoian tribes. Linguistic material is available for only two tribes, Tuscarora in North Carolina and Nottoway in Virginia, but it is probable that there were other Iroquoian tribes in the region, e. g. , the Coree and Neusiok in eastern North Carolina (Swanton 1946:15) and the Meherrin in Virginia. The Meherrin, according to colonial documents, were remnants of the Conestoga of upper Maryland (Mooney 1907e:839). To the west in the foothills and mountains of the Appalachians lived the Cherokee, the principal tribe bordering the southern colonies. The Cherokee occupied a leading place in all the treaty negotiations and were considered as owners of a large territory to which they had no real claim (Powell 1891a:78).

Comparison of vocabularies of the northern Iroquoian languages revealed immediately their close relationships. It was also clear that Tuscarora and Nottoway were related to the northern languages, although Tuscarora (and Nottoway) are in a separate subgroup (Chafe 1973:1177).[23] Tuscarora and Nottoway were classified by Gallatin (1836:80-83, 305-67) without hesitation as Iroquois. Gallatin (1836:91-92) agreed with Barton (1797) that Cherokee "belonged to the Iroquois family" (p. 91) but kept Cherokee as a separate family for lack of sufficient knowledge of the languages (p. 92). Barton (1797: xlv, lxvii) was the first to suggest a Cherokee-Iroquois relationship and pointed out a few similarities. Hale (1883a:27) presented about thirty cognate words in Iroquois and Cherokee and removed "the doubt which has existed as to the connection of the two languages" (p. 28). Gatschet (1886b:xlii-xliv) provided additional evidence, both lexical and grammatical, of a relationship of Cherokee to the other Iroquoian languages. J. N. B. Hewitt wrote a manuscript in 1887 "for the purpose of placing the Iroquoian affinity of this language [Cherokee] beyond question" (Pilling 1888:81), but never published it. Very little comparative work has been published on the Iroquoian languages. According to Chafe (1973:1177), Lounsbury has done some comparative work on Iroquoian but has not published it. Lounsbury (1961) has published one paper on glottochronological time depths for branchings within Iroquoian and suggested a "more complete, though not earlier, separation" of Cherokee from the other Iroquoian languages (p. 17).

Cherokee

The first white encounter with the Cherokee was in 1540 when the De Soto expedition passed through the central region of their country in the foothills and mountains of South Carolina, North Carolina, and Tennessee. In the Portuguese narrative of the De Soto expedition, published in 1557, they are referred to as Chalaque. The term Cheraqui is applied to them in a French document of 1699. The present spelling, Cherokee, dates from 1708 (Mooney 1900:15).[24] In the late 1600's the Cherokee were mentioned in accounts by visitors to their country from the coastal settlements of Carolina and in the record of a visit of a Cherokee party to Charleston (Swanton 1946:111). English traders began to establish themselves in the Cherokee country in 1711. The French made contacts with the Cherokee from the west as early as 1701. In 1736 the English captured a Jesuit priest, supposedly a Frenchman, by the name of Christian Priber, who had come among the Cherokee, had learned their language, and, so it was claimed, had written a dictionary of Cherokee designed for publication in Paris (Mooney 1900:36-37). The English, thinking that the French had political designs, increased their own pressure for influence among the Cherokee. The Cherokee were more favorably disposed to the French than to the English and maintained a tenuous peace with the latter only for the advantages of trade (Timberlake 1765:73-74). The Cherokee believed they had more to fear from the English than from the

French, who were farther away from their country. The English were coming upon the Cherokee from Virginia and the Carolinas and "encroached daily so far upon them, that they not only felt the bad effects of it in their hunting grounds, which were spoiled, but had all the reason in the world to apprehend being swallowed up, by so potent neighbours, or being driven from the country" (Timberlake 1765:74). The Cherokee took sides against the colonists during the Revolutionary War and continued the struggle against the Americans until 1794. In their battles with the Americans the Cherokee suffered greatly. Their crops and towns were destroyed and large numbers were killed. The survivors were forced to cede much of their land to the Americans. In the year that peace was concluded, 1794, a party of Cherokee moved westward across the Mississippi (Swanton 1946:112).

The Cherokee, believing that their hope for peaceful relations with the Americans was adoption of their culture, began to acquire the rudiments of, and to make steady progress in, the arts of European civilization. Missions were established among the Cherokee, the first by the Moravians who came to them in 1801 (Swanton 1946:112). The flow of settlers toward their borders was constant and with demands for further cessions of land, which were granted in 1817. The Cherokee in 1820 adopted a form of government modeled on that of the United States. In 1821 Sequoyah's syllabary was approved by the chief men of the nation and was soon learned by many of the people. Parts of the Bible were printed in the syllabary and in 1828 the _Cherokee Phoenix_, a weekly paper in the syllabary and in English, began to appear.

Many Cherokee had as early as 1829 begun to move west to settle on a grant of land set aside for them in Texas. The discovery of gold in northern Georgia, near Dahlonega, increased the pressure for the removal of the remaining Cherokee to lands west of the Mississippi River. The treaty of New Echota, signed in 1835 by only a fraction of the tribe, called for the removal of all Cherokee from the lands in the east. The removal was accomplished in the winter of 1838-39 with intense suffering by the Cherokee and with the loss of one-fourth of their numbers. The Cherokee established themselves in the lands set aside for them in the northeastern part of Indian Territory. A few hundred Cherokee escaped removal by fleeing to the mountains of North Carolina and in 1842 were given the right to remain on lands purchased in their behalf. Descendants of those who escaped removal to the western ıands, the eastern Cherokee, live at present on and in the vicinity of the Qualla Reservation near Cherokee, North Carolina. Descendants of the western, or Oklahoma, Cherokee live in northeastern Oklahoma, mostly in the general vicinity of Tahlequah, the old capital of the western Cherokee Nation.

The earliest Cherokee vocabulary was taken by William Gerard De Brahm about 1756 while De Brahm was in the Cherokee country supervising the construction of Fort Loudoun in Tennessee. De Brahm's vocabulary was first published by De Vorsey (1971:115-31). Adair (1775) published several Cherokee words in 1775. Benjamin Hawkins about 1790 sent to Thomas Jefferson a vocabulary of Cherokee (Pilling 1888:76). Adair's Cherokee words were reprinted by Barton (1797). Bringier in 1821 published a vocabulary of Cherokee (Pilling 1888:19). In 1823 two vocabularies of Cherokee were published, by Say (Pilling 1888:149) and by Haywood (Pilling 1888:77). John Pickering published a grammar of Cherokee in 1830 and some comments on Cherokee verbs in 1831 (Pilling 1888:134). In 1825 Rev. Samuel Austin Worcester began missionary work among the Cherokee in eastern Tennessee. Worcester moved to New Echota, in Georgia, in 1828 and began the publication of Biblical and secular materials in the Cherokee language. Worcester's opposition to the laws of Georgia forced his return to Tennessee in 1834. In 1836 Worcester moved to Park Hill, his mission in Indian Territory, and continued his work among the Cherokee. Worcester had in Georgia both a grammar and dictionary of Cherokee "in a forward state of preparation" but lost them when a steamboat sank on the Arkansas River (Pilling 1888:174). Worcester produced many publications in Cherokee, mostly Bible translations, tracts, and almanacs. He published also a few articles on Cherokee grammar in 1836 and 1852 (Pilling 1888:171-72).

Cherokee words used by Gallatin (1836:307-67) were written by Boudinot and Ridge, both native Cherokee, with some help from Worcester (Gallatin 1836:91). Gabelentz' grammar of Cherokee was published in 1852 (Pilling 1888:67). While among the Catawba in 1881, Gatschet collected a Cherokee vocabulary from a visiting Cherokee and in 1885 obtained additional vocabulary and linguistic material from Cherokee delegations in Washington (Pilling 1888:68). Gatschet (1886b) published some of his Cherokee material in an article which sought to examine the merits of Hale's (1883a:26-28) proposal for a connection between the "Iroquois dialects" and Cherokee. In 1887 J. N. B. Hewitt, a native Tuscarora, prepared a manuscript which contained much Cherokee material (Pilling 1888:81). James Mooney in 1887 obtained considerable linguistic material on Cherokee, including a vocabulary of the upper dialect (Pilling 1888:124). Mooney also obtained a vocabulary of the middle dialect and one from the last speaker of the lower dialect of Cherokee (Pilling 1888:187-88). Numerous short Cherokee texts with translations were published by Mooney (1891) in his "Sacred formulas of the Cherokees". Mooney (1900) provided a glossary of Cherokee words (pp. 506-48) in his "Myths of the Cherokee". Much of Mooney's Cherokee linguistic material remains unpublished. Frank G. Speck recorded a few Cherokee texts in 1922 while searching for Catawba speakers among the Cherokee of North Carolina (Speck 1926). Frans M. Olbrechts (1931) published two texts, one written in the Cherokee syllabary, which he recorded in North Carolina in 1926-27. Some of Mooney's texts have been edited and published by Olbrechts (Mooney 1932).

Bender and Harris (1946) published an article on the phonemes of North Carolina Cherokee, based on material collected by Harris in 1941 and by Bender in 1945. Bender (1949) published several short analyzed texts which he collected in 1945. Haas (1948:244) gave a few examples from her Cherokee notes of the use of classificatory verbs in Cherokee. William D. Reyburn worked on Cherokee in North Carolina in 1951-52 and published three articles on Cherokee verb morphology (Reyburn 1953, 1954). Krueger (1963) translated Gabelentz' 1852 Cherokee grammar into English and published it together with Pickering's 1831 Cherokee grammar. A. G. Kilpatrick and J. F. Kilpatrick (1966) published several Cherokee texts and other Cherokee linguistic material based on Mooney's collections of 1888.[25] J. F. Kilpatrick and A. G. Kilpatrick (1970) have published additional Cherokee texts, with translations and analyses.

Recent field work has been conducted on North Carolina Cherokee by William Cook and Duane H. King.[26] William Pulte has been involved in preparing teaching materials in Cherokee in the Cherokee Bilingual Education Program in Tahlequah, Oklahoma. Willard Walker of Wesleyan University has done recent work on Cherokee. A paper by Walker on the Cherokee language appears in this volume.

According to Chafe (1962:165) there are approximately ten thousand speakers of all ages of Cherokee, one thousand of whom speak the North Carolina or middle dialect. Walker, in the preface to his paper in this volume, puts the total number of speakers of Cherokee at fifteen thousand. King (1974, personal communication) has estimated there are about twelve hundred speakers of Cherokee in North Carolina.

Nottoway

The Nottoway lived in southeastern Virginia, south of present-day Petersburg, along the Nottoway River. They were a small tribe, but seemed to have preserved their independence and their numbers longer than the Powhatan. According to Beverley (Gallatin 1836:81) the Nottoway had 130 warriors at the end of the seventeenth century. In 1825 there were 47 Nottoway living on a reservation in Southampton County, Virginia (Mooney 1910a:87).[27]

In 1820 J. Wood obtained a vocabulary of Nottoway and forwarded it to Thomas Jefferson, who sent it on to Peter Duponceau (Gallatin 1836:81). Duponceau immediately recognized the language to be Iroquoian. It had earlier been supposed that the Nottoway were a Powhatan tribe (Gallatin 1836:81). Later, another Nottoway vocabulary was obtained by James Tresevant, who provided the information that the true name of the tribe is Cherohakah (Gallatin 1836:81-82). These two vocabularies are the only ones known for Nottoway. They were used by Gallatin (1836) in his comparative vocabularies (pp. 307-67) and again by Gallatin (1848) in a comparative table of 60 words from Onondaga, Seneca, Oneida, Cayuga, Tuscarora, and Nottoway (p. 115).

Tuscarora

First white contact with the Tuscarora, who lived in eastern North Carolina, was made by Edward Blande in 1650 (Swanton 1946:199).[28] Twenty years later, in July 1670, the Tuscarora were visited by John Lederer. The first detailed account of the Tuscarora is by John Lawson, who visited them in 1701 (Lawson 1709). Lawson was well received by the Tuscarora and by the other tribes he encountered. But during the decade following Lawson's visit, encroachments of settlers on Tuscarora lands and kidnappings of youth to be sold into slavery so aroused the Tuscarora that they, with aid from the neighboring Pamlico and other tribes, massacred some one hundred and thirty colonists in 1711. The colonists swiftly retaliated and defeated the Indians, with the aid of tribes hostile to the Tuscarora. The treaty of peace which followed was violated by the whites, who seized a number of Indians and sold them into slavery. The war was immediately resumed by the Tuscarora, who were again defeated, in 1713. The Tuscarora asked to be adopted into the League of the Iroquois and in 1722 they were incorporated into the confederation of the Five Nations, becoming the sixth nation. Many Tuscarora, particularly those most hostile to the colonists, moved north to the Juniata after their defeat in 1713. The movement northward of the entire tribe, according to Hewitt (1910:847), was not accomplished for 90 years. The Tuscarora who took the side of Great Britain during the Revolutionary War moved to Canada and settled on Grand River Reservation, Ontario. The Tuscarora in sympathy with the Americans remained in New York, in the vicinity of Niagara Falls. By authority of Congress in 1804 additional land was purchased for the Tuscarora about five miles northeast of Niagara Falls. This area today constitutes the Tuscarora Indian Reservation on which live 640 enrolled Tuscarora, of which some fifty persons, over fifty years of age, are native speakers of the Tuscarora language (Fickett 1967:35).[29]

The first known vocabulary of Tuscarora was taken about 1701 by Lawson (1709:225-230) and reprinted by Barton (1797). Shortly after 1800 Thomas Jefferson apparently collected a Tuscarora vocabulary (Wallace 1949:163-65, Freeman 1966:32). Gallatin (1836) used a Tuscarora vocabulary collected by two native Tuscarora, Nicholas and James Cusick (p. 83) in his comparative vocabularies (pp. 307-67). Schoolcraft published in 1846 a Tuscarora vocabulary in his report to the Secretary of State (of New York) (Pilling 1888:44). A few other short vocabularies and word lists were collected in Tuscarora in the nineteenth century (see Pilling 1888:162-63).

The largest collection of linguistic material in Tuscarora was made by Erminie A. Smith with the aid of a Tuscarora, J. N. B. Hewitt, in 1879-80 (Pilling 1888:156-57). Smith in 1880-82 with Hewitt's help compiled an English-Tuscarora dictionary and wrote a grammatical sketch of Tuscarora. These materials were in rough draft and uncompleted at the time of Smith's death in 1886. Hewitt continued Smith's work on the language and in 1886 began the preparation of a Tuscarora-English dictionary (Pilling 1888:81-82).

Neither the grammar nor the dictionaries of Smith and of Hewitt have been published. Prominent linguists and ethnologists such as Frank G. Speck, William N. Fenton, Arthur Parker, F. M. Olbrechts, and Floyd G. Lounsbury have collected linguistic materials in Tuscarora but have not published them (Wallace 1952:5). Anthony F. C. Wallace visited the Tuscarora in 1948 and 1949 for the purpose of studying the tribe. Wallace (1949) made numerous wire recordings of Tuscarora but, lacking linguistic training (p. 165), made no serious attempt to write down the language. William Reyburn listened to one of Wallace's recorded texts and later wrote down a second version of this text in the field directly from the informant (Waliace and Reyburn 1951: 43). The text with translation, a Tuscarora migration legend, was published by Wallace and Reyburn (1951).

Joan Gleason Fickett worked on the Tuscarora language and has published an article on the phonology of Tuscarora (Fickett 1967). Recent work has been done on Tuscarora by Marianne Mithun Williams.[30]

MUSKOGEAN

Languages of the Muskogean family were spoken by a large number of tribes whose lands were entirely within the southeastern United States. During the early period of white contact these tribes occupied the country from western and southwestern South Carolina across Georgia below the mountains, through Alabama and Mississippi into eastern Louisiana, southward into northwestern Florida, and northward from Mississippi into western Tennessee and Kentucky. Undoubtedly, there were several Muskogean languages which became extinct without being recorded. For example, the Abihka, Tukabahchee, Tuskegee, and Yamasee tribes probably spoke Muskogean languages. Since these tribes and others, whose names only have come down to us, were either exterminated or absorbed into other larger tribes, we must remain in ignorance of their languages. We do know something about nine Muskogean languages. For one, Apalachee, scarcely more is known than to permit its classification as Muskogean. For the remaining eight, a good bit is known, and even more can be learned about them, since seven Muskogean languages are still spoken. The seven extant Muskogean languages are: Alabama, Chickasaw, Choctaw, Creek, Koasati, Mikasuki, and Seminole. Hitchiti is now extinct. There are a few people who still remember a little of the Mobilian trade language, which once served as a lingua franca in the lower Mississippi valley region.

Not all these eight warrant the designation "language". Choctaw and Chickasaw are mutually intelligible and differ only slightly from each other. Indeed, there were, and are, dialects of Choctaw whose differences are not much less than the differences between Chickasaw and any one of the Choctaw dialects. At one time there may have been as many as six Choctaw dialects. Today there are dialectal differences between Choctaw spoken in Mississippi and that spoken in Oklahoma. Minor dialectal differences exist even in the Choctaw spoken in Mississippi. The Seminole language differs only slightly from Creek. Hitchiti was extremely close to Mikasuki. Alabama and Koasati are closer to each other than either is to any other language, differing mostly in lexical items, and are almost mutually intelligible. Apalachee was perhaps closer to Alabama and Koasati than to the other Muskogean languages.

Benjamin Smith Barton (1797:lxviii), as noted by Haas (1970:69), may have been the first to propose a relationship between Creek and Choctaw. Gallatin (1836), "in compliance with received opinions", arranged the vocabularies of Choctaw and Creek (pp. 307-67) as separate families, although he believed the similarities between the two were "sufficient to prove a common origin" (p. 101). Gallatin recognized the closeness of Choctaw and Chickasaw, noting that speakers of the two languages "understand each other without interpreters" (1836:99). Using a Hitchiti vocabulary collected by Ridge, a Cherokee, Gallatin (1836) concluded that the Hitchiti "who reside on the Chatahoochee [sic] and Flint rivers, though a distinct tribe, speak a dialect of the Muskhogee [Creek]" (p. 94), but that a "vocabulary is wanted in order to prove conclusively the entire identity of their language with the Muskhogee" (p. 95). Gallatin lacked vocabularies of Alabama and Koasati, but noted that they were "intimately connected together" and were part of the Creek confederacy, although they spoke "a language or a dialect distinct from that of the Muskhogees" (1836:96). Gallatin in his Introduction to "Hale's Indians of North-west America. . . " (1848) placed Choctaw and Creek in the same family, noting that the two tribes "though politically distinct, speak two almost identic [sic] dialects of the same language" (p. cv) and, as evidence of their close relationship, presented a comparative vocabulary of the two languages (p. cxii).

Daniel G. Brinton (1873) believed he had shown that Natchez was "a dialect of the Maskoke or Creek" (p. 498), in spite of a number of dissimilarities which he attributed to "a potent foreign influence" (p. 499). (Brinton [1867] previously had attempted to show Natchez to be related to Maya, having rejected Muskogean similarities in Natchez as "adventitious Choctaw words" [p. 16].)

Albert S. Gatschet (1884), using Alabama and Koasati material collected by General Albert Pike, supplemented by his own collection of Koasati (p. 57), presented a comparative table of 39 forms from the eight extant (in 1884) and the one extinct (Apalachee) Muskogean languages (p. 56) and proved conclusively that Alabama and Koasati were Muskogean. Gatschet observed that "Alibamu forms a dialect for itself, leaning more toward Cha'hta than Creek" (1884:57). Gatschet (1884) classified the Muskogean languages (actually, the Muskogean tribes) into four branches: Muskoki proper (Creek and Seminole), Apalachian, Hitchiti, Mikasuki, and Apalachee, Alibamu (Alabama and Koasati), and Western or Cha'hta (Choctaw and Chickasaw) (p. 52).[31] Gatschet's classification was accepted by Powell (1891a:94-95), who ignored Brinton's (1873) proposed Natchez-Muskogean connection.

Frank G. Speck (1907a) compared several morphological features of the Muskogean languages and concluded that "Lexically the greatest divergence is found between the two geographical extremes, the Choctaw-Chickasaw group and the Creek or eastern" (p. 483). John R. Swanton (1907b) compared Natchez and Muskogean and produced evidence "to confirm Brinton's position of 1873 and place the relationship of Natchez to the Muskhogean dialects beyond reasonable doubt" (p. 527). With more data on hand Swanton (1924-25) provided additional proof of a Muskogean connection for Natchez and set up sound correspondences between Natchez and Muskogean. Mary R. Haas (1941d), using for the most part her own field notes, presented cognate forms from the extant Muskogean languages, excluding only Apalachee, proposed Proto-Muskogean sounds to account for the sound correspondences of the cognates, reconstructed a considerable number of Proto-Muskogean words, and arrived at a classification of Muskogean into two divisions: Western and Eastern (p. 54). According to Haas, the Western division consisted of one language, Choctaw, and its subdialects, including Chickasaw, and the Eastern division consisted of three subdivisions: (1) Alabama and Koasati,

(2) Hitchiti and its subdialect Mikasuki, and (3) Creek and its subdialects, including Seminole (1941d:54-55). In subsequent papers Haas has treated with the internal relationships of Muskogean: noun incorporation in Muskogean (1941a), Muskogean subject pronoun affixes (1946a), the reflexes of Proto-Muskogean $*k^w$ (1947), and the development from Proto-Muskogean of (some) Creek long vowels (1950a). Haas (1956) reconstructed a large number of Proto-Muskogean forms to which she supplied Natchez cognates and, for a few words, proposed Proto-Natchez-Muskogean reconstructions. Haas (1966) reconstructed some Proto-Muskogean pronominal affixes and other forms in her essay "Historical linguistics and the genetic relationship of languages".

Alabama

When first encountered by whites, the Alabama were located on the Alabama River not far below the junction of the Coosa and Tallapoosa rivers, a few miles north of present-day Montgomery. They may have moved to this location at an earlier time, perhaps from northern Mississippi. The chroniclers of the De Soto expedition mention a "province" of Alibamo northwest of the Chickasaw. Soon after the French established themselves at Mobile Bay in 1702, they became involved in a war with the Alabama who were aided by the English. The hostilities lasted until 1712. In 1717 the French established Fort Toulouse at the junction of the Coosa and Tallapoosa to protect French traders and to hold the Alabama in check. Relations between the Alabama and French then became and remained friendly. When France ceded the area to England in 1763, the tribe began to break up. By 1806 a part of the Alabama had moved to Louisiana and were located about sixty miles north of New Orleans on the Mississippi River. They remained here until 1784, at which time they moved to western Louisiana, some to Calcasieu parish in southwestern Louisiana, some to central Louisiana, on Red River near the Caddo, and some to south central Louisiana northwest of Opelousas. Later some Alabama moved further west to Texas as far as the Sabine River. Eventually the greater portion of the tribe moved to Texas. In their attempts to escape white encroachments the Alabama and their kinsmen, the Koasati, had become homeless wanderers. As a result of their petition to the Texas state legislature in 1854, the Alabama were granted 1,280 acres of land and the choice of location, either in Polk or Tyler counties. The tribe chose Polk County and the state purchased the land 17 miles east of Livingston, the county seat (Rothe 1963:86). The Koasati were permitted to settle with the Alabama on the same reservation by a resolution of the next legislature.

Those of the Alabama who did not move west after the French cession in 1763 were compelled to leave their settlement on the Alabama River after the Creek War of 1813-14. Most resettled a short distance away at a town which took the name of Tawasa, the site of present-day Montgomery (Swanton 1946:190). The rest moved up the Coosa River and settled above Wetumpka. The Alabama who remained in the Creek Nation were removed to Indian territory along with the Creek tribes. Upon arrival at their new home, the Alabama settled in the general vicinity of Wetumka and Weleetka, at which latter place they still maintained a square ground in 1928 (Swanton 1946:88).[32]

The first vocabulary of Alabama seems to be one collected by General Albert Pike about 1861 (Pilling 1889:69). Gatschet in 1885 collected words, phrases, and sentences in Alabama at Wealaka [Weleetka (?)] in Oklahoma (Pilling 1889:38). Swanton was in Oklahoma and Texas in 1911 and 1912, as well as in subsequent years, during which time he collected materials in Alabama (Swanton 1928a:31-32).[33] Swanton (1928a:91) presented a few Alabama kin terms which differ from those in Koasati. In 1934 Mary R. Haas and Morris Swadesh recorded a vocabulary of Alabama (Haas 1973:1214). Alabama forms were cited by Haas in several publications (e. g., 1941d, 1950a). In the fall of 1960 Earl Rand made two field trips to the Alabama in Texas and collected four hours of tape recordings. His master's thesis, awarded in 1961, dealt with the phonology of Alabama and was the basis of his article on Alabama phonology which appeared several years later (Rand 1968). In 1969 Muriel Saville did work on the Alabama language for about four months.[34] In August 1970 I collected an Alabama vocabulary of several hundred words. In summer 1971 Mary E. McCall began an intensive study of Alabama, which is still in progress.[35] McCall has reported that recent work was done on Alabama by Karen Lupardus, both in Texas and in Kansas with an Alabama student at the University of Kansas.

According to Chafe (1962:164), there are two hundred to four hundred speakers of Alabama of all ages living in Texas. Rand (1968:94) wrote there are about four hundred Alabama Indians. According to Rand, "the younger generation uses Alabaman [sic] less than the older generation, and in a generation or two the language may be extinct" (1968:94). McCall (personal communication) has reported that Alabama and Koasati have become so intermixed that Alabama speakers, particularly the young to middle-aged, are unsure whether the linguistic material they provide is Alabama or Koasati. According to McCall, there are 500 Alabama and Koasati, 80 per cent of whom consider themselves to be Alabama.[36] For some reason Koasati has become the more prestigious language. Claude Medford believes that "Alabama is rapidly losing ground to Koasati at the reservation in Texas".[37]

Apalachee

The Apalachee inhabited the coastal region of northwest Florida from the Pensacola Bay area to the Aucilla River, about thirty miles east of Tallahassee. The Apalachee were visited in 1528 by Narvaez and in 1539 by De Soto, who made their country his winter headquarters. The Apalachee resisted the intrusion of the Spanish into their country, but were finally subdued about 1600 and were completely Christianized during the next half-century. During the winter of 1703-1704 the Apalachee were totally disrupted when their country was invaded by a South Carolina force under Colonel James Moore, who killed hundreds and took back to South Carolina some thirteen hundred Apalachee along with their slaves. The Apalachee who escaped Moore's army went to Pensacola and later to Mobile, probably about 1705, where they hoped to find safety under the French. Those who had been taken to South Carolina eventually made their way back to their old country, some settling near San Marcos on the coast south of Tallahassee, others settling in the vicinity of Pensacola. The Mobile and Pensacola bands maintained a separate existence until at least 1758. When the territory was ceded to Great Britain, they moved westward. By 1764 the Apalachee, along with the Taensa and the Pakana, had become settled on Red River in Louisiana. Gatschet (1884:76) noted there were 14 Apalachee families in 1815 on the Bayou Rapide in Louisiana. The Apalachee appear to have remained in this region, where they either died out or merged with other tribes. A few families may have remained in the east and gone west with the Creeks during the removal. Swanton (1946:91) wrote that Gatschet found three Apalachee families living in Indian Territory on the North Canadian River.[38]

Our knowledge of the Apalachee language is based almost entirely on a letter written in Apalachee and in Spanish by some Apalachee chiefs in 1688, addressed to Ferdinand IV, king of Spain, complaining of the hard treatment received from some governors of the province. Buckingham Smith reproduced the letter in facsimile in 1860 (Haas 1973:1213).[39] In the February 1860 number of the Historical Magazine, Smith (1860b) presented a passage taken from the letter in Apalachee, together with the Spanish translation and a translation into English from the Spanish. Gatschet (1884:76) reported that other documents written in Apalachee are preserved in the archives of Havana.[40] According to Gatschet (1884), "the Hitchiti, Mikasuki and Apalachi languages form a dialectic group distinct from Creek and the western dialects" (p. 74). Mooney (1907b:67) stated that Apalachee is closer to Choctaw than to Creek. Swanton (1922) expressed the opinion that Apalachee is "an independent dialect" (p. 130). Toomey (1918) presented a specimen of the Apalachee text, a glossary which compared Apalachee with other Muskogean languages, and an analyzed portion of the text, which included more than the specimen. Toomey noted that Apalachee is etymologically related to Choctaw, but resembles Hitchiti morphologically and differs phonetically "from Northern Choctaw very much as does Hooma and Alibamu" and concluded that Apalachee "became separated from Old Choctaw at least several centuries before the Columbian discovery" (p. 8). Haas (1949) examined Apalachee and presented evidence to show that it belongs in the Eastern division of Muskogean and that it seems to be closest to the Alabaman subdivision (Alabama and Koasati) (pp. 126-27).

Chickasaw

The first white contact with the Chickasaw was the De Soto expedition in 1540. De Soto encountered the Chickasaw in northeastern Mississippi, in an area northwest of present-day Tupelo, where most of their villages were located throughout the 1700's. The Chickasaw claimed as their territory the area west to the Mississippi River, a vast area to the north in Tennessee and Kentucky as far as the junction of the Tennessee and Ohio rivers, and an indeterminate area south and southwest of their central site near Tupelo. British traders entered the Chickasaw country very early in the eighteenth century and enlisted the tribe in the British interest. The Chickasaw were noted for their warlike disposition and were constantly fighting with neighboring tribes. French writers attributed to the Chickasaw the responsibility for much of the disturbance along the lower Mississippi River. The Chickasaw remained bitter enemies of the French throughout the French occupation of Louisiana. The incessant warfare weakened the Chickasaw and they "at times talked of moving over into the Creek country" (Swanton 1946:117). Some Chickasaw did move eastward and settle among the Creeks. In 1723 a Chickasaw band settled on the South Carolina side of the Savannah River. Official relations with the United States government began in 1786 at the treaty of Hopewell, which fixed the northern boundary of the Chickasaw at the Ohio River. Pressure from white settlers increased toward the end of the eighteenth century and the Chickasaw were forced to cede portions of their land in 1805, 1816, and 1818. In 1832 the Chickasaw signed a treaty by which they agreed to give up all their lands east of the Mississippi River. The Chickasaw moved to Indian Territory between 1837 and 1847 and settled in the western section of the Choctaw Nation. In 1855 this section was separated from the Choctaw Nation and given to the Chickasaw.[41]

Numerous Chickasaw forms were given by James Adair (Adair 1775). Adair seems to have been the first to attempt to take down words in the language. Pilling (1889:44) wrote that Benjamin Hawkins collected a Chickasaw vocabulary of some three hundred words about 1790. Adair's Chickasaw words were used by Barton (1797) in his comparative vocabularies. In 1800 General D. Smith of Tennessee took down a vocabulary of Chickasaw from a family who passed an evening at his house (Pilling 1889:85). The Chickasaw vocabulary used by Gallatin (1836:307-67) was written down in Gallatin's presence by a Chickasaw boy (p. 99). No further recordings of any consequence seem to been made until about 1861 when Mrs. A. E. W. Robertson obtained a vocabulary of Chickasaw from Daniel Austin, a half-breed Creek who grew up with the Chickasaw. Mrs. Robertson inserted her Chickasaw vocabulary into the vocabularies of General Albert Pike (Pilling 1889:69). George Gibbs in 1866 collected a vocabulary of 200 Chickasaw words (Pilling 1889:40). About 1875 Mrs. Robertson prepared another Chickasaw vocabulary with the aid of Daniel Austin and his sister, Pollie Fife (Pilling 1889:77). Gatschet (1884) made use of Gibbs' vocabulary in preparing his "comparative table" (p. 56) and cited a few additional Chickasaw forms from Gibbs' vocabulary (pp. 96-97). In 1889 Gatschet himself took down "words, phrases, and grammatic elements" from Judson Dwight Collins, a delegate of the Chickasaw tribe to the United States government (Pilling 1889:39). Swanton (1928c:186) presented an outline of Chickasaw kinship terms. Haas (1941d) in her article on the classification of the Muskogean languages made use of Chickasaw forms from Gatschet (1884). William Pulte worked on Chickasaw in the late 1960's (personal communication). A paper by Pulte concerning the relationship of Chickasaw to Choctaw appears in this collection.

According to Chafe (1962:165), there are two thousand to three thousand speakers of Chickasaw of all ages living in Oklahoma.

Choctaw

The Choctaw were, next to the Cherokee, the largest tribe in the Southeast. The Choctaw were encountered by De Soto, although they appear in the De Soto narratives by other names (Swanton 1922:421, 1946:121). The Choctaw are seldom mentioned in the literature before 1699, when the French settled Louisiana. Soon after the French arrival, they became important to the French as a buffer between the latter and the English to the east and north. Throughout the French occupation of Louisiana the Choctaw on the whole were kept in the French interest. However, several of the Choctaw towns favored the English and this resulted in a civil war which ended in 1750 with the defeat of the English faction. Individuals among the Choctaw joined the Creek in their uprisings, but the Choctaw tribe itself was never at war with the United States. After the American Revolution white settlers moved into their country and there was increasing pressure for removal of the Choctaw to lands across the Mississippi. In 1830 the Choctaw finally agreed to move to lands granted them in southwestern Indian Territory. Most of the Choctaw made the move between 1831 and 1833, with smaller numbers moving west in subsequent years. A considerable portion of Choctaw did not move, but remained in the recesses of the back country of Mississippi and Louisiana. Descendants of those who did not cross the Mississippi live today in the general vicinity of Philadelphia, Mississippi. There are several families of Choctaw in a few locations in Louisiana. There is a sizable band of Choctaw living near Golddust, Tennessee, on the Mississippi River, about fifty miles north of Memphis. This band is said to have come here from Mississippi.[42]

Choctaw towns were located throughout central and southern Mississippi and southeastern Louisiana. There seem to have been several dialects of Choctaw in the various towns, although "this difference [in dialects] seems to have been confined mainly to certain words" (Byington 1915:ix). There are a number of tribes in the region which are believed to have spoken Choctaw dialects or languages very close to Choctaw, e. g. , the Acolapissa and Houma. But, in general, linguistic evidence to support this belief is lacking. Complications arise in interpreting even the bit of linguistic evidence that does exist because of the fact that a second language was spoken by some members of all the tribes of the Gulf region from Alabama to Texas. This language, a lingua franca which served as the medium of communication throughout the lower Mississippi Valley region, went by the name of the Mobilian, or Chickasaw, trade language and was based on one, or possibly several, of the Choctaw dialects. It is possible that many of the tribes in the region received the names that have come down to us from this trade language. Furthermore, it is impossible to know if the few words and vocabularies recorded from speakers of various tribes are from their native languages or are from the trade language. For example, Swanton met two brothers of Pascagoula descent living with the Alabama and Koasati in Texas. From them Swanton got about ten words used either by their mother, a Pascagoula, or by their father, a Biloxi (they could not remember which). As Swanton acknowledges, the words are not Biloxi. They may be Pascagoula, but, what is more likely, the words belong to the Mobilian trade language (Swanton 1911:32). Swanton also collected about eighty words from an old Houma woman (1911:28-29). All the words look like Choctaw and could be taken as proof that Houma is a dialect of Choctaw. But it is equally possible that the words are from the Mobilian trade language and are not at all representative of the language of the Houma.

The first words in Choctaw were taken down in 1715 and consist of the four words 'father', 'heaven', 'land', and 'bread' from the Lord's prayer (Pilling 1889:21). In 1748 four words from Choctaw were published in a short vocabulary of several Indian languages (Pilling 1889:35). Several Choctaw words and numerals were given by James Adair (Adair 1775). In 1788 a list of 45 Choctaw words appeared in the account of a traveler through the French colonies (Pilling 1889:11). About 1790 Benjamin Hawkins prepared a vocabulary of some three hundred words and phrases of several Muskogean languages, including Choctaw, for Thomas Jefferson (Pilling 1889:44). From about the end of the eighteenth century on, a large number of word lists and vocabularies were collected, many of which were published. The Choctaw, and other Muskogean, words taken by Adair were published by Barton (1797).

In the early nineteenth century missionaries began to enter the Choctaw country. Among the first band of missionaries to the Choctaw was Loring S. Williams, who wrote numerous tracts and Bible stories in Choctaw (Pilling 1889:93-95). Williams went west with the Choctaw, but retired in 1838, not long after their arrival in Indian Territory. Missionaries were active among the Choctaw throughout the nineteenth century. Many of the Choctaw learned to read and write their language. Bibles, hymns, and innumerable tracts were printed in the Choctaw language, some of which were prepared by native speakers of Choctaw. Cyrus Byington, perhaps the most active and well-known of the Choctaw missionaries, left his home in Massachusetts in 1819 for the Choctaw country in Mississippi. Upon his arrival Byington immediately began the task of learning Choctaw and preparing a grammar of the language. The first draft of his grammar was completed by 1834 (Byington 1870:319, 1915:viii; Pilling 1889:17). Byington's last draft of the grammar was completed about 1865 (Pilling 1889:16) and was edited by Daniel G. Brinton and published two years after Byington's death in 1868 (Byington 1870). Byington had completed a Choctaw-English dictionary in manuscript by about 1865. John R. Swanton and Henry S. Halbert edited the manuscript, adding an English-Choctaw index, and published it a half-century later (Byington 1915). In 1880 the Presbyterian Publishing Company in St. Louis printed a "Chahta lexsikon—a Choctaw in English definition", prepared by Rev. Allen Wright, a native Choctaw (Pilling 1889:102). Gatschet (1881-82) wrote a review of Wright's lexicon and noted that this was the first Choctaw dictionary ever published. A "Complete Choctaw definer—English with Choctaw definition" by Ben Watkins (1892) was published, on newsprint, in Van Buren, Arkansas.[43] In 1887 the Presbyterian missionary, Rev. John Edwards, prepared a manuscript dictionary of Choctaw (Pilling 1889:32).

Albert S. Gatschet collected Choctaw words and phrases in Louisiana north of Lake Pontchartrain in 1881-82 (Pilling 1889:38). Gatschet (1884) used this material in preparing his comparative table of Muskogean languages

(p. 56). Gatschet returned to Louisiana in 1886 and collected additional linguistic material from Choctaw speakers living in Catahoula Parish, about twenty-five miles west of Natchez, Mississippi (Pilling 1889:39). In 1908-9 David I. Bushnell, Jr. (1909) was in Louisiana where he studied the two settlements of Choctaw northeast of Lake Pontchartrain. Bushnell (1909) reported that the Indians of Bayou Lacomb may be descendants of the Acolapissa, or they may be Choctaw who moved in later, or they may be a mixture of Acolapissa and Choctaw (p. 3). Bushnell (1909) cited Choctaw forms and gave a list of about sixty Choctaw words (pp. 16-17).[44]

John R. Swanton made several trips to Louisiana and Oklahoma (in 1911-12 and subsequent years) and collected Choctaw material. Swanton (1931) cited many Choctaw forms in his monograph on the Choctaw, using both his own material and forms from Byington (1915) and Morgan (1871:293-382) in preparing a table of Choctaw kinship terms (pp. 85-86). Eggan (1937) noted changes in the Choctaw kinship system. Read (1940) described a manuscript with a Choctaw glossary prepared by an anonymous writer in Opelousas, Louisiana in 1862. Mary R. Haas collected Choctaw vocabularies in the late 1930's, both in Louisiana and in Oklahoma (Haas 1973:1212) and cited Choctaw forms in several articles.[45]

T. Dale Nicklas of the University of Kansas worked on Choctaw in Oklahoma in 1967-68 and presents in this volume a paper on some of the grammatical features of Choctaw. H. A. Badger (1971) did some work on Choctaw and wrote a transformational grammar of the language, using material "gathered from three native Mississippi Choctaws" (p. 2). Jeffrey Heath of the University of Chicago made several visits to the Choctaw in Mississippi in 1972 and 1973 and presented a paper entitled "Choctaw cases" at the 1973 meeting of the American Anthropological Association. I worked in 1972-73 with a Choctaw speaker, a student from Philadelphia, Mississippi, and collected considerable lexical and grammatical material.

According to Chafe (1965:346), there are approximately ten thousand Choctaw speakers of all ages living in Oklahoma, Mississippi, and Louisiana.

Creek

During the early historic period the Creek, or Muskogee,[46] claimed as their territory the greater part of Alabama and Georgia, as well as lands adjoining in Mississippi, northern Florida, and South Carolina. Their residences were located chiefly in northern Alabama on the Coosa and Tallapoosa rivers, in Georgia and Alabama along the Chattahoochee River, and in Georgia on the Flint River. The former were known as the Upper Creeks. Those living at the latter two locations were called the Lower Creeks. The Creek tribes were the dominant element of the Creek Confederation, an association of diverse tribes for purposes of defense. By the time of their removal to the west, the Creeks had drawn into the confederation some fifty towns in which were spoken at least seven distinct languages in addition to Creek: Alabama, Chickasaw, Hitchiti, Koasati, Natchez, Shawnee, and Yuchi. The Creek language apparently served as a lingua franca throughout the confederation (Adair 1775: 267, Sturtevant 1971:96).

The first white contact with the Creek was De Soto's passage through their country in 1540. From 1703 to 1708 they were on the side of the English in the Apalachee wars. The Creek afterwards remained allied by treaties with colonists of South Carolina and Georgia. The only serious revolt against the settlers was in 1813-14, the so-called Creek Wars, in which Andrew Jackson took a prominent part and in which the Indians were completely defeated. With the encroachment on their lands by the settlers, pressure increased for their removal to the west. By 1840 the last of the tribes of the confederation moved to lands which had been set aside for them in Indian Territory. In their new home the old confederation took on a new form as the Creek Nation and preserved its identity as such until 1907.[47]

A few words in the Creek language (from the Lord's Prayer) were published as early as 1715 (Pilling 1889:21). The first vocabulary of any significance taken of Creek was some three hundred words recorded by Benjamin Hawkins about 1790 (Pilling 1889:44). James Adair, fifteen years before, in 1775, published a few terms and numerals from Creek, as well as from Choctaw and Chickasaw, which were reprinted by Barton (1797).

Intensive missionary work did not begin among the Creek until after their removal. Soon after the arrival of the Creek tribes in Indian Territory, the missionaries came among them and devised a writing system for the Creek language, established schools, and taught a large number of Creeks to write and read their language. The missionaries, aided by educated and pious members of the tribe, began translations of the Bible into Creek. Printing presses in Muskogee, the capital of the Creek Nation, and in Eufaula turned out religious tracts, hymnbooks, and books of the Bible in the Creek language. In 1860 a grammar of Creek was published by the Baptist missionary, H. F. Buckner, with help from a Creek, Goliah Herrod (Pilling 1889:14). Several periodicals written in Creek appeared during the 1870's and 1880's. Of all the missionaries to the Creek, the ones who made the greatest contributions were Rev. William Schenck Robertson, his wife, Ann Eliza Worcester Robertson (daughter of Rev. Samuel A. Worcester, missionary to the Cherokee), and Rev. Robert McGill Loughridge. Robertson in 1870 began the publication of the periodical _Our Monthly_, which was circulated widely and greatly stimulated the Creeks to learn to read their language. Mrs. Robertson continued the work of her husband after his death in 1884. In 1887 Mrs. Robertson printed privately a glossary to accompany a translation of the New Testament into Creek (Pilling 1889:76). Loughridge translated portions of the Bible into Creek, published hymns, catechisms, and other religious materials in Creek, and completed in 1882 an English-Creek dictionary in manuscript (Pilling 1889:55). Loughridge's dictionary was published in 1890 in St. Louis (Swanton 1928a:472) and reprinted in 1964 in Okmulgee, Oklahoma (Loughridge and Hodge 1964).[48]

Numerous vocabularies were collected in Creek during the nineteenth century. Gallatin (1836:97) noted their abundance in the preparation of his comparative vocabularies. In 1861 General Albert Pike collected verb forms and a vocabulary of fifteen hundred to seventeen hundred words (Pilling 1889:69). George Gibbs in 1866 collected a vocabulary of some two hundred words (Pilling 1889:40). Excluding the work of the missionaries, the vocabularies of Gibbs and Pike are the only ones worthy of mention until Albert S. Gatschet obtained phrases and sentences in Washington in 1879-80 from two Creek delegates of the Creek Nation, General Pleasant Porter and D. M. Hodge (Pilling 1889:38). In 1885 Gatschet went to the Creek Nation and obtained additional Creek material at Eufaula (Pilling 1889:38).

Daniel G. Brinton (1870) published a translation into English from the German of a Creek migration legend.[49] Gatschet took Brinton's English translation of the legend to a Hitchiti, George W. Stidham, judge of the supreme court of the Creek Nation, and employed him in the translation of the legend into Creek and Hitchiti. Gatschet (1884) published the Creek version, along with a description of southeastern tribes, the languages of the tribes, a comparative vocabulary of the languages, and brief sketches of Hitchiti and Creek grammar. Gatschet (1892) published the Hitchiti translation, a corrected version of the Creek translation, and provided Creek and Hitchiti glossaries.[50]

Frank G. Speck began his work with the Yuchi in 1904 and made return visits in 1905 and 1908 (Speck 1909:5). In spare time during the course of his work on Yuchi, Speck collected linguistic, ethnographic, and other information on Creek (1907-15:106) and recorded Creek (and Yuchi) songs (1911). Numerous Creek words and phrases are given in his monograph "The Creek Indians of Taskigi town" (Speck 1907-15).[51]

John R. Swanton was among the Creeks for about eight months in 1911-12 and for shorter periods in subsequent years (Swanton 1928a:31). In numerous publications Swanton has reported upon Creek culture, history, and language.[52] Swanton (1928a) presented relationship terms in Creek, also in Koasati, Alabama, and Natchez, with a few in Hitchiti, (pp. 80-95), Creek war names (pp. 103-105), Creek boys' names (pp. 105-106), and the names of the seasons in Creek (pp. 400-402). Most of Swanton's Creek linguistic material remains unpublished.

Mary R. Haas did considerable field work on Creek, historical and ethnological as well as linguistic, during the 1930's, mostly in the years from 1936 to 1939 (Haas 1940a:141). Haas has published several descriptive articles on Creek, e. g. , on Creek geminate consonant clusters (1938), on the function of ablaut in Creek (1940a), on a Creek etymology (1941b), on Creek dialects (1945), and on Creek classificatory verbs (1948).[53]

According to Chafe (1962:165), Creek is spoken by seven thousand to eight thousand people of all ages in Oklahoma. Chafe (1965:346) raised the estimate of the number of Creek speakers to ten thousand.

Hitchiti

At one time the Hitchiti, according to Swanton (1922:173), were probably the most important tribe in the southern half of Georgia, from the Chattahoochee River to the Atlantic Ocean. The Hitchiti language, with dialectal variations, is believed to have been spoken by other tribes in this region, e. g. , by the Apalachicola, Sawokli, Okmulgee, and Oconee (Swanton 1922: 12), although we have no linguistic data on the languages of these tribes for confirmation of the belief. The Mikasuki language is known, however, to be close to Hitchiti (Swanton 1922:401) and, in fact, Hitchiti and Mikasuki are only subdialects of one language (Haas 1941d:42). Swanton (1922: 174, 1946:138) believed the Hitchiti appear in the De Soto narratives under the name Ocute, or Ocuti, on the lower Ocmulgee River in Georgia. The tribe is not often mentioned in history (Gatschet 1907b:551). Its first mention seems to have been in 1733, as Echetas, when two Hitchiti war-captains, accompanied by four attendants, and several head warriors from the Lower Creek towns, with their attendants, met with Governor Oglethorpe in Savannah (Jones 1868:28). When Benjamin Hawkins was in the Lower Creek country in 1799, he found one Hitchiti town on the Chattahoochee River, another on the Flint River some sixty miles east of the Chattahoochee, and another on a creek just west of the Flint. The Hitchiti accompanied the Creeks and other tribes of the confederation to their new lands in Indian Territory, where they settled in the center of the Creek Nation near Okmulgee and Hitchita, the latter about twenty miles southeast of Okmulgee (Swanton 1922:178). Some Hitchiti migrated back to the East, to Florida, but returned with the Seminole and settled in the northern part of the Seminole territory (Swanton 1946:138).

The first vocabulary of Hitchiti seems to be the small specimen taken by the Cherokee, Mr. Ridge, in 1825-26, at Gallatin's request from a chief of the tribe who was part of a delegation to Washington (Gallatin 1836:97) and published by Gallatin in his comparative vocabularies (1836:307-67). A few Hitchiti numerals were recorded by Captain J. C. Casey and were published by Schoolcraft (1852:220-21). The first vocabulary of any size, fifteen hundred to seventeen hundred words, was taken by General Albert Pike about 1861 (Pilling 1889:69). George Gibbs collected a vocabulary of 200 words in 1866 (Pilling 1889:40). In 1886 Albert S. Gatschet recorded Hitchiti names and terms from a native Hitchiti, Judge G. W. Stidham, and in 1887, also from Judge Stidham, a text with added glossary (Pilling 1889:39). Gatschet (1884) published "A migration legend of the Creek Indians" in which he gave a specimen of female speech in Hitchiti and a "hunter's song" with English translation (p. 79) and some notes on Hitchiti morphology (pp. 80-85). In 1888, as a sequel to the preceding, Gatschet published privately "Tchikilli's Kasi'hta legend in the Creek and Hitchiti languages, with a critical commentary and full glossaries to both texts", which was reprinted in volume five of the Transactions of the Academy of Science of St. Louis (Gatschet 1892). In this volume Gatschet described (pp. 36-37) how he had Judge Stidham translate into Hitchiti and Creek Brinton's (1870) English translation from German of the "national legend of the Chahta-Muskokee tribes". Gatschet (1892) then presented a corrected version of the Creek text with English translation (pp. 40-51) and a Hitchiti version of the legend (pp. 52-57). Following explanatory and critical remarks (pp. 58-103), Gatschet gave a Creek glossary (pp. 106-62) and a Hitchiti glossary (p. 166-211).

In 1911-12 and subsequent years John R. Swanton visited the Creek Nation and collected extensive ethnographic and linguistic material. Swanton published a few Hitchiti terms of relationship (1928a:88). The larger part of Swanton's Hitchiti linguistic materials, including 150 pages of texts (Goddard 1914:587) and a sketch of the language (Haas 1973:1214), remains unpublished.

Mary R. Haas worked a few days with a speaker of Hitchiti in 1937 and prepared a manuscript containing Hitchiti notes and vocabulary (Haas 1973: 1214). Some of Haas' material on Hitchiti verb inflection has been published (Haas 1946a). Sturtevant (1962) listed a few Hitchiti forms of Spanish origin he collected in 1950-53 in Florida (p. 51).

The Hitchiti language is undoubtedly extinct. Haas probably worked with the last speaker. Hitchiti was virtually extinct thirty years ago (Haas 1973:1211). Chafe (1962, 1965) has no entry for Hitchiti in his articles on present speakers of North American Indian languages.

Koasati

The Koasati are equated by Swanton (1946:145) with the Coste, Acoste, Costehe, and Acosta, names of tribes mentioned in the De Soto narratives and encountered by De Soto in northeastern Alabama on the Tennessee River. According to Swanton (1946:145), the Tennessee River was sometimes called "River of the Cussatees". By 1686 a portion of the Koasati had settled just west of the junction of the Coosa and Tallapoosa rivers, "where most of the tribe soon gathered" (Swanton 1946:145). A reminder of their presence near where these two rivers join to form the Alabama River is the community Coosada, about ten miles north of Montgomery, Alabama. In 1763 part of the tribe moved from here to western Alabama and settled on the Tombigbee River, but soon returned because of maltreatment by the neighboring Choctaw. Between 1793 and 1795 a band of Koasati moved to Louisiana and settled on Red River. The Koasati who remained in Alabama were eventually absorbed by the Creek tribes. Those who went west settled in several places and remained in no place for very long. In 1805 there were Koasati on the Sabine River 80 miles south of Natchitoches, Louisiana (Swanton 1907a:719). By 1820 some Koasati had settled on the Trinity and Neches rivers in Texas. Some of the latter united with the Alabama after having suffered severely from pestilence (Swanton 1946:145). A few of the Texas Koasati returned to Louisiana to join those of their tribe who had remained.

Descendants of the Louisiana Koasati live at the present time about three miles north of Elton, Louisiana, having come to this location about 1884 (Jacobson 1960:106). The Koasati in Texas live on the eastern side of the Alabama-Coushatta reservation between Woodville and Livingston.[54]

General Albert Pike seems to have been, about 1861, the first collector of a Koasati vocabulary, which consisted of some fifteen hundred to seventeen hundred words (Pilling 1889:69). Pilling does not say, but Pike's vocabulary most likely was taken from a Koasati speaker who had remained with the Creeks in Alabama and had moved west with them to Indian Territory. Albert S. Gatschet at some time before 1884 collected a few Koasati terms at the Indian school at Carlisle, Pennsylvania (Gatschet 1884:57). In 1885 Gatschet located a Koasati speaker, an old woman, at Muskogee, Oklahoma, and obtained from her Koasati words, phrases, and sentences (Pilling 1889:38). John R. Swanton obtained ethnographic and linguistic material on Koasati, probably in 1911-12 (Swanton 1928a:31-32), and published some Koasati terms of relationship (1928a:89-90). Goddard (1914) stated that Swanton obtained 100 pages of Koasati texts (p. 587).

No further work was done on Koasati until 1934 when Mary R. Haas recorded vocabularies in Texas and, with Morris Swadesh, in Louisiana (Freeman 1966:211, Haas 1973:1214). Haas in 1938-39 collected considerable material on Koasati (Haas 1941d:41, fn. 4). In her article on the classification of the Muskogean languages Haas (1941d) cited numerous Koasati forms. Considerable material on the language was given by Haas (1944) in her article on men's and women's speech in Koasati. Koasati forms were cited in other articles by Haas (e. g., 1947, 1950a, 1956). Much of Haas' Koasati material has not been published.

Chafe (1962:166) estimated there are from one hundred to two hundred speakers of Koasati of all ages in Texas and Louisiana.[55]

Mikasuki

An early notice of the Mikasuki is by Benjamin Hawkins in 1799 when he listed them as one of seven Seminole towns in the country bordering the Gulf of Mexico (Hawkins 1848:25). Hawkins (1848:26) wrote that these people abandoned their former towns and moved to this region on account of the abundance of game, mildness of the climate, and richness of the soil. The Mikasuki were located in 1799 near the lake which bears their name (Swanton 1946:150), Lake Miccosukee, about twenty miles northeast of Tallahassee, Florida. The Mikasuki suffered heavily during the First Seminole War, 1817-18. When Andrew Jackson and his men approached, as many as were able to do so abandoned their houses, crops, and livestock and fled, some west toward Pensacola, some east to the Alachua region, and many southward into the peninsula (Sturtevant 1971:106). During the Second Seminole War, which began in 1835 and ended seven years later with a truce, not a treaty, the Mikasuki, and other Indians, underwent even greater hardships. Large numbers were killed in battle. The Indians who surrendered or were captured were deported to Indian Territory. Those who were successful in concealing themselves from the American army by retreating into the swamps of southern Florida were finally left in peace after the Third Seminole War, 1858-59, during which some twenty

Indians in the Big Cypress Swamp area were killed and 240 were deported (Sturtevant 1971:110-11).[56]

The first vocabulary of Mikasuki, identified as such, was recorded in Washington, D. C., by Buckingham Smith, who took down also a Seminole vocabulary from a Mikasuki member of a Seminole delegation from Arkansas.[57] The two vocabularies were published (Smith 1866a:239-43) along with a short vocabulary of Hitchiti recorded by Gallatin and Hitchiti numerals taken down by Captain Casey in Tampa (Smith 1866a:239). Smith's (1866a) vocabularies were reprinted in 1877 and 1880 (Pilling 1889:85). The Mikasuki delegate gave Smith his version of the Lord's Prayer, written by him in Mikasuki, which Smith sent to George Gibbs "to be verified" and which, upon being rewritten and partially translated by Gibbs, was published by Smith (1866b).

William C. Sturtevant spent 18 months in field work among the Mikasuki and Seminole in 1950-53. Sturtevant has published nothing specifically on the language, but often has cited Mikasuki words in his articles (e. g., 1954, 1971). John David West of the Summer Institute of Linguistics spent nine months of each year from 1955 to 1959 on Big Cypress Reservation in Florida working on the Mikasuki language and published an article on Mikasuki phonology (1962). West has recently returned to resume his work on the Mikasuki language (personal communication). Martha Hardeman-de-Bautista and her students at the University of Florida worked with a Mikasuki speaker in 1973 (personal communication from Roger W. Cole).

Chafe (1962:167) listed approximately seven hundred Mikasuki speakers of all ages in Florida. West (1962:77) wrote there were about seven hundred and fifty Mikasuki speakers who live mainly on the Dania and Big Cypress Reservations and in small groups in the Everglades west of Miami. The latter comprises "the Miccosukee Reservation which consists of scattered plots along U. S. Highway 41, called the Tamiami Trail by the Indians (Garbarino 1972:1).[58]

Mobilian

There were in the Southeast several languages which served as media of communication among tribes who spoke mutually unintelligible languages. One was Creek, which was spoken as a second language by tribes of non-Creek origin in the Creek Confederation. This fact was noted by Adair (1775: 267), who stated that the remains of seven nations living within six miles of the "late Alebahma garrison [Fort Toulouse at the junction of the Coosa and Tallapoosa rivers]" understood Creek, in addition to their own languages. Beverley (1705) wrote that the tribes of Virginia had a "general Language" which they used for purposes of intercommunication, "as Latin is [used] in most parts of Europe, and Lingua Franca quite thro the Levant" (p. 24, Book 3). This general language, according to Beverley, was "that of the Occaneeches" (p. 24, Book 3), who lived in central Virginia near the North Carolina line.[59] The Tuscarora language, according to Lawson (1709), was understood by several tribes in eastern North Carolina. Lawson wrote that "the most powerful Nation of these Savages scorns to treat or trade with any others (of few Numbers and less Power) in any other Tongue but their own, which serves for the Lingua of the Country, with which we travel and deal; as for Example, we see that the Tuskeruro's are most numerous in North-Carolina, therefore their Tongue is understood by some in every Town of all the Indians near us" (p. 225). Le Page du Pratz (1758) observed that the "Cadodaquioux" and the "Nactchitoches" have "une Langue particuliere; cependant il n'y a point de villages dans ces deux Nations, où il n'y ait quelqu'un qui parle la Langue Tchicacha, comme dans toutes les autres Nations de la Louisiane; on a nomme la Langue vulgaire; elle est dans cette Province ce qu'est la Langue Francque dans le Levant" (p. 242, vol. 2). Le Page du Pratz wrote that the Taensa were a branch of the Natchez and "ont conservé leur Langue naturelle, quoiqu'ils parlent tous la langue Tchicacha corrompue, que nos François nomment la Langue Mobilienne" (1758:219, vol. 2). As for the Choctaw, "ils ont conservé leur Langue en partie, dans laquelle ils entremêlent quelques mots de la Langue Tchicacha; quand ils m'ont parlé, c'étoit en cette derniere Langue" (Le Page du Pratz 1758:219, vol. 2).[60] Sibley (1832:724-25) listed eight tribes in Louisiana which spoke, in addition to their own languages, "Mobilian, which is spoken by all the Indians, from the east side of the Mississippi" (p. 724). The tribes named by Sibley as speaking Mobilian are: Boluscas [Biloxi], Apalachies, Alabamas, Pakanas, Tunicas, Pascagoulas, Tenisaws [Taensa], and Chactoos [Chatot].[61]

That the lingua franca which developed in the lower Mississippi Valley region was based on a language of the Western division of Muskogean (Haas 1941d:54) is evidence that Choctaw or Choctaw-like languages, including Chickasaw, were prestigious and widespread in the region. It has been called "the Chicasa trade language" (Gatschet 1884:96) and categorically stated that the "Chicasa language served as a medium of commercial and tribal intercourse to all the nations inhabiting the shores of the... Lower Mississippi river" (Gatschet 1884:95), although there is no evidence that the lingua franca derived from the speech of the Chickasaw tribe. It is possible that the trade language had its origin in the numerous Choctaw dialects spoken south of the Chickasaw. That the French called the common language Mobilian is an indication that it was similar to, although not necessarily identical to, the language of the Mobile tribe which lived on Mobile Bay. The language was used by whites, as well as by Indians. Woodward (1859), writing from Wheeling, Louisiana, in 1858, said "There is yet a language the Texas Indians call the Mobilian tongue, that has been the trading language of almost all the tribes that have inhabited the country. I know white men that now speak it. There is a man now living near me that is fifty years of age, raised in Texas, that speaks the language well. It is a mixture of Creek, Choctaw, Chickasay, Netches and Apelash" (p. 79). According to Gatschet (1884), the language "adopted a few terms from northern languages" (p. 96).[62] Swanton (1911:32) in 1908 recorded at Livingston, Texas, nine words from two brothers of Biloxi and Pascagoula parentage, words which, according to Swanton, may be Pascagoula, but more probably belong to the Mobilian trade language.

Having heard from Mary R. Haas and from Claude Medford that there were people on the Alabama-Coushatta Reservation in Texas and among the Koasati of Louisiana who still spoke the Mobilian trade language, I took the opportunity to search out these speakers in the summer of 1970, with the help of Mr. Medford. I recorded a few Mobilian words in Texas from Mrs. Maggie Poncho, an Alabama lady of about eighty years of age. In Louisiana, near Elton, I discovered three people who knew varying amounts of the language. The person who knew the most was Mrs. Arzelie Langley, a Choctaw lady over one hundred years of age who had married a Koasati. Mrs. Langley spoke no English and was almost deaf. It was necessary to communicate with her through an interpreter. Mrs. Langley spoke alternately Choctaw, Koasati, and Mobilian, being well aware of the similarity of Mobilian to Choctaw, which fact she pointed out.[63] I recorded on tape the entire session with Mrs. Langley and later attempted with the aid of Koasati speakers to extract the Mobilian from the Choctaw and Koasati, a task not yet completed. Another person who remembered a large number of words and short phrases was Leonard Lavan, a Negro man in his late seventies who had lived for many years among the Koasati. The third person who remembered a few Mobilian words was a white man, Davis La Fleur, about eighty years of age. Mr. La Fleur had learned to speak "the Indian language" as a young man "over 60 years ago" when he worked with his father who operated a sawmill and employed Indians. All the Mobilian material was turned over to Dr. Haas who examined it and wrote a paper on Mobilian for this volume.[64]

Seminole

The Seminole Indians, who now live in southern Florida and in Oklahoma, are descendants of several tribes of the Creek Confederation, whose nucleus consisted of the Oconee Indians living on the Oconee River in Georgia about 1695-1715 (Swanton 1946:181). The Oconee moved to the Lower Creek country about 1715. Between 1740 and 1750 the Oconee and other tribes, including some Hitchiti, moved into upper central Florida. The dominant language of these groups in Florida was Hitchiti (Sturtevant 1971:103).[65] After the Creek War of 1813-14 many Creek-speaking refugees joined these groups in northern Florida, having come mainly from the Upper Creek towns. As a result of the Seminole Wars of 1817-18 and 1835-42, the greater part of these Florida Indians, which were called Seminole, were removed to Indian Territory, just west of the Creeks. Those who refused to make the journey west retreated into the swamps of southern Florida, where they and their descendants have since remained.[66]

The Indians of southern Florida speak two languages, Creek and Mikasuki (West 1962:77). The Seminole Indians "in Oklahoma speak Creek for the most part, but a very few also understand the Hitchiti tongue" (Swanton 1946:182). Haas (1945) does not consider Seminole a separate language, but only the name for a group "who broke away from the main body of the Creeks in the eighteenth century" (p. 69, fn. 2). Thus, in linguistic usage, Seminole is the name of one of the Creek dialects and, for this reason, does not merit the rank of a separate language. "The distinction between... Creek and Seminole is of a political rather than of a linguistic order" (Haas 1941d: 42).

Pilling (1889:82) lists twelve vocabularies and word lists of Seminole, several of which are taken from earlier publications and are not original. The first Seminole vocabulary seems to be one collected by an unnamed traveler and published in 1822 (Pilling 1889:64).[67] Another Seminole vocabulary was collected by an unknown lieutenant in the Seminole War and published in a sketch of the war in 1836 (Pilling 1889:83). In 1837 a glossary of about one hundred and fifty Seminole words was published in a book describing the Florida territory (Pilling 1889:93).[68] Buckingham Smith (1866a) published a list of Seminole, along with Hitchiti and Mikasuki, words taken down by him in Washington from members of a Seminole delegation, some of which were reprinted by Gatschet (1884) in his "comparative table" of Muskogean languages (p. 56).[69] Francis Wilson procured a vocabulary of Seminole in 1889 from a pupil at Carlisle, Pennsylvania (Pilling 1889:95). Mary R. Haas collected linguistic material in Seminole in Oklahoma in 1938-39 (Haas 1941d:41, fn. 4). According to Haas (1973:1216), William C. Sturtevant has collected vocabulary materials among the Florida Seminole.[70]

According to Chafe (1962:168) there are approximately three hundred speakers of all ages of Seminole, the "Florida dialect of Creek". The Florida Seminole live on the Brighton Reservation in south Florida northwest of Lake Okeechobee (Garbarino 1972:1; West 1962:77). The Oklahoma Seminole, of whom there were 2,070 in 1950, live in Seminole County, Oklahoma (Wright 1951:228).

SIOUAN

The Siouan languages east of the Mississippi River for which we have linguistic material were all in the Southeast. They are: Biloxi and Ofo in Mississippi, Catawba in the Carolinas, Woccon in North Carolina, and Tutelo in Virginia. All are now extinct. It is probable that several other tribes in Virginia and the Carolinas, such as the Occaneechi, Saponi, Santee, and Sewee, also spoke Siouan languages. However, arguments in favor of their Siouan linguistic affinity cannot establish such a connection in view of the absence of specimens of their languages. Siouan tribes west of the Mississippi probably migrated there from the east, perhaps from the Ohio Valley. Legends of the western Siouan tribes support the theory of an eastern origin. Linguistic support for this theory is the relatively close relationship of Tutelo to the western Siouan languages and the even closer relationship of Tutelo to Biloxi and Ofo. The Biloxi and Ofo tribes may have come south by way of the Mississippi and Ohio rivers.[71] A western Siouan language, Quapaw, was spoken in Arkansas.

Quapaw is very close to the languages of four other tribes: Omaha, Ponca, Osage, and Kansa, once spoken to the northwest of the Quapaw in the central plains. Dorsey (1885:919, 1890:xv) is responsible for the term Ȼegiha, later written Dhegiha,[72] as the name for this linguistic group, as well as the name of the language of the Omaha and Ponca tribes. Dorsey (1885) published comparative vocabularies of four Siouan languages: Dakota, Ȼegiha (Ponca, Kansa, Osage), Čiwere (Iowa, Oto, Missouri), and Hotcañgara (Winnebago).[73] According to Fletcher and La Flesche (1911), the Ȼegiha "languages as yet have hardly differentiated into distinct dialects" (p. 35). Fletcher and La Flesche (1911) wrote also that "the five cognate tribes... bear a strong resemblance to one another, not only in language but in tribal organization and religious rites" (p. 34). Voegelin (1941b:25-26) considered the languages of the five tribes as more or less dialects of one language, but quoted Fortune (1932:9), who wrote that Osage, Kansa, and Quapaw are dialectally different from the language of the Omaha and Ponca, "who speak the same language". Wolff (1950) took note of the possibility that mutual intelligibility may not exist between members of the group, but treated them as dialects rather than separate languages (p. 64) in his series of articles on comparative Siouan (1950, 1951b). Wolff noted the importance, from a comparative viewpoint, of phonological differences which occur in Osage and joined Omaha with Ponca as one language (1950: 64). Using what he called the "ask the informant method", Wolff (1952) discovered that "speakers of Osage consider Kansa completely intelligible, though somewhat 'faster' than Osage; Omaha and Ponca barely intelligible but containing a small percentage of 'Osage' words; Quapaw completely unintelligible and 'very different' "(p. 63).

As noted by Siebert (1945:100), Lewis H. Morgan (1870:54) in suggesting a Siouan connection for Catawba was the first to propose the presence of Siouan peoples on the Atlantic seaboard. Adelung and Vater in 1816, according to Siebert (1945:100), were the first to note the relationship between Catawba and Woccon.[74] In the same year that Morgan's article appeared, Horatio Hale collected a vocabulary from an old man of the Tutelo tribe in Ontario, a tribe which had moved northward from Virginia in the mid-eighteenth century. An examination of this vocabulary showed clearly that Tutelo was not Iroquoian, as had been assumed (Gallatin 1836:81), but was related to the language of the Dakota tribes of the plains. The discovery was announced to the scholarly world in 1871 (Anderson 1872) and later demonstrated by a comparative vocabulary (Hale 1883c:36-45).

In 1886 Albert S. Gatschet located a remnant of the Biloxi tribe in Louisiana and, upon obtaining a vocabulary of the language, established the presence of a Siouan tribe in the Gulf region. John R. Swanton in 1908 found yet another Siouan language in the Gulf region when he collected material from the last speaker of Ofo. C. F. Voegelin (1939) compared Ofo and Biloxi, setting up sound correspondences between them "which indicate that the Ofo and Biloxi at one time spoke a single language" (p. 23), and noted that Ofo appeared to be the more archaic (p. 24). Voegelin (1941a) stated that on the basis of linguistic evidence Tutelo, Biloxi, and Ofo form one group which he proposed calling Ohio Valley Siouan, with the implication that the group dispersed from the Ohio Valley (p. 247). Holmer (1947) compared Ofo with other Siouan languages and noted its importance to comparative Siouan. Siebert (1945) demonstrated conclusively the Siouan affinity of Catawba. In a series of four articles on comparative Siouan, Wolff (1950, 1951b) affirmed Voegelin's grouping of Biloxi, Ofo, and Tutelo (1950:64-65), illustrated the close relationship of the Ȼegiha languages (1950:63-64), and made numerous reconstructions of Proto-Siouan from a comparison of the various Siouan languages. Wolff (1950) stated that Catawba was either strongly divergent Siouan or a remnant of a larger pre-Siouan stock (p. 66). G. H. Matthews dealt with the reconstruction of Proto-Siouan (1958, 1959, 1970) but omitted "any consideration of Catawba" (1970:98). According to Haas (1969c:286, fn. 6), T. S. Kaufman prepared a master list of Siouan sound correspondences. Haas (1968) compared Biloxi recordings made by her and Morris Swadesh in 1934 with Dorsey's Biloxi recordings and presented about thirty reconstructed forms of Ohio Valley Siouan (Biloxi, Ofo, and Tutelo), which she proposed be renamed Southeastern Siouan (p. 84). Haas (1969c) has made a few Proto-Siouan reconstructions (pp. 289-90). Other Proto-Siouan reconstructions remain unpublished (Haas 1973:1235).

Biloxi

The Biloxi lived on, and to the east of, the Pascagoula River in southern Mississippi in the early eighteenth century. The first direct notice of the tribe is that by Iberville, who found them near Biloxi Bay in 1699 (Biloxi 1907:147). The Biloxi moved to the west shore of Mobile Bay in 1702. In 1784 there was a Biloxi village in Louisiana on the west side of the Mississippi. According to Sibley (1832:724) some Biloxi came west with French families from near Pensacola about 1763, when it was taken by the English, settling first at Avoyelles, then moving to Rapide Bayou, about forty miles from Natchitoches. In 1828 there were 20 Biloxi families on the Neches River in Texas (Biloxi 1907:147). In 1829 about sixty-five Biloxi were living with the Caddo and a few other tribes on Red River, in Louisiana (Biloxi 1907: 147). In 1846 a Biloxi camp was found in Texas on Little River, a tributary of the Brazos (Biloxi 1907:147). In 1886 Gatschet visited the Biloxi living in Avoyelles Parish and reported that there were Biloxi living among the Choctaw and Caddo (Biloxi 1907:147). In 1892 Dorsey found about twelve Biloxi near Lecompte in Rapides Parish, Louisiana, but none in Avoyelles (Biloxi 1907:147). A few Indians of part Biloxi blood live among the Tunica near Marksville, Louisiana and probably in other places of Louisiana and southeastern Texas.[75]

The Biloxi were presumed to be Muskogean and it was with some surprise that Gatschet discovered, in 1886, the language to be Siouan (Dorsey and

Swanton 1912:9). In the fall of 1886 Gatschet was in Rapides Parish, Louisiana, near Lecompte, and located a small band of Biloxi. Gatschet collected a vocabulary of their language and submitted it to James Owen Dorsey, the chief authority of the Siouan languages. Dorsey visited the Biloxi in January and February 1892 and again in February 1893, during which time he reviewed and corrected Gatschet's material and collected additional material, including several texts. Dorsey's Biloxi material was the basis for his vice-presidential address before Section H of the American Association for the Advancement of Science in August 1893. The address, which gave a brief sketch of the Biloxi Indians and the grammar of their language, was published in the proceedings of the association the following year (Dorsey 1894). Dorsey died of typhoid fever on February 4, 1895,[76] two years to the month after his last visit to the Biloxi. After Dorsey's death John R. Swanton edited Dorsey's Biloxi material and published it in 1912 (Dorsey and Swanton 1912). In September 1934 Mary R. Haas and Morris Swadesh made a trip through southern Louisiana, east Texas, and eastern Oklahoma in a search for speakers of languages of remnant groups of Indians reported in this area in the latter part of the nineteenth century (Haas 1968:77). Haas and Swadesh succeeded in finding one woman in Port Arthur, Texas, who remembered a few words of Biloxi. They were able to obtain from her 54 Biloxi words (Haas 1968:78-80). So far as is known, the Biloxi language is now extinct.

Catawba

According to Mooney (1907c:214), the first notice of the Catawba is probably that of Vandera in 1579, who calls them Issa, in his narrative of Pardo's expedition. The Catawba by all accounts were a populous and powerful tribe in the piedmont region of upper South Carolina and adjacent North Carolina. Their towns and villages were centered on the Catawba River and its tributaries southeast of present-day Charlotte, North Carolina. They were visited by John Lawson, who passed through their country in 1701 (Lawson 1709). The Catawba were allies with the Yamasee in the Yamasee War in 1715. With this exception they were uniformly friendly to the English and, later, to the Americans. However, the Catawba were constantly at war with the Cherokee and northern tribes such as the Iroquois, Shawnee, Delaware, and other tribes of the Ohio Valley. The northern tribes made long journeys into the Carolinas to attack them and the Catawba retaliated by sending parties north into Ohio and Pennsylvania. The ceaseless attacks by their enemies reduced their numbers steadily. Several epidemics of smallpox and other diseases introduced by the whites accelerated their destruction. An epidemic of smallpox in 1759 destroyed about half the Catawba tribe.

The Catawba were assigned a reservation, confirmed by law in 1763, of some 15 miles square on the Catawba River in York and Lancaster counties, South Carolina. When British troops approached in 1780 during the American Revolution, the Catawba fled into Virginia but returned later and established themselves in two villages on opposite sides of the Catawba River. At the end of the war white men began to enter their country and encroach on their lands. In 1840 the Catawba signed a treaty with South Carolina ceding their lands to the state and agreeing to move to Haywood County, North Carolina. But North Carolina refused to sell them lands and after 18 months in that state, most returned to their old home where they were able to secure a reservation of 800 acres. Not all returned to the Catawba River. Some went to live with the Cherokee in western North Carolina, although many who did so eventually rejoined the tribe in South Carolina. One body of Catawba went to the Choctaw Nation in Indian Territory and settled near Sculleyville. A few families settled in other parts of Indian Territory. Some Catawba ended up in Arkansas, Utah, and Colorado, where they were gradually absorbed into the local Indian and white populations. A few Catawba may still be living with the Cherokee. The remainder live on their lands near Rock Hill, South Carolina.[77]

Barton (1798), according to Siebert (1945:100), was apparently the first to offer a specimen of Catawba.[78] The next Catawba vocabulary was collected in 1835 by J. L. Miller (Gallatin 1836:88) and published by Gallatin (1836) in his comparative vocabularies (pp. 307-67). Oscar M. Lieber (1858) collected a Catawba vocabulary in 1856 from his camp-servant and published it along with some grammatical notes on the Catawba language. Albert S. Gatschet visited the Catawba in November 1881 and collected texts, sentences, and about fifteen hundred words (Powell 1884:xxii). Gatschet (1900) published 19 years later a brief sketch of the language. Gatschet (1902) published a brief article on place and river names of the

Catawba River basin. In 1913 Frank G. Speck collected Catawba texts from a Catawba woman married to a Cherokee and living among the Cherokee in North Carolina (Speck 1934:x). The same year Speck (1913) published some of these texts, with interlinear and free translations, and their analyses in the form of grammatical notes. John R. Swanton was on the Catawba reservation in South Carolina in 1918 and recorded grammatical and lexical material in Catawba (Speck 1934:x), about two dozen words of which he published in his "Catawba notes" (1918). According to Speck (1934:xi), Truman Michelson attempted field work on Catawba. Speck returned in 1921 to resume his work with the Catawba woman in North Carolina. Additional trips were made by Speck in 1922 and 1923 and included visits to the Catawba reservation in South Carolina. Between 1928 and 1931 Speck made several trips to the Catawba reservation to work with the few remaining speakers of the Catawba language (Speck 1934:xi). Speck (1934) published the Catawba texts he had collected, with interlinear and free translation. Speck and Schaeffer (1942) coauthored an article on Catawba kinship and social organization and presented 40 Catawba kinship terms (pp. 556-57). Speck (1946) published another short Catawba text, with translation but no analysis, which he collected in 1944.

Morris Swadesh visited the Catawba in 1937 (Swadesh 1948:233) and collected texts, word lists, and paradigms (Freeman 1966:93). Swadesh's Catawba material remains unpublished. Raven I. McDavid, Jr., collected considerable Catawba material in 1940 and 1941. McDavid's material has not been published.[79] Frank T. Siebert, Jr., in 1941 worked with three Catawba speakers, "the only Catawbas who retain knowledge of their language" (Siebert 1945:211, fn. 1). Siebert (1945) published some of the results of his work and demonstrated convincingly a Siouan connection for Catawba. G. Hubert Matthews and Red Thunder Cloud (1967) published an article on Catawba, based on Red Thunder Cloud's knowledge of the Catawba language.

So far as is known, the Catawba language is extinct.

Ofo

The Ofo, or Ofogoula, were first mentioned, according to Swanton (1909: 478), by Iberville in 1699 in the journal of his first expedition to Louisiana.[80] Iberville did not visit the Ofo, but was told that there were villages of this tribe, and of other tribes, "on the river of the Chicachas, [the Yazoo River]" (Swanton 1909:478). They were mentioned by Pénicaut in 1700 and were visited the same year by the Jesuit Gravier, who referred to them under their Tunica name, Ounspik. The Ofo were spoken of by Charlevoix in 1721 and by La Harpe in 1722 (Swanton 1909:479). The Ofo were mentioned by Le Page du Pratz, who called them "Oufé Ogoulas, or the Nation of the Dog" (Swanton 1909:479-80).[81] According to Swanton (1910:108), at the outbreak of the Natchez war the Yazoo and Koroa tried to persuade the Ofo, their neighbors on the Yazoo, to join them in fighting the French alongside the Natchez. The Ofo refused and descended the Mississippi to live with the Tunica, where they remained until they disappeared from history. Hutchins stated in 1784 that the Ofo had a small village on the west bank of the Mississippi, eight miles above Pointe Coupée, Louisiana (Swanton 1910:108).

It was believed that the Ofo spoke a Muskogean language. Swanton (1910) stated in the Handbook of American Indians: "Their language being similar to that of the Choctaw, it is probable that the remnant has become confused with that tribe" (p. 108). Over two years before the Handbook appeared, Swanton himself discovered that the language of the Ofo was not Choctaw. During a visit to the Tunica Indians near Marksville, Louisiana, in May 1907, Swanton made inquiries about tribes known to have been associated with the Tunica, in particular, about the Ofogoula, who, along with the Tunica, had formerly lived on the Yazoo River in Mississippi, about twelve miles upstream from the Mississippi. Swanton met with little success in his inquiries. He succeeded in eliciting from a Tunica informant a word which he believed was the Tunica term for the Ofogoula. In May 1908 Swanton was again with the Tunica. His interpreter, whom he was using for the purpose of communicating through French to a Tunica informant, revealed that the name of her language was Ofo. Swanton, as soon as convenient, obtained a few words from his interpreter's language and discovered that the language was Siouan. In December 1908 he interviewed the Ofo speaker more carefully and collected all the words she was able to remember.

Swanton learned that she had not spoken her language since she was a girl of seventeen, when all her people died, and that her grandmother had told her that the name of her tribe was Ofo. On the basis of this information, Swanton shortened the name of the tribe and language from Ofogoula to Ofo. Swanton (1909) reported upon the details of his discovery of the last speaker of Ofo and presented a short vocabulary of the language (p. 485). Swanton later published all his Ofo material in the same volume with Dorsey's Biloxi materials (Dorsey and Swanton 1912).[82]

Quapaw

The Quapaw, also known as Arkansa, were living near the mouth of the Arkansas River in the late seventeenth and early eighteenth centuries.[83] If the Quapaw were the same as the Capaha encountered by De Soto in 1541, they apparently had moved down the Mississippi during the intervening century and a half.[84] The traditional home of the Quapaw was said by them to have been on the Ohio River. The name Quapaw derives from a word meaning 'with the current' or 'downstream', indicating a movement to the south along the Mississippi, as opposed to Omaha which signifies 'against the current' or 'upstream' (Fletcher and La Flesche 1911:36).

Soon after the Louisiana Purchase, the rich bottomlands of the Quapaw were wanted by settlers. In 1818 the Quapaw exchanged their lands between the Arkansas, Canadian, and Red rivers for a tract south of the Arkansas and Washita rivers. They were forced in 1824 to relinquish their newly acquired lands to the government and to move to a small tract in southeastern Kansas and northeastern Oklahoma (Fletcher and La Flesche 1911:67).[85] In 1867 the Quapaw ceded their lands in Kansas and part of their lands in Oklahoma. In 1877 the Ponca were brought to live with them. When the Ponca moved to their own reservation, most of the Quapaw accompanied them (Swanton 1946: 176). Some Quapaw settled also on the Osage reservation (Dorsey 1897:230).

The first Quapaw vocabulary apparently was one collected by General George Izard in 1827 and used by Gallatin (1836) in his comparative vocabularies (pp. 307-67).[86] The next Quapaw vocabulary was collected in 1882 by Lewis Francis Hadley (Pilling 1887:30). At about the same time (November 1882 to February 1883), James Owen Dorsey "was in Indian Territory, collecting similar [to Omaha and Ponca] information in the cognate

Ȼegiha dialects, Kansas, Osage, and Quapaw" (Pilling 1887:25). According to Powell (1887), "Rev. J. Owen Dorsey was engaged during the year [1883-84] on an English-Winnebago vocabulary; a Kwapa-English vocabulary; Osage and Kansa texts, local and personal names; and the socialization of the Dakota" (p. xxxii). Except for a few Quapaw village names and names of Quapaw gentes (Dorsey 1897:229-30 [published posthumously]), the only Quapaw material published by Dorsey are the "principal kinship terms" and numerals 1-12, 19, 100, and 1,000, which appear in the preface by Dorsey (pp. xviii-xxi, xxiii-xxix) to Riggs (1893). Swanton (1923:37) listed 48 Quapaw forms in a comparative table of words from several Siouan languages. Swanton did not give the source for the Quapaw words, but they were probably taken from Dorsey's manuscripts in the Bureau of American Ethnology. Wolff (1950, 1951b) cited Quapaw forms in his articles on comparative Siouan but did not identify their source. Frank T. Siebert, Jr., collected a vocabulary of Quapaw in Oklahoma in 1940 (Siebert 1967b:59).

Very little work seems to have been done on Quapaw, or on Kansa, both of which may still be spoken.[87]

Tutelo

When first encountered by whites in 1671, the Tutelo were living on the Roanoke River in Virginia (Hale 1883c:2).[88] In 1701 Lawson (1709:47) referred to some Tutelo who had come "down from the Westward Mountains, to the *Saponas*" to ask for captured Seneca warriors, in order to return the prisoners to the Seneca tribe in gratitude for civil treatment previously accorded the Tutelo by the Seneca. After the Tuscarora war with the Carolina settlers, which began in 1711 and ended in 1712 with the complete defeat of the Tuscarora and their allies, the Tutelo and Sapona, who had suffered greatly in the war, decided to move northward and place themselves under the protection of the Six Nations, as the major portion of the Tuscarora had done earlier to become the sixth nation of the Iroquois confederacy. By 1745 the Tutelo tribe had congregated at what was then Shamokin, Pennsylvania, where were also gathered fragments of Nanticoke, Delaware, and other tribes. In 1750 the Iroquois decided to admit the Tutelo and the Nanticoke to full honors of the confederacy. The Tutelo were considered the special friends and allies of the Cayuga and established themselves near the Cayuga at the south end of Cayuga Lake in New York. When the Iroquois confederacy was destroyed in 1779 by General Sullivan, many of the members of the broken tribes went to Canada, including the greater part of the Cayuga, who were accompanied by their Tutelo friends. The Cayuga and Tutelo settled on Grand River in Ontario. The Tutelo located their town in an area, near Brantford, which brought them into direct contact with white settlements. Two visitations of the Asiatic cholera, in 1832 and in 1848, virtually annihilated the Tutelo tribe. The few survivors fled their town and took refuge among the Cayuga.

When Horatio Hale visited the Cayuga in 1870, he found among them only one full-blooded Tutelo, by the name of Nikonha, who was married to a Cayuga. Hale acquired from Nikonha a vocabulary of nearly one hundred words, plus a few more words on a second visit. Hale's vocabulary of Tutelo "showed beyond question that the language was totally distinct from the Huron-Iroquois tongues, and that it was closely allied to the languages of the Dacotan family" (Hale 1883c: 10). Hale sent accounts of his discovery and lists of Tutelo words to Rev. Joseph Anderson. Anderson (1872) presented extracts from Hale's letters on the Tutelo tribe and language in a paper before the American Philological Association in 1871. After Nikonha's death in 1871, Hale returned to the Indian Reserve and obtained from several Indians ("children of Tutelo mothers by Iroquois fathers") "a sufficient number of words and phrases of the language to give a good idea of its grammatical framework" (Hale 1883c: 10, 11). Hale (1883c) presented a detailed description of what was known of the history of the Tutelo tribe and provided a sketch of Tutelo grammar and a comparative vocabulary of Tutelo, Dakota, and Hidatsa.[89]

In July 1907 Leo J. Frachtenberg was on the Grand River Reservation and collected a brief Tutelo vocabulary from an old Tutelo woman with the aid of a Cayuga interpreter. Edward Sapir in August 1911 obtained a few Tutelo words from the Cayuga interpreter Frachtenberg had used with the old Tutelo woman. Sapir (1913) and Frachtenberg (1913) presented their short Tutelo word lists without discussion or analysis.

Woccon

Practically all that is known of the Woccon was written by John Lawson who visited them about 1701 in eastern North Carolina, probably on the Neuse River, "perhaps about the present Goldsboro, Wayne co." (Woccon 1910:967). Lawson, in his book published in London in 1709, wrote that the Woccon lived about two leagues from the Tuscarora and that "their Speech differs [from that of the Tuscarora] in every Word thereof, except one, which is Tsaure, Cockles, which is in both Tongues the same, and nothing else" (p. 231). Lawson (1709:234) listed the Woccon as having 120 "Fighting Men" in two towns with the names: Yupwauremau and Tooptatmeer. Nothing further is known of the Woccon except for incidental references in colonial documents, stating that the Woccon joined the Tuscarora against the whites in the war of 1711-13 (Woccon 1910:967-68).

Lawson (1709) took down 150 words in the Woccon language (pp. 225-230). There are no other known recordings of Woccon.

LANGUAGE ISOLATES

Atakapa

The Atakapa lived in the region bordering the Gulf coast of Louisiana and Texas, from Vermilion Bay, below Franklin, Louisiana, to about the Trinity River at Galveston Bay, Texas. Their name means 'man-eater' in Choctaw and was applied to them by the Muskogean tribes who were acquainted with their anthropophagous habits. The first white contact with the Atakapa was probably in 1703 when Bienville sent three men to discover what nations of Indians lived in that region of southern Louisiana. Two of the Frenchmen Bienville sent out returned to report that they had found seven different nations and that while among the last nation, that of the Atakapa, their comrade had been killed and eaten (Hewitt 1907:114).

The Atakapa were never a large tribe, in spite of the immense extent of their country. Swanton (1946:94) questioned whether there ever were as many as one thousand Atakapa. There were several bands of the Atakapa, who spoke at least three dialects. The easternmost band lived on Vermilion River and Bay, with their main village near Abbeville. From 1760 until about the time of the transfer of Louisiana to the United States, most of the Atakapa lands were sold to white settlers. Most of the eastern band moved further to the west, although there were still Atakapa in the Vermilion village in the early 1800's (Swanton 1911:361). Another Atakapa band had villages on Mermentou River and its branches, 25 to 30 miles east and southeast of Lake Charles. This was the westernmost band of the Eastern Atakapa. There were Atakapa living in this vicinity at least until 1836 (Swanton 1911:362). Some of these latter Eastern Atakapa went west after 1836 to live with the Calcasieu band. The Calcasieu band lived along the Calcasieu River near Lake Charles. These were the Western Atakapa. Most of the Atakapa who survived into the twentieth century belonged to the Calcasieu band. Survivors of the Atakapa who lived about Lake Charles were visited by Gatschet in 1885 and by Swanton in 1907 and 1908. Little is known of the Atakapa who lived farther to the west. According to Swanton (1911), it may be "that the Bidai, hitherto supposed to be of Caddoan stock, were affiliated with the Atakapa" (p. 363).

The first vocabulary of Atakapa was collected in 1721 by Jean Bérenger, who also recorded a Karankawa vocabulary. The vocabulary was of Akokisa, an Atakapa dialect, and contained 45 words which Bérenger took down from prisoners captured near Galveston Bay while they were making the voyage back to Louisiana. The document containing the two vocabularies lay undiscovered in the national archives in France until 1919, when it was published by Villiers du Terrage and Rivet (1919).[90] In addition to Akokisa, there were two other dialects of Atakapa: Eastern Atakapa and Western Atakapa.[91] Our knowledge of the eastern dialect is dependent on a vocabulary of 287 entries recorded in 1802 at the Attacapas Post (present-day Franklin, Louisiana) by Martin Duralde, or by someone from whom Duralde copied the entries (Gatschet and Swanton 1932:3). This vocabulary was published by Vater (1821:63-84) and in part by Gallatin (1836:307-67).

The bulk of the linguistic material on Atakapa, representing the western dialect and constituting over nine-tenths of the total, about two thousand words and a few texts, was collected by Albert S. Gatschet in 1885 at Lake Charles, Louisiana. John R. Swanton visited the Atakapa near Lake Charles in 1907 and 1908 and found there were nine people who still remembered something of their language (Swanton 1911:362) and collected a few words in Atakapa (Gatschet and Swanton 1932:5). Swanton examined all the

Atakapa manuscript material and published a sketch of Atakapa grammar along with an analyzed text (1929b) and, a few years later, a dictionary of Atakapa accompanied by the texts Gatschet had collected (Gatschet and Swanton 1932). Swanton (Gatschet and Swanton 1932) presented "all the Atakapa linguistic material now known to be in existence and, since no speakers of Atakapa remain and there is slight prospect of amplifications from manuscript sources, our appreciation of the language itself and its relations to other Indian tongues must rest upon this" (p. 7).

A few last words of Atakapa were taken down by Mary R. Haas and Morris Swadesh in September 1934 (Freeman 1966:80; Hymes 1971:240).

Chitimacha

When first encountered by the French about 1700, the Chitimacha were living in southern Louisiana on the shores of Grand Lake and the banks of Grand River (Gatschet 1907a:286). From almost the beginning of their contact with the French, the Chitimacha became engaged in protracted wars with them and with Indian tribes allied with the French. The Chitimacha were a great annoyance to the French settlers along the Mississippi. Peace was concluded between them and the French in 1718, after which the tribe dispersed. Some settled on Bayou La Fourche and as far north as present Plaquemine. Others settled on Bayou Teche (Swanton 1911:45, 1946:120). Very little is known of the history of the Bayou La Fourche band. According to Swanton (1946), "the last of the Mississippi band appear to have settled finally near Plaquemine, where a few years ago there was a single survivor" (p. 120). The descendants of the Bayou Teche band are now located at Charenton, Louisiana.[92] There may have been other tribes in southern Louisiana whose languages were close to Chitimacha. Swanton (1917-20:49) believed that the Washa and Chawasha tribes spoke languages related to Chitimacha.

The first record of linguistic material taken down in Chitimacha is a vocabulary obtained by Martin Duralde in 1802, along with an Atakapa vocabulary, at the Attacapas Post (now Franklin), Louisiana (Freeman 1966:109) and printed by Gallatin (1836:307-67) in his comparative vocabularies. Nothing more seems to have been collected in Chitimacha until 1881-82 when Albert S. Gatschet recorded material in the language. Gatschet recorded the material in December 1881 and January 1882 from an old Negro who had lived so long with the Chitimacha as to speak their language fluently (Swanton 1919a:10).[93] Gatschet (1883a) reported on the Chitimacha, presented about twenty Chitimacha words, and illustrated the process of compounding in the language. Swanton visited the Chitimacha in 1907 and in 1908 and went over all of Gatschet's material, making corrections, and collected texts and other material (Swanton 1919a:10). The Chitimacha materials collected by Gatschet and by Swanton were used by the latter in his comparative article on Tunica, Chitimacha, and Atakapa (Swanton 1919a). Morris Swadesh worked with the last two speakers of Chitimacha during the summers of 1932 and 1933, and for a shorter period in 1934 (Swadesh 1934b:345, fn. 2, 1948:230; Hymes 1971:240, fn. 18). Swadesh (1933) published an article on Chitimacha verbs of derogatory or abusive connotation. The next year Swadesh (1934b) wrote on Chitimacha phonemes. In another article which appeared earlier in 1934 Swadesh (1934a) treated briefly with Chitimacha phonemes. Swadesh (1937) dealt with Chitimacha long stops (p. 5). Haas (1939) made use of Swadesh's 1932 and 1933 Chitimacha material in her article "Natchez and Chitimacha clans and kinship terminology". Swadesh's (1946a) "Chitimacha" appeared in the collection of grammatical sketches of American Indian languages entitled "Linguistic structures of Native America". Swadesh (1946b, 1947) presented Chitimacha material in two articles comparing Atakapa and Chitimacha. Most of Swadesh's Chitimacha material remains in manuscript in the library of the American Philosophical Society (Freeman 1966:110).

Chitimacha is now extinct. Swadesh's main informant, Benjamin Paul, died in 1934. The only other person who could still speak the language, Delphine Ducloux, died in 1940 (Swadesh 1948:230). Swadesh (1948:231) reported that in 1934 there were a few other people who knew a few Chitimacha words. In the summer of 1969 I recorded 14 Chitimacha words from Mr. Emile Stouff, the tribal chairman.

Natchez

The first notices of the Natchez appeared in the accounts of La Salle's expedition of 1682.[94] The Natchez in the eighteenth century occupied eight or nine villages along St. Catherine's Creek east and south of present-day Natchez, Mississippi. The Natchez attracted much attention on account of their relatively populous towns and their proximity to the French settlements. The French regarded their religious customs, centering in a highly developed sun worship, with great interest. The early French writers of Louisiana have left detailed descriptions of their customs, religious practices, form of government, and accounts of French relations with the Natchez.[95]

The Natchez were engaged in three wars with the French, in 1716, 1722, and 1729. The last one, ending in 1731, proved fatal to the tribe. Not half the Natchez remained alive after the final battle in 1731 at Natchitoches, Louisiana. Those who were not killed when captured were sold into slavery. They could not return to their old home on the Mississippi (at Natchez), since the French had now occupied it. Nor could they take refuge with the tribes allied with the French, such as the Choctaw, Tunica, Caddo, Atakapa, and Quapaw. The smaller tribes nearby who would have been willing to give them asylum were in similar straits as the Natchez. The only recourse of the Natchez was to go to the tribes in the English interest, the Chickasaw, Creeks, and Cherokee, or to the English settlers in the Carolinas. In fact, some did go to the English. In 1736 a delegation of 26 Natchez applied to the government of South Carolina for permission to settle on the Savannah River. Permission apparently was given, for in 1744 the Natchez were mentioned, in connection with the Pedee, as having killed some Catawba in a drunken quarrel, as a result of which the Natchez and Pedee fled to the white settlements to escape Catawba vengeance (Mooney 1894:84). This Natchez group on the Savannah eventually moved north to join the Cherokee. Other Natchez bands also joined the Cherokee, having come by way of the Chickasaw, and settled in Tennessee. Some Natchez who were earlier with the Creeks in Alabama came from the south and joined the Cherokee. The Cherokee appear to have been especially receptive of the Natchez and to have regarded them as a race of wizards and conjurers (Mooney 1899:517). The greatest portion of the Natchez remnants probably joined and remained with the Creeks, going west with them when the Creeks left Alabama in 1832.

Many Natchez went to Indian Territory with the Cherokee at the final removal in 1838. Some Natchez remained behind and became intermixed with the eastern Cherokee in North Carolina. In 1890 Mooney (1899:518) found one full-blooded Natchez and several of mixed blood in North Carolina.[96]

The first vocabulary of Natchez of which we have record was written down by Albert Gallatin (Gallatin 1836:97) and appeared in his comparative vocabularies (1836:307-67). General Albert Pike collected a Natchez vocabulary about 1861 (Pilling 1889:69). A vocabulary collected by Mrs. A. E. W. Robertson (daughter of Rev. Samuel A. Worcester, missionary to the Cherokee) in 1873 was used by Daniel G. Brinton (1873), along with the Natchez vocabulary of Gallatin, in his paper attempting to show a relationship between Natchez and Creek. Albert S. Gatschet collected Natchez linguistic material in 1885 (Swanton 1907b:514, 1924-25:46).[97] John R. Swanton (1907b) in 1906 examined the material in the two longest vocabularies, those of Pike and of Gatschet (p. 514), and presented numerous Natchez forms and forms from several Muskogean languages as evidence of a relationship between Natchez and Muskogean. In 1907 Swanton went to Oklahoma and visited a band of Natchez who were living near Braggs, southeast of Muskogee, and discovered five persons who spoke the Natchez language. Swanton returned to Braggs in the fall of 1908 and recorded a number of pages of Natchez texts and other material (Swanton 1911:256-57). In the fall of 1915 Swanton collected 113 pages of Natchez texts from one of the three surviving speakers of the language (Hodge 1923:10). Swanton (1924-25) published a portion of his Natchez material in a second paper comparing Natchez with the Muskogean languages. Swanton (1928a:80-95) published some Natchez (and Muskogean) kinship terms. In 1934 Mary R. Haas visited the Natchez living near Braggs and found two speakers still living of those five found by Swanton in 1907 (Haas 1939:598). Using her Natchez material and Swadesh's Chitimacha material, Haas (1939) reported on the kinship terminology of Natchez and Chitimacha and provided new information on Natchez and Chitimacha clans. Haas (1956) described Natchez phonemes and phonological processes and cited Natchez forms in her article on Natchez and Muskogean.

So far as is known, no further field work has been done on Natchez and the language is undoubtedly extinct.

Timucua

The Timucua Indians were represented by about a half-dozen tribes who spoke dialects of the same language and who lived in the region extending from southeastern Georgia into Florida as far west as the Aucilla River, east of Tallahassee, and as far south as Tampa Bay on the Gulf coast and Cape Cañaveral on the Atlantic Ocean. The first white encounter with the Timucua was by Ponce de León in 1513 near present-day St. Augustine. In 1528 Pánfilo de Narváez went from Tampa Bay northward along the coast through Timucua country. In 1539 Hernando de Soto entered Florida at Tampa Bay and traveled north through Timucua lands by way of a more interior route before turning west just below the Georgia line.[98] In 1562-64 French Huguenots under Ribault and Laudonnière attempted settlements at the mouth of St. Johns River (east of Jacksonville) and became acquainted with Timucua tribes along and to the west of the river. The Spanish drove the French out in 1565 and began a permanent colonization of the country, founded missions, and established garrisons. The principal mission was founded near St. Augustine and the most noted missionary was Father Francisco Pareja, who came to Florida in 1594. Pareja remained at the mission for 16 years and retired to Mexico City, where he wrote a Timucua grammar, dictionary, and several devotional works. Pareja died in 1628.

About 1703 the English from South Carolina, with aid from their Creek, Catawba, and Yuchi allies, began a series of invasions and destroyed the missions, killing hundreds of Timucua and capturing thousands whom they carried off into slavery. With the decline of Spanish power and the continuous southerly advances of Creek tribes, the Timucua rapidly dwindled in numbers. Only a handful of Timucua remained in 1821, living among the tribes in the southern end of the peninsula, when the United States took possession of the Florida territory. According to Mooney (1910e:754), the Spanish may have shipped the remnants of the mission tribes to Cuba, as they had done with the Calusa of southern Florida in 1753.[99]

Except for a number of place and other names, there are only nine sources for information on the Timucua language, five of which are the works of Father Pareja.[100] Interest in the Timucua language was aroused when Buckingham Smith reported having found in Spain a copy of Pareja's Confessionario (Smith 1858) and a copy of Pareja's two 1612 Cathecismos

(Smith 1860a). Smith's invaluable acquisitions were placed in the library of the Historical Society of New York.[101] Albert S. Gatschet made a careful examination of the contents of the two volumes and in a series of three papers read before the American Philosophical Society (1877, 1878, 1880) reported upon Timucua culture, history, and language. Gatschet was not successful in his attempts to find linguistic affinities for Timucua, but noted the similarities of a few Timucua words to words in Creek, Carib, and Arawak and suggested that the words were probably loans (1880:477-78).

In 1881 during the session of the Congrès des Américanistes in Madrid, Charles Leclerc found there (in Madrid) a copy of Pareja's grammar which, known from its mention in Pareja's Confessionario, was thought to have been lost. Leclerc exhibited his discovery to the assembled scientists at the Congress (Gatschet 1883b:283, 1886a:187).[102] Plans were immediately begun by Leclerc for publishing Pareja's grammar. Lucien Adam copied the volume with his own hands while Julien Vinson was in charge of revising Adam's copy and reading the proofs (Vinson 1883:363). The grammar was published as the eleventh volume of Bibliothèque Linguistique Américaine (Pareja 1886), with an introduction by Vinson. Raoul de la Grasserie, having studied Pareja's grammar and Confessionario and Gatschet's three papers (1877, 1878, 1880), published a sketch of Timucua grammar (Grasserie 1888a), followed in the same year by a paper which reproduced several of Gatschet's texts with literal translations and a Timucua-French vocabulary (Grasserie 1888b). The vocabulary, with minor revisions and without comment, was reprinted a year later (Grasserie 1889). Gatschet and Grasserie (1889) collaborated in the presentation, without comment, of selected Timucua sentences and texts with sometimes free, sometimes literal, translations.

John R. Swanton devoted much attention to Timucua (Milanich and Sturtevant 1972:7). By about 1925 Swanton had prepared a sketch of the Timucua language and by 1945 had completed a lexical file of items with a tentative index (Milanich and Sturtevant 1972:121). Swanton's only publication on Timucua was his report on the Tawasa language, in which he made comparisons among Tawasa, Timucua, Natchez, and the Muskogean languages (Swanton 1929a). In 1955 Julian Granberry examined Pareja's (1886) grammar, a letter published in facsimile by Buckingham Smith in 1860,[103] the articles by Gatschet and Grasserie mentioned above, and some unpublished

Timucua material on microfilm (Granberry 1970:606). After an analysis of these materials, Granberry (1956) published an article on Timucua prosodics and phonemics. Granberry (1970:606) reported that Swanton in 1956 turned over his Timucua materials to him for further analysis. Granberry completed his examination of the Timucua materials in 1967 and stated that several articles on the linguistic structure and genetic affiliations of Timucua were in progress (Granberry 1970:606). Granberry's primary purpose for undertaking a detailed study of Timucua was to determine its affiliations with other American Indian languages (Granberry 1970:607). After having compared Timucua "carefully on every level of structure with languages of every phylum, stock, and family of the Gulf and Circum-Caribbean areas", Granberry reported that "it can be stated with at least moderate confidence that Timucua seems to show closest genetic relationship with Warao, of the Orinoco Delta region of Venezuela and Guyana" (1970:607).[104]

Swadesh (1964) placed Timucua in "Macro-Arawackan", which "includes Timucuan of North America and many languages of the Antilles and South America" (p. 547), and provided 25 sets as justification for doing so (p. 548). Haas (1971) noted that "Siouan resemblances of a similar nature [to those provided by Swadesh] can also be found" (p. 51, n. 2).

Milanich and Sturtevant (1972) published a volume which reproduces in facsimile selected pages of Pareja's 1613 Confessionario, with Spanish and Timucua transcription and an English translation, for which ethnographic notes are provided. The volume contains also a bibliography of manuscripts and publications on the Timucua Indians and an introductory chapter on Pareja and the Timucua.

Tunica

The Tunica were living on the Yazoo River in Mississippi when they first came to the notice of the French at the close of the seventeenth century. Their villages were located about twenty miles upstream from the junction of the Yazoo with the Mississippi, near present-day Vicksburg. Two tribes living near the Tunica, the Yazoo and the Koroa, and a third tribe living with the Natchez, the Grigra, may have spoken languages related to Tunica (Swanton 1921-23:1). The Tunica were prominent in the early history of the lower Mississippi region on account of their attachment to the French and their alliance with the French in wars with other Indian tribes. In 1706 the Chickasaw and Alabama drove the Tunica from their villages. The Tunica sought refuge with the Houma, whose territory they occupied after killing more than half the tribe (Tunica 1910:838). In 1730 the Tunica themselves suffered a defeat at the hands of the Natchez. At some time between 1784 and 1803 the Tunica moved up the Red River as far as Marksville Prairie where they settled on the south side of the river in Avoyelles Parish, near present-day Marksville. Some Tunica went farther west and joined the Atakapa. Some others moved to the Chickasaw Nation and established themselves on Red River. Both these latter bands were entirely lost sight of (Swanton 1946:108).[105]

In late 1886 while Albert S. Gatschet was searching out the Biloxi settlement in Rapides Parish, Louisiana, he was told there were about twenty-five of the Tunica tribe still living on Marksville Prairie (Powell 1891b:xxi). Gatschet visited the Tunica and collected a vocabulary and some texts. Except for one article (Gatschet 1889), in which he illustrated the use of masculine and feminine gender in Tunica nouns, Gatschet published nothing on the Tunica language. After Gatschet's death in 1907 (Mooney 1907f), John R. Swanton began an examination of Gatschet's Tunica material and himself visited the Tunica, in 1907, 1908, and 1910 (Swanton 1921-23:1). Swanton checked Gatschet's material with Tunica speakers and collected a few additional texts. Several years later, Swanton (1921-23) published a grammatical sketch of the Tunica language.

Mary R. Haas worked with the last fluent speaker of Tunica during the summer of 1933 and in the course of four visits between 1933 and 1938-39 (Haas 1950b:1, 9; 1953:175). From this last Tunica speaker Haas "obtained as much linguistic material... as it is possible to obtain" (Haas 1940c:10). In 1935 Haas completed a grammar of the Tunica language which served as her doctoral dissertation. Haas subsequently enlarged and revised the grammar and it appeared as volume four of the Handbook of American Indian Languages (Haas 1940c).[106] Haas (1946b) later presented a sketch of Tunica based on her earlier grammar. Haas (1947-48) published a description of French words in Tunica. Haas published her collection of Tunica texts (1950b) and, three years later, a Tunica dictionary (1953).

A few of the old Tunica people can cite perhaps a half-dozen words of their language.[107] But so far as is known, there are no Tunica who can speak the language. Approximately one hundred and fifty members of the Tunica tribe live at the present time in the general vicinity of Marksville, Louisiana.[108]

Yuchi

Very little is known about the early history of the Yuchi. They do not appear in history by this name before the eighteenth century.[109] One of the earliest references to the tribe (by the name Hughchees) is in a legend on a map in Jefferys' Atlas, published in 1776, which places them on the Savannah River above Augusta, Georgia, and reads: "Hughchees or Hogoleges Old Town deserted in 1715" (Swanton 1922:288). This reference appears to equate the Yuchi with the Hogoleges, a tribal name which in various spellings appears also in early literature. Gatschet (1884:19) wrote that the Yuchi were called Yuchi by all surrounding tribes, but were called Tahogaléwi by the Delaware. This latter name in various spellings appears also in the literature (Speck 1910:1007). The Yuchi undoubtedly were known by other names which we are unable to identify definitely as Yuchi. There have been attempts, on the basis of inferences from historical evidence, to identify as Yuchi such tribes as Chisca, Chichimeca, Tomahittan, Taharea, Stono, and Westo.[110]

There are several references to the Yuchi during the eighteenth century. An early reference is in the notice of the trip by boat up the Savannah River by General Oglethorpe in July 1739 to "the Uchee town, five and twenty miles above Ebenezer [Ebenezer is about thirty miles above Savannah], where he had engaged Indian traders to meet him with saddle and sumpter horses, [and] entered upon his journey of three hundred miles through a trackless wilderness" (Jones 1868:117). At some time before Oglethorpe's visit the Yuchi and other tribes began to abandon their settlements on the Savannah River and to move westward, probably to escape the encroachment of white settlers. When Benjamin Hawkins was in the Creek country of central and southwestern Georgia in 1798 and 1799, he found Yuchi towns and settlements on the Flint and Chattahoochee rivers. In his description of the Yuchi town on the Chattahoochee River below Columbus, Georgia, Hawkins (1848: 61-62) wrote that the Yuchi here were settled formerly in villages at Ponpon,

Saltketchers, and Silver Bluff (south of Augusta on the Savannah River), and at Ogechee (on the Ogeechee River which parallels the Savannah some thirty to forty miles to the west) and had moved to the Chattahoochee River in 1729. Hawkins (1848:63) reported that other Yuchi had settled with the Shawnee in a town among the Upper Creeks. There were in addition Yuchi settlements about fifty miles east of the Chattahoochee on the Flint River (Hawkins 1848: 66, 1916:171-72).[111]

In 1776, some twenty years before Hawkins, William Bartram was in the Creek country and left a description of the Yuchi town on the Chattahoochee River. Bartram (1791) noted that the Yuchi and Creek languages were radically different, that the Yuchi did not mix with the Creek, and that the Yuchi "on account of their numbers and strength, are of importance enough to excite and draw upon them[selves] the jealousy of the whole Muscogulge confederacy, and are usually at variance, yet are wise enough to unite against a common enemy, to support the interest and glory of the general Creek confederacy" (p. 389).

There were Yuchi farther to the north in Georgia, Alabama, and Tennessee. Hawkins (1916:41) reported a Yuchi village, a remnant of the Yuchi on the Chattahoochee, located in 1796 among the Upper Creeks on the Tallapoosa River in Alabama. Mooney (1900:385) was told by a Cherokee that, before the removal to the west, a number of Yuchi lived among the Cherokee near Cleveland, Tennessee, and on Chickamauga, Cohutta, and Pinelog creeks in Georgia, south of present-day Chattanooga, Tennessee. In his section on the "Aborigines of Tennessee" Ramsey (1853) devoted a short paragraph to the Yuchi: "A small tribe of Uchees once occupied the country near the mouth of Hiwassee [River, about fifteen miles north of Cleveland]. Their warriors were exterminated in a desperate battle with the Cherokees. Little else is known of them" (p. 81). In his description of the Cherokee Ramsey wrote that the Cherokee "met the entire tribe of the Uchees, at the Uchee Old Fields, in what is now Rhea county, and, exterminating all its warriors, compelled the surviving remnant of that brave race to retreat to Florida, where they became incorporated with the Seminoles" (p. 84). In another reference to the Yuchi Ramsey wrote: "It is fabled that a fleet of Indian canoes, rowed by Uchee warriors, and destined for an invasion of the Shawnees, at the mouth of the Ohio, was engulphed in the Whirlpool, now known as the Suck [on the Tennessee River near Chattanooga]" (pp. 183-84).

Morse (1822:364) reported a Yuchi town near the Mikasuki tribe in Florida. In 1821 Morse (1822:306-308), in an enumeration of Seminole towns, placed a Yuchi town above Lake George in Florida. According to Swanton (1922:312), the Yuchi south of Lake George, "at Spring Garden, east of Dexters Lake, in Volusia County", moved here from their town near the Mikasuki in west Florida. The Yuchi in Florida became involved in the Seminole wars and as late as 1847 there were four Yuchi warriors among the Seminole (Swanton 1922:312).

A few Yuchi went west in 1825, before the mass removal of the Indians began, and settled at the spot where Tahlequah, the Cherokee capital, was to be located (Mooney 1900:385-86). The greater portion of the Yuchi were living among the Creek tribes and moved with them in the 1830's to Indian Territory, settling in the northwestern part of the Creek Nation, in the general vicinity of present-day Sapulpa and Bristow, Oklahoma.

The first Yuchi vocabulary is the one in Duponceau's collection (Gallatin 1836:97, Pilling 1889:36), taken down by Nathaniel A. Ware about 1820 (Freeman 1966:387). Not long afterwards a Yuchi vocabulary was taken by Mr. Ridge, a Cherokee (Gallatin 1836:91), from a Yuchi chief at Washington, D. C. (Gallatin 1836:97).[112] The vocabularies of Ridge and Ware were used by Gallatin (1836:307-67) in his comparative vocabularies. The next Yuchi vocabulary was taken by General Albert Pike about 1861 (Pilling 1889:69). Jeremiah Curtin was in Indian Territory from late 1883 to June 30, 1884 and collected myths and vocabularies in Yuchi (Powell 1887:xxxi).[113] Albert S. Gatschet collected a Yuchi vocabulary in Indian Territory in March 1885.[114] Gatschet published four Yuchi myths (1893) and wrote a brief sketch of the Yuchi tribe (1884:17-24). Although Gatschet published nothing on the language, he studied all the Yuchi linguistic materials in the Bureau of American Ethnology and wrote a manuscript entitled "Some grammatic comments of the Yuchi language".[115]

At the suggestion of Franz Boas, Frank G. Speck undertook an investigation of the Yuchi in the summer of 1904 for the purpose of collecting ethnological material. Speck returned to the field in the summer of 1905 and again in the winter of 1908. Speck (1909) published a monograph on Yuchi culture. Speck gave very little information on the Yuchi language, but throughout the monograph cited Yuchi names for numerous cultural items. Speck (1911) soon afterwards published a volume of Creek and Yuchi songs.[116] Except for the entry in the Handbook of American Indians (Speck 1910), Speck published nothing else on Yuchi other than a note on Yuchi kinship terminologies (1939) in reply to Eggan (1937).

Boas sent Günter Wagner to Oklahoma in the summer of 1928 to work on the Yuchi language. Wagner returned to Oklahoma for additional work in the winter of 1929, for a total period of about five months' work on the language. Wagner lived in the home of his major informant, where he recorded considerable textual material. Wagner published his Yuchi texts (1931) and a grammatical sketch of the Yuchi language (1934). Wagner prepared an English-Yuchi dictionary, but this remains in manuscript (Voegelin and Harris 1945:33). In 1940 Mary R. Haas collected Yuchi material (Haas 1964:499). Hans Wolff was in Sapulpa, Oklahoma, briefly in the summer of 1947 and took down a Yuchi text and other linguistic material. Wolff published an article on Yuchi phonemes and "person markers" (1948) and a Yuchi text with analysis (1951b). Émile Benveniste examined the two negative morphemes in Yuchi, as described by Wagner (1934) and as found in Wagner's (1931) texts, and published an article on the separate functions of the two morphemes (1950).

I began work on the Yuchi language in the summer of 1970 in Sapulpa, Oklahoma. I returned to Oklahoma for additional field work in the summer of 1971. I was there for two days in August 1972 and again, for one week, in July 1973.[117] W. L. Ballard, Georgia State University, worked with a Yuchi speaker in 1970-71, commuting regularly between Atlanta and Columbus, Georgia, where his informant was temporarily employed. In the summer of 1971 Ballard worked on the Yuchi language in Sapulpa, Oklahoma. In late 1973 Ballard prepared a mimeographed English-Yuchi lexicon. Professor Ballard has contributed a paper on some aspects of Yuchi grammar for this volume.

About five hundred Yuchi are now living in Oklahoma, in the general vicinity of Sapulpa, about ten miles west of Tulsa. My Yuchi informant told me in August 1972 that only about thirty-five Yuchi, all old people, speak the language with any degree of fluency.

THE TAENSA LANGUAGE HOAX

Earliest accounts place the Taensa west of the Mississippi River near present-day St. Joseph, Louisiana.[118] According to the records of early French missionaries and travelers, the Taensa spoke the same language as the Natchez, although no missionary or traveler, so far as is known, took down any words in the Taensa language. Were it not for the publication in 1880, 1881, and 1882 of linguistic material alleged to be taken from manuscripts found in France and to be in the language of the Taensa Indians, the Taensa tribe would have played no more prominent role in American Indian studies than numerous other tribes for which bits of historical and ethnographic information are preserved.

The 1880 publication was an article in _Revue de Linguistique et de Philologie Comparée_ which gave a sketch of the sounds and grammar of the Taensa language (Parisot 1880). The 1881 publication was called "Cancionero americano" and consisted of seven songs, without translation, supposedly in the Taensa language.[119] Neither the Taensa songs nor the sketch of the Taensa language attracted much attention. However, in the following year Lucien Adam published as volume nine of _Bibliothèque Linguistique Américaine_ (Haumonté, Parisot, and Adam 1882) what was purported to be a grammar, a vocabulary, and texts in the Taensa language. With endorsements by Adam and Gatschet in the introduction to the volume, the publication was accepted as a valuable contribution to American Indian linguistics. The "discovery" was soon attacked by Daniel G. Brinton (1885), who branded the grammar and texts as "deceptions practiced on the scientific world" (p. 113). Gatschet was the strongest champion of the genuineness of the material, with Brinton the principal challenger of its scientific credentials. After a few exchanges between the two (Brinton 1888a, 1888b; Gatschet 1888), the argument was dropped. Gatschet apparently never waivered in his belief in the authenticity of the Taensa material and continued to suggest evidence in favor of its genuine origin (Gatschet 1891:252-54).

Failure to produce the original manuscript aroused skepticism as to the genuineness of the material. The fact that the manuscript was in Spanish increased the skepticism, since the Taensa were constantly under French observation from the time of their discovery by La Salle in 1682 until their disappearance about 1740. Suspicion of forgery increased upon a close examination of the content of the songs and texts.[120]

In a brief article Swanton (1908) reviewed the history of the appearance of the Taensa material and the subsequent controversy and presented newly acquired documentary material asserting the sameness of the languages of the Natchez and the Taensa. Later, Swanton (1911) reviewed the episode in detail (pp. 9-26), noting that he had searched for a living representative of the tribe, one who might know a few words of the Taensa language, among the Chitimacha, in which tribe the Taensa remnants are last known (pp. 17, 23). Swanton found an old woman who had once spoken Taensa, but from whose memory he was able to extract only a single form, a Chitimacha word which the woman claimed meant something different in Taensa. Swanton was informed that other Chitimacha had once spoken Taensa, even the informant from whom Gatschet collected most of his Chitimacha material in 1881 and 1882. "Thus, by a curious irony of fate, in the same year in which the grammar which occasioned so much discussion appeared, its principal American defender was in communication with a man who possessed information which would have nipped the controversy in the bud, and yet he [Gatschet] never appears to have been aware of the fact" (Swanton 1911:23).

RELATIONSHIPS BEYOND THE FAMILY LEVEL

Since Sapir (1921, 1925:525-26, 1958) proposed his grouping of North American languages and language families into a relatively small number of stocks, there has been increasing interest in establishing relationships among these languages beyond the family level. Attempts to demonstrate the less obvious and more distant relationships began in earnest when scholars in the early part of this century acquired more material on the languages of California and Oregon and pondered the large numbers of languages and language families in so small a geographic region. Linguistic diversity in the southeastern United States was probably never as great as on the west coast, but here too, particularly along the Gulf coast, there were numerous apparently unrelated languages spoken in a relatively small area.

John R. Swanton, most of whose work was devoted to the southeastern Indian tribes, was the prominent early figure in attempting to group the southeastern languages into smaller numbers of related units. Influenced by Brinton's (1873) article, Swanton (1907b) compared Natchez and Muskogean and concluded they were related "beyond reasonable doubt" (p. 527). Swanton (1915) examined Atakapa, Tonkawa, and the Coahuiltecan languages of Texas and northeastern Mexico and found resemblances pointing to a genetic relationship. Swanton (1915) noted that the relationship might be shown eventually to include Chitimacha, Natchez, and Muskogean (p. 40). Swanton (1919a) compared Tunica, Chitimacha, and Atakapa and concluded that the three were "merely widely divergent dialects of one stock", which he called Tunican, and remarked that "It remains to be seen whether the connection ends here, or whether the newly identified group is affiliated with the Muskhogean stock to the east or the smaller stocks of central and southern Texas" (p. 56). Swanton (1924-25) reinforced the thesis of a Natchez-Muskogean relationship and set up correspondences between Natchez and Muskogean. In an article on the Tawasa language Swanton (1929a) attempted to show that Tawasa is Timucuan and that Timucua and Muskogean are related (pp. 450-53). Swanton apparently had worked at demonstrating a relationship between Siouan and Muskogean, as evidenced by an intriguing statement: "There is evidence, which has not yet been thoroughly marshaled, that the Siouan and Muskhogean linguistic families are related and that the Catawba tongue occupies an intermediate position between the extreme branches of each" (Swanton 1936:380).

Morris Swadesh (1946b) followed up "Swanton's thesis of a relationship (although a widely divergent one) between Tunica, Chitimacha and Atakapa" (p. 113) with a detailed comparison of Atakapa and Chitimacha. Swadesh (1947) provided additional evidence for an Atakapa-Chitimacha relationship.

Mary R. Haas (1951) proposed that Atakapa, Chitimacha, Natchez, Tunica, and the Muskogean languages be treated on a par, even though "the total number of cognates that can be arrived at when all are compared is much less than that which can be arrived at by comparing any two of them" (p. 72). In her 1951 paper Haas adopted the term "Gulf" to refer to Atakapa, Chitimacha, Natchez, Tunica, and Muskogean and examined the words for 'water' in the Gulf languages, with a brief consideration of words for 'water' in Timucua, Siouan, and Yuchi. Haas (1951) concluded by presenting four additional (to 'water') possible cognates between Siouan and Yuchi (p. 79). Haas (1952) presented more evidence for a Gulf stock by comparing the words for 'land' in Atakapa, Chitimacha, Natchez, Tunica, and Muskogean and suggested that Siouan words for 'ground, earth' may be cognate to Gulf words for 'land'.[121] Haas (1956) provided considerable phonological and some morphological evidence for a Natchez-Muskogean relationship and pointed out that Natchez is not a Muskogean language, "because Natchez must be compared with Proto-Muskogean and not directly with the separate Muskogean languages" (p. 61).

Haas (1958b) presented considerable evidence to demonstrate a relationship between the Gulf languages and the Algonquian languages and suggested that the time depth for Algonquian-Gulf may be no greater than that for the Gulf languages themselves: "The relationship of the various Gulf languages to one another is already quite remote and Algonkian simply forms another affiliate of the group" (p. 231). Haas (1959) set forth "the preliminary results obtained by comparing Tonkawa directly with Proto Central Algonkian (PCA) reconstructions" (p. 1) and wrote that

> The implications of the Algonkian-Gulf-Tonkawa relationship are clearly of such a nature as to make it entirely meaningless to speak of a Hokan-Siouan superstock in the terms in which it was proposed by Sapir. While this does not mean that the relationships subsumed under Hokan-Siouan have been invalidated, it does mean that any future validation of such relationships (of those which can be validated) can only be made in terms of a much wider context which will have to include, among other things, Algonkian, Ritwan [Wiyot and Yurok], and probably even Mosan [Wakashan, Chemakuan, and Salishan]. (p. 4)

Haas (1960) proceeded to examine some of these relationships in a wider context, with comparisons between Algonquian and Ritwan,[122] Algonquian and Mosan, Algonquian and Gulf, Algonquian and Tonkawa, and suggested "that all these languages are probably related to one another" (p. 989). In a brief note, Haas (1963) removed a doubt previously expressed by her (1958b:251) regarding the cognation of 'skunk' in Algonquian and Gulf, upon discovering a little-used Chickasaw form recorded by Gatschet in 1889.

Haas (1964) presented "a preliminary list of comparisons", a total of 34 (pp. 497-98), to suggest the possibility of "a genetic relationship between the Athapaskan family and Tlingit, on the one hand, and Yuchi and the Siouan family, on the other" (p. 495).[123]

William Elmendorf (1963) presented numerous sets of lexical similarities between Siouan (mainly Biloxi) and Yukian (mainly Wappo) and a few sets showing Wappo resemblances to Yuchi and Siouan. Elmendorf (1964) documented further his hypothesis for the genetic affinity of Yukian, Siouan, and Yuchi in an "item and set" comparison.

Karl-Heinz Gursky (1965a) provided a large number of possible cognate sets as evidence of a relationship between the "Hoka-Subtiaba", "Algonkin-Golf", and Tonkawa languages. The same year, Gursky (1965b), assuming that "the existence of this [Algonquian-Gulf] phylum has been proved by M. R. Haas" (p. 108, note 3), listed about sixty forms showing lexical similarities between Caddoan and this phylum, noting that some may be borrowings or chance resemblances, although "chance certainly cannot account for all these similarities" (p. 107). Gursky (1966) compared grammatical elements of Gulf and Hokan-Subtiaban. Gursky (1968) provided additional sets of resemblant forms between the Gulf languages and Hokan-Subtiaban in further substantiation "of a genetic relationship between the Hokan-Subtiaban-Jicaquean grouping and the Gulf stock" (p. 22). Gursky (1969) presented new lexical material for showing the relationships among three of the Gulf languages in "three binary comparisons: namely Atakapa and Chitimacha, Tunica and Chitimacha, and Atakapa and Tunica" (p. 85).

Chafe (1973:1190) has noted that Latham (1846:44) perhaps implied a relationship between Siouan and Iroquoian and later explicitly stated it (Latham 1860:327). It was Morgan's (1851) belief that the Iroquois were "an early offshoot" of the Sioux (Chafe 1973:1190). Latham (1860), as Chafe (1973:1190) noted, suggested also a connection between Siouan and Caddoan, as well as a relationship between the Caddo language and Iroquoian (p. 327). Sapir in his three classifications (1921, 1925:525-26, 1958:172-73) linked Iroquoian to Caddoan, with no hint of a connection of either to Siouan, except that all three were within his Hokan-Siouan stock. Louis Allen (1931) made some comparisons between the Siouan and Iroquoian languages, illustrated some morphological similarities, and hypothesized (p. 193) that a connection between the two families could eventually be established. Chafe (1964) presented 67 comparative sets as further evidence of a Siouan-Iroquoian relationship and pointed out some general similarities between Siouan and Iroquoian grammatical patterns (pp. 860-61). Chafe (1973) has published for the first time evidence which demonstrates a relationship between Caddoan and Siouan (pp. 1190-93) and between Caddoan and Iroquoian (pp. 1193-97), thus strengthening the supposition of a Macro-Siouan phylum, consisting of Siouan, Iroquoian, and Caddoan (see C. F. and F. M. Voegelin 1966). Chafe (1973) noted that if Siouan is related to the Gulf languages, as suggested by Haas (1951, 1952), "and the latter in turn are related to Algonquian (Haas 1958[b]), there is essentially but one superstock of languages east of the Rocky Mountains" (p. 1198). Chafe (1973) concluded with a reminder (p. 1199) of the speculativeness of proposed relationships between Siouan and Nadene (Haas 1964) and between Siouan and Yukian (Elmendorf 1963, 1964).

NOTES

1. Lawson (1709), in his description of the "Congerees", interjected a comment on the differences of speech of the Indians: "Altho' their Tribes or Nations border one upon another, yet you may discern as great an Alteration in their Features and Dispositions, as you can in their Speech, which generally proves quite different from each other, though their Nations be not above 10 or 20 Miles in Distance" (p. 29).

2. Eliot was a missionary to the Massachusetts Indians in the 1600's. Eliot published a grammar and primer and a translation of the entire Bible in Massachusetts, as well as numerous religious tracts (Pilling 1891:127-84). Pareja was a Franciscan missionary among the Timucua of Florida from 1595 until sometime in the early 1600's. Pareja published a Timucua grammar and several catechisms in Timucua (Milanich and Sturtevant 1972:15-21).

3. Neither Dorsey nor Gatschet survived for long in the "second period". Dorsey died in 1895 at the age of forty-seven (Dorsey 1897:207). Gatschet died in 1907 at the age of seventy-five (Mooney 1907f:561).

4. Another much longer article was published by Trumbull (1870b) on Algonquian geographical names.

5. Bloomfield's 1946 article was the final version of his earlier work in Proto-Algonquian. See Siebert's section on comparative Algonquian phonology in his paper in this volume for a description of previous work by Bloomfield.

6. See Siebert's section on Proto-Eastern Algonquian in his paper in this volume.

7. Hockett (1957) in his "first installment of a Central Algonquian comparative dictionary" (p. 247) cited a small number of Shawnee forms in making reconstructions, although "no reconstruction has been made solely on the basis of a correspondence between Sh[awnee] and one of the other languages" (p. 249).

8. The papers published were: Day (1967), Frantz (1967), Goddard (1967a, 1967b), Haas (1967), Salzmann (1967a, 1967b), Siebert (1967a, 1967b), Taylor (1967a, 1967b), and Teeter (1967a, 1967b).

9. The information given here on the Pamlico is about all that is known of this tribe and is from Mooney (1910b:197) and Swanton (1946:170). See also Speck (1924), who has written on the Pamlico, Powhatan, and other presumably Algonquian tribes of Virginia and North Carolina. Quinn (1955) has

brought together into two volumes all the documents concerning the attempt of the British to establish a colony in North Carolina, including Har[r]iot's "A briefe and true report... " (pp. 317-87). (Harriot [1972] is a facsimile edition by Dover Publications of the 1590 edition.) In Appendix II of the second volume, James A. Geary (1955) has attempted to place this southernmost Algonquian language within the Algonquian family and to assign meanings to the words from Harriot and a few other words from Spanish and English sources.

10. Lawson's spelling is Pampticough. For other spellings see Mooney (1910b:197).

11. Speck (1928) used the spelling Mattaponi. The name of the reservation is also spelled this way on the 1970 official highway map of Virginia. The older spelling appears to be Mattapony, but was used by Swanton (1946: 175).

12. This brief sketch of the Powhatan is based primarily on Mooney (1907a, 1910c) and Swanton (1946:175-76). Additional references on the Virginia Indians are Willoughby (1907), Speck (1924), Bushnell (1940), Speck and Schaeffer (1950), and Barbour (1969). In Barbour (1969) are reprinted all the documents relating to the foundation of the Jamestown colony from 1606 to 1609, including Captain John Smith's "A true relation . . . " (Smith 1969a) and "A map of Virginia . . . " (Smith 1969b).

13. Emphasis in original.

14. The Shawnee may have been met by De Soto in 1540 in western North Carolina. There may have been Shawnee in northwestern North Carolina in 1514. Shawnee may have been in New Jersey as early as 1614. See E. W. Voegelin (1939) for an examination of some possible early locations of the Shawnee.

15. For accounts of the early migrations of the Shawnee, see Brinton (1866), Swanton (1922:317-20, 1946:184-86), and Mooney (1910d). For a description of the Shawnee in Ohio, see Johnston (1820:273-76).

16. Pilling (1891:354) reproduced the Shawnee alphabet used by Lykins, with the English equivalents.

17. The three dialects of Shawnee are: Absentee, between Norman and Shawnee (southeast of Oklahoma City), Eastern, in the neighborhood of Miami (in the extreme northeastern corner of Oklahoma), and Loyal, or Cherokee, in the hills south of Vinita (in northeastern Oklahoma about fifty

miles northeast of Tulsa) (Voegelin 1935:23). Voegelin was in Oklahoma in 1933 and 1934, accompanied by Erminie W. Voegelin (C. F. and E. W. Voegelin 1935:617, Nettl 1953:279). The Voegelins collected about sixty Shawnee songs on phonograph records (Nettl 1953:279), five of which are analyzed by Nettl (1953). E. W. Voegelin has published on Shawnee music (1942), on Shawnee agriculture (1941) and on Shawnee mortuary customs (1944). C. F. and E. W. Voegelin have coauthored two articles on the Shawnee, one on name groups (1935) and one on the female deity (1946). C. F. Voegelin (1936a) has also written on the Shawnee female deity.

18. These notes on Caddoan are based primarily on Taylor (1963a).

19. This brief sketch of Caddo history is based on Fletcher (1907) and Swanton (1946:98-100).

20. The Adai, living at first white contact about fifteen miles southwest of Natchitoches, Louisiana, and the Eyeish, living in San Augustine County, Texas, were two tribes not attached to one of the three Caddo confederations: Kadohadacho (Caddo proper), Hasinai, and Natchitoches. All these tribes spoke more or less close dialects of the same language, except possibly the Adai, for which there exists only the meager vocabulary collected by Sibley and published by Gallatin (1848:95, 97).

21. See Swanton (1942), who has assembled material from original sources bearing on the Caddo tribes, for all that is known of Caddo history and culture.

22. Douglas R. Parks, who has a paper in this volume on Shawnee, has recently done extensive work on another Caddoan language, Pawnee.

23. The Nottoway may have been an offshoot of the Tuscarora (Powell 1891a: 79).

24. This brief sketch of Cherokee history is based mostly on Mooney (1900, 1907d) and Swanton (1946:110-15).

25. Bureau of American Ethnology Bulletin 196, in which this article appears, contains other articles on the Cherokee. See J. F. Kilpatrick and A. G. Kilpatrick (1966), J. F. Kilpatrick (1966), and Kupferer (1966). See also Fenton and Gulick (1961), which contains 25 papers and comments on papers from a symposium on Cherokee and Iroquois culture held in 1958. The paper by Lounsbury (1961:9-17) and the comment on Lounsbury's paper by Haas (1961:19-23) are of linguistic nature.

26. Cook's work has been conducted under the auspices of Yale University. King's work has been supported by Grant No. GS-28812 from the National Science Foundation to the University of Georgia.

27. Binford (1967) has compiled from the literature all that is known of the Nottoway.

28. This brief sketch of Tuscarora history is based primarily on Hewitt (1910) and Swanton (1946:199).

29. See Wallace (1949, 1952) for an account of recent work with the Tuscarora.

30. Personal communication from Floyd G. Lounsbury, March 29, 1973.

31. Without any linguistic evidence, Gatschet listed a few other tribes as belonging to one or the other of these branches, e. g. , Biloxi, Witumka, and Pascagoula. In 1886 Gatschet himself discovered that Biloxi was Siouan, not Muskogean.

32. This brief sketch of Alabama history is based on a reading of Mooney and Thomas (1907), Swanton (1946:86-88), and Rothe (1963). For more on the Alabama, see Smither (1932), Malone (1960), Folsom-Dickerson (1965), Swanton (1922:191-201), and Densmore (1937).

33. Goddard (1914:587) reported that Swanton collected 250 pages of texts in Alabama, a similar number in Natchez, 100 in Koasati, and 150 in Hitchiti.

34. Personal communication from Mrs. Maggie Poncho, August 24, 1970. Mrs. Poncho, an Alabama, said that Muriel Saville had a word list 42 years old and compared it with present-day Alabama. I was also told by Mrs. Poncho that Mrs. Marjorie M. Randall had recently visited her for the purpose of studying Alabama genealogies.

35. McCall returned to the field in summer 1972 and again in summer 1973. Her work on Alabama is supported in part by Grant No. GS-28812 from the National Science Foundation to the University of Georgia for the study of southeastern Indian languages.

36. McCall obtained this information in 1973 from the superintendent of the Alabama-Coushatta Reservation.

37. Personal communication from Mr. Medford in 1970. Claude Medford, Jr. , has been a source of much useful information to me and to others who have attempted linguistic and other field work among the Indians of Texas, Louisiana, and Oklahoma. Mr. Medford, being himself part Choctaw, has

taken great interest in the Indians of the Gulf states and has traveled extensively throughout the region, searching for and studying remnants like the Atakapa, Chitimacha, Houma, and Tunica. Mr. Medford is to be credited for informing Haas and me of several people in Louisiana and Texas who still remembered some the Mobilian trade language. In a reconnaissance of Indian tribes in Oklahoma, Texas, Louisiana, and Mississippi in August 1969, I discovered that each group I visited either had heard of Mr. Medford or knew him personally. I had not met Mr. Medford before this trip and was determined to meet him before returning to Athens. When I finally caught up with him at Marksville, Louisiana, he was engaged in helping the Tunica prepare handicrafts for sale at their "trading post". Mr. Medford, who has married a Koasati, Rosaline Langley, is now residing in Elton, Louisiana, where he has been influential in expanding and publicizing the crafts of the Louisiana Koasati.

38. This sketch of the Apalachee has been based primarily on a reading of Mooney (1907b), Swanton (1946:89-91), and Gatschet (1884:74-76). Other sources consulted were: Boyd (1949, 1952, 1953) and Boyd, Smith, and Griffin (1951).

39. Haas' (1973) bibliographic entry to the facsimile reproduction of the letter is (p. 1245): [Smith, Buckingham], compiler. [1860a]. [Documents in the Spanish and two of the early tongues of Florida, Apalachian and Timuquan.] [Washington, D. C.]. I have not seen a copy of this item.

40. Pilling (1889) commented in regard to these other documents: "Mr. Gatschet informs me further that M. Pinart saw these documents at Havana; but their nature I am unable to learn" (p. 3).

41. This sketch of Chickasaw history is based on Swanton (1922:414-20, 1946:116-19) and Gatschet and Thomas (1907). For a description of the Chickasaw before 1775 by a British trader, see Adair (1775). See Speck (1907b) on Chickasaw folklore. Swanton (1928c) is the best single source for Chickasaw history and culture.

42. I am grateful to Dr. Choong S. Kim, University of Tennessee, Martin, for information about the Golddust Choctaw. This sketch of Choctaw history is based on Swanton (1922:420-21, 1946:121-23) and Swanton and Thomas (1907). See Swanton (1931) for a description of Choctaw history and culture

and for additional references to the Choctaw. See Densmore (1943b) on Choctaw music.

43. Watkins' Choctaw definer was reprinted in 1972 by Southeastern Antiquities Survey, Nashville, Tennessee. Pilling (1889) did not list this item.

44. There are some minor differences in the Choctaw of Bayou Lacomb, an interesting one being okwa 'water', as opposed to oka in other dialects (Byington 1915:291).

45. E. g., Haas 1941a, 1941c, 1941d, 1946a, 1949.

46. Creek is the more contemporary of the two terms. There are numerous spellings of the older term, for which see Creek (1907:365).

47. This summary of Creek history is based for the most part on Creek (1907) and Swanton (1946:153-54). See Swanton (1928a, 1928b) on Creek culture and social organization.

48. The 1964 reprint has as first part a Creek-English dictionary and as second part an English-Creek dictionary, with no other date than 1964. Swanton's (1928a:472) bibliographic entry has as title: "English and Muskokee dictionary". The wording of the title pages of the two parts of the 1964 reprint (p. 95 for the title page to the Creek-English part) indicates that the two parts appeared separately. Haas (1938) gave the Creek-English dictionary as a reference, with "last edition" added, publication date 1914, by Westminister Press, Philadelphia (p. 61, fn. 2). Haas (1938) praised Loughridge's work: "his dictionary... is far superior to much work done in his day along similar lines" (p. 62, fn. 4).

49. This legend was in the form of a speech delivered to General Oglethorpe at Savannah in 1735. The speech was written on buffalo skin and was presented by the Indians to the British who framed it and apparently took it to England and hung it in the Georgia Office. The speech had been written down in English as it was interpreted to General Oglethorpe. Neither the buffalo skin nor the English translation has been found. But a translation into French of the speech (from the English translation) was made by von Reck, who was Commissary of the German emigrants from Salzburg and who visited Georgia in their interest. It was translated into German and published by Samuel Urlsperger at Halle, Germany, in 1741, as part of Urlsperger's Nachrichten (Brinton 1870:119).

50. Gatschet's "Tchikilli's Kasi'hta legend in the Creek and Hitchiti languages. . . " was printed privately in St. Louis in 1888 and was reprinted in Transactions of the Academy of Science of St. Louis (1886-91), Vol. 5, in 1892.

51. Speck published additional cultural and linguistic articles on Creek (and Muskogean). For these, see his bibliography in Hallowell (1951).

52. Swanton's publications on Creek and Muskogean are far too numerous to be listed here. Two important ones should be mentioned: Swanton (1922), "The early history of the Creek Indians and their neighbors", and Swanton (1928a), "Social organization and social usages of the Indians of the Creek Confederacy". A complete list of Swanton's publications was given by Steward (1960).

53. Creek forms and other descriptive material on Creek were given by Haas in other articles which are either ethnological (1940b) or deal with the Muskogean languages as a whole, e. g. , 1941a, 1941d, 1946a, 1947, and 1950a, as well as in her publications on the distant connections of Muskogean, which will be mentioned later. Much of Haas' Creek material remains unpublished.

54. This sketch of the Koasati is based largely on Swanton (1907a, 1946: 145-46). See Jacobson (1960) for a history of the Louisiana Koasati. For a description and a history of the Texas Koasati, and the Alabama, whose history in Texas parallels that of the Koasati, see Folsom-Dickerson (1965), Malone (1960), Rothe (1963), and Swanton (1922:201-207).

55. I was in Elton, Louisiana, in 1969 and was told there were about fifty Koasati families there, about two hundred people, all of whom speak Koasati. I was told by a Koasati in Texas, also in 1969, that of three hundred Alabama and Koasati, only about thirty-five are Koasati. Mary McCall visited the Koasati in Louisiana in 1973 and informed me there are 230 Koasati near Elton, all of whom speak Koasati. McCall told me that about 20 per cent of the 500 people at the Alabama-Coushatta reservation in Texas consider themselves Koasati, although most of the Alabama speak Koasati. McCall said that the two languages have become "very much mixed, except in the speech of very old speakers of both groups".

56. For a detailed account of the Seminole (and Mikasuki) Indians of Florida see Sturtevant's (1971) article "Creek into Seminole". For further

reading consult Sturtevant's references (1971:125-28).

57. Since the term _Seminole_ was applied indiscriminately to many Florida Indians, particularly to the Mikasuki and the Creek-speaking Seminole, it may be that there were earlier recordings of Mikasuki. A vocabulary of the "Seminole language" was included in the account of a traveler among the Seminole of Florida, published in 1822 (Pilling 1889:64). Another "Seminole" vocabulary appeared in 1836 in a sketch of the Seminole war by an anonymous lieutenant (Pilling 1889:83). A book published in 1837 describing the Florida territory has a glossary of about 150 "Seminole words" (Pilling 1889:93). All three vocabularies indeed may be linguistically "Seminole", i. e. , Creek, since the Seminole language is a dialectal variant of Creek. But it is possible, because of the loose application of the term _Seminole_, that the vocabularies may, on the other hand, be Mikasuki. There is a copy of the 1822 book (Pilling 1889:64) in the Boston Public Library. Copies of the 1836 and 1837 books are in the Library of Congress (Pilling 1889:83, 93). Examination of the vocabularies should identify them as either Mikasuki or Seminole.

Not long before this volume was to go to press, I discovered in the Wymberley Jones De Renne library at the University of Georgia a copy of the 1837 book ("The territory of Florida: or sketches of the topography, civil and natural history, of the country, the climate, and the Indian tribes, from the discovery to the present time, with a map, views, &c. ", by John Lee Williams, New York: A. T. Goodrich, 1837) and made a quick examination of the glossary (pp. 276-77). Most of the words, if not all of them, are Creek Seminole, not Mikasuki. The De Renne library does not have the 1822 and 1836 books mentioned by Pilling. See n. 67.

58. See Sturtevant (1971:114) for a map showing locations of the reservations.

59. Underlined words indicate italics in the original. Hale (1883c:13) was convinced the "general language" Beverley spoke of was the Tutelo language.

60. The first English edition of Le Page du Pratz was published in two volumes in 1763 in London. Another English edition appeared in 1774. An undated reprint of the 1774 edition was published about 1947 by Pelican Press, New Orleans.

61. The Chactoos were Chatot, not Choctaw. (See Swanton 1946:107-108).

62. Gatschet (1884) gave four examples (p. 96):

píshu lynx, from Odshibwē pishīu; also an Odshibwē totem-clan.

piakímina persimmon, changed in the French Creole dialect to plaquemine.

shishikushi gourd-rattle or drum, Margry IV, 175.

sacacuya war-whoop, la huée.

The second form is identical with Miami piakimina (Voegelin 1938-40:100). I have so far been unable to identify the source of the last two forms.

63. The Indians of Texas and Louisiana do not use the term Mobilian. They call the language alternately "the old language" and yamá, which they say means 'yes' in the old language.

64. In the summer of 1971 I was in Elton again and transcribed a few more Mobilian words from the tape made the year before. My informant did not know Choctaw very well and was not able to specify as Mobilian or Choctaw many words used by Mrs. Langley. Mrs. Langley was unfortunately ill at the time of my visit and could not work with me. I visited Mr. Lavan but found him also very ill. Claude Medford has written me that Mr. Lavan died in December 1973 at the age of eighty-three. In 1971 I was told by the Koasati that there are other Indians, and possibly a few white people, around Elton who remember some of "the old language", but I did not have the time to attempt to locate them.

65. A part of them "soon came to be known as Mikasuki, though under what circumstances is unknown" (Swanton 1946:181).

66. See Sturtevant (1971) for a history of the Seminole Indians of Florida. See MacCauley (1887) for a description of their life in 1880-81 and Skinner (1913) for a report of a visit among them in 1910. Capron (1953) has described their green corn ceremonies.

The name Seminole is from Spanish cimarrón 'wild, runaway' (Sturtevant 1971:105).

67. A vocabulary of the Seminole language, according to Pilling (1889:64), appears on pp. 97-105 in a book by an anonymous author, entitled "Notices of east Florida . . . ", and printed in Charleston in 1822, seen by Pilling in the Boston Public Library. Dr. Frank T. Siebert, Jr., has informed me that the author is Dr. W. H. Simmons and that there are copies in the New York Public and the St. Augustine Historical Society libraries, as well as in other libraries.

68. It is possible that the words in these three vocabularies are Mikasuki. See n. 57.

69. Gatschet may have collected Seminole linguistic material, perhaps from a member of a delegation to Washington. Mooney (1907f:565) lists Seminole as one of the nearly one hundred languages among Gatschet's manuscript linguistic material deposited with the Bureau of American Ethnology.

70. Sturtevant provided me with following information in a letter dated April 9, 1974:

> In my Florida fieldnotes for 1951-53 I find the following materials in Creek Seminole: 200-word Swadesh list; lexical materials amounting to several hundred words, with emphasis on plant and animal names, personal names, and cultural vocabulary; two small notebooks with phrases, some sentences, but no texts. The only part of this that is available is about 210 Creek Seminole plant names that appear in the Catalog of Plants at the back of my unpublished (but on University Microfilms) PhD thesis: "The Mikasuki Seminole: Medical Beliefs and Practices", Yale Anthrop. , 1954.

71. Hale (1883b) believed that Tutelo was the most archaic Siouan language and thought that this antiquity of Tutelo was evidence of a migration of the Siouan tribes from the east. Dorsey (1886) has written of western Siouan migrations in historical times. Mooney (1894) has presented strong circumstantial evidence for identifying numerous Virginia and Carolina tribes as Siouan. Swanton (1923, 1936) and Speck (1935) have written on the eastern Siouan tribes. Miller (1957) attempted to prove there were no Siouan tribes east of the Mississippi. Sturtevant (1958) replied to Miller and noted that nonlinguistic considerations cannot be used for determining linguistic relationships (p. 741). Miller (1957) had both ignored linguistic evidence (of Ofo and Biloxi) and challenged the reliability of the Tutelo material of Hale and others in arguing for an Algonquian identity of several eastern tribes.

72. Wolff (1950, 1951b) wrote it θegiha.

73. Dorsey had over a thousand Quapaw words but did not make use of them, since he was "unwilling to publish any of this [Quapaw] material at present" (1885:920).

74. Gallatin (1836:87) illustrated the more striking similarities between Catawba and Woccon in a brief comparative vocabulary.

75. Haas and Swadesh found a woman of Biloxi descent living in Port Arthur, Texas, in 1934 (Haas 1968:77). In the summer of 1969 I met several

women at Marksville, Louisiana, of Biloxi parentage, none of whom remembered any of the Biloxi language.

76. P. 207, biographic sketch of Dorsey by Mooney in Dorsey (1897).

77. This brief sketch of Catawba history is based on Mooney (1907c) and Swanton (1946:104-105). For more on their history, see Brown (1966). For a study of Catawba society by a social anthropologist, see Hudson (1970).

78. Barton's (1798) specimen of Catawba consisted of some thirty-one words collected by Barton upon the arrival of two Catawba Indians in Philadelphia "while this [1798] edition was in the press" (p. 22 of separately paginated appendix). Barton (1797) wrote in his first edition that he had "not been able to procure any word in the language of the Katahba" (p. lxix), but nevertheless in his vocabularies entered "Katahba" 31 times followed by asterisks to indicate no Catawba words were available. The numerous entries of "Katahba" apparently led Pilling (1885:61) to assume a "Katahba" vocabulary in Barton (1797), when not a single Catawba word is given.

79. In 1964 McDavid sent all his Catawba materials to Mary R. Haas. Dr. Haas has kindly turned over McDavid's notebooks and other materials to me. Duplicates were made of all the material and sent to Dr. Haas. Judith Crawford has begun an analysis of McDavid's material. When time permits, I expect also to begin work on it.

80. This brief account of the Ofo is from Swanton (1909, 1910, 1946: 164-66).

81. The Choctaw word for 'dog' is ofi. 'Nation, people' in Choctaw is okla.

82. See Haas (1969c) for a description of Swanton's manner of editing Dorsey's materials and for an understanding of Swanton's methods of arrangement and analysis in the preparation of dictionaries.

83. According to Dorsey (1886), the latter name was what the Illinois tribes called the Omaha, Ponca, Osage, Kansa, and Quapaw when these five tribes lived together as one nation on the Ohio River: "Five of these peoples, the Omahas, Ponkas, Osages, Kansas and Kwapas, were then together as one nation. They were called Arkansa or Alkansa by the Illinois tribes, and they dwelt near the Ohio river" (p. 215). Dorsey has also identified Arkansa as the Algonquian name for the Quapaw only; Gatschet (1884) wrote: "From Rev. J. Owen Dorsey, who makes a special study of all the Dakota tribes, I

obtained the following oral information, founded on his personal intercourse with individuals of the Káppa tribe: 'Ákansa is the Algonkin name by which the Kápa, Quápa were called by the eastern Indians, as Illinois, etc. They called themselves Ugáxpa. . . ' " (pp. 29-30). French explorers and missionaries of the eighteenth century referred to the Quapaw by their Algonquian name (Thomas 1910:336).

84. Swanton (1946) believed the Quapaw "were probably distinct from the Pacaha met by De Soto, with whom they have sometimes been identified" (p. 176), e. g. , by Cyrus Thomas (1910:336).

85. Swanton (1946:176) reported that the acquisition of the Kansas and Oklahoma lands occurred in 1833.

86. Pilling (1885:62, 1887:4) stated that Barton (1798) published an "Arkanzas" vocabulary from Bossu. I was able to find only one Akanzas [sic] word in Barton (1798): Coyocopchill, translated as "God" (p. 2), which is similar to the Natchez word for "God": Coyococop-chill (Barton 1797:2, 1798:2). The Arkansas word Coyocopchill can be found in Bossu (1962:60) and is said by Bossu to mean "Great Spirit" or the "Master of Life".

87. Voegelin (1941b:25) listed Kansa as extinct, followed by a question mark. C. F. and F. M. Voegelin (1964) wrote that there are "fewer than 10 speakers of Quapaw (Chafe) out of a total population of 720 in Oklahoma (Tax); and 10 to 100 speakers of Kansa, now in Oklahoma" (pp. 115-16). If Chafe's (1962) figures for Kansa (p. 166) and for Quapaw (p. 168) are correct, Quapaw seems closer to extinction than Kansa. According to Chafe (1962) speakers of both languages are all over fifty years of age.

Before the volume goes to press, it has been possible to insert the following item seen in Conference on American Indian Languages Clearinghouse Newsletter, Vol. 2, No. 2, April, 1974, James L. Fidelholtz, ed. , p. 18:

From Bob Rankin:

> ". . . I spent the summer working on the Quapaw language and have informants lined up for Kansa (Kaw). Both are near extinction. There is only one (senile) speaker of Quapaw and only about 6 of Kansa (hopefully nonsenile). The other Dhegiha Siouan languages are in better shape. . . "

Rankin's address, according to Fidelholtz (p. 22), is: Ling. Dept. , U. of Kansas, Lawrence, KS 66045.

88. Mooney (1910f) wrote that "they are first mentioned by Captain John

Smith in 1609 under the names of Monacan and Mannahoac, with many subtribes, occupying the upper waters of James and Rappahannock rs., Va." (p. 855).

89. These notes on Tutelo are based primarily on Hale (1883c) and Mooney (1894, 1910f).

90. John R. Swanton located a copy of this same document in the Newberry Library, Chicago, and prepared it for publication in IJAL, but withdrew it from the editor of the journal after learning of the publication of the material from the original document (Gatschet and Swanton 1932:3).

91. According to Swanton (1919a), Akokisa may have been of the western dialect, since it, "to judge by the Bérenger vocabulary, differed but slightly from the dialect of Lake Charles [the western dialect]" (p. 10).

92. For a sketch of Chitimacha history and culture see Swanton (1911: 337-60, 1946:119-21). Swanton (1911:45) estimated about fifty Chitimacha living at Charenton, reduced from 2,625 in 1698. Swadesh (1933:192) wrote there may be as many as one hundred Chitimacha in St. Mary's Parish, the parish in which Charenton is located. Swadesh (1948:230, n. 10) gave the "present" population as 65. Densmore (1943a:6) estimated about fifty Chitimacha. I visited the Chitimacha in August 1969 and was told that on the 400 acres of land owned by the tribe there lived about two hundred Chitimacha, mostly of mixed blood from intermarriage with whites.

93. Swadesh (1946a:313) wrote that Gatschet recorded Chitimacha material in 1886. Swadesh has made an error in the date. Powell (1884:xxii-xxiii), in reporting on Gatschet's activities for 1881-82, wrote that Gatschet left in November 1881 for South Carolina to investigate the Catawba. After leaving the Catawba, Gatschet visited the Choctaw north of Lake Pontchartrain and from there went to Charenton, where he spent two weeks collecting "phrases, sentences, and terms" in Chitimacha (p. xxiii). Gatschet did go to Louisiana in the late months of 1886, during which time he obtained vocabularies of Biloxi and Tunica (Powell 1891b:xx-xxi), but he did not visit the Chitimacha.

94. See Swanton (1911) for a summary of all that is known about the history and culture of the Natchez. Pp. 45-257 deal specifically with the Natchez. There are numerous references to the tribe elsewhere in the book.

95. See Swanton (1911) for a complete list of references. A Dutchman,

Antoine Simon Le Page du Pratz, arrived in Louisiana in 1718 and spent 16 years there. Le Page du Pratz left an interesting account of the Natchez in a book published in Paris in 1758 and translated into English in 1763 and 1774. An undated edition (printed in or before 1947) of the 1774 English translation was published by the Pelican Press, New Orleans.

96. This sketch of Natchez history is based primarily on Mooney (1894: 83-84, 1899).

97. In 1884-85, according to Pilling (1889:39).

98. See the map facing p. 348, Final Report of the United States De Soto Expedition Commission (1939) for de Soto's route through Florida.

99. This sketch of Timucua history is based primarily on Mooney (1910e) and Milanich and Sturtevant (1972:1-6). See pp. 115-21 of the latter for references to Timucua history and culture.

100. See Milanich and Sturtevant (1972:7-9, 15-21), Granberry (1956:98), and Vinson (1886:v-xi) for a description of these sources. Pareja may have prepared a Timucua dictionary and two other religious tracts, but none of these have been discovered (Milanich and Sturtevant 1972:16). Two religious texts were written by Frey Gregorio de Movilla in Timucua and Spanish and published in 1635 and 1636 (Milanich and Sturtevant 1972:7-9). There are two other works in Timucua, both of which are letters by Timucua chiefs written in Timucua and Spanish (Milanich and Sturtevant 1972:9). One letter signed by six Timucua chiefs in 1688, was reprinted by Smith (1860c) with English translation.

101. Smith (1860a:40) wrote that a duplicate copy of the Confessionario is known to exist in a private library in Spain.

102. Leclerc's discovery of the copy of Pareja's grammar appears not to have been "announced" to the Congress until the Copenhagen session in 1883 when Julien Vinson (1883) reported that he and Lucien Adam were preparing the grammar for publication. Milanich and Sturtevant (1972) wrote that "evidently misled by a remark on p. 365 [apparently Vinson's (1883:365) statement: 'Mais j'ai suffissamment traité ce sujet au Congrès de Madrid.'], Gatschet said in Pilling 1885:568 that the discovery was first announced at the 1881 Madrid Congress of Americanists" (p. 7). The impression left by Milanich and Sturtevant (1972:7) is an ignorance of Leclerc's discovery by the scientists until Vinson's formal announcement in Copenhagen in 1883.

Gatschet's two notes in the American Antiquarian state clearly that the volume was exhibited before the assembled scientists.

103. See n. 39. This letter was reprinted by Smith (1860c). Milanich and Sturtevant (1972:9) wrote that the letter was first printed by Smith in 1859.

104. Warao (Guarauan) is placed by C. F. and F. M. Voegelin (1965) in the (B) group of the Macro-Chibchan phylum, with about ten thousand speakers (pp. 25-26, 39).

105. This sketch of the Tunica is based mostly on Tunica (1910) and Swanton (1946:197-99). Swanton (1911:306-26) has provided considerable detail on the history and culture of the Tunica. Haas (1943) has written on the female solar deity of the Tunica. Haas (1950b:1-8) has given more information on Tunica myths in the introduction to her "Tunica texts".

106. I use Haas (1950b:10, line 5) as authority for 1940 as the date of publication, although the volume did not appear until 1941. As noted by Trager (1941:357) in his review of Haas' Tunica grammar, there is no date on the title page. The only date given in the grammar is July 1940 on p. 11, supplied by Haas at the end of the introduction to the grammar.

107. I obtained eight Tunica words in 1969 from an old woman of Tunica and Biloxi descent and about the same number from an old Tunica man.

108. Personal communication from Claude Medford and Joseph Pierrite, August 1969.

109. "Yuchi" is the modern spelling of the name of the language and tribe, used first by Gatschet (1884:17). Powell (1891a:126-27) followed Gatschet in this spelling of the tribal name; but, in line with his principles for naming language families (pp. 10-11), Powell placed the Yuchi language in the "Uchean" family (p. 126), following Gallatin (1836) who had used the spelling "Uchee", e. g. , pp. 95, 96, 97, and 119, but "Utchees" p. 306. Some other spellings of the tribal name in early literature are: Uche, Euchee, Yuchee, Yutchi, and Hughchee (Speck 1910:1007).

110. John R. Swanton was foremost in making such identifications. For a summary of Swanton's views concerning tribes synonymous with Yuchi, see Swanton (1922:286-312). See Bauxar (1957) for a more recent discussion of Yuchi identifications. Other articles which deal with the identification of tribes believed by Swanton and others to be Yuchi are: Crane (1918, 1919),

Swanton (1919b), Neill (1955), Mason (1963), and Juricek (1964).

111. The Yuchi seem to have been dispersed throughout central Georgia, from the towns on the Chattahoochee River eastward to the white settlements southeast of Milledgeville. They may have been, in the 1730's, the exclusive occupants of the land above Ebenezer between the Ogeechee and Savannah rivers, as far north as Bryar Creek, which enters the Savannah about halfway between Augusta and Savannah. The Yuchi village on the Savannah was called Mount Pleasant (De Vorsey 1961:143). Hawkins' (1916) letters contain about thirty references to the Yuchi and their activities. The Yuchi seem to have obtained a reputation for mischief. The Yuchi living with the Shawnee were blamed for stealing two horses from some Cherokee traders (Hawkins 1916:259). The Yuchi received the blame for killing a man and injuring his wife in Washington County (Hawkins 1916:185), for "killing one Allen at Long Bluff" (p. 299), and for having "killed one white man and one white woman, [and] burnt three houses and the fences on the frontiers about 12 miles above Carr's Bluff" (p. 463). Much mischief was done also to the Indians by the whites who entered the Indian country. Troops were needed on occasion to keep the white people "from coming over the line" (p. 464). There was resentment among all Indians to encroachments by whites, but Hawkins' letters give the impression that the Yuchi may have resisted white pressure more vigorously than did the Muskogean tribes of the region.

112. The Yuchi vocabulary was probably recorded in 1825-26 when Ridge and others collected vocabularies from two Creek delegations in Washington (Gallatin 1836:97). The Yuchi chief was probably in one of the Creek delegations.

113. See also Foreman (1948), who quoted Curtin as having learned Yuchi from "Sam Brown, a half-breed Yuchi" (pp. 349-50). Curtin's Yuchi vocabulary may have been lost or misplaced. The BAE catalogue of manuscripts does not list a Yuchi vocabulary by Curtin. A few, probably not all, of Curtin's myths are in BAE Ms. Cat. No. 1293. A few Yuchi words appear in the text of the myths.

114. Gatschet's vocabulary is in the Powell schedule, BAE Cat. No. 1440.

115. BAE Cat. No. 1440. Gatschet (1885) did publish a one-page notice of the Yuchi tribe and language and reported briefly on the sounds and structure of Yuchi.

116. Yuchi songs are on pp. 201-10.

117. My work on Yuchi was supported by two grants from the National Science Foundation, Grant Numbers GS-3056 and GS-28812. I have published an article on Yuchi phonology (Crawford 1973) and am preparing texts, grammar, and dictionary for publication.

118. See Swanton (1911:20-26) for a discussion of and references to accounts of white contacts with the Taensa.

119. I have not seen a copy of this. According to Brinton (1890:453), there is a copy in the Bureau of American Ethnology in Washington.

120. For example, the sugar maple, potato, rice, apple, banana, and white birch all were said to grow in southern Louisiana. For a description of the absurdities and impossibilities found in the Taensa texts and songs, see Brinton (1890).

121. It might be noted that, whenever possible, Haas made reconstructions in the proto-language which was parent to a family of languages before making comparisons for further reconstructions. For example, she reconstructed Proto-Muskogean forms by comparing the individual Muskogean languages. Proto-Muskogean was then compared to Atakapa, Chitimacha, Natchez, and Tunica. Proto-Gulf forms were reconstructed from a comparison of Proto-Muskogean, Atakapa, Chitimacha, Natchez, and Tunica. Proto-Siouan forms, reconstructed from a comparison of the individual Siouan languages, were then compared with Proto-Gulf forms. See Haas (1969b:60-62) for a recent description of the methodology employed in reconstruction.

122. Haas (1958a) had previously demonstrated conclusively a relationship between Algonquian and Ritwan.

123. A suggestion of a Siouan connection for Yuchi had been made by Sapir (1921, 1925:526, 1958:173).

REFERENCES

Abbreviations

AA	American Anthropologist
ARSI	Annual Report of the Board of Regents of the Smithsonian Institution
BAEAR	Bureau of American Ethnology Annual Report
BAEB	Bureau of American Ethnology Bulletin
FHQ	Florida Historical Quarterly
IJAL	International Journal of American Linguistics
PAAAS	Proceedings of the American Association for the Advancement of Science
PAPA	Proceedings of the American Philological Association
PAPS	Proceedings of the American Philosophical Society
RLPC	Revue de Linguistique et de Philologie Comparée
SIL	Studies in Linguistics
SMC	Smithsonian Miscellaneous Collections
TAPS	Transactions of the American Philosophical Society
VFPA	Viking Fund Publications in Anthropology

Adair, James. 1775. The history of the American Indians .... London: Edwar[d] and Charles Dilly. Reprinted in 1930 by Watauga Press, Johnson City, Tenn. and edited by Samuel Cole Williams.

Allen, Louis. 1931. Siouan and Iroquoian. IJAL 6:185-93.

Anderson, Rev. Joseph. 1872. The newly discovered relationship of the Tuteloes to the Dakotan stock. PAPA 2:15-16.

Badger, H. A. 1971. A descriptive grammar of Mississippi Choctaw. Ph. D. dissertation, 77 pages. Hattiesburg: University of Southern Mississippi.

Barbour, Philip L. , ed. 1969. The Jamestown voyages under the first charter 1606-1609. The Hakluyt Society, 2nd. ser., nos. 136, 137. Cambridge: The Hakluyt Society.

——. 1973. The function of comparative linguistics in the study of early transcriptions of Indian words. SIL 23:3-11.

Barton, Benjamin Smith. 1797. New views of the origin of the tribes and nations of America. Philadelphia: John Bioren.

___. 1798. New views of the origin of the tribes and nations of America. [2nd ed.] Philadelphia: John Bioren.

Bartram, William. 1791. Travels through North and South Carolina, Georgia, East and West Florida.... Philadelphia: James and Johnson.

Bauxar, J. Joseph. 1957. Yuchi ethnoarchaeology. Ethnohistory 4:279-301, 369-464.

Bender, Ernest. 1949. Cherokee II. IJAL 15:223-28.

Bender, Ernest, and Zellig S. Harris. 1946. The phonemes of North Carolina Cherokee. IJAL 12:14-16.

Benveniste, Émile. 1950. La négation en Yuchi. Word 6:99-105.

[Beverley, Robert]. 1705. The history and present state of Virginia, in four parts [each part, or "Book", separately paginated].... London. Reprinted in 1947 by University of North Carolina Press, Chapel Hill, edited with an introduction by Louis B. Wright.

Biloxi. 1907. BAEB 30, Part 1:147-48.

Binford, Lewis R. 1967. An ethnohistory of the Nottoway, Meherrin and Weanock Indians of southeastern Virginia. Ethnohistory 14 (3-4):103-218.

Bloomfield, Leonard. 1925. On the sound system of Central Algonquian. Language 1:130-56.

___. 1946. Algonquian. In Linguistic Structures of Native America, VFPA 6:85-129.

Bossu, Jean-Bernard. 1962. Travels in the interior of North America 1751-1762, translated and edited by Seymour Feiler. xvii, 243 pages. Norman: University of Oklahoma Press.

Boyd, Mark F. 1949. Diego Peña's expedition to Apalachee and Apalachicolo in 1716. FHQ 28(1):1-27.

___. 1952. Documents describing the second and third expeditions of Lieutenant Diego Peña to Apalachee and Apalachicolo in 1717 and 1718. FHQ 31:109-31.

___. 1953. Further consideration of the Apalachee missions. Americas 9:459-79.

Boyd, Mark F., Hale G. Smith, and John W. Griffin. 1951. Here they once stood: the tragic end of the Apalachee missions. Gainesville: University of Florida Press.

Brinton, D. G. 1866. The Shawnees and their migrations. Historical Magazine 10:1-4.

___. 1867. The Natchez of Louisiana, an offshoot of the civilized nations of Central America. Historical Magazine, 2nd ser., 1:16-18.

___. 1870. The national legend of the Chahta-Muskokee tribes. Historical Magazine, 2nd ser., 7:118-26.

___. 1873. On the language of the Natchez. PAPS 13:483-99.

___. 1885. The Taensa grammar and dictionary: a deception exposed. American Antiquarian 7:108-13.

___. 1888a. Linguistique américaine. RLPC 21:54-56.

___. 1888b. Rejoinder to M. Gatschet. RLPC 21:340-41.

___. 1890. The curious hoax of the Taensa language. In Essays of an Americanist, by Daniel G. Brinton, pp. 452-67. Philadelphia: Porter & Coates. Reprinted by Johnson, 1970.

___. 1891. The American race: a linguistic classification and ethnographic description of the native tribes of North and South America. xvi, 392 pages. New York: N. D. C. Hodges. Reprinted by Johnson, 1970.

Brown, Douglas Summers. 1966. The Catawba Indians, the people of the river. viii, 400 pages. Columbia: University of South Carolina Press.

Bushnell, David I., Jr. 1909. The Choctaw of Bayou Lacomb, St. Tammany Parish, Louisiana. ix, 37 pages. BAEB 48.

___. 1940. Virginia before Jamestown. SMC 100:125-58.

Byington, Cyrus. 1870. Grammar of the Choctaw language, ed. D. G. Brinton. PAPS 11:317-67.

___. 1915. A dictionary of the Choctaw language, John R. Swanton and Henry S. Halbert. xi, 611 pages. BAEB 46.

Capron, Louis. 1953. The medicine bundles of the Florida Seminole and the green corn dance. BAEB 151:155-210 (Anthropological Papers, No. 35).

Chafe, Wallace L. 1962. Estimates regarding the present speakers of North American Indian languages. IJAL 28:162-71.

___. 1964. Another look at Siouan and Iroquoian. AA 66:852-62.

___. 1965. Corrected estimates regarding speakers of Indian languages. IJAL 31:345-46.

___. 1973. Siouan, Iroquoian, and Caddoan. In Linguistics in North America, Part 2, Current Trends in Linguistics 10, ed. Thomas A. Sebeok, pp. 1164-1209. The Hague: Mouton.

Conference on Algonquian Linguistics. 1967. Contributions to Anthropology: Linguistics (Algonquian), National Museum of Canada Bulletin No. 214, Anthropological Series No. 78.

Crane, Verner W. 1918. An historical note on the Westo Indians. AA 20: 331-37.

___. 1919. Westo and Chisca. AA 21:463-65.

Crawford, James M. 1973. Yuchi phonology. IJAL 39:173-79.

Creek. 1907. BAEB 30, Part 1:362-65.

Dalrymple, Rev. Mr. 1858. [Pamunkey words]. Historical Magazine 2:182.

Day, Gordon M. 1967. Historical notes on New England languages. In Contributions to Anthropology: Linguistics (Algonquian), National Museum of Canada Bulletin No. 214, Anthropological Series No. 78:107-12.

Densmore, Frances. 1937. The Alabama Indians and their music. In Straight Texas, Publications of the Texas Folk-lore Society 13:270-93.

___. 1943a. A search for songs among the Chitimacha Indians in Louisiana. BAEB 133:1-15 (Anthropological Papers No. 19).

___. 1943b. Choctaw music. BAEB 136:101-88 (Anthropological Papers, No. 28).

De Vorsey, Louis, Jr. 1961. The Indian boundary in the southern colonies, 1763-1775. Chapel Hill: University of North Carolina Press.

___, ed. 1971. De Brahm's report of the general survey in the southern district of North America. Columbia: University of South Carolina Press.

Dorsey, J. Owen. 1885. On the comparative phonology of four Siouan languages. ARSI, 1883, pp. 919-29. Washington, D. C.

___. 1886. Migrations of Siouan tribes. American Naturalist 20:211-22.

___. 1890. The Ȼegiha language. Contributions to North American Ethnology 6. U. S. Geographical and Geological Survey of the Rocky Mountain Region. xviii, 794 pages. Washington, D. C.

___. 1894. The Biloxi Indians of Louisiana. PAAAS, 42nd Meeting, 1893, pp. 267-87.

___. 1897. Siouan sociology, a posthumous paper. BAEAR 10 (1893-94): 205-44.

Dorsey, James Owen, and John R. Swanton. 1912. A dictionary of the Biloxi and Ofo languages, accompanied with thirty-one Biloxi texts and numerous Biloxi phrases. v, 340 pages. BAEB 47.

Eggan, Fred. 1937. Historical changes in the Choctaw kinship system. AA 39:34-52.

Elmendorf, William W. 1963. Yukian-Siouan lexical similarities. IJAL 29:300-09.

___. 1964. Item and set comparison in Yuchi, Siouan, and Yukian. IJAL 30:328-40.

Fenton, William N., and John Gulick, ed. 1961. Symposium on Cherokee and Iroquois culture. BAEB 180:3-8.

Fickett, Joan Gleason. 1967. The phonology of Tuscarora. SIL 19:33-57.

Final Report of the United States De Soto Expedition Commission. 1939. House Document No. 71, 76th Cong. 1st Sess. xvi, 400 pages, with maps. Washington, D. C.

Fletcher, Alice C. 1907. Caddo. BAEB 30, Part 1:179-82.

Fletcher, Alice C., and Francis La Flesche. 1911. The Omaha tribe. BAEAR 27 (1905-06):17-672.

Folsom-Dickerson, W. E. S. 1965. The White path. iv, 148 pages. San Antonio, Tex.: Naylor.

Foreman, Carolyn Thomas. 1948. Jeremiah Curtin in Indian Territory. Chronicles of Oklahoma 26:345-56.

Fortune, R. F. 1932. Omaha secret societies. Columbia University Contributions to Anthropology 14, vi, 193 pages. New York: Columbia University Press.

Frachtenberg, Leo J. 1913. Contributions to a Tutelo vocabulary. AA 15: 477-79.

Frantz, Donald G. 1967. Blackfoot paradigms and matrices. In Contributions to Anthropology: Linguistics (Algonquian), National Museum of Canada Bulletin No. 214. Anthropological Series No. 78:140-46.

Freeman, John F. 1966. A guide to manuscripts relating to the American Indian in the library of the American Philosophical Society. Philadelphia: The American Philosophical Society.

Garbarino, Merwyn S. 1972. Big Cypress, a changing Seminole community. x, 132 pages. New York: Holt, Rinehart, and Winston.

Gallatin, Albert. 1836. A synopsis of the Indian tribes of North America. Transactions and Collections of the American Antiquarian Society 2:1-422.

___. 1848. Hale's Indians of North-west America, and vocabularies of North America. Transactions of the American Ethnological Society 2:xxiii-clxxxviii, 1-130.

Garvin, Paul L. 1950. Wichita I: phonemics. IJAL 16:179-84.

Gatschet, Albert S. 1877. The Timucua language. PAPS 16:626-42.

___. 1878. The Timucua language. PAPS 17:490-504.

___. 1879-80. Caddo. American Antiquarian 2:236-37.

___. 1880. The Timucua language. PAPS 18:465-502.

___. 1881-82. Review of: Chahta Leksikon, by Allen Wright, Presbyterian Publishing Company, St. Louis, 1880. American Antiquarian 4:338-39.

___. 1883a. The Shetimasha Indians of St. Mary's parish, southern Louisiana. Transactions of the Anthropological Society of Washington 2:148-58.

___. 1883b. Pareja's Timucua grammar. American Antiquarian 5:283-84.

___. 1884. A migration legend of the Creek Indians, with linguistic, historic and ethnographic introduction. Brinton's Library of Aboriginal American Literature Number IV, pp. vii, 251. Philadelphia: D. G. Brinton.

___. 1885. The Yuchi tribe of Indians, and its language. Science 5:253.

___. 1886a. Timucua of Florida. American Antiquarian 8:187.

___. 1886b. On the affinity of the Cheroki to the Iroquois dialects. PAPA 16:xl-xlv.

___. 1888. Réplique à Mr. D. G. Brinton au sujet de son article "Linguistique américaine". RLPC 21:199-208.

___. 1889. Sex-denoting nouns in American languages. TAPS 20:159-71.

___. 1891. Two Indian documents (I. Migration of the Wichita Indians. II. Removal of the Taensa Indians). American Antiquarian 13:249-54.

___. 1892. Tchikilli's Kasi'hta legend in the Creek and Hitchiti languages, with a critical commentary and full glossaries to both texts. Transactions of the Academy of Science of St. Louis 5 (1886-91):33-239.

___. 1893. Some mythic stories of the Yuchi Indians. AA 6:279-82.

___. 1900. Grammatic sketch of the Catawba language. AA 2:527-49.

___. 1902. Onomatology of the Catawba River Basin. AA 4:52-56.

___. 1907a. Chitimacha. BAEB 30, Part 1:286.

___. 1907b. Hitchiti. BAEB 30, Part 1:551.

Gatschet, Albert, and Raoul de la Grasserie. 1889. Textes Timucua, traduits et analysés (1). RLPC 22:320-46.

Gatschet, Albert S. , and John R. Swanton. 1932. A dictionary of the Atakapa language, accompanied by text material. v, 181 pages. BAEB 108.

Gatschet, Albert S. , and Cyrus Thomas. 1907. Chickasaw. BAEB 30, Part 1:260-62.

Geary, James A. 1953. Strachey's vocabulary of Indian words used in Virginia, 1612. In The historie of travell into Virginia Britania (1612), ed. by Louis B. Wright and Virginia Freund, The Hakluyt Society, 2nd series, no. 103, pp. 208-14. London: The Hakluyt Society.

___. 1955. The language of the Carolina Algonkian tribes (A. An introductory study of the position of the Indian language of Virginia and North Carolina in the Algonquian family. B. List of Indian words found in the documents, with notes on their meaning). The Hakluyt Society, 2nd series, no. 104 (The Roanoke Voyages, Vol. 2), pp. 873-900. London: The Hakluyt Society.

Gerard, William R. 1904. The Tapehanek dialect of Virginia. AA 6:313-36.

___. 1905. Some Virginia words. AA 7:222-49.

Goddard, Ives. 1967a. Notes on the genetic classification of the Algonquian languages. In Contributions to Anthropology: Linguistics I (Algonquian), National Museum of Canada Bulletin No. 214, Anthropological Series No. 78:7-12.

___. 1967b. The Algonquian independent indicative. In Contributions to Anthropology: Linguistics (Algonquian), National Museum of Canada Bulletin No. 214, Anthropological Series No. 78:66-106.

Goddard, Pliny Earle. 1914. The present condition of our knowledge of North American languages. AA 16:555-601.

Granberry, Julian. 1956. Timucua I: prosodics and phonemics of the Mocama dialect. IJAL 22:97-105.

___. 1970. Abstract of Granberry's work on Timucua, entitled: Grant No. 4633—Penrose Fund (1967), $500. Final collation of texts, vocabulary lists, grammar, of Timucua for publication. American Philosophical Society Yearbook, 1970, pp. 606-607.

Grasserie, Raoul de la. 1888a. Esquisse d'une grammaire du Timucua, langue de Florida. RLPC 21:209-34, 295-313.

___. 1888b. Textes analysés et vocabulaire de la langue Timucua. International Congress of Americanists 7:403-37.

___. 1889. Vocabulaire timucua. RLPC 22:168-83.

Gursky, Karl-Heinz. 1965a. Ein lexikalischer Vergleich der Algonkin-Golf-und Hoka-Subtiaba-Sprachen (1). Orbis 14(1):160-215.

___. 1965b. Lexical similarities between Caddoan and Algonkian-Gulf. Anthropological Linguistics 7(4), Pt. II:104-109.

___. 1966. Ein Vergleich der grammatikalischen Morpheme der Golf-Sprachen und der Hoka-Subtiaba-Sprachen. Orbis 15(2).

___. 1968. Gulf and Hokan-Subtiaban: new lexical parallels. IJAL 34:21-41.

___. 1969. A lexical comparison of the Atakapa, Chitimacha, and Tunica languages. IJAL 35:83-107.

Haas, Mary R. 1938. Geminate consonant clusters in Muskogee. Language 14:61-65.

___. 1939. Natchez and Chitimacha clans and kinship terminology. AA 41:597-610.

___. 1940a. Ablaut and its function in Muscogee. Language 16:141-50.

___.. 1940b. Creek inter-town relations. AA 42:479-89.

___. 1940c. Tunica. In Handbook of American Indian Languages 4:1-143. New York: J. J. Augustin.

___. 1941a. Noun incorporation in the Muskogean languages. Language 17:311-15.

___. 1941b. A popular etymology in Muskogee. Language 17:340-41.

___. 1941c. The Choctaw word for "rattlesnake". AA 43:129-32.

___. 1941d. The classification of the Muskogean languages. In Language, Culture and Personality, Essays in Memory of Edward Sapir, ed. Leslie Spier et al., 41-56. Menasha, Wisconsin.

___. 1943. The solar deity of the Tunica. Papers of the Michigan Academy of Science, Arts, and Letters 28 (1942):531-35.

___. 1944. Men's and women's speech in Koasati. Language 20:142-49.

___. 1945. Dialects of the Muskogee language. IJAL 11:69-74.

___. 1946a. A Proto-Muskogean paradigm. Language 22:326-32.

___. 1946b. A grammatical sketch of Tunica. In Linguistic Structures of Native America, VFPA 6:337-66.

___. 1947. Development of Proto-Muskogean $*k^w$. IJAL 13:135-37.

___. 1947-48. Some French loan-words in Tunica. Romance Philology 1:145-48.

___. 1948. Classificatory verbs in Muskogee. IJAL 14:244-46.

___. 1949. The position of Apalachee in the Muskogean family. IJAL 15: 121-27.

___. 1950a. On the historical development of certain long vowels in Creek. IJAL 16:122-25.

___. 1950b. Tunica texts. University of California Publications in Linguistics 6:1-174.

___. 1951. The Proto-Gulf word for water (with notes on Siouan-Yuchi). IJAL 17:71-79.

___. 1952. The Proto-Gulf word for land (with a note on Proto-Siouan). IJAL 18:236-40.

___. 1953. Tunica dictionary. University of California Publications in Linguistics 6:175-332.

___. 1956. Natchez and the Muskogean languages. Language 32:61-72.

___. 1958a. Algonkian-Ritwan: the end of a controversy. IJAL 24:159-73.

___. 1958b. A new linguistic relationship in North America: Algonkian and the Gulf languages. Southwestern Journal of Anthropology 14:231-64.

___. 1959. Tonkawa and Algonkian. Anthropological Linguistics 1(2):1-6.

___. 1960. Some genetic affiliations of Algonkian. In Culture in History: Essays in Honor of Paul Radin, pp. 977-92. New York: Columbia University Press.

___. 1961. Comment on Floyd G. Lounsbury's "Iroquois-Cherokee linguistic relations". In Symposium on Cherokee and Iroquois Culture, ed. William N. Fenton and John Gulick. BAEB 180:21-23.

___. 1963. The Muskogean and Algonkian words for skunk. IJAL 29:65-66.

___. 1964. Athapaskan, Tlingit, Yuchi, and Siouan. In Sobretiro del XXXV Congreso Internacional de Americanistas, México, 1962, Actas y Memorias, pp. 495-500.

___. 1966. Historical linguistics and the genetic relationship of languages. In Current Trends in Linguistics 3, ed. Thomas A. Sebeok, pp. 113-53. The Hague: Mouton.

___. 1967. The Proto-Algonkian word for 'sun'. In Contributions to Anthropology: Linguistics (Algonquian), National Museum of Canada Bulletin No. 214, Anthropological Series No. 78:60-65.

___. 1968. The last words of Biloxi. IJAL 34:77-84.

___. 1969a. Grammar or lexicon? The American Indian side of the question from Duponceau to Powell. IJAL 35:239-55.

___. 1969b. The prehistory of languages. Janua Linguarum, series minor, 57. The Hague: Mouton.

___. 1969c. Swanton and the Biloxi and Ofo dictionaries. IJAL 35:286-90.

___. 1970. Review of: New Views of the Origin of the Tribes and Nations of North America, by Benjamin Smith Barton, Ann Arbor, Michigan: University Microfilms, a Xerox Company, 1968 (Originally Philadelphia: John Bioren, 1797), pp. cix, 83. IJAL 36:68-70.

___. 1971. Southeastern Indian linguistics. In Red, White and Black: Symposium on Indians in the Old South, ed. Charles M. Hudson, SAS Proceedings No. 5:44-54. Athens: University of Georgia Press.

___. 1973. The Southeast. In Linguistics in North America, Part 2, Current Trends in Linguistics 10, ed. Thomas A. Sebeok, pp. 1210-49. The Hague: Mouton.

Hale, Horatio. 1883a. Indian migrations, as evidenced by language. Part I. the Huron stock. American Antiquarian 5:18-28.

___. 1883b. Indian migrations, as evidenced by language. Part II. the Dakota stock, the Algonkins, the Chahta-Muskoki stock, the mound-builders, the Iberians. American Antiquarian 5:108-24.

___. 1883c. The Tutelo tribe and language. PAPS 21:1-47.

Hallowell, A. Irving. 1951. Frank Gouldsmith Speck, 1881-1950. AA 53: 67-87.

Harrington, John P. 1955. The original Strachey vocabulary of the Virginia Indian language. BAEB 157:189-202 (Anthropological Papers, No. 46).

Harriot, Thomas. 1972. A briefe and true report of the new found land of Virginia (the complete 1590 edition with the 28 engravings by Theodor de Bry after the drawings of John White and other illustrations), with a new introduction by Paul Hulton. xv, 91 pages. New York: Dover.

Haumonté, J.-D., Parisot, and L. Adam. 1882. Grammaire et vocabulaire de la langue Taensa avec textes traduits et commentés. Bibliothèque Linguistique Américaine 9. xix, 111 pages. Paris: Maisonneuve et Cie. Reprinted by Kraus Reprint, 1968.

Hawkins, Benjamin. 1848. A sketch of the Creek country. Collections of the Georgia Historical Society 3, Pt. I. 85 pages.

___. 1916. Letters of Benjamin Hawkins 1796-1806. Collections of the Georgia Historical Society 9, 500 pages, 1 map.

Hewitt, J. N. B. 1907. Attacapa. BAEB 30, Part 1:114-15.

___. 1910. Tuscarora. BAEB 30, Part 2:842-53.

Hickerson, Nancy P. 1958. An acoustic analysis of Shawnee: I, II. IJAL 24:20-29, 130-42.

___. 1959. An acoustic analysis of Shawnee: III, IV. IJAL 25:22-31, 97-104.

Hockett, Charles F. 1957. Central Algonquian vocabulary: stems in /k-/. IJAL 23:247-68.

Hodge, F. W. 1923. Report of the ethnologist-in-charge. BAEAR 37 (1915-16):1-31.

Hoijer, Harry. 1973. History of American Indian linguistics. In Linguistics in North America, Part I, Current Trends in Linguistics 10, ed. Thomas A. Sebeok, pp. 657-76. The Hague: Mouton.

Holmer, Nils M. 1947. An Ofo phonetic law. IJAL 13:1-8.

Hudson, Charles M. 1970. The Catawba nation. University of Georgia Monographs, No. 18. x, 142 pages. Athens: University of Georgia Press.

Hulton, Paul, and David Beers Quinn. 1964. The American drawings of John White .... 2 volumes. Chapel Hill: University of North Carolina Press.

Hymes, Dell. 1971. Morris Swadesh: from the first Yale school to world prehistory. In The Origin and Diversification of Language, by Morris Swadesh, ed. Joel Sherzer, pp. 228-70. Chicago: Aldine.

Jacobson, Daniel. 1960. The origin of the Koasati community of Louisiana. Ethnohistory 7:97-120.

Johnston, John. 1820. Account of the present state of the Indian tribes inhabiting Ohio. Transactions and Collections of the American Antiquarian Society 1:271-99.

Jones, Charles C., Jr. 1868. Historical sketch of Tomo-chi-chi, mico of the Yamacraws. Albany, N. Y.: Joel Munsell.

Juricek, John T. 1964. The Westo Indians. Ethnohistory 11:134-73.

Kilpatrick, Anna Gritts, and Jack Frederick Kilpatrick. 1966. Chronicles of Wolftown: social documents of the North Carolina Cherokees, 1850-1862. BAEB 196:1-111 (Anthropological Papers, No. 75).

Kilpatrick, Jack Frederick, ed. 1966. The Wahnenauhi manuscript: historical sketches of the Cherokees, together with some of their customs, traditions, and superstitions. BAEB 196:175-213, 4 plates (Anthropological Papers, No. 77).

Kilpatrick, Jack Frederick, and Anna Gritts Kilpatrick. 1966. Eastern Cherokee folktales: reconstructed from the field notes of Frans M. Olbrechts. BAEB 196:379-447 (Anthropological Papers, No. 80).

___. 1970. Notebook of a Cherokee shaman. Smithsonian Contributions to Anthropology, vol. 2, num. 6. v, 83-125.

Krueger, John R. 1963. Two early grammars of Cherokee. Anthropological Linguistics 5(3):1-57.

Kupferer, Harriet Jane. 1966. The "principal people", 1960: a study of cultural and social groups of the eastern Cherokee. BAEB 196:215-325 (Anthropological Papers, No. 78).

Latham, Robert G. 1846. Miscellaneous contributions to the ethnography of North America. Proceedings of the [London] Philological Society 2: 31-50.

___. 1860. Opuscula: essays chiefly philological and ethnographical. London: Williams and Norgate.

Lawson, John. 1709. A new voyage to Carolina .... London.

Le Page du Pratz. 1758. Histoire de la Louisiane .... 3 volumes (separately paginated). Paris.

Lesser, Alexander, and Gene Weltfish. 1932. Composition of the Caddoan linguistic stock. SMC 87(6):1-15.

Lieber, Oscar M. 1858. Vocabulary of the Catawba language, with some remarks on its grammar, construction and pronunciation. Collections of the South Carolina Historical Society 2:327-42.

Loughridge, R. M., and David M. Hodge. 1964. English and Muskokee dictionary [and, beginning on p. 95] Dictionary of the Muskokee or Creek language in Creek and English. Okmulgee, Oklahoma: B. Frank Belvin, General Missionary to Creek and Seminole Indians, Baptist Home Mission Board.

Lounsbury, Floyd G. 1961. Iroquois-Cherokee linguistic relations. BAEB 180:11-17.

MacCauley, Clay. 1887. The Seminole Indians of Florida. BAEAR 5 (1883-84):469-531.

Malone, Prairie View. 1960. Sam Houston's Indians: The Alabama-Coushatti. xiv, 63 pages. San Antonio, Texas: Naylor.

Mason, Carol Irwin. 1963. A reconsideration of Westo-Yuchi identification. AA 65:1342-46.

Matthews, G. Hubert. 1958. Handbook of Siouan languages. Ph. D. dissertation. University of Pennsylvania.

___. 1959. Proto-Siouan kinship terminology. AA 61:252-78.

___. 1970. Some notes on the Proto-Siouan continuants. IJAL 36:98-109.

Matthews, G. Hubert, and Red Thunder Cloud. 1967. Catawba texts. IJAL 33:7-24.

Michelson, Truman. 1912. Preliminary report on the classification of Algonquian tribes. BAEAR 28 (1906-07):37-813.

___. 1933. The linguistic classification of Powhatan. AA 35:549.

___. 1935. Phonetic shifts in Algonquian languages. IJAL 8:131-71.

Milanich, Jerald T., and William C. Sturtevant. 1972. Francisco Pareja's 1613 _Confessionario_, a documentary source for Timucuan ethnography. Tallahassee, Florida: Division of Archives, History, and Records Management, Florida Department of State.

Miller, Carl F. 1957. Revaluation of the eastern Siouan problem with particular emphasis on the Virginia branches—the Occaneechi, the Saponi, and the Tutelo. BAEB 164:115-211.

Miller, Wick R. 1959. An outline of Shawnee historical phonology. IJAL 25:16-21.

Mooney, James. 1891. The sacred formulas of the Cherokees. BAEAR 7 (1885-86):301-97.

___. 1894. The Siouan tribes of the east. 101 pages. BAEB 22.

___. 1896. The Ghost-dance religion and the Sioux outbreak of 1890. BAEAR 14 (1892-93), Part 2:641-1110.

____. 1899. The end of the Natchez. AA 1:510-21.

____. 1900. Myths of the Cherokees. BAEAR 19 (1897-98), Part 1:3-548.

____. 1907a. The Powhatan confederacy, past and present. AA 9:129-52.

____. 1907b. Apalachee. BAEB 30, Part 1:67-68.

____. 1907c. Catawba. BAEB 30, Part 1:213-16.

____. 1907d. Cherokee. BAEB 30, Part 1:245-49.

____. 1907e. Meherrin. BAEB 30, Part 1:839.

____. 1907f. Albert Samuel Gatschet——1832-1907. AA 9:561-70.

____. 1910a. Nottoway. BAEB 30, Part 2:87.

____. 1910b. Pamlico. BAEB 30, Part 2:197.

____. 1910c. Powhatan. BAEB 30, Part 2:299-302.

____. 1910d. Shawnee. BAEB 30, Part 2:530-38.

____. 1910e. Timucua. BAEB 30, Part 2:752.

____. 1910f. Tutelo. BAEB 30, Part 2:855-56.

____. 1932. The Swimmer manuscript: Cherokee sacred formulas and medicinal prescriptions, reviewed, completed, and edited by Frans M. Olbrechts. xvii, 319 pages. BAEB 99.

Mooney, James, and Cyrus Thomas. 1907. Alibamu. BAEB 30, Part 1:44-45.

Morgan, Lewis H. 1851. League of the Ho-dé-no-sau-nee, Iroquois. Rochester: Sage and Brother. Reprinted 1962 by Corinth Books, New York.

____. 1870. Indian migrations. North American Review 110:33-82. Reprinted by AMS Press, 1968.

____. 1871. Systems of consanguinity and affinity of the human family. Smithsonian Contributions to Knowledge 17. xii, 590 pages, 14 plates.

Morse, Jedidiah. 1822. A report to the Secretary of War of the United States, on Indian affairs, comprising a narrative of a tour performed in the summer of 1820. New Haven.

Neill, Wilfred T. 1955. An historic Indian burial from Columbia County, Georgia. Southern Indian Studies 7:3-9.

Nettl, Bruno. 1953. The Shawnee musical style: historical perspective in primitive music. Southwestern Journal of Anthropology 9:277-85.

Olbrechts, Frans M. 1931. Two Cherokee texts. IJAL 6:179-84.

Pareja, Francisco. 1886. Arte de la lengua timvqvana compvesto en 1614 por el Pe Francisco Pareja y publicado comforme al ejemplar original único por Lucien Adam y Julien Vinson. Bibliothèque Linguistique Américaine 11.

xxxi, 132 pages. Paris: Maisonneuve Frères et Ch. Leclerc. Reprinted by Kraus, 1968.

Parisot, J. 1880. Notes sur la langue des Taensas (ancienne Louisiane). RLPC 13:166-86.

Parsons, Elsie Clews. 1941. Notes on the Caddo. Memoirs of the American Anthropological Association 57:1-76.

Pilling, James Constantine. 1885. Proof-sheets of a bibliography of the languages of the North American Indians. Bureau of American Ethnology Miscellaneous Publication 2. Reprinted by Central Book Co., Brooklyn, N. Y., 1966.

___. 1887. Bibliography of the Siouan languages. v, 87 pages. BAEB 5.

___. 1888. Bibliography of the Iroquoian languages. vi, 208 pages. BAEB 6.

___. 1889. Bibliography of the Muskhogean languages. v, 114 pages. BAEB 9.

___. 1891. Bibliography of the Algonquian languages. x, 614 pages. BAEB 13.

Pollard, Jno. Garland. 1894. The Pamunkey Indians of Virginia. 19 pages. BAEB 17.

Powell, J. W. 1884. Report of the director. BAEAR (1881-82) 3:xii-lxxiv.

___. 1887. Report of the director. BAEAR (1883-84) 5:xvii-lii.

___. 1888. Report of the director. BAEAR (1884-85) 6:xxiii-lviii.

___. 1891a. Indian linguistic families north of Mexico. BAEAR 7 (1885-86):1-142, map.

___. 1891b. Report of the director. BAEAR (1886-87) 8:xiii-xxxvi.

Quinn, David Beers. 1955. The Roanoke Voyages 1584-1590, documents to illustrate the English voyages to North America under the patent granted to Walter Raleigh in 1584. The Hakluyt Society, 2nd. ser., nos. 104, 105 (2 vols.), London.

Ramsey, J. G. M. 1853. The annals of Tennessee.... Charleston, S. C.: Walker and Jones. Reprinted 1967, with the addition of a biographical introduction, annotations and index for the East Tennessee Historical Society, Knoxville, Tennessee, by Kingsport Press, Kingsport, Tennessee.

Rand, Earl. 1968. The structural phonology of Alabaman, a Muskogean language. IJAL 34:94-103.

Read, William A. 1940. Notes on an Opelousas manuscript of 1862. AA 42: 546-48.

Reyburn, William D. 1953. Cherokee verb morphology I, II. IJAL 19:172-80, 259-73.

___. 1954. Cherokee verb morphology III. IJAL 20:44-64.

Riggs, Stephen Return (ed. James Owen Dorsey). 1893. Dakota grammar, texts, and ethnography. Contributions to North American Ethnology 9. xxxii, 239 pages. U. S. Geographical and Geological Survey of the Rocky Mountain Region, Dept. of the Interior, J. W. Powell in charge.

Rothe, Aline. 1963. Kalita's people: a history of the Alabama-Coushatta Indians of Texas. xxiii, 141 pages, 13 illustrations. Waco, Tex. : Texian Press.

Royce, C. C. 1880-81. An inquiry into the identity and history of the Shawnee Indians. American Antiquarian 3:177-89.

Salzmann, Zdeněk. 1967a. Some aspects of Arapaho morphology. In Contributions to Anthropology: Linguistics (Algonquian), National Museum of Canada Bulletin No. 214, Anthropological Series No. 78:128-34.

___. 1967b. On the inflection of transitive animate verbs in Arapaho. In Contributions to Anthropology: Linguistics (Algonquian), National Museum of Canada Bulletin No. 214, Anthropological Series No. 78:135-39.

Sapir, Edward. 1913. A Tutelo vocabulary. AA 15:295-97.

___. 1921. A bird's-eye view of American languages north of Mexico. Science 54:408.

___. 1925. The Hokan affinity of Subtiaba in Nicaragua. AA 27:402-35, 491-527.

___. 1958. Central and North American languages. In Selected Writings of Edward Sapir in Language, Culture and Personality, ed. David G. Mandelbaum, pp. 169-78. Berkeley: University of California Press. First published in 1929 in Encyclopaedia Britannica (14th ed.)5:138-41.

Schoolcraft, Henry R. 1852. Information respecting the history, condition and prospects of the Indian tribes of the United States: collected and prepared under the direction of the Bureau of Indian Affairs, per act of Congress of March 3d, 1847. Part 2. Philadelphia: Lippincott, Grambo.

___. 1853. Information respecting the history, condition and prospects of the Indian tribes of the United States: collected and prepared under the direction of the Bureau of Indian Affairs, per act of Congress of March 3d, 1847. Part 3. Philadelphia: Lippincott, Grambo.

Sibley, John. 1832. Historical sketches of the several Indian tribes in Louisiana, south of the Arkansas River, and between the Mississippi and River Grande. In American State Papers, Class II, Indian Affairs, vol. 1, pp. 721-43. (Also in Ann. Cong., 9th Cong., 2d Sess., cols. 1076-88).

Siebert, Frank T., Jr. 1941. Certain Proto-Algonquian consonant clusters. Language 17:298-303.

___. 1945. Linguistic classification of Catawba: Part I, Part II. IJAL 11: 100-104, 211-18.

___. 1967a. The original home of the Proto-Algonquian people. In Contributions to Anthropology: Linguistics I (Algonquian), National Museum of Canada Bulletin No. 214, Anthropological Series No. 78:13-47.

___. 1967b. Discrepant consonant clusters ending in *k in Proto-Algonquian, a proposed interpretation of saltatory sound changes. In Contributions to Anthropology: Linguistics I (Algonquian), National Museum of Canada Bulletin No. 214, Anthropological Series No. 78:48-59.

Skinner, Alanson. 1913. Notes on the Florida Seminole. AA 15:63-77.

Smith, Buckingham. 1858. The Timuquana language. Historical Magazine 2:1-3.

___. 1860a. Books printed in the Timuquan language. Historical Magazine 4:39-40.

___. 1860b. Specimen of the Appalachian language. Historical Magazine 4:40-41.

___. 1860c. [Sentences in Timucua]. Historical Magazine 4:180-81.

___. 1866a. Comparative vocabularies of the Seminole and Mikasuke tongues. Historical Magazine 10:239-43.

___. 1866b. Lord's prayer in Mikasuke. Historical Magazine 10:288.

Smith, Captain John. 1969a. A trve relation of such occurences and accidents of noate as hath hapned in Virginia. . . . In Jamestown Voyages Under the First Charter, 1606-1609, Vol. 1, ed. Philip L. Barbour. The Hakluyt Society, 2nd. ser., no. 136, pp. 165-208. Cambridge: Cambridge University Press. First published in 1608 in London.

Smith, Captain John, and others. 1969b. A map of Virginia with a description of the covntrey, the commodities, people, government and religion.

In The Jamestown Voyages Under the First Charter, 1606-1609, Vol. 2, ed. Philip L. Barbour. The Hakluyt Society, 2nd ser. , no. 137, pp. 327-464. Cambridge: Cambridge University Press. First published in 1612 by Joseph Barnes in Oxford.

Smither, Harriet. 1932. The Alabama Indians of Texas. Southwestern Historical Quarterly 36(2):83-108.

Speck, Frank G. 1907a. Some comparative traits of the Maskogian languages. AA 9:470-83.

___. 1907b. Notes on Chickasaw ethnology and folklore. Journal of American Folk-lore 20:50-58.

___. 1907-15. The Creek Indians of Taskigi town. Memoirs of the American Anthropological Association 2:99-164.

___. 1909. Ethnology of the Yuchi Indians. University of Pennsylvania Anthropological Publications of the University Museum 1(1):1-154. 1 plate.

___. 1910. Yuchi. BAEB 30, Pt. 2:1003-1007.

___. 1911. Ceremonial songs of the Creek and Yuchi Indians. University of Pennsylvania Anthropological Publications of the University Museum 1(2):157-245.

___. 1913. Some Catawba texts and folk-lore. Journal of American Folk-lore 26:319-30.

___. 1924. The ethnic position of the Southeastern Algonkian. AA 26:184-200.

___. 1926. Some eastern Cherokee texts. IJAL 4:111-13.

___. 1928. Chapters on the ethnology of the Powhatan tribes of Virginia. Indian Notes and Monographs 1(5):225-455. New York: Museum of the American Indian, Heye Foundation.

___. 1934. Catawba texts. Columbia University Contributions to Anthropology. Volume 24. xviii, 91 pages.

___. 1935. Siouan tribes of the Carolinas as known from Catawba, Tutelo, and documentary sources. AA 37:201-25.

___. 1939. Eggan's Yuchi kinship interpretations. AA 41:171-72.

___. 1946. Catawba text. IJAL 12:64-65.

Speck, F. G. , and E. E. Schaeffer. 1942. Catawba kinship and social organization with a resume of Tutelo kinship terms. AA 45:555-75.

Speck, Frank G., and Claude E. Schaeffer. 1950. The deer and the rabbit hunting drive in Virginia and the Southeast. Southern Indian Studies 2(1): 3-20.

Spier, Leslie. 1924. Wichita and Caddo relationship terms. AA 26:258-63.

Steward, Julian H. 1960. John Reed Swanton, February 19, 1873—May 2, 1958. National Academy of Sciences, Biographical Memoirs 34:329-49.

Sturtevant, William C. 1954. The medicine bundles and busks of the Florida Seminole. Florida Anthropologist 7(2):31-70.

___. 1958. Siouan languages in the east. AA 60:738-43.

___. 1962. Spanish-Indian relations in southeastern North America. Ethnohistory 9:41-94.

___. 1971. Creek into Seminole. In North American Indians in Historical Perspective, ed. E. B. Leacock and N. O. Lurie, pp. 92-128. New York: Random House.

Swadesh, Morris. 1933. Chitimacha verbs of derogatory or abusive connotation with parallels from European languages. Language 9:192-201.

___. 1934a. The phonemic principle. Language 10:117-29.

___. 1934b. The phonetics of Chitimacha. Language 10:345-62.

___. 1937. The phonemic interpretation of long consonants. Language 13: 1-10.

___. 1946a. Chitimacha. In Linguistic Structures of Native America, VFPA 6:312-66. Reprinted 1963 by Johnson Reprint.

___. 1946b. Phonologic formulas for Atakapa-Chitimacha. IJAL 12:113-32.

___. 1947. Atakapa-Chitimacha $*k^w$. IJAL 13:120-21.

___. 1948. Sociologic notes on obsolescent languages. IJAL 14:226-35.

___. 1964. Linguistic overview. In Prehistoric Man in the New World, ed. Jesse D. Jennings and Edward Norbeck, pp. 527-56. Chicago: University of Chicago Press.

Swanton, John R. 1907a. Koasati. BAEB 30, Part 1:719-20.

___. 1907b. Ethnological position of the Natchez Indians. AA 9:513-28.

___. 1908. The language of the Taënsa. AA 10:24-32.

___. 1909. A new Siouan dialect. In Putnam Anniversary Volume, Anthropological Essays Presented to Frederic Ward Putnam in honor of his 70th birthday, April 16, 1909, by his friends and associates, pp. 477-86. New York: G. E. Stechert.

____. 1910. Ofogoula. BAEB 30, Part 2:108-109.

____. 1911. Indian tribes of the lower Mississippi Valley and adjacent coast of the Gulf of Mexico. viii, 387 pages. BAEB 43.

____. 1915. Linguistic position of the tribes of southern Texas and northeastern Mexico. AA 17:17-40.

____. 1917-20. Unclassified languages of the Southeast. IJAL 1:47-49.

____. 1918. Catawba notes. Journal of the Washington Academy of Science 8:623-29.

____. 1919a. A structural and lexical comparison of the Tunica, Chitimacha, and Atakapa languages. 56 pages. BAEB 68.

____. 1919b. Identity of the Westo Indians. AA 21:213-16.

____. 1921-23. The Tunica language. IJAL 2:1-39.

____. 1922. Early history of the Creek Indians and their neighbors. 492 pages, 10 pocket maps. BAEB 73.

____. 1923. New light on the early history of the Siouan peoples. Journal of the Washington Academy of Sciences 13(3):33-43.

____. 1924-25. The Muskhogean connection of the Natchez language. IJAL 3:46-75.

____. 1928a. Social organization and social usages of the Indians of the Creek confederacy. BAEAR 42 (1924-25):31-472.

____. 1928b. Religious beliefs and medical practices of the Creek Indians. BAEAR 42 (1924-25):473-672.

____. 1928c. Social and religious beliefs and usages of the Chickasaw Indians. BAEAR 44 (1926-27):169-273.

____. 1929a. The Tawasa language. AA 31:435-53.

____. 1929b. A sketch of the Atakapa language. IJAL 5:121-49.

____. 1931. Source material for the social and ceremonial life of the Choctaw Indians. vii, 282 pages. BAEB 103.

____. 1934. Newly discovered Powhatan bird names. Journal of the Washington Academy of Sciences 24:96-99.

____. 1936. Early history of the eastern Siouan tribes. In Essays in Anthropology Presented to A. L. Kroeber, pp. 371-381. Berkeley: University of California Press. Reprinted 1968 by Books for Libraries Press, Freeport, New York.

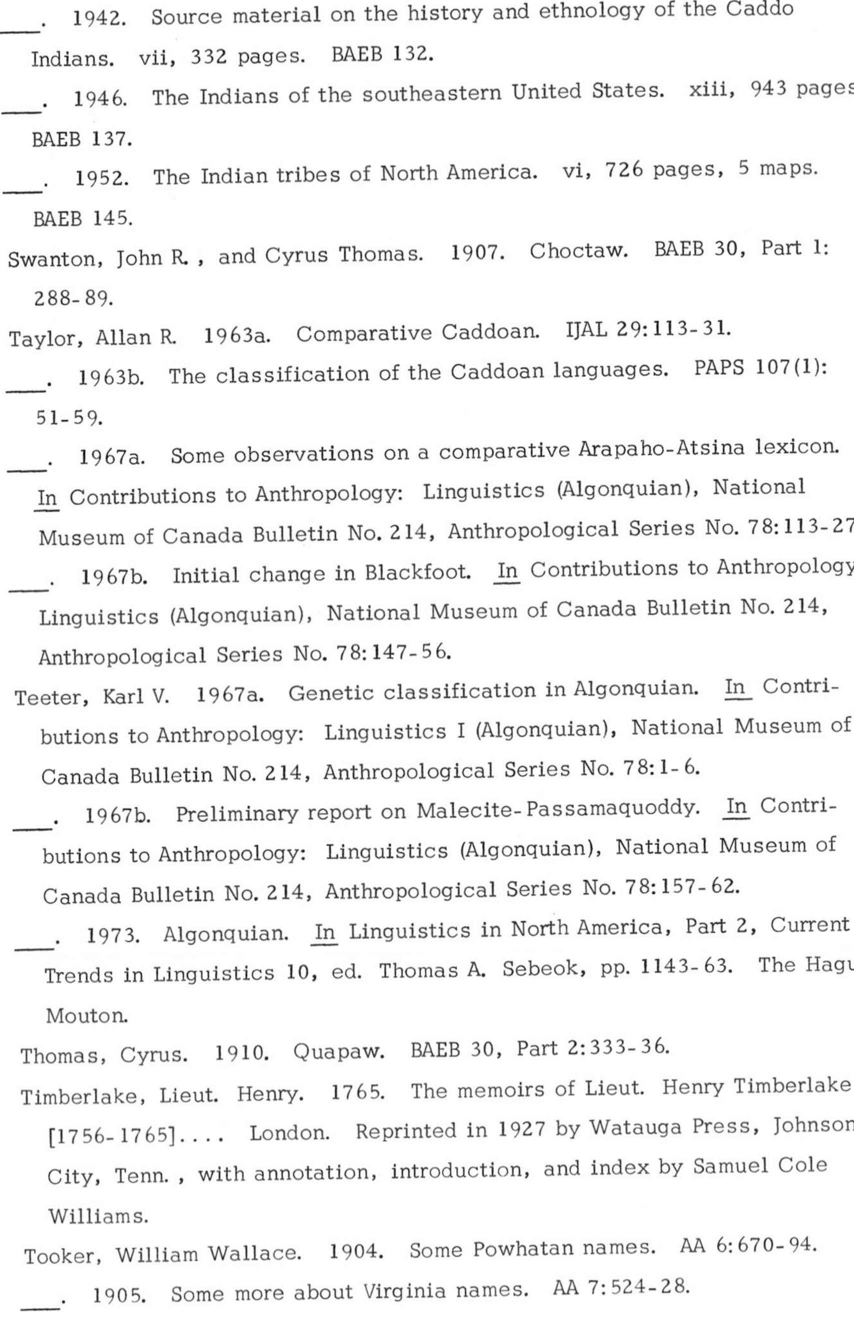

___. 1942. Source material on the history and ethnology of the Caddo Indians. vii, 332 pages. BAEB 132.

___. 1946. The Indians of the southeastern United States. xiii, 943 pages. BAEB 137.

___. 1952. The Indian tribes of North America. vi, 726 pages, 5 maps. BAEB 145.

Swanton, John R., and Cyrus Thomas. 1907. Choctaw. BAEB 30, Part 1: 288-89.

Taylor, Allan R. 1963a. Comparative Caddoan. IJAL 29:113-31.

___. 1963b. The classification of the Caddoan languages. PAPS 107(1): 51-59.

___. 1967a. Some observations on a comparative Arapaho-Atsina lexicon. In Contributions to Anthropology: Linguistics (Algonquian), National Museum of Canada Bulletin No. 214, Anthropological Series No. 78:113-27.

___. 1967b. Initial change in Blackfoot. In Contributions to Anthropology: Linguistics (Algonquian), National Museum of Canada Bulletin No. 214, Anthropological Series No. 78:147-56.

Teeter, Karl V. 1967a. Genetic classification in Algonquian. In Contributions to Anthropology: Linguistics I (Algonquian), National Museum of Canada Bulletin No. 214, Anthropological Series No. 78:1-6.

___. 1967b. Preliminary report on Malecite-Passamaquoddy. In Contributions to Anthropology: Linguistics (Algonquian), National Museum of Canada Bulletin No. 214, Anthropological Series No. 78:157-62.

___. 1973. Algonquian. In Linguistics in North America, Part 2, Current Trends in Linguistics 10, ed. Thomas A. Sebeok, pp. 1143-63. The Hague: Mouton.

Thomas, Cyrus. 1910. Quapaw. BAEB 30, Part 2:333-36.

Timberlake, Lieut. Henry. 1765. The memoirs of Lieut. Henry Timberlake [1756-1765].... London. Reprinted in 1927 by Watauga Press, Johnson City, Tenn., with annotation, introduction, and index by Samuel Cole Williams.

Tooker, William Wallace. 1904. Some Powhatan names. AA 6:670-94.

___. 1905. Some more about Virginia names. AA 7:524-28.

Toomey, Noxon. 1918. Analysis of a text in the Apalachi language (Muskhogean stock). Hervas Laboratories of American Linguistics, St. Louis. Bulletin. Vol. 6, pp. 1-8.

Trager, George L. 1941. Review of: Tunica, by Mary R. Haas, Handbook of American Indian Languages, Vol. 4, pp. 143, New York: J. J. Augustin, 1941. Language 17:353-57.

Troike, Rudolph C. 1964. The Caddo word for "water". IJAL 30:96-98.

Trumbull, J. Hammond. 1870a. Indian names in Virginia. Historical Magazine, 2nd. ser. 7:47-48.

___. 1870b. The composition of Indian geographical names, illustrated from the Algonkin languages. Collections of the Connecticut Historical Society 2:1-50.

Tunica. 1910. BAEB 30, Part 2:838-39.

Vater, Johann S. 1821. Analekten der Sprachenkunde. Leipzig.

Villiers du Terrage, de, and P. Rivet. 1919. Les indiens du Texas et les expéditions française de 1720 et 1721 a la "Baie Saint-Bernard". Journal de la Société des Américanistes de Paris 11:403-42.

Vinson, Julien. 1883. Sur la langue timucua. Congrès International des Américanistes, compte-rendu de la cinquième session, Copenhague 1883, pp. 362-65.

___. 1886. Introduction [to Arte de la lengua timuquana compuesto en 1614 por el Pe Francisco Pareja]. Bibliothèque Linguistique Américaine 11:v-xxxi.

Voegelin, C. F. 1935. Shawnee phonemes. Language 11:23-37.

___. 1936a. The Shawnee female deity. Yale University Publications in Anthropology Number 10. 21 pages. Reprinted by Human Relations Area Files Press, New Haven, 1970.

___. 1936b. Productive paradigms in Shawnee. In Essays in Anthropology, Presented to A. L. Kroeber in celebration of his sixtieth birthday, June 11, 1936, pp. 391-403. Berkeley: University of California Press. Reprinted 1968 by Books for Libraries Press, Freeport, New York.

___. 1938-40. Shawnee stems and the Jacob P. Dunn Miami dictionary. Indiana Historical Society, Prehistory Research Series 1:63-108, 135-67, 345-89, 409-78.

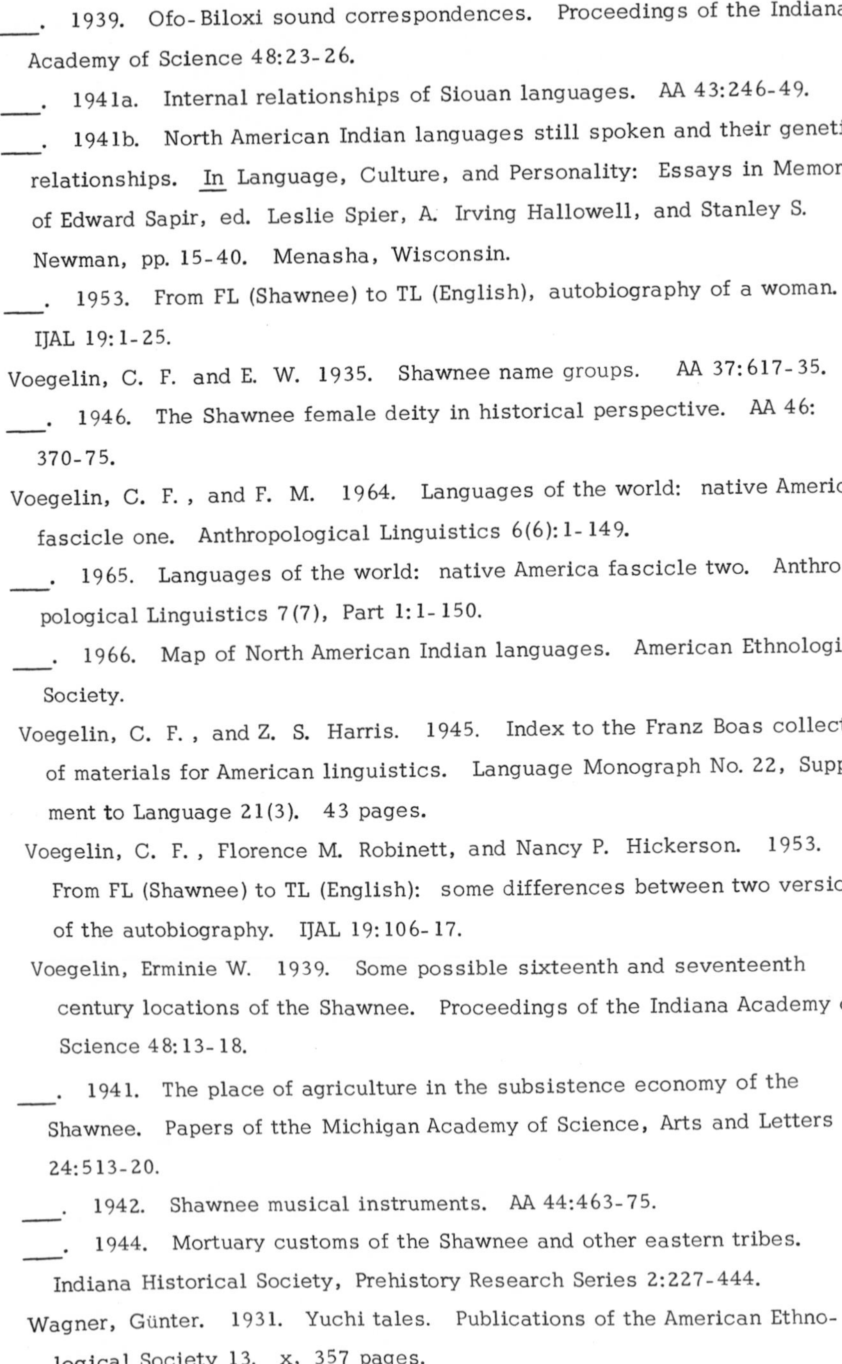

___. 1939. Ofo-Biloxi sound correspondences. Proceedings of the Indiana Academy of Science 48:23-26.

___. 1941a. Internal relationships of Siouan languages. AA 43:246-49.

___. 1941b. North American Indian languages still spoken and their genetic relationships. *In* Language, Culture, and Personality: Essays in Memory of Edward Sapir, ed. Leslie Spier, A. Irving Hallowell, and Stanley S. Newman, pp. 15-40. Menasha, Wisconsin.

___. 1953. From FL (Shawnee) to TL (English), autobiography of a woman. IJAL 19:1-25.

Voegelin, C. F. and E. W. 1935. Shawnee name groups. AA 37:617-35.

___. 1946. The Shawnee female deity in historical perspective. AA 46: 370-75.

Voegelin, C. F., and F. M. 1964. Languages of the world: native America fascicle one. Anthropological Linguistics 6(6):1-149.

___. 1965. Languages of the world: native America fascicle two. Anthropological Linguistics 7(7), Part 1:1-150.

___. 1966. Map of North American Indian languages. American Ethnological Society.

Voegelin, C. F., and Z. S. Harris. 1945. Index to the Franz Boas collection of materials for American linguistics. Language Monograph No. 22, Supplement to Language 21(3). 43 pages.

Voegelin, C. F., Florence M. Robinett, and Nancy P. Hickerson. 1953. From FL (Shawnee) to TL (English): some differences between two versions of the autobiography. IJAL 19:106-17.

Voegelin, Erminie W. 1939. Some possible sixteenth and seventeenth century locations of the Shawnee. Proceedings of the Indiana Academy of Science 48:13-18.

___. 1941. The place of agriculture in the subsistence economy of the Shawnee. Papers of tthe Michigan Academy of Science, Arts and Letters 24:513-20.

___. 1942. Shawnee musical instruments. AA 44:463-75.

___. 1944. Mortuary customs of the Shawnee and other eastern tribes. Indiana Historical Society, Prehistory Research Series 2:227-444.

Wagner, Günter. 1931. Yuchi tales. Publications of the American Ethnological Society 13. x, 357 pages.

___. 1934. Yuchi. In Handbook of American Indian Languages 3:291-384. New York: Columbia University Press.

Wallace, Anthony F. C. 1949. The Tuscaroras: sixth nation of the Iroquois confederacy. PAPS 93:159-65.

___. 1952. The modal personality structure of the Tuscarora Indians as revealed by the Rorschach test. viii, 120 pages. BAEB 150.

Wallace, Anthony F. C., and William D. Reyburn. 1951. Crossing the ice: a migration legend of the Tuscarora Indians. IJAL 17:42-47.

Watkins, Ben. 1892. Complete Choctaw definer, English with Choctaw definition. Van Buren, Arkansas: J. W. Baldwin. Reprinted 1972 by Southeastern Indian Antiquities Survey, Box 12392, Nashville, Tenn. 37212.

West, John David. 1962. The phonology of Mikasuki. SIL 16(3-4):77-91.

Whipple, Lieut. A. W. 1855. Report upon the Indian tribes. Part 3 [separately paginated] of Reports of Explorations and Surveys, to ascertain the most practicable and economical Route for a Railroad from the Mississippi River to the Pacific Ocean... 1853-4.... Vol. III. H. R. Executive Document No. 91, 3d Cong., 2d Sess., 1856. Washington, D. C.

Whorf, Benjamin L. 1938-40. Gestalt technique of stem composition in Shawnee. Indiana Historical Society, Prehistory Research Series 1:391-406.

Willoughby, Charles C. 1907. The Virginia Indians in the seventeenth century. AA 9:57-86.

Woccon. 1910. BAEB 30, Part 2:967-68.

Wolff, Hans. 1948. Yuchi phonemes and morphemes, with special reference to person markers. IJAL 14:240-43.

___. 1950. Comparative Siouan I, II, III. IJAL 16:61-66, 113-21, 168-78.

___. 1951a. Yuchi text with analysis. IJAL 17:48-53.

___. 1951b. Comparative Siouan IV. IJAL 17:197-204.

___. 1952. Osage I: phonemes and historical phonology. IJAL 18:63-68.

Woodward, Thomas S. 1859. Woodward's reminiscences of the Creek, or Muscogee Indians, contained in letters to friends in Georgia and Alabama. Montgomery, Alabama: Barrett & Wimbish. Reprinted in 1939 by Alabama Book Store, Tuscaloosa, Ala. and Birmingham Book Exchange, Birmingham, Ala. 168 pages.

Wright, Louis B. , and Virginia Freund, ed. 1953. The historie of travell into Virginia Britania (1612) by William Strachey, gent. The Hakluyt Society, 2nd ser. no. 103. xxxii, 221 pages. London: The Hakluyt Society.

Wright, Muriel H. 1951. A guide to the Indian tribes of Oklahoma. xvii, 300 pages. Norman: University of Oklahoma Press.

Wichita Verb Structure: Inflectional Categories

David S. Rood

A theory of language structure which suggests that semantics, not syntax, is the place to begin language description has recently been outlined by Wallace L. Chafe (1970b). Moreover, Chafe has also given us good examples of the way this method works for Onondaga (1970a) and English (1970b). I wish to explore an intermediate stage in the derivation of Wichita sentences according to the model Chafe has outlined. While doing this, I have two separate goals in mind: first, to present part of the morphology of this largely undescribed language, and second, to illustrate that at least some semantic analysis is possible even if one is not a native speaker of the language analyzed.

Because of the newness of this approach to language, however, I want to begin with a very brief sketch of the first part of the theory. Semantically, the sentence is said to center around the verb. Verbs are characterized by three kinds of semantic units. The first is called selectional, the second lexical, and the third inflectional. Selectional units are rarely symbolized in the surface structure – they are usually realized simultaneously with the root instead. They include such things as whether a verb is an action, a state, a process, or some combination of these. Moreover, selectional units have very important consequences for the rest of the sentence, for they determine the number and kind of nouns that will occur in the sentence. An action verb, for instance, will have an agent noun with it. An example is the root *come* in English — it demands that some sort of actor accompany it. A state verb, or a process, on the other hand, will have accompanying patient nouns. Thus in "the house is burning" the house isn't really *doing* anything — it is not an agent; rather, it is undergoing a process. Likewise, the wood in "the wood is dry", a sentence with a state verb, is simply said to be in a specific state — it is not doing anything. Various languages have different ways of indicating the differences between agents, patients, and other nouns in other roles — but these are all postsemantic processes, ways of symbolizing the semantic facts in sound.

Lexical units are the roots, things like the meanings *come*, *burn*, *dry* in the preceding examples. Selectional and lexical units can, therefore, be said to be inherent in the individual verbs. Unless a root which is inherently one thin has been derived to be another, none of the selectional units will be apt to hav a surface structure representation.

Another property of selectional units is that they limit the choice of specific roots which can occur in a given structure. For instance, a verb selectionally marked state would not permit the lexical unit *come* to occur with it. Inflectional units, on the other hand, have nothing to do with the choice of a root. They are not inherent in the verb, but are rather added optionally to verbs to express meanings which can occur with almost any root. In English they inclu such things as *past*, *perfect*, and *progressive*. In most languages most of thes receive some sort of overt surface structure representation, often in the form of bound morphemes attached to verb roots. It is these inflectional units in Wich which I wish to discuss, but before beginning a semantic analysis of this inflectional system it would seem appropriate to be clear about the surface struct system which symbolizes it. Let us therefore make a simple, taxonomic description of Wichita inflectional morphology.

The morphemes I have in mind occur as either initial prefixes or final suffixes in the polysynthetic verb complex. Each complete verb has both a prefix and a suffix from this set. The grammatical categories expressed include tens aspect, evidential, and mood, although there is no consistent correlation betw grammatical category and morpheme position.

The category I call "mood" has two members, represented in the surface stru ture by the choice of one or another set of suffixes. Subordinate verbs — thos which can occur only in constructions with other verbs — have one of the endings listed in Illustration 1. The prefixes which occur with these suffixes, together with labels and approximate meanings, are in the list in Illustration 2. The prefixes in Illustrations 2a and 2e also occur with nonsubordinating suffixes, as will be seen below (Illustrations 4g and 4j). The debetative participle (Illustration 2e) does not have an imperfective.

ILLUSTRATION 1.

a. h 'perfective subordinate'

b. skih 'imperfective subordinate'

ILLUSTRATION 2.

	Prefix	Label	Meaning
a.	hi/i	conditional	'if...; when...'
b.	ha...ki	infinitive subjunctive	'for... to...' 'that... would or might...'
c.	ra	general participle	'the one who...; ...ing'
d.	ki	past participle	'the one who...ed'
e.	kara	debetative participle	'the time... ought to have or was supposed to...'

This is all I want to say here about subordinate verbs, since further analysis depends on our conclusions about simple, one-verb sentences.

Nonsubordinate or independent verbs may have one of five suffixes, chiefly showing aspectual features, as listed in Illustration 3. Illustration 4 lists the prefixes which occur with these suffixes, again with labels. Glosses and/or

ILLUSTRATION 3.

	Suffix	Label
a.	zero (has phonetic effect of devoicing preceding vowels)	perfective
b.	s	imperfective
c.	staris	intentive
d.	:ss	habitual
e.	i:hi:ʔ	contrary-to-fact

alternative labels are given in cases where the exact meaning is uncertain. Th first three of these obligatorily occur with evidential morphemes — the forms listed in Illustration 4 are used when the speaker witnessed the event himself; the variants in Illustration 5 indicate reported facts, usually translated 'I hear that . . . '

ILLUSTRATION 4.

	Prefix	Label	Meaning
a.	a . . . ki	aorist	
	ki	aorist interrogative	
b.	keʔe	future	
c.	ara	perfective (recent past?)	
d.	ta/ti	indicative (present? nonfuture?)	
	ra/ri	indicative interrogative	
	ʔa/ʔi	indicative negative	
e.	iskiri	exclamatory	
f.	a/i	directive	'and then one. . . s'
		durative (timeless? coextensive?)	'all the time. . . '
g.	hi/i	imperative	
h.	kiʔi	future imperative	
i.	kaʔa	optative	'I wish. . . '
j.	kara	debetative	'. . . ought to. . . '

ILLUSTRATION 5.

a.	kiya . . . ki a:ʔa . . . ki	past quotative
b.	ehe:	future quotative
c.	a:ra	recent (perfective) quotative

Not all the possible combinations of prefixes and suffixes occur, but Illustration 6 gives examples of sentences translating those combinations which are possible, using the causative of the root cook and the third person singular subject pronoun as illustrations.

All of this serves as a complete inventory of the combinations of mood, aspect, tense, and evidential inflections available to Wichita speakers. But it is not a coherent description of the actual choices a speaker must make. I believe that, instead of selecting prefixes and suffixes, a speaker selects meanings to communicate. One arrangement of the inflectional meanings available to Wichita speakers is given in Illustration 7. Each branch of the tree, followed to a terminal node, represents what might be claimed to be the total semantic make-up of one prefix-suffix combination.

Let us examine this analysis in detail by following the various branches of this tree. The first division corresponds to what may be the first decision a speaker must make: will the event be reported objectively, or will there be some subjective opinion about the event, some commentary, added? Let us suppose, first, that there is to be commentary and follow the left branch of the tree.

The Commentary can be simple amazement — in which case no further decisions are needed; the exclamatory branch is chosen, and the tense/aspect structure of the sentence is complete. Alternatively, the commentary may involve some kind of attitude to be expressed toward the agent of the reported event; in this case, the speaker seems to have four choices.

First, he may wish to command the subject to do something. If this is so, we see from the tree that he must choose between two methods of commanding: direct ordering, or instructing. If the command is a true imperative, the left branch from the imperative node shows that the speaker must also specify whether the order is to be carried out in the future or at once. If future is his choice, he must additionally state whether the action is to be habitual or nonhabitual. Nonhabitual does not necessarily mean punctual; it is simply not obligatorily habitual. At this point, then, we have specified the semantic components of four more prefix-suffix combinations: the habitual future imperative, the regular future imperative, the plain imperative, and the directive, the latter used when giving instructions rather than orders.

Continuing to examine attitudes which a Wichita speaker may express inflectionally, we find that instead of commands he may state wishes about events. Within this attitude, he can choose between a wish that past events might have been otherwise, and one that concerns only nonpast events. The

ILLUSTRATION 6.

	perfective (-Ø)	imperfective (-s)
aorist aki-	She cooked it.	She was cooking it.
aorist quot a:ʔaki-	I heard that she cooked it.	I heard . . .
future keʔe-	She will cook it.	She'll be cooking it.
future quot ehe:-	I heard she'll cook it.	I heard . . .
perfect ara-	She cooked it.	
perfect quot a:ra-	I heard she cooked it.	
indicative ta-/ti		She's cooking it/She is the one who cooked it.
exclamatory iskiri-		Look! She's cooking it!
durative a/i-		(And yet,) all the time she was cooking it.
directive a-/i-		(And then) one cooks it.
imperative hi-/i-	Let her cook it.	
future imperative kiʔi-	And then you must let her cook it.	
optative kaʔa-	I wish she would cook it.	I wish she'd be cooking it.
debetative kara-		She ought to cook it.

ILLUSTRATION 6.

intentive (-staris)	habitual (-:ss)	contrary-to-fact (-i:hi:?)
She was going to cook it, but she didn't.	She always used to cook it.	
I heard . . .	I heard . . .	
	It will be her job to cook it every time.	
	I heard . . .	
I heard she was going to cook it, but I don't know whether or not she did.		
She's going to cook it.	She (is always the one who) cooks it.	
	Let her always be the one to cook it.	
I wish she'd plan to cook it.	I wish she'd always cook it.	I wish she had cooked it.
	She ought to always be the one to cook it.	She should have cooked it.

English equivalent to past wishes is usually a sentence with had: "I wish she had cooked it (even though I know it's too late for that now)".

If the wish concerns a nonpast event, the speaker must select an aspect for the sentence, too. This may be an unmarked, or neutral aspect – one which indicates the normal, expected state of affairs. Or it may be one of three semantically marked aspects. Imperfective indicates that the event is not necessarily wished to reach a conclusion; habitual implies that the event should be repeated regularly; intentive indicates that the speaker wishes the agent of the event to intend to carry it out ("I wish she would plan to cook it"). Expressing these ideas in English involves numerous complex predications, whereas in Wichita the whole set of semantic units can be realized simultaneously, simply by choosing the appropriate surface prefix-suffix set.

Besides commands and wishes, a Wichita speaker expresses some expectations inflectionally. Parallel to wishes, he may expect something about a nonpast or a past event. If the event is nonpast, the expectation may be for habitual action, or not; if the event is past, the expectation is clearly a should-have-been kind of situation ("She ought to have been the one to cook it").

As the final option on the subjective side of our tree, we find that a speaker can mention hearing of another's plans, again simply by choosing the appropriate affixes. Here we maintain that the semantics of the utterance do not correspond very closely to the more common meanings of the morphemes used — but more about that in a moment.

Starting back at the top of the tree again, and this time following the branch labeled "objective", we notice that, in Wichita, an objective reporter must decide whether or not time is important to his description. If time is to be part of his statement, it must be either past or future, and furthermore, the reporter must indicate something about the source of his information. Moreover, having decided to mention the time of the event, the speaker must also decide whether the aspect is unusual or not. If it is not unusual, he selects a neutral affix. With past events, he may instead select a habitual, an imperfective, or an intentive aspect. With intentive, in this case, the intention as well as the event are clearly past; the event is unambiguously one which did not actually occur ("She was going to cook it, but she didn't"). There is no future intentive, but otherwise the aspect choices with future events parallel those for past.

ILLUSTRATION 7.

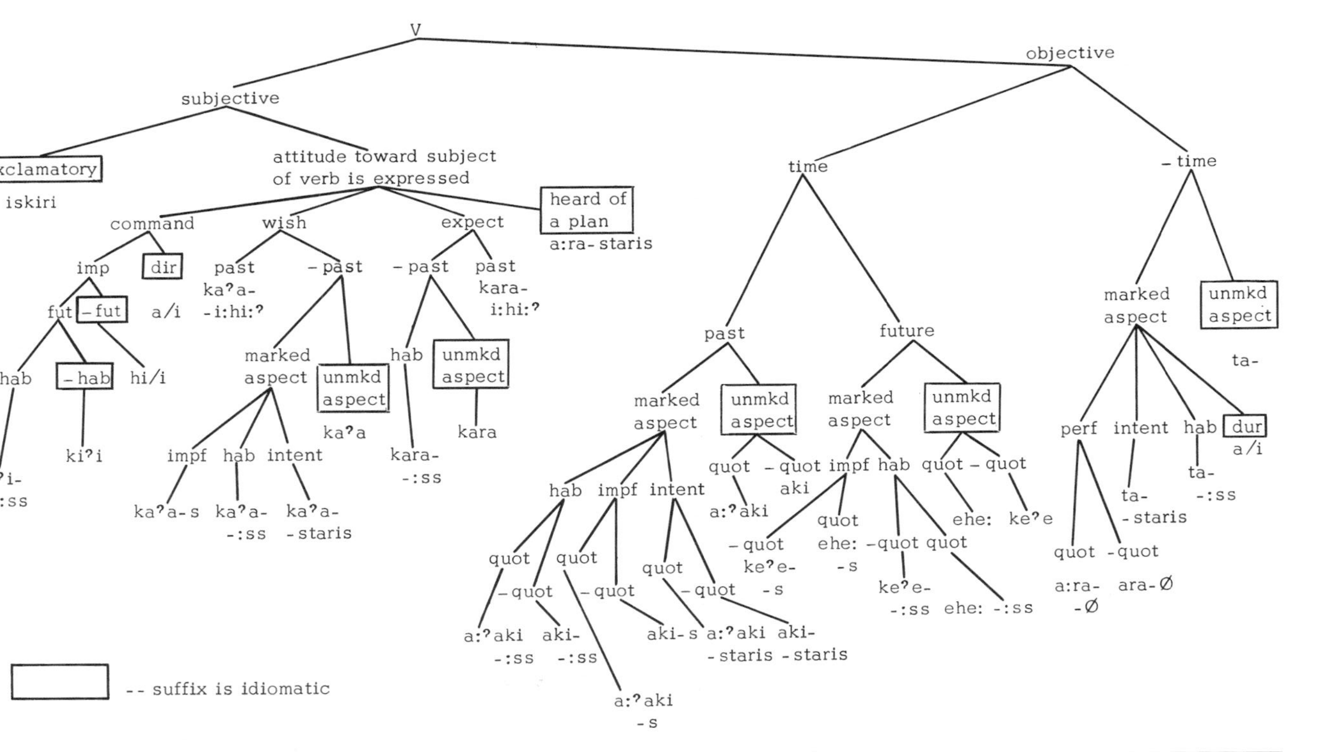

If time is not an important part of the report, aspect may nevertheless be marked. Again, lack of marking or neutrality may be chosen, but one of four marked aspects may be selected instead. These include intentive and habitual which have appeared elsewhere, but also perfective and durative, which are unique to this part of the tree. Perfective requires an evidential and implies the completion of an event; durative implies that the event occurred simultaneously with something else. Perhaps "coextensive" would be a slightly better label.

There are of course alternatives to some of the preceding suggestions. Most surprising in Illustration 7 is probably the lack of a "present time" node parallel to "past" and "future" on the objective side of the tree. Two candidates for such a node seem to exist: the whole "–time" branch, or the "exclamatory" node. But the unmarked aspect on the "–time" branch can refer to either past or present time, and it is indeed the aspect, rather than present time, which is emphasized through the use of any of the marked aspects. For this reason, I reject the suggestion that time is at all relevant to the speaker employing these affixes. As for "exclamatory", it is a rare form, and has always occurred in contexts where the speaker is conveying surprise at an event. To call it "present" just to have a present tense node in the system seems to stretch the facts.

One of Chafe's most frequently repeated points is that surface structures will probably not reflect semantic structures with anything like a one-to-one correspondence. That is, we may expect to find one surface structure representing many different semantic structures. There are two examples in this analysis of the same surface structure appearing at rather different places in the hierarchy of semantic relationships. First, I have separated two meanings for the prefix which symbolizes the "durative" and the "directive": the latter appears under "command" on the tree; the former under "objective, –time." I think that the meaning difference alone is enough to justify this kind of identification of homonyms, but there is also a syntactic justification for this particular decision. In the directive usage, this prefix occurs only with second or third person pronouns; in the durative usage, it may also take first person pronouns. Thus each sentence with this prefix is unambiguous for the first person, ambiguous for the others.

The second departure from an analysis in which surface structure identity would be seen to reflect semantic identity is in the separation of "perfective intentive" from "perfective" alone. "Perfective intentive" (see Illustration 6) occurs only when the "quotative" is also used; "perfective" alone can occur with either evidential. For this reason, "perfective intentive" has been placed on the subjective side of the tree as "heard of a plan"; it is always a matter of hearsay, and always deals with someone else's plans. The other perfective is included as the timeless perfective on the objective side of the tree. This separates, again, one occurrence of a prefix from another instance of the same prefix, but again for what seem to me to be very sound reasons – here the gross difference in meanings, depending on the suffix, plus the syntactic impossibility of nonquotative with intentive.

I would now like to conclude this analysis with the presentation of a formal summary of it via semantic structure and idiom literalization rules as in Illustration 8. They are necessarily incomplete, because they do not express the limitations placed on inflectional units by selectional units. For example, verbs such as *want* and *see* – those which Chafe describes as selectionally

ILLUSTRATION 8.

S1. V
root ⟶ { subjective / objective }

S2. V
root
objective ⟶ time

S3. V
root
objective
– time ⟶ { perfective / durative / intentive / habitual }

S4. V
root
objective
– time
perfective ⟶ quotative

S5. V
root
time ⟶ { past / future }

S6. V
root
time ⟶ (quotative
{ habitual / imperfective })

S7. V
root
time
past
– imperfect
– habitual ⟶ intentive

S8. V
root
subjective ⟶ { attitude expressed / exclamatory }

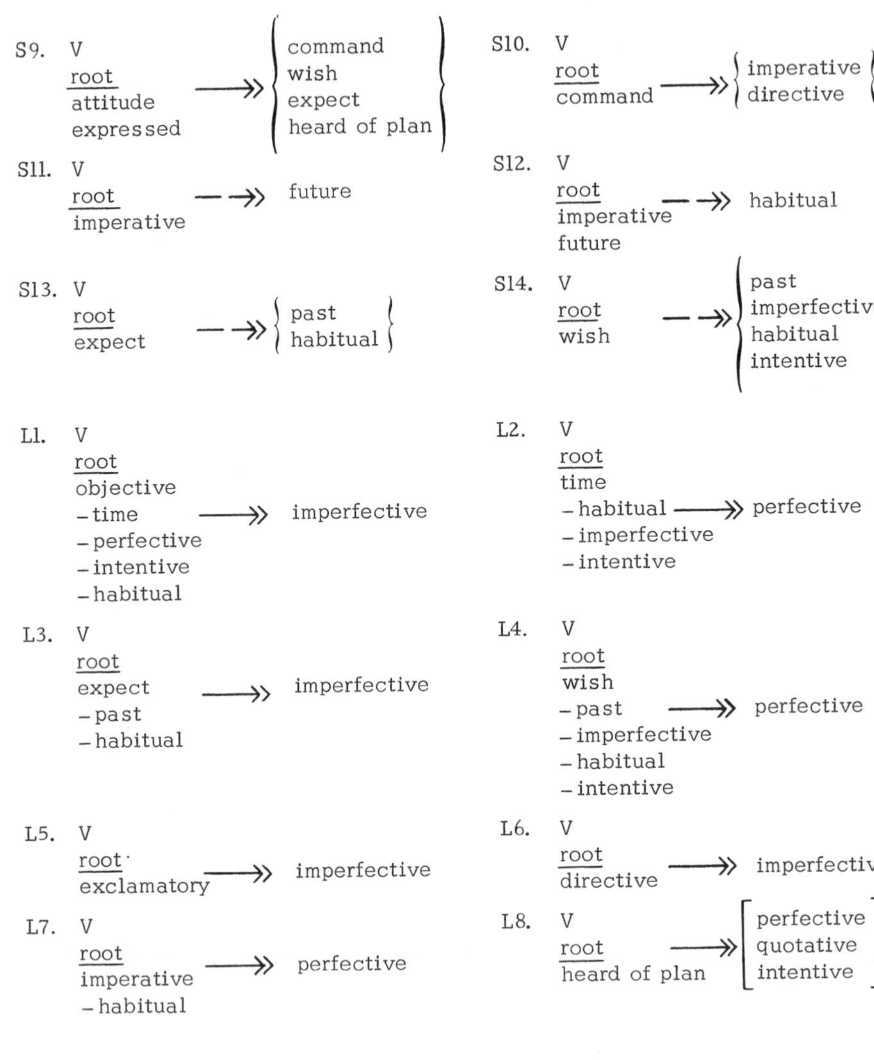

Rule conventions:

braces: either/or

parentheses: and/or

square brackets: both/and

double-headed arrow: 'is further specified as', rather than 'is rewritten as'

broken-shafted arrow: rule is optional

solid-shafted arrow: rule is obligatory

-: absence of

calling for an experiencer noun rather than an agent or patient noun — do not take the imperfective inflection (the -s suffix) under any circumstances. Surely there are other restrictions of this type to be built into a complete description.

The conventions for these rules are listed at the end of Illustration 8. The rules are of two types. Those whose numbers are prefixed with S are semantic structure rules; the L rules are idiom literalization rules. It is claimed here, then, that the use of perfective or imperfective with the unmarked aspect of a given form is purely idiomatic — that the suffix, so to speak, has no particular meaning in this construction, but is nevertheless required by surface structure constraints. By the same token, the use of "quotative", "intentive", and "perfective" with "heard of plan" is said to be idiomatic in the same way.

One goal of this paper has been purely descriptive; another has been to illustrate that semantic analysis is possible without native insight into the underlying structures of a language. If I were a native speaker of Wichita, I might easily be able to expand on this list of inflectional semantic features by including many which have no overt surface structure representation. As a descriptivist dependent on data from informants, however, I feel I must limit myself largely to attempts to organize observable, surface structure phenomena. Abstracting such units as "objective", "subjective", and "time" in the preceding analysis is illustrative of the possibilities. The coherence they lend to the whole range of surface possibilities seems to me to confirm the hypothesis that they are part of at least one segment of Wichita semantic structure.

REFERENCES

Chafe, Wallace L. 1970a. A semantically based sketch of Onondaga. IUPAL Memoir 25.

____. 1970b. Meaning and the structure of language. Chicago: University of Chicago Press.

Shawnee Noun Inflection

Douglas R. Parks

INTRODUCTION

Shawnee nouns, in contrast with those of many Algonquian languages, appear to have a large number of irregularities in their inflection. In fact, however, they do not: Shawnee noun inflection is quite regular. This paper is first a description of the inflection of the noun, giving the forms of the nominal affixes, and second a presentation of a set of ordered phonological rules which attempt to eliminate the seeming irregularities of that inflection.[1]

The material upon which the description is based comes from two sources: a stem list for Shawnee compiled by Carl F. Voegelin (1937-40), and two short periods of field work with Shawnee undertaken by the author.[2] The first source, Voegelin's stem list, contains a large number of nouns in both their singular and plural forms and frequently in other forms as well. In my own field work I sought to supplement this published data with as much complete paradigmatic material as I could, obtaining not only plurals but all other forms as well.

Published descriptive studies of aspects of the grammar of Shawnee consist of two papers, one a phonemic description[3] and the other an analysis of paradigms,[4] both by Voegelin (1935, 1936). In the latter paper Voegelin gives the forms of the affixes occurring with nouns. (These forms are given in note 4 of this paper, so that one can compare them with the forms that I give below.) Finally, in addition to the above two papers, Voegelin has published the stem dictionary already mentioned and, more recently, a small collection of texts (1953).

1. NOUN INFLECTION

The inflectional categories for the noun in Shawnee are those typical for Algonquian languages, and many of the peculiarities of inflection that occur in the other languages occur also in Shawnee.

Each noun stem belongs to one of two gender classes, the _animate_ or the _inanimate_. Nouns are inflected for two numbers, the _singular_ and the _plural_; and, in addition, animate nouns inflectionally distinguish between two third persons, a _proximate_ and an _obviative_. All noun stems may be inflected for the _locative_, and kin term stems may further be inflected for _vocative_ forms. Finally, noun stems may occur in _possessed_ as well as unpossessed forms, the exception being a class of _dependent_ noun stems which always occur in possessed, and never in unpossessed, form.

1. 1. _Number and obviation._

Noun stems are inflected for the singular and plural numbers, and there are different sets of suffixes for the two genders. Animate noun stems further distinguish an obviative which has its own suffixes for the singular and plural. The suffixes for number and obviation are given in Table 1.

TABLE 1: Number-Gender Suffixes

		Animate	Inanimate
Proximate	Singular	-a	-i
	Plural	-aki	-ali (-a)
Obviative	Singular	-ali	
	Plural	-hi	

Examples of animate stems with their suffixes are:

/mkw-/ 'bear'

/mkw + a/ → mkwa 'bear'

/mkw + aki/ → mkwaki 'bears'

/mkw + ali/ → mkwali 'bear (obv.)'

/mkw + hi/ → mkwhi 'bears (obv.)'

/hokima·-/ 'chief'

/hokima· + a/ → hokima 'chief'

/hokima· + aki/ → hokima·ki 'chiefs'

/hokima· + ali/ → hokima·li 'chief (obv.)'

/hokima· + hi/ → hokimahi 'chiefs (obv.)'

/-simi·θ-/ 'niece'

/ki + simi·θ + a/ → kisimi·θa 'your niece'

/ho + simi·θ + ali/ → hosimi·θali 'his niece (obv.)'

/ki + simi·θ + wa· + aki/ → kisimi·θwa·ki 'your nieces'

/ho + simi·θ + wa· + hi/ → hosimi·θwahi 'their nieces (obv.)'

Examples of inanimate stems with their suffixes are:

/miye·w-/ 'road'

/miye·w + i/ → miye·wi 'road'

/miye·w + ali/ → miye·wali 'roads'

/ma·neʔθ-/ 'knife'

/ma·neʔθ + i/ → ma·neʔθi 'knife'

/ma·neʔθ + ali/ → ma·neʔθali 'knives'

The inanimate plural suffix -ali has a variant form -a (indicated in parentheses in Table 1). This variant is conditioned in certain cases by the phonological environment, in other cases by the syntactic environment.

Inanimate stems which end with an n, a consonant plus w, or the sequence ya take the variant -a. Examples are:

/hote·wen-/ 'town, village'

/hote·wen + ali/ → hote·wena 'towns'

/pi·ta·kan-/ 'sack, bag'

/pi·ta·kan + ali/ → pi·ta·kana 'sacks'

/-ʔski·sekw-/ 'eye'

/-ʔski·sekw + ali/ → ski·seko 'eyes'

/msiskya-/ 'leaf'

/msiskya + ali/ → msiske 'leaves'

The syntactic features conditioning the variant -a are the diminutive suffix -e·θ and possessed themes. Examples are:

/howa·w-/ 'egg'

/howa·w + e·θ + ali/ → howa·wale·θa 'little eggs'

/tika·n-/ 'field'

/tika·n + e·θ + ali/ → tika·ne·θa 'little fields'

/-ola·kan-/ 'dish'

/ni + ola·kan + em + ali/ → no·la·kanema 'my dishes'

1\. 2. Locative.

All noun stems of both genders freely take the locative suffix -eki. This element translates as 'in, on'. Examples are:

/mi·kon-/ 'feather'

/mi·kon + eki/ → mi·koneki 'on the feather'

/ka·kw-/ 'groundhog'

/ka·kw + eki/ → ka·koki 'on the groundhog'

/-ʔkan-/ 'bone'

/ho + ʔkan + eki/ → hoʔkaneki 'on the bone'

/wiʔka·-/ 'camp'

/wiʔka· + eki/ → wiʔkaki 'in the camp'

1\. 3. Vocative.

Kinship term stems, which occur only in possessed forms, freely add a vocative suffix. There are two of these, -ehi 'vocative singular' and -eti 'vocative plural', and they occur with the first person possessive form of the stem. Examples are:

/-kwiʔθ-/ 'son'

/ni + kwiʔθ + ehi/ → nikwiʔθehi '(my) son!'

/ni + kwiʔθ + eti/ → nikwiʔθeti '(my) sons!'

/-oʔθ-/ 'father'

/ni + oʔθ + ehi/ → noʔθehi '(my) father!'

/ni + oʔθ + eti/ → noʔθeti '(my) fathers!'

/-ta·ne·θ-/ 'daughter'

/ni + ta·ne·θ + ehi/ → nita·ne·θehi '(my) daughter!'

/ni + ta·ne·θ + eti/ → nita·ne·θeti '(my) daughters!'

1. 4. Possession.

Possessed themes are formed from noun stems by means of the personal pronominal prefixes, the possessive suffix -em, and optionally one of the two plural possessor suffixes. Such themes are then inflected for number, obviation, and the locative.

There are three personal pronominal prefixes. They are ni- 'first person', ki- 'second person', ho- 'third person'. The possessor is pluralized in the first person by -ena· and in the second and third persons by -wa·. In first person plural forms a distinction is made between inclusive and exclusive possessors. The first person exclusive plural possessor is formed by using ni- and -ena·; the first person inclusive is formed by using ki- and -ena·.

An example of a possessive paradigm for an animate noun is that in Table 2.

TABLE 2: Possessive Paradigm of Animate Noun

/kosko·-/ 'hog'			
/ni + kosko· + em + a/	→	nikosko·ma	'my hog'
/ki + kosko· + em + a/	→	kikosko·ma	'your hog'
/ho + kosko· + em + ali/	→	hokosko·mali	'his hog'
/ni + kosko· + em + ena· + a/	→	nikosko·mena	'our (excl.) hog'
/ki + kosko· + em + ena· + a/	→	kikosko·mena	'our (incl.) hog'
/ki + kosko· + em + wa· + a/	→	kikosko·mwa	'your (pl.) hog'
/ho + kosko· + em + wa· + ali/	→	hokosko·mwa·li	'their hog'
/ni + kosko· + em + aki/	→	nikosko·maki	'my hogs'
/ki + kosko· + em + aki/	→	kikosko·maki	'your hogs'
/ho + kosko· + em + hi/	→	hokosko·mhi	'his hogs'
/ni + kosko· + em + ena· + aki/	→	nikosko·mena·ki	'our (excl.) hogs'
/ki + kosko· + em + ena· + aki/	→	kikosko·mena·ki	'our (incl.) hogs'
/ki + kosko· + em + wa· + aki/	→	kikosko·mwa·ki	'your (pl.) hogs'
/ho + kosko· + em + wa· + hi/	→	hokosko·mwahi	'their hogs'

It should be noted that (in the paradigm in Table 2 and) whenever an animate noun with an animate third person possessor occurs, the noun takes the obviative suffix. If, however, the locative suffix occurs, the third person possessor is not obviative, e. g. ,

/-ʔta·waka·-/ 'ear'

/ho + ʔta·waka· + em + eki/ → hoʔta·waka·meki 'on his ear'.

An example of a possessive paradigm for an inanimate noun is that in Table 3.

TABLE 3: Possessive Paradigm of Inanimate Noun

/-owa·w-/ 'egg'			
/ni + owa·w + em + i/	→	nowa·wemi	'my egg'
/ki + owa·w + em + i/	→	kowa·wemi	'your egg'
/ho + owa·w + em + i/	→	howa·wemi	'his egg'
/ni + owa·w + em + ena· + i/	→	nowa·wemena	'our (excl.) egg'
/ki + owa·w + em + ena· + i/	→	kowa·wemena	'our (incl.) egg'
/ki + owa·w + em + wa· + i/	→	kowa·wemwa	'your (pl.) egg'
/ho + owa·w + em + wa· + i/	→	howa·wemwa	'their egg'
/ni + owa·w + em + ali/	→	nowa·wema	'my eggs'
/ki + owa·w + em + ali/	→	kowa·wema	'your eggs'
/ho + owa·w + em + ali/	→	howa·wema	'their eggs'
/ni + owa·w + em + ena· + ali/	→	nowa·wemena	'our (excl.) eggs'
/ki + owa·w + em + ena· + ali/	→	kowa·wemena	'our (incl.) eggs'
/ki + owa·w + em + wa· + ali/	→	kowa·wemwa	'your (pl.) eggs'
/ho + owa·w + em + wa· + ali/	→	howa·wemwa	'their eggs'

Many possessed themes, including most dependent nouns, do not take -em. Examples of such nouns include:

/maʔkiθen-/ 'moccasin'

/ni + maʔkiθen + i/ → nimaʔkiθe 'my moccasin'

/-ca·s-/ 'nose'

/ho + ca·s + i/ → hoca·si 'his nose'

/-miʔθ-/ 'older sister'

/ni + miʔθ + a/ → nimiʔθa 'my older sister'

1. 5. Dependent nouns.

Certain noun stems, termed dependent nouns, occur only in possessed form and never in unpossessed form, i. e. , absolutely. Dependent nouns include body part terms, kinship terms, and certain other nouns denoting personal possessions. Examples of the latter include:

/-oˀkwa·kan-/ 'pipe'

/ho + oˀkwa·kan + a/ → hoˀkwa·ka 'his pipe'

/-kotepiθowen-/ 'breechcloth'

/ho + kotepiθowen + i/ → hokotepiθowe 'his breechcloth'

/-ola·kan-/ 'dish, plate'

/ho + ola·kan + i/ → ho·la·ka '(his) dish, plate'

1. 6. Diminutivization.

The formation of explicit diminutives is a productive process. One is formed with any noun by the addition of the diminutive suffix -e·θ, which adds the meaning 'little' to that of the stem. After -e·θ is suffixed, the diminutive theme then takes the inflectional suffixes for number and obviation, or the locative suffix, or the suffixes of the possessive theme. Examples of -e·θ with stems are:

/hameˀkw-/ 'beaver'

/hameˀkw + e·θ + a/ → hameˀko·θa 'little beaver'

/haya·pe·-/ 'buck'

/haya·pe· + e·θ + a/ → haya·pe·θa 'little buck'

/hapato·wen-/ 'cane, walking stick'

/hapato·wen + e·θ + ali/ → hapato·wene·θa 'little canes'

/-ce·nina·-/ 'brother'

/ni + ce·nina· + e·θ + a/ → nice·nina·θa 'my little brother'

A variant form of -e·θ occurs with singular inanimate noun stems. In this environment the form of the diminutive is -eh. Examples are:

/tika·n-/ 'field'

/tika·n + e·θ + i/ → tika·nehi 'little field'

/-wi·si·-/ 'head'

/ho + wi·si· + e·θ + i/ → howi·sihi 'his little head'

/ko·ta·-/ 'skirt'

/ko·ta· + e·θ + i/ → ko·tahi 'a small skirt'

Still another variant of -e·θ is -ale·θ (undoubtedly a compounded form of -ali + e·θ). This variant occurs after inanimate stems which end in a vowel or are monosyllabic and precedes the plural morpheme. Examples are:

/pikimi·-/ 'cherry'

/pikimi· + e·θ + ali/ → pikimi·wale·θa 'small cherries'

/wiʔka·-/ 'camp'

/wiʔka· + e·θ + ali/ → wiʔka·wale·θa 'small camps'

/-ʔka·t-/ 'leg'

/ho + ʔka·t + e·θ + ali/ → hoʔka·tale·θa 'small legs'

1.7. Summary.

The preceding information on the inflection of the noun can be summarized in a succinct way by means of several sets of rather informal rules. The first set consists of phrase structure rules; these give the categories which enter into the inflection of the noun and, with the addition of a transformational rule, the order of elements in that inflection. After the phrase structure rules, a set of lexical rewrite rules introduces the phonological, or underlying, forms of the morphemes for each category. Then, finally, a set of readjustment rules will account for variant forms of morphemes which are syntactically or morphologically conditioned.

Phrase structure rules. The first rule states that a noun consists of a noun stem followed by one of the number suffixes or the locative suffix; further, that the noun is optionally marked for personal possession (PP). Thus,

(PS 1) $$\text{Noun} \rightarrow (\text{PP}) \quad \text{N} \begin{Bmatrix} \text{Num} \\ \text{Loc} \end{Bmatrix}$$

Noun stems are either animate or inanimate and are optionally followed by the diminutive morpheme. Thus,

(PS 2) $$\text{N} \rightarrow \begin{Bmatrix} \text{N}_{\text{an}} \\ \text{N}_{\text{in}} \end{Bmatrix} \quad (\text{Dim})$$

For all nouns the category of number is composed of two features: plurality and obviation. Nouns are marked singular or plural and nonobviative (proximate) or obviative. Kinship nouns, in addition, have a feature vocative. Vocative forms distinguish singular and plural forms. The rule for number, then, is:

$$\text{(PS 3)} \quad \text{Num} \rightarrow \begin{Bmatrix} [\pm \text{Pl}, \pm \text{Obv}] & \\ [\pm \text{Pl}, \pm \text{Voc}] & / \quad [\text{Kin } \overline{\text{term}}] \end{Bmatrix}$$

Personal possession is marked by three sets of elements: a pronominal prefix (Pn), a possessive suffix (Poss), and an optional element marking pluralization of the pronominal possessor (PnPl):

$$\text{(PS 4)} \quad \text{PP} \rightarrow \text{Pn} \quad \text{Poss} \quad \text{(PnPl)}$$

Finally, there are three pronominal prefixes, ones for first, second, and third persons. In the first person plural a distinction is made between inclusive and exclusive. These pronominal distinctions can be indicated by means of two features, first person and second person. The rule for the pronouns is:

$$\text{(PS 5)} \quad \text{Pn} \rightarrow \begin{Bmatrix} \begin{bmatrix} +1 \\ -2 \end{bmatrix} \\ \begin{bmatrix} +1 \\ +2 \end{bmatrix} \\ \begin{bmatrix} -1 \\ +2 \end{bmatrix} \\ \begin{bmatrix} -1 \\ -2 \end{bmatrix} \end{Bmatrix}$$

In addition to the foregoing phrase structure rules, a transformational rule is necessary to give the correct order of the morphemes in a possessive theme. Thus,

$$\text{(T 1)} \quad \begin{array}{llllll} \text{SD:} & \text{Pn} - & \text{Poss} + \text{(PnPl)} - & \text{N} - & \begin{matrix}\text{Num}\\ \text{loc}\end{matrix} & \\ \text{SC:} & 1 & 2 & 3 & 4 & \Rightarrow \quad 1\ 3\ 2\ 4 \end{array}$$

This rule permutes the order of the possessive morpheme followed by the optional pronominal pluralizer so that the two elements come immediately after the noun stem and precede the number/locative suffixes.

<u>Lexical rewrite rules.</u> The lexical rewrite rules, which introduce the underlying forms of the morphemes for each category, are the following:

(L 1)
$$\begin{bmatrix} -\text{pl} \\ -\text{obv} \end{bmatrix} \rightarrow \begin{Bmatrix} \text{a} \;/\;]_{\text{N}_{\text{an}}} - \\ \text{i} \;/\;]_{\text{N}_{\text{in}}} - \end{Bmatrix}$$

(L 2)
$$\begin{bmatrix} -\text{pl} \\ +\text{obv} \end{bmatrix} \rightarrow \begin{Bmatrix} \text{ali} \;/\;]_{\text{N}_{\text{an}}} - \\ \text{i} \;/\;]_{\text{N}_{\text{in}}} - \end{Bmatrix}$$

(L 3)
$$\begin{bmatrix} +\text{pl} \\ -\text{obv} \end{bmatrix} \rightarrow \begin{Bmatrix} \text{aki} \;/\;]_{\text{N}_{\text{an}}} - \\ \text{ali} \;/\;]_{\text{N}_{\text{in}}} - \end{Bmatrix}$$

(L 4)
$$\begin{bmatrix} +\text{pl} \\ +\text{obv} \end{bmatrix} \rightarrow \begin{Bmatrix} \text{hi} \;/\;]_{\text{N}_{\text{an}}} - \\ \text{ali} \;/\;]_{\text{N}_{\text{in}}} - \end{Bmatrix}$$

(L 5) Loc → eki

(L 6) Poss → em

(L 7)
$$\begin{bmatrix} \begin{bmatrix} +1 \\ -2 \end{bmatrix} \\ \begin{bmatrix} -1 \\ +2 \end{bmatrix} \\ \begin{bmatrix} +1 \\ +2 \end{bmatrix} \\ \begin{bmatrix} -1 \\ -2 \end{bmatrix} \end{bmatrix} \rightarrow \begin{bmatrix} \text{ni} \\ \text{ki} \\ \text{ki} \\ \text{ho} \end{bmatrix}$$

(L 8)
$$\text{PnPl} \rightarrow \begin{Bmatrix} \text{ena·} \;/\; \begin{Bmatrix} +1 \\ \pm 2 \end{Bmatrix} - \\ \text{wa·} \end{Bmatrix}$$

(L 9) $\begin{bmatrix} +\text{voc} \\ -\text{pl} \end{bmatrix} \rightarrow \text{ehi}$

(L 10) $\begin{bmatrix} +\text{voc} \\ +\text{pl} \end{bmatrix} \rightarrow \text{eti}$

(L 11) $\text{Dim} \rightarrow \text{e·θ}$

Readjustment rules. The following rules account for the syntactically conditioned morpheme variants previously described.

(R 1) $\text{ali} \rightarrow \text{a} \ / \left\{ \begin{matrix} \left\{ \begin{matrix} \text{n} \\ \text{Cw} \\ \text{ya} \end{matrix} \right\} \\ \text{Dim} \\ \text{Poss} \quad (\text{PnPl}) \end{matrix} \right\} \ \_$

(R 2a) $\text{e·θ} \rightarrow \text{eh} \ / \ ]_{N_{an}} \ \_ \quad [-\text{Pl}]$

(R 2b) $\text{e·θ} \rightarrow \text{ale·θ} \ / \left\{ \begin{matrix} \ldots \text{V}(\cdot) \\ \text{C}_o\text{VC}_o \end{matrix} \right\}]_{N_{in}} \ \_ \quad [+\text{Pl}]$

2. PHONOLOGICAL RULES

For each morpheme, i. e. , each noun stem and affix, a base form is set up. The base forms of the nominal affixes have been presented in the previous section. In many instances the phonological, or underlying, shape of an affix or the noun stem to which it is added does not undergo any phonetic modifications when it combines with another element. But in most cases these base forms do undergo one or more phonetic changes in the formation of words. The modifications that occur are basically of three types: insertion of an element; deletion or loss of an element; and contraction of elements. The nine rules presented below explicitly state these changes for the nominal suffixes and their preceding noun stems; and when applied in the given order when the specified conditions are met, will give the actual phonetic shapes for Shawnee noun forms.

The phonological rules that have been formulated are based only upon noun forms and are not based upon any others, e. g. , verb forms. Thus, some of the rules may no doubt lack the generality that they would have if the language as a whole had been studied. Further, the rules apply specifically to the phonological processes involving nominal suffixation; no attempt has been made to give rules that would apply to processes involving prefixation.

2. 1. Glide insertion.

A large proportion of inanimate noun stems end in a vowel when the singular suffix or the locative suffix is added. When the plural suffix is added, however, a glide w precedes the plural morpheme. If the diminutive suffix also occurs with the plural, the glide precedes the diminutive. Thus, it might appear that the glide is a final element in the stem. But its presence is predictable if the base form of the stem is set up with a final vowel. All inanimate noun stems with a final vowel, optionally followed by length, insert the glide w before the plural suffix or insert it before the diminutive suffix if it is followed by the plural. This rule can be symbolized thus:

(P 1) $\emptyset \rightarrow w \ / \ \ldots V\,(\cdot)\,]_{N_{in}} \ \_\_ \ (\text{Dim})\ \text{Pl}$

Examples are the following:[5]

/wiʔka· + ali/ 'camps'

wiʔka·wali (P 1)

/wiʔka· + e·θ + ali/ 'small camps'

wiʔka· + e·θ + a (R 1)

wiʔka· + ale·θ + a (R 2b)

wiʔka·w + ale·θa (P 1)

wiʔka·wale·θa

/ki·mi·we· + ali/ 'gifts'

ki·mi·we·w + ali (P 1)

ki·mi·we·wali

/ki·mi·we· + e·θ + ali/ 'small gifts'

ki·mi·we· + e·θ + a (R 1)

ki·mi·we· + ale·θ + a (R 2b)

ki·mi·we·w + ale·θ + a (P 1)

ki·mi·we·wale·θa

Nearly half of the inanimate noun stems in Shawnee end in a vowel and hence are affected by this rule. Furthermore, most of the recent loanwords from English which are inanimate end in a vowel and thus take the epenthetic w when the plural morpheme follows. Examples of such loanwords include:

/ke·pici· + ali/ 'cabbages'
  ke·pici·w + ali (P 1)
  ke·pici·wali
/poki· + ali/ 'books'
  poki·w + ali (P 1)
  poki·wali

2. 2. Vowel raising (optional).

In two morphemes, viz., -e·θ 'diminutive' and -eki 'locative', the vowel e is frequently raised to i. There does not seem to be any clear environmental factor (or factors) conditioning this change, and in some cases both vowels have been recorded in forms having these suffixes. Hence, for the present an optional rule raising the e in these two morphemes is set up. This rule may be symbolized thus:

(P 2) $\begin{bmatrix} \text{e·θ} \\ \text{eki} \end{bmatrix} \rightarrow \begin{bmatrix} \text{i·θ} \\ \text{iki} \end{bmatrix}$

Examples are the following:

/wi·n + eki/ 'on the kernel'
  wi·n + iki (P 2)
  wi·niki
/wi·n + e·θ + i/ 'small kernel'
  wi·n + eh + i (R 2a)
  wi·n + ih + i (P 2)
  wi·nihi
/wapakko·θ + eki/ 'on the can'
  wapakko·θ + iki (P 2)
  wapakko·θiki
/θakkika·n + eki/ 'on the nail'
  θakkika·n + iki (P 2)
  θakkika·niki

2. 3. ya contraction.

For a number of noun stems a hypothetical syllable ya has been set up to account for an alternation between e· and Ø in final postconsonantal position in those bases.[6] By postulating this syllable and the contractions of it under the conditions discussed below, it is possible to account for certain "irregularities" otherwise common to at least some dozen nouns of both genders.

The syllable ya becomes zero after a consonant and before the singular suffix. The diminutive suffix may precede the singular suffix, and ya still becomes zero. With animate nouns, however, ya does not drop if the singular suffix is obviative. The rule accounting for these facts may be given thus:

(P 3a) $$\text{ya} \rightarrow \text{Ø} \ / \ \text{C}\_(\text{Dim}) \begin{bmatrix} +\text{sing} \\ -\text{obv} \end{bmatrix}$$

Examples of rule (P 3a) are:

/ho + skasya + a/ 'nail (of an animal)'
ho + skas + a (P 3a)
hoskasa

/hane·piyya + i/ 'elm'
hane·piy + i (P 3a)
hane·pi + i (P 4)
hane·pi + Ø (P 7)
hane·pi

/hane·piyya + e·θ + i/ 'little elm'
hane·piyya + eh + i (R 2a)
hane·piy + eh + i (P 3a)
hane·pi + eh + i (P 4)
hane·pi + h + i (P 7)
hane·pihi

In all other environments, i. e. , everywhere except before the (non-obviative) singular suffix, ya after a consonant becomes e·. Thus,

(P 3b) $$\text{ya} \rightarrow \text{e·} \ / \ \text{C}\_$$

Examples of this rule are:

/hane·piyya + ali/ 'elms'

hane·piyya + a	(R 1)
hane·piye· + a	(P 3b)
hane·piye· + Ø	(P 7)
hane·piye + Ø	(P 9)
hane·piye	

/hane·piyya + e·θ + ali/ 'little elms'

hane·piyya + e·θ + a	(R 1)
hane·piye· + e·θ + a	(R 3b)
hane·piye· + θ + a	(P 7)
hane·piye·θa	

/hane·piyya + eki/ 'on the elm' (cf. also 2.4 below)

hane·piye· + eki	(P 3b)
hane·piye· + ki	(P 7)
hane·piye + ki	(P 9)
hane·piyeki	

/ho + skasya + aki/ 'nails'

ho + skase· + aki	(P 3b)
ho + skase· + ki	(P 7)
hoskase·ki	

/ho + skasya + ali/ 'nails (obv.)'

ho + skase· + ali	(P 3b)
ho + skase· + li	(P 7)
hoskase·li	

2. 4. <u>y loss.</u>

This rule is tenuous and is set up to account for the loss of y in several forms which have the hypothetical syllable ya in the base. In these forms base final y is lost between i's and is lost between i and the suffixes -eh and -eki.[7] The rule accounting for this may be set up as follows:

(P 4) $$y \rightarrow \emptyset \;/\; i\_\left\{\begin{array}{c} i \\ \left\{\begin{array}{c} eh \\ eki \end{array}\right\} \end{array}\right\}$$

An example of this rule is:

/hane·piyya + eki/ 'on the elm'

hane·piy + eki	(R 3a)
hane·pi + eki	(P 4)
hane·pi + ki	(P 7)
hane·piki	

In order to derive this alternate form of 'on the elm' (cf. 2. 3 for the derivation of the other form), rule (P 3a) had to be applied in spite of the fact that ya is not ordinarily lost before the locative.

Other examples of the application of this rule are the derivations of 'elm' and 'little elm' in 2. 3 above.

2. 5. Nasal insertion.

Under certain conditions n is inserted at the end of a stem. This occurs with bases which end in the sequence kwi when the diminutive suffix is added; with the same stems it also optionally occurs when the locative suffix is added. The rule for nasal insertion may be symbolized thus:

(P 5) $$\emptyset \rightarrow n \,/\, kwi \_ \left\{ \begin{matrix} \text{Dim} \\ \text{(Loc)} \end{matrix} \right\}$$

It should be noted that this rule is of rather limited application, since there are only some half-doẓen different stems in which this nasal insertion occurs (There also is one exception to the rule, viz. , the stem /kawaskwi·/ 'wheat'.)

Examples are:

/wa·pikwi + e·θ + i/ 'small pumpkin'

wa·pikwi + eh + i	(R 2a)
wa·pikwin + eh + i	(P 5)
wa·piko·n + eh + i	(P 8)
wa·piko·nehi	

/wa·pikwi + eki/ 'on the pumpkin'

wa·pikwin + eki	(P 5)
wa·piko·n + eki	(P 8)
wa·piko·neki	

/tetepaʔtekwi + e·θ + ali/ 'small vines'

tetepaʔtekwi + e·θ + a (R 1)

tetepaʔtekwin + e·θ + a (P 5)

tetepaʔteko·n + e·θ + a (P 8)

tetepaʔteko·ne·θa

2. 6. Nasal loss.

A very large number of noun stems, especially inanimate ones, end in n or n plus vowel sequence. If such a stem has three or more syllables, the final n or nV sequence is regularly deleted when the singular suffix (with animate nouns, the nonobviative singular only) follows. It is optionally deleted when the diminutive suffix is followed by the singular suffix. The rule accounting for this can be formulated as follows:

(P 6) $$n\,(V\,(\cdot)) \rightarrow \emptyset \,/\, (C_o V\,(\cdot))_3 \underline{\quad} \left\{ \begin{matrix} \begin{bmatrix} -\text{Pl} \\ -\text{Obv} \end{bmatrix} \\ \left(\text{Dim} + \begin{bmatrix} -\text{Pl} \\ -\text{Obv} \end{bmatrix}\right) \end{matrix} \right\}$$

Examples of nasal loss before the singular suffix are the following:

/pakama·kan + i/ 'war club'

pakama·ka + i (P 6)

pakama·ka + Ø (P 7)

pakama·ka

/ho + tapkakane· + i/ '(his) chin'

ho + tapkaka + i (P 6)

ho + tapkaka + Ø (P 7)

hotapkaka

/pa·piʔsa·ka·n + a/ 'bat'

pa·piʔsa·ka· + a (P 6)

pa·piʔsa·ka· + Ø (P 7)

pa·piʔsa·ka + Ø (P 9)

pa·piʔsa·ka

/mkita·ka·n + a/ 'pillow'

mkita·ka + a (P 6)

mkita·ka· + Ø (P 7)

mkita·ka + Ø (P 9)

mkita·ka

Examples of the optional loss of the nasal element before the diminutive plus singular suffixes are the following:

/siʔsi·kwan + e·θ + i/ 'small gourd rattle'

siʔsi·kwan + eh + i	(R 2a)	siʔsi·kwan + eh + i
siʔsi·kwa + eh + i	(P 6)	
siʔsi·kwa + h + i	(P 7)	
siʔsi·kwahi		siʔsi·kwanehi

/ka·θe·min + e·θ + i/ 'small pecan'

ka·θe·min + eh + i	(R 2a)	ka·θe·min + eh + i
ka·θe·mi + eh + i	(P 6)	
ka·θe·mi + h + i	(P 7)	
ka·θe·mihi		ka·θe·minehi

Examples of monosyllabic and dissyllabic stems with final n which is retained before the singular suffix include:

/mi·n + a/ 'blackberry'

mi·na

/mi·kon + a/ 'feather'

mi·kona

/wi·n + i/ 'marrow; kernel'

wi·ni

2. 7. Vowel loss.

When a noun stem has a final vowel and is followed by a suffix with an initial vowel, the initial vowel of the suffix drops. The rule for this vowel loss can be given thus:

(P 7) V → Ø / V(·)_

/kosko· + aki/ 'hogs'

kosko· + ki (P 7)

kosko·ki

/ko·ta· + eki/ 'on the skirt'

ko·ta· + ki (P 7)

ko·ta + ki (P 9)

ko·taki

/mse·we· + ali/ 'horse (obv.)'

mse·we· + li (P 7)

mse·we·li

2. 8. <u>w + vowel contraction.</u>

Certain sequences of the glide w plus a vowel regularly contract to o· when any consonant immediately precedes w. Stem final w contracts with both initial e(·) and a of suffixes. Also the stem final sequence wi(·) contracts when it is postconsonantal. The rule for these contractions can be symbolized as:

(P 8) $$\left\{\begin{matrix} w + \\ wi(\cdot) \end{matrix}\right\} \left\{\begin{matrix} e(\cdot) \\ a \end{matrix}\right\} \rightarrow o\cdot \ / \ C\_$$

For contraction of the sequence w + e (·), the following examples are given:

/mkw + e·θ + a/ 'small bear'

mko· + θ + a (P 8)

mko·θa

/wa·pakkw + eki/ 'in the bucket'

wa·pakko· + ki (P 8)

wa·pakko + ki (P 9)

wa·pakkoki

/ki·saʔθw + e·θ + a/ 'small clock'

ki·saʔθo· + θ + a (P 8)

ki·saʔθo·θa

Examples of w + a contracting are:

/wa·pakkw + aki/ 'buckets'

wa·pakko· + ki (P 8)

wa·pakko·ki

/hameʔkw + ali/ 'beaver (obv.)'

hameʔko· + li (P 8)

hamʔko·li

When w and e(·) or a are not separated by morpheme boundary, they apparently do not contract. For example:

/menikwe· + aki/ 'bunches (of brush, flowers, etc.)'

menikwe· + ki (P 7)

menikwe·ki

/kato?hwa· + aki/ 'Cherokees'

kato?hwa· + ki (P 7)

kato?hwa·ki

Examples of postconsonantal wi(·) contracting are:

/wa·pikwi + e·θ + ali/ 'small pumpkins'

wa·pikwi + e·θ + a (R 1)

wa·pikwi + θ + a (P 7)

wa·piko· + θ + a (P 8)

wa·piko·θa

/pθika?kwi + e·θ + ali/ 'small boards'

pθika?kwi + e·θ + a (R 1)

pθika?kwin + e·θ + a (P 5)

pθika?ko·n + e·θ + a (P 8)

pθika?ko·ne·θa

/hinenalwi· + ali/ 'arrows'

hinenalwi·w + ali (P 1)

hinenalo·w + ali (P 8)

hinenalo·wali

2.9. Length loss.

Vowels followed by length lose that length in three different environments: word finally, i.e., before juncture; before h; and before the locative suffix. The rule for this can be symbolized as:

(P 9) $$V\cdot \rightarrow V \ / \ \_ \left\{ \begin{array}{l} \# \\ h \\ \text{Loc} \end{array} \right\}$$

Examples of the loss of length in word final position are:

/wi?si· + a/ 'dog'

wi?si· + Ø (P 7)

wi?si + Ø (P 9)

wi?si

/ne·naw?to· + a/ 'warrior'

ne·naw?to· + Ø (P 7)

ne·naw?to + Ø (P 9)

ne·naw?to

/ko·ta· + i/ 'skirt'

ko·ta· + Ø (P 7)

ko·ta + Ø (P 9)

ko·ta

The loss of length before h is illustrated by the following:

/haya·pe· + hi/ 'bucks (obv.)'

haya·pe + hi (P 9)

haya·pehi

/wi?si· + hi/ 'dogs (obv.)'

wi?si + hi (P 9)

wi?sihi

/wi?tona· + e·θ + i/ 'small facial hair'

wi?tona· + eh + i (R 2a)

wi?tona· + h + i (P 7)

wi?tona + h + i (P 9)

wi?tonahi

Finally, length loss before the locative suffix is illustrated by:

/ko·ta· + eki/ 'on the skirt'

ko·ta· + ki (P 7)

ko·ta + ki (P 9)

ko·taki

/le·mo·kwe· + eki/ 'on the mole'

le·mo·kwe· + ki (P 7)

le·mo·kwe + ki (P 9)

le·mo·kweki

/wi?ka· + eki/ 'in the camp'

wi?ka· + ki (P 7)

wi?ka + ki (P 9)

wi?kaki

3. SUMMARY REMARKS

The inflection of animate nouns is in nearly all cases regular. There is only one readjustment rule (i. e., [R 2a]) that is specific to animate stems; this rule simply gives a syntactically conditioned variant for the diminutive morpheme when the singular suffix follows. There are no phonological rules that are specific to animate stems. The same, however, is not the case with inanimate stems; here there are a number of innovations that have occurred.

Two changes in the suffixes occurring with inanimate stems are syntactically conditioned. One of these is the abbreviation of the plural suffix -ali to -a under the conditions specified above (see 1. 1). The other change is that in which the diminutive morpheme has taken the form -ale·θ (a compound it was noted previously, of -ali 'inan. sg.' plus -e·θ 'diminutive') when the plural morpheme follows either monosyllabic stems or stems ending in a vowel.

One important phonological change affecting inanimate stems is the glide insertion rule (P 1), which introduces w at the end of vowel final stems when the plural morpheme or diminutive plus plural sequence follows. For some of the forms to which this rule applies, reconstructed Proto-Algonquian forms have a base final w (e. g., *-wi·θaniw- (Ha) 'tongue'; *-ano·na·w- (Ha) 'cheek'; *si·pi·w 'river').[8] For the Shawnee forms which are reflexes of these Proto-Algonquian forms, it is not necessary to set up a final w in their stems, however, for the w is predictable by simply allowing a stem final vowel and then inserting w after the vowel in those forms taking the plural suffix. For many of the Shawnee forms, on the other hand, to which the w insertion rule applies, the reconstructed Proto-Algonquian forms do not have final w (e. g., *wi·yawehs- (Ha) 'meat': Sh. wiyawʔθi·). It might seem then that glide insertion came about on the analogy of those stems having a final w.

That the insertion of w is the result of analogical reshaping is supported by several additional facts. First, some nouns which are reflexes of Proto-Algonquian forms are recorded in two forms for the plural: one, the regular reflex, adds the suffix -ali to a stem ending in a consonant; the other form, actually a reshaping, has after the consonant a base final vowel (viz., i· < -i 'inan. sg.' plus length before w), which then takes w before -ali. For example:

/-lec + ali/ → -lecali; /-leci· + ali/ → -leci·wali 'hands'

/-θit + ali/ → -θitali; /-θiti· + ali/ → -θici·wali 'feet'

Note that all inanimate stems taking the epenthetic w do not have stem final i·; other final vowels occur, e. g. ,

/hapa?kwe·-/ 'roof'

/hapikamite·-/ 'soup'

/ko·ta-/ 'skirt'

/pa?pi?se·ya·-/ 'rag'

Second, all of the few English loanwords which are inanimate employ the glide insertion rule to a base that has final i·. Such loanwords include:

/poki·-/ 'book'

/ke·pici·-/ 'cabbage'

/ci·si·-/ 'cheese'

/stovi·-/ 'stove'

Thus, glide insertion is a productive process in the plural formations of inanimate nouns.

NOTES

1. This paper is a revised version of a seminar paper done in 1967 for Mary R. Haas while I was a graduate student at the University of California, Berkeley. Professor Haas had suggested to me that I work through the noun forms in Voegelin's dictionary (cited below) and try to establish regularity in their inflection for number since that inflection seemed to be quite irregular. This I was able to do. I then wanted to check my solution and expand the paper to take in other nominal inflectional processes. When I was in Oklahoma during the course of my dissertation field work on Pawnee, I managed to squeeze in a limited amount of informant work with Shawnee.

The data that I utilized from Voegelin's printed sources and that I collected myself were restricted to nouns. Because of time limitations, I have not had the opportunity to collect or work through other Shawnee material; hence, this paper suffers from a definitely restricted view of Shawnee, in that the description I provide is not excerpted from a fully integrated grammatical description of the language.

2. My field work consisted of a week in August 1966 followed by another week in July 1967. The Survey of California and Other Indian Languages, University of California, Berkeley, supported the field work, for which I wish to express grateful acknowledgment. The informants I worked with were: Mary Spoon of Shawnee, Oklahoma; and Eunice, Mary, and Robert Williams, all of Norman, Oklahoma.

3. The phonemes of Shawnee, as presented by C. F. Voegelin (1935), are as follows:

Consonants:	p	t	c	k	
		θ	s		
	m	n			
		l			
Glides:	w		y		ʔ
Vowels:	i	o			
	e	a			
Length:	V·				

In addition to these, Voegelin sets up three "defective" phonemes, symbolized as P, T, K. Since I found none of these, I have not included them in this chart.

For the consonants several features of phonetic variation should be mentioned. The nasals and the lateral phonemes are devoiced when they occur before a consonant at the beginning of a phrase. The semivowels w and y are also devoiced in the same position and are devoiced between voiceless consonants in syllable-final position phrase-medially and in syllable-initial position phrase-initially. In addition, the glottal stop has a variant, the glottal spirant [h]. Note that even though [ʔ] and [h] constitute a single phoneme, I have used both symbols in underlying phonemic forms. This is simply a notational convenience. The vowels have both open and close variants, but otherwise demonstrate no notable variation.

4. C. F. Voegelin (1936) lists the forms of the suffixes occurring with nouns as follows:

	Animate	Inanimate
Singular	-θ	-i
Plural	-ki	-li, -a
Diminutive sing.		-hhi
plural		-θa (-)
Obviative sing.	-li	
plural	-hhi	
Locative	-ki	-ki
Vocative sing.	-hi	
plural	-ti	

The pronominal prefixes he gives as follows:

First person	ni-
Second person	ki-
Third person	hw-

In addition, the forms of the possessive plurals are:

First person	-naa-
Second person	-waa-

5. In the derivations in these and subsequent examples, two kinds of rules are cited as applying in each derivation: readjustment rules, indicated

by (R) followed by the number of the rule as given in section 1. 7; and the phonological rules described in this section and indicated by (P) followed by the number of the rule.

6. The setting up of a hypothetical syllable ya was suggested to me by Mary R. Haas. She, of course, is not responsible for my use of it.

7. This rule points to a more general process, viz. , that y is lost when it occurs after i and before a front vowel; but whether such a general rule obtains for Shawnee is not presently known.

8. The Proto-Algonquian reconstructions given here come from the personal file of Mary R. Haas. She is not, however, responsible for my use of them.

REFERENCES

Haas, Mary R. Proto-Algonkian file. MS.

Voegelin, Carl F. 1935. Shawnee phonemes. Language 11:23-37.

___. 1936. Productive paradigms in Shawnee. In Essays in anthropology, presented to A. L. Kroeber in celebration of his sixtieth birthday, June 11, 1936, 391-403. Berkeley: University of California Press. (Reprinted 1968 by Books for Libraries Press, Inc. , Freeport, N. Y.)

___. 1937-40. Shawnee stems and the Jacob P. Dunn Miami dictionary. Indiana Historical Society, Prehistory Research Series 1:63-108, 135-67, 289-341, 345-406, 409-78.

___. 1953. From FL (Shawnee) to TL (English). IJAL 19:1-25.

Aspects of Yuchi Morphonology

W. L. Ballard

From April 1970 until March 1972 I spent approximately 200 hours interviewing a Yuchi informant, Mrs. Addie George.[1] During the summer of 1971, I spent approximately six weeks in Sapulpa, Oklahoma,[2] interviewing Yuchis there and in the vicinity for ethnographic and linguistic information. Besides field notes, a number of tapes of conversations in Yuchi were made and these have been transcribed. It is hoped that processing these materials will soon yield a description of Yuchi, an English-Yuchi lexicon, a Yuchi morpheme lexicon, and a Yuchi chrestomathy. This paper will touch on some of the more interesting aspects of Yuchi morphonology that have come to light during this research.

Yuchi has the following phonemic consonantal system:

This paper is based on a talk presented _in absentia_ at the Southern Anthropological Society Annual Meeting, April 1971, Dallas, Texas.

	labials	alveolars	alveolar affricates	palatal affricates	velars
voiceless unaspirated	p	t	ts	tʃ	k
voiceless aspirated	ph	th	tsh	tʃh	kh
voiced	b	d	dz	dʒ	g
voiceless fricatives	f	ɬ	s	ʃ	
resonants		n, l			
glides			h, ʔ, j, w		

As Wolff (1948) notes, the voiceless unaspirated consonants sound vaguely preaspirated when following a vowel on some occasions. Since the manner of articulation is auditorily identical with that of the consonants /p, t, k/ in clusters after /s/ and /ʃ/ the underlying form for this series might appear to be /hC/. However, so little of the /h/ remains in most contexts that this form had best be treated as a free variant; an underlying /hC/ cluster is probably only available to internal reconstruction. The analysis of the native speaker's system as containing just the plain stops and affricates is also mor symmetrical in that the latter do not cluster with /s/ and /ʃ/.

The voiceless unaspirated obstruents (stops, affricates, and fricatives) occur in clusters with /ʔ/ in the order /Cʔ/. /n, l/ and perhaps /j, w/ occur in clusters with /ʔ/ in the order /ʔC/. Previous studies (Wagner 1934; Crawford, personal communication) have treated these consonants as a glottalized series, but this approach does not seem appropriate for Yuchi.[3]

In the first place, when noninitial the obstruents and glottal stop appear to separate phonetically as a result of syllabification rules that assign the obstruent to the preceding syllable and the glottal stop to the following syllable. Secondly, the glottal stop and the obstruent may be separated by a morpheme boundary. Thus 'I cry' /ditsʔa/, but 'she cries' /seʔa/ where /ʔa/ is the verb stem. Both of these phenomena stand in contrast to the aspiration of the voiceless aspirated series. The third argument for the cluster treatment is based on the syllable canon. For Yuchi at the phonological level this is:

{s, ʃ, (h)} C (ʔ) (j, w) V[4]

with the following constraint: a preconsonantal fricative never co-occurs with a postconsonantal /ʔ/. Thus /Cʔ/ functions differently from the aspirated series in the canon. On the basis of these three considerations, the system is described as having consonantal clusters with /ʔ/. Thus the following four items are distinct:

weti	'their name'
wethi	'they ask'
wetʔi	'their urine'
wedi	'theirs'

Additional constraints on the phonological syllable canon are: (1) /s/ and /ʃ/ can precede just the three plain stops /p, t, k/; (2) /j, w/ can follow all of the consonants (though such clusters are relatively rare) except /h, l, n, ɬ/ and the labials (there are a few derived /bj/ clusters); (3) only voiceless unaspirated consonants can occur with a glottal stop. Thus it would be possible to posit one voiceless stop/affricate series. The obstruents treated as plain here could be phonemicized as /hC/; then the voiceless stops and the affricate would be aspirated if they were not preceded by a fricative or followed by a glottal stop. (Note that the only fricative preceding the affricate would be /h/.) For the reasons presented above this economy appears to be spurious for Yuchi.

The vowels are somewhat more difficult to analyze. The underlying system appears to contain:

i	u		
e	o	ẽ, jẽ	õ
æ	a	æ̃	ã

but there are a number of problems. First of all, /ẽ/ is realized phonetically as [ɛ̃] so that the phonetic/phonological distinction /ẽ/ versus /æ̃/ is at best marginal (in the sense of Labov 1972:1122). In a few words speakers regularly produce an [ɛ̃], in other words regularly an [æ̃]. However, for the majority of words with either underlying vowel (hypothetically), the vowel may be pronounced either as [ɛ̃] or as [æ̃]. Moreover, for the one possible minimal pair, I have found that speakers cannot regularly produce or hear the distinction: /ʔẽ/ 'first person plural inclusive' and 'elderly female third person singular' versus /ʔæ̃/ 'second person plural' — where both are pronominal prefixes that could occur with the same verb. Thus /ʔẽkʔæ/ 'we/she laugh' should contrast with /ʔæ̃kʔæ/ 'you all laugh'.[5] A similar situation occurs between /ã/, realized as [ʌ̃] and /õ/ which can be more or less rounded freely in its realizations. Again the distinction is marginal, but there is one possibly minimal pair: /nõnã/ 'we have' versus /nãnã/ 'creek'. We might hypothesize that the system once had more clear contrasts and that a gradual merger of the structurally parallel front and back series is occurring.[6]

But there are some additional vowels phonetically: [ɔ, ɔ̃, ĩ, ũ] and [ã]. All of these appear to arise as the result of the application of morphonological rules. There is a general rule in Yuchi:[7,8]

(1)
$$\begin{bmatrix} +\text{voc} \\ -\text{cons} \\ -\text{fl} \\ \alpha\text{nas} \\ -\text{gr} \\ \beta\text{diff} \\ \gamma\text{comp} \end{bmatrix} \begin{bmatrix} -\text{voc} \\ -\text{cons} \\ +\text{vcd} \\ +\text{fl} \\ +\text{gr} \end{bmatrix} \begin{bmatrix} +\text{voc} \\ -\text{cons} \\ -\text{fl} \\ -\text{nas} \\ -\text{gr} \\ -\text{diff} \\ -\text{comp} \end{bmatrix} \rightarrow \begin{bmatrix} +\text{voc} \\ -\text{cons} \\ +\text{fl} \\ \alpha\text{nas} \\ +\text{gr} \\ \beta\text{diff} \\ \gamma\text{comp} \end{bmatrix}$$

i + we → u
e + we → o
{æ + we, a + we} → ɔ

i. e., an unrounded vowel plus the morpheme /we/ 'third person non-Yuchi' becomes a back rounded vowel with features of height and nasalization preserved. This is the only source for [ɔ] even though in one or two forms its provenience is no longer clear to the native speaker: /kʔɔlafæ/ 'flower' < /kʔa/ 'something' + /we/ '(indefinite) third person' pronominal prefix + /lafæ/ 'burst, bloom.' Since nasalization is retained, this rule also accounts for [ɔ̃].

Velars in general tend to have a glide [j] optionally inserted before the front vowel /æ/. When rule (1) above is applied to these forms the glide is obligatory. In addition, when rule (1) applies to the underlying sequence /ewe/ after velars, the same glide is always inserted. Thus the following rule:[8]

(2)
$$\begin{bmatrix} +\text{cons} \\ +\text{gr} \\ -\text{diff} \end{bmatrix} \rightarrow \begin{bmatrix} +\text{cons} \\ +\text{gr} \\ -\text{diff} \end{bmatrix} \begin{bmatrix} -\text{cons} \\ -\text{voc} \\ -\text{gr} \\ +\text{vcd} \end{bmatrix} \Big/ \_\_ \begin{bmatrix} -\text{cons} \\ +\text{voc} \\ -\text{gr} \\ -\text{diff} \end{bmatrix}$$

$$\text{Velars} \rightarrow \text{Velars} + \text{j} \;/\; \_\_\; \underset{(\text{e})}{\text{æ}}$$

must apply before rule (1). In addition it must be constrained to apply optionally (if [1] is not to apply) to the [+ compact] vowel and obligatorily (if [1] is to apply) to the [−diffuse] vowels. (In addition, rule [1] must be modified to reflect the presence of a glide.) Thus these rules yield the following contrast: /kh(j)æwe/ > /khjɔ/ but /khawe/ > /khɔ/.

The most interesting aspect of rule (1), however, is the number of constraints under which it operates. If the sequence is in close juncture (within a word) the rule must apply. Hence, the form for 'flower'. The rule does not apply (ever) across certain syntactic boundaries that are not clear yet. It is applied optionally within some permissible environments with no semantic effect; the coalescence here is probably related to the speech rate. Finally, in one particular syntactic environment it has a semantic function: when the first vowel ends a noun and the /we/ that follows is part of the plural demonstrative, then the absence of rule application means 'plural indefinite', whereas presence of rule application means 'plural definite'. (The form without a demonstrative means 'singular indefinite'.) Thus, /dzenẽ/ 'dog'; /dzenẽwenã/ 'dogs'; /dzenõnã/ 'the dog'.

The two high nasalized vowels [ĩ] and [ũ] arise due to the application of another less obvious rule in Yuchi:[8]

(3) $$\begin{bmatrix} -\text{cons} \\ +\text{voc} \\ \alpha\text{gr} \\ \beta\text{diff} \\ \gamma\text{comp} \\ \delta\text{fl} \end{bmatrix} \begin{bmatrix} +\text{cons} \\ +\text{nas} \end{bmatrix} \begin{bmatrix} -\text{cons} \\ +\text{voc} \\ -\text{gr} \\ -\text{diff} \\ -\text{comp} \end{bmatrix} \rightarrow \begin{bmatrix} -\text{cons} \\ +\text{voc} \\ +\text{nas} \\ \alpha\text{gr} \\ \beta\text{diff} \\ \gamma\text{comp} \\ \delta\text{fl} \end{bmatrix} \quad / \_\_ X$$

$$\text{V} + \text{ne} \rightarrow \tilde{\text{V}}$$

(where X may not be null or a word boundary)

This rule is more difficult to analyze than the earlier rule because it is never variable or functional. On the same grounds it is also more dubious as a rule in the synchronic grammar. Thus /tʃhine/, generic for 'melon' or 'gourd', appears in the names of several different kinds of melon as [tʃhĩ] : [tʃhĩᵑkˀo] 'pumpkin'. Similarly /kˀagojune/ 'sickness' becomes [kˀagojũ] in [kˀagojũtshole] 'hospital' (=sick home). This coalescence is sometimes perspicuous to the native speaker; Mrs. George recognized the source /wedine/ 'cow' for the [wedĩ] of [wedĩᵑkˀãdi] 'beef'.

Finally, [ã] and frequently non-nasal [a] are derived as free variants from /æ̃/ and /æ/, respectively, in the pronominal prefixes indicating second perso plural.

My preliminary analysis has yielded no contrast based on length, stress, pitch, or intonation. It does appear that stressed vowels are long, especially if nonfinal. In isolation words tend to be stressed as follows:

Monosyllabic:	CV̀	falling stress
Disyllabic:	CV̄	long level stress (first syllable)
	CV̀	falling stress (second syllable)
Trisyllabic:	CV̄	long level stress (first syllable)
	CV̌	zero stress short (second syllable)
	CV̀	falling stress (third syllable)

The verbal paradigms show several interesting morphonological and semantic features, both with respect to the subject prefixes and with respect to the stem (There are also object and combined subject/object paradigms; these will not be discussed here.) Approximately the same prefixes occur before nouns as possessors; we shall make only passing reference to these forms.

In the paradigms below the only marker for the third person shown will be that which means 'third person, male, singular, Yuchi, women's speech'. By and large the other markers do not participate in the morphonological and sema operations that will interest us here. They include:

hõ (~hẽ)[9]	'third person, Yuchi, male, men's speech'
ˀo (~ˀi)[9]	'third person, plural, Yuchi, women's speech'
go (~ge)[9]	'one, a person, everyone'
se[10]	'third person, singular, Yuchi, female'
ˀẽ	'third person, singular, Yuchi, female, elder'
we	'third person, non-Yuchi, animate'
jõ[11]	'third person, plural, non-Yuchi, animate'

These glosses are minimally distinctive; all of these prefixes have additional uses. For example, a husband uses se, etc. for females other than his wife, hõ for his wife. Similarly, a Yuchi wife calls males generally sˀe, but refers to her husband as ˀo.

The prefix paradigms will be arranged in a standard format. The left-hand column indicates singular subjects, the right, plural. The right-hand column in the first row also distinguishes inclusive (to the left) from exclusive (to the right). The three rows indicate first, second, and third person subjects, respectively.

Ia. The <u>di</u> paradigm:

difæ	ˀõfæ	nõfæ	
næ̃fæ	ˀæ̃fæ		'beat'
sˀefæ	ˀofæ		

Ib. The <u>do</u> paradigm:

dofæfæ	ˀõfæfæ	nõfæfæ	
jofæfæ	ˀæjofæfæ		'beat' (for someone)
sˀjofæfæ	ˀofæfæ		

Most verb stems take one or both of these prefixes as subjects; they may also take direct or indirect object pronoun prefix paradigms. A partial list of the stems and their various combinatory possibilities and glosses follows.

Stems with <u>di</u> with direct object prefixes or <u>do</u> with indirect object prefixes:

di	do	Stem
'dress up'	'dress up for someone; dress up in someone else's clothes'	ˀæ̃__dʒi
'bite'	'bite off someone else's thing'	__wa
'care for'	'care for on someone else's behalf'	__kˀæha
'listen'	'listen to someone else's phonation'	__tʃˀuda
'buy'	'buy from, for someone else'	(kˀa)__wãdʒi
'pull out (one at a time)'	'pull off of someone else'	ˀæ__wæ̃
'speak to'	'speak to someone'	__ˀwede
'throw'	'throw to someone'	__pha
'chase'	'drive for someone'	__ɬˀæ̃tʃhi
'punch, stick'	'pound for someone'	__ʃi
'see'	'show someone else's thing'	__ˀnæ̃ˀnæ̃

And the following where the do + indirect object prefix form always means 'fo someone':

'carry on the back'	__hi	'chop; cut'	__pha
'fight'	__k?ahã	'hang out'	łahe__bã
'push'	__ł?ãge	'pull'	__dithæ̃
'supervise'	__tã(tã)	'remember'	__k?jãwã

Stems with di with no direct object prefix or do with an indirect object prefix:

di	do	Stem
'breathe'	'smell someone else's thing'	__hæ
'drink'	'drink for someone, drink someone else's fluid'	__p?e
'wear, hang around the neck'	'hang around someone else's neck'	__phæ?æ
'put on'	'put on for someone; put on someone else's thing'	__thoʃ?i
'be awake'	'dream of, about someone'	__wæ̃
'send'	'send to someone, send on someone else's behalf'	__k?wæ̃
'tell about'	'order someone to'	__?jagwa
'ask a question'	'ask a question of someone'	__?ænẽ
'lie'	'lie to someone'	__tiʃæ̃
'look back'	'look back at someone'	{kele, jale}__p?a
'offer'	'offer to someone'	__lahæ̃
'steal'	'steal from someone'	(hi)__ʃa

And the following where the do + indirect object prefix form always means 'for someone else':

'be afraid'	__thafa	'bake'	__ł?o
'braid'	__thæthæ	'call (to)'	__ge
'complete'	__?atʃha	'cook'	__gã
'hurry'	__khægæ	'kill'	__ʃe
'peel'	tʃhwa__thi	'plant'	__ho
'run'	s?æ__the	'scrape'	__sathæ̃
'sweep'	(?ju, s?æ)__dathæ̃		

A few verbs take di with no direct object prefix or do with a direct object prefix:

di	do	Stem
'cover'	'cover someone'	__hæne
'hunt'	'hunt for someone (look for)'	__ʔade
'be angry'	'be angry at someone'	__thjã
'turn (around, intransitive)'	'turn someone (around, transitive)'	__piɬi

One verb takes di with no direct object prefix, do with a direct object prefix, or do with an indirect object prefix:

di	do + direct object	do + indirect object	Stem
'take a bath'	'bathe someone else'	'bathe on someone else's behalf'	ha__hæ̃

Most verbs take just di or do prefixes and a subset of each takes the object prefixes. Stems with di only with no direct object prefix:

'alive'	__hæle	'asleep, sleep'	__tsa
'be born'	__pʔa	'chew'	__wawa
'close the eyes'	__dæ̃	'be cold'	__dã
'come'	__de	'be cold'	__ʃpa
'be crazy'	__kʔjãwi	'dance'	__(kʔa)ʃti
'die'	__wado	'finish'	khæ__(kʔã)wi/ʃtu
'die'	__wile	'fly'	__sta
'go'	__wi	'be hungry'	__ʔjãhã
'go'	{ʔa(he) / ke} __dʒi	'jump'	__tʃha
'lay down'	__ʔẽ	'lie down'	sʔæ__ʔe
'lick'	__tʔẽkha	'live (in a certain place)'	__kʔu
'be lost'	__wi	'get married'	go__kʔatã
'be a member of'	keʔæ__de	'be noisy'	__datsʔã
'get old'	go__ha	'pile up'	sʔæ__wi/ʃtu
'play'	__wãhã	'play ball'	(kʔa)__the
'be in power'	kʔala__se(se)	'read'	__kʔãʔwede
'be selfish, stingy'	__thjẽʃʔjẽ	'be sleepy'	__tsjaspa
'sneeze'	__hætshi	'stand'	__fa
'study'	__kʔæha	'turn summersaults'	__wejupʔædæske

'suspect'	(hi)__khi	'swim'	__stã
'take'	__kʔãdʒi	'be thirsty'	tse__kʔotʃha
'walk'	__fafa		

Stems with di only with a direct object prefix:

'depend on'	__thæʔæ	'favor, mock, look like'	__ʔnõʃã
'go with'	__to	'hate, be mad at'	__tʔasʔjẽ
'help'	__thjã	'hold'	hi__ta
'hug'	__kʔajuhã	'jealous of'	__thæʃʔjẽ
'laugh at'	__kʔæ	'love'	__thjæju
'paint'	__baba	'talk to'	__ʔwede
'visit (look back)'	__kʔæ̃ʔnæ̃	'wake (a person)'	__lawæ̃
'want'	__thæ	'be with'	__kʔada
'wrestle with'	__kʔæłæ		

Stems with do only with an indirect object prefix:

'agree with'	__(ho)ʔnẽga	'ask for something'	__thi
'bury'	{ʔahe / ke}__tʔæ	'call for'	__pʔæ
'close for'	__ʃtã	'precede'	taha__gã
'count for'	kʔa__ʔã	'eat up for'	__laha
'fix for'	__kʔãle	'give to'	__wã
'kill for (slaughter)'	__ʃe	'make for, build'	__da
'open for'	kho__tha	'paddle'	__phæ̃phæ̃
'pluck for'	__tʃhwã	'quit on'	__tʔæle
'receive'	__kʔi	'sew for'	__pʔa
'show to'	__ta	'sing'	ʔja__kʔwæ̃
'stir for'	kʔahi__ʃigæ̃	'take away from'	__wałæ̃
'tan'	tʔonẽ__sãdi	'tear'	tʔa__kwæ̃
'wash for'	__di	'weave'	__ła
'work for'	kʔa(la)__kʔã	'write to'	__łʔi
'sift for'	hi__kʔakʔa		

Stems with do only with a direct object prefix:

'burn'	__lagæ̃	'feel, notice'	__ʔwæ̃ha
'give up on'	__wãlæ̃	'kiss'	__tsʔu
'like'	__thæʃʔa	'look for'	__wage

'pay'	hoti__k?ã	'pity'	__ʃi
'scared of'	__łæ̃	'touch'	__do
'wait for'	__ʃ?æ̃ (ʃ?æ̃)		

Stems with do only with both object prefixes possible:

do + direct object	do + indirect object	Stem
'pick up'	'pick up from (take); pick up for someone else'	__hã
'teach to'	'teach for someone else'	__ta
'catch'	'catch for someone else'	__hãle
'hear'	'hear of'	__tʃ?wæ
'know'	'learn from'	__ju?õta

It should be obvious that if the subject is from the do paradigm, the verb will probably be able to take an object prefix and more indirect object prefixes than direct. In addition, in most cases the direct object belongs to someone else and the indirect object indicates a recipient of the action. These generalizations apply to verbs that take both subject paradigms as well. However, di paradigm only verbs tend to be intransitive and hence object-less; where they do take an object prefix it is a direct object and is usually another person taken as a whole.

Generally, then, if the subject is to come from these two paradigms, di is preferred for intransitive verbs whereas do is preferred for transitive verbs and those situations where the verb affects something pertaining to someone other than the subject.

A number of verbs take subject prefix paradigms that are rather different from the di and do paradigms above in the first and second persons (though the third person forms are identical and the remarks above for di and do third persons apply to dze and dzo, respectively, below). None of these paradigms may take any object prefixes. These paradigms exhibit the following typical forms:

IIa. The dze paradigm

dzeju[12]	?õdzeju nõdzeju	
næ̃dzeju	?æ̃dzeju	'be sick, ache'
s?eju	?oju	

IIb. The dzo paradigm

	dzonã[12]	ʔõdzonã	nõdzonã	
sæ̃le 'good' +	sonã	ʔasonã		'feel good, be well'
	sʔjonã	ʔonã		

IIc. The dzjo paradigm

dzjoʃʔæ̃le	ʔõdzjoʃʔæ̃le	nõdzjoʃʔæ̃le	
næ̃dzjoʃʔæ̃le	ʔ[ã]dzjoʃʔæ̃le		'be skinny'
sʔjoʃʔæ̃le	ʔoʃʔæ̃le		

The first of these is by far the most common; it occurs with stems with the following glosses:

'accustomed to'	__kʔaʃo	'ache'	__ju
'be big'	__ʔæ	'be broke (penniless)'	__dade
'face (stand before)'	__jatafa	'be fat'	__danẽ
'have a fever'	__dzafa	'be a few' (plural only)	__kʔætʔe(le)
'be folded over (doubled up)'	__tʃʔa	'be full'	__ʔopa
'be good'	__sæ̃le	'have with'	__kʔadʒu
'be heavy'	__haɫi	'be light (in weight)'	__sogaʔæ̃
'be naked'	__sʔule	'quiver'	__sasahæ̃
'be ready'	(kede)__ʃæ̃ʃæ̃	'recover (get well)'	__ʃæ̃læ̃
'be slow'	__ʃu	'smell (stink)'	__sole
'smell good'	__sodi	'straighten up'	__tsabile
'be strong'	__baga	'be strong'	__safi
'be sweet'	__dabisæ̃	'be swollen'	__khaba
'be tall'	__gjẽ	'be tired (wrinkled up)'	__ʃʔo
'wet (damp)'	__ʃpi	'be hit (struck)'	__tawi
'wet (soaked)'	__ʃo		

dzo occurs with only three stems: 'to feel good' sæ̃le__nã; 'to have (be, stay)' __nã; and 'to pray' __sæ̃ɫʔæ̃tʃi; the last of which may be a special denominative, and the first two of which utilize the same stem, nã 'have, be'.

dzjo is likewise restricted to just a few verbs: 'bleed', __ʔi; 'bloom' __lafæ; and 'be skinny' __ʃʔæ̃le.

More than one of these three paradigms and the two earlier ones can sometimes occur with the same verb stem. Thus in the negative, dze (etc.) + nã means 'not be (here)', whereas dzo (etc.) + nã means 'not have'. Similarly næ 'negative' + dze + gwæ̃ˀæ̃ means 'I am not present', whereas næ + dzo + gwæ̃ˀæ̃ means 'I do not have'. dzjo (etc.) + wæ 'to be left' means that the subject 'got left (behind)', whereas dzo (etc.) + wæ means either that the subject 'has some left' or that an object belonging to the subject 'was left behind'. di (etc.) + gæ̃ 'reach' means 'come up to, reach (a place), arrive', whereas dze (etc.) + gæ̃ means to 'reach (up to) an object'.

The dze and dzo subject paradigms are in fact very similar in form to the direct object paradigms for di and do paradigm verbs, respectively. Thus the first person objects are /dze, ˀõdze, nõdze/ with the di subjects and /dzo, ˀõdzo, nõdzo/ with the do subjects. Both subject paradigms take /næ̃dze/ and /ˀæ̃dze/ as the second person direct objects.

Finally, in order to have an idea of the complete range of variation in Yuchi subject prefix paradigms, we need to examine a number of irregular paradigms. These fall into a small number of patterns:

The ts/tʃ/X type A:

(di)tsˀæ̃ ~ ˀadiˀæ̃	ˀõˀæ̃	nõˀæ̃	
(næ̃)tʃˀæ̃ ~ ˀanæ̃ˀæ̃	ˀæ̃tʃˀã ~ ˀæ̃ˀaˀæ̃		'think'
ˀasˀeˀæ̃	ˀaˀoˀæ̃		

ˀa(he)	tsˀã	--	nẽˀã	'have (a large object)'
+	tʃˀã	ˀætʃˀã		'have plural objects (large and small)'
'there'	sˀeˀã	ˀoˀã		

tsˀa	ˀõˀa	nõˀa	
(næ̃ˀa)[13]	(ˀæ̃ˀa)	(ˀatʃha 'cry out')	'cry'
sˀeˀa	ˀoˀa		

The ts/tʃ/X type B:

tshe	ˀõthe	nõthe	
tʃhe	ˀatʃhe		'beat, hit, win'
sˀethe	ˀothe		

tshwa	ʔõthwa	nõthwa	
tʃhwa	--		'kill'
sʔethwa	ʔothwa		

One verb shows a remnant of this pattern in the second person plural:

nẽ(ke)	tʔotʃi	ʔẽha	nẽha	
	+ jotʃi	ʔætʃa		'be here'
'here'	sʔetʃi	ʔiha		

The dz/ʃ/ł pattern:

dzæ	ʔõłæ	nõłæ	
ʃæ	--		'find'
sʔełæ	ʔiłæ		
dzi	ʔõłi	nõłi	
	(ʔẽłi)	(nẽłi)	
ʃi ~ næ̃łi	ʔæʃi ~ ʔæłi		'come here'
sʔełi	ʔiłi		

The d/ʃ/ł pattern:

kʔãda	ʔõkʔãła	nõkʔãła	
kʔãʃa	ʔækʔãʃa		'carry'
sʔekʔãła	ʔokʔãła		
kʔadæ	kʔaʔõłæ	kʔanõłæ	
kʔɔʃæ ~ dzekʔɔłæ	ʔæ̃dzekʔɔłæ		'eat'
kʔasʔełæ	kʔaʔołæ		

(This root in the invariant form łæ can occur with do subject prefixes and the preverbal particle kʔa 'something'. It seems to mean that the subject ate by himself.)

The following verb, the very common causative verb, may show a defective form of the above paradigm:

diʃa	ʔõła	nõła	
næ̃ʃa	ʔæ̃ʃa		'cause, do'
sʔeła	ʔoła		

Note that if it followed either of the irregular paradigms above, the first and second persons singular would be just da, ʃa, respectively. The two irregula verbs are protected from this monosyllabicity by the prefix. Another apparently similar verb is differently "protected":

weda	ʔõɬa ~ ʔõfe	nõɬa ~ nõfe	
weʃa ~ dzeweɬa	ʔafe		'go, precede'
sʔjoɬa	ʔofe		

But other irregularities (such as dzeweɬa, sʔjoɬa, and the ɬa~fe alternation) affect it as well; and it will not be further treated here.

Two more verbs show irregular patterns:

dzã	ʔõgã	nõgã	
dʒã	ʔægã ~ ʔædʒã		'come'
sʔegã	ʔogã		

(This verb can also take a direct object or a do subject and an indirect object.)

dã	ʔõnã	nõnã	
jã	ʔæjã		'be, stay'
sʔjonã	ʔinã		

We are now in a position to examine the basic patterning of the Yuchi verbal subject prefixes in both form and meaning.

The irregular verbs seem best distinguished from the regular verbs by positing vowel-less prefixes. Thus the ts/tʃ/X types and the verb 'come' (dzã, etc.) could be characterized as taking dz, dz prefixes from the dze paradigm; the dz/ʃ/ɬ type, dz, s from the dzo paradigm; 'be' (dã, etc.), d/j from the do paradigm; and the d/ʃ/ɬ type from the variant of the do paradigm that occurs as a noun (possessive) prefix, i. e. , do, so, ʔaso, etc. (The di, dze, and dzo paradigms are the same before both verbs and nouns.) The palatal forms in the second person seem best explained as showing palatalization of underlying alveolars before j, apparently from the do, jo paradigm. Finally, there is the obvious consonant cluster assimilation in voicing and aspiration and consonant cluster simplification.

To formalize these hypotheses, we may posit the following rules, underlying forms, and typical derivations:[8]

(4) $$\begin{bmatrix} +\text{cons} \\ -\text{voc} \\ +\text{diff} \\ +\text{stri} \\ (-\text{gr}) \end{bmatrix} \begin{bmatrix} -\text{cons} \\ -\text{voc} \\ -\text{gr} \\ +\text{vcd} \end{bmatrix} \rightarrow \begin{bmatrix} +\text{cons} \\ -\text{voc} \\ -\text{diff} \\ +\text{stri} \\ (-\text{gr}) \end{bmatrix}$$

dz + j → dʒ

s + j → ʃ

(i. e. , strident alveolars become alveolopalatals by absorption of j)

(5) $$\begin{bmatrix} +\text{cons} \\ -\text{voc} \end{bmatrix} \rightarrow \begin{bmatrix} \alpha\text{vcd} \\ \beta\text{ten} \end{bmatrix} \;/\; \underline{\quad} \begin{bmatrix} -\text{voc} \\ -\text{cont} \\ \alpha\text{vcd} \\ \beta\text{ten} \end{bmatrix}$$

$$\text{C} \rightarrow \begin{matrix} \text{C} \\ \text{vcl} \\ \text{asp} \end{matrix} \;/\; \underline{\quad} \begin{matrix} \text{C} \\ \text{vcl} \\ \text{asp} \end{matrix}$$

(i. e. , a consonant assimilates to the following consonant in voicing and aspiration. Why does this rule group ɫ with g, n rather than with ʔ, th?)

(6) $$[+\text{cons}]_1 \; [+\text{cons}]_2 \rightarrow [+\text{cons}]_1$$

$$C_1 \, C_2 \rightarrow C_1$$

(i. e. , consonant clusters reduce unless the second consonant is ʔ)

Application of rules (4), (5), and (6) is illustrated by the following paradigr

Gloss	Underlying forms	Rule 4 Palatal-ization	Rule 5 CC assi-milation	Rule 6 CC reduction
'think'				
1st sg	dz+ʔæ̃	--	ts+ʔæ̃	tsʔæ̃
2nd sg	dz+j+ʔæ̃	dʒ+ʔæ̃	tʃ+ʔæ̃	tʃʔæ̃
2nd pl	ʔæ+dz+j+ʔæ̃	ʔæ+dʒ+ʔæ̃	ʔæ+tʃ+ʔæ̃	ʔætʃʔæ̃
(plus: sʔe, ʔõ, nõ, ʔo + ʔæ̃)				
(and similarly 'cry' and 'have')				
'beat'				
1st sg	dz+the	--	tsh+the	tshe
2nd sg	dz+j+the	dʒ+the	tʃh+the	tʃhe
2nd pl	ʔæ+dz+j+the	ʔæ+dʒ+the	ʔæ+tʃh+the	ʔætʃhe
(plus: sʔe, ʔõ, nõ, ʔo + the)				
(and similarly 'kill')				

Gloss	Underlying forms	Rule 4 Palatalization	Rule 5 CC assimilation	Rule 6 CC reduction
'come here'				
1st sg	dz+łi	--	--	dzi
2nd sg	s+j+łi	ʃ+łi	--	ʃi
2nd pl	ʔæ+s+j+łi	ʔæ+ʃ+łi	--	ʔæʃi
(plus: sʔe, ʔõ, nõ, ʔo + łi)				
(and similarly 'find')				
'carry'				
1st sg	d+ła	--	--	da
2nd sg	s+j+ła	ʃ+ła	--	ʃa
2nd pl	ʔæ. . . s+j+ła	ʔæ. . . ʃ+ła	--	ʔæ. . . ʃa
(plus: sʔe, ʔõ, nõ, ʔo + ła)				
(and similarly 'eat', 'go, precede')				
'come'				
1st sg	dz+gã	--	--	dzã
2nd sg	dz+j+gã	dʒ+gã	--	dʒã
2nd pl	ʔæ+dz+j+gã	ʔæ+dʒ+gã	--	ʔædʒã
(plus: sʔe, ʔõ, nõ, ʔo + gã)				
'be, stay'				
1st sg	d+nã	--	--	dã
2nd sg	j+nã	--	--	jã
2nd pl	ʔæ+j+nã	--	--	ʔæjã
(plus: sʔjo, ʔõ, nõ, ʔi + nã)				
(note here that the form sʔjo reinforces a <u>do</u> origin for the subject forms)				

The forms underlying the irregular prefixes in these verbs, then, appear to be the following:

	1st sg	2nd sg	2nd pl	Parallel regular paradigm
'think', etc. and 'come'	dz	dz + j	ʔæ + dz + j	<u>dze</u>
'come here', etc.	dz	s + j	ʔæ + s + j	<u>dzo</u>
'carry', etc.	d	s + j	ʔæ + s + j	<u>do</u> (with nouns)
'be, stay'	d	j	ʔæ + j	<u>do</u> (with verbs)

Rule (4) in a fashion parallel to other rules in this paper is of dubious synchronicity on this slim a basis; in addition it may have (or may have had) a semantic function: note the difference between /tshjała/ 'red' and /tʃhała/ 'pink' (but only /tsjaso/ 'money').

If the analysis above is at all correct, then it reveals vowel-less person markers. What do the vowels signify in the di, do, dze, and dzo paradigms I suspect that the vowel-less irregular verbs are archaic and that the vowelat forms are more productive; hence analogical leveling may make it impossible discover the original function of the presence versus absence of a vowel. Bu there are ways to approach the difference between the i/e vowels of the di/d paradigms where they contrast with o vowels in the do/dzo paradigms, as well as the d versus dz distinction itself.

While the assignment of given verbs to given subject paradigms is probably largely arbitrary at the present time, we can discern some general semantic properties of the classes that may be remnants of an earlier stage of the language. Regular verbs that take only dze subject prefixes tend to be translat as predicate adjectives or passives in English and they cannot take objects. The irregular dz verbs can be transitive and take objects but the focus is on the subject, e. g. , compare 'find' versus 'look for, hunt'. Thus, the Yuchi dz forms may represent a third option to the choice between passive and ergative voice systems: a subject focus category. The d, di, and do forms are either neutral or focused on the object. Thus the d versus dz distinctio appears to be one of focus.

To approach the semantic value of the vocalic i/e versus o distinction we need to look at another set of forms. Some sentences in Yuchi take verbs in an absolute form; these absolute verbs show either a prefixed hi or a prefixe ho. Some examples of each follow:

hithjã	'it's attached, hanging from the ear'
hibo	'it's bent'
hiʔopa	'it's full'
hikhi	'strange'
hiłi	'slick'
haʃʔæ̃	'burned up' (< hi + ʔaʃʔæ̃ ?)
hoʃʔo	'withered' (compare 'tired')

hoʃˀule 'bare'
hoˀi 'it bleeds, is bleeding' (compare 'bleed')
holafæ 'it blooms' (compare 'burst, bloom')
hodʒu 'burnt, scorched'
hoʃtãle 'closed up' (compare 'close')
hopˀalæ̃ 'cloud up' (compare hopˀa 'cloud')
hoɬo 'deep' (of water)
hohæle 'empty'
hoʃˀæ̃le 'it's skinny' (compare 'skinny')
hotho 'it's short'
hoʃu 'tied up' (compare ʃu 'string' ?)

(Forms other than verbs take hi and ho but they do not concern us here. For example, hisala 'everything', hiʃahi 'hot', hithohe 'later', hidzã 'green, blue', hitˀe 'one', hophati 'pale', hodofa 'in the midst of', X + hojuʃtæ̃le 'X's road'.)

In addition some verbs which take a subject prefix paradigm may also take hi or ho. Thus:

hi+dz+ɬæ 'find out' (compare 'find')
hi+di+ta 'hold'
hi+di+ʃa 'steal' (or just do)
kˀahi+do+ʃigæ̃ 'stir' (or just do + ju)
hi+do+kˀakˀa 'sift'
hi+di+khi 'suspect'
hi+do+ˀnæ̃ˀnæ̃ 'try'
(hi)+do+juˀõta 'know' (ju only in the third person and plural forms)
do+(ho)ˀnẽga 'agree with, believe'
do+hojuˀõta 'learn (from)' (compare 'know')
do+hokˀwæ̃ 'send for' (compare di+kˀwæ̃ 'send' and do+kˀwæ̃ 'send to')
do+hoˀnæ̃ 'show for' (compare do+ˀnæ̃ 'show mine', etc.)
dzjowæ 'left' (NB: < dze + ho + wæ)

By and large, hi seems to collocate with the di paradigm, ho with the do. (Where hi occurs with do there is an at present unanalyzed particle ju present as well; otherwise there is one hi + dz and one ho with dze.) Note that hi normally precedes the subject prefix whereas ho follows. But more important for almost any verb with a do prefix and an indirect object prefix indicating for whom the action was performed or whose property was affected, there is an alternate form with ho. Thus do + pˀe 'I drink', do + ho + pˀe 'I drink (theirs)'. Thus ho seems bound up with the primary benefactive focus of do or with the fact of nonsubject possession of the affected object. The particle hi, on the other hand, seems to be associated with a neutrally focused di or with an inanimate object. Thus we may surmise that the basic subject prefixes may have been vowel-less in Yuchi at an earlier period; that the dz versus d systems indicated a difference in focus (subject versus other); and that the vowels of the now regular paradigms arose ultimately from the particle ho which emphasized the object especially as animate benefactive or as other possession and hi which was unmarked as to focus but which perhaps emphasized an inanimate unpossessed object.

It is worth pointing out here that for the dz paradigms as noun prefixes (they occur much more frequently as noun prefixes than as verb prefixes), we can get the following distinctions: /dzehi/ 'my sinews' (in my body) and /dzeʃˀæ̃/ 'my bones' (in my body) versus /dzohi/ 'my sinews' (that I bought at the grocery store) and /dzjoʃˀæ̃/ < /dzehoʃˀæ̃/ 'my bones' (that are in this bag). Again e seems to state subject (inalienable) possession whereas o shows alienable possession, or possession by other than the subject.

The synchronic morphonology of the regular verbs is now rather apparent; it exhibits similarities to the phenomena with we and nẽ discussed earlier.

First of all, if a pronominal prefix ending in e precedes the underlying particle ho, the sequence coalesces to jo:[8]

$$(7)\quad \begin{bmatrix} -\text{comp} \\ +\text{voc} \\ -\text{comp} \\ -\text{diff} \\ -\text{gr} \\ -\text{fl} \end{bmatrix} \begin{bmatrix} -\text{cons} \\ -\text{voc} \\ -\text{vcd} \end{bmatrix} \begin{bmatrix} -\text{cons} \\ +\text{voc} \\ -\text{comp} \\ -\text{diff} \\ +\text{gr} \\ +\text{fl} \end{bmatrix} \rightarrow \begin{bmatrix} -\text{cons} \\ -\text{voc} \\ -\text{comp} \\ +\text{diff} \\ -\text{gr} \\ -\text{fl} \end{bmatrix} \begin{bmatrix} -\text{cons} \\ +\text{voc} \\ -\text{comp} \\ -\text{diff} \\ +\text{gr} \\ +\text{fl} \end{bmatrix}$$

e + ho → jo

The intervocalic glide h appears to impart its glide quality to the preceding vowel. This accounts for the dzjo prefix paradigm and for the sˀjo third person forms in the do and dzo paradigms. These third person forms, then, further support a basic underlying *ho* in these paradigms. But this *ho* is subject to another coalescence rule:[8]

$$(8)\quad \begin{bmatrix} -\text{cons} \\ +\text{voc} \\ -\text{comp} \\ -\text{diff} \\ +\text{gr} \\ +\text{fl} \end{bmatrix} \begin{bmatrix} -\text{cons} \\ -\text{voc} \\ -\text{vcd} \end{bmatrix} \begin{bmatrix} -\text{cons} \\ +\text{voc} \\ -\text{comp} \\ -\text{diff} \\ +\text{gr} \\ +\text{fl} \end{bmatrix} \rightarrow \begin{bmatrix} -\text{cons} \\ +\text{voc} \\ -\text{comp} \\ -\text{diff} \\ +\text{gr} \\ +\text{fl} \end{bmatrix}$$

o + ho → o

This change, like the one for *we*, also demonstrates a semantic control: lack of application (and thus the appearance of *ho* on the surface) emphasizes the benefactive meaning; application (and thus the absence of *ho* on the surface) emphasizes ownership.

Note that rule (7) would apply to /ʔ/ as well as /h/; in fact the collapse /e + ʔa/ > /ja/ also occurs; this would occasion the removal of [-diff] and [+fl] from the right-hand matrix of the input to (7). This coalescence is demonstrated in the following forms:

dzjaʃpa ←	dze + ʔaʃpa	'I'm cold'
næ̃dzjaʃpa ←	næ̃dze + ʔaʃpa	'you're cold'
sʔjaʃpa ←	sʔe + ʔaʃpa	'he's cold'

Finally, from the verbal prefix paradigms it would appear that the surface 'second person plural' marker /ʔæ̃/ should be analyzed as being composed of /næ̃/ 'second person' plus an /ʔæ/ meaning 'plural for second person'. The rule generating /ʔæ̃/ would parallel our rule (3) for nẽ:[8]

$$(9)\quad \begin{bmatrix} -\text{cons} \\ +\text{voc} \\ +\text{comp} \\ -\text{gr} \end{bmatrix} \begin{bmatrix} +\text{cons} \\ -\text{voc} \\ +\text{nas} \end{bmatrix} \begin{bmatrix} -\text{cons} \\ +\text{voc} \\ +\text{comp} \\ -\text{gr} \\ +\text{nas} \end{bmatrix} \rightarrow \begin{bmatrix} -\text{cons} \\ +\text{voc} \\ +\text{comp} \\ -\text{gr} \\ +\text{nas} \end{bmatrix}$$

ʔæ + næ̃ → ʔæ̃

But unlike the situation with the *nẽ* rule, this rule is always applied; one again wonders if it should be a synchronic, i. e., competence, rule at all.

Some of the rules discussed in this paper obviously share two formal properties but they are probably collapsible only in an obscurantist fashion. One shared property involves vowel syncope: an underlying VCV sequence surfaces with one full vowel. The other shared property involves the assignment of phonological features from the medial nonvowel to the preceding vowel. Thus in rules (1), (3), and (9) ($\begin{bmatrix} \mathrm{V} \\ -\mathrm{gr} \end{bmatrix} + \mathrm{we} \rightarrow \begin{bmatrix} \mathrm{V} \\ +\mathrm{gr} \\ +\mathrm{fl} \end{bmatrix}$, V + nẽ → Ṽ, ʔæ + næ̃ → ʔ

the second vowel disappears and the medial n or w assigns its value to the preceding vowel (n appears as vowel nasalization; w as vowel backing and rounding). In rule (7) (e + ho → jo and e + ʔa → ja), the medial nonvocalic glide transforms the preceding vowel into a vocalic glide and only the rightmost vowel surfaces. In both cases the medial consonant features are moved to the preceding vowel.

In addition some rules show similar constraints on their operations. The vow coalescence rules (1) and (8) are both subject to controls with a semantic differ ential function. These two rules and the nasal collapsing rules (3) and (9) als show considerable variation in the extent to which the native speaker can recover the underlying forms; this makes the synchronic status of such rules difficult to ascertain. Should they be regarded as competence rules or as internally reconstructed changes, or as partly both?

In summary, the examination of these morphonological phenomena in Yuchi leads us to a view of rules and items that is at variance with present theory: neither are they absolutely discrete nor do they belong to closed systems either within the synchronic grammar (are phonological rules phonologically automatic?) or diachronically (to what extent are rules known by native speakers?).

The continuum fascinates.

NOTES

1. Acknowledgment is here gratefully extended to Mrs. George for her generous and patient assistance throughout this project.

2. Acknowledgment is here gratefully extended to Georgia State University for making possible the field work in Oklahoma. Acknowledgment is also gratefully extended to the Yuchi Indians of Sapulpa for their generous hospitality and selfless cooperation.

3. To what extent are we led to posit /Cˀ/ as a co-articulation because of the existence of the notion glottalization? Why don't we posit dentalized stops for [ækt] 'act' and [æpt] 'apt' in English? The analysis here agrees with Wolff (1948).

4. Thus phonetically some syllables can have final consonants. Also note that Yuchi is unusual in having one basic syllable type: CV.

5. Even this example is dubious since, as we shall see, /ˀæ̃kˀæ/ is composed of the following morphemes: /ˀæ/ 'second person plural' + /næ̃/ 'second person' + /kˀæ/ 'laugh'.

6. One interesting note: some previous studies (Wagner 1934) have assumed an /m/ for Yuchi; actually both [m] and [ŋ] occur briefly and epenthetically when a nasalized vowel precedes a labial or a velar consonant, respectively.

7. With no alternation condition on the formulation of morphonological rules, this rule could be used to produce all surface back rounded vowels from underlying front vowels plus /we/, surely an undesirable result even though it would reduce the vowel inventory to just /i, e, æ, a/.

8. Abbreviations used in rules are: asp = aspirated, C = consonant, comp = compact, cons = consonantal, cont = continuant, diff = diffuse, fl = flat, gr = grave, nas = nasal, stri = strident, ten = tense, V = vowel, vcd = voiced, vcl = voiceless, voc = vocalic.

9. /hõ, ˀo, go/ occur with most paradigms; some di and dze paradigms show /hẽ, ˀi, ge/. These last should probably be regarded as irregular residues of an earlier di(dze)/hẽ/ˀi/ge versus do(dzo)/hõ/ˀo/go contrast.

10. se operates exactly as does its sexually opposite prefix sˀe shown with the paradigms.

11. There is some very vestigial tendency for di verbs to prefer we and for do verbs to prefer jõ. However, there also appears to be a tendency to use we

for singular, jõ for plural and/or for we to be more frequent with non-Yuchi humans and jõ with animals.

12. The /dze/ and /dzo/ first person singular forms sometimes alternate with /didze/ and /dodzo/, respectively.

13. /næ̃ˀa/ probably is the result of leveling by analogy.

REFERENCES

Labov, William. 1972. On the use of the present to explain the past. Preprints for the Eleventh International Congress of Linguists. Bologna, Italy.

Wagner, Günter. 1934. Yuchi. Handbook of American Indian Languages 3:291-384. New York: Columbia University Press.

Wolff, Hans. 1948. Yuchi phonemes and morphemes with special reference to person markers. IJAL 14:240-43.

Cherokee

Willard Walker

PREFACE

The purpose of the following sketch is to give a general description and overview of what is currently known of written and spoken Cherokee, a language spoken by some 15,000 people of all ages who live, for the most part, in northeastern Oklahoma and in the vicinity of Cherokee, North Carolina. There are no full-length published grammars of Cherokee and only one dictionary (Alexander 1971), but several vocabularies and texts with translations have appeared in print and a number of books printed in Cherokee are available. Cherokee is taught, as a second language, only at Wesleyan University in Middletown, Connecticut, and at Northeastern State College in Tahlequah, Oklahoma. It is related to six other Iroquoian languages (Cayuga, Mohawk, Onondaga, Oneida, Seneca, and Tuscarora) which are spoken chiefly in New York, Ontario, and Oklahoma. These Iroquoian languages are generally

---

This essay is based on data collected in 1964-1966 when the writer was a research associate of the Carnegie Corporation Cross-Cultural Education Project of the University of Chicago, a project funded by the Carnegie Foundation and directed by Sol Tax and Robert K. Thomas.

considered to be remotely related to the Siouan and Caddoan languages, which are now spoken, for the most part, in the Plains states.

THE SYLLABARY

The Cherokee writing system was invented by a monolingual and formerly illiterate Cherokee named Sequoyah. It was perfected in about 1819, learned and used by the majority of the tribe throughout the remainder of the nineteenth century, and remains in use in many communities today. Sequoyah's system includes 85 letters, of which one represents the sound of English s and six others represent vowel sounds. The remaining 78 letters, however, represent neither vowels nor consonants, but combinations of consonant-plus-vowel.

KEY TO SEQUOYAH'S SYLLABARY

Ꭰ [a, ʔa]	Ꭱ [e, ʔe]	Ꭲ [i, ʔi]	Ꭳ [o, ʔo]	Ꭴ [u, ʔu]	Ꭵ [ɨ, ʔɨ]
Ꭶ ga	Ꭸ ge, ke	Ꭹ gi, ki	Ꭺ go, ko	Ꭻ gu, ku	Ꭼ gɨ, kɨ
Ꭷ ka					
Ꭽ ha	Ꭾ he	Ꭿ hi	Ꮀ ho	Ꮁ hu	Ꮂ hɨ
Ꮃ la, ła	Ꮄ le, łe	Ꮅ li, łi	Ꮆ lo, ło	Ꮇ lu, łu	Ꮈ lɨ, łɨ
Ꮉ ma	Ꮊ me	Ꮋ mi	Ꮌ mo	Ꮍ mu	
Ꮎ na	Ꮑ ne, hne	Ꮒ ni, hni	Ꮓ no, hno	Ꮔ nu, hnu	Ꮕ nɨ, hnɨ
Ꮏ hna	Ꮐ (not used)				
Ꮖ gwa, kwa	Ꮗ gwe, kwe	Ꮘ gwi, kwi	Ꮙ gwo, kwo	Ꮚ gwu, kwu	Ꮛ gwɨ, kwɨ
Ꮝ s					
Ꮜ sa	Ꮞ se	Ꮟ si	Ꮠ so	Ꮡ su	Ꮢ sɨ
Ꮣ da	Ꮥ de	Ꮧ di	Ꮩ do, to	Ꮪ du, tu	Ꮫ dɨ, tɨ
Ꮤ ta	Ꮦ te	Ꮨ ti			
Ꮬ dla	Ꮮ dle, tle	Ꮯ dli, tli	Ꮰ dlo, tlo	Ꮱ dlu, tlu	Ꮲ dlɨ, tlɨ
Ꮭ tla					
Ꮳ [ja, dza] [ca, ča]	Ꮴ [je, dze] [ce, če]	Ꮵ [ji, dzi] [ci, či]	Ꮶ [jo, dzo] [co, čo]	Ꮷ [ju, dzu] [cu, ču]	Ꮸ [jɨ, dzɨ] [cɨ, čɨ]
Ꮹ wa, hwa	Ꮺ we, hwe	Ꮻ wi, hwi	Ꮼ wo, hwo	Ꮽ wu, hwu	Ꮾ wɨ, hwɨ
Ꮿ ya, hya	Ᏸ ye, hye	Ᏹ yi, hyi	Ᏺ yo, hyo	Ᏻ yu, hyu	Ᏼ yɨ, hyɨ

Sequoyah's Cherokee syllabic characters with phonetic values for each. All sequences which are not enclosed in square brackets are phonemically distinct. The letter Ꮙ (gwo, kwo) is often used in place of expected Ꮚ (gwu, kwu). Note that many of the characters represent more than one sequence of phonemes. Note also that the phonetic values of characters bear no relation to those of similar letters of the English alphabet.

Many of Sequoyah's letters resemble English capital letters; others seem to have been borrowed from Greek or Cyrillic; still others appear to have no precedent in other writing systems. Those that resemble English capitals have phonetic values that are quite unlike their English counterparts. Thus A, B, C, D, E, for example, are pronounced go, yɨ, tli, a, and gɨ, respectively. The allocation of these phonetic values to such traditional European letters indicates that Sequoyah was in no sense literate in English or any other European language when he incorporated European letters into his syllabary, for he was clearly ignorant of their phonetic values in the European languages.

To become fully literate in Cherokee, it is necessary to learn certain spelling conventions as well as the phonetic values of the 85 letters. Most words consisting of alternating vowels and consonants may be encoded into the writing system without difficulty. The word amageʔi' 'hominy', for example, is written with a sequence of letters representing a (or ʔa), ma, ge, and i (or ʔi), respectively. A few words, however, consist of identical sequences of vowels and consonants, but differ in vowel length, a distinction which cannot be indicated by the writing system. Thus ama' 'salt' and a:ma' (with long vowel) 'water' are spelled alike in Cherokee, though pronounced differently. Words such as nasgi' 'that one' are easily spelled, since the letter representing s may be inserted between the syllabic letters for na and gi. Problems arise, however, in the spelling of such words as kodesdi' 'spade', for there is no letter used specifically for the syllable ko or for a number of other low-frequency syllables. A single letter, resembling English A, is used to represent both ko and go. Likewise, other letters are assigned to both to and do, g^{w}e, and k^{w}e, gɨ and kɨ, etc. In reading, of course, it is necessary to choose between alternative phonetic values in order to pronounce such words as kodesdi' 'spade' correctly. A few letters have as many as four phonetic values, e. g., ja, dza, ča, and tsa or ji, dzi, či, and tsi. The most difficult words to spell, however, are those which include consonants other than s without an intervening vowel, for they must be written as though a vowel were present; and which of the six vowels must be indicated is dictated by convention. Thus the word tsg^{w}i'sdi 'many' (inanimate things) is written as though it were pronounced $tsig^{w}$isdi (or jig^{w}isdi, or $dzig^{w}$isdi, or $čig^{w}$isdi). Likewise, dinełdi' 'dolls' is conventionally written as though it were pronounced dinelodi, and taʔlsgo' 'twenty' is spelled as though it were pronounced talisgo or talisko. The spelling conventions of Cherokee are much easier for a fluent speaker of the language to acquire than are the spelling and reading conventions of English for English-speaking Americans. The Cherokee conventions are relatively few in number and are quite easily learned. Many of them may be ignored without adversely affecting communication.

LITERACY AND LITERATURE

Sequoyah's syllabary was the end product of some twelve lonely, frustrating years of trial and error. Obsessed with his notion that Indians, like the more educated of the white people, might learn to communicate with "talking leaves", Sequoyah let his farm go to ruin, neglected his family, defied tradition, and was ultimately tried for witchcraft as the predictable result of his eccentric and antisocial behavior. By 1819, however, he had perfected the syllabary and taught his daughter to read, so that when asked to demonstrate his system before a committee of Cherokee elders he wrote a dictated statement that was subsequently read aloud by his daughter. His achievement was one of the most remarkable intellectual _tours de force_ in American history. Equally remarkable, however, was the fact that within a few years thousands of tribal Cherokees became literate in their native language. People wrote letters, kept accounts, and copied the sacred songs and curing formulas. A weekly newspaper called _The Cherokee Phoenix_ was printed by a Cherokee national press as early as 1828. John K. White's "On the Revival of Printing in the Cherokee Language" describes the history of Cherokee printing:

> Between 1828 and 1835 the press at New Echota, the Cherokee Capital, also issued a number of portions of the Bible, copies of the laws passed by the National Council, various political pamphlets, 4 editions of a Cherokee Hymn Book, temperance tracts, and religious documents. Copies of correspondence between the Cherokee Nation and the United States Government were always printed in the newspaper. (White 1962:511)

When in 1839 the last contingents of Cherokees were "removed" by United States troops and forced to migrate over the "trail of tears" to Indian territory, they found a Cherokee printing press already set up in what came to be called the New Nation. "Between 1835 and 1861," according to White,

> this press printed 13,980,000 pages of books, tracts, pamphlets, and passages from the Bible. . . . An Annual Almanac was published for many years in English and Cherokee. The Cherokee Messenger, a bi-monthly religious magazine, was printed, as well as numerous tracts, primers, spelling books, arithmetics, Bible passages, a complete New Testament, hymn books, and other miscellaneous publications. The Constitution and laws of the Cherokee Nation were printed in various editions. Resolutions of the National Council, messages of the Chiefs, even current acts of the legislative council were printed and promptly circulated among the people. (White 1962:511-12)

After the Civil War, which left virtually every building in the New Nation gutted or in ashes, the Cherokee National Press was brought from its wartime hiding place, and from 1870 until 1906, when the press was evidently confiscated by the United States government as a prelude to the incorporation of the Nation into the new state of Oklahoma, a newspaper, The Cherokee Advocate, and a number of religious and educational books were printed. More recently, Cherokee language publications have been made available by the American Bible Society and, in the 1960's, by Cherokee Phoenix Publications, by the Carnegie Corporation Cross-Cultural Education Project of the University of Chicago, by the Laboratory of Anthropology of Wesleyan University, and by the Original Cherokee Community Organization. A large proportion of the existing Cherokee literature, however, consists of manuscripts. These are, for the most part, church records, curing formulas, unpublished Christian songs, and personal correspondence. The largest collections of these manuscripts are probably those of the Smithsonian Institution and the American Philosophical Society.

A Cherokee manuscript often contains a variety of clues as to the background of its author. It normally contains considerable evidence as to his mastery of the spelling conventions and also reflects the vagaries of his penmanship; but, more importantly, it may contain words, or forms of words, which are associated with regional dialects. If, in a manuscript from Oklahoma, h is indicated where one would expect the glottal stop ʔ, the document may have originated in the vicinity of the present Oklahoma-Missouri border. If, on the other hand, ʔ is indicated where one would expect h, the writer may have grown up near Porum, in Muskogee County. When words ending in a are spelled as though the final vowel were ɨ, a dialect such as that spoken south of Stilwell, in southern Adair County, is indicated. Special orthographic conventions may also be significant, e. g. , the letters representing no (or hno) and g^wa (or k^wa), which in print and in most manuscripts appear as Z and I , respectively, are sometimes written ˙/. and :|: , particularly, perhaps, in Delaware County. Another useful cue is the appearance of a redundant s, i. e. , when such a word as sako'nige 'blue' is spelled s-sa-ko-ni-ge. This spelling convention dates from the earliest days of written Cherokee; for Sequoyah, himself, signed his name not si-g^wo-ya but s-si-g^wo-ya, with a redundant s at the beginning. In later times, when Worcester and Boudinot translated the *New Testament* and printed it in Cherokee, the redundant s was omitted; and for this reason many generations of Christian Cherokees have learned, by reading the Bible, the more recent (and more streamlined) tradition of indicating s-plus-vowel with a single letter. The redundant s persists, however, in manuscripts written by native doctors and others associated with non-Christian "Nighthawk" communities, for theirs is a manuscript tradition that dates from the pre-Removal period and has succeeded in maintaining its redundant s down to the present time.

THE CHEROKEE LANGUAGE TODAY

In general, the ability to read Cherokee is functional in only two major aspects of contemporary Cherokee life — participation in religious activities and the practice of Indian medicine. To participate fully in a Cherokee church congregation, one must be able to read aloud from the Bible. In a Sunday school class, for example, each participant is required to read a verse from the New Testament or, if illiterate, is expected to repeat after someone who reads for him. Each Sunday school class, then, is a test of each participant's ability to decode written Cherokee into spoken Cherokee.

A large number of adult Cherokee men are semiprofessional Indian doctors; and the practice of Cherokee medicine entails the ability to read. The doctor, unlike the church member, reads written as opposed to printed Cherokee, reads in privacy rather than in public, and reads for content, as opposed to reading aloud without necessarily understanding the text.

Cherokees associate literacy with *knowledge*, and knowledge is prerequisite to the full acceptance of an individual as a mature and responsible member of the Cherokee community. Cherokee society has a long tradition of literacy, and the ability to read either Cherokee or English has been highly valued by generations of Cherokees.

Modern Cherokees, then, learn to read Cherokee to participate more fully in church activities, to become competent doctors, to acquire generalized knowledge, or for some combination of these three objectives. Since young people are relatively unconcerned with religion, medicine, and knowledge, many Cherokees do not become literate in their native language until they become adults. For this reason, the fact that most readers of Cherokee are over thirty does not necessarily mean that literacy is declining. Alternatively, it may simply reflect the fact that young people have less incentive to learn than their elders.

A survey of the Oklahoma Cherokee communities was made during the period 1963-1965 by Albert L. Wahrhaftig and his interpreter, Fines J. Smith. The results of this survey are reported in both English and Cherokee in Wahrhaftig's The Cherokee People Today (1966). According to this report, there are sixty-seven named Cherokee communities in eastern Oklahoma, each of which is identified with a particular Christian church or non-Christian (Nighthawk) stompground. Forty-seven of these communities are listed as having a stable or slowly growing population, eleven are in decline, and nine are "new and growing". The table below gives statistical information on the extent to which Cherokee is spoken, heard, and read by individuals and households in four widely separated and multiply diverse communities. These are the Cherokee community in and around the town of Hulbert, in Cherokee County, and the rural communities of Cherry Tree, in Adair County, Marble, in Sequoyah County, and Bull Hollow, in Delaware County. The figures on "people younger than 18" indicate that Cherokee may well continue indefinitely as a viable language.

Cherokee Bilingualism and Native Literacy (after Wahrhaftig 1966)

	Hulbert	Cherry Tree	Marble	Bull Hollow
		(percentages)		
Households in which:				
English is spoken exclusively	17	6	11	6
Cherokee is spoken exclusively	53	59	72	83
English and Cherokee are spoken	30	34	17	11
Heads of households who speak no English at all	40	14	24	42
People younger than 18: who speak only English	59	44	20	22
who speak Cherokee and English	42	55	80	78
who hear Cherokee spoken at home	67	98	98	100
People over 30 who read Cherokee	36	43	46	65
Cherokee households with at least one reader of Cherokee	40	63	83	83

THE SOUND SYSTEM

The sound system of Cherokee has six basic vowels, of which five resemble those of the English words he, hay, harm, who, and hoe. The sixth, which is always nasalized, resembles the French word un. While this sixth vowel is always nasalized, the other five are nasalized only at the ends of words and in certain other positions.

Each of the six vowels occurs with either strong or weak stress, and each may have either long or short duration. Long vowels take about twice as much time to pronounce as short vowels. A long vowel may have increasing stress, decreasing stress, weak stress throughout, or (rarely) strong stress throughout:

i	as in beet	i:	(long) as in bead
e	as in rate	e:	(long) as in raid
a	as in art	a:	(long) as in arm
o	as in lock	o:	(long) as in log
u	as in loot	u:	(long) as in lewd
ɨ	as in French un	ɨ:	(same, but longer)

An apostrophe (') indicates strong stress on the preceding vowel. Before a colon, it indicates falling stress and pitch; after a colon, it indicates rising stress and pitch; both before and after a colon, it indicates continued strong stress and high pitch.

Cherokee has consonants resembling English j, s, t, d, k, g, m, n, l, y, w, and h. It also has a glottal stop (ʔ), a voiceless l (ɫ), a voiceless, lateral affricate (tl), ts, and three other consonants which resemble those written ch, qu, and gw in English. Like other Iroquoian languages, Cherokee has no consonants resembling English p, b, f, or v.

t as in English tip

d as in English dip

k as in English cap

g as in English gap

m as in English map

n as in English nap

s as in English sop, occasionally (in some dialects) as in English shop

ts as in English eats (rarely heard in Cherokee)

l as in English late

h as in English hate

w as in English woo

y as in English you

j as in English jump or like the dz of English adz

ʔ pronounced by contracting the vocal cords as in the middle of the English expression oh-oh!, used when someone has goofed.

ɫ a voiceless l, often preceded by an h sound, can be approximated by trying to say English h followed immediately by l.

tl like an English l, but with the tip of the tongue in the position it assumes to make a t sound

č like the ch of English church

k^w like the qu of English queen

g^w like the gw of English Gwendolin

GRAMMAR

Cherokee is a highly inflected language. The following description of its complex grammar is in no sense complete. It is intended merely as a brief, and necessarily superficial, introduction to certain of the more prominent grammatical patterns of the language.

Inanimate nouns are often formed by the addition of an instrumental suffix, -sdi, to a verb stem, e. g., goksdi 'cigarette', literally 'that which is used for smoking'. Inanimate nouns take a plural prefix, usually di-, e. g., goksdi' 'cigarette', digoksdi' 'cigarettes'. Other suffixes also occur, e. g., gasgilo' 'table, bench, chair', gasgila' 'that table, bench, chair', gasgiłi' 'on (in, by) the table, bench, chair'. The so-called animate nouns take the singular prefix a- or u- and the plural prefix ani- or uni-, e. g., aji'łisgi' 'flower', aniji'łisgi' 'flowers', uji'łisgi' 'bud' (potential flower), uniji'łisgi' 'buds'. All four of these words are derived from ajila' 'flame, fire' by the addition of the suffix -sgi 'one who' 'one which'. Literally, then, the Cherokee word for flower may be translated as 'that which flames'.

Many English nouns have no exact equivalent in Cherokee. The word brother, for example, must be translated in one of a number of different ways, according to whose brother is referred to. Thus u:do' may be translated either as 'her brother' or as 'his sister', since it actually means 'some third person's sibling of opposite sex'. Additional prefixes generate such forms as ju:do' 'his sisters, her brothers', unido' 'their (women's) brother, their (men's) sister', etc. When a man translates the phrase 'my brother' into Cherokee, he must say josdada:nitli, which seems literally to mean 'I and one other person (not you) are brothers to one another'. Like so many other Cherokee words, this may function either as the subject or object of a verb, perhaps in a very long sentence, or it may occur alone as a complete sentence in itself.

From the preceding example, it will be apparent that many Cherokee words, even some of those which are often translated by English nouns or noun phrases, are actually verb forms, often of considerable complexity. Cherokee verbs, in general, fall into one or the other of two major categories, active and stative. Active verbs refer to some definite action performed by someone. They occur with one of ten prefixes indicating the person and number of the performer, or subject. From the first person singular form (the "I" form) of the verb, all other forms can be predicted. It is this form, then, that should be learned or entered in a dictionary. Active verbs have first person singular forms with either the prefix j-, as in jiwo'niha' 'I'm talking', or g-, as in geli?a' 'I guess'. Verbs with j- for first person take ga- for third person singular, e. g. , gawo'niha' 'he (or she) is talking'. Those with g- in the first person, however, have no prefix indicating the third person singular, e. g. , eliʔa' 'he (or she) guesses'. All other forms are predictable regardless of the first and third person forms; thus h(i)- 'you' (singular), (i)sd- 'you two', (i)j- 'you all', etc. as in hiwo'niha' 'you (singular) are talking', isdeliʔa' 'you two guess', ijiwo'niha' 'you all are talking'. The table below indicates all of the personal subject prefixes associated with active verbs.

	one person involved	two people involved	more than two people involved
Prefixes which include 'you' and perhaps others, but not 'I'	h(i)-	(i)sd-	(i)j-
Prefixes which include 'I' and perhaps others, but not 'you'	j-/g- *	osd-	oj-
Prefixes which include 'you' and 'I' and perhaps others	—	(i)n-	(i)d-
Prefixes which include one or more people, but not 'you' or 'I'	ga- *	an(i)-	an(i)-

*Verb stems which take j- 'I', also take ga- 'he, she'. Those which take g- 'I', have no prefix indicating the third person singular.

Stative verbs refer to passive states or to actions performed by an unspecified actor on some recipient or group of recipients of the action. These verbs take one of twelve personal prefixes indicating the person and number of the recipient of the action or of whoever is in the indicated state. Often these forms are translated into English as active verbs, but not without some distortion of their meaning in Cherokee. The form ag^{w}adu:li', for example, is normally translated 'I want it', but it has a stative prefix indicating that someone ('I') is in a state of wanting, or to put it another way, that 'something is being wanted by me'. Likewise, agilɨ'k^{w}di, though it is usually translated as 'I like it', might more accurately be translated as 'I am in a state of liking something (or someone)' or 'he (she, it) is liked by me'. The table below gives all of the stative personal prefixes, which in many cases resemble the corresponding active prefixes in the preceding table.

	one person involved	two people involved	more than two people involved
Prefixes which include 'you' and perhaps others, but not 'I'	j-	(i)sd(i)-	ij(i)-
Prefixes which include 'I' and perhaps others, but not 'you'	ag(i)- ak(i)- * ag^{w}-	ogin(i)-	og(i)-
Prefixes which include 'you' and 'I' and perhaps others	—	(i)gin(i)-	(i)g(i)-
Prefixes which include one or more people, but not 'you' or 'I'	u-	un(i)-	un(i)-

*The first person, singular, stative prefix is ag^{w}- before stems beginning with a or ɨ and ak(i)- when the first consonant of the stem is h, s, t, or k or when the first consonant of the stem is n and the second is h, s, t, or k. Elsewhere, this prefix is ag- (before vowels other than a and ɨ) or agi- (before consonants). Examples are ag^{w}adu:li' 'I want it', akinohiselɨ:gi' 'he (or she) told me', and agilɨ'k^{w}di 'I like it'.

In addition to the active and stative personal prefixes, which have been presented in the preceding tables, there are combination prefixes which specify both the actor and the recipient of such actions as giving, telling, killing, etc. Some, but by no means all, of the components of these combination prefixes resemble the prefixes in the preceding tables. The combination prefixes are illustrated below by forms of the verb -nɨ'hsi' 'just now gave a flexible object'. Inflected forms of this verb are used when the object is a rope, string, dead animal or corpse, cloth, piece of paper, article of clothing, etc. It contrasts with -no'hɨsi' 'just now gave a liquid', -ka':si' (with long a accompanied by decreasing stress) 'just now gave a living thing', etc.

gada:nɨ'hsi'

'I just now gave myself a flexible object'

gɨ:nɨ'hsi'

'I just now gave you a flexible object'

ji:nɨ'hsi'

'I just now gave him, her a flexible object'

gaji:nɨ'hsi'

'I just now gave them a flexible object'

isdɨ:nɨ'hsi'

'I just now gave you two a flexible object'

or 'we two just now gave you a flexible object'

or 'we two just now gave you two a flexible object'

or 'we all just now gave you two a flexible object'

o:sdinɨ'hsi'

'he (or she) and I just now gave him (or her) a flexible object'

do:sdinɨ'hsi'

'he (or she) and I just now gave them a flexible object'

o:jinɨ'hsi'

'they and I just now gave him (or her) a flexible object'

do:jinɨ'hsi'

'they and I just now gave them a flexible object'

sginɨ'hsi'

'you just now gave me a flexible object'

hada:nɨ'hsi'

'you just now gave yourself a flexible object'

či:nɨ'hsi'

'you just now gave him (or her) a flexible object'

sgini:nɨ'hsi'

'you just now gave him (or her) and me a flexible object'

sgi'nɨ'hsi'

'you all just now gave me a flexible object'

or 'you just now gave me and them a flexible object'

aginɨ'hsi

'he (or she) just now gave me a flexible object'

dzanɨ'hsi'

'he (or she) just now gave you a flexible object'

ajinɨ'hsi'

'he (or she) just now gave someone a flexible object'

e:sdinɨ'hsi'

'he (or she) just now gave you two a flexible object'

or 'they just now gave you two a flexible object'

or 'you two just now gave him (or her) a flexible object'

ogini:nɨ'hsi'

'he (or she) just now gave him (or her) and me a flexible object'

e:ji:nɨ'hsi'

'he (or she) just now gave you all a flexible object'

or 'you all just now gave him (or her) a flexible object'

ogi:nɨ'hsi'

'he (or she) just now gave me and them a flexible object'

e:gini:nɨ'hsi'

'he (or she) just now gave you and me a flexible object'

e:gi:nɨ'hsi'

'he (or she) just now gave you, me and others a flexible object'

gɨ:ginɨ'hsi'

'they just now gave me a flexible object'

ge:janɨ'hsi'

'they just now gave you a flexible object'

gɨwanɨ'hsi'

'they just now gave him (or her) a flexible object'

gogini:nɨ'hsi'

'they just now gave him (or her) and me a flexible object'

ge:ji:nɨ'hsi'

'they just now gave you all a flexible object'

gogi:nɨ'hsi'

'they just now gave me and others a flexible object'

ge:gini:nɨ'hsi'

'they just now gave you and me a flexible object'

ge:gi:nɨ'hsi'

'they just now gave you, me and others a flexible object'

ge:jinɨ'hsi'

'they just now gave others a flexible object'

or 'he (or she) just now gave them a flexible object'

de:sdi:nɨ'hsi'

'you two just now gave them a flexible object'

jisgini:nɨ'hsi'

'you two just now gave me and another a flexible object'

isgi:nɨ'hsi'

'you two (or you all) just now gave me and others a flexible object'

eni:nɨ'hsi'

'you and I just now gave him (or her) a flexible object'

geni:nɨ'hsi'

'you and I just now gave them a flexible object'

edi:nɨ'hsi'

'you, he (or she) and I just now gave another a flexible object'

gedi:nɨ'hsi'

'you, he (or she) and I just now gave others a flexible object'

In addition to the personal prefixes, Cherokee verbs take other prefixes indicating negation, doubt, plural object, future tense, distant position, direction of motion, or the fact that an action is still forthcoming. Each of the prefixes which precede the personal prefixes occurs in one of five positions. The first position is occupied exclusively by yi- 'negation, doubt' which occurs at the beginning of every word in which it occurs. The second position is occupied exclusively by wi- 'distant action, motion away from speaker' which precedes all prefixes other than yi-. The third position is occupied exclusively by ni- 'still, yet, not yet' and the fourth position by do- 'plural object'. The fifth position, immediately before the personal prefix, is occupied either by da- 'future' or di- 'distant position'. The sequence, then, is as follows: (yi) + (wi) + (ni) + (do) + (da/di) + personal prefix.

Future tense is indicated by the prefix da-. Before e, o, or u, however, da- becomes day-; and where a would be expected to follow da-, da- plus a becomes dɨ-. Examples are:

daje:si'

'you all will go'

dɨne':si'

'they will go'

daye:'si

'he (or she) will go'

The future prefix requires the suffix -i, which is preceded by one of several consonants, the particular consonant used being determined by the verb stem. The following examples have the future prefix and the suffix -i preceded by s, l, n, and j, respectively.

daye:'si

'he (or she) will go'

daji:li'

'I'll kill it'

dago:'tlɨ:ni'

'I'll make it'

dodɨni'lawiji'

'they will meet' (them)

The future prefix da- may be preceded by do- (plural object) as in the last example cited or in dodago:'tlɨ:ni' 'I'll make them'. Otherwise it seems to occur only at the beginnings of words and is followed directly by one or another of the personal prefixes. da- 'future' never occurs in the same word with yi- 'negative, doubt', wi- 'distant action', or ni- 'still, yet, not yet'; it always seems to indicate that something will definitely be done right away or after an interval.

The prefix indicating distant position is normally di-; in many dialects, however, e- or e:- replaces di- at the beginning of a word used as an imperative. This prefix indicates that something is out of reach or entirely out of sight of the speaker and often occurs in verbs indicating motion toward the speaker. Examples:

diskine'hɨsi' or eskine'hɨsi'

'Give me the (container of) liquid yonder!'

gaduhɨ'

'town' (in which the speaker is located)

digaduhɨ'

'town' (distant from speaker)

The prefix di- 'distant position' may be preceded by do- 'plural object', by ni- 'not yet', or by both:

sɨkta' dodiskɨ'hsi'

'Pass me the apples!'

ahsi' nidisgi'nelɨ'nag^{w}u'

'while you have still not passed it to me'

ahsi' nidodisginelɨ'nag^{w}u'

'while you have still not passed them to me'

The prefix indicating plural of inanimate nouns and plural object of verbs appears as d- or, less frequently, j- before vowels, do- before other nonpersonal prefixes, di- or de- elsewhere. Examples are:

dunadu:li'

'they want them'

dodago:'tlɨ:ni'

'I'll make them'

josdi'hihi'

'he (or she) and I kill things, are killers'

diginesdi'ʔi

'for me to get flexible things'

dejaha'

'you have things' (not on your person, but in an unspecified place)

In some words, the plural object prefix is indistinguishable from the first component of certain of the combination (active-stative) personal prefixes listed above. Thus o:jinɨ'hsi' may always be translated 'they and I just gave him (or her) a flexible object'; but do:jinɨ'hsi' is ambiguous, since it may be translated 'they and I just gave them a flexible object', 'they and I just gave him (or her) the flexible objects', or 'they and I just gave them the flexible objects'.

The plural object prefix precedes da- 'future' and di- 'distant position', but follows ni- 'not yet', wi- 'distant action', and yi- 'negation'. Examples:

dodago:'tlɨ:ni'

'I'll make them'

dodida'naʔnɨ'

(distant) 'stores'

ahsi' nidag^{w}o'tlɨnɨ'nag^{w}u'

'while I still haven't made them'

widisgigi':si'

'go get them for me' (spherical objects, etc.)

tla yiduni'naʔa'

'they don't have any' (flexible objects)

When the plural object prefix occurs in verbs with the active personal prefix h(i)- ('you', singular), and without an intervening prefix, it combines with h(i)- to form ti- or t- just as wi- 'distant action' combines with h(i)- to form hwi- or hw-. Compare:

sɨkta' higi'

'Pick up the apple!'

sɨkta' hwigi'

'Go get the apple!'

sɨkta' tigi'

'Pick up the (container of) apples!'

sɨkta' witigi'

'Go get the (container of) apples

The prefix ni- 'still, yet, not yet' (n- before vowels) occurs after yi- 'negation, doubt' and wi- 'distant action' but before do-, di-, de-, etc. 'plural object'. Examples:

ahsi' winagi'gi?eli'nag^{w}u'

'before he goes and gets it for me, while he still hasn't gone and gotten it for me'

tla' yinag^{w}a'lsdahne:ha'

'I don't need to'

ahsi' nidisgi'neli'nag^{w}u'

'before you pass it to me', etc.

ahsi' nidijo:tlini'nag^{w}u'

'before you make them', etc.

ahsi' nido:disgi'neli'nag^{w}u'

'before you pass them to me', etc.

The prefix wi- 'distant action' or 'motion away from the speaker' occurs as w- before vowels and combines with hi- 'you' to form hwi- or hw- in verbs whose subject is the person addressed and in which there is no intervening prefix such as di- 'plural object'. Examples:

witiya'

'Go get the long, rigid objects!'

we:do:ha'

'he (or she) is (moving around) in a distant area'

hwigi'

'Go get it!' (a spherical object, or the like)

hwedo':hi'hno

'and when you're (moving around) over there' (in a distant area)

wi- 'distant action' may be preceded by yi- 'negative, doubt,' but by no other prefix:

yiwige:do:ha'

'I might be over there' (later on)

ahsi' winihi?sgi:'na

'before you take it over there'

witihi':ga'

'Take them over there!'

The prefix yi- 'doubt', or (after tla) 'negative', precedes all other prefixes and hence is the first component of all words in which it appears. It occurs as y- before vowels. Examples:

yiwige:do:ha'

'I might be over there' (later on)

tla yinag^{w}a'lsdahne:ha'

'I don't need to'

tla yiduni'na?a'

'they don't have any flexible items'

yi'gi

'it may be'

(Cf. i:gi' 'it is')

ya:ga:na'

'it may rain'

(Cf. aga:sga' 'it's raining')

iʔ- 'also, too' (i- before consonants) occurs at the beginnings of verbs and seems always to be followed directly by a personal prefix. It is used when someone is said to be doing the same thing that someone else has just been said to be doing.

ja:ni' ulɨ'k^{w}di
'John likes it'

ja:li' na:sg^{w}u' i'ʔulɨk^{w}di
'Charlie likes it too'

jigohtiha'
'I see it'

nihi'sg^{w}u ihi'gohti'
'Do you see it too?'

In addition to the personal prefixes and the prefixes which precede them, there are also certain prefixes which may be inserted between the personal prefixes and certain verb stems. These include such items as -tla- 'resting on a raised surface', but consist mainly of the object classifiers, which indicate whether the verb's object is liquid, living, flexible, long and rigid, or none of these. Examples of the object classifiers are given below as they occur in verbs meaning 'bring me' (as you come from a distance, later on), 'hand me' (right away), and 'I have' (not on my person, but somewhere around).

sɨkta' esgihyɨ'sdanɨ:ha'
'Bring me an apple!'

gohwe:li' esgihyɨ'sdane:lɨ:ha'
'Bring me a (sheet of) paper!'

ama' esgi'ʔjɨsdane:lɨ:ha'
'Bring me some water!'

jita:ga' ek^{w}sdi'nɨsdane:lɨ:ha'
'Bring me a (live) chicken!'

galo:g^{w}e' esgi:nɨ'sdane:lɨ:ha'
'Bring me the gun!'

sɨkta' eskɨ'hsi'
'Hand me an apple!'

gohwe:li' eskine'hɨsi'
'Hand me a (sheet of) paper!'

ama' eskine'hɨsi'
'Hand me a (glass of) water!'

jita:ga' esgi:ka':si'
'Hand me a (live) chicken!'

galo:g^{w}e' esgidi':si'
'Hand me the gun!'

sɨkta' agiha'
'I have an apple'

gohwe:li' a:gi'ʔna'
'I have a (sheet of) paper'

ama' agine:ha'
'I have some water'

jita:ga' agi:kaha'
'I have a (live) chicken'

galo:g^{w}e' ag^{w}ɨ:ya'
'I have a gun'

Cherokee verbs take suffixes as well as prefixes; and these may be added to verb stems either singly or in complex sequences to indicate an astonishing variety of subtle and precise shades of meaning. The suffix system is by no means fully understood, but clearly it provides grammatical machinery for specifying actions or states which are currently in progress, which either may happen or may have happened at any future or past time, which definitely have occurred or will occur in the immediate past or future, which are repeated or continued, which definitely will happen sometime in the future, which might happen sometime in the future, which definitely happened in the remote past, and which reportedly (or evidently) happened in the remote past. By way of illustrating some of these distinctions, we give below various forms of the verb to be, which incidentally may be used as an auxiliary in Cherokee, as in English, in complex verbal constructions. The English glosses which accompany these verb forms are, of course, reliable for only some contexts in which the forms may occur.

i:gi'
'he, she, it is'

yi'gi
'it may be'

geso:ʔi'
'it is often the case that'

gese:sdi'
'it will be' (probably)

jigese:'sdi
'it will be' (almost certainly)

gesɨ'ʔi
'it (probably) was' (and may still be)

jigesɨ'ʔi
'it used to be' (and may still be)

gesɨ:gi'
'it evidently was'

jigesɨ:'gi
'it certainly was'

The following forms show a variety of suffixes combined with the verb stem -noh- 'to tell' and the stative first person prefix aki-. Note that the definite future and the doubtful future are indicated by prefix-suffix combinations.

akinohise:ha'
'he (or she) is telling me'

yaki'nohise:la
'he (or she) may tell me, if he (or she) tells me'

akinohise:hoʔi'
'he (or she) often tells me'

akinohisehe':sdi'
'he (or she) will be telling me'

dɨki'nohise:li'

'he (or she) will tell me'

akinohisi'

'he (or she) just told me, will tell me right away'

akinohise:hɨ:gi'

'he (or she) was (in the process of) telling me'

akinohise:lɨ:gi'

'he (or she) told me' (in full)

akinohise:lɨ'ʔi

'whenever he (or she) tells me'

a:kinohise:hɨ'

'while he (or she) was telling me'

akinohisehdi'ʔi

'for him (or her) to tell me'

Each Cherokee verbal suffix appears in several different forms depending on the class of the verb stem to which it is attached and on the presence or absence of other adjacent suffixes. The paradigm given above is intended to establish the existence of a suffix system of considerable semantic significance. As this system has never been adequately analyzed, however, even a superficial description of its forms, arrangements, and functions cannot now be attempted.

TEXTS

The following texts are given first in the syllabary, next in transcription, and finally in translation. The numbers which follow each word in the transcribed texts refer to footnotes which give English glosses and morphemic analyses.

Text I: Object classifiers

ᏥᎻ, ᎡᎦᏔ ᏘᎩ ᏗᏍᎩᎾᏛᏏ ᎷᏏᎱ ᎾᏘᎥᏏ.
ᏌᏉᎲᏃ ᎧᎱᏎᏥ ᏗᏍᎩᏰᏍᏓᏁᎸᏍ, ᎤᏙᏧ. ᏗᏱᎱᏍᎩ ᏙᏓᎪᏢᏂ.

Ꭷ, ᎱᎾ, ᎠᏓ ᎾᏘᏑ ᎠᏏᏓᏝᎲ ᏘᏘᎦ ᎤᎧᏏᏛᎢ.
ᏴᎱᎹ ᏑᎦᎾ ᎪᎯ ᎤᏒᎢ. ᎠᏏ ᏂᏙᎤᏓᎹ ᎠᎼᎱᏙ ᎡᏍᎬᏏ.

Ꮍ. ᎠᏏᎹ ᏗᏋᏗᏰᏗ ᎾᏆᎱᏍᏓᏁᏍ. ᎤᏙᎯᏳ ᏥᏘᏍᏗ
ᎠᎩᏍ ᏗᎩᎸᎾᏍᏓᏗ ᎠᏏ ᏧᏂᏔᎾᏍᏗ ᏂᏱᎤᏓ ᎪᎯ ᎤᏒᎢ.

ᏚᏔᎩ ᏂᎦᏓ Ꮎ ᏘᎪᏌᎱ ᎦᏍᎩᎸ ᏗᏍᎩᎵᎥᏏ,
ᎤᏙᏧ ᏌᎩ.

jimi' (1) sɨkta' (2) tigi' (3) disgiwi':'dɨ:si' (4) lu:si:l(i') (5) witi'ʔɨsi' (
hwedo':hɨ'hno (7) kal(i)se:ji' (8) (d)esgihyɨ'sdane:lɨ:ha' (9) (u)do:'ju (10). dige:li'sdgi (11) dodago:'tlɨ:ni' (12).

ka' (13) li:wi' (14) aʔda' (15) witiya' (16) ayo:da'tlahɨ' (17) tidi':ga' (18) ukahyo:dɨ'ʔi (19). ye:li'g^{w}u (20) ya:ga:na' (21) kohi' (22) uhsɨ'(ʔi) (23). ahsi' (24) nije:nɨ'dag^{w}u' (25) (ah)telido' (26) eskɨ'hsi' (27).

ha' (28) asi:g^{w}u' (29) dig^{w}ɨdi'ye:di'(ʔi) (30) na'g^{w}alsda'hne:ha' (31). (u)dohiyu' (32) tsg^{w}i:'sd(i) (33) a:giha' (34) digilɨ'w(i)sdahdi'(ʔi) (35) ahsi' (24) junilaw(i)sdi'(ʔi) (36) nige:nɨ'da (37) kohi' (22) uhsɨ'ʔi (23).

tu:tagi' (38) niga:'da (39) na (40) digohwe:li' (41) ga:sgilɨ' (42) disgitlɨ'ʔ(ɨh)si' (43) (u)do:'ju (10) we:g(i') (44).

Jimmie, pick up the apples over there and take them to Lucille for me. Wh you're there, get a cup of sugar and bring it back for me, will you? I'm goin to make some pies.

Now, Levi, go get some wood and put it on the porch in a dry place. It might rain tonight. Before you go, hand me that dish.

Oh! I have some more dishes to wash. I sure have a lot of things to do before we go to church tonight.

Pick up all those papers and put them on the table for me, will you Becky?

---

(1) jimi' 'Jimmy'.

(2) sɨkta' 'apple, apples'.

(3) tigi' 'pick them up!' This word is used for items which are not on a raised surface and are not living, flexible, or long and rigid, and when referring to not more than two items or when several items are together in a container. di- 'plural object' plus -hi- 'you' (singular, active) becomes ti-; -gi 'pick up' (right away).

(4) disgiwi':'dɨ:si' 'take them away for me right away!' This word is used when referring to items which are not living, liquid, flexible, or long and rigid. di- 'plural object'; -sgi- 'you (singular) with reference to me'; -wi:d- (unanalyzed); -ɨ(h)si 'give, move (it) right away'.

(5) lu:si:li' 'Lucille'.

(6) witi'ʔɨsi' 'take them away right now!' This word is used when referring to items which are not living, liquid, flexible, or long and rigid. wi- 'distant action' or 'motion away from speaker'; -di- 'plural object' plus -hi- 'you' (singular active) becomes -ti-; -ʔɨ(h)si 'give, move (it) right away'.

(7) hwedo':hɨ'hno 'and when you're over there'. h(i)- 'you' (singular, active); -w(i)- 'distant action' or 'motion away from speaker'; -e(:)- 'go', -do:- 'motion in more than one direction' becomes -do:h- before vowels; -ɨ(:ʔi) 'potential action' becomes -ɨ- before -hno 'and then, and when'.

(8) kal(i)se:ji' 'sugar, sugar cane, candy' (or anything sweet). Compare kal(i)se:ji' jo:dalɨ'ʔi 'Sugar Mountain', a community in eastern Cherokee County.

(9) (d)esgihyɨ'sdane:lɨ:ha' 'bring it to me!' (later on), used when referring to an item which is out of sight and which is neither living, liquid, nor long and rigid. (d)e- 'distant position', -sgi- 'you (singular) with reference to me', -hyɨ- 'not living, liquid, or long and rigid', -sda(h)- 'cause to happen', -ne- 'give' becomes -ne(:)l- before -ɨ:(ʔi) 'potential action', -ha 'present' or, in this case, 'at the same time' (that you are over there).

(10) (u)do:'ju 'Will you do it?, will you, please?' That this is a question is indicated by the question marker -ju. Compare (u)do(:)hiyu' 'that's true, that's right, sure enough!' and do'ka 'isn't that right?'

(11) dige:li'sdgi 'pies'. di- 'plural' (inanimate), ge:li'sdgi 'pie'.

(12) dodago:'tlɨ:ni' 'I'm going to make them'. This word may be used regardless of what class of objects are to be made. do- 'plural object', -da- 'future', -g- 'I', -o:tlɨ:- 'make' becomes -o:tlɨ:n- before vowels, -i (required by -da- 'future').

(13) ka' 'now then!'

(14) li:wi' 'Levi'

(15) aʔda' 'wood, piece of wood'.

(16) witiya' 'go get the long rigid objects!' wi- 'distant action' or 'motion away from speaker'; -di- 'plural object' plus -hi- 'you' (singular active) becomes -ti-; -ya 'pick up a long rigid object'.

(17) ayo:da'tlahɨ'(ʔi) (at, on the) 'platform, porch'.

(18) tidi':ga' 'put the long rigid objects down!' (on the floor or ground).

di- 'plural object' plus -hi- 'you' (singular, active) becomes ti-; -di: 'long rigid object'; -ga 'put down' (right away).

(19) ukahyo:dɨ'ʔi 'in a dry place, where it's dry'. u- 'he, she, it' (stative -kahyodɨ- 'dry'; -ʔi 'location'.

(20) ye:li'g^{w}u 'it's possible'.

(21) ya:ga:na' 'it may rain'. This word is normally preceded by ye:li'g^{w}u 'it's possible'. y(i)- 'doubt'; -a- 'he, she, it' (active); -(:)ga:na 'rain' (nonpresent). Compare aga:sga' 'it's raining'.

(22) kohi' 'this' (unit of time). This word occurs in such phrases as kohi' i:ga' 'today' and kohi' uhsɨ'(ʔi) 'tonight'.

(23) uhsɨ'(ʔi) 'night'. Compare uhsɨ'hi 'last night'.

(24) ahsi' 'while'. When this word introduces a dependent clause, the following verb form has the prefix n(i)- 'not yet' which precedes the personal prefixes.

(25) nije:nɨ'dag^{w}u' 'you have yet to go, still haven't gone'. n(i)- 'not yet' -j(a)- 'you' (singular, stative); -e:- 'go' becomes -e:n before vowels; -ɨda- (unanalyzed); -g^{w}u 'emphatic'.

(26) (ah)telido' 'dish, plate, bowl'.

(27) eskɨ'hsi' 'give me something' (which is out of reach and which is not living, liquid, flexible, or long and rigid). (d)e- 'distant position'; -sg(i)- 'you (singular) with reference to me' often becomes -sk(i)- before h or vowel plus h; -ɨhsi or -ɨʔsi 'give an object which is not living, liquid, flexible, or long and rigid'.

(28) ha' term of disgust used mostly by women.

(29) asi:g^{w}u' 'more'.

(30) dig^{w}ɨdi'ye:di'(ʔi) 'for me to wash dishes, that I wash dishes'. This word is used when referring to washing dishes after a meal, as opposed to dishes which are merely dusty or have become dirty through some mea other than their use as food containers. di- 'plural object'; -(a)g^{w}- 'I' (stative); -(a)diye- 'wash' (a dirty dish used for cooking or eating) -diʔi 'that, for'.

(31) na'g^{w}alsda'hne:ha' 'I must, I have yet to cause myself' (to). n(i)- 'not yet'; -agw- 'I' (stative); -al(i)- (with reference to) 'oneself'; -sda(h)- 'cause'; -ne:- 'some time ago, later on'; -ha 'present'.

(32) (u)do(:)hiyu' 'that's true, that's right, sure enough'.

(33) tsg^{w}i:'sd(i) 'many' (things which are not living, liquid, flexible, or long and rigid). Compare uni'jati' 'many' (living things).

(34) a(:)giha' 'I have' (not on my person, but in an unspecified place) something which is not living, liquid, flexible, or long and rigid. agi- 'I' (stative); -ha 'present'.

(35) digilɨ'w(i)sdahdi'(ʔi) 'my job, that I work, for me to work'. di- 'plural object' (?); -(a)gi- 'I' (stative); -lɨw(i)sda- 'work, cause something to be done' becomes -lɨw(i)sdah- before -diʔi 'that, for'.

(36) junilaw(i)sdi'(ʔi) (their) 'church, meeting, that they meet, for them to meet'. j- 'distant position'; -uni- 'they' (stative); -law(i)- 'meet' becomes -law(i)s- before -diʔi 'that, for'.

(37) nige:nɨ'da 'you, I, and one or more others have yet to go, still haven't gone'. ni- 'not yet'; -(i)g(i)- 'you, I, and one or more others' (stative); -e:- 'go' becomes -e:n- before vowels; -ɨda (unanalyzed). The emphatic suffix -g^{w}u is often added to this word to form nige:nɨ'dag^{w}u' 'while we still haven't gone, before we finally go, while we're still waiting to go', etc.

(38) tu:tagi' 'pick them up!' (items scattered on the ground or floor which are not living or long and rigid). di- 'plural object' plus -h(i)- 'you' (singular, active) becomes t(i)-; -u:tagi 'pick up flexible items or scattered objects which are not living, liquid, or long and rigid'.

(39) niga:'da 'all of them, of it'.

(40) na 'that, those'.

(41) digohwe:li' 'papers, book, magazine'. di- 'plural' (inanimate); gohwe:li' 'paper'. Compare gowe:li^{ʔ}a' 'I'm writing'.

(42) ga:sgilɨ' 'on, at the table, bench, chair'.

(43) disgitlɨ'ʔ(ɨh)si' (also pronounced dikstlɨ'hsi') 'put the flexible items on a shelf, table, or other raised surface for me!' di- 'plural object'; -sgi- 'you (singular) with reference to me'; -tla- 'on a raised surface' becomes -tlɨ- before -ʔɨ-; -ʔɨhsi 'give' (right away).

(44) we:g(i') 'Becky, Rebecca'.

Text II: Active Personal Prefixes

ᏗᎦᏚᎲᏧ ᏓᏙᏏ ᎪᎯ ᎢᎦ.

ᎥᎥ, ᏌᎻ ᎾᎱ ᎠᏴ ᏓᏥᏙᏏ. ᏑᏓᎤᏏᏍᎪ

ᏙᎤᏍᏗᎢ.

ᎨᏣ, ᎢᏕᎾ. ᎪᎯᎩ ᏕᏥᎪᎥᎢ ᏌᎻ. ᏥᎣᏍᏗ ᏦᏍᏗᎯᎯ

ᎨᏒᎩ ᏌᎶᎱ.

ᏑᎵ ᏕᏍᏗᏧᎢ ᏌᎶᎱ.

ᏎᎳᎻ ᎾᎥᎢ. ᎤᏂᏣᏘ ᎠᏁᎲᎢ ᎤᎿᎢ.

ᎾᏁᏙᏄᎢ ᎵᎵᏴ.

ᎨᏣ, ᏌᎻᏧ ᏴᏒᎾ.

digaduhɨ'ju (1) daje:si' (2) kohi (3) i:ga' (4).

i:' (5) sami' (6) wili' (7) ayɨ' (8) dayoje':si' (9). hadantesgo' (10) jenɨsdi'ʔi (11).

howa' (12) ide':'na (13). gohi:gi' (14) gajigoʔɨ'ʔi (15) sa:mi' (6).

tsgwi:'sdi (16) josdi'hihi' (17) gesɨ:gi' (18) salo:li' (19).

hadlɨ' (20) de'sdiɫe' (21) salo:li' (19).

selami (22) naʔɨ'ʔi (23). uni'jati (24) anehɨʔi (25) uhna:ʔi' (26).

winedo'lɨʔi' (27) dlɨdlɨ'yɨ (28).

howa' (12). samile (29) y(ɨʔ)e:na' (30).

Are you all going to town today?

Yes, Sam, Willie and I are going. Are you thinking about going?

Okay, let's (you, I and others) go. It's a long time since I've seen Sam. We (another and I) used to kill lots of squirrels together.

Where did you (two) kill the squirrels?

Around Salem. There used to be a lot of them around there.

Let's (you and I) go sometime.

Okay. Maybe Sam will go.

---

(1) digaduhɨ'ju (distant) 'town?'. di- 'distant', gaduhɨ' 'town', -ju 'question marker'. To inflected verbs or nouns or simple lexical forms -ju, -jɨ, or -sgo may be added to form questions. Thus o:si' 'pretty good', o:siju', o:sijɨ', or o:sisg(o') 'is it okay?'.

(2) daje:si' 'you all are going, will go'. da- 'future', -(i)j- 'you all', -e:- 'go' becomes -e:s- before vowels, -i automatic suffix required by da- 'future'.

(3) kohi' 'this' (unit of time). This word occurs in such phrases as kohi' i:ga' 'today' and kohi' uhsɨ'(ʔi) 'tonight'.

(4) i:ga' 'day'.

(5) ɨ:' (also ɨ: and ɨ:ʔɨ') 'yes'.

(6) sami' 'Sam, Sammie'.

(7) wili' 'Willie'.

(8) ayɨ' 'I, me'.

(9) dayoje':si' 'they and I are going, will go'. da- 'future' becomes day- before e, o, or u; -oj- 'they and I'; -e:s- 'go' (see 2, above); -i required by da- 'future'.

(10) hadantesgo' 'are you thinking' (to yourself)? h(i)- 'you', adan(ɨ)te 'think', -sgo 'question marker'. Compare adante' 'he, she is thinking' gadanɨte' 'I'm thinking'. Compare also uda:n(ɨ)ta' 'he, she feels' (goo tired, happy, etc.).

(11) jenɨsdi'ʔi 'that you go, for you to go'. j- (with reference to) 'you', -e(:)- 'go', -(nɨ)sdi'ʔi 'that (someone) should' or 'for (someone) to'. Compare agiwonihisdi'ʔi 'for me to talk', digine:sdi'ʔi 'for me to get some' (flexible items).

(12) howa' 'okay, all right'.

(13) ide':'na 'let's (you, I, and one or more others) go'. id- 'you, I, and one or more others', -e:- 'go', -na 'may it be' (right away).

(14) gohi:gi' 'long ago'.

(15) gajigoʔɨ'ʔi 'since I saw him'. ga- 'since', -ji- 'I', -goʔ- 'see', -ɨʔi action which continued for a period in the past and which the speake witnessed personally. Compare gajigoʔe'ʔi 'since I saw him without realizing it', that is, 'since the time when I seem to have seen him, although I was not aware that it was him at the time'.

(16) tsgwi:'sdi 'many' (things which are not alive, not liquid, not flexible, and not long and rigid). Some speakers use this word when referring to animals, but it is never used with reference to human beings. Compare uni'jat(i') 'many' (living things, especially humans).

(17) josdi'hihi' 'he and I are killers, kill living things'. j- 'plural object', -osdi- 'he or she and I', -hi- 'kill' -hi 'one(s) who'. Compare sudaldi'hihi' 'Sixkiller', composed of sudal(i') 'six', -di- 'plural object', -hi- 'kill', -hi 'one(s) who'.

(18) gesɨ:gi' 'it used to be'. Compare i:gi' 'he, she, it is', yi'gi 'it might be'. Before vowels 'be' is indicated by ges-. The suffix -ɨ:gi indicate action or a state of being which existed for some time in the past and which the speaker was aware of at the time.

(19) salo:li' 'squirrel(s)'.

(20) hadlɨ' 'where?'.

(21) de'sdiɫe'(ʔi) 'you two killed them'. di- 'plural object' becomes de-

before (i)sd- 'you two', -ih(i) 'kill' becomes iɫ- before vowels, -e(ʔi) action reported to have happened in the past although the speaker did not personally witness the event. Compare desdi'ɫɨ:gi' 'you two killed them' (in view of the speaker).

(22) selami 'Salem' (a district in Adair County).

(23) naʔɨ'ʔi 'near'.

(24) uni'jati 'many' (living things). See tsgwi:'sdi (16), above.

(25) anehɨʔi' 'they used to live, be alive'. an(i)- 'they', -e- 'live' becomes -eh- before vowels, -ɨʔi action which continued for a period in the past and which the speaker witnessed personally.

(26) uhna:ʔi' 'there'.

(27) winedo'lɨʔi' 'let's (you and I) go' (later on). w(i)- 'distant action', -in- 'you and I', -e(:)- 'go', dolɨʔi 'may it be sometime'. Compare ine:na' 'let's (you and I) go' (now) and winedo'lido'lɨʔi' 'let's (you and I) go' (from place to place sometime).

(28) dlɨdlɨ'yɨ 'sometime, later on'.

(29) samile 'maybe Sam'. The suffix -le may be added to names of people or to other nouns to indicate doubt, just as -sgo, -ju, and -jɨ are added to indicate a question. When nouns with -le are the subjects of verbs, the verb has the prefix y(i)- which indicates 'negative' after tla but 'doubt' after -le.

(30) y(ɨʔ)e:na' 'he, she might go'. y(i)- 'negative' after tla, 'doubt' elsewhere. (ɨʔ) seems to contribute nothing to the meaning of the word and does not usually occur in spoken Cherokee, but is indicated by the conventional spelling of the word. -e:- 'go', -na 'may it be' (right away). Compare ide':'na (13), above, 'let's (you, I, and others) go' (right away).

Text III: Stative Personal Prefixes

ᎵᏏ ᎦᎤᏙᎠ ᎠᎩᏍᏓᏴᎲᏍᎩ. ᏕᎵᏤᎩ ᏗᏂᏲᎵ ᏙᎩᏂᏯᏭ. ᏣᎳᎩ ᏧᎩᏇᏤᏗ ᏧᎩᏬᏂᎯᏍᏗᎢ ᏏᏓᏁᏇ ᏧᏕᏙᏢᏒᎢ ᎠᎴ ᎠᎢᏚᎵ ᏗᏂᏲᎵ ᏣᎳᎩ ᎤᏂᎪᎵᏰᏗᎢ ᎠᏎᏃ Ꮭ ᏳᎾᏚᎵᏭ ᎤᏂᎪᎵᏰᏗᎢ.

ᎦᏍᏗᏲᏏᏑᏍᎪ.

ᎨᎵᎠ. ᏌᎻ ᏣᏲᏏᏍᎪ.

ᎢᏕᎢ ᎠᎩᏲᏏ. ᎤᏙᎯᏳ ᎢᎩᏂᏇᏤᏗ ᎡᎩ ᎢᎾᎨ ᎡᎯ, ᏙᏯ ᏣᏂ.

ᏕᎳᏛ ᎢᎩᏝᏭ. ᎠᎵᏍᏓᏴᏗ. ᏌᎻ ᏭᎵᏍᏛᏑᏕ. ᏨᏌᏊ ᏭᎵᏍᎦᎳ. ᎦᏥᏲᏏᏍᎨᏍᏗ ᎢᏣᎵᏍᏓᏴᎲᏕᏊ.

li:s(i') (1) d(e'ˀ)udoˀ(a') (2) aksdayɨ'hɨsg(i') (3). gałgwog(i') (4) diniyo'łi (5) dogini:kaha' (6). jalag(i') (7) ogilɨ'kwdi (8) ogiwonihisdi'ˀi (9) sidanelɨ' (10) ogadotlɨ'sɨ'ˀi (11) ale' (12) agwadu:li' (13) diniyo'łi (5) jalagi' (7) unigoliye':di'ˀi (14) a:sehno' (15) tla (16) yuna'du:liha' (17) unigoliye':di'ˀi (14).

desdiyo'siha'sg(o) (18).

geliˀa' (19). sami' (20) jayo'sisg(o) (21).

iga'(ˀi) (22) agiyo'si (23). (u)doh(i)yu' (24) iginilɨ'kwdi (25) sɨ:gi' (26) inage (27) e'hi (28) do'ka (29) ja:n(i) (30).

galadɨ (31) igitlaha' (32) ałsday(ɨ)di' (33). sami' (20) hałsdɨ:tluga' (34) jɨsagwu' (35) hałsde:la' (36). de'jiyo'sisge'sdi (37) ijałsdayɨhɨgagwu' (38).

My wife's name is Lizzie. She and I have seven kids. We all like to talk Cherokee at home and I want the kids to read Cherokee, but they don't want to yet.

Are you two hungry?

I guess so. Are you hungry, Sam?

I sure am hungry! We sure like wild onions (too), don't we Johnny? We already have the food on. Sam, sit down. Help yourself. If you all are hungry, you all eat.

---

(1) li:s(i') 'Lizzie'.

(2) d(e'ˀ)udoˀ(a') 'his, her name is; he, she is called'. This word is used when the speaker is talking about someone well known to him. Often it is used when only the given name is mentioned. When the reference is to a stranger, however, and particularly when both the given and the family names are mentioned, one uses judo'ˀid(a') 'his, her (full) name is', digwado'ˀid(a') 'my (full) name is', etc. de- 'plural' (?), -u- (with reference to) 'him, her', -do- 'call, name', -ˀa 'present'.

(3) aksdayɨ'hɨsg(i') 'my wife, my cook'. agi- (with reference to) 'me' may become ak- before h, s, t, or k; -sdayɨ- 'feed', -hɨ- probably the alternate of -ha- 'present' (regularly, all the time) which occurs before certain other suffixes, -sgi 'one(s) who'. Compare jasdayɨ'hɨsgisgo'

(is it) 'your wife?'.

(4) gałgwog(i') 'seven'

(5) diniyo'łi 'children'. dini- 'plural', (a)yo'łi 'child'. Compare gayo'łi 'a little, a few'.

(6) dogini:kaha' 'we two' (not including you) 'have some' (living things). d(i)- 'plural object', -ogini- (with reference to) 'me and one other' (but not you), -ka- 'animate object', -ha 'present'. The sentence diniyo'łi dogini:kaha' 'we have some children' does not necessarily mean that the children are the speaker's offspring. It may be that they are someone else's children who happen to be with the speaker temporarily. Compare dagi:kaha' 'I have some' (living things, not on my person but somewhere around).

(7) jalag(i') 'Cherokee' (language), 'Cherokee' (thing). Compare dijalagi' 'Cherokee things', ajalagi' 'Cherokee person', jalagiha' 'pure Cherokee The English word Cherokee is no doubt derived from some form of this wo

(8) ogilɨ'kwdi 'others and I like' (it). ogi- (with reference to) 'others and me', -lɨkwdi 'be liked'.

(9) ogiwonihisdi'ʔi 'that we (others and I) talk, for us (others and me) to talk'. ogi- (with reference to) 'others and me', -woni- 'talk', -hisdiʔ 'that, for'. Compare agiwonihisdi'ʔi 'for me to talk'.

(10) sidanelɨ' 'household, family'.

(11) ogadotlɨ'sɨ'ʔi 'our organization' (which includes me and others, but not you). og(i)- (with reference to) 'me and others, but not you', -adotlɨ- 'society, association, organization', -sɨʔi 'potential'.

(12) ale' 'and, but'.

(13) agwadu:li' 'I want' (it). agw- (with reference to) 'me', -adu:li 'be wanted'. Compare (17), below.

(14) unigoliye':di'ʔi 'that they read, for them to read'. uni- (with reference to) 'them', -goliy- 'read', -e- 'from time to time', -diʔi 'that, for'.

(15) a:sehno' 'but, but probably, but yet, nevertheless'. a:se' 'probably', -hno 'and, but'.

(16) tla (also ɨ'tla) 'no, not'.

(17) yuna'du:liha' 'they don't want' (it). y(i)- 'negative' after tla, un(i)- (with reference to) 'them', -adu:li- 'be wanted', -ha 'present'.

(18) desdiyo'siha'sg(o) 'are you two hungry?' di- 'plural object' becomes

de- before -(i)sdi (with reference to) 'you two', -yosi- 'there is hunger' -ha- 'present', -sgo 'question'.

(19) geli?a' 'I guess, I am thinking'. g- 'I', -eli- 'guess, think', -?a 'present'.

(20) sa(:)m(i) 'Sam, Sammie'.

(21) jayo'sisg(o) 'are you hungry?' ja- (with reference to) 'you', -yosi 'there is hunger', -sgo 'question'.

(22) iga'(?i) 'amount, number of'.

(23) agiyo'si 'I'm hungry'. agi- (with reference to) 'me', -yosi 'there is hunger'.

(24) (u)doh(i)yu' 'that's true, that's right, sure enough!'

(25) iginilɨ'kwdi 'you and I like' (it). igini- (with reference to) 'you and me', -lɨkwdi 'be liked'.

(26) sɨ:gi' 'onion(s)'.

(27) inage 'woods, boondocks'.

(28) e'hi 'he, she, it lives, is usually located; one(s) who, or one(s) which, live, are located' (somewhere). e- 'live, be located', -hi 'one(s) who'. The phrase inage e'hi may be translated as (something) 'wild', (something that) 'lives in the woods'.

(29) do'ka 'Isn't that right?'

(30) ja:n(i) 'John, Johnnie'.

(31) galadɨ 'already'.

(32) igitlaha' 'we (you, I, and others) have something which is not flexible, living, or long and rigid on a raised surface'. igi- (with reference to) 'you, me, and one or more others', -tla- 'be on a raised surface' (such as a table, shelf, bed, etc.) -ha 'present'. Compare igitla'?a 'we have a flexible object on something', igitla' 'we have a long rigid object on something', igitlaha' 'we have something liquid on something', edinisiha' 'you, I, and one or more others have a living thing lying horizontally on the ground, the floor, or on a raised surface out of sight'.

(33) ałsday(ɨ)di' 'food'. ali- 'oneself, oneselves' often becomes ał- before s, -sdayɨ- 'feed', -(s)di 'something with which to'. Compare a'gwałsday(ɨ)di' 'my food' (something for me to feed myself with), agwałsda'yɨhɨsga' 'I'm being eaten' (something is feeding itself on me), galisda'yɨhɨsga' 'I'm eating' (I am feeding myself), aksdayɨ'hɨsgi' 'my

cook, my wife' (the one who feeds me), found in (3) above, aksda'yɨhɨs[e] 'he, she is cooking for me'.

(34) hałsdɨ:tluga' 'sit down'. h(i)- 'you', -ali- (with reference to) 'oneself' may become -ał- before s, -sdɨ:tlu- 'sit down on a raised surface' (not on the ground or floor), -ga 'imperative'.

(35) jɨsagwu' 'you yourself!' ja- (with reference to) 'you' plus a becomes jɨ-, -asa- 'oneself', -gwu 'emphasis'. Compare uwa'sa 'he himself', agwɨ'sa(gwu') 'I myself'.

(36) hałsde:la' 'help yourself!' h(i)- 'you', ali- (with reference to) 'oneself' may become -ał- before s, -sde:- 'help', -la 'may it be' (right away). Compare galisde:liha' 'I'm helping myself', a'ksde:liha' 'he's helping me', deji'sde:liha' 'I'm helping them'.

(37) de'jiyo'sisge'sdi 'if you all are hungry'. di- 'plural object' becomes de- before -(i)ji- (with reference to) 'you all', -yosi- 'there is hunger -sgesdi 'should it be that, whenever it may be that'. The stem -yosi- requires the prefix de- before all personal object prefixes which include more than one person.

(38) ijałsdayɨhɨgagwu' 'you all eat!' ij(i)- 'you and others' (but not me), -ali- (with reference to) 'oneself, oneselves' may become -ał- before s, -sdayɨ- 'feed', -hɨ- probably the alternate of -ha- 'present, regularly, all the time' which occurs before certain other suffixes, -ga 'imperative', -gwu 'emphasis'.

Text IV: Prefixes Which Precede Personal Prefixes

ᎦᏙ ᎤᏍᏗ.

ᏥᏔᎦ. ᏣᏂᎢ ᎾᎨᏙᎸᎩ ᎪᎯ ᎢᎦ.

ᎾᏍᎩᎩ.

ᏧᏁᎳ ᏥᏔᎦ ᏙᏥᏄᎩ. ᎤᎾᏕᎵᏍᎬᏃ ᎢᎦᏓ

ᏥᏔᎦ ᏗᎨᎩᏅᏁᏗᎢ.

ᎠᏲ ᎡᏍᎬᏏ.

ᏥᏍᏕ ᏣᎭ ᎠᎩᏃᎯᏎᏄᎩ ᎢᎾᎨ ᎡᎯ ᎡᎩ ᎡᏤ

ᎤᏍᏗ ᎠᏲ ᎠᏰᎵ ᎤᏔᏃᎢ ᎤᏬᏰᎢ ᎾᎥᎢ.

ᎠᏲᎨᎢ ᎡᏍᎩᏁᎸᏏ... ᏩᏙ. ᎠᏏᎲᏍᎪ ᏟᏕᎵ ᎧᎾ.

Ꮭ. ᎤᎦᏲ ᎠᏆᏕᎵᏤ.... ᎦᏙᏃ Ꮭ ᏐᏍᎩᏁᏁᏤ

ᎠᏲᎨᎢ ᎦᏥᏁᏁᏗᎢ ᎠᏂᏣᎭ ᏋᎾᏧ. ᏥᏍᏕ ᎤᏙᎯᏳ

ᏟᏄᏉᏓᏁᏤ ᎠᏲᎨᎢ.

ᎰᏩ. ᏋᎾᏧ ᎬᏁᏁᏄᎢ. ᎯᏁᏁᏄᏃ ᏬᏙᏄᎢ.

ga?do (1) u:sdi' (2).

jita:ga' (3). wahyo'?(i) (4) wige:do':hɨ:(gi') (5) koh(i') (6) i:ga' (ɨ)sgigi' (8).

čane:la' (9) jita:g(a') (3) do:jiłɨ:gi' (10). unadu:lisgɨhno' (11) iga':'da (12) jita:ga' (3) dige:gi:nɨnehdi'?i (13).

a:m(a') (14) eskɨ'hsi' (15).

ji:sdu' (16) wahya' (17) akinoh(i)se:lɨ:gi' (18) inage' (19) e'hi (2 sɨ:g(i') (21) eha' (22) uhsdi' (23) am(a') (24) ayeł(i') (25) utano'(?i) (26) uwe:yɨ'(?i) (27) na?ɨ'?i (28).

amage?(i') (29) eskine'hɨsi' (30) . . . wado' (31). (a)sigwu'sgo (32) jadu:li' (33) kahwi' (34).

tla (35). u:gam(a') (36) agwadu:liha' (37) . . . ga?do':hno' (38) tla' yisgine'neha' (39) amage?i' (29) gaji:ne:'nehdi'(?i) (40) ani:wahya' (41) suna:le' (42). ji:sdu' (16) udoh(i)yu' (43) jalɨ'kwdaneha' (44) amage?i' (29).

howa' (45) suna:le'?(i) (42) gɨ:ne:nelɨ:?i' (46) hine:nelɨhno' (47) hwedo':lɨ:'?i (48).

What's that?

Some chickens. I was over at the Wolfes' today.

Is that so?

We killed eight chickens. And they wanted to give us a few (dead) chickens.

Pass the salt.

Rabbit Wolfe told me that there are some wild onions growing over on the island in the river.

Pass the hominy. . . . thanks. Do you want some more coffee?

No. I want some soup. . . . Why don't you give me some hominy to give the Wolfes in the morning? Rabbit sure likes your hominy.

Okay, I'll give you some tomorrow and you can give it to him when you go over there.

---

(1) ga?do 'why?'. This word may occur in such phrases as ga?do u:sdi' 'what is it?' and ga?do u:'sdi 'which is it?'. See also ga?do':hno' (38), below.

(2) u:sdi' This word occurs most frequently in the phrase ga?do u:sdi' 'what is it?' Compare uhsdi' 'small', uhsdi'?i 'baby', ga?do u:'sdi 'which is it?'.

(3) jita:ga' 'chicken(s)'.

(4) wahyo'?(i) (in) 'wolf country', (at) 'the Wolfes' place'. wahya' 'wolf, wolves', like all stems ending in -a, changes -a to -o- before -?i 'location'. Compare gita:ya' 'cherry', gita:yo'?i (at) 'Cherry Tree community', utano'?i (26), below.

(5) wige:do':hɨ:(gi') 'I was moving about in a distant area'. wi- 'distant action' or 'motion away from the speaker', -g- 'I', -e:- 'go', -do:- 'motion in more than one direction' becomes -do:h- before -ɨ:gi' 'past completed action witnessed by the speaker'. Compare we:do:ha' 'he, she is (moving around in an area distant from the speaker).

(6) koh(i') 'this', used with units of time as in the phrases kohi' i:ga' 'today' and kohi' uhsɨ'(?i) 'tonight'.

(7) i:ga' 'day'.

(8) (ɨ)sgigi' 'Is that so? Is that a fact?' Compare do'ka 'Isn't that right?'. The word given here as ɨsgigi is usually pronounced either as ɨsgi or sgigi, depending on dialect. In formal speech it is na:sgigi.

(9) čane:la' 'eight'. In some dialects this word is pronounced čune:la'. The standard spelling of the word in syllabic texts reflects the latter pronunciation.

(10) do:jiƚɨ:gi' 'they and I killed them' (all at one time). do:ji- 'they and I (with reference) to others', -h(i)- 'kill' becomes -ƚ- before vowels, -ɨ:gi' 'past completed action witnessed by the speaker'.

(11) unadu:lisgɨhno' 'and they wanted' (it). un(i)- (with reference to) 'them', -adu:li- 'be wanted', -sgɨ- 'past continued action or state', -hno 'and, but, and so, and then'.

(12) iga':'da 'some, a few, a portion'. Compare niga:'da 'all of them, all of it'.

(13) dige:gi:nɨnehdi'?i 'for them to give more than one flexible item to you, me, and one or more others'. di- 'plural object', -ge:gi:- 'they (with

reference) to you, me, and one or more others', -nɨ- flexible object(s), -ne- 'give' becomes -neh- before certain suffixes including -di'ˀi 'that, for'. Note that dead animals require verb forms with the flexible object classifier.

(14) a:m(a') 'salt'.

(15) eskɨ'hsi' 'give it to me' (something beyond reach which is not living, not flexible, not liquid, and not long and rigid). e- 'distant position' (out of reach), -sg(i)- 'you (with reference) to me' becomes -sk(i)- before h or vowel-plus-h, -ɨhsi or -ɨˀsi 'give an object which is not living, flexible, liquid, or long and rigid'.

(16) ji:sdu' 'rabbit(s)', a common man's given name.

(17) wahya' 'wolf, wolves', a common surname. Compare wahyo'ˀi (4), above and ani:wahya' (41), below.

(18) akinohise:lɨ:gi' 'he told me'. agi- 'he, she (with reference) to me' becomes aki- when followed by h or by n-plus-vowel-plus-h, -nohise:- 'tell' becomes -nohise:l- before vowels, -ɨ:gi' or -ɨ:ˀi' 'past completed action witnessed by the speaker'. Compare ɨkinohise:lɨ:gi' 'I was told, someone (unspecified) told me'.

(19) inage' 'woods, boondocks'.

(20) e'hi 'he, she, it lives, is usually located; one(s) who, or one(s) which, live, are located' (somewhere). e- 'live, be located', -hi 'one(s) who'. The phrase inage e'hi may be translated as (something) 'wild', (something that) 'lives in the woods'.

(21) sɨ:g(i') 'onion(s)'.

(22) eha' 'he, she is alive, is living'. e- 'live', -ha 'present'. The absence of a subject prefix indicates a third person singular subject.

(23) uhsdi' 'small, little'. Compare uhsdi'ˀi 'baby' and u:sdi' (2), above.

(24) am(a') 'water'. See ayehl(i') (25) and amageˀi' (29), below.

(25) ayeɬ(i') 'the center, fifty cents' (half, or the midpoint of, a dollar). The phrase am(a') ayeɬi' is pronounced as though it were a single word, amayeɬi'. Literally, this means 'something in the center of or surrounded by water'. It can usually be translated as 'island, continent', or often 'America'.

(26) utano'(ˀi) 'at the big one'. u'tana' 'big around' becomes utano'- before -ˀi 'location'. See uwe:yɨ'(ˀi) (27), below.

(27) uwe:yɨ'(ʔi) 'creek, stream'. The phrase utano'(ʔi) uwe:yɨ'(ʔi) is used for 'at, to, in the river'. Literally, it means 'at the big one flowing'. Compare uhsdi' uwe:yɨ'(ʔi) 'at the small branch'.

(28) naʔɨ'ʔi 'near'.

(29) amageʔ(i') 'hominy' (which is served by Cherokees as a liquid to be drunk rather than eaten). Notice that the first component is ama' 'water', (24) above.

(30) eskine'hɨsi' 'give me the (container of) liquid yonder'. e- 'distant position' (out of the speaker's reach), -sgi- 'you (with reference) to me' becomes -ski- before h or before n-plus-vowel-plus-h, -ne- 'liquid object', -hɨsi' 'give' or 'just now gave'. Some Cherokees use the word diskine'hɨsi' for 'give me the liquid' (either within or beyond their reach).

(31) wado' 'thank you'.

(32) (a)sigwu'sgo 'more?' (a)si:gwu' 'more', -sgo 'question marker'.

(33) jadu:li' 'you want' (it). ja- (he, she, it with reference) 'to you', -(a)du:li 'be wanted'. The rule which normally converts a plus a to ɨ does not apply to this form. Compare agwadu:liha' (37), below.

(34) kahwi' 'coffee'. This word, of course, is one of the few which have been borrowed from English.

(35) tla, also ɨ'tla 'no, not'.

(36) u:gam(a') 'soup, juice'. Compare ama' (24), above.

(37) agwadu:liha' 'I want it' (right now). agw- (with reference) 'to me', -adu:li- 'be wanted', -ha 'present'. Compare jadu:li' (33), above.

(38) gaʔdo':hno' 'and why?', so why?, why then?'. gaʔdo- 'why?', -hno 'and'. See gaʔdo (1), above.

(39) (tla) yisgine'neha' 'you're not giving me the liquid'. yi- 'negative' (after tla), -sgi- 'you (with reference) to me', -ne- 'liquid object', -ne- 'give', -ha 'present'. This word may be pronounced either as yisgine'neha' or with emphatic stress on the second syllable, yisgi'neneha' 'you're not giving <u>me</u> the liquid'.

(40) gaji:ne:'nehdi'(ʔi) 'for me to give a liquid to them'. gaji:- 'I (with reference) to them', -ne- 'liquid object', -ne- 'give' becomes -neh- before -di'ʔi 'that, for'. Compare gaji:nenelɨ:gi' 'I gave them a liquid', dagaji':'nene:li' 'I'll give them a liquid'.

(41) ani:wahya' 'Wolfes, the wolf clan'. ani:- 'they', -wahya 'wolf'. One of the seven Cherokee clans is referred to by this term.

(42) suna:le'(ʔi) 'tomorrow', (in the) 'morning'.

(43) udoh(i)yu' 'that's true, that's right, sure enough'.

(44) jalɨ'kwdaneha' 'he, she likes something of yours or something about you'. In formal speech this word is pronounced jalɨgwo'daneha', and this pronunciation is reflected in its spelling in the syllabary. ja- (he, she, it with reference) 'to you', -(i)lɨkwd(i)- 'be pleasing', -ane- (see below) -ha 'present action or state'. The -ane- component in this word and elsewhere seems to mean 'to him, her' and takes precedence over the prefix ja-, which must then be translated (with reference) 'to you' rather than 'by you' as in the case of jadu:li' (33), above, 'by you it is wanted' (you want it). This component may be of some significance to historical linguists, as its function and position relative to the stem seem to be similar to those of the "inverse theme sign" of Algonquian languages.

(45) howa' 'okay, all right'.

(46) gɨ:ne:nelɨʔi' 'when I give you a liquid, should I give you a liquid'. gɨ: 'I (with reference) to you', -ne- 'liquid object', -ne- 'give' becomes -nel- before vowels, -ɨ:ʔi 'potential action'.

(47) hine:nelɨhno' 'and you can give a liquid' (to him, her later on). hi- 'you', -ne- 'liquid object', -ne- 'give' becomes -nel- before vowels, -ɨ(:ʔi) 'potential action', -hno 'and, and then'. Compare hine'hɨsi' 'give him the liquid!' (right now).

(48) hwedo':lɨ:'ʔi 'when you go'. h(i)- 'you', -w(i)- 'distant action', -e:- 'go', -do:- 'motion in more than one direction' (in this case, a trip to a place and return) becomes -do:l- before certain suffixes including -ɨ:ʔi 'potential action'.

BIBLIOGRAPHY OF PUBLICATIONS ON AND IN THE CHEROKEE LANGUAGE

1830. Pickering, John. A grammar of the Cherokee language. Boston (reprinted in Krueger 1963).

1833. Boudinot, Elias, trans. Poor Sarah, or the Indian woman. New Echota: United Brethren's Missionary Society. (Financed by the American Tract Society, Wheeler & Candy, printers; printed in the syllabary.)

1836. Gallatin, Albert. A synopsis of the Indian tribes of North America. Transactions and Collections of the American Antiquarian Society 2:87-93 (history and writing system), 239-50, 276, 291-94 (grammar), 301 (syllabary), 399-404 (word list), and 415-21 (sentences and texts).

1849. Worcester, Samuel A., and Stephen Foreman, trans. Selections from the Book of Isaiah. Park Hill, Indian Terr.: Park Hill Mission Press. (Printed in the syllabary.)

1850. Worcester, Samuel A., and Elias Boudinot, trans. The Gospel of St. Matthew. 5th ed. Park Hill, Indian Terr.: Park Hill Mission Press. (Printed in the syllabary.)

1852. Von der Gabelenz, Hans Georg Connor. Kurze grammatik der Tscherokesischen sprache. In Zeitschrift für die Wissenschaft der Sprache 3:257-300. Greifswald. (English translation in Krueger 1963.)

1853. Schoolcraft, Henry R. Information respecting the history, condition and prospects of the Indian tribes of the United States. Pt. 2. Philadelphia: Lippincott, Grambo & Co. (See pp. 209-11, number systems; 228, syllabary and sample text; and 443-56, Rev. S. A. Worcester's grammatical notes.)

1856. Worcester, Samuel A., and Stephen Foreman, trans. The Book of Genesis. Park Hill, Indian Terr.: Park Hill Mission Press. (Printed in the syllabary.)

1860. Greenleaf, Ben. Cherokee almanac. Park Hill, Indian Terr.: Park Hill Press.

1860. Worcester, Samuel A., Elias Boudinot, et al. The Cherokee New Testament. New York. (Printed in the syllabary. Current edition, New York: American Bible Society, available through John Roberts, Stilwell, Oklahoma.)

1885. Foster, George Everett. Se-quo-yah, the American Cadmus and modern Moses. Philadelphia.

1888. Pilling, James C. Bibliography of the Iroquoian languages. Smithsonia Institution, Bureau of Ethnology Bulletin 6. (References to all previou publications on Cherokee and other Iroquoian languages.)

1891. Mooney, James. Sacred formulas of the Cherokees. Smithsonian Institution, Bureau of American Ethnology, 7th Annual Report, pp. 307-97.

1899. Foster, George Everett. A story of the Cherokee Bible. Ithaca, N. Y.

1900. Mooney, James. Myths of the Cherokee. Smithsonian Institution, Bureau of American Ethnology, 19th Annual Report, Pt. 1, pp. 3-548. (Includes historical sketch and glossary.)

1926. Speck, Frank G. Some Eastern Cherokee texts. IJAL 4 (1):111-13. (Phonetic transcriptions, close and free translations.)

1931. Olbrechts, Frans M. Two Cherokee texts. IJAL 6 (3-4):179-84. (Phone transcriptions, close and free translations, one text in the syllabary.

1932. Mooney, James, and F. M. Olbrechts. The Swimmer Manuscript: Cherokee sacred formulas and medicinal prescriptions. Smithsonian Instit ution, Bureau of American Ethnology Bulletin 99. (Classic study of native Cherokee medicine, theory of disease, therapy, texts of curin formulas with translations, reproductions of original Cherokee manuscripts, linguistic notes, key to phonetic transcription, photographs, etc.)

1944. Bloomfield, Leonard. Secondary and tertiary responses to language. Language 20 (2):45-55.

1946. Bender, Ernest, and Zellig Harris. The phonemes of North Carolina Cherokee. IJAL 12:14-21.

1949. Bender, Ernest. Cherokee II. IJAL 15:223-28. (Texts, translations, word lists, morphemes.)

1953. Reyburn, William D. Cherokee verb morphology I. IJAL 19:172-80.

1958. Gulick, John. Language and passive resistance among the Eastern Cherokees. Ethnohistory 5:60-81.

1961. Lounsbury, Floyd G. Iroquois-Cherokee linguistic relations, with commentary by Mary R. Haas. In Symposium on Cherokee and Iroquois culture, Smithsonian Institution, Bureau of American Ethnology Bulletin 180.

1961. Yamachika, Raymond. Cherokee literature; printing in the Sequoyan Syllabary since 1828 with a bibliography. MS. Norman: University of Oklahoma.

1962. Kilpatrick, Jack F. An etymological note on the tribal name of the Cherokees and certain place and proper names derived from Cherokee. Journal of the Graduate Research Center (Southern Methodist University 30(1):37-41.

1962. ___. The Siquanid Dil'tidegi collection. Dallas: Bridwell Library, Southern Methodist University.

1962. White, John K. On the revival of printing in the Cherokee language. Current Anthropology 3 (5):511-14.

1962. White, John K., ed. The Swiss peasant. Chicago: Cherokee Phoenix Publications, 5425 S. Woodlawn Ave. (New edition of a nineteenth-century Christian morality story; printed in the syllabary.)

1963. Chafe, Wallace L., and Jack F. Kilpatrick. Inconsistencies in Cherokee spelling. _In_ Garfield, Viola E., and Chafe, eds., Symposium on language and culture, Proceedings of the 1962 Annual Spring Meeting of the American Ethnological Society. Seattle: University of Washington.

1963. Krueger, John R. Two early grammars of Cherokee. Anthropological Linguistics, March 1963. (Includes the Pickering grammar of 1831 and the von der Gabelenz grammar of 1852.)

1963. Shive, Richard. Cherokee reading grammar. 11 pp. Mimeographed. Chicago: Cherokee Phoenix Publications, 5425 S. Woodlawn Ave. (Sentences in the syllabary with translations.)

1964. Kilpatrick, Jack F. Folk formulas of the Oklahoma Cherokees. Journal of the Folklore Institute (Indiana University) 1(3):214-19. Reprinted The Hague: Mouton & Co., Box 1132. (Text, translation, notes.)

1964. ___, and Anna Gritts Kilpatrick. Cherokee burn conjurations. Journal of the Graduate Research Center 33 (1):17-21. (Text, translation, notes.)

1964. ___. A Cherokee conjuration to cure a horse. Southern Folklore Quarterly (University of Florida), Sept. 1964, pp. 216-18. (Text, translation, notes.)

1964. __. "The Foundation of life": the Cherokee national ritual. American Anthropologist 66 (6):1386-90. (Text, translation, notes.)

1964. __. Friends of thunder: folktales of the Oklahoma Cherokees. Dallas. (Reviewed by Alice Marriott, American Anthropologist 67 (1):143.

1965. __. Walk in your soul: love incantations of the Oklahoma Cherokees. Dallas: Southern Methodist University Press. (English translations, one short text on p. 43; reviewed by James Howard, Plains Anthropologist 2 [33]:233-34 [1966].)

1965. __. The shadow of Sequoyah: social documents of the Cherokees 1862 1964. Norman: University of Oklahoma Press. (English translations notes, a few photos of original manuscripts; reviewed by Paul Kutsch American Anthropologist 68 [5]:1291-92 [1966]. Reviewed also by Willard Walker, IJAL 33 [1]:82-84 [1967]. See also James Howard's review of both The Shadow of Sequoyah . . . and Walk in your Soul . . in Plains Anthropologist 2 [33]:233-34 [1966].)

1965. Kilpatrick, Jack F. , and Anna Gritts Kilpatrick. Sequoyah of earth and intellect. Austin: Encine Press.

1965. __. Verbs are kings at Panther Place: the Cherokee tongue versus "English". Southwest Review 50:372-76.

1965. Anonymous. P. H. S. Indian Hospital, Tahlequah, Oklahoma. Tahlequ Oklahoma: Social Service Dept. , Public Health Service Indian Hosp. (Description of hospital procedures, printed in the syllabary and in English.)

1965. Walker, Willard. Cherokee primer. First printing March 1965, 2nd printing Oct. 1965, rev. ed. Dec. 1965. Tahlequah, Okla. [Box 473 Carnegie Cross-Cultural Education Project of the University of Chic (Words and texts in the syllabary and in English translation, illustrations, some phonetic transcriptions. Primarily for Cherokee-speaking readers.)

1965. __. An experiment in programmed cross-cultural education: the import of the Cherokee primer for the Cherokee community and for the behavioral sciences. Mimeographed. March 1965. (An explanation o the purposes of the Cherokee Primer and the rationale for its design, with relevant information on Cherokee literacy, learning patterns, roles of the school, church, family, etc.)

1966. Kilpatrick, Anna Gritts, and J. F. Kilpatrick. Chronicles of Wolftown: social documents of the North Carolina Cherokees, 1850-1862. Smithsonian Institution, Bureau of American Ethnology Bulletin 196:1-111.

1966. Kilpatrick, Jack F., ed. The Wahnenauhi manuscript: historical sketches of the Cherokees, together with some of their customs, traditions, and superstitions. Smithsonian Institution, Bureau of American Ethnology Bulletin 196:175-213.

1966. ___, and Anna Gritts Kilpatrick. Eastern Cherokee folktales: reconstructed from the field notes of Frans M. Olbrechts. Smithsonian Institution, Bureau of American Ethnology Bulletin 196:379-447.

1966. Spade, Rev. Watt, and Willard Walker. Cherokee stories. Middletown, Conn.: Laboratory of Anthropology, Wesleyan University. (Seven stories printed in the syllabary with translations.)

1966. Wahrhaftig, Albert L. The Cherokee people today, trans. Calvin Nakedhead. Tahlequah, Oklahoma [Box 473, 74464]: Carnegie Cross-Cultural Education Project of the University of Chicago. (Statistics, map of the Oklahoma Cherokee communities, illustrations, printed in the syllabary and in English.)

1967. The Cherokee report, periodical, first issue dated Dec. 15, 1967, sponsored by The Original Cherokee Community Organization, 605 E. Downing St., Tahlequah, Okla. (Printed in the syllabary and in English.)

1967. Kilpatrick, Jack F., and Anna Gritts Kilpatrick. Muskogean charm songs among the Oklahoma Cherokees. Smithsonian Contributions to Anthropology 2 (3). (Curing songs, translations, notes.)

1967. ___. Run toward the nightland: magic of the Oklahoma Cherokees. Dallas: Southern Methodist University Press.

1967. ___. Concerning Kutsche's review of "The Shadow of Sequoyah". American Anthropologist 69 (5):515-16.

1967. Kutsche, Paul, Kutsche responds. American Anthropologist 69 (5):516.

1968. Indian Education Hearings before the Special Subcommittee on Indian Education of the Committee on Labor and Public Welfare. U. S. Senate, 90th Congress, 1st and 2nd sess., Pt. 2. Feb. 19, 1968. Twin Oaks, Okla.

1968. Kilpatrick, Jack F., and Anna Gritts Kilpatrick. New Echota letters, contributions of Samuel A. Worcester to the Cherokee Phoenix. Dall Southern Methodist University Press.

1969. Tax, Sol, and Robert K. Thomas. Education "for" American Indians: threat or promise? The Florida Fl Reporter, Spring/Summer 1969.

1969. Walker, Willard. Notes on native writing systems and the design of native literacy programs. Anthropological Linguistics 11 (5):148-66.

1970. Kilpatrick, Anna G. An introduction to Cherokee. Tahlequah, Okla.: Cherokee Bilingual Education Program, Northeastern State College. 67 pages.

1971. Alexander, J. T. Dictionary of the Cherokee Language. 359 pages. (Cherokee in syllabics to English and English to Cherokee in syllabi and in transliteration of syllabics, based on the Levi Gritts MS, n. d below.)

n. d. Cherokee hymn book, compiled from several authors and revised. Philadelphia: American Baptist Publication Society. (Currently available through John Roberts, Stilwell, Okla. 134 hymns printed in the syllabary.)

n. d. Gritts, Levi. Cherokee-English dictionary. MS. ca. 1950. Gilcrease Museum, Tulsa, Okla. (Cherokee word list in the syllabary with English translations, mostly nouns.)

n. d. Walker, Willard. Conversational Cherokee. MS. (144 pages on phonology, conversations, grammatical analysis.)

Choctaw Morphophonemics

Thurston Dale Nicklas

We present here the morphophonemics of Choctaw as spoken by a middle-aged woman raised in the vicinity of Stigler, Oklahoma, now living in Talihina, Oklahoma. This analysis is based on the most productive paradigms, leaving untouched stem formation. It consists of a list of ordered rules for affixation, internal change, and phonological processes. The processes of affixation described are intended only to provide sufficient illustrative material, and are hence incomplete. The rules for internal change are apparently complete; the phonological rules are sufficient to produce a broad phonetic transcription.

Forms are cited in systematic, intermediate, and phonetic notations. In systematic notations the infix -l- 'passive' is capitalized, and prefixes and suffixes are set apart with hyphens. Forms following > are intermediate, being closer to the phonetic as one progresses through the rules. Forms in square brackets are broad phonetic.

SOUNDS

The following sounds occur in systematic notations: p, t, č, k, b, f, ł, s, š, h, m, n, l, y, w, a, i, o, a., i., o., and high pitch accent sign (´).

In addition to the above, intermediate and phonetic notations include nasalized counterparts to the oral vowels, the marginal phonemes [ɛ] and [ɛ.], and a falling pitch accent written with the circumflex accent sign (ˆ). The symbol h represents a velar fricative in systematic notations, a faucal spirant in phonetic notations.

AFFIXATION[1]

Some verb stems are inflected for active and passive voice in one of the following three ways: (1) by adding -l- after the first stem vowel in the passive, (2) by adding -a in the passive and -li in the active, (3) by applying both (1) and (2). Examples: abani 'to barbeque', aLbani; baš-li 'to gash', baš-a; awaš-li 'to fry', aLwaš-a. Causatives add -či, occasionally -li. Examples: pisa 'to see', pisa-či 'to show'; okča 'to awaken (intr.)', okča-li 'to awaken (causative)'.

There are several series of pronominal affixes, which we list in the following order: first singular, second singular, third singular, first dual inclusive, first plural, second plural, third plural, reciprocal (where relevant). These may be reduced to two basic series, I and II. In listing the basic series we indicate morpheme boundaries; otherwise these prefixes are treated as unitary. Series I affixes are sa- (si-/_a, o), či-, i-, pi-, ha-pi, ha-či-, i-. Series II affixes are -li (the only suffix), iš-, zero, il- (i.-/_C), il-oh- or i.-hoh- (i.-ho-/_C), ha-iš- (the i is lost by a late rule), zero.

Series I is used to indicate inalienable possession, often with -h increment. Examples: sa-naksi 'my rib'; sah-foni 'my bone'. Series Ia has a- in place of sa-; it is used with a few kin terms, sometimes with the increment -h. Examples: a-ški 'my mother'; ah-pókni 'my grandmother'. Series Im is formed by adding the increment -m to Ia: am- (sam-/C_), čim-, im-, pim-, hapim-, hačim-, im-, ihtim-. Series Im is used for alienable possession and to indicate the indirect object of verbs. Examples: am-ófi 'my dog'; am-anompo-li 'to talk to me', ihtim-anompo-li 'to talk to each other'. Series I-zero differs from I by having no third person forms. It indicates the subject of passive verbs, stative verbs, and adjectives, and the object of transitive, active, and causative verbs. Examples: pisa 'to see him', sa-pisa 'to see me'; čito 'he is big', či-čito 'you are big'; ihti-pisa 'to see each other'.

Series II indicates the subject of active verbs. Examples: pisa-li 'I see', iš-pisa, pisa, i·-pisa, i·ho-pisa, haš-pisa, pisa.

When more than one series occurs with a verbal stem, the order of prefixes is II, Im, I-zero.

The negative is formed by suffixing -o and prefixing k-. Series II pronominals combine with k- as follows: a-k-, či-k-, i-k-, k-il- (k-i·-), k-iloh- (k-i·ho-), hači-k-, i-k-. Examples: a-k-pí·sa-o 'I don't see', či-k-pí·sa-o, i-k-pí·sa-o, k-i·-pí·sa-o, k-i·ho-pí·sa-o, hači-k-pí·sa-o, i-k-pí·sa-o. In the absence of a series II affix in the affirmative, i- is added to k-. Examples: i-k-čí·to-o 'he isn't big', i-k-či-čí·to-o 'you aren't big'.

There are approximately fifteen particles which are used in various combinations to form both conjunctions and article constructions. These include ma 'that', pa 'this', and the less easily defined o·ka and o·. In a sequence of particles, the last is inflected for case, -t (-š/o_) 'nominative' and -n 'oblique'. Examples: ma-t, ma-n, o-š, o-n. After -t and -n, but not -š, -o 'emphatic' may be affixed. Examples: ma-t-o, ma-n-o. When used as pronouns, ma and pa usually take ila- or ya- with the increment -h. Examples: ya-h-ma-t, ila-h-ma-t, ya-h-pa-t, ila-h-pa-t (all in the nominative).

The suffixes -óši 'diminutive' and -óba 'similar to, but larger' are added to nouns. Examples: čokfi 'rabbit', čokfi-óši 'young rabbit'; čokka 'house', čokka-óši 'small house'; yala 'grubworm', yala-óba 'tadpole'; issi 'deer', issi-óba 'horse', issi-óba-óši 'young horse'.

Enclitics include -tok 'recent past', -tto·k 'remote past', -a·či-n 'future', -a·či-ki 'future request', -a·hi 'subjunctive', and -ahínla 'potential'.

In what follows, we use the term 'theme' for verbal and noun themes. A verbal theme is a verbal stem plus (if present) the infix -l- 'passive' and the suffixes -li 'active', -a 'passive', -li 'causative' and -či 'causative'. A noun theme is a noun stem plus (if present) the suffixes -óši 'diminutive' and -óba 'similar to, but larger'.

PROSTHESIS

As all verb themes end in vowels, the shortest possible verb themes have the forms V, CV, and VCV. VCV themes include ani 'to fill', iši 'to take', iya 'to go', ona 'to arrive there', and osi 'little'. Three themes, a· 'to give', a· 'to say', and a 'copula', have the form V.[2] The existence of V and VCV types suggests the existence of the intermediate CV type.

Possible CV themes are bi 'to kill', la 'to arrive here', mo 'to harvest, mow', and pa 'to eat'. In the presence of a prefix, these themes have the form CV; in the absence of a prefix they appear with an initial a, presumably a prosthetic vowel. Examples: abi 'to kill', sa-bi 'to kill me', abi-li 'I kill', či-bi 'to kill you', iš-bi 'for you to kill'. Compare ani 'to fill', ani-li 'for me to fill', iš-ani 'for you to fill'.

Prosthesis precedes the infixation of -l- 'passive': amo 'to harvest', aLmo 'to be harvested'.

INTERNAL CHANGE

Verbals are subject to five internal changes giving a maximum of six forms which we call unchanged, n-grade ('continuative'), h-grade ('instantaneous'), hn-grade ('iterative'), y-grade ('completive'), and the lengthened grade, which replaces the unchanged form in the negative and before the conjunctions na and ča 'and then next'. Internal change follows affixation and prosthesis. We discuss the changed grades in turn. Forms of the following themes will not be glossed: takči 'to tie', falama 'to return', kobafa 'to break', wa·ya 'to grow', pisa 'to see', ona 'to arrive there', a· 'to say', bi 'to kill', isso 'to hit'.

The n-grade is formed by infixing -n- after the penultimate theme vowel; subsequently this vowel is accented. Examples: tánkči, falánma, wá·nya, pínsa, ónna. Themes of the form V suffix the -n to that vowel. Themes of the form CV infix the -n after the preceding prefix or prosthetic vowel. Examples: á·n, ánbi, čínbi.

The h-grade is formed by infixing -h-, with subsequent accentuation, placed as with the n-grade. Examples: táhkči, faláhma, wá·hya, píhsa, óhna, áhbi, číhbi.

The hn-grade is formed by (1) infixing -n-, (2) infixing -h-, and

(3) accentuation, in that order. Examples: táhnkči, faláhnma, wá·hnya, pínhsa, óhnna, áhnbi, čínhnbi, á·hn.

The first process in the formation of the y-grade is the expansion of verbals with short themes. Long themes have the form . . . $VC^1VC^2V\#$, where . . . may be null, C^1 is a single consonant, and C^2 is one or more consonants. All other themes are short. Verbals with short themes are expanded by changing the penultimate theme vowel, whether long or short, to VyV; verbals with CV themes change the prosthetic or prefix vowel. The following rules are then applied: (1) the penultimate theme vowel, or prosthetic or prefix vowel in the case of CV themes, is lengthened if followed by a single consonant; (2) the antepenultimate theme (prosthetic, or prefix) vowel is accented; (3) the consonant following the accented vowel is doubled. Examples: táyyakči, óyyo·na, fálla·ma, kóbba·fa, áyya·bi, sáyya·bi. Where the changed vowel of a short theme verbal is i, one would expect to find íyyi(·) in the y-grade. However, a phonological rule following rule (2) above deletes y between two i's, and the two i's then form a long vowel with a falling accent. Examples: pisa > piyisa > piyi·sa > píyi·sa > píi·sa > pî·sa. Similarly, čî·bi, î·šbi, î·sso.

The lengthened grade is formed by lengthening as in rule (1) immediately above, with subsequent accentuation of the lengthened vowel. Examples: tákči, falá·ma, wá·ya, pí·sa, ó·na, á·, á·bi, čí·bi (before ča and na); i-k-tákči-o, i-k-falá·ma-o, i-k-wá·ya-o, i-k-pí·sa-o, i-k-ó·na-o, í-k-bi-o, i-k-čí·bi-o (negatives).

To summarize, the following rules have been discussed up to this point:

(1) Affixation

(2) Prosthesis

(3) Infixation of -n- (n- and hn-grades)

(4) Infixation of -h- (h- and hn-grades)

(5) Expansion of verbals with short themes (y-grade)

(6) Vowel lengthening (y- and lengthened grades)

(7) Accentuation of the antepenultimate (y-grade) or penultimate (other changed grades) theme, prosthetic, or prefix vowel

(8) Contraction of íyi(·) to î.

(9) Doubling of post-accent consonant (y-grade)

PHONOLOGICAL RULES

We continue now with the remainder of the phonological rules, numbered in sequence to the summary above.

(10) The sequence N^1N^2C is reduced to N^2C, if C is a stem consonant. The longer sequence results from rule (3). Examples: omba 'to rain', ónmba > ómba, óhnmba > óhmba; impa 'to dine', ínmpa > ímpa, íhnmpa > íhmpa; čany-li 'to saw', čánny-li > čány-li; ačonw-li 'to sew', ačónnw-li > ačónw-li; but fánm-li (fam-li 'to spank, beat') remains unreduced, since l is not a stem consonant.

(11) Long vowels are shortened before hC and lC. The h results from rule (4), and the l is the passive infix. Examples: wa.ya 'to grow (of plants)', wá.hya > wáhya, wá.hnya > wáhnya; a.Lfoh-a > aLfoh-a 'to be wrapped around'; a.Lpitta > aLpitta 'to be put into a container'; the active forms of the last two examples are a.foh-li and a.pitta.

(12) The sequence V^1V^2 is reduced to V^2, when V^2 is the initial vowel of a suffix or enclitic. Examples with -óši 'diminutive' and -óba 'augmentative': čokfi-óši > čokfóši 'young rabbit', yala-óba > yalóba 'tadpole'. Examples with the negative suffix -o: a-k-pí.sa-o > akpí.so 'I don't see', i-k-čí.to-o > ikčí.to 'he isn't big'. Examples with enclitics: takči-a.čin > takča.čin 'he will tie', takči-ahínla > takčahínla 'he can tie', takči-li-a.čin takčila.čin 'I will tie', takči-li-ahínla > takčilahínla 'I can tie', a-k-tákči-o-a.čin > aktákča.čin 'I won't tie'.

(13) The basic form of the vowel-lengthening rule is as follows: In a sequence of short syllables $S^1S^2S^3 \ldots S^n$, the vowels of even-numbered syllables are lengthened, except in final position. A short syllable is V or CV, where V is short. Examples with habina 'to receive a present' and pisa 'to see' with či- 'you (object)', -či 'causative', and -li 'I (subject)', [habi.na], [čiha.bina], [habi.nali], [čiha.bina.li], [habi.nači], [čiha.bina.či], [habi.nači.li], [čiha.bina.čili]; [pisa], [čipi.sa], [pisa.li], [čipi.sali], [pisa.či], [čipi.sači], [pisa.čili], [čipi.sači.li].

The scope of the vowel-lengthening rule is the sequence of short syllables to which it may apply. There are phonological and morphological limitations on the scope. All theme vowels are within the scope. Lengthening follows (12), so that initial suffix and enclitic vowels are within the scope. Examples:

čokfi 'rabbit', čokfi-óši > čokfóši 'young rabbit', but ópa 'owl', opa-óši > opóši > opó.ši 'young owl'; yala [yala] 'grubworm', yala-óba > yalóba > yaló.ba 'tadpole', but issi 'deer', issi-óba > issóba > issóba 'horse'; takči-ahínla > takčahínla 'he can tie', but pisa-ahínla > pisahínla > pisa.hínla 'he can see'. A vowel followed by a consonant initial enclitic is word final, hence never lengthens. Examples: pisa-li > pisa.li 'I see', but pisa-tok > pisatok 'he saw'.

With prefixes the situation is more complicated. The scope does not extend beyond the final syllable of a sequence of prefixes; that is, the last prefix syllable, if short, can count as S^1 of the scope, but cannot itself be lengthened.[3] Examples: pisa 'to see', i.ho-pisa > i.hopi.sa 'we see', či-pisa > čipi.sa 'to see you', ha-či-pisa > hačipi.sa (not hači.pisa) 'to see you (pl.)', i.ho-či-pisa > i.hočipi.sa (not i.hoči.pisa) 'we see you (pl.)'; iši 'to take (pick up)', im-iši > imi.ši 'to take it for him', iš-iši > iši.ši 'you take it', iš-im-iši > išimi.ši (not iši.miši) 'you take it for him', čim-iši > čimi.ši 'to take it for you', ha-čim-iši > hačimi.ši (not hači.miši) 'to take it for you (pl.)'. In addition, the scope does not extend beyond an initial theme vowel if the theme is longer than two syllables. Examples: apila 'to help him', iš-apila > išapi.la (not iša.pila) 'you help him' im-apila > imapi.la (not ima.pila) 'to help him for him'. (Compare the treatment of iši above.) The same limitation applies to noun themes.[4] Examples: ofi 'dog', čim-ófi[5] > čimó.fi 'your dog', ha-čim-ófi > hačimó.fi 'your (pl.) dog'; ohoyo > oho.yo 'woman', čim-ohóyo > čimohó.yo (not čimo.hóyo) 'your wife'; notakfa 'jaw', či-notakfa > čino.takfa 'your jaw', ha-či-notakfa > hačino.takfa (not hači.notakfa) 'your (pl.) jaws'.

A prefix final consonant outside the scope of vowel-lengthening, followed by a vowel, ranges in length from short to the length of geminates; this lengthening is more pronounced in slow speech. Examples: iš(š)imi.ši, iš(š)api.la, im(m)api.la (glossed above), iš-im-apila > iš(š)im(m)api.la 'you help him for him'; čim(m)ohó.yo (glossed above).

(14) The sequence C^1C^1-li is reduced to C^1C^1-i, where C^1 is not a nasal, and -li is the active suffix. Examples: fokk-li > fokk-i 'to put inside', fokk-a 'to be inside'; kočč-li > kočč-i 'to put outside', kočč-a 'to go outside'.

(15) The sequence $V^1C^1C^2C^3$ is subject to epenthesis, yielding $V^1C^1V^1C^2C^3$, if C^1 is not a nasal. The accent, if any, shifts to the epenthetic vowel. These three-consonant clusters result from the infixation of passive -l- and -h- of the h- and hn-grades. Examples: taLkči > talakči 'to be tied', hoLyya > holoyya 'to be dripping'; táhkči > tahákči, hóhyya > hohóyya, h-grades of takči 'to tie' and hoyya 'to drip'; táhnkči > tahánkči píhnsa > pihínsa, hn-grades of takči 'to tie' and pisa 'to see'.

(16) The sequence V^1-i is reduced to V^1, this V^1 having the length and tonal features of i. Examples of the grades of isso 'to hit him' and sa-issc 'to hit me': isso, ínsso, íhsso > ihísso, íhnsso > ihínsso, íyisso > î·sso, ísso; sasso, sánsso, sahísso, sahínsso, sâ·sso, sásso.

(17) The sequence V·N (N = nasal) changes to V̨(·). The sequence VN changes to V̨· before a single consonant, V̨ elsewhere. These changes occur in certain environments, which we now enumerate.

(a) It occurs finally, except in nouns. Examples: ma-n > mą 'that objective', ma-n-o > mano 'that objective emphatic', -a·či-n > -a·čį 'future tense enclitic', am issi-hákšop 'my deer hide' > ą issi-hákšop (before compound nouns the possessive prefixes are not affixed; compare amissi 'my deer'). This final nasal is always an affix of some sort. A very few nouns, and no other parts of speech, end in a nasal, always n. This cannot be treated as basic m, as it remains n before the diminutive suffix -óši; it is not nn for the same reason. Examples: niškin 'eye' (a loanworc from Algonquian), tákkon 'peach' (a loanword from Siouan apparently), yołkc 'mole', čołkan 'spider'; takkonó·ši 'plum'.

(b) It also occurs before a non-nasal consonant within morpheme boundaries. If these nasals can be considered homorganic with the followin consonant, the one exception, łamko 'strong' (Byington writes łampko, łimpko) is accounted for. Examples: ámpo > [ą́·po] 'dish', onsi > [ǫ·si] 'eagle', okčank > [okčą·k] 'melon', hánwa > [hą́·wa] 'locust', lonssa > [lǫssa] 'river bottom land', hallons > [hallǫ·s] 'leech', biyónkko > [biyǫ́kko] 'strawberry', tínškila > [tį́škila] 'bluejay', impa > [į·pa] 'to eat', łabanka > [łabą·ka] 'to snore'. Examples of VN before nasal consonants: onna 'to dawn', homma 'red'.

(c) Nasalization occurs before any consonant if the nasal is the last consonant of an affix. Examples with Im series prefixes: [amissi] 'my deer', [ą·pala] 'my lamp', [ą·tabi] 'my cane', [ą·čókka] 'my house', [ą·kofi] 'my guinea fowl', [ą·bina] 'my camphouse', [ą·mį·ko] 'my chief', [ą·naki] 'my bullet', [ą·lowak] 'my fire'. Examples of the n-grade: ona 'to arrive there', ónna > [ǫ́·na] (compare onna > [onna] 'to dawn'); homi 'bitter', hónmi > [hǫ́·mi] (compare homma > [homma] 'red'); takči 'to tie', tánkči > [tą́kči]; ši·p-li > [ši·bli] 'to stretch', ší·np-li > [šį́·bli]; nokšo·p-li > [nokšo·bli] 'to scare', nokšó·np-li > [nokšǫ́·bli]. The hn-grades of the last two examples are ši·hnp-li > šíhnpli > šihínpli > šihį́pli > [šihį́bli] and [nokšohǫ́bli]. It is apparent that all nasal vowels are long before single consonants, while long and short nasal vowels contrast before two consonants; examples of length contrasts among nasal vowels exist for all three vowel qualities.

(18) y is lost before l; w is lost before l if preceded by a high back vowel. Examples of active and passive forms of čany 'to saw', ačonw 'to sew', anow 'to tell', and kow- 'to spank': čany-li > čąyli > čą.li, but čany-a > čą.ya; ačonw-li > ačǫwli > ačǫ.li, but aLčonw-a > alčǫ.wa; anow-li > ano.li, but aLnow-a > alnowa; kow-li > ko.li, but kowa. Apparently the loss of a semivowel is accompanied by compensatory lengthening.

(19) The sequence Bl becomes BB, where B is b, f, m, or w. Examples: atob-li > atobbi 'to pay', kobaf-li > kobaffi 'to break', akam-li > akammi 'to stopper', tiw-li > tiwwi 'to open'.

(20) The sequence ƚl becomes ƚƚ. Examples: naƚ-li > naƚƚi 'to sting', haƚ-li > haƚƚi 'to kick'.

(21) The sequence ln becomes nn. Examples: taLna > tanna 'to be woven', aLnow-a > annowa 'to be told'.

(22) The sequence lC becomes ƚC when C is voiceless. Examples: aLkam-a > aƚkama 'to be stoppered', aLtah-a > aƚtaha 'to be finished', aLpoš-a > aƚpoša 'to be parched'.

(23) The sequence ƚF becomes hF, where F is a fricative or č. Examples: aLčifa > aƚčifa > ahčifa 'to be washed', a.Lfoh-a > alfoha > aƚfoha > ahfoha 'to be wrapped around', aLčonw-a > aƚčǫ.wa > ahčǫ.wa 'to be sewn'.

(24) The sequence hC may become CC. There are several examples of this sequence, which we enumerate.

(a) The -h increment always assimilates in the articles and in inalienable nouns with bound stems. Examples: ya-h-ma-t > yammat 'that nominative', ila-h-pa-t > ilappat 'this nominative'; i-h-bak > ibbak 'his hand', i-h-yi > iyyi 'his foot', i-h-takka > ittakka 'his mouth'. It always assimilates in the reciprocal prefix; i-h-ti > itti-. In inalienable nouns with free stems, it always assimilates to a resonant, but assimilates optionally to an obstruent. Examples: nali 'back', i-h-nali > innali 'his back'; fóni 'bone', i-h-fóni > ihfóni or iffóni 'his bone'; tahči 'shoulder', i-h-tahči > ihtahči or ittahči 'his shoulder'; čonkaš 'heart', i-h-čonkaš > ihčǫ.kaš > ihčǫ.kaš or iččǫ.kaš 'his heart'. A few of the obstruent initial stems always seem to undergo the assimilation, while a few others never seem to undergo it.

(b) h which is derived from l by (22) and (23), and the infix -h- optionally assimilate only to following fricatives and to č. Examples: ahčǫ.wa or aččǫ.wa 'to be sewn'; ahfoha or affoha 'to be wrapped around', nosi 'to sleep', nóhsi > nóhsi or nóssi; pisa-či 'to show', pisáhči > pisáhči or pisáčči.

(c) There is comparative evidence for other assimilations of hC, but these result in no doublets in the present dialect. For example, Byington gives fohka and kohcha for fokka and kočča of the present dialect.

(25) The sequences pl and tl become bl and dl, respectively; d subsequently becomes l. Examples: ši.p-li > ši.bli 'to stretch' (passive: ši.pa); bičot-li > bičodli > bičolli 'to bend' (passive: bičo.ta).

(26) The sequences ihV and ohV becomes iyV and owV, respectively, when V is not accented. This rule is optional, leading to doublets. Examples: ni·ha or ni·ya 'fat', ačaffoha or ačaffowa 'few'; [a·fohli] 'to wrap around', [ahfowa] 'to be wrapped around'.

(27) The sequence šs becomes ss. This assimilation is also optional, being more usual in faster speech. Examples: iš-sakki > issakki 'you overtake'; iš-sa-pisa > išsapi.sa > issapi.sa 'you see me'.

(28) The sequence Vyy becomes iyy after š or č. Many examples occur in the y-grade. Examples: ša·.li 'to carry', šáyya.li > šíyya.li; čomi 'somewhat', čóyyo.mi > číyyo.mi.

(29) The sequence ayy becomes ɛyy; this always occurs in the y-grade of verbals, sporadically elsewhere. Examples: táyyakči > tɛ́yyakči, from

takči 'to tie'; *hayyip > hɛyyip 'lake', *bayyi > bɛyyi 'nephew'; but sa-h-yi > sayyi 'my foot', *kayya > kayya 'full after eating'. The following derivations are of some interest: ša > aša > áyya.ša (y-grade) > ɛ́yya·ša or íyya·ša; *iláyyo·ka > ilíyyo·ka 'various'. (Note these contrasts: [hɛyyip] 'lake', [kayya] 'full after eating', [čiyyi] 'your foot', [hoyya] 'to drip'; this list is easily expanded.)

(30) There are two more sources for an ɛ-like sound. When the first person prefix si- is followed by a, and to some extent when followed by o, it is lowered. Examples: si-ačokma > sɛačokma 'I am good', si-abika > sɛabi.ka 'I am sick'.

When ki or hi follow a or o, i commonly breaks to ɛy. Examples: akínli > akį́.li > akį́.li or akɛ̨́yli 'indeed', waki-li > waki.li or wakɛyli 'to raise'.

In a single word ia has become ɛ., this being the only occurrence of ɛ. and the only vowel which can be used in this word: ihti-álbi > ittɛ́.lbi 'eyelid'.

OTHER CHANGES

The rules given above are sufficient for converting systematic representations into broad phonetic notations.[6] Two more rules are of some interest, namely weak epenthesis and weak nasalization.

Weak epenthesis occurs between k or h and a following resonant or b. The epenthetic vowel has the quality of the preceding vowel. Examples: ikbi > $ik^{i}bi$ 'to make', hokli > $hok^{o}li$ 'to catch', tahli > $tah^{a}li$ 'to finish'. After nasal vowels, instead of epenthesis, voicing and nasalization occur. Examples of the n-grades: [į́ŋbi], [hǫ́ŋli], [tą́.li].

Weak nasalization occurs in the vicinity of nasal consonants; it is strongest when both of the following conditions are met: the vowel is long or final and follows the nasal consonant.

NOTES

1. Labels for inflectional categories give approximate meanings only.

2. All three verb stems of the form V seem to derive from proto-Muskogean roots of the form *ka. As far as I know, there are no cognates for the Choctaw copula in the other Muskogean languages. However, if the copula a is etymologically related to the passive suffix -a, as seems likely, then it is derived from *ka. Compare the passive suffixes Choctaw -a, Koasati -ka, Creek -k. The root *ka 'to say' also occurred with the suffixes *-či and *-li. Compare Choctaw a·, a·či, a·li with Koasati ka and Creek keyč- (*ka-či > kaič- > kayč- > keyč-). The root *ka 'to give' always occurs with a series Im prefix. With *im-ka we derive Choctaw im-a·, Alabama iŋ-ka. In Miccosukee the Im prefix has become part of the root, and a new prefix is added: im-iŋka-.

3. An exception to this restriction is the reflexive prefix i-li-, which we have not considered. The morpheme li- is lengthened: ili-pisa-li > ili·pisa·li 'I see myself'.

4. We have at hand no data on VCV noun stems with either -óši or -óba which would indicate whether they admit prefixes in the scope of lengthening. However, the following is suggestive: ofi 'dog' forms a diminutive with osi 'little' in the n-grade, and a general nominal suffix -k, giving ofónsik. The scope of lengthening does not extend to prefixes with this word.

5. A few inalienably possessed nouns are accented. The most common are -čókka 'home' from čokka 'house', -ohóyo 'wife' from ohoyo 'woman', and -ófi 'dog' from ofi 'dog'. Usually there is a change of meaning, as indicated. The accent on the possessed form of ofi is unexpected. However, according to Byington, in the last century ofi could not be inflected for possession; the root -pʋf was used instead. This feature is reminiscent of some Algonquian languages.

6. While these rules appear to exhaust the morphophonemic variations of this dialect, their formulation and ordering can be improved. In particular, a cycle in the application of two rules must be provided for, and rule (6) must be reformulated and placed after rule (13).

The rules involved in the cycle are (11) and (15). Rule (11) shortens a long vowel followed by hC or lC; rule (15) inserts an epenthetic vowel after h and l in the clusters hCC and lCC. Rule (11) must precede (15). These rules apply first to themes with the passive infix -l-; the passive of takči 'to tie' is taLkči > talakči. The epenthetic vowel is now the penultimate theme vowel which the infixes of the internal changes follow. The h-form of talakči is taláhkči > talahákči. Rule (15) applies first to the cluster lkč, then later to the cluster hkč.

Rule (6) as it applies to the lengthened grade, but not the y-grade, must follow rule (13). The only forms for which the order matters are verbals with the suffix -li 'I'. If the vowel preceding -li is lengthened by (13), then it is the vowel to which rule (6) and accentuation apply, rather than the penultimate theme vowel. For example, apa-li 'I eat' > apa·li by rule (13), with lengthened form apá·li, not á·pali.

REFERENCE

Byington, Cyrus. 1915. A dictionary of the Choctaw language. Smithsonian Institution, Bureau of American Ethnology Bulletin 46.

The Position of Chickasaw in Western Muskogean

William Pulte

Chickasaw, of all the Muskogean languages and dialects, has received perhaps the least attention from linguists.[1] Since Gatschet (1884), writing almost a century ago, reported the Chickasaw to be virtually identical to the Choctaw in language and culture, the Chickasaw dialect has apparently not been the object of further study.

It would seem desirable, however, to know more about the present-day status of Chickasaw and its relationship to Choctaw, since the reconstruction of Proto-Muskogean depends to a large extent on adequate knowledge of Western Muskogean, the branch of the Muskogean family consisting of Choctaw-Chickasaw, and of the dialect variation existing within it. The importance of Western Muskogean dialect forms has already been shown in one instance; Haas (1963) was able to complete the reconstruction of the Proto-Muskogean-Algonquian word for skunk only after consulting Gatschet's unpublished Chickasaw word list and finding a conservative variant form.[2]

The purpose of this paper is to present the results of a preliminary survey undertaken in Oklahoma in an attempt to determine the extent of dialect variation within Western Muskogean.[3] In particular, the question of the linguistic validity of the labels Choctaw and Chickasaw will be examined.

Gatschet (1884:117) noted the existence of several dialects within Choctaw, including "the Sixtown dialect, the ones spoken from Mobile bay to New Orleans, those heard on the Lower Mississippi River, and that of the Chicasa This description of the nineteenth-century dialect division within Choctaw does not give Chickasaw equal rank, but rather implies that Chickasaw is bu one of several Choctaw dialects; were this the case, it would be misleading to speak of Western Muskogean as being composed of Choctaw-Chickasaw, since these labels would then be indicative of political, but not linguistic, groupings.

The available data point toward the opposite conclusion, however. The results of the preliminary survey reveal that there is only slight dialect variation among Chickasaw speakers, and when word lists obtained from Choctaw informants from various areas of Oklahoma are compared,[4] the same conclusion is reached in the case of Choctaw. When Choctaw is compared with Chickasaw, however, relatively extensive lexical differences appear; in addition, certain differences are found in the phonologies of the two dialects.

The lexical data will be examined first.[5] Choctaw and Chickasaw have different terms for a number of body parts, e. g. , Choc. i-konla, Chick. nokistak 'neck' , Choc. i-bi-šakni, Chick. i-bi-čala 'nose' , Choc. i-yyi-kalaha, Chick. i-yyi-tonška 'knee' , Choc. i-nnali, Chick. nałcaba 'back' , and Choc. niškin, Chick. -škin 'eye' .[6] Other basic lexical differences include Choc. ohoyo, Chick. ehoo 'woman' , Choc. alla, Chick. čipota 'child' , Choc. čito, Chick. išto 'large' , Choc. iskitini, Chick. iškannosi 'small' , Choc. moma, Chick. katima 'still' (adverbial), Choc. čišno, Chick. išno 'you' , and Choc. pišno, Chick. pošno 'we' . The last item is of particular interest, since the Choctaw form pišno, contrasting with pošno in all the Eastern Muskogean languages, is one of the criteria employed by Haas (1950:123) in separating Eastern and Western Muskogean. The Chickasaw data show, however, that pošno occurs in both branches of Muskogean, with only Choctaw in the west and Apalachee in the east exhibiting the less common pišno.

Animal terms are different in a number of instances, including Choc. hoši, Chick. foši 'bird' , Choc. tolok-lonha, Chick. čoklowa 'turkey' , Choc. katos, Chick. kowi 'cat' , and Choc. šokhata, Chick. šokka čokyahanli 'possum' .[7]

A regular correspondence exists between Choc. final -ya and Chick. -ha; consider the following forms: Choc. falaya, Chick. falaha 'long', Choc. okčanya, Chick. okčanha 'alive', Choc. yaanya, Chick. yanha 'he cries'. It should be noted that an optional rule operates in Chickasaw to delete h in the above forms, giving rise to alternations such as [falaha]~[fala:].

In the phonetic data, a Choctaw long nasalized vowel corresponds to Chickasaw vowel plus nasal in certain environments, e. g., Choc. [tą:či], Chick. [tanči] 'corn', Choc. [ǫ:ba], Chick. [omba] 'to rain', Choc. [hasį:biš], Chick. [hasimbiš] 'tail'. These differences at the phonetic level can be explained by positing the presence of slightly different rules of vowel nasalization in the grammars of the two dialects. In Choctaw, the nasalization rule applies before a non-nasal consonant, before morpheme boundary followed by a consonant, and word finally. In Chickasaw, the process is more restricted, as the following examples reveal: /išonš/ [išǫ:š] 'worm', /takkonlo/ [takkǫ:lo] 'apple', /am+hattak/ [ą:hattak] 'my husband', /am+ehoo/ [amebo:] 'my wife', /am+waka/ [ą:waka] 'my cow', /tanči/ [tanči] 'corn', /akanka/ [akaŋka] 'chicken', and /hasimbiš/ [hasimbiš] 'tail'. Note that nasalization does not occur before stops in Chickasaw, as it does in Choctaw, but only before fricatives; nor does the Chickasaw nasalization rule apply before a morpheme boundary in Chickasaw unless a glide or liquid follows, as the forms for *my wife*, *my cow*, and *my husband* show. It is apparent that the more general rule is present in Choctaw. Assuming the correctness of the hypothesis advanced by King (1969:58-63) to the effect that rules tend to become more general as they spread from dialect to dialect,[8] it would seem likely that the process of vowel nasalization was innovated in Chickasaw and was later borrowed by Choctaw. Alternatively, it might be supposed that the rule existed in its more restricted form before the divergence of the two tribal groups, with subsequent generalization of the rule in Choctaw after the split.

A further difference between Choctaw and Chickasaw at the phonetic level involves the presence of glottal stop medially in Chickasaw in certain forms, in which a long vowel varies freely with a sequence of short vowel plus glottal stop, e. g., [to:wa] ~ [toʔwa] 'ball', [aliba:mo] ~ [alibaʔmo] 'Alabama Indian', and [čokyaha:li] [čokyahąʔli] 'grinning'. Such instances of medial glottal stop, which is never found in Choctaw, can perhaps best be accounted for by positing an optional rule in Chickasaw which converts a long vowel to the corresponding short vowel plus glottal stop in the correct set of environments.

In the light of the above data, it can be concluded that it is correct to speak of a single Western Muskogean language, Choctaw-Chickasaw, divided into the two dialects indicated by the compound name. Since the lexical differences between the two dialects are fairly extensive, further work toward the reconstruction of Proto-Muskogean should include an adequate study of the Chickasaw lexicon.

NOTES

1. I would like to thank Dale Nicklas for his comments, and for providing me with Choctaw data which helped make this paper possible. A special debt of gratitude is due Isaac Underwood for his hospitality and patience in attempting to teach me something of the Chickasaw language, and to the late Homer Alberson, who provided a number of texts and who was always eager to serve as informant.

2. The word list in question is deposited in the archives of the Smithsonian Institution.

3. The Chickasaw data was provided by informants from Tishomingo and Ada, Oklahoma; the Choctaw informants are from Madill, McAlester, Broken Bow, and Talihina, Oklahoma.

4. Unfortunately, no data from Mississippi Choctaw was available, and it is conceivable that former dialect differences in Choctaw have been leveled in Oklahoma. The conclusion reached below must therefore remain tentative until Mississippi Choctaw and Oklahoma Choctaw can be compared.

5. Throughout this study systematic phonemic representation is indicated by / /, or by absence of brackets. Phonetic representation is indicated by [ ].

6. The term for <u>eye</u> is an Algonquian loan; the Choctaw form retains the Algonquian prefix ni-, while the Chickasaw variant does not. I am indebted to Dale Nicklas for this observation.

7. The Chickasaw phrase for <u>possum</u> is, literally, 'grinning pig'.

8. The hypothesis in question, which might aptly be termed the "generalization hypothesis", was first suggested, I believe, in Bach (1968) and Harms (1967).

REFERENCES

Bach, Emmon. 1968. Two proposals concerning the simplicity metric in phonology. Glossa 2:128-49.

Gatschet, Albert S. 1884. A migration legend of the Creek Indians, vol. 1. Brinton's Library of Aboriginal American Literature, Number 4. Philadelphia.

Haas, Mary R. 1950. The position of Apalachee in the Muskogean family. IJAL 15:121-27.

___. 1963. The Muskogean and Algonkian words for skunk. IJAL 29:65-66.

Harms, Robert. 1967. Split, shift, and merger in the Permic vowels. Ural-Altaische Jahrbücher 39:161-98.

King, Robert D. 1969. Historical linguistics and generative grammar. Englewood Cliffs, N. J.: Prentice-Hall.

What is Mobilian?

Mary R. Haas

There are references in the literature for the past two hundred years or more to a trade language or jargon used by Indians of the southeastern part of North America. James Mooney, in 1900, gave a brief description of it as well as an estimate of the range of its use:

> This trade jargon, based upon Choctaw, but borrowing also from all the neighboring dialects and even from the more northern Algonquian languages, was spoken and understood among all the tribes of the Gulf states, probably as far west as Matagorda bay and northward along both banks of the Mississippi to the Algonquian frontier about the entrance of the Ohio. It was called Mobilienne by the French, from Mobile, the great trading center of the Gulf region. Along the Mississippi it was sometimes known also as the Chickasaw trade language... (p. 187).

Although Mooney's description of the jargon is rather precise, it is not known that he had any actual linguistic material to base it on. A century earlier John Sibley reported, according to Mooney (1900:187), that Mobilian "was spoken in addition to their native languages by all the Indians who had come from the east side of the Mississippi. Among those so using it he names the

Alabama, Apalachi, Biloxi, Choctoo, Pacana, Pascagula, Taensas, and Tunica." Thomas S. Woodward, writing in the middle of the nineteenth century, also commented on the jargon (p. 79): "There is yet a language the Texas Indians call the Mobilian tongue, that has been the trading language of almost all the tribes that have inhabited the country... It is a mixture of Creek, Choctaw, Chickasay, Netches [Natchez], and Apelash [Apalachi]."

When I worked on the Tunica language in the 1930's, Sesostrie Youchigant, my Tunica informant, also knew of the jargon, which he referred to by its French name, Mobilienne, and he was able to remember two or three words which appeared to be Choctaw or Chickasaw. I unfortunately did not make any inquiries about the jargon among the Koasati in western Louisiana or the Alabama in east Texas.

In the late 1960's I heard from Claude Medford that there were still some persons who speak the jargon among the Alabama and the Koasati and so I encouraged Dr. James M. Crawford to collect some information on it when he got a chance. The chance came in the summer of 1970 and he kindly sent me a few pages of the material he had collected. There is more material on tape but it has not yet been transcribed. He has given me permission to make use of the transcribed material to see if I could determine what the jargon is based on. This report gives the results of my preliminary investigation.

The jargon, at least as spoken by Crawford's informants,[1] appears to be a mixture of Choctaw[2] and Alabama.[3] Both of these languages are Muskogean and in addition probably share more lexical items than any two other Muskogean languages. But there are also many differences and it is among these that it is possible to determine which language is the source for any given lexical item. The kind of vocabulary mixture that has been found can be seen in the following list:[4]

	Alabama	Choctaw	Mobilian
fish:	łało	nani	šlašu
squirrel:	ipło	fani	fani
horse:	čičoba	(is)suba	suba
dog:	ifa	ofi	ofi
eat:	ipa	apa	apa
fire:	tikba	lowak	lowak
water:	oki	oka	oki
rain:	oyba	omba	hoyba
friend:	am-okla my ——	aŋ-ka·na my ——	mog(u)la fina good ——

The most interesting feature of the jargon, however, lies in the simplification of the morphology. In this it shows differences from both Choctaw and Alabama. Both of the latter languages distinguish inalienable possession (marked by one set of prefixes) from alienable possession (marked by another set of prefixes), both conjugate static verbs by means of the inalienable prefixes, and both use a discontinuous morpheme (though with different rules) in the formation of the negative. In all these respects Mobilian differs from both languages but has put together a simpler construction for each of these out of Alabama and Choctaw morphemes. These features are described next.

The independent personal pronouns of Mobilian are taken from Alabama,[5] not from Choctaw. They are:

	Alabama	Choctaw	Mobilian
I:	ino	ano	inu
you:	išno	čišno	išnu
we:	pošno	pišno, hapišno	pošnu

In Choctaw 'your father' is expressed by an alienable prefix plus stem, thus: činki. In Mobilian it is the independent personal pronoun 'you' plus 'his father', thus: šnu inke 'your father'. The static verb 'to want' is conjugated through the use of the inalienable prefixes in Choctaw (and Alabama) (left-hand column) but through the use of the independent pronouns in Mobilian, e. g.,

oki sabanna 'I'm thirsty'	oki inu bana 'I'm thirsty'
oki čibanna 'are you thirsty?'	oki šnu bana 'are you thirsty?'

The negative construction is quite complex in both Choctaw and Alabama. In Choctaw it consists of the discontinuous morpheme ik...o in which ik- is prefixed to the stem and -o is suffixed (accompanied by the regular vowel deletion rule, $...V\# \rightarrow \emptyset$ / __-V), e. g. ,

Choctaw Positive	Choctaw Negative
fala•ya 'long, tall'	ikfala•yo 'not long, tall'
lawa 'many'	iklawo 'not many'

In Koasati (and probably also in Alabama) the rules for forming the negative are more complex in that the element -ik- is sometimes infixed instead of being prefixed (and the rules can be stated), e. g. ,

Koasati Positive	Koasati Negative
alokpa 'sharp'	alokikpo 'dull'

In Mobilian all of this has been simplified. The discontinuous morpheme ik... o is not used. Instead the Choctaw independent negative ekšo 'it is not' follows the term being negated. There is also a vowel-deletion rule but it is the reverse of the usual Muskogean rules in that it deletes the first vowel of ekšo and the final vowel of the preceding word is retained, e. g. ,

$$\#V_2 \rightarrow \emptyset / V_1\_\_$$

Thus we have the following:

Mobilian Positive	Mobilian Negative
falaya 'tall'	falayakšu 'short' (or: falaya ekšu)
alokpa 'sharp'	alokpakšu 'dull'
lawa 'many'	lawakšu 'not many'
čito 'big'	čitokšu 'small'

The vowel-deletion rule given for Mobilian is not limited to the forms in the negative construction. It occurs in other constructions as well, e. g. , šna•pa bana (šnu apa bana) 'do you want to eat?' This latter example also illustrates the fact that active verbs in Mobilian are also conjugated by means of the independent personal pronouns instead of by special subject prefixes, as in Choctaw or Alabama.

In the material that has been examined so far I have not found any traces of the Algonkian ingredients mentioned by Mooney, but as more material becomes available, some may still turn up. On the other hand, Woodward's description of Mobilian can be seen to fit very well. He said that it was a mixture of Creek, Choctaw, Chickasaw, Natchez, and Apalachi. The only non-Muskogean language in his list is Natchez, but the Natchez Indians he knew probably spoke Creek most of the time. Of the remaining languages Choctaw and Chickasaw are only slightly differing dialects, Apalachi is very close to Alabama and Koasati, and Creek, while quite different, does have a number of words that are the same as Alabama, e. g., łałó 'fish', ifá 'dog'. Consequently the results arrived at in this paper are not really at variance with Woodward's statement of over a hundred years ago.

NOTES

1. Most of the Mobilian forms quoted here were recorded by Crawford in August 1970 near Elton, Louisiana, from a speaker named Leonard Lavan. Other materials were collected by Crawford at the Alabama-Coushatta Reservation near Livingston, Texas, but only a few words of these other materials have been transcribed.

2. Choctaw and Chickasaw are closely related dialects and the Mobilian material cited could probably be from either one. However, the unavailability of Chickasaw lexical materials made it necessary to use Choctaw sources. The most important of these is Byington's dictionary (1915). Some forms, however, are taken from my own brief unpublished notes collected in the late 1930's.

3. Alabama and Koasati are closely related languages, though they are not as close as Choctaw and Chickasaw. Alabama forms cited here are from brief vocabularies recorded by Morris Swadesh and me in 1934 (Haas 1968:77). Koasati forms are from more extensive materials which I collected a few years later.

4. There is no phonemic difference between u and o in any of these languages. The Alabama words have been normalized to o, the Choctaw and Mobilian words have been left unnormalized.

5. There is enough difference between the independent pronouns of Alabama and Koasati to enable us to determine that Alabama is the source of the Mobilian forms cited here. The corresponding Koasati forms are: ano 'I', išno 'you', and košno 'we'.

REFERENCES

Byington, Cyrus. 1915. A dictionary of the Choctaw language. Smithsonian Institution, Bureau of American Ethnology Bulletin 46.

Haas, Mary R. 1968. The last words of Biloxi. IJAL 34:77-84.

Mooney, James. 1900. Myths of the Cherokee. Smithsonian Institution, Bureau of American Ethnology, 19th Annual Report, Pt. 1.

Samarin, William J. 1968. Lingua francas of the world. _In_ Readings in the sociology of language, ed. Joshua A. Fishman, pp. 660-72. The Hague: Mouton.

Sibley, John. 1807. Historical sketches of the several Indian tribes in Louisiana south of the Arkansas River, and between the Mississippi and River Grand. _In_ Travels in the interior parts of America, by Captains Lewis and Clark, Doctor Sibley, and Mr. Dunbar, pp. 40-53. London: Richard Phillips.

Woodward, Thomas S. 1859. Woodward's reminiscences of the Creek, or Muscogee Indians. Montgomery: Barrett and Wimbish.

The Phonological Sequence *ya* in Words Pertaining to the Mouth in Southeastern and Other Languages

James M. Crawford

When comparing languages in the search for cognates, one ordinarily proceeds by examining forms with more or less the same meanings in the various languages. Upon finding several sets represented by a few recurrent correspondences, identities or nonidentities, one feels justified in positing a case for genetic relationship and in continuing the search for cognates by examining forms which show the previously discovered correspondences (at the same time looking for additional correspondences), but which have greater divergences in meanings. However, in dealing with meaning changes there are no rules or criteria to follow, as, on the other hand, there are for sound changes, which exhibit certain regularities. Regularities in meaning change are difficult to demonstrate and many scholars doubt if any exist (Ullman 1951:154).

Consequently, one is rather much on his own in attempting to show genetic relationships if the languages after a brief but careful inspection do not present a good case for common origin. Findings pointing to relationships much beyond the family level may be accepted by readers without reservation or they may be dismissed as personal vagaries of the writer. Or, a more rational attitude, they may be accepted tentatively with the expectation that additional evidence will be forthcoming to strengthen the case for the proposed relationships.[1] It is obviously difficult, and it may indeed be impossible, to demonstrate conclusively the common origin of languages whose relationship extends much pa the family level. Nevertheless, there are many who attempt to demonstrate these more distant relationships, searching painstakingly for sets with forms reasonably similar whose meanings can be linked in some logical fashion.

Americanists are intrigued and sometimes puzzled upon encountering words or partials of words with approximately the same form and meaning in languag for which there is otherwise scanty evidence to suggest common ancestry of the languages. It has been customary to take note of them, but to attribute little or no value to such concurrences for demonstrating genetic relationship The reasoning, it would seem, is that such identities and near identities of form and meaning, if not purely coincidental, can be due only to borrowing or to onomatopoeia, since, if the languages were related, the time depth of the relationship must surely be so great as to have effected at least a moderate degree of change in both sound and meaning. A few examples are given to illustrate the phenomenon referred to. Examples of identities in form and meaning:[2] Catawba (Catawba isolate) ya, Yana (Yanan, Hokan) -ya 'woman' Dakota (Siouan) le, Yuchi (Yuchi isolate) le- 'this'; Cocopa (Yuman, Hokan) má, Yana (Yanan, Hokan) ma- 'eat'; Biloxi (Siouan) hi, Maidu (Maiduan, Penutian) hí 'smell'.

Sets with only slight differences of form or meaning are much more numerou e. g.: Cocopa (Yuman, Hokan) -piṣ, Biloxi (Siouan) pis, psi 'suck'; Atakap pix 'die', Yavapai pi 'dead'; Biloxi pi 'liver cut out of a body', Yuchi -y̓ç Creek (Muskogean) lupi· 'liver'; Tunica (Tunica isolate, Gulf) yána 'to spea talk', Cupeño, Luiseño (Uto-Aztecan) ya-, Cahuilla (Uto-Aztecan) yá- 'say' Yana gayaa- 'to speak, talk', Yuchi y̓agwa 'say, tell', Central Sierra Miw (Miwokan, Penutian) jajumnu- 'to make a speech at someone'; Yuchi w̓ede 'speak', Maidu (Maiduan, Penutian) wéj, wéje 'speech, tell, talk, say', Maidu sìmí, Quechua (Quechuan) simi 'mouth'; Yuchi -dakha 'mouth' (-da 'face'), Choctaw (Muskogean) itakha 'inside of mouth, the voice' (iti 'mout front part of mouth').

Similarities of this sort in American Indian languages are not at all uncomm And they are far too numerous for the entire lot to be tossed aside as the resu of chance. Some similarities are undoubtedly due to chance, but it is conceivable that genetic affiliation can be adduced to explain many of the sets i we were able to treat semantic changes in the same systematic fashion that is possible for sound changes. It cannot be denied that meanings do change with time (perhaps even more readily than sounds), as is fully documented in languages with written records.

It is my belief that comparativists working with languages lacking written records have not sufficiently taken into account not only the possibility, but also the range and direction, of semantic change. We know that meanings can change erratically and in ways we least expect. I suggest that the search for cognates among languages would be more fruitful if the search was focused on specific semantic categories or "semantic fields" (Ullman 1951:152-70).[3]

Semantic changes which are of most concern to the comparativist are those which involve "transfers of names", either through "similarity between the senses" or through "contiguity between the senses" (Ullman 1951:220). Similarities between the senses include such "anthropomorphic transfers" as "leg of a table, foot of a hill, arms and mouth of a river, eye of a needle, bridgehead" (Ullman 1951:224). Contiguities between the senses, apparently a more common type of transfer, include changes which do not arise out of similarities alone, but from some other kind of connection, spatial, temporal, or causal, corresponding in general to the categories of metonymy and synecdoche, e.g., the use of crown, sceptre, or throne for royalty, pig-tails for Chinamen, bench for judge, steel for any weapon of steel (examples from Stern 1931:327-28).

In the present paper I am postulating a semantic category focusing on the body part mouth and am assuming the operation of the sort of semantic changes just mentioned. Specifically, I am assuming that it is possible that meaning can shift in the course of time from, e.g., 'mouth' to 'lips', to 'tongue', to 'speak', to 'eat', etc. and that meaning can be figuratively transferred, e.g., 'mouth' to 'house-mouth' (i.e., 'door') and to 'river-mouth'. I do not claim that shifts occurred in any particular sequence or even that the starting point for the shifts was 'mouth'. The latter may very likely be true, but does not appear to be capable of proof.

I am also assuming the "sameness" of the linguistic form which recurs in words fitting within the category 'mouth'. Such words are henceforth called mouthwords. The linguistic form symbolizing the concept of 'mouth' in mouthwords is denominated ya, which is used as a cover form for convenient reference to actual phonological segments in languages having the shape /ya/ or a variant of /ya/.[4] Variants include segments of the shape: consonant plus vowel, where the consonant is not /y/ in a given language, but is a consona which corresponds regularly to /y/ in some related language. For example, in Osage mouthwords is considered a variant since Osage /ð/ is a regular co spondence to Dakota /y/ (Wolff 1950:120-21).[5] No variant of /ya/ is consid in which the consonant is other than /y/, unless it has been shown that this consonant is the regular correspondence to /y/ in a related language.[6] Vari however, can include segments whose vowel is other than /a/, e.g. /a·/, / /o/, /e/, and /u/, even when no regular vowel correspondences have been demonstrated. From a historical viewpoint, treating as the "same" segment i mouthwords those sequences whose sounds show regular correspondences wc seem to demand no justification. However, inclusion of segments such as / /ye/, etc., which imply the operation of morphophonemic and/or morphologic processes, calls for some defense, which can be found in Dakota.

An examination of mouthwords in Dakota clearly indicates that a process, possibly morphophonemic, has operated to modify the vowel /a/ in words wh contain the prefix ya-, defined in Buechel's Lakota dictionary as "action by the mouth, literally and figuratively" (Buechel 1970:43). This affix is very pr ductive in Dakota and

> is prefixed to a large number of verbs and signifies that the action is done with the mouth by biting, talking, etc. Thus yaksa, To bite off. Affixed to adjectives, and sometimes to nouns, it makes of them verbs meaning to speak of as such, or to make so with the mouth: thus yawaŝte, To call good. Yawicaŝa, To speak of as a man (Buechel 1970:617).

Moreover, it is obvious that ya- has figured in the formation of such Dakota words as: iyóha 'jaw' (cf. ihá 'lips'), tiyópa 'door' (cf. típi 'house'), iyógnaka (also recorded as iógnaka) 'put into the mouth' (gnáka 'put'), iéŝn (interpreted as yéŝni) 'be dumb' (cf. iyásni 'become still, as a noise ceasir and iéksapa (interpreted as yéksapa) 'be wise in one's speech, be eloquent' (ksápa 'wise'). The influence of ya- may also have produced oyúte 'eating, food' and yúta (interpreted as yú·ta) 'eat anything'.

These same segments are found, not only in Dakota mouthwords, but also i numerous other American Indian languages, with /ya/, as a rule, the most frequent in a given language.[7] It would seem, not only possible, but rather likely, that processes analogous to those in Dakota could have operated to produce words such as: Creek yólketa 'suck with the tongue' (cf. yaca·k-it [Haas] 'chew'); Choctaw yopoma 'to mock', yopula 'to joke' (cf. yahapa 'rude, boisterous, noisy'); Tunica yɔ́wa 'silent' (cf. yána 'speak'); Lake Miwok jókku 'to be false, a lie' (cf. jájju 'to invite, want, ask for, call'), jólum 'to eat', jútte 'to chew' (cf. jáṣṣu 'to chew'); Nisenan ja·paj 'shout at' (cf. jaj 'scold'); and Tonkawa yoko- 'to curse' (cf. yakosa- 'to whistle' and nelʔaya- 'to spit out').

The presence of ya (which includes /ya/ and the variants) in mouthwords in languages throughout North America is indeed striking and is of such frequency and distribution that it is scarcely possible to dismiss the phenomenon as mere coincidence. One balks, however, at drawing the conclusion that this is a bit of evidence for relating the languages. One feels that, although there seems to have been a reasonable and acceptable degree of semantic change, there has not been sufficient sound change for languages whose common origin, if any, must extend back many millenia. One thinks of Siouan, a family of relatively shallow time depth, where Osage /ð/, Biloxi /č/, and Dakota /y/ have descended from the same Proto-Siouan sound (Wolff 1950:121). In view of these diverse changes within a language family, surely, one argues, the presence of ya in mouthwords in, e. g. , the Penutian languages Lake Miwok and Nisenan, which themselves are only distantly related,[8] can have no connection with its presence in Siouan!

If not taken as a token of evidence for common origin, then can the phenomenon find its explanation in diffusion or in onomatopoeia? Diffusion may indeed account for some of the interfamilial occurrences of ya, or for that matter, it may account for all the occurrences, but one can scarcely do more than invoke diffusion and there let the matter rest. The supposition of diffusion, as the sole explanation, introduces improbable hypotheses in regard to distribution and movement of peoples and, since the borrowings must be ancient, imposes so great a time depth that it is still necessary to assume the passing of many millenia without sound changes in this linguistic form. At any rate, borrowings of specific linguistic forms cannot usually be identified until the sound correspondences have been worked out. Therefore, I fail to see how diffusion can be offered, except on faith, as even a contributing cause for this widespread phenomenon.

Onomatopoeia cannot be ruled out quite as easily. Consider, for example, the number of mouthwords in English with ya having to do with the exercise of the vocal cords: yammer, yap, yawp, yell, yelp, yip, yodel, yow, yowl.[9] Does not such a set as this deflate any claims for ya in mouthwords as evidence of common origin, or even of diffusion? At first it does seem so, for here is clearly an example of sound symbolism, involving approximately the same sounds and meaning, operating in a language that no one has seriously proposed could be shown to share a common origin with any of the American Indian languages. And what about the presence of ya in mouthwords in Old World languages as, for example in Turkish: yalamak 'lick', yanak 'cheek', yaygara 'screaming', and yemek 'eat'?[10] Also, in songs of some American Indians there is a possibility of symbolism in the apparently meaningless sequences in which ya is frequent, e. g., Comecrudo: ayami, ketseyo, semeye, wenepayo (Swanton 1940:55-107) and Cocopa: wayomi·, wayawe, koyawi·, yanila·, n^{y}ayawi·, si·maya· (Crawford 1963-67). Certainly, sound symbolis as an explanation cannot be ruled out. There is more of a case here than for diffusion, but like diffusion, sound symbolism can be invoked, but once calle forth, and with the favorable evidence having been presented, one is in a cul-de-sac: nothing further can be adduced; one either believes or does not believe. The option for genetic relationship does carry at least the potential for further progress. That is, the search can be continued for additional, or different, clues for genetic relationship.

It does not follow that further search gives hope of demonstrating a genetic relationship between Turkish and English or between English and American Indian languages. There is nothing to suggest that it is other than accidenta that this feature found in numerous American Indian languages occurs also in English and Turkish.[11] It is not likely that a genetic relationship between English and the American Indian languages can ever be demonstrated. But it not totally unreal to believe that, at some distant time, most American Indiar languages can be shown to have descended, if not from one ancestral languag from a smaller number than is indicated by present difficulties in identifying cognate forms and positing sound correspondences in ultrafamily comparisons

I do not argue that all ultrafamilial instances of ya in mouthwords in Ameri Indian languages count as evidence for common origin. Just which ones can count must await additional studies. I suggest that studies of this sort, whi focus on a specific semantic category in the search for cognates, can accele our progress in revealing affiliations beyond the family level.

APPENDIX

The following is a list of <u>mouthwords</u> with <u>ya</u> (as defined in the body of the paper) selected from several American Indian languages. The arrangement is alphabetical by language. In parentheses following each language name are the Roman numeral designating the phylum and the lower case letter identifying the family or language isolate, followed by the name of the family or language isolate (Voegelin and Voegelin 1966).[2]

Achomawi (Vd Palaihnihan)

yawass	'singer'	opyāmə	'beard, mustache'

Alabama (IIId Muskogean)

yaska	'chew'	yahka	'cry'

Atakapa (IIIf Atakapa Language Isolate)

ya	'to eat'	yok	'to sing'

Biloxi (IVa Siouan)[12]

(a)yɛpeʔ	'door'	ihí yapí	'lips' (ihi 'mouth')
yatká	'jaw'	yátce, yatcí	'name'
yakudi	'feed' (ku 'give', ti 'eat')	yao^{n}ni	'sing'
yetcí	'tongue'	i^{n}ye	'food'
tayó	'cheeks'		

Cahuilla (VIIb Uto-Aztecan)

yá-	'say'

Catawba (IVb Catawba Language Isolate)

hį·yáp	'his teeth'

Chimariko (Vg Chimariko Language Isolate)

-isek-[13]	'swallow'	-sáxni	'cough'
wessa	'door' ('awa 'house')		

Chitimacha (IIIg Chitimacha Language Isolate)

yak(t)	'to weep, cry, mew, play on an instrument'

Choctaw (IIId Muskogean)

yahapa	'rude, boisterous, noisy'	yaiya	'to cry, weep, howl'
ya^{n}wa	'to cry, mew'	yopoma	'to mock'

yopula	'to joke, jest'	yukpa	'to laugh'
yuhapa	'noise, noisy'		

Chumash (Vk Chumashan)

oxyoko	'Adam's apple'	tiyep	'teach, show'

Coahuilteco (Vm Coahuiltecan Language Isolate)

xāmayā	'to make fun of'	wāyo	'to cry, weep'

Cocopa (Va Yuman)

i·yá	'mouth'	i·yáčkṣá	'chin'
syá·	'sing' (s- 'do with the mouth')		

Comecrudo (Vl Comecrudan)

máwayo	'singer, dancer'	yesó knem	'to nurse' [mamar las tetas]
yehau	'to vomit'	yáx	'nose'

Cotoname (Vl Comecrudan)

koyáma	'to sing'	yáx	'nose'

Creek (IIId Muskogean)[14]

yaca·k-itá	'chew'	yólkita	'suck with tongue'
yakíknita	'to giggle'	yanáwa	'cheek'
yátika[15]	'interpreter'		

Cupeño (VIIb Uto-Aztecan)

ya-	'say'		

Dakota (IVa Siouan)

yagwá	'bite off'	yamá	'gnaw'
čéya	'cry, weep'	oyák̓a	'relate, tell'
iyóhaḫ	'whiskers'	iyóhloke	'mouth of river'
iéška	'interpreter'		

Hopi (VIIb Uto-Aztecan)

ʔayá-ta	'tell, command'	yá:pa	'mockingbird'

Huchnom (VIIIb Yukian)

pōkeyaka	'shout'	hūlyo	'face' (hul 'eye')

Huichol (VIIb Uto-Aztecan)

-ʔiya	'drink'		

Kansa (IVa Siouan)

yesa	'tongue'		

Karankawa (VIIIe Karankawa Language Isolate)

yóta	'music'	owíya[16]	'to cry, weep'

Karok (Vj Karok Language Isolate)

ʔú·hyana	'to talk, speak'	tayáv[17]	'name'
ya:yá:hi	'to stutter'		

Kiliwa (Va Yuman)

ya·w	'teeth' (Hicks 1958)	ya·w/-ʔha·w	'teeth' (Mixco 1966)

Klamath (VIe Klamath-Modoc Language Isolate)

-yal	'speaking the language of the preceding noun'
yeqa	'(coyote) howls; rejoices, celebrates'

Luiseño (VIIb Uto-Aztecan)

ya-	'say'		

Maidu (VIb Maiduan)

jaký	'be named'	jawí	'call by name'
jawíti	'teach school' ('cause to read')	jakán	'saliva'
jomó	'invite, call to come'	wéje/wéj	'speech; tell, talk, say'
k̓ojó	'stranger' ['one who speaks strangely' (?)]		

Maricopa (Va Yuman)

ʔiyá	'mouth'	ʔiyavomé	'beard'
yaxal^{y}mé	'cheeks'	yatk^{w}iṣá	'chin'

Miwok, Central Sierra (VId Miwok-Costanoan)

jajúmnu-	'to make a speech at someone'	jáj·u-	'to demand'
jalá·k-	'to wail for the dead'	jejý·če-	'speaker'
jéj·a-	'to call'	júpse-	'to spit'
jýl·y-	'to bite'		

Miwok, Lake (VId Miwok-Costanoan)

jáalak	'to squeal, yell once, yell like a woman'		
jájju	'to invite, want, ask for, call for (vocally)'		
jákka	'to bark'	jáṣṣu	'to chew'
jóko	'to tell a lie'	jólum	'to eat'
jómu	'to laugh'	jóppu	'to feed'
júute	'to chew'		

Mohave (Va Yuman)

-iyá	'mouth'	ʔavoyá	'door' (ʔavá 'house'

Nisenan (VIb Maiduan)

jakan	'saliva'	jakba	'face'
jawi·	'call, name'	jom	'suck out disease'
ja·paj	'shout at'		

Ofo (IVa Siouan)

áye	'to cry'	téska iyónaki	'mockingbird' (tésk 'bird')
itcépi[18]	'door'	bitcápi	'my lips' (b- 'my')
itcóti	'throat, neck'	itcáhu	'to sing'
tcátka	'jawbone'	atcokfá	'to tell a lie'

Omaha-Ponca (IVa Siouan)

gθebe[19]	'vomit'

Osage (IVa Siouan)

wa-tho[19]	'to sing'	thatsé	'to eat'
thé-ba	'jaw'	ú-thage	'to tell a story'

Paiute, Southern (VIIb Uto-Aztecan)

yampa-	'mockingbird'

Pomo, Central (Vc Pomoan)

myá	'neck'

Pomo, Eastern (Vc Pomoan)

ya·ʔó	'tooth'

Pomo, Northeastern (Vc Pomoan)

batcoya	'sing'	matōya	'shout'

Pomo, Southeastern (Vc Pomoan)

myán	'throat'		

Pomo, Southern (Vc Pomoan)

mihya	'neck'		

Pomo, Southwestern [Kashaya] (Vc Pomoan)

mihya	'neck'		

Salinan, Antoniano (Vi Salinan)

ihaltéya	'saliva'	iyóhun	'bark, cry'
o·ye'	'respond, reply'		

Seneca (IVc Iroquoian)

-yas-	'name'		

Seri (Vb Seri Language Isolate)

yam	'throat'		

Shoshone (VIIb Uto-Aztecan)

yahne	'laugh'	muyahne	'smile'
yage/yake	'cry'		

Subtiaba (Vp Tlapanecan)

-mbi·ya	'cry'		

Tarahumara (VIIb Uto-Aztecan)

bayé	'call'	ʔoʔyó	'vomit'

Tepehuan, Northern (VIIb Uto-Aztecan)

ayəi	'drink'		

Tlappanec (Vp Tlapanecan)

skí·n·ya'	'mucus'	yá' ndɔ'	'saliva'
natabìya'	'you cry'	mąmbiyà'	'I cry'
maré·'nya	'I answer (him)'		

Tonkawa (IIIi Tonkawa Language Isolate)

yaxa-	'to eat'	nataya-	'to choose'
nelʔaya-	'to spit out'	yamas	'lips'
yakosa-	'to whistle'	yoko-	'to curse'

Tunica (IIIh Tunica Language Isolate)

yáha	'to open mouth, yawn, gape'	-yáhpa	'be hungry'
yána	'to speak, talk'	yápa	'(fish) to bite'

Wappo (VIIIb Yukian)

yáwe	'name'

Washo (Vh Washo Language Isolate)

ya·m	'to tell'	íyeg	'tooth'

Wintun, Southern (VIc Wintun)

Lēye	'laugh'

Yana (Vf Yanan)

gayaa-	'to speak, talk'	gayaamau(na)	'language, word, spee
yaagai-	'to ask' (gai- 'to hear')	yaa-	'blow a horn' (yaasinʔ 'I play a flute')

Yavapai (Va Yuman)

yá	'mouth'	yahapí	'cheeks'
yàvan^{y}imíya	'beard'	yà·vaˀí	'to say'
yó·qi	'to vomit'	ti·yé	'to tell a lie'
yá·wa	'loud (voice)'		

Yuchi (IVe Yuchi Language Isolate)

y̓agwa	'say, tell'	y̓ak'wę	'sing' (k'wę 'send')
y̓atik'e[15]	'interpreter'		

Yurok (IIIb Yurok Language Isolate)

teloyew-	'to tell a lie'	koˀoyew-	'to request, ask'
keˀyolew	'to spit'		

NOTES

1. For example, the two former reactions were expressed after publication by Sapir (1913) of evidence pointing to a genetic relationship of Wiyot and Yurok to Algonquian. Michelson (1914, 1915) rejected outright any possibility of such a relationship, declaring "the utter folly of haphazard comparisons unless we have a thorough knowledge of the morphological structure of the languages concerned" (1914:367). On the other hand, Kroeber (Dixon and Kroeber 1919), who had collected the Wiyot and Yurok material, did not have "the slightest hesitation in subscribing to Dr. Sapir's interpretation of Yurok and Wiyot" (p. 112); both Dixon and Kroeber "therefore accept his findings in full confidence, and merge their tentative Ritwan [Wiyot and Yurok] family in the Algonkin" (p. 113). The more rational attitude has been assumed by Haas who (1958) presented the additional evidence for demonstrating beyond reasonable doubt the genetic affiliation of Wiyot, Yurok, and Algonquian.

2. Sources of data are: Achomawi (Olmsted 1966), Alabama (Crawford 1970b), Atakapa (Gatschet and Swanton 1932), Biloxi (Dorsey and Swanton 1912, Haas 1968), Cahuilla (Bright and Hill 1967), Catawba (McDavid 1940-41), Chimariko (Harrington 1969), Chitimacha (Swanton 1919), Choctaw (Byington 1915), Chumash (Beeler 1970), Coahuilteco (Swanton 1940), Cocopa (Crawford 1963-67), Comecrudo (Swanton 1940), Cotoname (Swanton 1940), Creek (Haas 1956, Loughridge and Hodge 1964), Cupeño (Bright and Hill 1967), Dakota (Buechel 1970), Hopi (Miller 1967), Huchnom (Barrett 1908), Huichol (Miller 1967), Kansa (Wolff 1950), Karankawa (Gatschet 1891), Karok (Bright 1957), Kiliwa (Hicks 1958, Mixco 1966), Klamath (Barker 1963), Luiseño (Bright and Hill 1967), Maidu (Shipley 1963), Maricopa (Crawford 1963a), Miwok, Central Sierra (Freeland and Broadbent 1960), Miwok, Lake (Callaghan 1965), Mohave (Crawford 1972), Nisenan (Uldall and Shipley 1966), Ofo (Dorsey and Swanton 1912), Omaha-Ponca (Wolff 1950), Osage (La Flesche 1932), Paiute (Miller 1967), Pomo, Central, Southeastern, Southern, and Southwestern [Kashaya] (McLendon 1970), Pomo, Eastern (Moshinsky 1970), Pomo, Northeastern (Barrett 1908), Quechua (Harrington 1943), Salinan (Heizer 1952), Seneca (Chafe 1964), Seri (Moser 1961), Shoshone (Crawford 1967-68), Subtiaba (Sapir 1925), Tarahumara (Miller 1967), Tepehuan (Miller 1967), Tlappanec (Radin 1932-33), Tonkawa (Hoijer 1949), Tunica (Haas 1953), Wappo (Sawyer 1965), Washo (Jacobsen 1969), Wintun (Barrett 1908), Yana (Sapir and

Swadesh 1960), Yavapai (Crawford 1963b), Yuchi (Crawford 1970-71), Yurok (Robins 1958).

Forms are cited as they appear in the sources with these exceptions: č replaces c in Creek (Loughridge and Hodge) and in Dakota, a and i replace respectively, v and e in Creek (Loughridge and Hodge), accents following vowels are written over the vowels, breve (˘) is omitted, as well as certain diacritics used with consonants (as in Buechel's Lakota-English dictionary), and η following a vowel to indicate nasalization in Dakota is replaced by ˛ under the vowel. j and y in Maidu, Nisenan, and the two Miwokan langua are to be read respectively, as [y] and [ɨ].

3. Comparativists do allow, of course, for meaning shifts and changes (e at times far-fetched), particularly when a few sound correspondences have b established. In general, it seems, it is preferred that the Pandora's box of semantic change be opened at most only slightly.

4. Slanted brackets (/ /) enclose actual forms recorded in some languag The forms cited may or may not be phonemic. The brackets are used as a de for distinguishing attested forms from the abstract and synthetic form ya, wh is underlined.

5. According to Wolff (1950:120), Osage /ð/ corresponds to Santee Dakot /y/ and to Teton Dakota /l/. He cites as evidence Teton la 'go'. Wolff is error here. la is the second singular of the indefinite tense; ya is the third singular and the citation form of the irregular verb 'go' (Buechel 1939:75).

6. With the exception of /y̓a/ in Yuchi mouthwords. Yuchi shows strong indication of being related to Siouan, a relationship first suggested without evidence by Sapir (1921, 1929) and with slight evidence provided by Haas (19 79, 1964) and Elmendorf (1963, 1964). With considerable Yuchi material at h (my own field notes), I have begun a comparison of Yuchi with Siouan. Yuch /y̓/ is an occasional correspondence to Dakota /y/, although more often to Dakota /č/ (the reflex of Wolff's Proto-Siouan $*L^{Y}$ [1950:121] and Matthews $*y$ [1970:108-109] or ṙ, which he equates with Wolff's $*L^{Y}$ [p. 98]. [Matth replaces ṙ with $*y$ in his Proto-Siouan reconstructions]).

7. A selected sample of ya in mouthwords is given as an appendix. Only those languages were examined for which there was relatively abundant mate at hand or, if not abundant, in which there seemed good reason to expect ya mouthwords (i. e. , on account of occurrences of ya in sister languages for w

there is considerable material available). The search was not successful in some language families, e. g. , Algonquian, Athapaskan, and Iroquoian.

8. See Pitkin and Shipley (1958) and Shipley (1966) for a discussion of some of the difficulties encountered by Penutian scholars in attempts to validate this stock.

9. This list is from Webster's Collegiate Dictionary, 5th edition, 1946. Additional mouthwords with ya in English can be found in an unabridged dictionary.

10. Turkish undoubtedly has other mouthwords with ya. These four are from the Turkish-English vocabulary in Essentials of modern Turkish, by Herman H. Kreider, Washington, D. C. : Middle East Institute, 1954.

11. One does wonder, however, if there might not be a universal symbolic connection between this phonological sequence and action by the mouth. If such is indeed the case, it can be asked if the symbolic associations arose independently, with subsequent parallel semantic extensions, or if they date back to the primordial stages of human speech.

12. The first Biloxi form is from Haas (1968). The other forms are from Dorsey and Swanton (1912).

13. Chimariko s corresponds to y in Cocopa and other Yuman languages (Crawford 1970a).

14. yaca·k-itá is from Haas (1956). All other Creek forms are from Loughridge and Hodge (1964).

15. Yuchi y̓atik'e 'interpreter' is probably a borrowing from Creek yatíkita 'to interpret'.

16. Gatschet (1891:95) says owíya is onomatopoetic in origin.

17. Cf. Chumash tiyep 'teach, show' and Tonkawa nataya- 'to choose'.

18. Ofo tc [č] corresponds to Biloxi y (Voegelin 1929:24, Wolff 1950:65, 121).

19. Omaha-Ponca θ and Osage th [ð] correspond to Dakota y (Wolff 1950:64, 121).

REFERENCES

Abbreviations

UCPL	University of California Publications in Linguistics
UCPAAE	University of California Publications in American Archaeology and Ethnology
BAE-B	Bureau of American Ethnology Bulletin
AA	American Anthropologist
IJAL	International Journal of American Linguistics
JWAS	Journal of the Washington Academy of Sciences
UCAR	University of California Anthropological Records

Barker, M. A. R. 1963. Klamath dictionary. UCPL 31:1-550.

Barrett, S. A. 1908. The ethno-geography of the Pomo Indians. UCPAAE 6:1-

Beeler, Madison S. 1970. Topics in Barbareño Chumash grammar. 100 page Typescript.

Bright, William. 1957. The Karok language. UCPL 13:1-457.

Bright, William, and Jane Hill. 1967. The linguistic history of the Cupeño. In Studies in Southwestern Ethnolinguistics, ed. Dell H. Hymes with Willi E. Bittle, 351-71. Mouton: The Hague.

Buechel, Eugene, S. J. 1939. A grammar of Lakota. Saint Francis, S. D.: S Francis Mission.

___. 1970. A dictionary of the Teton Dakota Sioux language, ed. Paul Manh S. J. Pine Ridge, S. D.: Red Cloud Indian School, Inc., Holy Rosary Miss

Byington, Cyrus. 1915. A dictionary of the Choctaw language. BAE-B 46:1-

Callaghan, Catherine A. 1965. Lake Miwok dictionary. UCPL 39:1-287.

Chafe, Wallace L. 1964. Another look at Siouan and Iroquoian. AA 66:852-

Crawford, James M. 1963a. Maricopa field notes.

___. 1963b. Yavapai field notes.

___. 1963-67. Cocopa field notes.

___. 1967-68. Shoshone field notes.

___. 1970a. A Comparison of Chimariko and Yuman. Typescript.

___. 1970b. Alabama field notes.

___. 1970-71. Yuchi field notes.

Crawford, Judith G. 1972. Mohave field notes.

Dixon, Roland B., and A. L. Kroeber. 1919. Linguistic families of California. UCPAAE 16:47-118.

Dorsey, James Owen, and John R. Swanton. 1912. A dictionary of the Biloxi and Ofo languages. BAE-B 47:1-340.

Elmendorf, William W. 1963. Yukian-Siouan lexical similarities. IJAL 29:300-309.

___. 1964. Item and set comparison in Yuchi, Siouan, and Yukian. IJAL 30:328-40.

Freeland, L. S., and Sylvia M. Broadbent. 1960. Central Sierra Miwok dictionary with texts. UCPL 23:1-71.

Gatschet, Albert S. 1891. The Karankawa Indians, the coast people of Texas. Archaeological and Ethnological Papers of the Peabody Museum, Harvard University 1:2. 1-103.

Gatschet, Albert S., and John R. Swanton. 1932. A dictionary of the Atakapa language. BAE-B 108:1-181.

Haas, Mary R. 1951. The Proto-Gulf word for water (with notes on Siouan-Yuchi). IJAL 17:71-79.

___. 1953. Tunica dictionary. UCPL 6:175-332.

___. 1956. Natchez and the Muskogean languages. Language 32:61-72.

___. 1958. Algonkian-Ritwan: the end of a controversy. IJAL 24:159-73.

___. 1964. Athapaskan, Tlingit, Yuchi, and Siouan. In Sobretiro del XXXV Congreso Internacional de Americanistas: México, 1962. Actas y Memorias. 495-500.

___. 1968. The last words of Biloxi. IJAL 34:77-84.

Harrington, John P. 1943. Hokan discovered in South America. JWAS 33:334-44.

___. 1969. A Chimariko word list from Harrington's field notes compiled under the direction of Mary R. Haas. Typescript.

Heizer, R. F., ed. 1952. California Indian linguistic records: the mission Indian records of Alphonse Pinart. UCAR 15:1-84.

Hicks, Judith Joël. 1958. Kiliwa word list. 5 pages. Manuscript.

Hoijer, Harry. 1949. An analytical dictionary of the Tonkawa language. UCPL 5: 1-74.

Jacobsen, Jr., William H. 1969. Washo stem lists. 12 pages. Typescript.

La Flesche, Francis. 1932. A dictionary of the Osage language. BAE-B 109:1-406.

Loughridge, R. M., and David M. Hodge. 1964. English and Muskokee dictionary. B. Frank Belvin, General Missionary to Creek and Seminole Indians, Okmulgee, Okla.: Baptist Home Mission Board. 1-236.

Matthews, G. H. 1970. Some notes on the Proto-Siouan continuants. IJAL 3
98-109.

McDavid, Jr., Raven I. 1940-41. Catawba notebooks. Manuscript.

McLendon, Sally. 1970. Proto-Pomo phonology. 149 pages. Typescript.

Michelson, Truman. 1914. Two alleged Algonquian languages of California. AA 16:361-67.

___. 1915. Rejoinder [to: Sapir, E. 1915. Algonkin languages of California a reply. AA 17:188-94.] AA 17:194-98.

Miller, Wick R. 1967. Uto-Aztecan cognate sets. UCPL 48:1-83.

Mixco, M. J. 1966. Kiliwa phonology I. 46 pages. Typescript.

Moser, Edward, and Mary B. Moser. 1961. Seri-castellano/castellano-seri. Serie de vocabularios indigenas mariano y aceves Num. 5. Instituto lingüís de Verano. México, D. F.

Moshinsky, Julius. 1970. Historical Pomo phonology. 49 pages. Typescrip

Olmsted, D. L. 1966. Achumawi dictionary. UCPL 45:1-158.

Pitkin, Harvey, and William Shipley. 1958. A comparative survey of Califor Penutian. IJAL 24:174-88.

Radin, Paul. 1932-33. Notes on the Tlappanecan language of Guerrero. IJAL 45-72.

Robins, R. H. 1958. The Yurok language: grammar, texts, lexicon. UCPL 1

Sapir, Edward. 1913. Wiyot and Yurok, Algonkin languages of California. A 617-46.

___. 1921. A bird's-eye view of American languages north of Mexico. Scien 54:408.

___. 1925. The Hokan affinity of Subtiaba in Nicaragua. AA 27:402-527.

___. 1929. Central and North American languages. In Encyclopaedia Britann (14th ed.) 5:138-41. (Reprinted in Selected Writings of Edward Sapir in Lang Culture and Personality, ed. David G. Mandelbaum, 169-78, Berkeley and Los Angeles: University of California Press.

Sapir, Edward, and Morris Swadesh. 1960. Yana dictionary, ed. Mary R. Ha UCPL 22:1-267.

Sawyer, Jesse O. 1965. English-Wappo vocabulary. UCPL 43:1-128.

Shipley, William F. 1963. Maidu texts and dictionary. UCPL 33:1-261.

___. 1966. The relation of Klamath to California Penutian. Language 42:489

Stern, Gustaf. 1931. Meaning and change of meaning. 2nd printing, 1965. Bloomington: Indiana University Press.

Swanton, John R. 1919. A structural and lexical comparison of the Tunica, Chitimacha, and Atakapa languages. BAE-B 68:156.

___. 1940. Linguistic material from the tribes of Southern Texas and Northeastern Mexico. BAE-B 127:1-145.

Uldall, Hans Jørgen, and William Shipley. 1966. Nisenan texts and dictionary. UCPL 46:1-282.

Ullman, Stephen. 1951. The principles of semantics. 2nd ed. (with additional material), 1959. Oxford: Basil Blackwell.

Voegelin, C. F. 1929. Ofo-Biloxi sound correspondences. Proceedings of the Indiana Academy of Science 48:23-26.

Voegelin, C. F., and F. M. Voegelin. 1966. Map of North American Indian languages. American Ethnological Society.

Wolff, Hans. 1950. Comparative Siouan I, II. IJAL 16:61-66, 113-21.

Resurrecting Virginia Algonquian from the Dead: The Reconstituted and Historical Phonology of Powhatan

Frank T. Siebert, Jr.[1]

It is a matter of regret that the Algonquian languages indigenous to the Atlantic coast from New England southward to North Carolina were so inadequately recorded during the colonial period. This deficiency is especially true for the dialects once spoken in the region comprising the present states of Delaware, Maryland, Virginia, and North Carolina. Here the records are most fragmentary, and therefore an inventory of the isoglosses reflecting the dialectologic and grammatical features prevailing in this area will remain forever incomplete. On the other hand, Virginia Algonquian, commonly referred to as Powhatan, offers an opportunity to describe some of the characteristics of southeastern Algonquian. It is the purpose of this article to pursue such a line of inquiry and to sketch the relevant historical setting of Powhatan.

Shrouded in the romance of near-antiquity are the original inhabitants of Virginia and their language, both inextricably bound to the stirring narratives of early Jamestown, and to such legendary figures as Captain John Smith, Pocahontas, and Powhatan. The Virginia Algonquians had come into contact with Europeans half a century or more before the establishment of the first permanent English settlement in North America, heralded by the founding of

Jamestown in 1607. The New World had been divided with the approval of Pope Alexander VI between Spain and Portugal by the Treaty of Tordesillas in June 1494. In North America this agreement made the Cabot Strait the line of demarcation, and tacitly assigned to Spain the Atlantic coast from present Cape Breton Island southward to Florida. During the sixteenth century Spain played the major role on the American scene. Although Spanish penetrations into the southeastern section of present United States are well-known through the exploits of Ponce de León (1513), Nuñez Cabeça de Vaca (1526), Pánfilo de Narváez (1528), Hernando de Soto (1539-1541), Tristán de Luna (1559-1561), Pedro Menéndez de Avilés (1565), and Juan Pardo (1566-1567), Spanish activities to the north of Cape Fear have received little attention. There were unquestionably a series of explorations and attempts at colonization by Spain during the sixteenth century on the north and middle Atlantic coast, but most of these are unknown or have remained obscure because of poor documentation, official secrecy, or the fact that such efforts were considered marginal to the primary Spanish movements in the Caribbean and elsewhere that held the promise of greater riches. At any rate, it seems probable that there were at least temporary Spanish posts on the eastern coast as far north as Pemaquid, Maine. The chief recorded undertakings on the upper coast were the voyage of Estéban Gómez northward along the eastern seaboard from Florida to Nova Scotia in the spring and early summer of 1525 in which he sailed up the Penobscot River as far as present Bangor; and the ill-fated expedition of Luís Vasquez de Ayllón in 1526 which established the unsuccessful colony of San Miguel de Guadalupe on the middle Atlantic coast. The location of San Miguel is uncertain, but varying sites have been proposed, the suggestions ranging from the mouth of the Cape Fear River north to the lower Delaware Bay. Possibly San Miguel was somewhere in the Chesapeake Bay region, later called by the Spanish Bahía de Santa Maria.

In 1561 there were at least two other Spanish expeditions along the east coast, one of which kidnapped a prominent Virginia chieftain who was taken to the West Indies, Mexico, and Spain, and received the baptismal name of Don Luis de Velasco. In 1566 the governor of Florida, Pedro Menéndez de Avilés, made plans to establish a colony on the Chesapeake with the aid of

Don Luis, but the expedition that was sent out returned for unknown reasons. At Havana early in 1570 Don Luis persuaded the Jesuit Father Juan Baptista Segura to establish a mission on Chesapeake Bay. The project was encouraged by Menéndez at St. Augustine, and in 1570 Father Segura, a group of Jesuit friars, and Don Luis were transported to Virginia by Captain Vincente González. Father Segura founded the mission of Axacán or Ajacán somewhere along the estuary of the James River, probably at or near the present site of Jamestown. Soon after the departure of the caravel, Don Luis deserted the friars. Five months later the Indians, led by Don Luis, killed all the Spanish except for taking captive a boy, who was the son of one of the soldiers stationed at Santa Elena on the present South Carolina coast. During a return visit in 1571 González learned of the destruction of the mission, and in 1572 under the orders of Menéndez, he led a punitive expedition which recovered the boy, killed eight or nine Indians, carried off a few others as slaves, and failed to recapture Don Luis.[2]

Previous writers have overlooked evidence that identifies Don Luis de Velasco. It can be demonstrated that he was the father of Powhatan by the following quotation from Hamor[3] in which he described a treaty between the English and the natives of Virginia: "Thirdly, they should at all times be ready and willing to furnish vs with three or foure hundred bowmen to aide vs <u>against the Spaniards</u>, whose name is odious amongst them, for <u>Powhatans</u> father was driuen by them from the <u>west-Indies</u> into those parts . . . ."

It seems possible that the nine years of observation that Don Luis spent in the Spanish Empire may have provided the cultural source for the genesis of the conquest state that Don Luis and his son established among the Virginia Algonquians in the late sixteenth century. If not, his experience probably contributed to such a development. At the time of the death of Don Luis, presumably about 1583-1585, he ruled over a confederacy of six tribes. His son, Wahunsonacock, called by the English Powhatan from his principal seat of residence, succeeded to the chieftainship and expanded his inherited dominion by conquest to control some hundred or more villages. This fact is of linguistic significance, since the extant records of Virginia Algonquian made by Captain John Smith and William Strachey show dialectic divergence sufficient to indicate that the speech of the people of Powhatan's dominion who visited Jamestown to trade was not uniform.

After the destruction of Father Segura's mission in February 1571, the Spanish presence on the middle and north Atlantic coast was sustained for about two decades by frequent visits and probably by some temporary posts. As late as 1588 Captain González sailed up the Chesapeake Bay at least as far as the Potomac River. By this time the intrusion of the English on the Atlantic coast had started. In the summer of 1585 Sir Bernard Drake and George Raymond began their seizure and dispersal of the Spanish fishing fleet in north Atlantic waters from Newfoundland to the Azores, and in 1586 Sir Francis Drake unsuccessfully assaulted St. Augustine. Following the defeat of the Spanish Armada in 1588 Spain abandoned control of the middle and north coast to England and retired to the south of Cape Fear, although for decades many Spanish and Basque fishing vessels in times of peace continued to frequent the northern coast from Cape Cod to Newfoundland. It is incorrect to believe that the Spanish yielded the whole Atlantic coast north of St. Augustine following Francis Drake's attack of 1586, as has been stated by some writers. Control of the coast south of Cape Fear remained in Spanish hands until the time of English settlement in South Carolina, at Albemarle Point in 1670 and Charleston in 1680. In 1663 when Captain William Hilton[4] sailed along the southern coast as far north as Cape Fear he found the Spanish still in possession of Santa Elena and Edisto and met some Indians (Yamasee) speaking Spanish.

The Algonquian-Spanish contact in Virginia has some linguistic interest. There is evidence that ephemeral loans from Virginia Algonquian may have entered Caribbean or Floridian Spanish during the late sixteenth century. The early Spanish dictionaries of Stevens[5] and Pineda[6] give pemmenáu as "a sort of Rush in Virginia, so fine that the Indians spin and make good Thread of it." This seems to refer to the hemp dogbane plant (Apocynum cannabinum L. and variants) and is the Powhatan term for the plant or its fiber. Smith speaks of "a kind of grasse they call Pemmenaw; of these they make a thred" used for sewing apparel and making nets and lines for fishing. The correct gloss is probably /pi·mena·w/ 'hemp dogbane fiber or plant'. Strachey gives only the related /pi·menahko·n/ 'rope' (see the following lexicon).

Another result of the Spanish presence in Virginia was the accidental or deliberate introduction of two varieties of a poisonous weed from tropical America, the thorn-apple (Datura stramonium L. and D. innoxia Miller). The thorn-apple first appeared along the James River, perhaps at the site of Father Segura's mission, and from there spread throughout much of temperate eastern North America. At any rate, from the place of its first naturalization it was known to the early English settlers in Virginia and the Carolinas during the seventeenth century as the Jamestown-weed, later shortened to Jimsonweed. Because of the superficial similarity of the deadly thorn-apple to the harmless native balsam-apple and edible prickly pear (see PEAR in the lexicon), some Indians probably were poisoned. This may have been a minor factor among more certain and greater concerns that contributed to the extreme aversion felt by the Virginia Algonquians to the Spaniards.

Early contacts of the Virginia natives with the English call for a pertinent review. A few of Powhatan's people probably had their first contact with the English when explorations were undertaken from the unsuccessful Roanoke Island colony of Sir Walter Raleigh and Sir Richard Grenville in the period 1585-1587. For example, Ralph Lane visited the village of Chawanoac on the lower Meherrin River in March 1586, and about the same time may have reached the village of Nansemond or elsewhere on the lower Chesapeake Bay to the west of Cape Henry. The next English contact was the visit of Bartholomew Gilbert to Virginia in early 1603, but the natives were so enraged against all Europeans that he met his death at their hands on July 29, 1603.

With the settlement of Jamestown in May 1607 the first permanent English settlement in North America came into being, and following this there ensued an eventful era from 1607 to the death of Powhatan in 1618 which may be called the epochal period of early Virginia history. There were hardships, dissensions, and near-starvation during the early years until Captain John Smith returned to England in late 1609. Despite some initial altercations and displays of hostility, and the abduction of Pocahontas to Jamestown by Captain Samuel Argall in 1612, no incident between the Indians and English caused any general uprising. In April 1613 Pocahontas was married to an Englishman, John Rolfe, and thereafter relations took a peaceful turn. In 1613 the Powhatan confederacy entered into an alliance with the English against the Spaniards and other hostile tribes which has been described by

Hamor. Following the death of Pocahontas from smallpox in England in March 1617 and the death of Wahunsonacock (Powhatan) in 1618, relations again became strained. Opechancanough, the youngest half-brother of Powhatan, who had always been hostile toward the whites, gradually assumed the chieftainship over Opitchapan, an older half-brother and the rightful successor. On March 22, 1622, Opechancanough led a general surprise attack upon all the English settlers throughout Virginia. A bloody war of mutual extermination followed for fourteen years until peace was established in 1636 by the exhaustion of both sides. Opechancanough renewed the war on April 18, 1644, by a second attack, but he was later captured, taken to Jamestown, and shot by a guard. A peace was negotiated, and most of the Virginia Algonquians were assigned to several reservations. So far as is known, no considerable number migrated to the west. Many of them continued to speak their language until about the last decade of the eighteenth century but no one seems to have bothered to record it. From the beginning of the reservation period the Indians declined and this process was hastened by the rapid spread of the plantation-slavery system. An English visitor to Virginia in the period 1650-1655, Gatford,[7] was especially critical of the tobacco planters and accused the Virginians of robbing the Indians, of land frauds, and of murdering the Indians and their white neighbors in Maryland.

The natives of Virginia were the first Algonquians to have a prolonged intimate contact with speakers of English and for this reason Powhatan is the source of more loans into English than any other single Algonquian language. These loanwords include the English terms: *chinquapin*, *chum*, *hominy*, *matchcoat*, *moccasin*, *muskrat* (a loanblend), *opossum*, *persimmon*, *pone* (and *corn pone* as a loanblend), *puccoon*, *raccoon*, *terrapin*, *tomahawk*, *tuckahoe*, and *wicopy* (*Dirca palustris* L.). All or most of them entered English during the first two decades of contact and probably before the outbreak of hostilities in 1622. Other Algonquian loans in English are mostly from various New England and northeastern languages and include: *caribou* (from Micmac), *moose*, *sachem* (from Narragansett), *sagamore* (from Abenaki), *skunk*, *wampum*, and *wigwam* (from Abenaki). Some others are from various central Algonquian languages, all of them of a much later date: *pecan*, pemmican (from Cree), totem (from Ojibwa), and wapiti (from Shawnee). No loanwords from English into Powhatan have been recorded, but there probably were some.

SOURCES FOR POWHATAN

The first source for Virginia Algonquian is a brief vocabulary collected by Captain John Smith[8] in the period 1607-1609 and published in 1612 and again in 1624. He does not tell us what dialect it is or where he secured it, and the chief usefulness is to supplement Strachey's materials.

The only other source for Powhatan is the vocabulary collected by William Strachey, the first secretary of the Virginia colony. Little is known of Strachey's life or education except that he was a native of London and that he was still alive in 1618 when he tried to interest Francis Bacon in the publication of his manuscripts on Virginia. He sailed on May 15, 1609 for Virginia, but was shipwrecked on the Bermudas by a storm in July 1609 and did not arrive at Jamestown until May 23, 1610. As secretary of the colony he met Indians from different villages who came to Jamestown to trade. He sailed from Jamestown for England in October 1611, having spent about seventeen months in Virginia. In England during the years 1612 and 1613 Strachey composed his "The Historie of Travaile into Virginia Britannia" to which he appended a vocabulary of the Virginia Indian language, all probably rewritten from rough notes made in America. This has remained in the Bodleian Library at Oxford as Ashmole Ms. 1754. In 1618 Strachey made a second copy which is inscribed to Francis Bacon in the hope of securing his aid for projected publication. No interest was forthcoming and later this second copy was deposited in the British Museum as Sloane Ms. 1622. It differs in some particulars from the earlier copy in the Bodleian. In 1849 the Hakluyt Society published the British Museum copy which was edited by Richard Henry Major.[9] In general it is a creditable performance. Not until 1955 was the linguistic material from the earlier Bodleian copy published by John P. Harrington[10] which is fortunately accompanied by facsimile reproductions of the sixteen original sheets of vocabulary. The chief value of Harrington's edition lies in these reproductions of Strachey's earliest extant version of the Powhatan recordings. I have used Harrington's reproductions but have disregarded his interpretations of Strachey's handwriting. References to the Bodleian manuscript sheets in Harrington's edition are made with such symbols as (H6) for sheet six.

THE CHARACTER OF STRACHEY'S VOCABULARY

Strachey's Powhatan material collected in the years 1610 and 1611 is the earliest recording in quantity (that has survived) of any Algonquian language and is to be viewed as a fruit of the charismatic and epochal period of early Virginia history. Among Strachey's virtues were the fact that he was generous and diversified in his linguistic sampling, and that he often rendered the same gloss two or more times in varying recordings so that it is possible to form a reasonable opinion of the probable pronunciation. In comparison with most of his contemporaries, his "ear" for an exotic language appears to have been of a superior order, but in common with other English writers of his period he had little conception of consistency in sound representation or of uniform orthography.

On the opposite side of the ledger, there are two major difficulties with Strachey's recordings which have created nearly all the problems in using his material. These are his execrable and multifarious script and his many mistranslations which range from minor deviations to unequivocal howlers. Both are understandable but troublesome. The errors in rendered meaning are misleading and can be attributed to a communication barrier since the Powhatan speakers had little or no knowledge of English and misunderstandings were inevitable. For example, Strachey must have indicated by signs to one of his informants that he was hungry, to which the Indian replied /ketassame/ 'I will give you food', and Strachey thought he was calling him "a beggar" and recorded Cuttassamais "a Begger" (see sheet H3). A gust of wind stirred up some dust, and blew a speck in the eye of Strachey's Indian associate who commented /nepensen/ 'I have something (dust, a foreign body, a mote) in my eye', but Strachey misunderstood him and wrote down Nepensun "Dust" (see sheet H5). There are numerous examples of this type of error throughout.

Most exasperating of all is Strachey's cramped handwriting which sometimes defies certain interpretation and which was considerably below the average in legibility when compared to that of his contemporaries. Since the two extant copies of Strachey's vocabulary were written after a lapse of time and far removed from Virginia and Indian speakers, some of the variations in spelling lead one to believe that Strachey himself was not certain of some features of his own handwriting in his original notes. His "small" letters frequently seem to have from two to four variants that are used haphazardly. Some of the "small" letters subject to confusion or in which the orthographic contrasts are sometimes difficult or even impossible to distinguish are listed below:

u : n	m : nn
u : a	t : r
o : e	s : t
c : e	s : r
m : n	s : h
k : h	t : h

Some of the difficulties arise from the uncertainties inherent in fine writing with a quill point. The contrasts of "small" o : e and t : r in some of their variants are especially subject to misinterpretation so that reliability can be approximated only by a sensitive comparison of all recordings and a correlative cryptanalysis. Many examples of e which are indistinctly or closely looped at the top have the appearance of an o. Similarly a variety of t is readily confused with a type of r, although in general, but by no means serving as an invariable criterion, the r has a stroke at the base extending to the right, which is often lacking in the t. The inconsistencies can be attributed to careless copying, so that correlation alone provides sound solutions. For example, Strachey recorded <u>Oteingeis</u> "feet of a hawke" (see sheet H6) and <u>Meteengass</u> "a shooting glove" (sheet H13), in both of which the t conforms more closely to one of the usual patterns of an r. However, the more frequent listings of this morpheme with a distinct t (see the lexicon under HAND and MITTEN) confirms that they are to be taken as /otenči·s/ 'his hands' and /metenče·ss/ 'someone's glove, mitten'. Two distinct types of "small" written t appear in the same word in <u>Matowtam</u> "to Burne as if a sparke light on any (thing)" (sheet H3) and <u>Ahtut</u> "It stinketh" (sheet H8), for /mato·tam/ (see KINDLE) and /atet/ (see ROTTEN). Convincing proof that /t/, from PA /*θ/, and /r/ from PA /*l/, are distinct phonemes in Powhatan and are not distinguished by any unfounded or dubious interpretation of the handwriting is established by a comparison of their word initial occurre[nces] where Strachey writes capital letters clearly and consistently. For example, word initial /t-/ (Powhatan root /ta·t-/ from PA /*θa·θ-/) is found in the lex[icon] under CRACK, and instances of unequivocal initial /r-/ occur in MEAL (Powha[tan] root /ro·hk-/ from PA /*lo·xk-/ 'soft') and in SAND (Powhatan /re·kaw/ from PA /*le·kawi/ 'sand').

RECONSTITUTED PHONOLOGY OF POWHATAN

The purpose of reconstituted phonology is to determine by empirical method[s] which of several alternative phonological interpretations is valid in projecting the surface phonological entities or phonemes of an impressionistically record[ed] but defunct linguistic system. This procedure is justified only when pertinent direct observation and analysis are inaccessible. Despite the difficulties pre[-]sented by Strachey's script and the vagaries of his orthography, there are som[e] consistencies and prevailing regularities of representation that can be detecte[d] in his recordings. The trends of these consistencies are utilized in conjuncti[on] with comparative data from other Algonquian languages and the painstaking sleuthing of a trial-and-elimination method to evolve a working hypothesis, which when tested and found reasonable, leads to a determination of the reconstituted phonology of this poorly recorded dead language.

Strachey's chief orthographic representations of vowels in declining order o[f] frequency from 1 to 6 are tabulated below. Solitary, rare, and aberrant notati[ons] are not listed. Representations 1 and 2 are the most frequent, 3 and 4 less common, and 5 and 6 uncommon.

	1	2	3	4	5	6
/i/	i	-	e	-	-	ei
/i·/	e	ei (ey)	i	ÿ	ie	ea
/e/	e	u	i	ei	a	ai (ay)
/e·/	a	-	e	ai	ao (au)	aa
/o/	o	-	u (v)	-	-	ou

	1	2	3	4	5	6
/o·/	o	ou (ow, au)	-	ū (uu, u)	oa	oo
/a/	a	-	au	u (v)	-	o (ou, uw)
/a·/	a	aw (av, au)	o	aa (ā, ah)	-	oo (ou)

Therefore the most cogent hypothesis projects the following syllabic phonemes for Powhatan, with a contrast of long and short vowels throughout:

Front			Back	
i·	i	(strong)	o	o·
e·	e	(weak)	a	a·

The nonsyllabic phonemes are:

OBSTRUENTS	Labial	Alveolar	Palatal	Laryngeal
Plosive	p	t	k	
Affricate		č		
Spirant		s		h
SONORANTS				
Tap		r		
Nasal	m	n		
Glide	w		y	

The spirant /s/ is a voiceless lenis sibilant, but after a front vowel seems to be in free variation phonetically with the corresponding shibilant. Geminated /ss/ occurs only after vowels and is a voiceless fortis sibilant which in intervocalic position is ambisyllabic. Other geminated fortis consonants do not appear to occur in Powhatan except secondarily as a result of syncope.

DIALECTS OF VIRGINIA ALGONQUIAN

No evidence of any grammatical differences in Strachey's materials has come to my attention, but there is convincing proof of minor phonological disparity and considerable lexical diversity. These findings indicate that the speech of the Powhatan confederacy was not homogeneous and that at least two and probably more dialects were recorded. Since the original authors (Smith and Strachey) made no mention of such differences we have no way of assigning any given feature to any particular dialect and therefore can note only the variations as contrasts without even being able to sort them properly. Presumably the Indians who most often frequented Jamestown were from Paspahegh, the nearest village, situated somewhat to the west on the north side of the James River. It is reasonable to assume that the major dialect represented in the sources was Chickahominy, and the other Pamunkey, but even this is doubtful without specific information. Some of the lexical contrasts are listed below, but my proposed dialectic assortment is not guaranteed. For fuller details on each gloss consult the lexicon.

	Dialect A	Dialect B
'sun'	/ki·so·ss/	/nepass/
'roe'	/wa·hk/	/osi·ka·n/
'copper'	/matassen/	/osa·wa·ss/
'he is asleep'	/nepe·w/	/kawi·w/
'(his) thigh'	/opo·m/	/wi·kkway/
'arrow'	/ato·ns/	/askwiwa·n/
'muskrat'	/ossaskwe·ss/	/mossaskwe·ss/
'raccoon'	/a·re·hkan/ (?)	/e·sepan/

Among phonological variations which appear to be of dialectic origin the following merit mention. If Strachey's recordings can be relied upon, in most Powhatan dialects /o-/ is the reflex of Proto-Algonquian initial /*we-/, and /a·-/ is the reflex of initial /*wa·-/ before a nonfinal labial consonant. However, in Strachey's material there appear to be a few exceptions to both changes which may represent a different dialect, for example, in such glosses as /weski·k/ 'his (fish's) gill', /wesekwan/ 'his tail', and /wa·passak/ 'white heron'.

ALGONQUIAN COMPARATIVE PHONOLOGY

There have been a number of misunderstandings regarding the perspective of Algonquian comparative studies.[11] The major features of the phonological system of what later became known as Proto-Algonquian (PA) were reconstructed by Leonard Bloomfield[12] in 1925 by a brilliant application of the comparative method on the basis of four languages, namely Fox, Cree,

Menomini, and Ojibwa. At that time only two of these languages, Cree and Menomini, were personally familiar to Bloomfield, and he supplemented his own knowledge of Cree with some data drawn from Lacombe.[13] For Fox he used the published materials of William Jones and Truman Michelson, relying heavily upon Jones' texts.[14] Bloomfield never did hear Fox in the field and his extensive knowledge of that language was derived entirely from his complete and meticulous analysis of Jones' Fox texts, supplemented by a similar study of some of Michelson's publications, especially his Owl Sacred Pack.[15] For Ojibwa he used the work of William Jones,[16] and the missionary fathers Baraga[17] and Cuoq.[18] Since at that time the other languages of the stock were considered by Bloomfield to be inadequately recorded, he gave the reconstructed forms based on these four languages the name Primitive Central Algonquian (PCA) as a cover-term. He did not use the term Proto-Central Algonquian or define such a group as a specific genetic entity with features held in common as opposed to other Algonquian languages, and said "the exact grouping is doubtful". However, he did employ the expression "pre-Central Algonquian" in passing to project a theoretical earlier stage of general Algonquian.[19] It was Michelson who gave the first impetus to the Proto-Algonquian thesis when in several papers he demonstrated that Bloomfield's reconstructions largely satisfied the requirements of other Algonquian languages and especially of the Plains languages, Arapaho and Cheyenne. He used the term from 1926 on, but made his major summary in 1935.[20] Bloomfield himself came to use the term Proto-Algonquian in his papers published in 1939 and 1941.[21] In the period from 1937 to 1941 Bloomfield went on to make a detailed investigation of Ojibwa. Based on his own work on Ojibwa, Michelson's comparative studies, his examination of the materials of Voegelin on Shawnee and Delaware, and this writer's on Penobscot and Munsee at the 1939 Linguistic Institute at Ann Arbor, and the demonstration that the Eastern Algonquian languages are revelant for determining some original consonant clusters,[22] Bloomfield in 1946 made his final version[23] of his reconstruction of what he then called Proto-Algonquian. In his revision Bloomfield set up postconsonantal /*-wi/ and /*-yi/, eliminated the pseudo-cluster /*θš/, adopted /*θk/ as a valid cluster, and recognized the status of initial /*we-/ which was projected from his perusal of the Eastern Algonquian materials. A model of condensation and clarity, it became the standard reference on Algonquian.

Today Bloomfield's final version seems to require a few minor revisions and additions.[24] His PA cluster /*št/, supported only by Cree and Ojibwa and found only in one example /*weštekwa·ni/ 'his head', is isolated and appears to be of tenuous validity. Some other consonant clusters should be recognized in addition to /*θk/. For example, /*θp/, which Bloomfield did not describe, had seemed probable ever since /*θk/ was described, but at that time only one example was known to me, namely /*naθpyi/ 'with, together', as shown by Cree (eastern dialect) /aspiy/, Massachusee <u>nashpe</u> /naspi/, Delaware /naxpi/, and Penobscot /nspi/ (morphophonemically |nəspi|) 'at the same time, together'. There are a few additional examples of /*θp/, such as in the PA root /*weθpa·-/ 'rouse, wake from slumber', attested by Cree /waspa·-/, Ojibwa /oppa·-/ with conjunct /we·ppa·-/, and Penobscot |wəspɑ-| with conjunct /wespɑ-/.

Bloomfield's treatment (1946) of interconsonantal sequences of glide plus vowel (or nonsyllabic vowel plus syllabic vowel) also calls for minor revision and two additions. He described the interconsonantal sequences /*ya, *ya·, *yi, *yi·, *wi, *wi·, *we·, and *ye·/, but made no mention of the interconsonantal sequences /*we/ and /*ye/, both of which can be identified by reflexes in Eastern Algonquian. Failure to recognize these two sequences has caused some problems in reconstruction and both are of frequent occurrence.

The PA sequence /*we/ is common and is found in PA /*eškwete·wi/ 'fire' (Bloomfield's /*eškote·wi), F /aškote·wi/, C /iskote·w/, M /eskotɛ·w/, O /iškote·/, P /sk^{w}ə̀te/ (|askwəte|), and in PA /*no·hkwema 'my grandmother' (Bloomfield's /*no·hkomehsa/ dimin.), F /no·hkomesa/, C /no·hkom/, M /no·hkomɛh/, O /no·kkomiss/, P /nòhkəməss/ (before a labial consonant the P reflex of interconsonantal /*we/ is /ə/), mD /nó·həm/. Cree and Delaware use the nondiminutive form.

PA /*ye/ is found in many examples also, among them: PA /*a·čyemwiwa 'he narrates, tells anecdotes or news' (Bloomfield's /*a·čimowa/), F /a·čimowa/, C /a·čimow/, M /a·čemow/ (M /a·čemwan/ 'narrative'), O /a·čimo/, S /a·čimo/, and P /àčəmo/; PA /*no·hšyehsa/ 'my grandchild

(i. e., 'my little child', PA /*-o·hšy-/ 'child', plus diminutive PA /*-ehs-/), (Bloomfield's /*no·hšihsema/), F /no·šisema/, C /no·sisim/, M /no·hsehsεh/, D (all dialects) /nó·xwi·s/, Mh /nó·xi·s/, P /nòhsəss/ 'my kinsman' (usually 'my child of my niece or nephew', with semantic change; dependent stem |-ohsəhs|); PA /*nemyehsa/ 'my older sister' (Bloomfield's /*nemihsa/), F /nemise·ha/, C /nimis/, M /neme·h/, pl. /neme·hsak/, O /nimisse·nʔ/, S /nimiʔθa/, D (all dialects) /nəmí·s/, and P /nə̀məssis/ (dependent stem |-məhs|).

PROTO-EASTERN ALGONQUIAN

Eastern Algonquian forms no trenchant subdivision within general Algonquian as a whole, but does exhibit a few morphological and phonological innovations and some distinctive lexical features which apparently are not found elsewhere. The lexical specialities are probably preserved archaisms for the most part, and to a less degree neologisms. They are labeled Proto-Eastern Algonquian (PEA) but this does not imply any profound genetic divarication. Nevertheless, some characteristics of the eastern languages are sufficiently distinctive that one can speak of Proto-Eastern Algonquian as a latent subdivision of general Algonquian. Goddard in his brilliant paper on the Algonquian independent indicative[25] has pointed out that the chief morphological innovation of Proto-Eastern Algonquian was a thorough rebuilding of the transitive inanimate verb (TI) with its double paradigm of absolute and objective forms so that the original PA absolute third person singular ending /*-amwa/ was generalized in PEA throughout the entire TI paradigm, first in the PEA absolute paradigm and then analogically in the PEA objective paradigm, to make a functionally new PEA TI theme-sign /*-am/. The old PA TI objective singular ending /*-en-/, found also in the inanimate subject verb forms, was then taken to be a suffix marking the objective TI paradigm, so that in PEA /*-en/ acquired a new function as a formal element signaling the PEA TI objective.

The phonological system of Proto-Eastern Algonquian was not radically different from that of Proto-Algonquian, one of the chief sound changes being the lenition of preglottalized consonant clusters to become preaspirated clusters. These changes can be schematized as follows:

PA		PEA	PA		PEA
/*ʔl/	>	/*hl/	/*ʔθ/	>	/*hθ/
/*ʔš/	>	/*hš/	/*ʔs/	>	/*hs/
/*ʔt/	>	/*ht/	/*ʔč/	>	/*hč/

The vowel phoneme inventory of PEA was identical with that of PA, but by the earliest period of PEA two vocalic sound changes had already occurred. PA word-initial /*e-/ became PEA /*a-/, and PA final /*-wa/ was lost following a nonsyllabic other than /*k/. Otherwise the final short vowels of PA, /*-i, *-e, *-a/, were retained in early PEA.

The PA prenasalized consonant clusters /*mp, *nt, *nč, *nk, *nl, *nθ, *nš, *ns/ were retained in the earliest period of PEA.

The original contrast of PA /*l/ and /*θ/ was preserved in the earliest stage of PEA, /*l/ being a voiced lateral, probably apico-alveolar, and /*θ/ a voiceless lateral or lateral fricative, probably apico-alveolar also.[2 The two phonemes in contrast shared all phonological features except the feature of voice, differing only by the presence or absence of one feature and establishing the unidimensional opposition of voiced/unvoiced. Phonem /*θ/ was then the unmarked member of the pair, and /*l/ the marked member with the feature of voice. The two were identical in their phonological behavior except that /*θ/ was replaced in alternation by /*š/ before /*i, *i·, *y/ in PEA, as Bloomfield[27] has shown to have occurred in PA.

Dialectic divergence within the whole PEA group evidently started early and followed different directions within a large area and over a long period of time. One large body of PEA speakers who later occupied a marginal geographical distribution in two large unconnected enclaves on the periphery of the Atlantic coast can, for this reason, be called the archaic coastal grou of Proto-Eastern Algonquians and their speech which has an unique feature not found elsewhere in Algonquian can be labeled tentatively as PEA-A. The distinguishing trait of the PEA-A group was a morphologically conditioned partial coalescence or merger of /*l/ and /*θ/, that is, phonemic change without loss of contrast. In word-final syllables of inflectional suffixes and particles /*l/ as the marked member of a pair of phonemes was neutralized, and unmarked /*θ/ appeared in the position of neutralization. In all other environments the contrast of /*l/ and /*θ/ remained unchanged and the opposition of voice and absence of voice persisted. This partial phonemic coalescence can be schematized as follows:

```
                         PEA          PEA-A
voiced (marked)          /*l/ ------> /*l/
                              \
                               \ . . . . . . . . . . . . (environment: final
                                \                          syllables of inflections
unvoiced (unmarked)      /*θ/ ------> /*θ/                 and particles)
```

Syllable final /*θ/ in inflections and particles was then treated as original /*θ/ elsewhere, and was replaced in alternation by /*š/ before /*i, *i·, *y/. Accordingly the suffix of the plural of the inanimate noun PA /*-ali/ > PEA /*-ali/ > PEA-A /*-aši/, and with loss of short final vowels became /-aš/, or /-as/ in languages where /*š/ and /*s/ fell together. The replacement of /*θ/ by /*š/ by alternation before short final /*-i/ was soon analogically extended in PEA-A so as to occur in all inflections and particles in word-final syllables before all short final vowels such as /*-e/ and /*-a/. In fact, by the operation of analogy the phonemic change of partial coalescence lost its phonological character and became a morphologically conditioned sound change in which inflectional syllable final /*θ/ became /*š/ regardless of whether its origin was PEA /*l/ or /*θ/. Thus the inflection of the transitive animate verb (TA) for first person singular-second person singular or 'I . . . thee' PA /*ke—eθe/ > PEA /*ke—eθe/ > PEA-A /*ke—eše/, and with later loss of short final vowels became Powhatan /ke—es/ and SNE /kə—əs/.

An example involving a particle is PEA /*aθa/ 'or', Penobscot /ȃla/, but giving PEA-A /*aša/, with Massachusee /asa/ 'or' (Eliot and Mayhew <u>asuh</u>, John 2:6), and Nipmuck-Pocumtuck /asa/ 'or' (Mathevet's Loup <u>asse</u>, p. 13).

The PEA-A or archaic coastal group of Proto-Eastern Algonquian is found in two discontinuous enclaves which share this special feature which seems unlikely to be due to a parallel development. The northern peripheral enclave comprises all the closely related languages of southern New England and Long Island (exclusive of Mahican) and may be called the SNE group of Eastern Algonquian. A group in the south embraces the Powhatan confederacy. The exact limits of the latter cannot be determined because of meager data.

At a later date PA and PEA /*θ/ disappeared in all Eastern Algonquian languages by one of three types of complete phonemic coalescence with other phonemes, often called "falling together". In many eastern languages, including Malecite-Passamaquoddy, Eastern and Western Abenaki, and all Delaware dialects, /*θ/ completely merged with /*l/ to give /l/, and for the most part the original alternation of /*θ/ to /*š/ was analogically restored almost without exception as /l/. However, a small residue of /*š/ as an alternation remnant of /*θ/ persisted in some languages. In Nipmuck-Pocumtuck as a member of the SNE and PEA-A groups /s/ remained in syllable final inflections and particles from former /*θ/ although it was an "l" dialect. In Penobscot a residue of the old alternation remained in a few forms, such as P /àso/ 'he fares so' (AI), but the II form is /àle/ 'it happens so', with the II conjunct /ésiwik/ and the TI conjunct passive or indefinite actor form /ésimək/. The PA root /*entaθ-/ 'there, in that place or time', with the Penobscot reflex /tal-/ and changed conjunct /etal-/, however has the derivative form PA /*netentašima·wa/ 'I speak or talk about him', Cree /nitihtasima·w/, Ojibwa /nitašima·/, and Penobscot /nətásimɑ/ in which the ancient alternation is preserved. The Penobscot changed conjunct is /etásimɑt/ 'when he spoke about him', reflecting PA /*e·ntašima·či/.

In some eastern languages (Mohegan-Pequot-Niantic-Montauk) there was a complete loss of PA and PEA /*l/ and /*θ/ which merged with /*y/ to give /y/, and in others (Massachusee-Nauset-Wampanoag) PA and PEA /*l/, /*θ/ and /*n/ coalesced to give /n/.

On the other hand, subsequent to the changes of the PEA-A group in which there was a morphologically conditioned partial merger of /*l/ and /*θ/ to /s/, Powhatan made a complete phonemic coalescence of /*θ/ and /*t/ to /t/, and underwent a complete loss of PA and PEA /*l/ without change in contrast so that /*l/ became Powhatan /r/ which was probably a voiced single tap liquid. The falling together of PEA /*θ/ and /*t/ to /t/ in Powhatan paralleled an identical phonetic change in Cree-Montagnais-Naskapi, but these changes were historically independent and occurred as separate movements after the separation of Eastern Algonquian, which maintained the contrasts of /*t/, /*θ/ and /*l/. This corrects the erroneous interpretation previously given by Michelson[28] and myself[29] that the coalescence of PA /*θ/ and /*t/ to /t/ in Cree and Powhatan was significantly related, when as a matter of fact it was no more than an independent parallel innovation perhaps contingent upon a similar phonetic drift.

THE NUMERALS OF PROTO-ALGONQUIAN AND POWHATAN

In the Algonquian languages the cardinal numerals are based on a primeval digital enumeration in which the hands were customarily held in pronation. The Proto-Algonquian language during at least part of the Proto-Algonquian period was not a homogeneous speech. Individual surviving Algonquian languages show a blending of three original numeral systems, an archaic quinary system, a decimal system, and a protean and surrogate descriptive system. Failure to recognize these facts has caused most of the difficulties that have been encountered in reconstructing the Proto-Algonquian numeral forms. In the quinary system the numeral particles from one to ten fall into two groups, lower numerals of the first hand from <u>one</u> to <u>five</u> which were formed from elementary roots, and the higher numeral particles of the second hand from <u>six</u> to <u>ten</u> which were formed by compounding the roots of the lower numbers with the PA complex final /*-a·šyeka/, consisting of the prefinal /*-a·θ-/ 'by the side, of the row of the second hand' and the abstract final /*-yeka/. To the quinary system belong PA /*nekwetwi/ 'one', /*nyi·šwi/ 'two' (from PA root /*nyi·šw-/ 'couple, pair'), and /*ne?θwi/ 'three', from which are formed the quinary system higher numeral particles PA /*nekwetwa·šyeka/ 'six', /*nyi·šwa·šyeka/ 'seven', and /*ne?šwa·šyeka/ 'eight' which was an analogical or perhaps an assimilative form in the PA period for expected and earlier /*ne?θwa·šyeka/.

In the decimal system there seems to be no clear division into lower and higher numbers. There are some problems of assignment, but the following belong to the decimal system: PA /*pe·šyekwi/ 'one' (from PA root /*pe·θ-/ 'single', supported by O /pe·šik/ 'one', P /pèsək^{w}/ and S /pe·leko/ 'once'; with decimal system abstract final /*-yekwi/), and PA /*ta·pawi/ 'two' (from the extended root or marked allomorph /*ta·paw-/ of the root /*ta·pw-/ 'alike, equal, identical').

The quinary abstract final is PA /*-yeka/ and the decimal system abstract final is /*-yekwi/, which probably is related or paired. The decimal system abstract final appears without a prefinal, but the quinary system abstract final is always preceded by the quinary prefinal /*-a·θ-/ 'of the row of the second hand, by the side'. In some languages the quinary prefinal often functions as a final without the abstract final /*-yeka/ in which case it assumes the form /*-a·ši/ which is evidently the deverbal /*-a·θ-/ of the PA root /*ma·θ-/ 'side by side, in a row', C /ma·t-/.

Throughout the various languages both systems often show replacement by substitute descriptive numeral forms. The descriptive system is disparate because of alternative digital identifications so that the same form may appear with a different meaning in another language. They indicate that the hands were held in pronation while counting. Examples are found in PA /*pe·yakwi/ "little finger" from root /*pe·yakw-/ 'alone, by itself', which appears in Cree as /pe·yak/ 'one' and as /payak/ 'ten' in all of the languages of southern New England and Long Island (SNE group) in which PA /*e·/ and /*a/ fell together to SNE /a/; and PEA /*wi·mpatwi/ which has the reflexes /wi·mpat/ 'one' in Pampticough (or Pamlico)[30] of the North Carolina coast and /wí·mpat/ 'ten' in the Munsee dialect of Delaware.[31]

In addition, the original numeral systems are obscured by frequent new formations, later rebuilding of forms so that elements from the originally separate three systems may be blended, and analogical reshaping, especially analogical alteration of endings. For example, the prevalent PEA /*ta·pawa·ši/ 'seven' is a blend of a decimal system root with the quinary prefinal functioning as a final, and compounded in the style of the quinary system.

Some doublets are found in which a minor contrast serves to distinguish the forms of the quinary and decimal systems, especially at the endpoints of both the lower and higher numeral sets. This has made the independent particles for five and ten confusing and difficult to attempt to reconstruct unless this fact is realized. The assignment of one or the other of each pair to the proper system is arbitrary. The quinary (?) system has PA /*nya·θanwi/ 'five', reflected in Shawnee /niya·lanwi/, Munsee Delaware /ná·lan/, and Arapaho /yóóθón/. The decimal system (?) has PA /*nya·nanwi/ 'five', based on Cree /niya·nan/, and with apocope, Micmac and Malecite-Passamaquoddy /nan/, and Penobscot (coastal dialect) /nɑn/. The Fox, Menomini, Ojibwa, and Mahican reflexes could belong to either system due to the merging of PA /*θ/ and /*n/ in these languages. The archetypes of the doublet for ten are more complicated, and Bloomfield's PA /*meta·tahθe/ and Michelson's /*meta·tahθwi/ do not satisfy the requirements of many languages.

The decimal (?) system has PA /*meta·hθwi/ 'ten' supported by Fox /meta·swi/, Ojibwa /mita·sswi/, and Shawnee /metaʔθwi/. The quinary (?) system has PA /*meta·tanθwi/ 'ten' posited by Cree /mita·taht/ and derived /mita·tahtwa·w/ 'ten times', Menomini /meta·tah/ with stem /meta·tahn-/, and Arapaho /béteetox/, where /x/ is the reflex of /*nθ/ as in Arapaho /wóoxé/ 'knife' from PA /*ma·nθehsi/ 'flint knife'. Eastern Algonquian deviated very early, but follows the quinary (?) pattern with PEA /*metaθanθwi/, and due to the ancient variation of PA and PEA /*a/ and /*e/, besides PEA /*metaθanθwi/, there are also the PEA variants /*metaθenθwi/ and /*meteθenθwi/. PEA /*metaθanθwi/ proceeds from PA /*meta·tanθwi/ by regressive assimilation in which the PEA adformate sequence /*-aθ-/ has replaced PA /*-a·t-/ before /*-anθ-/. PEA /*metaθanθwi/ 'ten' is posited by Penobscot (and other Abenaki dialects) /mə̀tala/ formed by dissimilatory suppression from pre-Abenaki /*mətalal/ from underlying morphophonemic |mətalahl| , Mahican /mtánit/ by syncope from morphophonemic |metanet| , Delaware (Unami) /télən/, and Micmac and Malecite-Passamaquoddy /mtə́lən/. The Penobscot cluster /hl/ and Mahican /t/ are the regular reflexes of PA and PEA /*nθ/. The reasons for final /-n/ in Delaware and Malecite-Passamaquoddy are not clear, but are perhaps of dissimilative origin, or may be due to a special treatment of word final /*-nθ/ in these languages. At any rate, common Abenaki and Mahican in agreement strongly affirm PEA /*metaθanθwi/, /*metaθenθwi/.

LEXICON

In the Powhatan lexicon we shall conform to the following procedure. To facilitate reference all glosses will be numbered and made under an English entry. Each item will then be presented in three sections. Section (a) will contain what I believe to be the phonemic representation of the Powhatan form; section (b) will give the recording(s) of Smith and Strachey with their English translations in modernized English spelling, together with reference the numbers of Harrington's sheets; and section (c) will present pertinent Pr Algonquian or Proto-Eastern Algonquian reconstructions and supporting comp data when available. Prior reconstructed forms given by Bloomfield not requ emendation are coded (Bl. 1925 or 1946) following the entry. Reconstruction made by myself from 1937 to 1941 and from 1964 to the present, only some of which have been published, are repeated or corrected when required.

Lexicon of Numbers

1. ONE

(a) /nekot/

(b) necut (Smith), nekut (H10), necut (H 11)

(c) PA /*nekwetwi/ 'one', of the archaic quinary s F /nekoti/, M /nekot/, S /nekoti/, uD /kwə́t·i/, mD /nkwə́ti/, Mh /nkwíta/ (from |nekweta| with vowel analogically reshaped).

2. TWO

(a) /ni·ns/, with unoriginal /n/ as in some Miami-I dialects.

(b) ningh (Smith), ninge (H10)

(c) PA /*nyi·šwi/ 'two', of the archaic quinary system, from PA root /*nyi·šw-/ 'couple, pair'. F /ni·šwi/, C /ni·so/, M /ni·s/, O /ni·š/, S / P /nis/, D /ní·ša/, Mh /ní·sa/, Mi /ni·šwi/ a /ni·nšenwi/ 'twice', Illinois (Boulanger and Gra /ni·nšwi/.

3. THREE

(a) /nass/, /nassa/, perhaps dialect difference.

(b) nuss (Smith), nussaugh (H10), nus (H14)

(c) PA /*neʔθwi/ (Bl46) 'three', of the archaic quin system. F /neswi/, C /nisto/ and /nistwa·w/ 't times', M /nɛʔniw/, O /nisswi/, S /nθwi/, P / D /náxa/, Mh /náxa/.

4. FOUR

(a) /ye·w/

(b) yowgh (Smith), yeough (H16)

(c) PA /*nye·wwi/ (Bl25) 'four', of the decimal syst F /nye·wi/, C /ne·wo/, Mt /ne·w/, M /ni·w/,

O /ni·win/, S /niye·wi/, P (and all EA dialects) /yew/, WA and all SNE languages /yaw/, Mh /náwa/, D /né·wa/, Mc /new/, Ml-Ps /new/, Mi and Illinois /ni·wi/.

It is interesting to note that word initial PA /*ny-/ in the chain of PEA languages from Newfoundland to North Carolina always occurs before historical PEA /*e·/, but is reduced to either /n-/ or /y-/, these features being distributed in four regions: (1) /n-/ in the north (Mc, Ml, Ps), (2) /y-/ in all Abenaki and SNE languages, (3) /n-/ in Mh and all Delaware dialects, and (4) /y-/ again in the south in Nanticoke, Powhatan, and Pamlico.

5. FIVE

(a) /pare·nsk/

(b) paranske (Smith), parance (H12)

(c) PEA /*pale·neθkwi/ 'five', of the PEA descriptive system, which is probably analogical for an earlier /*pale·neθki/ derived from the PA dependent noun /*-neθki/ 'hand', reshaped by analogy to the ending of the decimal system abstract final /*-yekwi/, and the PEA root /*pale·-/ of uncertain meaning. P (and all EA dialects except the coastal dialect of Penobscot) /pálenəsk^{w}/, uD /palé·naxk/.

6. SIX

(a) /ka·ma·tenč/

(b) comotinch (Smith), camatenge (H4)

(c) Pseudo-PA /*ka·ma·čihčini/ 'six' and by haplology PEA /*ka·ma·hčini/, of the descriptive system (i. e. "contrary or opposite thumb," confirming that the hands were held in pronation while counting). Ps-Ml /kamáhčin/ 'six', Powhatan /ka·ma·tenč/ with the relatively late substitution of final /-tenč/ from the PA dependent noun /*-θenčy-i/ 'hand, finger'. There is a cognate in Montauk of eastern Long Island but it is poorly recorded as conma.

The root is PA /*ka·ma·t-/ 'contrary, opposite sparingly attested in M /kama·č/ 'contrarily', a ently morphophonemic M |ka·ma·t-|. The final is /*-ihčin-i/ 'thumb', deverbal from the following PA /*nečihčini/ 'my thumb' INAN; C /ničihčin/; P /nə̀čihčin/.

7. SEVEN

(a) /ta·pawa·s/

(b) toppawoss (Smith), but not recorded by Strachey.

(c) PEA /*ta·pawa·ši/ 'seven', a blend of the decin system root PA /*ta·paw-/ 'two, two of a kind' extended form or marked allomorph of PA root /*ta·pw-/ 'alike, equal, identical') for which c pare Mc and Ml-Ps /tapo/ 'two', and the PA qui system prefinal /*-a·θ-/ functioning as the fina /*-a·ši/ 'of the row of the second hand'. Prefir /*-a·θ-/ is the deverbal of the PA root /*ma·θ- 'side by side, in a row'. P (and all EA dialects) /tȁpawɑs/, Mh /tá·pawa·s/, and equivalents ar found in the SNE dialects of central Long Island a in Pamlico of the North Carolina coast.

8. EIGHT

(a) /nasswa·s/

(b) nusswash (Smith), nuschawas (H10)

(c) PA /*neʔšwa·šyeka/ 'eight', of the archaic quin system, and probably analogical or assimilative an earlier form during the PA period from PA root /*neʔθw-/ 'three', positing early PA /*neʔθwa· If the change was analogical the source was in th act of counting from quinary PA /*nyi·šwa·šyeka 'seven', supported by Moose Cree /ni·swa·sik/ uD /ni·šá·š/, mD /ni·šwá·š/, and Ms /nisɑsək (Eliot nesáusuk, Cotton nēsasuk), or it may have been caused by regressive assimilation.

F /nešwa·šika/, M /suasek/ for expected /*nɛʔsuasek/, O /niššwa·sswi/ (ending analogi reshaped), S /nθwa·šikθwi/ (ending analogically reshaped), P (and all EA dialects) /nsàsək/ from underlying |nəhsɑsək| , D /xa·š/, Mh /xá·sa/.

9. NINE (a) /ke·ka·ta·s/

(b) kekatawgh (Smith), kykeytawc (H9)

(c) This is a descriptive system form with the quinary prefinal, suggesting the pseudo-PEA formation /*ke·kya·ta·ši/ 'nine' but there are no similar forms in other languages except C /ke·ka·t-mita·taht/ 'nine'. The root is /*ke·kya·t-/ found in PA /*ke·kya·ta/ 'almost, nearly', F /ke·kya·ta/, C /ke·ka·č/, O /ke·ka·/, P /kèkɑ/.

10. TEN (a) /ka·ski·k/

(b) kaskeke (Smith), koske (H9)

(c) There is a cognate in Pamlico (Pampticough cosh, Lawson 1709, p. 226; misprint for cosk or coshk?) which suggests a southeastern PEA /*ka·škyekwi/ 'ten' formed with the decimal system abstract final PA /*-yekwi/.

It is perhaps impossible to reconstruct the entire Proto-Algonquian number system with proper assurance by the strict comparative method of the neogrammarians without the aid of written records from antiquity. This can be attributed to the dying out of elements, extensive analogical changes, possibly some interlingual borrowing, and the fragmentation of a triadic nomenclature in the course of several millennia of attrition. It is probable that the quinary, decimal, and descriptive orders of numerals are, relatively speaking, of nearly equal age and reflect a social stratification among the Proto-Algonquian people in which each class manifested some speech differences. Diglossia is known to occur in some societies in which there are noble and ignoble castes, or, in which there is an absorbing sexual dichotomization. The latter is often based on a sexual division of labor and predisposing social attitudes reinforced by taboos, especially menstrual and pubertal customs requiring separate residence. The second situation would seem to correspond to the practices of the Proto-Algonquians, and had sociolinguistic consequences. The Proto-Algonquian language was not a uniform speech, and not only were there distinctions in the number systems, but also frequent doublets and multiple reconstructible lexical items with the same meaning. One can speculate with some reason but with absolute proof that there were socially standardized but mutually intelligible differences in the speech of men and women, and possibly of children as we Furthermore, it is suspected that the ancient innovations in the separate spe of children may account for the surviving descriptive number system. One c suggest too, without proof, that the quinary system represents the original usage of women and the decimal system that of men. Early atomization and widespread dispersal of the Algonquian peoples seems to have resulted in th disintegration of such age-sex distinctions in speech so that the descendent languages recorded in modern times show confused and haphazard patterns o retention of the number systems and other reconstructible doublets and dupli lexical items. Without ancient written records full explication of Proto-Algo by the comparative method is a sanguine prospect but has serious limitations A *de facto* archaism must persist in at least two adequately recorded descend languages even to be considered as reconstructible, and then the two cognat may not show the requisite sound distinctions to make a satisfactory reconstruction. Moreover, when two or more glosses in identical semantic catego are reconstructed so that there is a duplication of meaning, the temporal and sociolinguistic relations of these contrasting reconstructions are difficult to determine. On the other hand, an archaism surviving in only one language o stock usually cannot be identified as such by the neogrammarian method unle supported by internal reconstruction, and even more unfavorable, an original feature not persisting in any extant language is irretrievably lost. An incom quasi-idealized syllabus, in part speculative rather than demonstrably rigoro of the Proto-Algonquian number systems is epitomized below. The doublet n bers for *five* and *ten* of the quinary and decimal systems are arbitrarily assig since there are no obvious distinguishing criteria.

	Quinary	Decimal	Fused Quinary-Decim
1.	/*nekwetwi/	/*pe·šyekwi/	
2.	/*nyi·šwi/	/*ta·pawi/	
3.	/*ne?θwi/	....	
4.	/*ša·ka/	/*nye·wwi/	
5.	/*nya·θanwi/	/*nya·nanwi/	
6.	/*nekwetwa·šyeka/	....	
7.	/*nyi·šwa·šyeka/	....	/*ta·pawa·šyeka/

8.	/*ne?θwa·šyeka/	....
9.	/*ša·ka·šyeka/	/*no·lyiwi/
10.	/*meta·tanθwi/	/*meta·hθwi/

Descriptive System

1 or 10. ("little finger")	/*pe·yakwi/ (C, Mt, all SNE)
1 or 10.	/*wi·mpatwi/ (mD, Pamlico)
5. ("full (?) hand")	/*pale·neθki/ (EA, uD, Powhatan)
5. ("on one of two sides")	/*napaθe·θwi/ (Mt, most SNE, Nanticoke)
6. ("opposite thumb")	/*ka·ma·čihčini/ (Ml, Ps, Montauk, Powhatan)
7. ("pointer, forefinger")	/*eθwahikani/ (F, M, Ml, Ps, Mc)

Attention should be called to the fact that Fox /ša·ka/ and reshaped Menomini /sa·kε·w/ 'nine', found also in modified form in some eastern Cree dialects, are believed to represent original quinary four, and that these languages transferred digital identification to the other hand. This is supported by the Ojibwa and Shawnee numbers for nine which, although they have analogically reshaped endings, provide evidence of the quinary higher numeral pattern following the quinary root /*ša·k-/, Ojibwa /ša·nk-/ with unoriginal n-stop cluster as shown by eastern Cree and Menomini /sa·k-/.

Word Lexicon

It is probably impossible to disentangle all of Strachey's recordings because of errors in given meaning which are compounded with the difficulties that one encounters in interpreting his handwriting. This lexicon consequently is confined to glosses which the author believes are reasonably certain. Doubtlessly additional recordings can be solved by further investigation. However, the following lexicon will suffice to determine the major phonological features of Powhatan and to ascertain the reflexes of most of the Proto-Algonquian consonant clusters.

11. ABOVE
   (a) /oskič/
   (b) oskeitch "above" (H2)
   (c) PA /*weθkiči/, /*waθkiči/ 'above, on top (of), on the surface of, on the outside of', F /ahkwiči/ (reshaped by analogy to Fox root /akw-/ 'cover'), C /waskič/, M /wahke·č/, O /akkit-/ as in /akkita·kki/ 'on the land', P /wskíči/. However,

S /oškiči/ does not match. The PA root is /*we *waθkit-/ and shows the ancient variation of /* and /*a/.

A common form is PA /*waθkitaxkamikwi/ 'th world, the top of the ground expanse, the surfac the earth, the upperworld', C /waskitaskamik/, M /wahke·tahkamek/, P /wskítkamik^{w}/ with syncope, from |waskitahkamikw|.

12. ACORN (a) /ana·skimin/ INAN, pl. /ana·skimins/

(b) anaskemens "acorns" (H2), anaskimmens "acorn (H2)

(c) PEA /*ana·θkimini/ (?) 'acorn', cluster /*θk/ proven. P /anáskimin/, pl. /anaskíminal/, Np /anasčiminas/ (Mathevet p. 37 anechemanĕs "glands").

13. ANT (a) /e·rikwess/, pl. /e·rikwessak/

(b) arigwessac "ants" (H2)

(c) PA /*e·likwa/ 'ant', (PA /*-ikw-a/ 'gnawing creature, rodent'), F /e·nikono·sa/ dimin., C /e·yik/, pl. /e·yikwak/, M /ε·nek/, O /e·nik Mi /e·likwa/, mD /e·líkwəs/, pl. /e·líkwsak/, P /énik^{w}əss/, pl. /énik^{w}sak/ (borrowed from sor n-dialect since all other EA dialects have /élik^{w}

14. ARISE (a) /pasekwi·w/ (AI) 'he arises, gets up from his s /pasekwi·s/ (2 pers. sing. imper.) 'arise!, get up from your seat!'

(b) passaqueac "rise up" (H13)

(c) PA /*pasekwi·wa/ (AI) 'he arises, gets up from seat', F /pasekwi·wa/, C /pasiko·w/, O /pas S /paθekwi/. PA /*pasekwi·lwe/ (2 pers. sing imper.) 'arise!, get thou up from your seat!', F /pasekwi·no/, O /pasikwi·n/, S /paθekwi·lo/, Np /pasikwis/ (Mathevet pp. 14, 62, 114 passik8 "leve toy").

15. ARM (a) /nenesk/ 'my arm' INAN, pl. /neneskas/ 'my a

(b) nesc "arm" (H2), nneuscos "arms" (H2)

(c) PA /*neneθki/ 'my arm, hand' INAN, pl. /*neneθkali/, F /nenehki/, M /nenε·h/, pl. /nenε·hkan/, O /ninikk/, pl. /ninikkan/, S /ne?ki/, pl. /nine?kali/, uD /nnaxk/, Mh /nnisk/.

16. ARROW (a) /ato·ns/ 'arrow'; /askwiwa·n/ 'arrow'; /assawa·n/ 'fletched arrow with a head' AN, pl. /assawa·nak/

(b) attonce "arrows" (Smith); asgweowan "arrow" (H2), vsquion "arrow" (H15); assaovncawk "feathers of an arrow" (H6), assamvnh "head of an arrow that is round" (H7), with miswriting of m for w.

(c) PA /*aθwi/ 'arrow' (PA root /*aθw-/ 'round'), dimin. PA /*aθo·nsi/, C /atos/, M /ani·h/, pl. /ano·n/, O /anwi/, pl. /anwi·n/, S /alwi/, pl. /alo·li/, D /aló·ns/, P /ȃlos/ 'penis', but 'arrow' in other EA dialects. It is INAN in all languages except D which has pl. /aló·nsak/.

PA /*akaxkwa/ 'blunt or round-headed arrow' (gender doubtful); F /akahkwi/ 'arrow', pl. /akahko·ni/ INAN, C /akask/ 'round-headed arrow', pl. /akaskwak/ AN, P |-ahkw| in /énikahk^{w}/ 'fish-spear', pl. /eníkahk^{w}ak/; Powhatan /askw-/ in /askwiwa·n/ seems to be a root which appears as the deverbal noun final /*-axkw-/ in the other languages. It is not the same as PA /*-a·xkw-/ 'wood'.

PA /*a?θawa·na/ 'fletched arrow, arrow with a stone head and feathers' AN; O /assawa·n/, pl. /assawa·nak/; P /ssȁwɑn/, pl. /ssáwɑnal/ 'stone arrowhead(s)', /nətáhsawɑn/ 'my arrowhead'; compare C /astawe·w/ 'he fletches arrows'.

17. AWAKE (a) /amamo·w/ (AI) 'he awakes, wakes up'; /amamis/ (2 pers. sing. imper.) 'awake!, wake up!'

(b) vmamuū "waken" (H15), aumaumec "awake" (H2)

(c) PA /*amamwiwa/ (AI) 'he awakes, wakes up'; S /amamo/.

18. AWL

(a) /mekwess/ 'awl', /omekwessem/ 'his awl'.

(b) vmeqwussum "a stab" (H13)

(c) PA /*mekwehsi/ 'awl' (cluster /*hs/ not prove
since there is no Menomini cognate and it could
/*ʔs/), PA /*wemekwehsemi/ 'his awl'; F /me
pl. /mekosani/, /omekosemi/ 'his awl'; O /mik
pl. /miko·ssan/; P /mə̀kohs/, pl. /mə̀kohsal/,
/wəmə̀kohsəm/ 'his awl'; mD /məkó·s/; Ms an
/məkws/ (Ms mukqs Eliot, Exodus 21:6, Deutero
15:17; Np mĕk8s, pl. mĕk8ssak AN, Mathevet p.

19. BAG, BASKET

(a) /meno·te·/ 'bag, basket', pl. /meno·tas/; dimi
/meno·te·ns/ 'small basket'.

(b) manote "basket" (H10), mannottaihcaun "make a
ket"; manotyens "little baskets" (actually sg.)
(Smith)

(c) PA /*-mo·tayi/ (dependent noun) 'bag, basket,
M /nemu·ti·h/ 'my bag' dimin., pl. /nemu·ti·h
/omu·ti·h/ 'his bag'; O /nimo·te·ns/ 'my pock
dimin. (dependent noun).

PA and only PEA form /*meno·tayi/ 'someone'
bag; bag, basket, sack' with indefinite possess
prefix /*me-/ and with /m/ replaced by /n/ by
dissimilation; M /menu·ti·h/ dimin. (from /-mu
by dissimilation as Bloomfield showed, Menomin
Lang. 6.84, p. 131), pl. /menu·ti·hsan/; P /mə̀n
pl. /mə̀notal/, /nəmə̀note/ 'my bag' with the in-
definite prefix treated as part of the stem |mənota
mD /mənó·te·s/ 'pouch' AN dimin., pl.
/mənó·te·sak/.

20. BALL

(a) /atow/ 'ball', /atowetowe·w/ 'cymbling, summe
squash'.

(b) attowh "ball" (first t not crossed) (H2), autowta
"ear of wheat" (H5)

(c) PA /*atowa/ 'ball, mushroom' AN; M /wato·w/
'ball' AN, /wa·patow/ 'mushroom' (i.e., "whit

ball"); S /atowa/ 'mushroom', pl. /atowaki/; P /atówsak^{w}e/ 'jack-o'-lantern, false chanterelle' INAN (refers to phosphorescent mushrooms of genus *Clitocybe*), and P /atówətəwan/ 'crookneck or winter squash' (*Cucurbita moschata* Duchesne) INAN; |atow-əhs-akway|, |atow-ətow-an|.

PEA /*atowetowe·wa/ 'cymbling or summer squash' (*Cucurbita maxima* Duchesne) AN; P /atówətəwe/ 'cymbling' AN, pl. /atówətəwak/.

21. BAST

(a) /wi·kepi/ 'bast, wicopy, piece of inner fibrous bark of linden or leatherwood' (*Dirca palustris* L.), INAN, pl. /wi·kepi·s/.

(b) *weihkippeis* "hemp" (H8), (actually pl.)

(c) PA /*wi·kwepyi/ 'bast, piece of inner fibrous bark', pl. /*wi·kwepyali/; F /wi·kopi/, pl. /wi·kopye·ni/; M /we·kop/, pl. /we·kopyan/; O /wi·kop/, pl. /wi·kopi·n/; S /wi·kopi/, pl. /wi·kopiwali/; P /wìkəpi/, pl. /wìkəpəyal/. In addition to the above meanings, in Penobscot the term is used also for the sapwood splints of the black ash employed in making baskets. This is INAN, however, there is an AN form as follows: PA /*wi·kwepya/ 'tree ring (of annual growth), concentric layer of wood' AN; P /wìkəpi/, pl. /wìkəpəyak/; but unfortunately this has not been recorded in other languages.

22. BEARD

(a) /mi·ssetonowa·n/ 'beard' INAN, pl. /mi·ssetonowa·ns/ 'facial hairs, whiskers'.

(b) *weihsatonowans* "beard" (H2), *messetonoanse* "beard" (H10), *wisetonoans* "beard" (H15); the first and third examples evidently have an error of *w* for *m*.

(c) PA /*mi·ʔletona·kani/ 'beard'; F /mi·setona·kani/; M /me·ʔnetona·kan/ AN; C /mi·hyi·stowa·n/ (mi·hy- 'hairy', deverbal -i·stow-, PA /*-i·ʔtow-/, 'whisker', and abstract noun final -a·n); O /mi·ssitona·kan/. The PA elements are /*mi·ʔl- 'hairy', deverbal medial /*-eton-/ from dependen noun stem /*-eto·n-i/ 'mouth', and noun final /*-a·kan-i/ 'device, contrivance'.

The Powhatan word /mi·ssetonowa·n/ 'beard' has the same root or initial element and the same medial as the PA form, but a different prefinal /-ow-/ and final /-a·n/ similar to the Cree term, as if pseudo-PEA /*mi·hletonowa·ni/.

23. BEAVER

(a) /po·yawe·w/ 'young beaver, pup of any fur-bearing mammal up to one year of age'.

(b) pohkeuwh "otter or rather beaver" (H11), with mishearing or miswriting of what looks like a k but possibly could be intended for a y.

(c) PA /*po·yawe·wa/ 'beaver up to one year of age, pup of any fur-bearing mammal'; C /po·yawe·w/; O /apo·yawe·/ with prothetic unoriginal vowel; P /pəyáwehso/ dimin., |poy-awe-əhs-iw|.

24. BIG

(a) /manki/ (II) 'it is big'.

(b) aquintayne manggey "a great ship" (H2)

(c) PA root /*mank-/ 'big'; F /mak-/, /makekinwa/ 'he is big'; M /mahk-/, /mahka·hkosew/ 'he is big (as a wooden object)'; O /mank-/, /mankiška·/ 'it is big'; S /mak-/, /makiya·wi/ 'they (INAN pl.) are big'; uD /amánki/ 'it is big', with prothetic vowel.

25. BIRD

(a) /si·ssi·p/ 'bird, fowl, duck'.

(b) tshessip "bird" (H3)

(c) PA /*ši·ʔši·pa/ (B146) 'duck, fowl, large bird'; F /ši·ši·pa/; C /si·si·p/; M /se·ʔsep/; O /ši·šši·p/; S /šiʔši·pa/; P /ssìpəss/ dimin., /nətáhsipsəm/ 'my duck, bird, fowl', stem |ahsip-əhs|.

26. BITCH

(a) /askwe·ssem/

(b) vsqwausum "bitch" (H3)

(c) PA /*eθkwe·ˀθemwa/ 'bitch'; C /iskwe·stim/; P /sk^{w}èhsəmohs/ dimin., |askwehsəmw-əhs|.

27. BLACK (a) /mahkate·we·w/ (II) 'it is black'. See COAL, entry 52.

(b) mahcatawaiuwh "black" (H3)

(c) PA /*maxkate·we·wi/ 'it is black'; F /mahkate·wa·wi/; C /mahkate·wa·w/; M /mahka·tɛ·w-/ 'black' (prenoun); O /makkate·wa·/; S /mkate·wa/; P /mkasewi-/ and /mehkasayi-/ 'black' (paired prenouns), root |məhkasew-|, (reshaped by analogical contamination with PA /*maxkanšye·wi/, P /mkàse/ 'coal, ember'); mD /máhkate·w/.

There is some doubt about the cluster /*xk/ in this gloss, for Cree points to /*hk/, but Munsee supports /*xk/ which is the regular source of /hk/, and PA /*hk/ has the reflex /h/ in all Delaware dialects. Powhatan seems to have /sk/ as the reflex of /*xk/, but there are apparently some exceptions where /hk/ occurs. Since it can be shown that Strachey recorded more than one dialect of Powhatan it seems quite possible that one dialect had /sk/ as the reflex of /*xk/ and the other /hk/. Possible borrowing in one or more languages may account for some of the discrepancies.

For the alternation of /*a·/:/*e·/, leveled out in Fox, Cree, Ojibwa, and Shawnee see Bloomfield (1946; Section 35, p. 98).

28. BLOOD (a) /mesk/ 'blood'.

(b) miskc "heart" (H10); misunderstanding for 'blood'.

(c) PA /*meçkwi/ 'blood' (B125); F /meškwi/; C /mihkoh/, /nimihk/ 'my blood'; Mt /mohk/; M /mɛhki·h/; O /miskwi/; S /mškwi/; mD

/mohk/; Nr /məskwi/ (Roger Williams mishquè, msqui "blood").

29. BLOW (a) /nepo·ta·tamen/ 'I blow (on) it'.

(b) nepotatamen "to blow anything" (H3)

(c) PA /*nepo·ta·ta/ 'I blow it', /*po·ta·tamwa/ 'he blows it' (TI absolute); F /nepo·ta·ta/ 'I blow on it, I make a fire', /po·ta·tamwa/ 'he makes a fire, blows on it'; C /po·ta·tam/ 'he blows it'; M /po·tawɛw/ 'he builds a fire'; O /nipo·ta·ta·n/ 'I blow (on) it' from PA TI-objective /*nepo·ta·ta·ni/; S /nipo·ta·ta/ 'I blow on it'; P /nəpotáwαtamən/ 'I blow on it', /pótawe (AI) 'he blows, he (snake, cat) hisses'.

The simplex root is PA /*po·t-/ 'blow, hiss' but some languages (Menomini and Penobscot) use the extended root or marked allomorph /*po·taw-/.

30. BLOW NOSE (a) /saniko·w/ 'he blows his nose, sneezes'.

(b) zanekoue "sneeze" (H16)

(c) PA /*sanikwiwa/ 'he blows his nose'; M /sane·ko·w/; P /sániko/, /nəsánik^{w}i/ 'I blow my nose'. Since Ojibwa has /s/ rather than /š/ in a similar form, /*s/ is preferred to /*š/ in the reconstruction.

31. BOAT (a) /messo·t/ 'boat, ship, large watercraft', pl. /messo·tas/

(b) mushowt "ship" (H7), mussawutuc "ship" (H13), (actually pl.)

(c) PA /*meʔθo·ši/ 'boat, large watercraft', pl. /*meʔθo·θali/, with root PA /*meʔθ-/ 'big, great' (B146); C /misto·t/; Mi /misso·li/ with /l/ from /*θ/ analogically restored for reflex of expected /*š/ by analogy to the plural form, pl. /misso·la/; Ms /məsson/ (Eliot and Mayhew mishoon, mushoon, pl. mushoonash "boats",

John 6:23); Nr (Cowesit) /məsson/ (Roger Williams <u>mishoòn</u> "canoe, boat").

The dependent noun stem and noun final PA /*-o·θ-/ 'boat' shows that in the PEA-A languages (Powhatan, Narragansett, and Massachusee) the partial phonemic merger of syllable final /*-l, *-θ/ to /*-š/ or its reflexes did not affect derivational morphemes, but only inflectional suffixes and particle endings.

32. BONE

(a) /waskan/ 'bone'.

(b) <u>wuskan</u> "bone" (H3), <u>wauscan</u> "bone" (H15)

(c) PA /*waθkani/ 'bone', pl. /*waθkanali/; F /ahkani/, pl. /ahkanani/; C /oskan/; M /ohka·n/, pl. /ohka·nan/, /neto·hkanεm/ 'my bone'; O /okkan/, pl. /okkanan/; S /wʔkani/; WA /wskan/; uD /xkan/, mD /waxkán/; Ms /wəskan/, (Eliot <u>wuskon</u> John 19:36, <u>wuskonash</u> pl. Psalm 34:20).

33. BOW

(a) /ahta·p/ 'bow'.

(b) <u>attawp</u> (Smith), <u>auhtab</u> (H3), <u>hawtoppe</u> "bow" (H7)

(c) PA /*aʔta·pya/ 'bow' AN, from PA root /*aʔt-/ 'placed in position, set in place', and noun final /*-a·py-/ 'cord, string'; C /ahča·piy/ reshaped for expected /*asta·piy/ as shown by Montagnais, and with diminutive symbolism of /č/ for /t/ but AN in all dialects; Mt /ašča·piy/ AN, pl. /ašča·pi·č/; P /ttɑ̀pi/, pl. /ttɑ̀pəyak/, /nətáhtɑpi/ 'my bow', /wətáhtɑpəyal/ 'his bow', stem |aht-ɑpiy|; uD /hata·p·i/ AN.

34. BOWEL

(a) /otakes/ 'his bowel', pl. /otakesi·s/ 'his bowels'.

(b) <u>otakeisheheis</u> "guts of anything" (H7)

(c) PA /*-θakešyi/ 'bowel, entrail, gut, intestine' INAN dependent noun, pl. /*-θakešyali/; PA /*weθakešyi/ 'his bowel'; F /onakeši/ 'his bowel', pl. /onakešye·ni/; C /otakisiy/, pl. /otakisiya/; M /ona·kes/, pl. /ona·kesyan/;

O /onakiš/, pl. /onakiši·n/; P /wə̀lakəsi/, pl. /wəlákəsəyal/, dependent stem |-lakəsiy|.

35. BOWL
(a) /ora·kan/ 'bowl, dish'.
(b) ouracan "dish" (H5)
(c) PA /*wela·kani/ 'bowl, dish' (Bl25, Lang. 1:145, /*ula·kani/); F /ana·kani/, pl. /ana·kanani/; C /oya·kan/ INAN; M /ona·kan/; O /ona·kan/, pl. /ona·kanan/; S /ola·ka/, pl. /ola·kana/; P /wə̀lakan/ 'bowl' (not 'dish'), pl. /wəlákanak/ AN.

36. BOWSTRING
(a) /a·pi·s/ 'bowstrings', INAN pl.
(b) aupeis "bowstring" (H3), auppes "bowstring" (H2)
(c) PA /*aʔča·pyi/ 'bowstring' INAN; O /ačča·p/, pl. /ačča·pi·n/. One wonders whether Strachey did not miss an initial syllable since PA /*-a·py-/ does not seem to appear as a root elsewhere. See BOW, entry 33.

37. BOY
(a) /oska·pe·ss/
(b) vscapess "boy" (H3)
(c) PA /*weška·pe·wehsa/ 'young ceremonial attendant, boy attending a chief'; M /oska·pɛ·we
pl. /oska·pɛ·wehsak/; O /oška·pe·wiss/. Note contraction of /*-e·we-/ to /e·/ in Powhatan.

38. BREAD
(a) /apo·n/ 'bread' INAN, pl. /apo·ns, apo·nas/ 'loaves of bread'.
(b) apones "bread" (H2), appoans (H3), apetawh poan "broil or toast bread" (H3), ponas "bread" (pl.) (Smith)
(c) PA /*apwa·na/ 'roast of corn bread' AN, PA /*apwa·ni/ 'roast of meat, roasted haunch'; (F /apo·ne·wa/ 'he makes a roast for him'); C /apwa·n/ 'roast of meat' INAN; M /apuan/ AN 'roast of corn bread', INAN 'roast of meat, roasted haunch'; P /âpan/ 'loaf of bread, corn bread' AN, pl. /ápanak/ 'loaves of bread', dimin. AN

/ápanis/ 'biscuit, cake', pl. /apánisak/.

39. BREAST (a) /oto·ss/ 'her breast', dependent noun, INAN.

(b) otaus "woman's breast" (H16)

(c) PA /*-to·hša/ 'breast, teat, udder' AN dependent noun, PA /*weto·hšali/ 'her breast, teat'; C /mito·to·s/ 'someone's breast, udder' AN dependent noun, /nito·to·sim/ 'my breast'; Mt /oto·to·šim/ 'her breast', /nito·to·šim/ 'my breast'; M /to·to·hs-/ 'teat' in /to·to·hsapoh/ jest word for 'milk', labeled foreign by Bloomfield (Menom. Lang. 1962, 14. 39, p. 232); O /to·to·šš/, pl. /to·to·ššak/ AN, but independent noun, /oto·to·ššan/ 'her breast'.

Cree and Ojibwa have rebuilt the form with intercalated /t/ following the pronominal prefixes, and treated the original third person dependent noun as the remainder of the stem, Ojibwa going one step further than Cree and making a new independent root in /t-/. The Menomini term is probably a loan from Ojibwa. The Powhatan form seems to be the archaic one.

40. BRIAR (a) /ka·wins/ 'briar, bramble' INAN, pl. /ka·winsas/

(b) cawindgus "bramble or briar" (H3), (actually pl.)

(c) PA /*ka·winšyi/ 'bramble, briar, bur' INAN, but PA /*ka·winšya/ 'spine, thorn' AN; S /ka·wi/ 'thorn' AN, pl. /ka·wi·ki/, /ka·wi·ši/ 'briar plant or stalk' INAN; P /káwisi/ AN 'spine, thorn', but INAN 'bramble, briar, bur', pl. /káwisəyak/ 'thorns', /káwisəyal/ 'brambles, briars'; mD /ka·winši/ 'thorn' AN.

41. BROOM (a) /či·kkahikan/, pl. /či·kkahikanas/

(b) tshekehicannous "broom" (H3), (actually pl.)

(c) PEA /*či·kehkahikani/ 'broom'; P /čikkáhikan/; PA has /*či·katahikani/; M /če·katahekan/; O /či·kata?ikan/; S /či·kathika/.

42. BROTHER

(a) /ni·mat/ 'my brother' (man speaking), /ki·mat/ 'thy brother'.

(b) nemat "brother" (H3), kemotte (H8)

(c) PA /*-i·mata/ 'brother', dependent noun, man speaking, /*ni·mata/ 'my brother'; M /ne·mat/ 'my brother' (man speaking), pl. /ne·matak/; mD /ní·mat/ 'my brother' (man speaking); Ms /nimat/ (Eliot nemat "my brother", wematoh "his brother", First Chron. 1:19).

43. BRUSH

(a) /nepawahama/ (AI formed from an objectless TI) 'I do brushing'.

(b) vnepawahamma "brush" (H3)

(c) PA /*pawahamwa/ (TI absolute) 'he brushes it off, knocks it off by instrument'; M /pawa·ham/; PA /*nepawaha·ni/ (TI objective) 'I brush or knock it off by instrument'; M /nepa·wahan/; O /nipawaʔ

44. CANOE

(a) /akwinten/ INAN

(b) acquintan (Smith), aquintayne "canoe, boat" (H2), aqintān "boat" (H3), aqueintan "canoe" (H4)

(c) PEA /*akwintenwi/ 'canoe'; P /ák^{w}itən/, pl. /ák^{w}itənol/. Compare PA /*akwinte·wi/ 'it floats' (II).

45. CAPSIZE

(a) /kotapeska·w/ 'he capsizes, upsets in a boat, he keels or tips over'.

(b) cotappesseaw "overset or a boat to turn keel up" (H11). Note error of ss for sk.

(c) PA /*kweθapeška·wa/ (AI) 'he capsizes, upsets, keels over, tips over in a boat or canoe'; C /kotapiska·w/; O /konapiška·/.

There is also PA /*ko·θka·we·wa/ with the same meaning; F /ko·hka·we·wa/; M /ko·hkawɛw P /kóskawe/.

46. CHESTNUT

(a) /a·pimin/, pl. /a·pimins/ 'chestnuts', INAN

(b) opemens "chestnuts" (H11)

(c) PEA /*wa·pimini/ 'chestnut'; P (and all EA

dialects) /wápimin/ 'chestnut', pl. /wapíminal/ INAN. This term occurs in Fox and Menomini with the meaning 'maize' and in some Ojibwa dialects with the meaning 'apple'. Compare mD /wa·pim/ 'chestnut'.

47. CHILD (a) /neni·ča·n/ 'my child'.

(b) nechaan "child" (H4)

(c) PA /*-ni·čya·na/ 'child, offspring', dependent noun, /*neni·čya·na/ 'my child' (B146 gives only the dimin. PA /*neni·čya·nehsa/); F /neni·ča·nesa/, 'my child', /oni·ča·nesani/ 'his child'; M /neni·čianɛh/; O /nini·ča·niss/; S /nini·ča·na/, /oni·ča·nali/ 'his child'; P /nə̀ničan/, /wəníčanal/ 'his child'; uD /nní·č·a·n/ 'my daughter' with semantic change; Mh /nní·ča·n/, /wní·ča·nan/ 'his child'.

48. CHINQUAPIN (a) /či·hči·nkwe·min/ INAN, pl. /či·hči·nkwe·mins/, (Castanea pumila [L.] Miller), i.e., "prickly eye berry".

(b) chichiquamins "kind of grain to eat" (H4), chechinquamins "nut like a small acorn, good meat" (H11), chechinquamins "like a very small acorn" and "growing on little trees, husked like a chestnut" (Smith)

(c) Pseudo-PEA /*či·hči·nkwe·mini/; from root PA /*či·ˀt-/ 'jab, prick', C /či·st-/, M /če·ˀt-/, O /či·tt-/, and medial PA /*-i·nkwe·-/ 'eye', F /-i·kwe·-/, M /-e·hkwɛ·-/, O /-i·nkwe·-/, P /-ikwe-/, and PA final /*-min-i/ 'berry, grain, fruit, drupe'.

49. CLAW (a) /mehkas/ 'someone's claw, nail, hoof' AN; /nehkas/ 'my nail', pl. /nehkasi·k/

(b) mekouse "nail of fingers or toes" (H10)

(c) PA /*-škašya/ 'claw, nail' AN dependent noun; PA /*neškašya/ 'my nail'; F /neškaši/, pl.

/neškašye·ki/; C /niskasiy/, pl. /niskasiyak/; M /neska·s/, pl. /neska·syak/; O /niškanš/, pl. /niškanši·k/ with unoriginal nasal cluster; S /neškaša/, pl. /neškaše·ki/. However, Eastern Algonquian for obscure reasons reflects a different archetype.

PEA /*-xkašya/, /*nexkašya/ 'my nail'; P /nkàsi/, pl. /nkàsəyak/; uD /nhík·aš/; Ms /nəhkas/ (Eliot wuhkasoh "his nail(s)", Deuteron. 21:12).

50. CLAY (a) /asi·skiw/ 'clay, mud'.

(b) assesquewh "clay they make pipes of" (H2)

(c) PA /*ašyeškiwi/ 'clay, mud'; F /ašiškiwi/; C /asiskiy/; Mt /ašiščiy/; O /ašiški/; S /ašiški/; P /ásəsko/, but /asə́sko/ 'it is muddy' |asəskiw| .

51. CLOUD (a) /a·rahkwat/, pl. /a·rahkwatas/ 'clouds'.

(b) arrokoth "sky" (H2), arrahgwotuwss "clouds" (H4

(c) PA /*a·laxkwatwi/ (II) 'it is a cloud, it is cloudy F /nekwa·nahkwatwi/ 'it is overcast, the clouds lie low'; C /yikwaskwan/ 'it is overcast', as in F from PA root /*lekw-/ 'bury, cover under' (F /nekw-/, C /yikw-/, O /nikw-/, S /lekw-/); M /a·nahkwat/ (II) 'there is a cloud', also noun 'cloud', pl. /a·nahkwaton/; O /nikwakkwat/ 'the sky is buried in clouds, it is overcast', /a·nakkw 'cloud', pl. /a·nakkwato·n/; Mi /a·lahkwatwi/ 'it is cloudy'; Ps /alohkət/ 'it is cloudy'.

The primary PA form appears to be /*waxkwiwi 'cloud'; C /waskow/, pl. /waskowa/; northern O /wahkwi/ 'cloud' (Rogers 1963, p. 154); Cheyen /woˀe/; from which is derived the prevalent deverbal PA /*-axkw-/ 'cloud, sky'; F /-ahkw-/; C /-askw-/; M /-ahkw-/ (see Bl. 1962, Menomi Lang. 18. 149); O /akkw-/.

Some languages however reflect initial short vowel forms followed by the variant PA /*-exkw-/ 'cloud, sky'; F /menehkwatwi/ 'cloud', pl. /menehkwato·ni/; S /menʔkwatwi/ 'sky'; Mi /alihkwatwi/ 'cloud', pl. /alihkwatwa/; Arapaho /hónoʔ/ 'sky'; P /àlohk/ 'evening or night cloud', pl. /álohkal/, beside /àhsohk/ 'daytime cloud', pl. /áhsohkal/, (II) /áhsohkat/ 'it is cloudy'.

52. COAL

(a) /mahkate·s/ 'coal, ember'. See BLACK, entry 27.

(b) mahcateis "coal of fire" (H6)

(c) PEA /*maxkate·wi/ 'coal, ember'; mD /máhkate·w/. This is a formative of PA /*maxkate·we·wi/ 'it is black' for which see entry 27. However, the two common terms for 'coal, ember, charcoal' formed from separate roots for 'black' are as follows:

PA /*maxkanšye·wi/ 'coal, ember, charcoal'; M /mahka·hsiw/; P /mkàse/, pl. /mkàsal/, |mahkasay-|, dimin. /mkàses/ 'small ember or live coal', /mkàsehs/ 'charcoal, old or dead ember' (compare P /mkàsess/ 'crow'); Ms /mahkasa/, (Eliot mahkohsaash "coals" Psalm 18:8). The noun final is PA /*-anšye·w-i/ 'cinder, coal' which is found also in the following form.

PA /*kaxkanšye·wi/ or /*kaxkenšye·wi/ 'coal, ember, charcoal'; F /kahkeše·wi/; C /kaskase·w/; O /kakkanše·/ (also dialectic variants /akkakkanše·/, /kakkiše·/). The root is PA /*kaxk-/ 'black', found in C /kaskite·wa·w/ (beside C /mahkate·wa·w/) 'it is black'; P (coastal dialect) /káhkakohs/ 'crow'.

53. COAT

(a) /meskote·/ 'coat, matchcoat, robe, jerkin, mantle of fur', pl. /meskotas/. Probably a dependent noun, 'someone's coat'.

(b) mautchkoot "coat, jerkin, doublet" (H4), matchkote "stag skin" (H10), matchcores (misprint for matchcotas?) "skins or garments" (Smith). Strachey's recording was probably influenced by the English loan matchcoat, perhaps a Chesapeake trade jargon term. At least match coate is recorded as early as 1638 in the Maryland Archives (IV, 30, 1). Ojibwa /mačiko·te·/ 'petticoat, skirt' is not related and not the source of English matchcoat as has been often stated.

(c) PA /*-θkoθayi/ 'coat, jerkin, mantle or robe of fur', dependent noun; C /-skota·kay/ reshaped (?); M /-hkoney-/ 'robe' (Bl. 1962, Menomini Lang. 18.168); O /-kkonay-/ 'robe' as in O /wikkonaye·/ 'he has a robe', /okkona·ss/ 'his blanket, robe; peel of fruit', /nikkona·ss/ 'my blanket, robe'.

54. CODFISH (a) /ota·kome·k/

(b) vttacomaik "codfish" (H4)

(c) Pseudo-PEA /*weθa·kwame·kwa/ 'evening fish', as if from PA /*weθa·kw-/ 'evening' and /*-ame·kw-a/ 'fish'.

55. COME (a) /nepya·m/ 'I come', /nepya·m se·p/ 'I will come tomorrow', /ota kepya·m/ 'you (sing.) come here', /pe·w/ 'he comes', /oski-pe·w/ 'he comes quickly' (AI indicative).

/pya·k/ 'come ye!', /oski-pya·k/ 'come ye quickly!' (2 person pl. AI imper.)

/pya·č/ 'let him come', /na·ntake· pya·č/ 'if only he would come, would that he come' (3 person sg. injunctive). See ONLY, entry 144.

/pe·to·w/ 'he brings' (objectless-TI indicative

(b) neihpÿahm sab "I will come tomorrow" (H8), vske-pewh "come quickly" (H4), ota-cpÿam "come again or we will come again" (H4)

pÿak "come, being spoken from afar off to one" (H4), vske-pÿak "come quickly" (H4)

naantucah pyautch "come again" (H4)

patow "bring again" (H3)

(c) PA root /*py-/, (AI) /*pya·-/, extended root /*pye·t-/ 'hither' (B146). Some languages (for example Penobscot) use only the extended root form.

PA /*nepya/ 'I come'; F /nepya/; M /nepiam/; S /nipiya/; uD /mpa/, mD /mpa·m/; Mh /npa/; Ms /nəpəyɑm/, (Eliot nuppeam, nuppeyam John 5:43, 9:39, 10:10, 12:46).

PA /*pye·wa/ 'he comes' (B146); F /pye·wa/; M /pi·w/; S /piye·wa/; Mi /pi·wa/; D /pe·w/; Mh /paw/; Ms and Np /pəyaw/, (Eliot peyau John 11:20, 28, 38; peyaog "they come" John 11: 48, 20:3; Np pia8oc "they come" Mathevet p. 65).

PA /*pya·kwa/ 'come ye!' (2 person pl. AI imper.); F /pya·ko/; S /piya·ko/; Np /pəyɑkwa/, (Mathevet piang8̆a "venez icy!" p. 19).

PA /*pya·čye/ 'let him come' (3 person sg. injunctive); F /pya·če/.

PA /*pye·ta·wa/ 'he brings it' (TI indicative); F /pye·to·wa/ reshaped; C /pe·ta·w/; M /pi·ta·w/; S /piye·to/.

56. COME FROM THERE

(a) /ta·n nowa·m/ 'Where does he come from?', /ta·n kenowa·m/ 'From where do you come?', /ni·r nenowa·m/ 'I come from there'.

(b) near nowwam̄ "I have been" (H7), tan nowaam "Where have you been?" (H15) (with omission of pronominal prefix).

(c) PA /*nowawemwa/ and /*wemwa/ 'he comes from there' is an irregular and polymorphic verb, and with the irregular contraction of /*-awe-/ to

/*-a·-/ and /*-o·-/ (for which see Bl. 1946, Section 19, p. 92), there are /*nowa·mwa/ and /*nowo·mwa/ as early contracted forms. Compare F /nowi·wa/ 'he goes outside'.

From contracted PA /*nowa·mwa/ derives Powhatan /nowa·ˈm/ 'he comes from there'.

From PA /*wemwa/ are D /wəm/; Ms /om/, (Eliot oom "he comes out" Acts 28:3); Np /om/, (Mathevet 8m "il vient de" p. 18); PA /*wemwaki/ 'they come from there', D /mo·k/, Ms and Np /omak/, (Mathevet 8mak p. 18); PA /*neweme/ 'I come from there', D /no·m/, and Ms and Np /nom/, (Mathevet n8m "je viens de" pp. 18, 21).

From PA /*nowo·mwa/ by contraction is S /no·mwa/ 'he comes from there', but in the first person sg. S /nimo·me/ 'I come from there' is formed by dissimilation for expected Shawnee /*nino·me/. However, the Shawnee subjunctive forms are from the short PA form /*wemwa/ and not /*nowawemwa/. Thus there is S /we·meya/ 'where I come from' and /we·meki/ 'where he came from'.

57. COPPER (1)

(a) /osa·wa·ss/ 'brass, copper'.

(b) osawas "brass" (H3)

(c) Pseudo-PA /*wesa·wa·nθakwi/, reflected in northern PEA as /*wi·sa·wa·nθakwi/ 'copper' (see YELLOW, entry 251); P /wisáwahlak^{w}/ 'copper, brass', |wisaw-ahl-akw|. The medial and final PA /*-a·nθ-/ 'flint, ore, mineral, unsmelted metal' is the deverbal of PA /*ma·nθ-/ 'chert, flint' found in PA /*ma·nθehsi/ 'flint knife' (F /ma·tesi/, pl. /ma·tesani/; S /ma·neʔθi/, pl. /ma·nʔθali/; mD /máhləs/; compare P /màhsihpsk^{w}/ 'chert, flint', |mahsihpəskw| with /hs/ for /hl/ before /i/

as a residue of the alternation /*θ/:/*š/). PA /*-a·nθ-/ is found as O /-a·n-/, P |-ɑhl-|, and Powhatan /-a·ss-/, usually appearing with the abstract noun final /*-akw-i/. Thus, PA /*-a·nθakw-i/ 'flint, mineral, unsmelted metal, ore', and in modern times 'metal'; appears in Ojibwa as /-a·nakw/ (O /pi·wa·nak/ 'flint', pl. /pi·wa·nako·k/), and Eastern and Western Abenaki as |-ɑhlakw| (P /wápahlak^{w}/ 'silver', /álənahlak^{w}/ 'iron'). The PA cluster /*nθ/ has the reflexes F /t/, O /n/, P /hl/, mD /hl/, and Powhatan /ss/.

Omission of the abstract noun final /*-akw-i/ in concurrent forms is not unusual in the Eastern Algonquian languages, found in Powhatan /-a·ss/ from PA /*-a·nθ-akwi/. Another example is PEA /*-o·θakw-i/ 'watercraft' and PA /*-o·θ-/ beside /*-o·ši/ 'boat' found in P /ssànol/ 'raft' and /mósolak^{w}/ 'moosehide coracle'.

58. COPPER (2)

(a) /matassen/ 'copper'.

(b) <u>matassun</u> "copper" (H4), <u>mattassin</u> "copper" (Smith)

(c) Pseudo-PEA, from pseudo-PA /*matwaʔsenyi/ from PA root /*matw-/ 'uneven, jagged', and deverbal /*-aʔseny-i/ 'stone'. Compare mD /matasən/ 'pipe', perhaps originally a pipe of native copper or some other uneven ore or stone.

PA /*matw-/ 'uneven, irregular, jagged' is found in P, C, and S; P /mátahpəsk^{w}/ 'jagged rock, meteorite', /mátekən/ 'hide, skin'; C /mača·ča·w/ 'it is uneven ground', /mače·kin/ 'leather (for a tent)', Cree everywhere replacing /*mat(w)-/ with /mač-/ which is homophonous with /mač-/ 'bad'; S /mate·wa·mi/ 'it is a rough river' (S permits cluster /tw/ however).

59. COUGH

(a) (AI) /no·ssassom/ 'I cough', /ossassomo·w/ 'he coughs'.

(b) nussacom "bite" (H3), nussuccum "cough" (H4)

(c) PA root /*wehθaʔθw-/ 'cough', PA /*wehθaʔθwemwiwa/'he coughs'; C /ostastotam/ 'he coughs', by regressive assimilation for expected /*ohtastotam/; O /ossassotam/; M /ohnɛ·ʔnomow/ with the same final as Powhatan, and the ancient variation /ɛ/ and /a/.

60. COVER

(a) /kawassan/ 'cover, bottom skin of bed'.

(b) cawassan "covering to lay upon out" (H4)

(c) Pseudo-PA /*kawahθani/, derived from PA root /*kaw-/ 'lie prostrate' (B146), medial PA /*-ahθ- 'robe, pelt, skin' (F /-as-/, C /-aht-/, M /-ahn-/, S /-aʔθ-/, P /-ahs-/, mD /-ax-/), and abstract noun final /*-an-i/.

The medial /*-ahθ-/ is well attested in F /wa·pasaya/ 'white robe'; M /aska·hniy/ 'rawhide'; mD /askxay/ 'rawhide'; P /wəláhsew 'he is well clothed, robed'. The noun root is the same.

PA /*ahθaya/ AN 'robe, pelt, hide, skin'; F /asayi·hi/ dimin. 'buckskin'; C /ahtay/ 'skin', pl. /ahtayak/; S /aʔθaya/ AN; mD /xay/ Mh /xay/, /ntáxay/ 'my hide, skin'.

61. CRACK

(a) /ta·tasse·w/ (II) 'it is cracked, torn, split'.

(b) tatumsew "a crack or (it is) cracked" (H4), with m as a writing error for s (?); tuttasewh "rent or torn" (H12)

(c) PA root /*θa·θ-/ 'crack, rift, channel, crevice, fissure'; C /ta·t-/; S /la·l-/; P /nɑl-/, and extended root /nɑlɑ-/ which can be considered a marked allomorph; Powhatan /ta·t-/. Supporting forms are found in C /ta·tase·ka·w/ 'there is a crack, fissure', /ta·tapayiw/ 'it rends, tears', /ta·tapitam/ 'he rips, tears it'; S /la·lekwe·we/ 'he is ruptured', /la·lo?pe?še/ 'he has his ear lobes slit'; P /nálikən/ 'it is split, grooved', /nálαčəwan/ 'the current flows in a channel, crevice', /nαlápeke/ 'the water forms a channel'.

62. CRUSH

(a) /osekohamen/ or /osekwahamen/ (TI) 'he crushes it by tool or instrument'.

(b) vshuccohomen "beat corn into meal" (H3), vssequahamun "smooth" (H13), vssequahamuñ "rub a thing" (H13)

(c) PA /*šekwahamwa/ (TI absolute) 'he crushes it by tool or instrument'; C /sikoham/ or /sikwaham/. Root PA /*šekw-/ 'crush', C /sikw-/; O /šikw-/ as in O /nišikoštikwane·ška·/ 'I crush his head', /ošikopito·n/ 'he crumbles it'; P /səkw-əsk-/ usually with postradical /-əsk-/.

63. CUT

(a) /neki·skama·w/ 'I bite him through'.

(b) nekiskemuw "cut any thing" (H5)

(c) PA /*neki·škama·wa/ 'I bite, gnaw him through' (TA); F /neki·škama·wa/, C /niki·skama·w/, M /neke·skamaw/, O /niki·škama·/.

64. CUT HAIR

(a) /nemo·nsa·w/ (TA) 'I cut his hair', /kemo·nsa·w/ 'you (sg.) cut his hair', /mo·nsa·kan/ 'scissors, shears'.

(b) nummundgaw, cummundguw "cut the hair of a man's head" (H5), moundgsacañ "shears" (H13)

(c) PA /*nemo·nšwa·wa/ (TA) 'I cut his hair'; C /nimo·swa·w/; M /nemu·hsa·w/; O /nimo·nšwa·/; P /nə̀mosα/.

Pseudo-PA /*mo·nšwa·kani/ 'scissors, shears'; C /mo·swa·kan/; M /mo·hsokan/ or /mu·hswakan/; O /mo·nšwa·kan/.

65. DANCE

(a) /kenteke·w/ (AI) 'he dances'.

(b) kantekau "dance" (H9), kantikantie "sing and

dance" (H9), the latter probably a jargon term.

(c) PEA /*kenteke·wa/ (AI) 'he dances'; D /kə́ntke·w/. The AI final is PA /*-eke·-wa/ 'da as in PA /*pemeke·wa/ 'he dances along, by'; F /pemeke·wa/, P /pə̀məke/.

66. DEAF

(a) /kake·pehte·w/ (AI) 'he is deaf'.

(b) <u>cappetaw</u> "deaf" (H5), (first syllable probably missed by Strachey).

(c) PA /*kakye·pehte·wa/ (AI) 'he is deaf', derive from PA root /*kakye·p-/ 'impair, obstruct' an /*-eht-/ 'ear'; C /kake·pihte·w/; M /kaki·pɛhtɛw/. Other languages compound the same root with PA /*-ehš-/ 'ear'.

PA /*kakye·pehše·wa/ 'he is deaf'; F /kekye·peše·wa/; O /kaki·pišše·/; S /kake·pe?še/; P /kákepse/, |kakepəhse|.

67. DOE

(a) /no·nse·s/ 'doe, matron, female with young'.

(b) <u>noungas</u> "doe" (H5), <u>noungass</u> "wife" (H15)

(c) PA /*no·nšye·swa/ 'doe, matron, female quadruped with young', derived from PA root /*no·nšye·-/ 'have offspring, young' and the deverbal noun final PA /*-osw-a/ 'quadruped' from PA noun /*mo·swa/ 'moose' with vowel shortening in the deverbal as usual; O /no·nše· 'doe, mare, female of moose, deer, elk, bison, caribou', pl. /no·nše·sok/; mD /nó·nše·w/ 'd with young' without the deverbal final. Compar S /no·šeškata/ 'female with young, doe, matro

Compare PA /*no·nšye·?θemwa/ 'bitch with young' (PA deverbal noun final /*-a?θemw-a/ 'dog'); C /no·se·stim/; M /nu·hsi·?nem/; O /no·nše·ssim/.

68. DOG

(a) /atemoss/

(b) <u>attemoys</u> "dog" (H2), <u>attemous</u> "dog" (H5)

(c) PA /*aθemwa/ 'dog' (Bl25, Lang. 1:142);

Kickapoo /anemwa/; F /anemo·ha/ dimin. ; C /atim/; M /anɛ·m/; Ms /anəm/, (Eliot anum "dog" Proverbs 26:11; anumwog "dogs" Exodus 22:31). From this are derived a number of diminutives, Algonquian diminutives in general requiring further study.

PA /*aθemwehša/ 'little dog'; O /animošš/, Powhatan /atemoss/.

PA /*aθemwensa/ 'little dog'; O /animo·ns/, P /áləmoss/. The diminutive is PA /*-ens-/, O /-ins/(see Bl. Eastern Ojibwa 11.58 where O /-ins/ and secondary /-e·ns/ after stems ending in /-w/ show vowel lengthening), P /-əss/.

9. DUNG (a) /mo·wi·č/ INAN.

(b) moich "turd" (H14)

(c) PA /*mo·wi·čyi/ or /*mo·wi/ INAN, 'dung, manure'; F /mo·wi·či/, /nemo·wi·či/ 'my dung'; O /mo·/, /nimo·wan/ pl. 'my droppings'; S /mo·wi/, pl. /mo·wali/; mD /mowi/; Ms /mowi/. There also is another PA term.

PA /*mye·yi/ 'piece of dung, dropping', pl. /*mye·yali/; C /me·yi/, pl. /me·yah/; M /mi·h/, pl. /mi·yan/.

0. DUST (a) /penkwi/ 'dust, ashes' INAN.

(b) pungwe "ashes" (H2), pāgguy "ashes" (H11)

(c) PA /*penkwi/ 'dust, ashes, powder' INAN; F /pekwi/; C /pihko/; M /pɛhki·h/; O /pinkwi/; S /pekwi/; Mi /pinkwi/; P /pək^{W}/; mD /ponkw/; Np /pəkwi/, (Mathevet peg8i "cendre" p. 57).

1. EAGLE (a) /a·patane·w/ 'adult bald eagle', pl. /a·patane·wak/

(b) opatenaiok "eagle" (H5), (actually pl.)

(c) PA /*wa·paθanye·wa/ 'adult bald eagle' (i. e., "white tail"); S /wa·palanye/, /wa·palanyeʔθi/ dimin. ; mD /wa·paláne·w/; uD /ɔ·p·alániye/. Compare S /mškwalanye/ 'red-tailed hawk or buteo'.

The derivation is PA root /*wa·p-/ 'white', and the PA medial /*-aθany-/ 'bird's tail'. Th latter is a deverbal from the following dependent noun stem:

PA /*-aθanyi/ 'bird tail', PA /*waθanyi/ 'h (bird's) tail' INAN; C /wataniy, (/otaniy/ in some dialects); M /wana·n/, pl. /wana·nyan/ P /wálanəss/ 'his (bird's) tail' dimin.; Ms /wanani/, (Eliot wananeyeuash "their tails", Revelations 9:19).

72. EAR (a) /mehtawak/ 'someone's ear, an ear', /wehtawa 'his ear', /wehtawakos/ 'his ears'.

(b) meihtawk "ear of a man" (H5), weihtaws "ears of a hare or any other beast" (H5), metawke "ea (H10)

(c) PA /*-htawakayi/, PEA /*-htawakwi/ 'ear' IN dependent noun; PA /*wehtawakayi/ 'his ear', F /ohtawakayi/, C /ohtawakay/, M /ohta·wak O /ottawak/; PEA /*wehtawakwi/, P /wtàwak^{w} (pl. /wtáwakol/), Mh /wtawakw/, Ms /wihtawa (Eliot wehtauog "his ear" Proverbs 18:15).

73. EARTHWORK (a) /me·nesk/ 'earthwork, intrenchment'.

(b) manausk "little stone" (H14)

(c) PA /*mye·neθki/ 'earthwork, intrenchment'; C /me·nisk/; M /mi·nɛhk-/ in /mi·nɛhkɛ·hka 'graveyard'; uD /me·naxk/ 'fort'; Nr /omansk/ fort' (Roger Williams aumánsk "fort"; error for " fort"); Ms /mansk/ or /manəsk/ (Eliot mansk "stronghold", oomanskash "his strongholds" Psalm 89:40; Mayhew manushk "stronghold", oomonushkumash "his strongholds" Psalm 89:40

74. EAT (a) /mi·tasso·w/ (AI) 'he eats', /nemi·či·n/ (TI) 'I eat it', /mi·či·s/ 'eat (thou) it!' (2 person sg. imper.), /mi·či·hkas/ 'eat (thou) it then!' (2 person sg. delayed imperative).

(b) All (H5): meches "eat", nummechÿn "I will eat" (error for "I eat it, I will eat it"), meihtussuw "eat with me" (error for "he eats"), mechecusk "I'll eat by and by" (error for "eat thou it then, eat thou it by and by").

(c) PA /*mi·čyehswiwa/ 'he eats', C /mi·čiso·w/, M /me·čehsow/; but PEA /*mi·tahswiwa/ (AI) 'he eats', P /mìtso/ or archaistic style (used in formal speeches and myths) /mítahso/; mD /mi·tso/.

PA /*nemi·čyeni/ (TI) 'I eat it'; C /nimi·čin/ (/mi·čiw/ 'he eats it'); M /neme·čen/ (/mi·čwah/ 'he eats it'); O /nimi·čin/; P /nə̀mičin/; mD /nəmi·či·n/.

PA /*mi·čyilwe/ (2 person sg. TI imperative); F /mi·čino/; C /mi·čiy/; M /me·čeh/; O /mi·čin/; S /mi·či·lo/; P /mìči/; mD /mí·či·l/ 'eat thou it!'

The second person singular TI delayed or future imperative of Powhatan seems to have the suffixed inflection /-ehkas/, Cree /-ihkan/ (Swampy Cree form, generalized ?), and Ojibwa /-ikkan/.

PA /*mi·čyehkalwe/ 'eat thou it by and by, later'; O /mi·čikkan/; Powhatan /mi·či·hkas/.

5. EGG

(a) /wa·w/ 'egg', /owa·w/ 'his egg' INAN.

(b) wouwh "egg" (H5), owaugh "egg" (H11)

(c) PA /*wa·wani/ 'egg', pl. /*wa·wanali/; F /owa·wani/ 'egg', pl. /owa·wanani/ with prothetic vowel; C /wa·wi/, pl. /wa·wa/; Mt /wa·w/, pl. /wa·wač/ AN; M /wa·wan/, pl. /wa·wanon/; O /wa·wan/, pl. /wa·wano·n/; S /owa·wi/, pl. /owa·wali/ with prothetic vowel; Mi /wa·wi/, pl. /wa·wa/; P (and all EA dialects) /wàwan/, pl. /wáwanal/; mD /wa·hw/, pl. /wá·hwal/ and /wá·hwalal/; eastern SNE languages spoken to the east of the Blackstone River have the morphophonemic form |wawan-| (Ms, Eliot <u>wóóu</u>, pl. <u>wôanash</u>, Cotton <u>wou</u>, pl. wowănash); Np and Pq /wam/, pl. Np /wamanas Pq /wámanš/ (Mathevet p. 23, <u>8am</u>, pl. <u>8amanĕ</u> Prince and Speck 1904, Amer. Anthropol. 6. 44, wâ´mŭnsh "eggs") (Nipmuck-Pocumtuck and Mohegan-Pequot, both western SNE languages, have morphophonemic |waman-| with /*w/ replaced by /m/ by dissimilation, and retain fin /n/ from PA /*n/ which supports PA /*wa·wa since PA /*θ/ and /*l/ fall together to Np /l/ and Pq /y/ respectively; in all SNE languages the singular of nouns with final syllables of sho vowel plus sonorant regularly undergo apocope); Mh /wá·wan/, pl. /wá·wanan/.

Michelson (1935, IJAL 8. 134) and Goddard (196 IJAL 31. 219) have attempted reconstructions of th form, both rather opaquely.

In some languages singular forms are short innovations and all such languages seem to fall into either a northern tier (C, Mt, and Algon or into a southern tier (S, Mi, D, and Powhatan suggesting that this modification was not histor cally connected but represented two parallel developments which resulted from the same conditioning factor. The source of the modification seems to be analogical contamination with PA /*wa·hkwa/ 'fish egg, frog egg' (see ROE in this lexicon). In fact, the Munsee form /wa·hw is the exact phonological correspondent of /*wa·hkwa/ in which D /h/ is the reflex of PA /*hk/, and one dialect of Munsee went on t restructure the plural form as /wá·hwalal/ in a manner similar to the SNE languages.

Menomini and Ojibwa analogically reshaped the stem PA /*wa·wan-/ to /wa·wanw-/, but otherwise all the central tier of languages, including conservative Fox, Menomini, Ojibwa, all Abenaki dialects, Mahican, and all SNE languages are in agreement and point to /*wa·wani/ as the original lexeme. The shortened singular forms in the SNE languages are, of course, deceptive, but result from an apocope unrelated to the process of analogy to PA /*wa·hkwa/ 'fish or frog egg'. It is noteworthy too that all Abenaki dialects and the l-dialect (Np) of the SNE group which regularly have /l/ for PA /*θ/ and /*l/ uniformly attest PA /*wa·wan-/ and not /wa·wal-/. Borrowing from an n-dialect in this area, on the other hand, is relatively isolated as in the case of P /énik^{w}əss/ 'ant' for expected /élik^{w}əss/ which actually occurs in some Abenaki dialects (Caniba, etc.). Furthermore, collateral forms, for example P /mánɑwane/ 'he gathers, collects eggs' with deverbal /-ɑwan-/, support the original cast of the morpheme with /n/.

6. ELBOW

(a) /mi·skwan/ 'someone's elbow'.

(b) <u>meisquañ</u> "elbow" (H5)

(c) PEA /*-yeškwana/ 'elbow', AN dependent noun; PEA /*wyeškwana/ 'elbow'; P /wə̀sk^{w}an/, pl. /wə̀sk^{w}anak/; uD /wi·skon/, pl. /wi·skonak/; Ms /wisk/ (Eliot <u>weesk</u>). In PA the presumed cluster /*šk/ is discrepant.

7. ENTER

(a) /pi·ntike·s/ 'come (thou) in!' (2 person sg. AI imperative), /pi·ntike·w/ 'he enters'.

(b) <u>peintikec</u> "come in" (H4)

(c) PA /*pi·ntwike·wa/ 'he enters a dwelling' (B146) AI; F /pi·tike·wa/; C /pi·htoke·w/; M /pi·htikɛw/; O /pi·ntike·/; P /pítike/.

PA /*pi·ntwike·lwe/ 'come (thou) in!' (2 person sg. AI imper.); F /pi·tike·no/; C /pi·hto O /pi·ntike·n/; Mi /pi·ntiki·lo/; P /pítike'/.

78. EXTINGUISH FIRE

(a) /a·htawe·hass po·kete·w/ 'put out the fire!' (2 person sg. TI imperative), /ota·hte·hamen/ 'he extinguishes it (fire, flame)' (TI).

(b) otawiaac bocetew "fire is out" (H6), vtahtahamu "put out a candle" (H12)

(c) PA /*a·ʔte·hamwa/ or /*a·ʔtawe·hamwa/ 'he extinguishes it (fire, flame) by instrument or tool' (TI absolute); C /a·stawe·ham/; M /a·ʔtɛhaṁ/; O /ota·tte·ʔa·n/ (TI objective). PA /*a·ʔte·ha or /*a·ʔtawe·hanlwe/ 'put it (fire) out!' (2 per sg. imper. TI); C /a·stawe·hah/; M /a·ʔtɛhah/ O /a·tte·ʔan/. Some languages (M, O) reflect t root /*a·ʔt(e·)-/ 'extinguish fire' but others (C follow this with the postradical /*-awe·-/ whic is identical with the final /*-awe·-wa/ 'make f Powhatan apparently has both types, or perhaps the two forms reflect a dialect difference within Powhatan. The root with and without postradical is manifest in other forms also.

PA /a·ʔte·wi/ or /*a·ʔtawe·wi/ (II) 'it (fire goes out, is extinguished'; C /a·stawe·w/; M /a·ʔtɛw/; O /a·tte·/; S /aʔte/.

PA /*a·ʔte·škamwa/ or /*a·ʔtawe·škamwa/ 'he extinguishes it (fire) by foot, he extinguishe fire by stepping on it'; (TI absolute in C and M, TI objective in O); C /a·stawe·skam/; M /a·ʔtɛ·skam/; O /ota·tte·ška·n/.

79. EYE

(a) /meski·nsek/ 'someone's eye', pl. /meski·nse 'eyes', /neski·nsek/ 'my eye' (dependent noun INAN).

(b) muskiendguk "eye" (H5), muskiendgues "eyes" (H5), muskins "eyes" (H10)

(c) PA /*-ški·nšekwi/ 'eye' INAN dependent noun (B146); PA /*neški·nšekwi/ 'my eye'; F /neški·šekwi/; C /niski·sik/ and /miski·sik/ 'someone's eye'; M /neske·hsek/; O /niški·nšik/; S /nˀški·šekwi/; uD /nə́škinkw/; Mh /nski·skw/, pl. /nski·skwan/; Ms /nəskisək/ (Eliot nuskesuk). This has been reshaped (by dissimilation ?) in all Abenaki dialects, P /nsìsək^{w}/, pl. /nsìsəkol/.

80. FATHER (a) /no·ss/ 'my father', /ko·ss/ 'thy father', (not attested but expected) /o·ssah/ 'his father'.

(b) nows "father" (H6), kowse "father" (H8)

(c) PA /*-o·hθa/ 'father' (dependent noun), /*no·hθa/ 'my father', PA /*o·hθali/ 'his father' (B125, Lang. 1.152); F /no·sa/ 'my father', /o·sani/ 'his father'; C /no·hta·wiy/, /o·hta·wiya/ with reshaped ending; M /no·hnεˀ/, /o·hnan/; O /no·ss/, /o·ssan/; S /noˀθa/, /oˀθali/; mD /no·x/, /ó·xwal/; Mh /no·x/, /ó·xan/.

81. FEATHER (a) /mi·kwan/ 'quill, long feather' AN, pl. /mi·kwanak/; /opi·we·/ 'short feather, plume, down feather, bristle' AN, pl. /opi·wak/

(b) meqwanoc "long feather" (H6), ahpewk "feathers" (H6), (both are pl. forms).

(c) PA /*mi·kwana/ 'quill, long feather', pl. /*mi·kwanaki/ AN in all languages; F /mi·kona/, pl. /mi·konaki/; C /mi·kwan/; M /me·kon/; O /mi·kwan/, pl. /mi·kwanak/; S /mi·kona/, pl. /mi·konaki/; Ms /mikwan/ (Eliot and Mayhew umméqunoh "his feathers" Psalm 91:4, 139:9); mD /mí·kwan/.

PA /*wepi·waya/ 'plume, down or short feather, bristle', AN in all languages except C and O where INAN; F /opi·waya/, pl. /opi·wayaki/; C /opi·way/; M /ape·wε·way/ reshaped, compare /opε·wana·sken/ INAN 'plant down'; O /opi·way/ 'bristle, hair of fur', pl. /opi·wayan/; Mi /pi·wia/ 'feather', pl. /pi·wiaki/.

82. FEED, GIVE FOOD TO

(a) /ketassames/ 'I feed thee, I give you (sg.) food', (not attested but expected) /netassama·w/ 'I feed him, give him food'.

(b) cuttassamais "beggar" (H3)

(c) PA /*ketahšameθe/ 'I feed thee, I give you food' (TA); F /ketašamene/; C /kitasamitin/; M /keta·hsamen/; O /kitaššamin/; S /kitšamele/ with syncope of the first vowel of the TA stem /*ahšam-/; P /kətáhsaməl/; Ms /kətassaməš/, (Eliot and Mayhew kuttassamush Psalm 145:15).

PA /*netahšama·wa/ (TA) 'I feed him'; F /netašama·wa/; C /nitasama·w/; M /neta·hsamə O /nitaššama·/; S /nitšama/; P /nətáhsamɑ/.

83. FIRE

(a) /po·kete·w/ 'fire'.

(b) pokatawer "fire" (Smith), boketawgh "fire" (H2), bocuttaow, bocetew (H6), boketaw (H11), bocataoh (H14)

(c) PEA /*po·kete·wi/ 'fire'; Mc /pő·ktew/ 'fire'; uD /pó·ktay/ 'firebrand', dimin. /pó·kte·s/; WA /pokwəta/ 'firebrand' (evidently analogically reshaped on the model of WA /skwəta/ 'fire'); PA II reflexive /*-ete·wi/ 'by heat' (B146).

84. FISH

(a) /name·ss/ 'fish', pl. /name·ssak/

(b) noughmass "fish" (Smith), nammais "fish" (H6), namaske, nameche "fish of any kind" (H11)

(c) PA /*name·ʔsa/ 'fish' (B125, Lang. 1. 142); F /name·sa/; C /name·s/ 'fish' (about James Bay), 'small lake sturgeon' elsewhere; M /namɛ·ʔs/; O /name·/ 'sturgeon', pl. /name·wak/; S /nameʔθa/; P /nàmehs/; D (all dialects) /namé·s Mh /namás/; Ms /namas/, (Eliot namohsog "fishes" Exodus 7:18, 7:21).

85. FISH-HOOK

(a) /mekohkan/

(b) mowhkokañ "fish-hook" (H10)

(c) PA /*mekeçkani/ 'fish-hook'; Mt /mičihkin/; O /mikiskan/, pl. /mikiskanan/; P /mə̀kihkan/, pl. /məkíhkanal/. Initial /*me-/ is the indefinite possessor prefix.

The Powhatan form /mekohkan/ has been analogically reshaped, as has the Menomini form /kohka·n/ 'fish-hook' without the indefinite possessor prefix, by analogy to PA /*koxke·wa/ 'he angles, he fishes with a hook, he sets hooks for fish'; C /koske·w/ (also C /koskane·ya·piy/ 'fishing line'; M /kohkɛ·w/; O /-kokke·/ in /ota·čikokke·/ 'he fishes with a hook', /ota·čikokkan/ 'fishing line with a hook'.

There is another Algonquian term: PA /*wečkwani/ 'fish-hook'; Ms /ohkwan-aš/, (Eliot ukquonash "fishhooks" Amos 4:2); Nr /ohkwan/ (Roger Williams hoquaùn "hook", pl. hoquaûnash); M /kočkuan/ 'hook', analogical for expected /*očkuan/ (M /kohkɛ·w/ 'he angles, fishes with a hook'); uD /hók·ɔ·n/ 'hook'.

86. FLOUNDER

(a) /ki·skess/ (?)

(b) keiskis "plaice" (H12)

(c) The PA root is /*ki·šk-/ 'remove part, cut off'; F /ki·šk-/, C /ki·sk-/, M /ke·sk-/, O /ki·šk-/, S /kišk-/.

87. FLY

(a) /awe·sse·w/ (AI) 'he flies'.

(b) awassew "to fly" (H6)

(c) PEA /*awe·hle·wa/ 'he flies' (PA /*-ʔle·wa/ 'fly', B125, Lang. 1.149); P /áwehle/ 'hawk'; mD /awéhle·w/ 'hawk'; Ms /awassaw/, (Eliot pl. owóhshaog "hawks" Deuteron. 14:15).

88. FOAM

(a) /pi·hte·w/ 'foam, froth'.

(b) peihteah "froth" (H6), peihtaōh "scum" (H13)

(c) PA /*pi·ʔte·wi/ 'foam, froth'; F /pi·hte·wi/;

C /pi·ste·w/; M /pe·ˀtɛw/; O /pi·tte·/; S /piˀte/; P /pìhte/; Ms /pihtaw/, (Eliot pehteau).

89. FOOT

(a) /mesit/ 'someone's foot', pl. /mesitas/, /nesit/ 'my foot'.

(b) messets "feet by a general name" (H6), messeate "foot" (H10)

(c) PA /*-siči/ 'foot' INAN dependent noun, pl. /*-sitali/, /*nesiči/ 'my foot', pl. /*nesitali/ (B146); C /nisit/, /nisita/; M /nese·t/, /nese·t O /nisit/, /nisitan/; S /niθiči/, /niθitali/; P /nə̀sit/, /nə̀sital/; Ms /nəsit/, (Eliot nusseet "my foot" Psalm 94:18).

90. FRIEND

(a) /ni·ta·p/ probably a jargon term for proper /ni·ta·pe·w/ 'my fellow man, my friend', pl. /ni·ta·pe·wak/, given correctly by Strachey at (H8) and by Smith.

(b) netab "friend" (H6), netab, netapewk "friend" (H netap "my dear friend" (H10), netab "word of greeting" (H15), netoppew "friend" (Smith)

(c) PEA /*ni·ta·pe·wa/ 'my fellow man, my friend'; formed from the PA dependent or pseudo-root /*-i (see Bl. Lang. 17.292-297; B146 Sec. 100, p. 119) 'fellow', and PA /*-a·pe·w-a/ 'male, man'; P /nítɑpe/; Ms and Nr /nitɑp/, (Nr nétop "my friend" Williams).

91. FROST

(a) /takwaskwat/ (II) 'there is glazed frost on the ground or snow'.

(b) tacqwacat "frost" (H6), (error for tacqwacqwat).

(c) PA /*takwaškwatwi/ (II) 'there is glazed frost o ice on the ground or snow'; M medial /-askw-/ 'ice, frost' in M /pi·wana·skiˀtan/ 'there is ice floating in the water' (see M. Lang. 15. 317); O /kaškwe·we·/ 'there is glazed frost on the groun (Baraga p. 118 gives kaskwe·we· which is taken a an error); Mi /takwahkatwi/ 'it is frosting, there is frost', by dissimilation for expected /*takwahkwatwi/, and PA /*šk/ regularly gives /hk/ in Miami; P /ták^{w}ask^{w}at/ 'there is a crust of ice on the snow or ground'. Compare Ms /takwatən/, (Eliot togquodtin "it is frozen" Job 38:20).

The root is PA /*takw-/ 'among or between two particulars, together'; plus the medial PA /*-aškw-/ 'frost, ice' deverbal of root PA /*kaškw-/; and the II final PA /*-atwi/ 'state, condition'.

92. FULL OF FOOD (a) /ki·spo·w/ 'he is full of food', /neki·sp/ 'I am full'.

(b) geispuu "to be full" (H6), negeisp "I am full" (H6)

(c) PA /*ki·špwiwa/ 'he is full of food, he has his fill of food'; C /ki·spo·w/; uD /kí·spo/. The root PA /*ki·š-/ 'complete, finish' is compounded without connective /*-i-/ to the final PA /*-hpwi-/ 'eat'.

In F /ki·hpoče·wa/ 'his belly is full' and M /ke·hpow/ 'he suffers from indigestion' the /h/ has been analogically restored.

93. FUR (a) /wi·ssakan/ 'hair of fur', pl. /wi·ssakanas/ 'fur'.

(b wessacanoc "fur of raccoon" (H6), weisacannac "skin or fur of a hare" (H13)

(c) PEA /*wi·hθakani/ 'hair of fur', pl. /*wi·hθakanali/ 'fur'; Ms /wissakanaš/, (Eliot weshaganash "hairs" Exodus 25:4), from the following:

PA /*wi·ˀθayi/ 'body hair, hair of fur', pl. /*wi·ˀθayali/ 'fur'; S /wiˀθaya/ 'body hair', pl. /wiˀθayali/ 'body hairs, fur'; uD /wí·xa/ 'body hair' AN, pl. /wí·xak/. M /wɛ·ˀ/ 'single hair of fur or body hair' INAN, pl.

/wε·ʔnan/, and M /wε·ʔsekan/ 'furs', /wε·ʔnasikwan/ 'fur coat' have the first vowel modified by analogy to M /we·nεʔ/ 'his single hair of head'. The latter represents:

PA /*-i·θeʔši/ 'single hair of head' INAN dependent noun, pl. /*-i·θeʔθali/ 'head hairs'; PA /*mi·θeʔθali/ pl. 'human head hair, someone's head hairs', F /mi·nesani/, M /me·nεʔnε PA first person possessed plural /*ni·θeʔθali/ 'my head hair'; F /ni·nesani/; M /ne·nεʔnan/; O /ni·nississan/ dimin.; S /ni·leʔθa/, sg. /ni·leʔθi/.

94. GILL

(a) /oski·k/ or /weski·k/ 'gill' INAN, pl. /oski·kwas/ or /weski·kwas/ 'gills', really 'his (fish's) gills'.

(b) <u>woskeqwas</u> "gills of a sturgeon or any other fish" (H7)

(c) PA /*weçki·kwi/ 'his (fish's) gill' INAN dependent noun; C /ohki·k/; M /ohke·k/, pl. /ohke·kon/.

95. GNAT

(a) /penkwess/ 'gnat' dimin.

(b) <u>poengwus</u> "gnat" (H7)

(c) PA /*penkwehša/ dimin. of /*penkwa/ 'buffalo gnat' or 'black fly' (genus <u>Similium</u>), not the 'sand fly' (genus <u>Phlebotomus</u>); C /pihkos/; M /pεhko·hsεh/ with supra-added dimin.; O /pinkošš/, pl. /pinkoššak/; mD /ponkwəs/.

96. GO OFF

(a) /nema·ča·/ 'I go away, go off'; /kema·ča·/ 'you (sg.) go away'; /ma·či·w/ 'he starts off, goes away'.

(b) <u>nummacha</u> "I will go home" (H7, H8 and H16), <u>cumacha</u> "Will you go home?"

(c) PA /*ma·čyi·wa/ 'he goes away, starts off' (B125, Lang. 1. 144); /*nema·čya/ 'I go away, start off'; F /nema·čya/; M /nema·čiam/;

O /nima·ča·/; P /nə̀mači/; mD /nəmá·či/. Powhatan has analogic /-a·/ like Ojibwa. The alternation is /*ya·/ : /*yi·/ before /*w/.

7. GOOSE (1)
(a) /a·piki·ra·hk/ 'snow goose' (genus Chen).
(b) opykerough "brant, a fowl like a goose" (H11)
(c) PEA /*wa·piki·la·hkwa/ 'snow goose'; P /wapíkilahk^{w}/, |wap-i-kil-ahkw| .

8. GOOSE (2)
(a) /kaha·k/ 'Canada goose' (Branta canadensis L.), pl. /kaha·kak/
(b) kahaugoc "goose" (H7), actually pl.; kahauge "goose" (H9)
(c) This term, probably onomatopoetic from the bird's call, was used from North Carolina to southern New England. Compare uD /kha·k/, pl. /kha·kak/; Np (Mathevet p. 46, kank, pl. kankak "outarde").

9. GOURD
(a) /pe·me·sk/ 'gourd'.
(b) pamyack "gourd" (H11)
(c) PA /*pe·me·θkwi/(?) 'gourd'; M deverbal /-ɛ·mɛhkw-/ 'pulp, gourd' (see M. Lang. 18.157), as in M /wi·nɛ·mɛhkwan/ INAN 'squash', /aski·mɛhkwan/ 'watermelon'.

00. GROUNDNUT
(a) /ohpen/ 'groundnut, Indian potato, tuber' AN (Apios americana), pl. /ohpenak/.
(b) ouhpunnauk "groundnut" (H7), (actually pl.).
(c) PA /*wexpenya/ 'groundnut' AN, pl. /*wexpenyaki/; F /ahpenya/, pl. /ahpenye·ki/; M /ohpɛn/, pl. /ohpɛ·nyak/; O /oppin/, pl. /oppini·k/, /nito·ppini·mak/ 'my potatoes'; S /oʔpenya/, pl. /oʔpenye·ki/, /noʔpenye·ma/ 'my potatoes'; uD /hópəni·s/ dimin.; P /ppən/, pl. /ppə̀nak/, /nə̀tahpənak/ 'my groundnuts', /nətáhpənimak/ 'my testicles'.

01. GULL
(a) /kaya·hkwess/ 'herring gull' dimin.
(b) coiahgwus "gull" (H7)

(c) PA /*kaya·škwa/, /*keya·škwa/ 'herring gull' which reflects the ancient variation of /*a/:/*e F /akaya·škwa/ with prothetic vowel; C /kiya· Mt /čiya·škw/; O /kaya·šk/; Mi /kiya·hkwa/ in which Mi /hk/ is the regular reflex of /*šk/. This term was analogically reshaped in PEA and separately in some individual noneastern langua after the PA period by analogy to other bird name in /*-a·hkw-a/. For example, there are PA /*wetečya·hkwa/ 'crane' (genus Grus, two species); F /oteča·hkwa/; C /očiča·hk/; Mt /očiča·hkw/ 'great blue heron' with semantic change, since out of range of cranes; M /otɛ·či pl. /otɛ·čiahkok/; O /očiča·kk/; and PEA /*wa·piki·la·hkwa/ 'snow goose' (genus Chen

PEA /*kaya·hkwa/ 'herring gull'; Powhatan /kaya·hkw-/; Chowan /kaya·hk/, (John White, Roanoke Island 1585, kaiauk "gull"); pre-Abenak and one EA dialect (Sokoki-Pequaket ?) /kayahk (Rasles ms. p. 23 kaia·k8); P /kahk^{w}/, pl. /kàhk^{w}ak/ with contraction /-aya-/ > /-a-/, |kayahkw|. The same analogical change is foun in M /kaya·h/, pl. /kaya·hkok/; S /kayaʔko·θ dimin.

102. GUM (a) /pekiw/ 'gum, resin, pitch'.

(b) pickewh "gum that issueth out of a certain tree called the Virginia maple" (H7), pickuts "gum we hold balsam" (H12)

(c) PA /*pekiwa/ 'gum, pitch, resin', AN in all languages; F /pekiwa/; C /pikiw/; M /peke·w O /pikiw/; P /pə̀ko/, pl. /pə̀kəwak/, |pə̀kiw|; Np /pəčo/, (Mathevet pech8 "gomme" p. 22); Ms /pəto/, (Mayhew pittu "wax" Psalm 68:2).

PA /*k/ before /*i/ and /*e·/ is fronted to alveolar /t/ in the eastern group of SNE dialects spoken to the east of the Blackstone River, but in the western SNE languages including those spoken on Long Island this sound change proceeded further and was both fronted and affricated to /č/. However, there are some irregularities, for example, Ms /ahtihkanət/ 'in the field' (Eliot ohteakonit First Chron. 1:46), P |ahkihkanək| , and Ms /ahkihtaw/ 'he plants him' TA absolute (Eliot ohketeau Isaiah 44:14), and Ms /wito/ 'house' (Eliot wetu) and /wik/ 'his house' (Eliot week, Mayhew wék John 4:53). The latter is PA /*wi·ki/ 'his house, dwelling'; F /owi·ki/, C /wi·ki/, M /we·k/, Ms /wik/.

103. HAIR

(a) /ni·tess/ 'my single hair of head'. See FUR.

(b) netesse "hair of the head" (H7)

(c) PA /*-i·θeʔši/ 'single hair of head' INAN dependent noun, pl. /*-i·θeʔθali/, PA /*ni·θeʔši/ 'my single hair of head'; M /ne·nɛʔ/, pl. /ne·nɛʔnan/; O /ni·nissis/; S /ni·leʔθi/.

Compare PA /*wi·ši/ 'his head', F /owi·ši/, M /we·s/, S /wi·ši/.

104. HAND

(a) /metenč/ 'a hand, someone's hand', /netenč/ 'my hand', /otenč/ 'his hand', pl. /otenči·s/ 'his hands'.

(b) meihtinge "a hand" (H7), metenge "a hand" (H10), ohtindge "claw of a crab" (H4) (i.e. 'his hand'), oteingeis "feet of a hawk" (H6), (i. e. 'his hands').

(c) PA /*-θenčyi/ 'hand, finger' INAN dependent noun, pl. /*-θenčyali/; (Bl25, Lang. l. 145, /*-θšenčye·-/ 'hand, finger' later corrected to /*-θenčy-/); PA /*weθenčyi/ 'his hand'; C /očihčiy/; O /oninč/, pl. /oninči·n/; P /wə̀ləči/; PA /*meθenčyi/ 'someone's hand', C /mičihčiy/.

PA /*neθenčyi/ 'my hand'; C /ničihčiy/;

O /nininč/, pl. /nininči·n/; S /nileči/ 'my finger', pl. /nilečali/, and S /nileča/ 'my hand', pl. /nileče·ki/; P /nə̀ləči/ 'my finger', pl. /nə̀ləčəyal/.

105. HAVE

(a) /netayi·n/ (TI) 'I have it', /netayi·wa·w/ (TA) 'I have him', /mata netayi·wa·w/ (TA) 'I do not have him', /netayi·na/ (TI, INAN pl. object) 'I have them'.

(b) netainwh "have" (H7), natayhough "I have it" (H11) error for "I have him", matta natiayyough "I have it not" (H10), error for "I do not have him" ntayeina "I have it not" (H10), error for "I have them" (INAN pl.)

(c) PA /*netayi·wa·wa/ (TA) 'I have him'; C /nitaya·wa·w/; O /nitaya·wa·/; P /nə̀tayəwα/, |nətayiwα| ; Powhatan /netayi·wa·w/.

The Proto-Algonquian alternation /*ya·/ : /*yi before /*w/ has been leveled out in Cree and Ojibwa. For other examples of the alternation see GO OFF (entry 96) and SHARP (entry 182).

PA /*netaya·ni/ (TI, class 3) 'I have it'; C /nitaya·n/; O /nitaya·n/; P /nə̀tayin/; Powhatan /netayi·n/. Penobscot and Powhatan have stabilized the alternation, analogically extending the alternant /*yi·/ before other sonorants besides /*w/.

The theoretical simplex root PA /*ay-/ 'be there, exist, abide, remain, stay' appears only as the extended root PA /*aya·-/, and this assumes also the form of a TI stem in identity, forming TI verbs by the direct addition of the TI inflectional suffix /*-en-/. A TA stem is formed by appending the TA final /*-w-/ to the extended root, rendering with alternation the TA stem /*ayi·w-/ which is then followed by a TA inflection. Thus the TA absolute form is PA /*ayi·we·wa/ 'he has him'; C /aya·we·w/ with the alternation leveled out; O /otaya·wa·n/ in TA objective form. Both transitive stems entail some change of meaning to 'have there, possess, remain in possession', illustrated in the forms above.

It should be noted that in Fox and Menomini the extended root PA /*aya·-/, modified by stabilization of the alternation (as in Penobscot and Powhatan), has been further reshaped as F /awi·-/ and M /a·we-/, perhaps by analogical contamination with the PA root /*aw-/ and its extended form /*awe·-/ 'use'; F /awe·wa/ 'he uses him'; M /awɛ·w/ 'he uses him' and M /a·w/ 'he uses it'; O /otawa·n/ 'he uses him'; P /awe-/.

Intransitive stems (AI and II) also are projected from the extended PA root /*aya·-/ by directly appending, subject to alternation, the intransitive endings, as is shown in the following:

PA /*ayi·wa/ (AI) 'he exists, is there, he abides, remains, stays'; F /awi·wa/; C /aya·w/ with alternation leveled out; M /a·wew/ 'he is so-and-so'; O /aya·/ with analogic /a·/ as in O /ma·ča·/ 'he starts off, goes away', although some O dialects (Baraga's) have /awi·/ which may be a loan from Fox; P /àyo/, |àyiw|.

PA /*ayi·wi/ (II) 'it exists, is there, it remains'; C /aya·w/ with alternation leveled out; M /a·wew/ 'it is so-and-so, such-and-such'; O /aya·/; P /áyo/, |áyiw|. Only Penobscot distinguishes the AI and II forms, reflecting the original contrast of /*ayi·wa/ : /*ayi·wi/ by accent differentiation.

There is also PA /*aya·mekatwi/ (II) 'it exists, remains', formed by adding the II final /*-mekatwi/ to either AI or II stems; F /awi·mekatwi/; M /a·wemakat/ 'it is so-and-so' O /aya·makat/.

106. HEAR (a) /neno·ntamen/ (TI) 'I hear it'; /mata neno·ntamen/ 'I do not hear it'. See SEE, entry 178.

(b) nownuntamen "hear" (H8), mata nownontamen "not to hear" (H8)

(c) PA /*no·ntamwa/ 'he hears it' (B146); PA /*neno·nta/ 'I hear it' (TI absolute), F /neno·ta/; PA /*neno·nta·ni/ 'I hear it' (TI objective), M /neno·hta·n/, O /nino·nta·n/.

PEA /*neno·ntameni/ 'I hear it', P /nənòtamən/ Powhatan /neno·ntamen/.

107. HERON (a) /assak/ 'great blue heron' (genus Ardea); /wa·passak/ 'great white heron' (also genus Ardea), or perhaps and less likely the 'egret' (genus Casmerodius).

The great white heron formerly occurred north to Chesapeake Bay, but is now confined to southern Florida.

(b) ussac "crane" (H4), wopussouc "swan" (H14)

(c) PA /*ša?šakiwa/ 'great blue heron' (genus Ardea); C (Swampy Cree only) /sasakiw/; M /sa·?sakew/ (Menomini Lang. has /sa·?sakεw/ at 14.154, 368 and 20.15, but only /sā?sakiw/ uniformly appears several times in the Menomini Texts, pp. 494-496, which is certainly phonemic /sa·?sakew/); O /šaššaki/, pl. /šaššakiwak/; Ms /sassat/, (Eliot sassadt "crane" Isaiah 38:14); Powhatan /assak/. For PA /*k/ > Ms /t/ see under GUM, entry 102.

PA /*wa·pa?šakiwa/ 'great white heron', perhaps 'egret' also; M /wa·pahsa·kε·w/

'white heron' (personal name, with foreign /hs/ for standard Menomini /ʔs/, and with error of the last vowel ?); Powhatan /wa·passak/. Strachey's meaning 'swan' is certainly wrong.

108. HIGH (a) /aspe·w/ (II) 'it is high'

(b) uspeuwh "above" (H2)

(c) PA /*ešpe·wi/ (II) 'it is high'; (B125, Lang. 1.150 gives root PA /*išp-/ 'above, high', revised to /*ešp-/ B146, Sections 8, 101); C /ispa·w/; O /išpa·/; Powhatan /aspe·w/. For the alternation of PA /*a·/ : /*e·/ before /*w/, leveled out in Cree and Ojibwa, see Bl. 46, Section 35, p. 98.

109. HOMINY (a) /apohomin/ 'grain of parched corn' INAN, pl. /apohominas, apohomins/ 'hominy'.

(b) aphohomins "whelpes" (H15)

(c) Pseudo-PA /*apwahwemina/ AN 'grain of parched maize'; root PA /*apw-/ 'heat', /*-ahw-/ TA instrumental 'by tool or medium' (see Bl. 46, Section 84, p. 114), /*-min-/ deverbal noun final 'drupe, grain, berry'.

110. HORN (a) /wi·wi·r/ 'horn, antler' AN, pl. /wi·wi·rak/

(b) wawirak "horns of a deer" (H8), (I assume this to be a writing error for wewirak).

(c) PA /*-i·wi·la/ AN dependent noun, pl. /*-i·wi·laki/; PA /*wi·wi·la/ 'a horn', and restructured as nondependent in some languages; F /owi·wi·na/ 'horn', pl. /owi·wi·naki/, /owi·wi·nani/ 'his horn', /ni·wi·na/ 'my horn'; M /ne·wen/ 'my horn', /we·wenan/ 'his horn(s)', AN dependent noun; S /wi·wi·la/ 'horn', but as a deverbal /kaškwiwilaki/ 'sharp horns' (S /-iwila/ AN); Mi /awi·wi·la/ 'horn', pl. /awi·wi·laki/; mD /wi·lá·wan/ 'horn' (reshaped); EA (except Penobscot) /áwiwil/ 'horn, antler' AN, pl. /awíwilak/, but

/wətawíwilal/ or /wətawíwiləmal/ 'his horn' (P has this morpheme only in /wiwíləyamek^{w}/ 'snail'); Ms (Nauset dialect only) /wiwin/ 'horn (Cotton weween "horn", but not in Eliot or Mayhew).

There is also: PEA /*wešemowa/ 'antler, horn'; uD /wšə́mo/, pl. /wšə́mowak/; P /wə̀səm pl. /wə̀səməwak/, | wəsəmow- |.

111. HOT (a) /apete·w/ (II) 'it is hot, warm'; /apete·w apo· 'the bread is hot'. This shows that /apo·n/ is INAN in Powhatan.

(b) apetawh poan "broil or toast bread" (H3)

(c) PA /*apwete·wi/ (II) 'it is hot, warm'; M /apɛ·tɛ·w/; P /âpəte/; Powhatan /apete·w/.

112. HOUSE (a) /yi·ha·ka·n/ (?) 'house'

(b) yehacan "house" (H8), yeahaukan "house" (H16), yehawkans "houses" (Smith)

(c) Compare Nanticoke /ya·ha·k/ (?) (Heckewelder iahack "house"); uD /ya·k·á·ɔn/ 'shade house'

113. ISLAND (a) /menenak/ 'island', pl. /menenakos/

(b) mennunnakgus "island" (H8); actually pl.

(c) Pseudo-PEA /*menenakwi/ 'island'; PA root /*men-/ 'mass, pile', and PEA noun final /*-enakw-i/ 'island'; P /kı̀nənak^{w}/ 'large island', /màtənənak^{w}/ 'mountain island', |-ənakw| ; reshaped (?) in Cree as /-a·nak(w)/, C /awasa·nak/ 'the other side of the island', /iskwa·naka·w/ (II) 'the island is so long'. The usual PA term is:

PA /*menehsi/ 'island'; F /menesi/, pl. /menesani/; M /menɛ·s/, pl. /menɛ·hsyan/, with analogical /y/ (?); O /miniss/, pl. /minissan/; S /meneʔθi/, pl. /meneʔθi·wali/.

114. KINDLE (a) /mato·tam/ (Class 1, objectless-TI) 'he kindles a fire'.

(b) matowtam "burn as if a spark light on anything" (H3)

(c) PA root /*mato·t-/ 'strike fire, kindle' found without sound change in F /mato·tešiwa/ 'he takes a steam bath'; C /mato·tisiw/; O /mato·to·/ 'he takes a steam bath', all with semantic specialization; P /mátotawe/ (AI) 'he kindles a fire' with root |matot-| and final |-awe| from PA /*-awe·-wa/ 'make fire, make light'.

115. LEG (a) /meska·t/ 'someone's leg', /neska·t/ 'my leg'.

(b) mescot "leg" (H10)

(c) PA /*-xka·či/ 'leg' INAN dependent noun, pl. /*-xka·tali/; PA /*nexka·či/ 'my leg'; F /nehka·či/, pl. /nehka·tani/; C /niska·t/, pl. /niska·ta/; M /nɛhka·t/, pl. /nɛhka·tan/; O /nikka·t/, pl. /nikka·tan/; S /nka·či/, pl. /nka·tali/; P /nkɑt/, pl. /nkɑ̀tal/.

116. LIP (a) /neskese·/ 'my lip' INAN.

(b) nusskaih "lips" (H9), (actually sg.).

(c) PA /*-škešayi/ 'lip' INAN dependent noun; /*neškešayi/ 'my lip'; C /niskisay/; Mt /nisčišiy/; S /niškiša/, pl. /niškiša·wali/ 'my lips'.

117. LIZARD (a) /a·po·sse·ss/ dimin. 'slowworm', probably the 'slender glass lizard' (Ophisaurus attenuatus longicaudus).

(b) apouscase "slowworm" (H13)

(c) Pseudo-PA /*wa·po·hθe·hša/ dimin. 'little white worm'; root PA /*wa·p-/, and deverbal /*-o·hθe·wa/ 'worm', Powhatan /-o·sse·/ with PA dimin. final /*-ehš-a/, Powhatan /-ess/. See WORM.

118. LONG (a) /kene·w/ (II) 'it is long'.

(b) cunnaivwh "long) (H9)

(c) PA /*kenwe·wi/ (II) 'it is long' (B146); C /kinwa·w/; M /keni·w/; O /kinwa·/; S /kinwa·wi/. For the alternation of PA /*a·/ : /*e· before /*w/, leveled out in Cree, Ojibwa, and Shawnee, see Bl. 46, Sections 35, 75, pp. 98, 110.

119. LOON

(a) /akwimess/ 'loon' dimin., or with syncope /akwims/

(b) ockquims "watchet colored bird" (H11)

(c) Ps /əkwím/ 'loon'; the Powhatan form as if from Pseudo-PEA /*akwimehša/ dimin. 'loon', with PA dimin. /*-ehša/. The PA root is /*akwim-/ 'float motionless on or within the water'. PA /*akwimowa/ 'he (waterfowl, fish, man in a canoe) floats motionless on or within the water'; C /akomow/; O /akomo/; P /ák^{w}imo/.

120. LOST

(a) /newaniss/ (AI) 'I am lost, I go astray', /wanisse·w/ 'he is lost'.

(b) nowwanus "lost" (H9)

(c) PA /*wani?le·wa/ 'he is lost, he goes astray, he disappears'; F /wanise·wa/; C /wanihyow/ with reshaped ending; O /wanisse·/ 'he makes a blunder'; P /wánihle/.

121. LOUSE

(a) /metahkem/ 'a louse, someone's louse', /netahkem/ 'my louse', /ketahkemi/ 'you (sg.) have lice'.

(b) metacum "louse" (H9), cuttahcummeis "look one's head" (H9)

(c) PA /*ehkwa/ 'louse' (B146); F /ahkwa/; C /ihkwa/; M /ehkua/; O /ikkwa/; P /kkəm/ with syncope, and restructured from possessed forms. Fox /ihkwa/ given by Bloomfield does not exist.

PA /*netehkwema/ 'my louse' (Bl. /*netehkoma F /neto·hkoma/; C /nitihkom/; M /netɛ·hkom/; O /nitikkom/; P /nə̀tahkəm/.

PA /*ehkwemiwa/ 'he has lice, is lousy'; P /kkə̀mo/, |ahkəmiw| ; rebuilt in C, M, and O as /*wetehkomiwa/ (B146). PA /*netehkwemi/ 'I have lice'; P /nə̀tahkəmi/; Powhatan /netahkemi/; O /nitotikkom/.

22. LOVE

(a) /ko·wama·nes/ 'I love thee' (TA), /no·wama·tamen/ 'I love it' (TI)

(b) cuwumonais "you love" (H8), nouwmais "I love you" (?) (H8), nowamatamen "I must keep it or I love it" (H8)

(c) PEA /*ko·wama·neθe/ (?) 'I love thee'; Ms /kowamɑnəš/ (Eliot koowomonsh, Cotton koowomonŭsh, Mayhew koowomônush, koowamonish); Nr /kowamɑnəš/ (Williams cowàmmaunsh); but Np /nowamalɑ/ (?) 'I love him', (Mathevet pp. 11, 19 n8amanlan "je l'aime"). If recorded correctly Powhatan and Np do not match.

123. MAN

(a) /ni·mate·w/ 'man'.

(b) nematough (Smith; misprinted nemarough), nimatewh "man" (H10)

(c) PEA /*ni·maθe·wa/ 'man'; Mh /ní·manaw/.

124. MARROW

(a) wi·mp/ 'marrow'.

(b) wimpe "marrow" (H15), weimb "marrow of a bone" (H10)

(c) PA /*wi·mpikani/ 'bone marrow'; F /owi·pikani/ with prothetic vowel. Compare M /we·hpaham/ 'he hollows it out', and O /wi·mpašk/ 'hollow reed', pl. /wi·mpaško·n/; for PA root /*wi·mp-/ 'hollow'.

125. MAT

(a) /ana·ska·n/ 'mat, rug'.

(b) anauson "mat" (H2), anausacoon "mat made of reeds" (H10)

(c) PA /*ana·xkani/ INAN 'mat, rug', but AN in S and EA (including P); F /ana·hkani/, pl. /ana·hkanani/; C /ana·ska·n/ INAN with PA noun final /*-a·n-/ rather than /*-an-/ as in Powhatan; M /ana·hkyan/ INAN and reshaped by analogy to the verb form; O /ana·kkan/, pl. /ana·kkanan/; S /ana?ka/ 'pallet, mattress', pl. /ana?kanaki/; EA (except Penobscot) /ánahkan/, pl. /anáhkanak/, |anαhk-an| ; P /ánehkan/ 'mat, rug, floor or bed of a canoe', pl. /anéhkanak/, reshaped by analogy to P root /anehk-/ in /anehkáyi/ 'in low position, below' mD /anáa·hkan/, pl. /aná·hkanal/.

PA /*ana·xkye·wa/ 'he lays a mat, spreads a rug'; C /ana·ske·w/; M /ana·hkow/, reshaped by analogy to M /apa·hkow/ 'he thatches'; P /ánehke/ 'he lays a skin, rug or mat, spreads a quilt' (compare P /wəlánehke/ 'he makes, prepares a bed').

126. MEAL (a) /ro·hkahamen/ 'parched corn meal'.

(b) rokohamin "parched corn ground small" (H12)

(c) PEA /*lo·xkahameni/, P /nòhkhamən/ 'parched corn meal, flour', with syncope; compare Np /lohkik/ (Mathevet p. 22 18kik "farine"); S /lokha·na/ 'flour'.

The root is PA /*lo·xk-/ 'soft'; F /no·hk-/; C /yo·sk-/; M /no·hk-/; O /no·kk-/; P /nohk-/.

127. MEAT (a) /wi·ya·ss/ 'meat, flesh'.

(b) oiawhs, wiaaws "lean of any flesh" (H9), weyaus "lean of any thing" (H15), weghshaugh "flesh" (Smith).

(c) PA /*wi·yawehsi/ 'meat, flesh'; F /owiya·si/ pl. /owiya·sye·ni/ (with prothetic vowel and ending analogically reshaped); C /wiya·s/; O /wi·ya·ss/; S /wiyaw?θi/, pl. /wiyaw?θi·wa/ P /wə̀yohs/, pl. /wə̀yohsal/, |wiyohs| ; uD /wiyó·s/; Ms /wiyos/ (Eliot weyaus "flesh"

Exodus 29:32). This is a diminutive formative of the following:

PA /*wi·yawi/ 'his body, flesh' (B146, p. 91); F /wiyawi/; C /wiyaw/; M /we·yaw/; O /wi·yaw/; S /wiyawi/.

128. MIRE

(a) /passakwan/ 'mire, sticky mud'.

(b) pussagwun "clay" (H4)

(c) PEA /*pahsakwani/, /*pehsakwani/ 'mire, mud'; Ms /pəssakw/, pl. /pəssakwanaš/ (Mayhew pussogq "dirt" Psalm 18:42; Mayhew pussogquanit "in the mire", Eliot pissogquánuhtu Psalm 69:2); Np /pəssakwa/, pl. /pəssakwanas/ (Mathevet p. 98 pissag8̆a "vasé, boüe", pissag8an8h8 mai "chemin bourbeux").

The PA root is /*pahsakw-/ 'sticky, muddy, miry' (or /*pehsakw-/ assuming the cluster is /*hs/ rather than /*ʔs/ in the absence of a Menomini cognate), found in C /pasakwa·w/ (II) 'it is sticky', /pasakoče·sk/ 'mire'; O /passakwa·kami/ 'it is a thick, sticky liquid'; S /peθakwa/ 'it is sticky, muddy' (reshaped for expected S /*peʔθakwa/).

129. MITTEN

(a) /metenče·ss/ 'a glove, someone's mitten', /otenče·ss/ 'his glove, mitten', evidently INAN. See HAND, entry 104.

(b) meteingeies "fingers" (H6), oteingas "glove" (H7), meteengass "shooting glove" (H13)

(c) PEA /*meθenčye·nsa/ AN 'a glove, someone's mitten' with the indefinite possessor prefix /*me-/; P /mə̀ləčess/ 'glove, mitten', pl. /mə̀ləčessak/; Np /mələčass/ (Mathevet p. 53 melejas, pl. melejassak "mitaine"). Powhatan /metenče·ss/ seems to be from an expected and earlier Powhatan /*metenče·ns/ by progressive dissimilation, reinforced by the analogy of the more numerous examples of diminutives with this suffixed form.

130. MORNING (a) /waspa·sa·hk/ (II) 'it is morning'.

(b) papasawk "morning or sunrise" (H10), paspasak uscautewh "the morning is fair" (H10); (hearing error of initial p for w assumed).

(c) PEA /*waθpa·sa·xkiwi/ (?) (II) 'it is morning'; P /spɑsáhko/, changed conjunct /wespɑsáhkiwik/ 'when it is morning'.

The root is PA /*waθpa·-/ or /*weθpa·-/ 'awake, rouse'; C /waspa·-/ as in (TA) /waspa·we·me·w/ 'he wakes him by calling'; O /oppa·-/ as in /oppa·we·/ (AI) 'he keeps people awake'; Nanticoke /wespa·/ 'morning' (Heckewelder weschpa "morning").

131. MOTE IN EYE (a) /nepensen/ 'I have (dust, a mote, foreign body) in my eye'.

(b) nepensun "dust" (H5)

(c) PA /*nepensenli/ 'I have a mote or foreign body in my eye'; M /nepɛ·sɛhnem/; C /nipisinin/; O /nipinsin/; P /nəpə̀ssihli/ or with syncope /nə̀pəsli/ (both forms are used); (compare S /nipeθena/ (TA) 'I throw dirt in his eye'; (AI) S /nipeθene/ 'I have something in my eye').

PA /*pensenliwa/ 'he has a foreign body in his eye'; C (Swampy Cree) /pisiniw/; M /pesɛ·hnew/ (Menomini Language 14. 47) re-shaped for expected /*pehsɛ·hnew/; O /pinsini/; P /pə̀ssihlo/, |pəssəhliw|.

For the de-aspiration and lenition of word initial checked syllables in Menomini see PERSIMMON (entry 153), and compare M /seko·h/ 'weasel' for expected /*sehko·h/, and M /suasek/ 'eight' for expected /*nɛˀsuasek/. Some doubt exists concerning the length of the first vowel in the Ojibwa form; I have assumed it is short, but if long it is by analogical contamination with /*pi·nt-/ and assibilated /*pi·ns-/ 'enter, inside'. In Penobscot /ss/ from |ss| but not from |hs| is the reflex of PA /*ns/ following /*e/ and /*e·/, as in PA /*e·nsa/ 'bivalve mollusk' or 'shell', P /ess/ (see entry 183), and PA /*aθemwensa/ 'little dog', P /ǻləmoss/ (see entry 68).

132. MOTHER (a) /nek/ 'my mother', /kek/ 'thy mother'.

(b) kick "mother" (H8), neck "mother" (H10)

(c) PA /*nekya/ 'my mother'; F /nekya/; M /nekiah/ or /neki·yah/; S /nekiya/; Mi /ninkia/; mD /nkək/. PA /*wekyali/ 'his mother'; F /okye·ni/; M /okian/.

133. MOUSE (a) /a·pikwess/ 'mouse'.

(b) apegwas "mouse" (H10)

(c) PA /*a·pikwa/ or /*wa·pikwa/ 'mouse', the latter form probably due to analogical contamination with PA /*wa·p-/ 'white', and both with PA noun final /*-ikw-a/ 'gnawing animal, rodent'. In surviving languages the term always appears in diminutive form, often with a super-added diminutive. F /wa·pikono·ha/; C /a·pikosi·s/; O /wa·wa·pikono·či/ with reduplication; S /wa·pikoloʔθa/; P /ɑpíkʷsehso/, |ɑpikwəhsehsiw|.

134. MOUTH (a) /meto·n/ 'someone's mouth', /neto·n/ 'my mouth'.

(b) mettone "mouth" (H10), mehtoan "mouth" (H10)

(c) PA /*meto·ni/ 'someone's mouth' (Michelson 35); C /mito·n/; M /meto·n/. PA /*neto·ni/ 'my mouth'; F /neto·ni/; C /nito·n/; M /neto·n/; O /nito·n/; S /nito·ni/; P /nə̀ton/; uD /nto·n/; Mh /nto·n/; Ms /nəton/ (Eliot and Mayhew nutoon "my mouth" Psalm 17:3).

135. MUCUS (a) /makikw/ 'nasal mucus'.

(b) makigue "snot" (H10)

(c) PA /*makikwa/ or /*akikwa/ 'nasal mucus, catarrh', PEA having /*makikwa/; F /akikwa/; C /akik/, pl. /akikwak/; M (AI) /ake·kon/ 'he has a cold in the head, an obstructed nose'; O /akik/; P /màkik^{w}/ 'nasal mucus, catarrh' (not 'phlegm' or 'sputum'); AN in all languages.

136. MUSKRAT (a) /ossaskwe·ss/ dimin. 'muskrat', and in another Powhatan dialect /mossaskwe·ss/.

(b) osasqaws "muskrat" (H10), mosskwacus "marten" (H10), mussascus "water rat" and "smell exceedingly strong of musk" (Smith).

(c) PA /*we?šaškwa/ 'muskrat'; F /ašaškwa/; C /wačask/ with /č/ for expected /s/ by diminutive symbolism; M /o?sas/, pl. /o?saskw[illegible] or /o?saskok/; O /waššašk/ or /oššašk/, pl. /waššaškwak/ or /oššaškok/.

Some eastern languages reflect a PEA /*mohšaškwe·hša/ 'muskrat' (i. e. "little-gatherer-of-grass") or other diminutive variants, from an initial analogical alteration of the PA form; P (and all EA dialects) /móhssk^{w}ehso/, |mohsaskwehsiw| ; Powhatan (one dialect) /mossaskwe·ss/. The medial in both cases is PA /*-aškw-/ 'grass, herb', and the root is apparently /*mohš-/ (?) as in C /mosahkinam/ (TI) 'he gathers it, them up'. Trumbull's etymolo[illegible] of muskrat (Natick Dictionary, p. 299) from musqui-ôáás "red animal" is incorrect. Other eastern languages have different analogical forms such as Np /təmaskwass/ (Mathevet p. 106, temesk8as, pl. temesk8assak "rat musqué"), modeled after PEA /*tema·xkwe·wa/ 'beaver (severer-of-trees)' from root /*tem-/ 'sever, break in two' and medial /*-a·xkw-/ 'wood, tree'; P (and general EA) /tə̀mahk^{w}e/, |təmahkway-| 'beaver'; Nr /təmahk/ (Roger Williams tummòck "beaver", pl. tummockquaûog); uD /təmá·kwe/.

137. NAME

(a) /ke·/ or /ke·kway keteri-wi·ns ki·r/ 'What is your (sg.) name?',. /ari-wi·nso·w/ 'he calls himself, he is named so, thus'.

(b) ka katorawincs yowo "what call you this?" (Smith), caqwaih cacuttewaas yowk "what call you that?" (H15); cacutterewindg kear "what is my name?" (H15), cacutterewindg yowk "what is his name?" (H15), cacutterewindg keir "what is your name?" (H15), quequoy ternis quire "what is your name?" (H12)

(c) PA /*wi·nle·wa/ 'he names him' (B125, Lang. 1. 155), TA absolute; F /wi·ne·wa/; C /wi·he·w/; M /we·hnɛw/; and TA objective PA /*wewi·nla·wali/ 'he names him'; O /owi·na·n/; P /wətəlí-wihlal/.

PEA /*aši-wi·nswiwa/ 'he is named so, he calls himself thus'; P /alí-wiso/; Ms /asi-wiso/ (Eliot ussowesu "he is called, named" First Chronicles 1:19, 50); Powhatan /ari-wi·nso·w/.

PEA /*ke·kwayi *keteši-wi·nswi/ 'What is your (sg.) name?'; P /kek^{w} kətəlí-wisiʼ/; Powhatan /ke·kway keteri-wi·ns/.

138. NEST

(a) /wasi·sse·w/ 'nest', perhaps /wači·sse·w/

(b) wahchesao "nest of a bird" (H11)

(c) PA /*wasyeʔθanwi/ 'nest', INAN in all languages; F /wasisanwi/, pl. /wasisanwani/; C /wačistwan/ with /č/ for expected /s/ by diminutive symbolism; M /wasɛ·ʔ/, pl. /wasɛ·ʔnan/; O (varies with dialect, for example see Jones' Ojibwa Texts, Part II, p. 154) /wasisswan/, /wasissan/, and /asissan/, pl. of the first form /wasisswanan/; S /wθiʔθa/, pl.

/wθi?θaniwali/. Cree and some Ojibwa dialects show metathesis of /w/ as if pseudo-PA /*wasye?θwani/. The ending has been reshaped in Eastern Algonquian.

PEA /*wasyehθe·wi/ 'nest'; P /wàsəsse/, pl. /wásəssal/; Ms /wačiss/, (Eliot oowadjish "her nest" Job 39:27) with the same diminutive symbolism as Cree and perhaps Powhatan.

139. NET (a) /assap/ 'net, seine' AN; pl. /netassapi·k/ 'my nets'.

(b) aussab "net" (H11), nuttassapec "cobweb" (H4), (actually pl., "my nets").

(c) PA /*a?lapya/ 'net, seine' (B125, Lang. 1.149), AN in all languages; C /ahyapiy/; M /a?nap/, pl. /a?napyak/; O /assap/, pl. /assapi·k/; P /áhlapi/, pl. /áhlapəyak/; Ms /assap/, (Eliot ahshop "net" Psalm 140:35), /wətassapah/ 'his net', (Eliot wuttahshapoh "his net" Psalm 35:8).

140. NETTLE (a) /masa·n/ 'nettle' AN.

(b) mauhsaan "nettle" (H11)

(c) PA /*masa·na/ 'nettle', AN in all languages; F /masa·na/, pl. /masa·naki/; C /masa·n/, /masa·nask/ 'nettle plant or stalk' AN; M /masa·n/; O /masa·n/, pl. /masa·nak/, /masa·našk/ 'nettle stalk'; S /maθa·na/ 'nettle, thorn', pl. /maθa·naki/.

141. NEW (a) /oska·te·w/ (II) 'it is new, young'. See MORNING.

(b) uscautewh "it is fair" (H10)

(c) PA root /*wešk-/ 'new' (B146); pseudo-PA /*weška·te·wi/ 'it is new' (II); compare C /oska·tisiw/ 'he is youthful, a young person', /oska·w/, /oska·yiwa·w/ 'it is new'.

142. NOSE (a) /meskiwan/ 'someone's nose', or /mehkiwan/;

/nehkiwan/ or /neskiwan/ 'my nose' (dialect difference probably).

(b) mehkewh "bill, beak" (H3), meskewe "nose" (H10), nethkeon "nose" (H11), really "my nose".

(c) PA /*-xkiwani/ 'nose', INAN dependent noun; PA /*mexkiwani/ 'someone's nose'; C /miskiwan/; PA /*nexkiwani/ 'my nose'; F /nehkiwani/; C /niskiwan/; Mi /ahkiwani/ 'bill, beak, nose'; Mh /nkiwan/; uD /nhikí·yɔn/.

143. NUT

(a) /paka·n/ 'large nut', pl. /paka·ns/ or /paka·nas/ INAN.

(b) paucauns "walnut" (H15)

(c) PA /*paka·na/ or /*paka·ni/ 'nut' (B125, Lang. l. 143, /*paka·na/), but INAN in F, Mi, P, and Powhatan; AN in C, M, and O; and both AN and INAN in S); F /paka·ni/, pl. /paka·nani/; C /paka·n/, pl. /paka·nak/; M /paka·n/; O /paka·n/, pl. /paka·nak/; S /paka·na/ or /paka·ni/; Mi /paka·ni/; P /pàkɑn/ 'large nut, butternut', pl. /pákɑnal/.

144. ONLY

(a) /na·ntake·/ 'only, if only, would that'; /na·ntake· nekot/ 'only one'; /na·ntake· pya·č/ 'if only he would come, would that he come' (3 person sg. injunctive).

(b) naantucah necut "only one" (H11), naantucah pyautch "come again" (H4)

(c) Compare O /na·nta/ (particle) 'would that, possibly'; (AI) /na·ntake·nimo/ 'he does all in his power'.

145. OPOSSUM

(a) /a·passem/ 'opossum', English loan from Powhatan.

(b) aposoum "beast in bigness of a pig and in taste alike" (H2), opassom "hath an head like a swine. . . tail like a rat. . . of the bigness of a cat" (Smith).

(c) PA /*wa·pa?θemwa/ 'white dog or dog-like beast'; (B125, Lang. 1. 142, 149, PA /*-a?θemw 'dog', deverbal noun final); C /wa·pastim/; M /wa·pa?nεm/; O /wa·passim/; P /wápahsəmohs dimin. None of these terms refers to the opossu

146. OTTER (a) /ketate·w/ 'otter'.

(b) cuttate "otter" (H11)

(c) PA /*ketate·wa/ 'otter'; F /ketate·wa/; S /kitate/; Powhatan /ketate·w/.

147. PAROQUET (a) /maskawins/ 'Carolina paroquet', now extinct (i. e., "grain robber")

(b) maskawhingc "parrot" (H10), massacamwindg "parrot" (H12)

(c) Pseudo-PEA as if /*maθkawinsowa/ with cluster /*θk/ not proven; from PA root /*maθk-/ 'seize by force, rob', and deverbal /*-awinso-wa/ 'he gathers berries, fruit, grain'.

PA /*maθkantwe·wa/ (AI) 'he seizes somethi by force, he robs people, commits robbery'; C /maskahtwe·w/; M /mahka·htaw/; O /makkant PA /*maθkame·wa/ (TA absolute) 'he robs him, he takes something from him by force'; C /maskame·w/; M /mahka·mε·w/; O /omakkama (TA objective).

PA /*mawinsowa/ 'he gathers berries, fruit, grain, nuts'; C /mawiso·w/; M /mawe·hsow/ 'he (bear) gathers acorns'; O /mawinso/; S /mawiθo/; P /máwiso/.

148. PATH (a) /me·w/ 'path' INAN.

(b) mayu "going in a path" (H10)

(c) PA /*mye·wi/ 'path' INAN; F /mye·wi/, pl. /mye·wani/; M /mi·hekan/ with different or reshaped ending; O /mi·kkan/ with reshaped ending; S /miye·wi/, pl. /miye·wali/; Mi /mi·wi/, pl. /mi·wa/; Np /may/, (Mathevet

p. 37 mai "chemin", mat maiin8 "il n'y a pas de chemin"); Ms /may/, (Eliot and Mayhew may "way" John 14:4, 5, 6; mayut "in a path" Psalm 28:11; ummay "his way" Psalm 25:9; ummayash "his paths" Psalms 17:4, 25:10). There is also:

PA /*metemye·wa/ 'he follows a path or trail'; C /mitime·w/; M /metɛ·mow/; S /metemye/.

49. PAWPAW (a) /assi·min/ 'pawpaw' (Asimina triloba (L.) Dunal, the genus term being from Algonquian).

(b) assessemin "wheat plum" (H15), with dittographic copying error of Strachey's.

(c) PA /*ahši·mini/ 'pawpaw', with cluster /*hš/ not proven in the absence of a Menomini cognate; F /aši·mini/; O /ašši·min/; S /aʔši·mi/, pl. /aʔši·mi·wali/, and /aʔši·mini-ki·šθwa/ 'September' ('pawpaw month').

50. PEANUT (a) /assanta·min/ 'hog-peanut' INAN, pl. /assanta·mins/ or /assanta·minas/, /otassanta·minas/ 'his hog-peanuts'. This is almost certainly the hog-peanut, Amphicarpa bracteata, (L.) Fernald.

(b) assentammens "peas" (H2), ossantamens "peas" (H12), ottassantamens (H12), assentamens "peas" (Smith).

(c) Pseudo-PEA /*ahθanta·mini/ 'hog peanut'; the simplex root is PA /*aʔθ-/ 'put away, cache' which usually appears with a postradical as PA root /*aʔθant-/ 'conceal in ground'; C /astaht-/, O /assant-/, and Powhatan extended root /assanta·-/.

PA /*aʔθančikowa/ 'he conceals food in the ground, he makes a cache'; C /astahčiko·w/; O /assančiko/. Compare M /aʔnapa·hkow/ 'he puts away stores, makes a cache' in which the simplex root appears, PA /*aʔθ-/. The PA deverbal noun final /*-min-i/ 'berry, drupe, grain' is common.

151. PEAR (a) /matakask/ 'prickly pear' or 'Indian fig' (Opunt humifusa Rafinesque). In Powhatan this term was probably not species specific, but was used for the similar fruits of the prickly pear, the balsam-apple or prickly cucumber (Echinocystis lobata [Michaux] Torrey and Gray), and the introduced but deadly Jamestown-weed, Jimsonw or thorn-apple (Datura Stramonium L. and Datur innoxia Miller).

(b) matakuskc "leaf of a prickly pear" (H10)

(c) PEA /*matwakaškwi/ 'prickly pear' or 'balsam-apple', evidently with both meanings; P /mátakask/ 'balsam-apple' (Echinocystis lobata pl. /matákaskol/. The elements are:

PA root /*matw-/ 'uneven, jagged' (see COPPER); the deverbal medial /*-ak-/ 'capsule nut' from PA /*pak-/ 'nut'; and the noun final PA /*-aškw-i/ 'plant, herb, grass' deverbal from the root /*maškw-/. The PA root /*pak-/ 'capsule, nut' is paired with the PA root /*pak- 'strike' (B146 /*pakantamwa/ 'he strikes it'), as in (AI) PA /*pake·wa/ 'he strikes, pounds'; S /pake/ 'he pounds nuts'; P /pàke/ 'he taps, strikes without intent to destroy or injure'. The medial /*-ak-/ is deverbal from root /*pak-/ 'capsule, nut'. In a botanical sense Algonquian semantics classifies all fruits into two groups: /*pak-/ 'capsule, large nut' (deverbal /*-ak-/ and /*mi·n-/ 'drupe, berry, grain, legume' (deverbal /*-min-/). Compare O /paka·n/ 'nut' and O /pake·ssan/ 'plum', the latter classified as a 'capsule' because of the large size and thick covering.

152. PENIS (a) /netatakay/ 'my penis', /atakay/ 'penis',

apparently restructured as a nondependent noun. /neka·hpamatamen netatakay/ 'I feel a scraping or grating of my penis'. See SCRAPE.

(b) *vnegapamuttamen* *netatakÿ* "it hurts my leg or my legs ache" (H8)

(c) PA /*-i·θakayi/ 'penis', dependent noun; F /-i·nakayi/; C /-i·takay/; M /-e·nak/; uD /-í·lak·ay/ as in /wí·lak·ay/ 'his penis'. Apparently restructured as a nondependent noun in some languages: Mi /awi·lakay/ 'penis'; uD /alák·ay/; Powhatan /atakay/.

153. PERSIMMON (a) /pessi·min/ 'persimmon', English loan from Powhatan; pl. /pessi·minas/ INAN.

(b) *pichamins* "excellent plum" (H11), *pusheminas* "plum very delicious when it is ripe" (H12), *putchamins* "fruit like a medlar... red when it is ripe... as delicious as an apricot" (Smith).

(c) PEA /*pehši·mini/ 'persimmon' (*Diospyros virginiana* L.); uD /xí·mi·n/ (for expected /*pəxi·min/); Powhatan /pessi·min/. The root is PA /*pehš-/ 'peel, husk'; O /pišš-/; S /peʔš-/; P |pəhs-|. Compare M /pesε·kahεw/ (TA) 'he husks him' for expected /*pehsε·kahεw/, with de-aspiration of word initial checked syllable, for which see MOTE IN EYE (entry 131).

54. PIPE (a) /ohpo·kan/ 'tobacco pipe'.

(b) *apokan* "tobacco pipe" (H2), *vppocane* "tobacco pipe" (H12), *vhpoocan̄* "tobacco pipe" (H14)

(c) PA /*wexpwa·kana/ AN 'tobacco pipe'; F /ahpwa·kana/; C /ospwa·kan/; M /ohpuakan/; O /oppwa·kan/; Mi /pwa·kana/; uD /hopɔ́·k·an/.

55. PLAICE See FLOUNDER, (entry 86).

56. PLAY (a) /pa·hpiko·w/ 'he plays a flute' (?) (AI).

(b) *pawpecoou* "play on a pipe" (H12)

(c) PA /*pa·hpiwa/ 'he laughs' (B125, Lang. 1. 152);

C /pa·hpiw/, dimin. /pa·hpisiw/ 'he laughs a little'; O /pa·ppi/. However, in Eastern Algonquian and some other languages the term means 'play' rather than 'laugh'. F /pa·hpiwa/ 'he entertains'; Mi /pa·hpiani/ 'I play'; uD /pá·po/ 'he plays'; P /pàhpo/ 'he plays', |pahpiw|.

'Play, frolic, gambol' is the Penobscot meaning and one suspects that this is the original meaning rather than 'laugh'.

157. PLUM

(a) /po·skam/ 'plum' AN, pl. /po·skamak/. This is probably Prunus americana Marsh., with a fruit which has a thick skin. Despite Strachey's meaning it is probably not the red mulberry, Morus rubra L.

(b) poskamatk "mulberries" (H11)

(c) PA /*po·θkama/ 'wild American plum'; S /poʔkama/ 'peach' (modern meaning), dimin. /poʔkama·θa/ 'plum', /poʔkama·wi·ši/ 'plum tree', /poʔkamawi-ki·šθwa/ 'June' ('wild plum month'). Compare O /po·kkito·nš/ AN 'pear' with the same root, PA /*po·θk-/.

For the only native mulberry, Shawnee has /mtekwa·palwa/ 'red mulberry tree', Morus rubra L.

158. POT

(a) /ahkehkwassen/ 'copper kettle, metal or stone pot' (see COPPER); /ahkehk/ 'water-drum, pot' AN, pl. /ahkehkok/; /ahkehkwins/ 'small pot, kettle'.

(b) aucutgagwassun "copper kettle" (H4), ahqwehkc "drum" (really pl.) (H5), aucagmins "kettle" (H9) with writing error of m for w, aucagwins "pot" (H12)

(c) PA /*axkehkwa/ 'pot, kettle, water-drum' (B125, Lang. 1. 142, B146 Section 31, p. 96);

F /ahkohkwa/ 'pot, water-drum', pl. /ahkohko·ki/, with assimilation of /*e/ to /o/ before /hkw/ (see B146 Section 3, p. 86); C /askihk/; M /ahkɛ·h/, pl. /ahkɛ·hkok/; O /akkikk/, pl. /akkikko·k/; S /aʔkoʔkwa/, pl. /aʔkoʔko·ki/; Mi /ahkihkwi/, pl. /ahkihkwa/; P /kkohk/, pl. /kkòhkak/, /nə̀tahkohk/ 'my pot, my buttocks, rump'.

PA /*axkehkwinsa/ dimin. 'little pot'; C /askihkos/; M /ahkɛ·hko·hsɛh/; O /akkikko·ns/; Powhatan /ahkehkwins/.

59. POUR

(a) /oso·kenemen/ (TI) 'he pours it'.

(b) vsowcunnemun "pour in water" (H12)

(c) PEA /*weso·kenameni/ (TI) 'he pours it'; P /wəsókənəmən/. The PEA TI theme-sign /*-am-/ was assimilated (?) to /*-em-/ following /*-en-/ 'by hand' late in PEA times. The root is as follows:

PA /*so·k-/ 'pour, soak'; C /so·k-/ (C /so·kistita·w/ 'he soaks it'); O /so·k-/ as in O /so·kippo·/ 'it snows'.

60. PUCCOON

(a) /pakkan/ 'puccoon', English loan from Powhatan; 'Indian paint plant, red dye'. The plant is Lithospermum caroliniense (Walter) Macmillan.

(b) poughcone "red paint or dye" (H11), pokcoons "a red dye" (H5), pocones "small root that grows in the mountains, which being dried and beat in powder turns red" (Smith).

(c) PEA /*pakaxkanwi/ 'blood, red dye'; P /pákahkan/ 'blood', /pakáhkanok/ 'in the blood'; /nəpákkanom/ 'my blood' INAN, stem |pakahkanw-|; Mh /pkáhkan/ 'blood', by syncope from |pakahkanw-|; Nanticoke /pakahk/ 'blood' with apocope similar to that of the SNE languages.

Somehow related are Mi /ni·pikkanwi/ 'blood as if from /*ni·pekaxkanwi/, and Pq /nipakk/ (Roger Williams néepuck "blood") as if from /*ni·pakaxkanwi/.

161. PUMPKIN

(a) /mahkahk/ 'pumpkin' INAN (Cucurbita pepo L.).

(b) makawke "gourd" (H10), mahcawk "pumpkin" (H12), macaugscaunemes "grape's stone or the stone of any plum" (H7), macocks "pumpkins" (Smith).

(c) PA /*mahkahkwi/ 'tub, cask, calabash', with varying degrees of semantic change in the differ[ent] languages; F /mahkahkwi/ 'box', pl. /mahkahko·ni/; C /mahkahk/ 'tub, cask'; M /mahka·h/ 'box', pl. /mahka·hkon/; O /makkakk/ 'tub, box', pl. /makkakko·n/; S /mkaʔkwi/ 'box, tub, keg', pl. /mkaʔkowali/; mD (and some uD dialects ?) /máhkahkw/ 'pumpkin', pl. /mahkáhkwal/. The Delaware form is borrowed from the Algonquian languages to the south, from the more agricultural Nanticoke and Powhatan peoples of the Chesapeake Bay region, since /h/ is the reflex of PA /*hk/ in all Delaware dialects. The Powhatan form with the same meaning 'pumpkin' and the expected sound change in Delaware which did not occur point to certain borrowing from the south.

The other term given by Strachey is evidently mistranslated and should be /mahkahkoskanimin[/] 'pumpkin seeds'.

162. RACCOON (1)

(a) /a·re·hkan/ (?) 'raccoon', English loan from Powhatan.

(b) aroughcan (Smith), arathkone "beast like a fox" (H2), arratkcune (H6)

(c) The source of this is uncertain, but perhaps suggests a PA /*la·lwe·čkan-/ (?); M

/na·ni·čkanɛ·na·w/ legendary name of the 'raccoon'.

163. RACCOON (2)

(a) /e·sepan/ 'raccoon', pl. /e·sepanak/. This is another Powhatan dialect gloss, but what dialect we do not know.

(b) esepannauk "hare" (H7), actually plural. This is unquestionably the raccoon despite Strachey's mistranslation, perhaps due to viewing the animal at a distance in the brush.

(c) PA /*e·hsepana/ 'raccoon', evidently reshaped in Eastern Algonquian as PEA /*e·sepana/; F /e·sepana/; M /ɛ·hsepan/; O /e·ssipan/; P /ésəpanəss/ dimin., pl. /ésəpansak/; mD /é·span/ pl. /e·spának/ with syncope; Np /asəp/, (Mathevet p. 24 assep, pl. assebanak "chat sauvage"); Nr /asəp/, pl. /asəpanak/ (Roger Williams aûsup, pl. âusuppánnog).

164. RAIN

(a) /kemiwan/ (II) 'it rains, is raining'.

(b) komeyhon "rain" (H8), cameowan "rain" (H12)

(c) PA /*kemiwanwi/ 'it rains, is raining' (II) (Michelson, Lang. 13.73-75 [1937]; B146, p. 91); F /kemiya·wi/, analogically reshaped; C /kimiwan/; M /keme·wan/; O /kimiwan/; S /kimowa·nwi/, reshaped by analogy to S /kwtela·nwi/ 'it rains hard'.

165. RAW

(a) /askani·w/ 'it is raw' (II).

(b) ascanniewh "raw" (H12), vscannewh "not ripe" (H13)

(c) PA /*aškenwi/ and /*aškanwi/ (II) 'it is raw'; F /aškenwi/; C /aska·w/ (ending reshaped); M /askɛ·n/; O /aškin/; S /škinwi/ and /škanwi/.

Powhatan /askani·w/ suggests another archetype, probably PA or PEA /*aškanyi·wi/ (?).

166. REED (1)

(a) /atask/ 'reed, water weed', pl. /ataskwas/

(b) attasqwas "weeds" (H15), attasskuss "weeds or grass" (Smith).

(c) PEA /*aθwaškwi/ 'reed, water weed'; P /ȁlask/ 'reed', pl. /álaskol/. The root is PA /*aθw-/ 'round' (see ARROW, entry 16), with the noun final PA /*-aškw-i/ 'plant, herb, grass' deverb. from root /*maškw-/. There is also:

PA /*aʔθa·kanaškwi/ 'reed' (probably Phragmites communis, var. Berlandieri [Fournier] Fernald); C /asta·kanask/; O /assa·kanašk/, pl. /assa·kanaško·n/.

167. REED (2)

(a) /ni·ssa·kan/ 'reed, cane' (probably genus Arundinaria).

(b) nissakan "reed" (H10), nisake "cane" (H10), nehsaakan "reed" (H12)

(c) Pseudo-PA as if /*ni·ʔθa·kanaškwi/; the root is PA /*ni·ʔθ-/ 'shred'; M /ne·ʔn-/; O /ni·ss and extended root /ni·sse·-/; P |nəhse-| extend root.

168. ROE (1)

(a) /wa·hk/ 'fish or frog egg', pl. /wa·hkwak/ 'roe fish eggs'. See EGG.

(b) woock "caviar or the roe of sturgeon" (H4)

(c) PA /*wa·hkwa/ 'fish or frog egg' AN, pl. /*wa·hko·ki/; C /wa·hkwa/ 'fish or frog egg', pl. /wa·hkwak/ 'fish eggs, spawn, roe', also C /wa·hkwan/ 'roe' AN, pl. /wa·hkwanak/; M /wa·h/ 'fish egg' AN, pl. /wa·hkok/ 'roe, fish or frog eggs' (also M /wa·hkow/ 'female sturgeon with roe'); O /wa·kk/ 'egg of fish or frog' AN, pl. /wa·kkok/ or /wa·kkwak/ 'fish eggs, roe, spawn'.

169. ROE (2)

(a) /osi·ka·n/ 'roe' AN.

(b) vsecān "gristle of a sturgeon" (H7)

(c) PEA /*wešyeka·na/ 'roe' AN; P /wə̀səkan/

'roe', pl. /wə̀səkanak/ AN. This term is found in all EA dialects, and is similar to a dependent noun in other languages:

PA /*-šyi·kani/ 'rump', INAN dependent noun; PA /*wešyi·kani/ 'his rump'; F /oši·kani/; M /osi·kan/; Np /wəsik/, (Mathevet p. 95 8sik "croupe").

170. ROOT (a) /očapahk/ 'root' INAN.

(b) vtchapoc "root" (H13)

(c) PA /*wečye·pihki/ 'root' INAN, pl. /*wečye·pihkali/; F /oče·pihki/, pl. /oče·pihkani/; C /oče·pihk/; M /oči·pɛh/, pl. /oči·pɛhkan/; O /oči·pikk/, pl. /oči·pikkan/; S /oče·piʔki/ 'medicine, medicinal root', pl. /oče·pkali/, and /oče·pkaʔkatwi/ 'root'. This has been reshaped in Eastern Algonquian:

PEA /*wačapahkwi/ and /*wečapahkwi/ 'root'; P /wáčapahk/ 'plant root, medicinal root', /wáčapahk^{w}/ 'shrub or tree root, bole, lower trunk of tree below the limbs or leaf-line', pl. of both forms /wačápahkol/ (in the coastal dialect of Penobscot with partly different rules of syncope the forms are /wàčapk^{w}/, pl. /wáčapkol/); WA /wačápk^{w}/ with syncope as in coastal Penobscot. The PEA form /*wačapahkwi/ has been analogically reshaped partly on the model of PA /*watapya/ 'sewing root' as follows:

PA /*watapya/ 'fine spruce root, sewing root'; C /watapiy/; O /watap/, pl. /watapi·k/; P /wátapi/, pl. /wátapəyak/; Np /watap/, (Mathevet p. 22 8atap "racine a coudre").

The PEA noun final /*-ahkw-i/ contains a short vowel subject to syncope and is not the same as PA /*-a·xkw-/ 'wood, tree'.

171. ROPE (a) /pi·menahko·n/ 'rope, cord', dimin.

/pi·menahkwa·ne·ns/ 'small cord or line of twined thread'.

(b) peminak "rope" (H11), pemunakqweraneind "twined thread" (H15), peyminako~ "thread" (H11), pemanakaon "cord or small line or a thread (H4), pemunkuan "rope or cord" (H13)

(c) PA /*pyi·menahkwa·ni/ 'rope, cord'; C /pi·mina hkwa·n/; M /pi·mena·hkwan/; O /pi·minakkwa·n pl. /pi·minakkwa·nan/, dimin. /pi·minakkwa·ne 'small cord, twine'; S /pi·min?kwa/ 'thread'.

172. ROTTEN (a) /atet/ (II) 'it stinks, it is rotten, decayed'.

(b) ahtut "it stinketh" (H8), auutut "stink" (H14)

(c) PA /*aθetwi/ (II) 'it stinks, it is rotten, decayed'; F /anetwi/ 'it is rotten'; M /anε·t-/ in /anε·timyakwat/ 'it smells decayed', /anε·tipokwat/ 'it tastes decayed'; O deverbal /-anat/ in /kawanat/ 'it (wooden object) falls or lies from being rotten, it (clothing) decays'; S deverbal /-aletwi/ in /wiškaletwi/ 'it is rotting'; D (all dialects) /alə́t/ 'it is rotten'; Ms and Nr /ánət/, (Eliot anit "it stank" Exodus 16:20, matta anetunoo "it did not stink" Exodus 16:24; Roger Williams anit "it is putrified"); Np /alət/, (Mathevet p. 23 alet "pourri").

173. SALT (a) /sawa·n/ 'salt'.

(b) sawwehone "blood" (Smith), sawwone "salt" (H13); some sort of misunderstanding by Smith.

(c) The root is PEA /šaw-/, or extended root /*šawa·-/ 'sour'; P /saw-/ and /sawɑ-/, as in P /sawáhpokat/ 'it tastes sour' and /sawáskihko/ 'sour grass, wood sorrel' (Oxalis montana Rafinesque), pl. /sawáskihkəwal/. However, some eastern languages have the root following the form of the "central" languages, as in WA /siwan/ 'salt', mD /ší·wan/.

PA /*ši·w-/ 'sour'; C/si·w-/ (C /si·wa·w/ 'it is sour, salty'); M /se·w-/; O /ši·w-/ (O /ši·wan/ 'it is sour, salty').

174. SAND (a) /re·kaw/ 'sand'.

(b) racawh "sand" (H13)

(c) PA /*le·kawi/ 'sand'; F /ne·kawi/; C /ye·kaw/; M /nɛ·ka·w/; O /ne·kaw/; S /le·kawi/; Mi /ne·kawi/; uD /le·k·aw/; Mh /nakaw/; P root /nekaw-/ in P /nekáwɑkame/ 'it is a sandy lake', /nekáwihtək^{w}/ 'sandy river' (also the Penobscot name for the Tobique River in New Brunswick), /nekawámkimin/ 'sand cherry' or 'sand plum' (Prunus depressa Pursh).

175. SCAB (a) /meki/ 'scab', pl. /meki·s/ 'scabs'.

(b) meihkeih "sore" (H13), meihkeis "wart" (H15), actually pl.

(c) PA /*mekyi/ 'scab'; F /omeki/ with prothetic vowel; C /mikiy/ INAN; Mt /mičiy/; P /mə̀ki/, pl. /mə̀kəyal/. PA /*nemekyi/ 'my scab'; F /netomeki/ (restructured); C /nimikiy/; M /nemɛ·k/ (restructured as a dependent noun); Mt /nimičiy/; P /nə̀məkim/. There is also the AI verb:

PA /*wemekiwa/ 'he has scabs, is scabby'; F /omekiwa/; C /omikiw/; M /omɛ·ke·w/; O /omiki/; P /mə̀kəyo/, but /nəmə̀kiwi/ 'I have scabs'.

176. SCALE (a) /warahake·/ 'scale of a fish or reptile', pl. /warahakayak/

(b) woraihauk "scales of a fish" (H13), (actually sg.)

(c) PA /*walahakaya/ 'scale of fish or reptile' AN; C /wayakay/ AN, reshaped; M /wasa·hak/ AN, analogically reshaped with /s/ for expected

/n/; O /wanakaʔay/ AN; S /olʔhaka/; P (and all EA dialects) /wálahake/ 'scale of fish or reptile, shed snake skin', |walahakay|, pl. /wálahakak/.

The Cree, Ojibwa, and Menomini terms by two separate processes have been reshaped by analogical contamination with the dependent noun PA /*-ašakahaya/ 'skin' (of birds, fishes, reptiles, and man, but not of mammals) AN, as follows:

PA /*wašakahaya/ 'his skin'; C /wasakay/ INAN, with contraction; northern O /wašakay/ INAN; O /ošakaʔayan/ AN, /nišakaʔay/ 'my skin'. The Cree and Ojibwa words for 'scale' have been analogically reshaped following the model of the terms for 'his skin' in which there was a transposition of /*h/ and /*k/ so that the sound change falsely appears to be an example of independent metathesis but is in reality metathesis conditioned by the analogy between two terms of similar phonological sequence and related meanings. The Menomini form for 'scale' is different and shows substitution of /s/ for expected /n/ by analogy to the word for 'his skin', but no pseudo-metathesis. Another term for 'skin' is:

PA /*-θo·kayi/ 'skin', dependent noun; /*neθo·kayi/ 'my skin'; M /neno·k/; S /nilo·ka/ or /nilo·kaye/; Mi /nilo·kayi/.

Still another term for 'skin' is the dependent noun PA /*-θameškaya/ AN, 'inner skin or membrane' (refers to the elastic derma and the attached panniculus adiposus in both man and animals, that is, all structures between the epidermis and the muscular flesh, in both

Montagnais and Penobscot):

PA /*weθameškayali/ 'his inner skin'; F /onameškayani/ 'his skin'; Mt /otimiške·/; P /wə̀lamske/ INAN, |-laməskay|. PA /*neθameškaya/ 'my inner skin'; F /nenameškaya/ 'my skin'; P /nə̀lamske/ 'my inner skin'.

177. SCRAPE (a) /neka·hpamatamen/ (TI) 'I feel the scraping, grating of it'. See PENIS.

(b) vnegapamuttamen netataky̆ "it hurts my leg, or my legs ache" (H8)

(c) Root PA /*ka·xp-/ 'scrape, scrape bare or dry, grate, abrade'; C /ka·sp-/ (C /ka·spisam/ 'he makes it brittle, parches it'); M /ka·hp-/ (M /ka·hpahtam/ 'he scrapes it clean in eating it', /ka·hpiwɛw/ 'it makes a scraping sound'); O /ka·pp-/ (O /nika·ppina·/ 'I crumble him in my hand', /oka·ppisa·n/ 'he parches it').

PEA TI final /*-amat-/ 'feel'; P /nətahk^{w}ámatamən/ 'I feel the pain of it', with the PEA TI theme sign /*-am-/ and PEA TI objective suffix /*-eni/.

178. SEE (a) /onamen/ (TI class 3) 'he sees it'; /mata onamo·wen/ 'he does not see it'. The latter form gives the correct negative verb inflection of the TI, evidently given wrongly by Strachey in 'I do not hear it' (see HEAR, entry 106).

(b) vnnamuñ "see" (H13), mata namowuñ "not to see" (H13)

(c) PEA /*wenameni/ 'he sees it' (Class 3 TI); all SNE languages /wənamən/, (Quinnipiac, Pierson p. 28 wonaumen "he sees it"; Np, Mathevet p. 69 nikaten-naman m8liang "plut a dieu que je voye Montreal", pp. 21, 25 mat a8an nina8a or nena8a "je n'ai vu personne"), uD /wəné·mən/. In P and all EA dialects the root appears as Class

2 TI form, P /wənámihton/ 'he sees it' and negative /âta wənámihtowən/ 'he does not see it', but as a deverbal final it assumes the Class 3 TI form, as in P /wətəpínamən/ 'he examines, inspects it'.

179. SEED (1)

(a) /ami·nehka·n/ 'seed', pl. /ami·nehka·nak/ AN 'seeds', with prothetic vowel which circumvents syncope of /-eh-/.

(b) amenacanac "seeds" (H13)

(c) PA /*mi·nehka·ni/ 'seed (of grain, grass)'; O /mi·nikka·n/ 'seed', pl. /mi·nikka·nan/; S /mi·nʔka/, pl. /mi·nʔka·na/ and /mi·nʔka·na INAN and AN. The O form is also AN when reference is to seeds saved for future planting, O pl. /mi·nikka·nak/, positing PA /*mi·nehka· 'seed for sowing'. This is a formative of PA /*mi·nehke·wa/ (AI) 'he collects, saves seeds, berries' with the abstract noun final /*-a·n-/; with the semantic variations O /mi·nikke·/ 'he gathers whortleberries'; S /mi·nʔke/ 'he saves seeds for next year'.

180. SEED (2)

(a) /mahkahkoskaniminas/ 'pumpkin seeds' INAN pl. /waskanimin/ 'seed or stone of fruit, pit'.

(b) macaugscaunemes "grape's stone or the stone of any plum" (H7). See PUMPKIN.

(c) PA /*weθkanimini/ or /*waθkanimini/ 'seed or stone of fruit, pit' (PA /*waθkan-i/ 'bone', see BONE, entry 32; connective /*-i-/ or /*-e-/, and deverbal noun final /*-min-/ 'drupe, berry'); M /ohka·nɛ·men/ 'stone of fruit' with connective /*-e-/; P /skánimin/, pl. /skaníminal/; mD /waxkanim/; Np /wskanim (Mathevet p. 76 8skanimenĕs "graine de bled, semence"); Ms /oskanim/, (Eliot and Mayhew ooskannem "his seed" Psalm 89:29, 36) 'his seed', Ms and Nr /wskanim/ 'seed', pl. /wskaniminaš/.

181. SEINE — See NET, entry 139.

182. SHARP — (a) /ki·ni·w/ (II) 'it is sharp'. Note the sound contrast with /kene·w/ 'it is long' in entry 118.

(b) keneiwoh "sharp" (H13)

(c) The PA root appears in two forms, the simplex /*ki·n-/ and the extended root /*ki·nl-/ 'sharp, pointed'. Some descendent languages reflect both types, and some languages generalize one or the other. PA /*ki·n-/ is found exclusively in Fox and Cree as /ki·n-/, and /*ki·nl-/ alone appears in Menomini (M /ke·hn-/) and Miami (Mi /ki·nt-/). Since /*n/ and /*nl/ coalesce to give /n/ in Ojibwa, Massachusee, and Powhatan, these languages do not unequivocally reflect either root type, although the protoform may be indicated loosely by the accompanying features of whole words. General Abenaki and general Delaware employ reflexes of both types, and both have /hl/ as the reflex of /*nl/. Compare the following examples:

PA /*ki·nikenwi/ (II) 'it is pointed, sharp; it grows or tapers to a point'; C /ki·nika·w/ (Cree everywhere replaces other II finals with /-a·w/); M /ke·hnekɛn/ (Menomini everywhere replaces /*ki·n-/ with /ke·hn-/); P /kínikən/ 'it is sharp, pointed; it is big, prominent'.

PA /*ki·nye·wi/ (II) 'it is sharp, pointed'; C /ki·na·w/; O /ki·na·/; uD /kí·ne·w/. The PA alternation /*a·/: /*e·/ before /*w/ is leveled out as usual in Cree and Ojibwa.

PA /*ki·nlyi·wi/ (II) 'it is sharp, pointed'; M /ke·hn-/; Mi /ki·nta·wawi/ (ending analogically reshaped ?; Dunn kindawawi, who fails to distinguish vowel lengths; Mi /nt/ is the regula reflex of PA /*nl/); O /ki·na·/; Ms /kina/, but in Martha's Vineyard dialect /kini/ (Eliot keénu, Mayhew kene "it is sharp", Psalm 120:4); mD /kíhlo/, |ki·hli·w| 'he is pointed, has an erection'; P (and EA) |kihliw| in P /kəsí-kihlo/ (AI and II) 'he, it is sharp' (contrast /mačí-kihlo 'he, it is dull'); Powhatan /ki·ni·w/ (which corresponds better to this archetype rather than to /*ki·nye·wi/ unless one prefers to interpret Strachey's recording as /ki·ne·w/ which is improbable). The PA alternation /*ya·/ : /*yi· before /*w/ is leveled out in Miami, Ojibwa, and Massachusee (but apparently not in the Martha's Vineyard dialect).

183. SHELL

(a) /osaskway/ 'freshwater pearl mussel' or 'moquette' (of genus Lampsilis Rafinesque), pl. /osaskwayak/.

(b) osakescai "cockle" (H4), vsasgwoik "pearl mussel shells" (H12). Evidently Strachey has transposed the s in his first recording at (H4).

(c) PA /*wešaθkwaya/ 'freshwater pearl mussel' (apparently genus Lampsilis Rafinesque); O /ošakkwe·ss/ dimin., pl. /ošakkwe·ssak/; Powhatan /osaskway/. Other terms for mollusks are:

PA /*mi·kehsa/ 'spiral univalve mollusk, trumpet shell, conch, whelk; shell bead made from a univalve mollusk, wampum bead'; F /mi·kesa/; C /mi·kis/; M /me·kes/, pl. /me·kɛhsak/; O /mi·kiss/, pl. /mi·kissak/; S /mi·keˀθa/. As a general term for the morphologic type of spiral univalve mollusks, this PA word was originally applied to the larger species of freshwater or river snails of conch-like appearance, such as Io spinosa Lea, but later applied also to the marine whelks, and especially to Fulgur canaliculatus Say, found on the Atlantic coast southward from Cape Cod, from which wampum beads were made. The translation cowrie or cowry shell sometimes given for this term is incorrect since all species of cowrie are tropical marine types which extend no further north than the coasts of southern Florida and California.

PA /*e·nsa/ 'any bivalve mollusk; clam, bivalve shell', pl. /*e·nsaki/; F /e·si·ha/ dimin.; C /e·s/ or /e·sa/; Mt /e·š/; M /ɛ·hse·hsɛh/ dimin.; O /e·ns/ and in some dialects /e·ss/; P /ess/, pl. /ȇssak/.

The Shawnee term /mškwaheʔθa/ 'freshwater mussel' apparently refers to the genus Pleurobema, most of which have salmon red flesh. Their type distribution is in the Ohio, Cumberland, Tennessee, and Missouri rivers.

184. SHOE (a) /mahkesen/ 'shoe, moccasin' (English loan from Powhatan), pl. /mahkesens/ INAN.

(b) mockasins "shoes" (Smith), mawhcasuns "shoes" (H13)

(c) PA /*maxkeseni/ 'shoe, moccasin' (previously given wrongly as /*maxkesini/ by Bloomfield and myself), with noun final PA /*-esen-i/ 'footwear piece or section'; F /mahkese·hi/ dimin.; C /maskisin/; M /mahkɛ·sen/ or /mahkɛ·san/; O /makkisin/; S /mkiθe/, and /omaʔkiθe/ 'his shoe', /nimaʔkiθena/ 'my shoes'; Mi /mahkisini/; P /màhksən/, pl. /màhksənak/, AN |mahkəsən| (compare P /wak^{w}ánkəsən/ 'high or shank shoe, buskin'); Mh /mkisin/; Ms /mahkəs/, (Psalm 60:8, Eliot nummohkis "my shoe", Mayhew nummohkus).

The noun final /*-esen-i/ is found in other forms: PA /*ase·seni/ 'front top section of shoe, tongue or instep piece (of classical or original Algonquian moccasin)'; C /ase·sin/, pl. /ase·sina/; Mt /aše·šin/; eastern O and Algonkin /ase·sin/; P /ásesən/, pl. /ásesənal/; Mc /sesən/.

185. SHOOT

(a) /nepemotamen/ 'I shoot (at) it' (TI)

(b) nepomotamen "shoot" (H13)

(c) PEA /*nepemotameni/ (TI) 'I shoot (at) it'; P /nəpəmótamən/; Powhatan /nepemotamen/. PA /*nepemota/ 'I shoot it' (TI absolute); F /nepemota/; S /nipemota/; and in TI objective form, C /nipimote·n/; M /nepɛ·motan/; O /nipimota·n/.

PA /*pemotamwa/ (TI absolute) 'he shoots it' (B146, p. 114); or early-PA /*pemwetamwa/; F /pemotamwa/; C /pimotam/; M /pemo·tam/; S /pemotamwa/.

186. SHORT

(a) /tahkwesiw/ (AI) 'he is short'.

(b) tacqwaisuw "short" (H13)

(c) PA /*tahkwesiwa/ (AI) 'he is short'; F /čahkwihiwa/ with reshaped final; C /tahkosiw/; M /tasko·sew/ with discrepant /sk/ for expected /*hk/ as in SPOON; O /takko·si/; P /čáčahk^{w}əso/ with reduplicated root. The root is PA /*tahkw-/ 'short', or with consonantal diminutive symbolism /*čahkw-/. However, Munsee /čahkw-/ (mD /čahkwahkwší·šo/ dimin. 'he is short') suggests that the PA root could be /*taxkw-/. This noncorrespondence of clusters follows a similar pattern to that observed in PUMPKIN (entry 161) which is due to borrowing into Delaware, and in BLACK (entry 27) which is unexplained, although in these three examples Menomini diverges only in SHORT, and is unique in showing the same divergence in SPOON (entry 201).

187. SIT DOWN

(a) /nahapiw/ (AI) 'he sits down', /nahapis/ (2 person sg. imperative) 'sit (thou) down!'

(b) nehappeo "sit down" (H10), nawpiu "sit down" (H13); nahapuc "dwell" (H5), nehappec "sit further" (H11)

(c) PA /*nahapiwa/ 'he sits down' (AI); C /nahapiw/; O /naʔapi/; Powhatan /nahapiw/.

PA /*nahapilwe/ 'sit (thou) down!' (2 person sg. AI imper.); C /nahapiy/; O /naʔapin/.

188. SKIN

(a) /assay/ 'skin, hide, pelt' INAN, /otassayas/ 'his hides, skins', /neneskassayem/ 'my soiled or filthy hide', /matassay/ 'prepared fabric or dressed leather', pl. /matassayas/. See COVER, entry 60.

(b) vttocais "leather" (H9), nuscahsaiyam "tawny" (H14), matasaeih "apron of any kind of dressed leather" (H2), matassaish "napkin or any linen cloth" (H11)

(c) PA /*ahθaya/ 'skin, hide, pelt (of fur bearing mammal)'; F /asaya/, pl. /asayaki/, and F /asayi·h/ 'buckskin' dimin., pl. /asayi·hani/; C /ahtay/, pl. /ahtayak/; M /aska·hniy/ 'rawhide' (reshaped ?, but with cluster /hn/); O /aškattay/ AN 'green skin or rawhide' (evidently a loan from Cree); S /aʔθaya/, pl. /aʔθaye·ki/; mD /xay/, |axay| ; Mh /xay/, |axay| , /ntáxay/ 'my hide', /wtáxayan/ 'his hide'.

Pseudo-PA /*matwahθaya/ 'prepared fabric, dressed leather'; for root /*matw-/ 'uneven'; see COPPER, entry 58.

189. SLED

(a) /ota·pa·kan/ 'sled, toboggan' (English loan

from Eastern Algonquian, either Powhatan or Abenaki).

(b) atapakan "kixe" (H2), natapakan "kixe" (H9)

(c) PEA /*weta·pa·kani/ 'sled'; P /wətápakan/ INA

190. SLEEP (1)

(a) /nepe·w/ 'he sleeps, he is asleep' (AI), /nenepa·m/ 'I am asleep', /nema·či·-nepa·m/ 'I start to go to sleep'.

(b) nuppawv̄ "sleep" (H10), nepauū "sleep" (H13), nummacvshe nepam "I have been asleep" (H8)

(c) PA /*nepe·wa/ 'he sleeps, is sleeping' (B146, p. 97); F /nepe·wa/; C /nipa·w/; M /nepε·w/; O /nipa·/; S /nepe·wa/; Mi /nipe·wa/; Powhatan /nepe·w/. For the alternation of PA /*a·/ : /*e·/ before /*w/, leveled out in Cree and Ojibwa, see Bl 46, Sections 34, 35, and 75, pp. 97, 98, 110; and HIGH entry 108, and LONG entry 118. The alternation, as Bloomfield thought, seems to be best preserved in Menomini. Cree and most Ojibwa dialects regularly level it to /*a·/, and Fox and Shawnee seem to fluctuate in treatment subject to conditions which are not entirely clear. However from the data at hand, it is evident that in Fox and Shawnee the alternation of /*a·/ to /*e·/ regularly occurs before the third person suffix /*-wa/, but is leveled out to /*a·/ before the II suffix /*-wi/.

The /*a·/ : /*e·/ alternation is archaic in Proto-Algonquian, and the /*a·/ assumes a morphophonemic character. Since the AI verb of PA has a zero ending in the first and second persons singular, and since long final vowels are not permitted in PA phonology, AI verb stems ending in /*-a·/ such as /*pya·-/ 'come' and /*nepa·-/ 'sleep' shorten the vowel in the singular of the first and second persons of the

AI, attested by PA /*nepya/ 'I come' (see entry 55), and /*nenepa/ 'I sleep'. On the other hand, most languages with Goddard's long-*m pluralizing endings which are innovations (see Goddard 1967, Sections 2. 2, 3. 4, and 4. 2), namely Menomini, Massachusee, and Munsee-Delaware, have the first and second person singular AI forms reshaped to end in /-m/. The /m/ of the long-*m plural endings was segmented out and analogically extended to the singular where it functioned to preserve the long /*a·/ vowel. Since Powhatan has such forms (/nepya·m/ 'I come', /nenepa·m/ 'I sleep'), it can be assumed to have pluralizing suffixes similar to Munsee and Massachusee. The first person singular forms are:

PA /*nenepa/ 'I sleep' (B146, p. 97); F /nenepa/; C /ninipa·n/; M /nenɛ·pa·m/; O /ninipa·/; S /ninepa/; Mi /ninepa/ or /nepa·ni/; Powhatan /nenepa·m/.

191. SLEEP (2)

(a) /kawi·w/ 'he sleeps, is asleep'; of a different Powhatan dialect than /nepe·w/.

(b) kawwiu "sleep" (H9)

(c) PEA /*kawi·wa/ 'he sleeps, is sleeping'; P /kȁwo/, |kawiw| ; D (all dialects) /kawi·w/; Np /kawiw/, (Mathevet pp. 7, 25, 40, 107 ka8i8 "il dort"). The root is PA /*kaw-/ 'lie prostrate' (B146, p. 90) as in /*kawenkwaʔšiwa/ 'he is sleepy'.

192. SLEEP WITH

(a) /kewi·hpe·ntomen/ (AI) 'we (inclusive) sleep together', /newi·hpe·ma·w/ (TA) 'I sleep with him'.

(b) cowӯhpaantomun "lie together" (H9).

(c) PA /*kewi·hpe·ntoPena/ 'we (inclusive) sleep together'; M (exclusive) /newe·hpɛ·htomenaw/; uD /kəwi·péntomәna/; Ps /kəwihpetópən/.

PA /*newi·hpe·ma·wa/ 'I sleep with him'; F /newi·hpe·ma·wa/; C /niwi·hpe·ma·w/; M /newe·hpemaw/; O /niwi·ppe·ma·/; uD /nəwi·pé·ma/; Ps /nəwihpéma/.

This Powhatan form shows that the inflection for the AI first person plural inclusive is /ke—m agreeing with Delaware and Massachusee.

193. SLOWWORM — See LIZARD, (entry 117).

194. SMALLPOX
(a) /nemamiminiss/ 'I have smallpox'.
(b) nummamemennaus "pox" (H12)
(c) As if pseudo-PA /*ne-mam-i-min-i-ˀle/ "I chang to a condition of lumpy grains". The final with the AI 3 sg. ending is PA /*-ˀle·-wa/ 'go, change, proceed, fly'.

Disease terms deserve further study in Algonqu for there seems to have been extensive borrowing from language to language. There is pseudo-PA /*mamaθkesiwa/ 'he has smallpox'; M /mama·hkesew/; O /mamakkisi/; S /mamˀkiθi/.

195. SMELL (PERCEIVE ODOR)
(a) /nemera·ma·w/ (TA) 'I smell him', /nemera·nta·n/ (TI) 'I smell it'.
(b) numeramuw "smell" (H13), nummeraantaan "strew or cast" (H13)
(c) PA /*nemela·ma·wa/ (TA) 'I smell him, perceive his odor'; C /nimiya·ma·w/; M /nemɛ·na·ma·w O /nimina·ma·/; S /nimela·wa/; mD /nəməlá·wa·w/, with different final in S and mD.

PA /*nemela·nta·ni/ (TI) 'I smell it'; C /nimiya·hte·n/; M /nemɛ·na·htan/; O /nimina·nta·n/; S /nimela·ta/ (S is in TI absolute form); Powhatan /nemera·nta·n/.

196. SNAKE
(a) /asko·k/ 'snake', /kehtasko·k/ 'large snake', /ta·tasko·k/ 'crab' (?).
(b) keihtascooc "adder" (H2), tuttascuk "crab" (H4)

vscook "fine or small thread" (H6). Most of Strachey's meanings seem inaccurate.

(c) PEA /*aθko·ka/ 'snake'; P (and all EA dialects) /skok/, pl. /skòkak/, |askok|; uD /xko·k/; mD /áxko·k/; Np /skok/, (Mathevet p. 53 sc8g "serpent", pl. sc8gak); Ms /askook/ (John 3:14, Psalm 58:4, Eliot askook, Mayhew ashkook; in his grammar Eliot gives the pl. as askookquog, which, if correct, is analogical and does not correspond with the other languages).

PEA /*kehtaθko·ka/ 'large snake' is a compound of PEA /*keht-/ from PA /*keʔt-/ 'big, great, old' (B146, p. 89).

Powhatan /ta·tasko·k/ 'crab' (?) whether the meaning is correct or not, seems to attest the root /ta·t-/ from PA /*θa·θ-/ 'crack, rift' (see CRACK, entry 61).

197. SNAKE (SPECIES)

(a) /sa·ssa·kanaw/ genus Pituophis (?), perhaps the pine snake of the pine barrens, pl. /sa·ssa·kanawak/.

(b) sassaconuwak "adder" (H2), (actually pl.)

(c) PA /*ša·hša·kanawa/ 'snake species' (genus Pituophis); S /šaʔša·kanaweʔθi/ dimin. 'bullsnake' (Pituophis melanoleucus sayi, which does not occur east of the Ohio Valley); Powhatan /sa·ssa·kanaw/. Root PA /*ša·hša·k-/ 'bare, naked' and noun final /*-anaw-/ 'fox snake', extended root and deverbal of root /*anw-/, M /anuah/ 'fox snake'.

PA /*ša·hša·k-/ 'naked, bare'; C /sa·sa·k-/; M /sa·hsak-/; O /ša·šša·k-/; S /šaʔša·k-/; Powhatan /sa·ssa·k-/.

198. SNOW

(a) /ko·n/ 'snow'.

(b) coañ "snow" (H13)

(c) PA /*ko·na/ 'snow', AN in most languages; F /ako·ni/ with prothetic vowel and INAN, pl.

/ako·nani/ 'snowballs, lumps of snow'; C /ko·na/; M /ko·n/, pl. /ku·nyak/ 'lumps of snow', with analogic /y/; O /ko·n/ and /ako·r AN, the latter with prothetic vowel as in Fox; S /ko·na/; D (all dialects) /ko·n/; Pq /kon/; Ms /kon/, AN with obv. /konah/, (Eliot and Mayhew, Psalm 51:7, 68:14, 147:16, koon and ob koonoh).

199. SOUL (a) /nečehča·k/ 'my soul' AN.

(b) netshetsauk "soul or vital breath of man" (H13)

(c) PA /*nete?čya·kwa/ 'my soul' (a dependent noun in some languages as in M); C /nitahča·k/ /otahča·kwa/ 'his soul'; M /netɛ·?čyak/, and with indefinite possessor /metɛ·?čyak/ 'soul', pl. /metɛ·?čyakok/; O /ničičča·k/, /očičča·kw 'his soul'; Powhatan /nečehča·k/.

Reshaped nondependent forms are S /ničeča·la?kw/ 'my soul' and P /nə̀čəčahk^{w}/, |čəčahkw|. In Penobscot there is a progressive metathesis of /h/, so that there is preaspiration of /kw/ rather than /č/.

200. SPIT (a) /sehko·w/ (AI) 'he spits', /sehkwan/ 'spittle'.

(b) secoū "spit" (H13), tsehqwun "spit" (H13)

(c) PA /*sehkwiwa/ (AI) 'he spits'; F /sehkwiwa/; C /sihko·w/; M /sɛhko·w/; O /sikkwi/ or /sikko·/; Ms /səhko/, (Eliot suhkou Mark 7:33)

PA /*nesehkwa·θa·wa/ (TA) 'I spit on him'; F /nesehkwa·na·wa/; C /nisihkwa·ta·w/; M /nesɛ·hkwanaw/; O /nisikkwa·na·/.

201. SPOON (a) /e·mko·n/ 'spoon, ladle'.

(b) ampkone "frying pan" (H2), hamkone "ladle" (H7

(c) PA /*e·mehkwa·na/ 'ladle, spoon'; F /e·mehkwa·hi/ dimin.; C /e·mihkwa·n/ AN; M /ɛ·meskwan/ with discrepant cluster /sk/ for expected /*hk/ as in SHORT (see entry 186);

O /e·mikkwa·n/ INAN; S /e·m?kwa/, pl. /e·m?kwa·naki/; P /èmk^{w}an/, pl. /émk^{w}anak/, |eməhkwan| ; uD /e·mhɔ́·nəs/ AN; mD /e·mhwá·nəs/ AN.

202. SQUIRREL (a) /messani·k/ 'gray squirrel', or 'black squirrel' (a melanistic phase of the same species).

(b) moussonike "squirrel" (H10), mussanek "squirrel" H14)

(c) PA /*me?θanyikwa/ 'gray' or 'black squirrel'; (Menomini has /mɛ?sena·wanik/ 'gray squirrel' which is the same form except that it is compounded with the medial /*-inaw-/ 'body'); O /missanik/, pl. /missaniko·k/; uD /xáni·kw/ for expected /*məxani·kw/; Np /məssanikw/, (Mathevet pp. 6, 106 misanig8̆e "écureuil noir", pl. misanig8ak); Ms and Nr /məssanik/, pl. /məssanikwak/, (Roger Williams mishánneke, Cotton mishannek, pl. mishannekwog).

203. SQUIRREL (FLYING) (a) /assapani·k/ 'flying squirrel' (i. e., "net squirrel", see NET, entry 139)

(b) assapanick "flying squirrel" (Smith), aiossapanÿk "flying squirrel" (H6)

(c) Pseudo-PA /*a?lapanyikwa/ 'flying squirrel'.

204. STAR (a) /ata·nkwess/ dimin. AN 'star', pl. /ata·nkwessak/.

(b) attaangwassowk "star" (H14), (actually pl.)

(c) PA /*aθa·nkwa/ 'star' (B125, Lang. 1:138); F /ana·kwa/; C /ata·hk/, and /ača·hk/ with diminutive symbolism; M /ana·h/, pl. /ana·hkok/; O (some dialects) /ana·nk/; S /ala·kwa/; mD /alá·nkwew/ with reshaped ending. Powhatan points to a long second vowel also, and since Unami Delaware shortens all long vowels before /*nk/ clusters, uD /álankw/ 'star' is indeterminate. However, some languages seem

to reflect a short second vowel as if PA /*aθankw
C (Swampy Cree) /ačahk/ and dimin. /ačahkos/;
O (some dialects) /anank/, pl. /ananko·k/; Ms
/anakws/, pl. /anakwsak/, (Eliot Psalm 136:9
anogqsog "stars"); Np /alakws/, (Mathevet p. 9
alag8̌s); WA /alakws/.

205. STEAL (a) /kemo·to·w/ (AI) 'he steals (something)'.
(b) commotoowh "steal" (H14)
(c) PA /*kemo·twiwa/ (AI) 'he steals (something)';
F /kemo·twa/; C /kimotiw/; M /kemo·tew/
(Menomini Language 2. 58, 2. 60, given wrongly
elsewhere); O /kimo·ti/; S /kimo·twa/; P
/kə̀motəne/, ending reshaped with PA /*-en-/
'by hand'. Several languages have reshaped
the final, Fox and Shawnee by reduction; and
Cree has the second vowel short.

Powhatan /kemo·to·w/ and Ms /kəmoto/ (Eliot
kommooto; kummootowog "they steal" Matthew
6:20) posit /*kemo·twiwa/; otherwise a less likel
archetype is /*kemo·twa/ following Fox and
Shawnee. An unerring solution is not certain.
Reduction does occur in Shawnee, as in PA
/*wexkwe·wa/ 'maggot' > S /oʔkwa/, for
which see WORM, entry 248.

206. STRAWBERRY (a) /maski·hki·wimin/ INAN 'strawberry', pl.
/maski·hki·wiminas/
(b) muskeskiwimins "strawberries" (H10) (I assume
the second s of Strachey to be an error for h)
(c) PEA /*maškyihkyiwimin-a/ 'strawberry'; P
/mskíhkəwimin/ AN, pl. /mskihkəwíminak/.
This is derived from:

PA /*maškyihkyiwi/ 'herb, grassy plant';
F /maškihkiwi/; C /maskihkiy/; M
/maski·hkiw/; O /maškikki/, pl. /maškikkiwan/;
P /mskìhko/ 'blade of grass, herb, grassy

plant', pl. /mskìhkəwal/, |maskihkiw|.

207. STRIKE

(a) /nepakama·w/ (TA) 'I strike him'.

(b) nepacamaū "strike with a sword" (H14)

(c) PA /*nepakama·wa/ 'I strike him' (B146, p. 113); F /nepakama·wa/; M /nepa·kamaw/; P /nəpákamɑ/; mD /mpákama·w/.

208. STRIP

(a) /peri·w/ (II) 'it is torn off, stripped'.

(b) perew "broken or cracked" (H3), perewh "naught, broken or cracked" (H11)

(c) Root PA /*pel-/ 'strip, remove surface, tear off'; F /pen-/ (F /peninawi·wa/ 'he undresses'); C /piy-/ (C /piyawe·w/ 'he scales him [a fish]'); S /pel-/, (/nipeleše·na/ 'I ripped the seam of it', /peleše·tone/ 'he has his mouth torn up at the sides'). This more commonly appears with a postradical:

PA /*pelak-/ 'peel, husk'; C /piyak-/ (C /piyakinam/ 'he peels it'); O /pinak-/ (O /pinaki·ška·/ 'the skin peels off' (II), (TA) /opinakikkona·n/ 'he peels him'); P /pəlak-/ (P /pəlakihátahso/ 'he hulls, husks corn').

209. SUN (1)

(a) /ki·so·ss/ 'sun' AN

(b) keshowghes "sun" (Smith), keshowse "sun" (H14)

(c) PA /*ki·seʔθwa/ 'sun, moon, luminary, month' AN; F /ki·šeswa/, pl. /ki·šeso·k/ 'months'; M /ke·soʔ/, pl. /ke·soʔnak/ 'sun and moon, luminaries, months'; O /ki·siss/; S /ki·šθwa/; P /kìsohs/, pl. /kísohsak/ 'months'; D (all dialects) /ki·šo·x/; Mh /ki·so·x/; Np /kisos/ (Mathevet p. 9 kiz8s, kis8s "soleil"); Mi /ki·lʔswa/. The /š/ in the F, S, and D forms is probably analogical, and the Miami term seems to show that metathesis of /*s/ and /*θ/ occurred, as Haas has suggested (Nat. Mus. of Canada Bul. 214:60-65, Ottawa, 1967).

210. SUN (2)

(a) /nepass/ 'sun' AN, of a different Powhatan diale

(b) nepausche "sun" (H10)

(c) PEA /*nepahθ/, as if pseudo-PA /*nepaʔθwa/ (?); Ms /nəpas/, (Eliot and Mayhew, Psalm 19:4 nepauz; Psalm 74:16 nepauz; Psalm 121:6 Eliot nuppáuz and Mayhew nuppaz); Nr /nəpas/, (Roger Williams nuppaŭus "sun"); Powhatan /nepass/.

211. SWALLOW

(a) /kwentamo·w/ (AI) 'he swallows', /nekontamen/ (TI) 'I swallow it'.

(b) necoondameñ "it is good meat" (H7), quantamū "swallow" (H14)

(c) PEA /*kwentamwiwa/ 'he swallows' (AI formed from an objectless-TI); compare P /k^{w}əsihátamo (AI) 'he swallows'.

PA /*kwentamwa/ 'he swallows it' (TI absolute); F /kotamwa/; C /kohtam/; M /ko·htam/; O /okonta·n/ (TI objective); S /kotamwa/; compare Mi /kwentama·ni/ 'I swallow it'.

PEA /*nekwentameni/ (TI) 'I swallow it'; Powhatan /nekontamen/; uD /nkwə́ntamən/.

212. SWAN

See HERON

213. SWEEP

(a) /či·kkahike·w/ (AI) 'he sweeps'. See BROOM

(b) tsekehica "sweep" (H14)

(c) PEA /*či·kehkahike·wa/ 'he sweeps'; P /čikkáhike/; Powhatan /či·kkahike·w/. Compare PA /*či·katahike·wa/ 'he sweeps'; M /če·katahekɛw/; O /či·kataʔike·/.

214. TAIL (OF BIRD)

(a) /otani·ss/ 'his (bird's) tail', dimin. INAN.

(b) otanneis "train of a bird" (H14)

(c) PA /*-aθanyi/ 'bird tail', INAN dependent noun; PA /*waθanyi/ 'his (bird's) tail'; C /wataniy/, pl. /wataniya/; M /wana·n/, pl. /wana·nyan/, dependent stem /-ana·ny/ (see Bl. Menom. Lang.

18. 1); P /wálanəss/ dimin. , pl. /walánəssal/; Ms /wanani/ (Eliot wananeyeuash "their tails", Revelations 9:19). Powhatan and some Cree dialects, following the ancient variation of PA /*a/ : /*e/ have restructured the form as a nondependent noun, as though PA /*weθanyi/; C (Swampy Cree) /otaniy/. The diminutive form is:

PA /*waθanyehši/ 'his small (bird's) tail'; P /wálanəss/; Powhatan /otani·ss/. See EAGLE.

215. TAIL (a) /wesekwan/ or /osekwan/ 'his tail', INAN. Used for fish and mammals.

(b) wushagwan "single of a deer" (H13), wushaqwun "tail of anything" (H14)

(c) PA /*-šekwanayi/ or /*-šekwani/ 'fish tail', INAN dependent noun; C, P, and Np reflect the first variant, and F, M, O, and Ms the second archetype. The Eastern Algonquian languages have generalized the meaning to varying degrees, originally confined to the tail of fishes and limited to this sense in F, C, M, and O.

PA /*wešekwanayi/ or /*wešekwani/ 'his (fish's) tail'; F /ošekwani/, pl. /ošekwanani/; C /osikwanay/; M /osɛ·kwan/ and /osɛ·kwanan/ INAN and AN (M /nesɛ·kwan/ 'my [fish's] tail'); O /ošikwan/; P /wə̀səkʷəne/, |-səkwənay| , /nə̀səkʷəne/ 'my tail'; Ms /wəsəkwən/, (Eliot wussukqun "his tail" Job 40:17, Isaiah 9:14); Np /wəsəkwəna/, (Mathevet p. 35 8ssig8na "queue de bette a quatre pieds ou des poissons").

216. TAKE (a) /nemamen/ (TI) 'I take it, pick it up', /omamen/ 'he takes it, picks it up'.

(b) mammun "take hold of anything" (H4) (pronominal prefix missing), nummaumen "pull" (H12), vummaumun "take up" (H14)

(c) PA /*nemameni/ (TI objective, class 3) 'I take it, I pick it up'; F /nemameni/ (/mamiwa/ 'he takes it'); M /nema·men/ (/mamuah/ 'he takes it'); O /nimamo·n/, with ending reshaped; S /nimame/; Mi /nimame/; Powhatan /nemamen/.

PA /*nemamawa·wa/ (TA) 'I take it from him' F /nemamawa·wa/; M /nema·muawa·w/; O /nimamawa·/; S /nimamawa/.

217. TAKE FROM THERE

(a) /ontenass/ 'take (thou) it, them (INAN) from there' (2 person sg. TI class 1 imperative), /o·ntenamen/ (TI) 'he takes it from there'.

(b) vntenugh "take it" (H14), vndensc "take it" (H15

(c) PA /*wentenanlwe/, PEA-A /*wentenanθwe/ 'take (thou) it, them (INAN) from there' (2 person sg. TI class 1 imper.); F /otenano/; C /ohtinah/; M /ohtɛ·nah/; O /ontinan/; P /wə̀təne'/; mD /wə́ntənah/. Penobscot imperati form a partly altered paradigm. The Powhatan form follows the PEA-A pattern.

PA /*wentenamwa/ (TI absolute) 'he takes it from there' (B146); F /otenamwa/; C /ohtinam/; M /ohtɛ·nam/.

218. TASTE GOOD

(a) /wi·nkan/ (II) 'it tastes good'.

(b) wingan "good" (H7), wingañ "good" (H15)

(c) PA /*wi·nkanwi/ (II) 'it tastes good'; M /we·hkan/; S /wi·kanwi/; uD /wínkan/; Mh /wi·kan/; Nr /wikan/ (Roger Williams weékan "it is sweet").

219. TERRAPIN

(a) /to·repe·w/ 'terrapin', English loan from Powhatan, 'sea turtle, loggerhead' (genus *Caretta*), the chief reference. The loggerhead nests on the southern Atlantic coast as far north as the southern end of Chesapeake Bay, and strays northward to the coasts of New England and Newfoundland. Pl. /to·repe·wak/.

(b) *towruppewk* "sea turtle" (H14), (actually pl.)

(c) PEA /*to·lepye·wa/ 'loggerhead' (genus *Caretta*), 'sea turtle, terrapin' (original PEA meaning, later generalized in many Eastern Algonquian languages to include all species of large turtles); P /tòləpe/ 'turtle, tortoise', as a general term, pl. /tòləpak/, (P /kčí-toləpe/ 'loggerhead', or other species of 'sea turtle'); Mh /to·npaw/, |to·nepaw| ; mD /tó·lpew/; uD /tó·lpe/; Ms /tonəp/, dimin. /tonəpas/, (Eliot *toonuppasog* "tortoise" pl. dimin., Leviticus 11:29); Unquachog (Long Island, Siebert in July 1932) /tórəp/ 'sea turtle, loggerhead'.

220. TESTICLE

(a) /netessiwe·/ 'my testicle' AN, /otessiwah/ 'his testicle(s)' as an obv. sg. or pl.

(b) *vtshewwah* "stones of any male thing" (H14)

(c) PA /*-θeʔšiwaya/ 'testicle', AN dependent noun (Michelson 35; with revisions and additions); PA /*neθeʔšiwaya/ 'my testicle'; F /nenešiwa/; C /nitisiway/; M /nenɛ·ʔseway/; S /nilʔšiwe/, pl. /nileʔši·ki/; Powhatan /netessiwe·/, pl. /netessiwak/.

221. THIGH (1)

(a) /opo·m/ 'his thigh', /nepo·m/ 'my thigh'.

(b) *apome* "thigh" (H2)

(c) PA /*-pwa·mi/ 'thigh', INAN dependent noun; PA /*nepwa·mi/ 'my thigh'; C /nipwa·m/; M /nepuam/, pl. /nepuamyan/ 'my thighs', with analogic /y/; O /nipwa·m/, pl. /nipwa·man/; Mi /nipwa·mi/, pl. /nipwa·ma/; S /nipwa·mi/, pl. /nipwa·mali/; uD /mpɔ·m/, pl. /mpɔ́·ma/; Powhatan /nepo·m/.

222. THIGH (2)

(a) /wi·kkway/ 'his thigh', pl. /wi·kkwas/ 'his thighs', INAN, of a different Powhatan dialect.

(b) *wÿkgwaus* "thigh" (H14), (actually pl.)

(c) PEA /*-i·kahkwayi/ 'thigh', INAN dependent

noun; PEA /*wi·kahkwayi/ 'his thigh'; P /wìkk^{w}e/, pl. /wìkk^{w}al/, |-ikahkway| (P /nìkk^{w}e/ 'my thigh', pl. /nìkk^{w}al/); Powhatan /wi·kkway/, pl. /wi·kkwas/.

223. THROAT (a) /wekwenta·kan/ or /okwenta·kan/ 'his throat', /nekwenta·kan/ 'my throat'. See SWALLOW, entry 211.

(b) vegwantaak "throat" (H14) (I assume that Strachey omitted the end of the word by writing error.)

(c) PA /*kwenta·kani/ 'throat', /*nekwenta·kani/ 'my throat'; F /nekota·kani/; C /nikohta·kan/; M /neko·htakan/; O /nikonta·kan/; S /nikota·ka P /nək^{w}ə̀takan/; uD /nkwəntá·k·an/.

224. THUMB (a) /okehtekwayetenč/ 'his thumb'.

(b) vketeqwaiutteindg "thumb" (H14)

(c) Pseudo-PEA /*wekehtekwayeθenčyi/ formed with a medial, otherwise similar to PA /*neke?teθenčyi 'my thumb'; M /nekɛ·?čenɛh/, pl. /nekɛ·?čenɛ·hčyan/; O /nikiččininč/; uD /nki·tə́lənč/ AN, pl. /nki·təlә́nčak/.

225. TOOTH (a) /mi·pit/ 'a tooth, someone's tooth', /ni·pit/ 'my tooth', pl. /ni·pitas/ 'my teeth'.

(b) mepit "teeth" (H10), actually sg., neputts "tooth" (H11), actually pl., "my teeth".

(c) PA /*-i·piči/ 'tooth' INAN, pl. /*-i·pitali/ 'teeth', dependent noun (B146, p. 119); PA /*ni·piči/ 'my tooth', pl. /*ni·pitali/ 'my teeth'; F /ni·piči/, pl. /ni·pitani/; C /ni·pit/, pl. /ni·pita/; M /ne·pet/, pl. /ne·petan/; O /ni·pit/, pl. /ni·pitan/; S /ni·piči/, pl. /ni·pitali/; P /nìpit/, pl. /nípital/; Mh /ni·pit/, pl. /ni·pitan/.

226. TREE (a) /mehtek/ 'tree', pl. /mehtekok/; /mehtekos/ 'sticks', /mehtekwins/ 'little stick'.

(b) meihtuc "tree" (H14), metucs "bridge" (H3),

mehtacouc "stalk" (H14), actually pl. , mehteqweins "grass" (H7)

(c) PA /*me?tekwa/ 'tree', pl. /*me?teko·ki/; but PA /*me?tekwi/ 'stick' (B146); F /mehtekwi/ 'tree', pl. /mehteko·ni/; C /mistik/; M /mɛ?tek/ 'tree' AN, pl. /mɛ?tekwak/; O /mittik/, pl. /mittiko·k/; S /me?tekwi/ 'tree', pl. /mteko/; uD /hít·okw/, pl. /hítko·k/; mD /míhtək/, pl. /míhtəkwak/; Mh /míhto·kw/; Ms /mihtək/, pl. /mihtəkwaš/, (Eliot mehtug "tree", mehtugquash "trees" Psalm 105:33, and Grammar).

227. TUBER — See GROUNDNUT, (entry 100).

228. TUCKAHOE — (a) /takwahahk/ 'green arum' (plant or root), 'tuckahoe', the latter an English loan from Powhatan (Peltandra virginica, (L.) Schott and Endlicher, the root of which is inedible in raw state, but when baked is used for breadstuff and as a starchy vegetable), /takwahapo·n/ 'bread made of green arum root or tuckahoe', pl. /takwahapo·nas/ 'loaves of tuckahoe bread'. See BREAD, (entry 38).

(b) tockwhogh, tocknough, tockawhoughe "chief root they have for food . . . like a flag in low muddy freshes . . . of the greatness and taste of potatoes . . . raw it is no better than poison . . . roasted . . . in summer they use this ordinarily for bread" (Smith), taccahoappoans "bread made of a wort called —" (H3)

(c) The root is PA /*takw-/ 'pound fine, bray, beat to a powder' found in identical form in C, O, S, Mi, D, Mh, Np, and Powhatan. This is homophonous with and perhaps related by semantic extension to the PA root /*takw-/ 'among or between two particulars, together' (see FROST, entry 91). Following this is the transitive INAN final or instrumental PA /*-ah-/ 'by instrument or tool' and the noun final PEA /*-ahkw-i/ 'taproot, bole, large root and trunk' (see ROOT, entry 170), as if pseudo-PEA /*takwahahkwi/ 'green arum, tuckahoe'. Other examples are:

PA /*takwahamwa/ (TI absolute) 'he pounds it fine, brays it, beats it to a powder by tool'; C /takwaham/; O /otakwaʔa·n/, TI objective; Mi /takwahamwa/; uD /takɔ́ham/; Np /takwham/ (Mathevet nitak8am "je pile" pp. 90, 93).

PA /*netakwahwa·wa/ (TA) 'I pound him (maize) fine, beat him to a powder by tool'; C /nitakwahwa·w/; O /nitakwawa·/ (when /*w/ of the transitive AN instrumental final (PA /*-ahw-/ 'by instrument or tool') is not merged with a following /*e/ to /o/, Ojibwa drops the preceeding /ʔ/ from PA /*h/, for which see B146, footnote 14, p. 114); S /nitakhwa/ 'I pound him (maize) for bread' (haplologic for expected S /*nitakwahwa/).

PA /*takwahwa·na/ originally 'bread baked from flour prepared from the root of Peltandra virginica', later extended in some languages (Shawnee, Mahican) to mean also 'bread made from corn meal or pounded maize'; S /takhwa/ 'bread', pl. /takhwa·na/ 'loaves of bread', |takwahwa·n|; Mh /tkwax/, |takwax|, /ntákwxam/ 'my bread', pl. /tkwáxak/ 'loaves of bread', /wtákwxaman/ 'his bread'. The distribution of the green arum from Florida and Texas northward to southern Maine and New Hampshire, and to northern New York and southern Ontario, together with the linguistic evidence, suggests that the roots were used for breadstuff among the Algonquian peoples before the introduction of maize.

229. TURKEY (a) /mo·nesse·w/ 'turkey cock'.

(b) <u>monnagh</u> "turkey" (H10), <u>monassaw</u> "turkey" (H15)

(c) PEA /*mo·nehle·wa/ 'turkey cock' from PA /*mo·n-/ 'dig into, scratch out' and noun final PA /*-ʔle·w-a/ 'bird'; Ms /monəšš/ 'cock', (Eliot <u>monsh</u>, Mayhew <u>monish</u> "cock" John 13:38, 18:27); Powhatan /mo·nesse·w/.

230. UNDERSTAND (a) /nenenohtawa·w/ 'I understand him', /kenenohto·s/ 'I understand thee', /mata kenenohto·ro·w/ 'I do not understand thee'.

(b) <u>kennenautows</u> "I understand well" (H15), <u>mata kennenutorowh</u> "I understand not" (H15)

(c) PA /*nenenohtawa·wa/ 'I understand him (his speech)'; F /nenenohtawa·wa/; M /nenε·nohtawa·w/; S /nineno?tawa/; Powhatan /nenenohtawa·w/.

PA /*kenenohto·θe/ 'I understand thee'; F /kenenohto·ne/; M /kenε·nohtonen/; S /kineno?to·le/; Powhatan /kenenohto·s/.

The Powhatan negative /mata kenenohto·ro·w/ results from a late analogical restoration of /r/ as the projected source of alternant /s/, by analogy to the much more commonly used positive form /kenenohto·s/, subsequent to the falling together of /*θ/ and /*t/ to /t/ in Powhatan and the change of /*l/ to /r/.

231. URINATE (a) /sekiw/ 'he urinates'.

(b) <u>shekÿu</u> "piss" (H12)

(c) PA /*šekiwa/ 'he urinates' (B125, Lang. 1. 146); F /šekiwa/; C /sikiw/; M /seke·w/; S /šekiwa/; P /sə̀ko/, |səkiw|.

232. VAGINA (a) /meta·ske·/ 'vagina', /neta·ske·/ 'my vagina'.

(b) <u>muttask</u> "woman's secret" (H5)

(c) PA /*-θa·çkaya/ (?) 'vagina', dependent noun, with /*θ/ not proven; C /mita·hkay/ 'vagina', /nita·hkay/ 'my vagina'.

233. VINE (a) /wa·pa·pe·mins/ 'vine' (species ?, perhaps the scuppernong (Vitis rotundifolia Michaux) with cream-colored grapes), pl. /wa·pa·pe·minsas/

(b) wapapamindgas "vine" (H15), actually pl.

(c) Pseudo-PA as if /*wa·pa·pye·minšyi/ "white vine bush"; from PA /*wa·p-/ 'white'; PA /*-a·pye·-/ 'string, vine'; and PA /*-eminšy-/ 'drupe-bearing bush or tree'. Compare F /ki·wa·pye·hi/ 'creeping vine'.

234. WALNUT (a) /assena·mins/ 'black walnut tree' (?), more probably the 'mockernut hickory tree'; /asseni·na 'mockernuts' (?); /paka·ns/ 'black walnuts' (?), pl.

(b) assunnomeindg "walnut tree" (H14), assinenans "walnut" (H15), paucauns "walnut" (H15)

(c) PA /*aˀsena·minšya/ 'rock or sugar maple tree'; F /asena·miši/, pl. /asena·mišye·ni/; O /assina·mi·šš/; mD /asəná·minši/, pl. /asəna·mínšəyak/. The sugar maple is not found near Jamestown, consequently this PA term was transferred to some other species, possibly the mockernut hickory. The noun root formative is:

PA /*aˀsenyi/ 'rock, stone' (given as AN by Bloomfield, B125, Lang. l. 139, l. 149, and B146, p. 93, as /*aˀsenya/, largely following Cree and Menomini); F /aseni/, pl. /asenye·ni/; C /asiniy/, pl. /asiniyak/; M /aˀsɛn/, pl. /aˀsɛnyak/; O /assin/, pl. /assini·n/ INAN in Eastern Ojibwa, but AN, pl. /assini·k/ in Central, Western and Northern Ojibwa; but INAN in all Eastern Algonquian languages, WA /ssən/, pl. /ssənal/; Ms /assən/, (Eliot Grammar hassun "stone", pl. hussunash); mD /asə́n/, pl. /asə́nal/. The final is PA /*-eminšy-/ 'drupe-bearing bush or tree'.

For /paka·ns/ or /paka·nas/ 'large nuts, black walnuts' (?), see NUT, entry 143.

235. WASH (a) /kesi·nkwe·w/ 'he washes his face', /kesi·tenče·w/ 'he washes his hands'.

(b) keseigwaau "wash the face" (H15), with prestop n omitted by Strachey (see CHINQUAPIN, entry 48), keseitendcheo "wash the hands" (H15)

(c) PA /*kesi·nkwe·wa/ 'he washes his face'; F /kesi·kwe·wa/; O /kisi·nkwe̩·/ 'he wipes his face'; P /kə̀ssik^{w}e·/; Powhatan /kesi·nkwe·w/.

PA /*kesi·θenčye·wa/ 'he washes his hands'; F /kesi·neče·wa/; O /kesi·ninči·/ 'he wipes his hands'; S /kiθi·leče/; P /kə̀ssiləče/; uD /kəši·lə́nče/; Powhatan /kesi·tenče·w/.

236. WATER (a) /nepi/ 'water'.

(b) neppe "wet" (H15)

(c) PA /*nepyi/ 'water' (B146, p. 93); F /nepi/; C /nipiy/; M /nepe·w/ with reshaped ending; O /nipi/; S /nepi/; P /nə̀pi/, pl. /nə̀pəyal, |nəpiy|.

237. WATER RECEDES (a) /wenseskat/ 'the water recedes, flows back, ebbs', negative /mata wenseskato·w/ 'the water does not ebb'.

(b) seiscatuwh "ebbing water" (H5) (evidently a negative form, with the first part missing), wenssicket "running brook" (H15)

(c) PEA /*wensexkatwi/ (II) 'the water level goes down, the water ebbs or recedes, the current or water flows back or out, there is a condition of receding water'; P /wə̀sihkat/, |wəsəhkat|. The morphemes are: PA root /*went-/ 'from there' (for the irregular alternation of PA /*t/ : /*s/

before /*a·/ and /*e/ see B146, Section 21, p. 92); the PA medial /*-exk-/ 'flood, high water' deverbal from PA root /*lexk-/ given below; and the II final PA /*-atwi/ 'state, condition'.

PA /*lexkepye·wi/ (II) 'it is flooded, under water; there is a flood, the water level rises'; C /yiskipe·w/; O /nikkipi·/; P /nkə̀pe/, |nəhkəpe|. Root /*lexk-/ and the deverbal /*-exk-/ are not to be confused with the following:

PA /*eçka?te·wi/ (II) 'it (body of water) dries up'; F /aškahte·wi/; C /ihkaste·w/; M /ehka·?tɛw/; O /iskatte·/. Here the final is the PA II reflexive /*-a?te·wi/ 'be in place, lie in position'.

238. WEED (SEAWEED)

(a) /a·skarask/ 'seaweed', pl. /a·skaraskwas/ 'seaweeds'.

(b) ascarasqwus "seaweeds" (H13)

(c) PEA /*a·škalaškwi/ or /*a·škalenšyi/ 'seaweed, weed growing under water'; Powhatan /a·skarask/ following the first, and P /áskaləsi/ 'seaweed' (general term), pl. /askáləsəyal/, |ɑskaləsiy| the second, which differ only as to noun finals. Massachusee at least has the same term without a medial in Ms /askaskw/ 'meadow or water (?) grass', (Eliot askoshq, Mayhew askasquash "grass" pl., Psalm 72:16; the usual word in Ms being moskeht "grass, herb" Eliot Grammar, from PA /*maškyihkyiwi/ 'herb, grassy plant' for which see STRAWBERRY, entry 206). The morphemes of /*a·škalaškwi/ are: PA root /*a·šk-/ 'downward, below' (F /a·šk-/, P |ɑsk|); medial PEA /*-al-/ 'water' (?, meaning uncertain); and noun final PA /*-aškw-/ 'herb, plant'. The other form is:

PEA /*a·škalenšyi/; P /ə́skaləsi/ with PA noun final /*-enšy-i/ 'weed' which occurs as: C /-isiy/ (C /asisiy/ INAN 'seaweed, grass growing under water'); M /-εhsy-/ (M /wasε·hsyan/ pl. 'water weeds', see Menom. Lang. 14.190, 14.213); O /-inšy-/ (O /aninawi·nš/ 'milkweed'); Mi /-enšy-/ (Mi /ke·kkenša/ 'weed', pl. /ke·kkenši·ki/, Mi /leninši/ 'milkweed', pl. /leninša/); P |-əsiy|.

239. WHISKER — See BEARD, (entry 22).

240. WHISTLE — (a) /kwi·skwesso·w/ 'he whistles'.

(b) qweisgwesuw̄ "whistle" (H15)

(c) PA /*kwi·škwehšwiwa/ (AI) 'he whistles·; C /kwi·skosiw/; M /ki·skihsow/ 'he whistles a call or signal'; O /kwi·škwišši/; P /k^{w}ìk^{w}so/, |kwikwəhsiw|, reshaped without /sk/ cluster by dissimilation (?); Powhatan /kwi·skwesso·w/.

241. WHITE — (a) /a·pe·w/ and with dialect variation /wa·pe·w/ (II) 'it is white'.

(b) opaivwh "white" (H15)

(c) PEA /*wa·pe·wi/ (II) 'it is white' (PA root /*wa·p-/ 'white' (Bl25, Bl46); PA probably also had /*wa·pe·wi/ since a Cree form agrees with Eastern Algonquian, and Bloomfield's (Bl46, p. 121) PA /*wa·peškye·wi/ 'it is white' is either merely concurrent or a new formation of some antiquity; C /wa·pa·w/, Mt /wa·pa·w/, with the ancient alternation /*a·/ : /*e·/ before /*w/ leveled out as usual in Cree (see Bl46, Section 35, p. 98); mD /wá·pe·w/; uD /ɔ́·p·e·w/; Mh /wá·payo/; Pq /wɑpáyo/; Powhatan /a·pe·w/ or /wa·pe·w/.

242. WICOPY — See BAST, (entry 21).

243. WIFE — (a) /wi·wah/ 'his wife or wives' (obv. sg. and pl.), /mata wi·wiw/ 'he does not have a wife'.

(b) wiowah "husband" (H8), with meaning error, mata wiowÿh "a bachelor" (H2)

(c) PA /*-i·wa/ 'wife' dependent noun; PA /*ni·wa/ 'my wife'; PA /*wi·wali/ 'his wife' and /*wi·wahi/ 'his wives'; F /ni·wa/ 'my wife'; M /ne·w/; S /ni·wa/; mD /ni·w/; Mh /ni·w/.

F /owi·wani/ 'his wife' with prothetic vowel; M /we·wan/; O /wi·wan/; S /wi·wali/ and /owi·wali/, the latter with an analogical prothetic vowel as in Fox; mD /wí·wal/; Mh /wí·wan/.

F /owi·wahi/ 'his wives' obv. pl.; Powhatan /wi·wah/ 'his wife or wives'. Powhatan has generalized the obviative plural, as in Cree, Western Abenaki, and all the SNE languages; Nr /wiwa/ 'his wife' (Roger Williams weewo "his wife"); C /wi·wah/ 'his wife or wives' (Bl. Cree Texts 1934, pp. 54, 102).

PA /*wi·wiwa/ (AI) 'he has a wife'; F /owi·wiwa/ with prothetic vowel; C /wi·wiw/; M /we·wew/; O /wi·wi/; Powhatan /wi·wiw/.

244. WINTER

(a) /pepo·no·w/ (II) 'it is winter'.

(b) popanow "winter" (Smith), puppoannoh "winter" (H16)

(c) PA /*pepo·nwi/ (noun) 'winter', (II) 'it is winter'; F /pepo·wi/, reshaped by analogy to F /mehpo·wi/ 'it snows' from PA /*mexpo·wi/; C /pipon/; M /pepo·n/; O /pipo·n/; S /pepo·ni/ with reshaped ending: Mi /pipo·nwi/; P /pə̀pon/; Ms /pəpon/, (Eliot popón, Mayhew puppoon, Psalm 74:17). In addition to PA /*pepo·nwi/ there is a longer and perhaps more archaic form:

PA /*pepo·no·wi/ (II) 'it is winter'; M /pepo·no·wew/ with regularized or reshaped final; P /pə̀pono/; Powhatan /pepo·no·w/.

Compare also the three PA terms for 'it snows':

PA /*mexpo·wi/ (II) 'it snows'; F /mehpo·wi/; C /mispon/ reshaped by analogy to C /pipon/ 'it is winter'; Ms /məhpo/ and /məhpowi/, (Eliot muhpoo I Chron. 11:22, muhpoowi "it snows" Cotton).

PA /*so·kexpo·wi/ (II) 'it snows'; O /so·kippo·/; Nr /sóčihpo/, (Roger Williams sóchepo "it snows"); Pq and Unquachog /sóčpo/ with syncope, (Stiles souch'pouu, Speck súčpu, Jefferson soáchpo).

PA /*peʔθa·nwi/ (II) 'it snows'; M /pɛ·ʔnan/; P /psan/, changed conjunct /pèhsak/ 'when it snows', |pəhsan|; Mh /pxa·n/, changed conjunct /pa·xá·k/ 'when it snows', |pexa·n| (initial change in Mahican provides that morphophonemic |e| and |a| are replaced by |a·|); Ml and Ps /psán/. The root is PA /*peʔθ-/ 'in small particles'; C /pist-/ (C /pistahipe·w/ 'it drifts lightly'); O /piss-/.

The II verb PA finals of the above are: /*-expo·wi/ 'snow'; and /*-a·nwi/ 'weather, air condition', the former being deverbal from /*mexpo·wi/. The latter forms with a prefinal the complex II final PA /*-ela·nwi/ 'rain'; S /-ela·nwi/; Mi /-ila·nwi/; P /-əlan/; Mh |-ena·n|; Pq /-əyan/; Ms /-ənan/ (Eliot sokanon "it rains" Exodus 9:34).

245. WOMAN (a) /metemsiss/ dimin. 'old woman'.

(b) mtumpseis "old woman" (H11), tumpseis "old woman" (H16)

(c) PA /*metemwa/ 'old woman', dimin. PA /*metemwehsa/ and with super-added dimin. PA /*metemwehsihsa/ 'little old woman'; from the last is Powhatan /metemsiss/ with syncope of the third syllable; F /metemo·ha/ 'old woman' dimin.; M /metɛ·moh/ 'woman' but of dimin. origin, pl. /metɛ·mohsak/; O /mintimo·ye·nʔ/ 'old woman' dimin., with unoriginal /nt/ cluster; Mi /mitemsa/ 'woman' but in dimin. form with syncope of the third syllable, pl. /mitemsaki/; Ms /mətəmwossis/ 'woman' with super-added diminutive (Eliot mittamwossis "woman", Mayhew muttumwussis John 2:4, 4:7); Nr /mətəmos/ 'wife' (Roger Williams mittummus "a wife", nummittamus "my wife").

246. WOLF

(a) /nantom/ 'wolf' (i.e., "the hunter"), if correctly recorded by Strachey with an unoriginal /nt/ cluster as in the Ojibwa root.

(b) naantam "wolf" (H16)

(c) The root is PA /*natw-/ 'seek, hunt', and in extended form /*nataw-/ (B146, Sections 78, 85, 104); F /natw-/; C /natw-/; M /natw-/; O /nantw-/; S /natw-/ (S /ninatoneha/ 'I search for it'); P /natw-/ and /nataw-/ (P /nátawat/ 'it is scarce').

Evidently some other Eastern Algonquian languages have this root in terms for 'wolf', for example the Martha's Vineyard dialect of Massachusee (Mayhew nattoohqus "wolf" John 10:12), and one dialect of Narragansett (Cowesit ? where it is recorded as natóqus "wolf" by Roger Williams.

247. WOOD

(a) /messiw/ 'piece of firewood, fuel-wood, faggot' INAN, pl. /messi·s/.

(b) mushe "wood" (H4), meihtusmusheis "post" (H12) with the first s for intended c, musheis "wood" (H16), musheis-ni-ourewh "wood all along" (H16) (actually the last three are pl.), musses "woods" (Smith).

(c) PA /*mehši/ 'piece of firewood, fuel-wood, faggot' (Michelson 35, but incompletely rendered); pl. /*mehθali/; F /mese·hi/ dimin. and analogical from the plural for expected /*meše·hi/, pl. /mese·hani/; C /mihtiy/ or /miht/, pl. /mihta/ (compare C /mihto·t/ 'raft'); M root |mɛhN-| as in /mɛhno·s/ 'raft'; Mt /miht/, pl. /mihta/; O /mišši/, pl. /missan/, but some Ojibwa dialects have the sg. /missi/ (see Rogers p. 151) which is analogical from the pl. as in Fox.

The PA form posited by some languages almost certainly represents an older archetype:

PA /*mehšiwi/, pl. /*mehšiwali/; M /mɛhse·w/, pl. /mɛhse·wan/; Powhatan /messiw/, pl. /messi·s/, the latter for |messiw-as| , with contraction of /-iwa-/ to /i·/ before a nonsyllabic. Compare O /miššiwa·ttik/ 'stick of firewood', reflecting PA /*mehšiw-i/ and /*-a·htekw-i/ 'stick, stem', and PA /*mehšiwa·xkwa/ 'dead tree' (i. e. "firewood tree"); F /mešiwa·hkwa/ and P /msə̀wahk^w/, |məhsiwahkw| . There are also verb forms with the deverbal medial /*-ehθ-/ 'wood' from the noun root /*mehθ-/ 'firewood':

PA /*manehθe·wa/ (AI) 'he gathers firewood'; F /manese·wa/ 'he cuts wood'; M /manɛ·hnɛw/; O /manisse·/ 'he chops wood'; S /man?θe/ 'he chops wood'; P /mànəsse/; mD /manáxe·w/. M, P, and mD preserve the original meaning.

248. WORM (a) /mo·sse·w/ 'worm'. See LIZARD, entry 117.

(b) <u>mowsah</u> "little worm or maggot" (H16)

(c) PA /*mo·hθe·wa/ 'worm'; C /mo·hte·w/, pl. /mo·hte·wak/; Mt /mo·hte·w/, pl. /mo·hte·wač/; M /omo·hnɛw/ with prothetic vowel; O /mo·sse·/, pl. /mo·sse·k/; Mi /mo·sia/, pl.

/mo·siaki/; uD /mo·xwe·s/ dimin.; Powhatan /mo·sse·w/. There is also:

PA /*wexkwe·wa/ 'maggot'; Mt /oškwe·w/; M /u·hkiw/; O /okkwe·/, pl. /okkwe·k/; S /oˀkwa/ (in words of three or more syllables word final postvocalic /*-wV/ is dropped in Shawnee, but in word final sequences of /*-wVwV/ reduction occurs so that the vowel of the last syllable is retained; for another example of possible reduction in Shawnee see STEAL, entry 205); Ms /ohkw/, (Eliot oohkq "worm", oohquou "it bred worms" Exodus 16:20, matta oohquánoo "there was no worm therein" Exodus 16:24).

249. WRAP UP

(a) /newi·skwe·pita·w/ (TA) 'I wrap him up with cords, I tie him up'.

(b) nuwweisquaput "wrap or wind up any thing" (H16) (with inflectional suffix missing).

(c) PA /*newyi·xkwe·piθa·wa/ (TA) 'I tie him up, wrap him up with cords'; F /newi·hkwe·pina·wa/; C /niwi·skwe·pita·w/; M /wi·hkw-/ in /wi·hkiho·htam/ 'he carries it on his back wrapped in a bundle'; S /niwiˀkwe·pila/; P /nəwihk^{w}épilα/. The root appears in unextended form in Ojibwa, as O /niwi·kkopina·/ 'I tie him', but in most languages appears in extended form as PA /*wyi·xkwe·-/ 'bundle, wrap up'; F /wi·hkwe·-/; C /wi·skwe·-/; S /wiˀkwe·-/; P /wihk^{w}e-/. The TI absolute form would be:

PA /*wyi·xkwe·pitamwa/ 'he binds it, wraps it up with cords'; F /wi·hkwe·pitamwa/; C /wi·skwe·pitam/.

250. YAWN

(a) /ta·watetone·w/ (AI) 'he yawns, gapes, opens his mouth'.

(b) tawatuttoneo "yawn or gape" (H16)

(c) Pseudo-PA /*ta·waθetone·wiwa/ 'he opens his

mouth', with AI prefinal and final complex PA /*-etone·wiwa/ 'move mouth'; C /-itone·yiw/; P |-ətonewiw| (P /ɑpk^{w}ətónewo/ 'he opens his mouth'). The PA root is /*ta·waθ-/ 'yawn, gape'; Powhatan /ta·wat-/, found as follows:

PA /*ta·waθwa/ 'he yawns, gapes' (AI); C /ta·watiw/; M /ta·wanɛw/; O /ta·wani/; S /ta·walwa/; the endings of the C, M, and O forms being reshaped.

251. YELLOW (a) /osa·we·w/ (II) 'it is yellow', /o·sa·wa·k/ (II participle) 'that which is yellow', with initial change of /o-/ to /o·-/.

(b) oussawauk "yellow" (H16)

(c) PA /*wesa·wye·wi/ (II) 'it is yellow'; F /asa·wa·wi/; C /osa·wa·w/; M /osa·wi·w/; O /osa·wa·/; S /oθa·wa/; Powhatan /osa·we·w/. In some languages (not following any "eastern" or "central" Algonquian distribution) the root of the form has been analogically reshaped, as if to represent pseudo-PA /*wi·sa·wye·wi/; Mt /wi·ša·wa·w/; P root /wisɑw-/ (P /wisɑ́wikən/ 'it is yellow'); D (all dialects) /wi·sá·we·w/; Mh /wi·sá·wayo/ where /a/ is the reflex of /*e·/; Np /wisɑway/, (Mathevet p. 33 8isan8ai "jaune"); Unquachog /wisɑwayo/ (Jefferson weesawayo); Nr root /wisɑw-/, (Roger Williams wesaûi "yellow"). The ancient alternation of PA /*a·/ : /*e·/ before /*w/ has been leveled out in Fox, Cree, Montagnais, Ojibwa, and Shawnee.

PA /*we·sa·wya·ki/ (II participle) 'that which is yellow, yellow thing'; C /we·sa·wa·k/; M /wɛ·sa·wi·k/; O /we·sa·wa·k/; S /we·θa·wa·ki/; Powhatan /o·sa·wa·k/.

The analogy of the modified root /*wi·sa·w-/

is to the following two nouns, representing items of yellow color:

PA /*wi·si/ 'belly fat'; C /wi·si/; Mt /wi·š/; Ms /wis/, (Eliot wees "fat" Exodus 29:13, 22).

PA /*wi·swi/ 'bile'; F /owi·swi/ with prothetic vowel; P /wìsi/; uD /wi·shwi/; Ms /wiswi/, (Eliot and Mayhew weswe "gall" (for bile) Psalm 69:21).

Addenda

252. BUTTOCKS

(a) /mesket/ 'someone's buttocks, breech', /nesket/ 'my buttocks', /kesket/ 'thy buttocks', /osket/ 'his buttocks'.

(b) musket "run" (H10), kehsekit "arse" (H2), with Strachey's second e apparently orthographic.

(c) PA /*-çkečyi/ 'buttocks, breech' INAN dependent noun; S /-ˀkiči/, pl. /-ˀkičiwali/, reshaped with discrepant /ˀk/ cluster for expected /šk/; P |-hkəčiy|; Ms /-skət/; Powhatan /-sket/; as in PA /*neçkečyi/ 'my buttocks'; P /nkə̀či/; Powhatan /nesket/.

PA /*weçkečyi/ 'his buttocks'; S /oˀkiči/ with discrepant cluster; P /wkə̀či/, |wəhkəčiy|; Ms /wəskət/, (William Wood (1634) mouskett "the breech" for /məskət/ 'someone's breech'); Powhatan /osket/. There is also:

PA /*-čyexki/ 'buttocks' INAN dependent noun; PA /*wečyexki/ 'his buttocks'; C /očisk/; M /oče·h/, dependent stem /-čehk/.

253. COB

(a) /ohkit/ 'cob of maize, corncob' INAN, pl. /ohkiči·s/.

(b) okishec, okiicshec "bob of the Virginia wheat without corn" (H3), actually pl.

(c) PA /*wexkičyi/ 'spike, spadix, inflorescent

plant stem' (apparent original PA meaning), and secondarily by semantic extension 'cob of maize, corncob', and 'pipestem'; C /oskičiy/ 'pipestem', pl. /oskičiya/; O /okkič/ 'pipestem', pl. /okkiči·n/; Powhatan /ohkit/ 'cob'. There is also:

PA /*weθemeθkwi/ 'bud, catkin'; C /osimisk/ (with assibilation in which expected /t/ is replaced by /s/ before /*e/); O /onimikk/, pl. /onimikko·n/; P /wə̀ləməsk^{w}/, pl. /wə̀ləmskol/.

54. LEAF

(a) /ma·nkwipak/ 'compound leaf', pl. /ma·nkwipakos/.

(b) maangwipacus "leaves" (H9)

(c) PEA /*ma·nkwipakwi/ 'compound leaf'; P /mák^{w}ipak^{w}/, pl. /mak^{w}ípakol/; Powhatan /ma·nkwipak/. The root is PEA /*ma·nkw-/ 'toward a point, converge'; P |makw-|, and extended root |makwe-|, as in P /mák^{w}ihle/ 'it goes together', /mák^{w}ehle/ 'it accumulates'. The noun final is PA /*-pakw-/ 'leaf'; F /-pakw-i/; M /-pakw-/; Mi /-pakw-/; P /-pak^{w}/.

55. NIGHT

(a) /tepahkat/ (II) 'it is night'.

(b) toppquough "night" (Smith), tapocot "night" (H11)

(c) PA /*tepexkatwi/ or /*tepaxkatwi/ (II) 'it is night'; F /tepehkatwi/; C /tipiska·w/, with generalized II final; M /tepɛ·h/ 'last night', /wani·tepɛ·hkat/ 'it is night'; O /tipikkat/; S /tepeˀki/; P/tə̀pahkat/, /ak^{w}ané-təpahkat/ 'it is the early or fore part of the night', /nawí-təpahkat/ 'it is the late part of the night, far into the night'; Ms /naw-təpahkat/ 'it is late at night', (Cotton nouttippohkod "late at night'); Nr (Roger Williams nanashowa-típpocat "midnight").

256. PADDLE, ROW

(a) /či·me·w/ (AI) 'he paddles, rows', /či·me·s/ 'paddle thou!' (2 person sg. AI imperative)

(b) tchÿmaac "row" (H13)

(c) PA /*či·me·wa/ (AI) 'he paddles'; C (deverbal final with shortened vowel) /nihta·wičime·w/ 'he paddles well, swims well'; M (deverbal final with short vowel) /peme·čemɛw/ 'he paddles or swims along'; O /či·me·/; Ms and Nr /čimaw/, (Eliot chemáu "he paddles, rows" Ezekiel 27:29, menuhke chemáog "they toil in rowing" Mark 6:48).

PA /*či·me·lwe/ 'paddle thou!' (2 person sg. AI imper.); O /či·me·n/; Powhatan /či·me·s/; Ms and Nr /čimaš/, (Roger Williams chémosh "paddle thou").

PA /*či·me·kwa/ 'paddle ye!' (2 person pl. AI imper.); O /či·me·k/; Powhatan /či·me·k/; Ms and Nr /čimak/, (Roger Williams chémeck "paddle ye").

Penobscot has this root in /čìmse/, |čiməhse| 'he collects firewood by canoe, while paddling along a stream'.

257. PADDLE, OAR

(a) /či·ma·kan/ 'paddle, oar' INAN, pl. /či·ma·kan

(b) tshemacans "oar" (H11), actually pl.

(c) PEA /*či·ma·kani/ 'paddle'; C /či·ma·kan/ 'companion in a canoe'; mD /či·má·kan/; Powhatan /či·ma·kan/.

258. SUMMER

(a) /ni·peno·w/ (II) 'it is summer'.

(b) nepinough "summer" (Smith)

(c) PA /*ni·penwi/ (noun) 'summer', (II) 'it is summer'; F /ni·penwi/; C /ni·pin/; M /ne·pe O /ni·pin/; Mi /nipinwiki/; P /nìpən/; mD /ni·pən/; Ms and Nr /nipən/, (Eliot népun

Genesis 8:22, Roger Williams néepun). There is also the longer and probably archaic form:

PA /*ni·peno·wi/ (II) it is summer'; M /ne·penowew/ with regularized or reshaped ending (?); P /nìpəno/; Powhatan /ni·peno·w/.

59. WAVE

(a) /akwa·ska·w/ sg., pl. /akwa·ska·was/ 'breakers, waves dashing on the shore, surf'.

(b) agwaskawwaus "waves of the sea" (H15)

(c) Pseudo-PA as if /*akwa·ška·wi/ 'breaker, wave dashing on the shore'; root PA /*akw-/ 'ashore, out of the water', and PA /*-a·ška·-/ 'wave'. An example is:

PA /*mama·nka·ška·hanwi/ (II) 'it runs in big waves, the waves run high'; C /mama·hka·ska·han/; O /mama·nka·ška·/.

60. BLOODROOT

(a) /meskwaspen/ AN, pl. /meskwaspenak/ 'bloodroot' (Sanguinaria canadensis L.).

(b) musquaspenne "a root of the bigness of a finger, and as red as blood . . . in drying, it will wither almost to nothing . . . they use to paint their mats, targets, and such like" (Smith).

(c) Pseudo-PA as if /*meçkwaxpenya/ 'red tuber', for which see BLOOD (entry 28) and GROUNDNUT (entry 100). If Smith has recorded the term correctly, it provides an example of PA /*xp/ reflected as Powhatan /sp/ rather than the usual /hp/, in the same manner that Powhatan has the reflexes /hk/ and /sk/ both from PA /*xk/. This is almost certainly the result of differences between various Powhatan dialects.

PA /*maθkwaxpenya/ "bear potato"; F /mahko·hpenya/; O /makko·ppin/, pl. /makko·ppini·k/; is not the same as the Powhatan word, despite the suggestion of Michelson (1933, reference cited in note 28).

The bloodroot is mildly poisonous if eaten and the "bear potato" is described by Baraga and others as edible. The latter is probably the huge, yam-like, and edible man-of-the-earth or wild-potato-vine (*Ipomoea pandurata* [L.] G. F. W. Meyer).

261. RICE

(a) /mato·min/ 'wild rice, water oats' (*Zizania aquatica* L. and variants)

(b) *mattoume* "groweth as our bents do in meadows . . . seed is not much unlike to rye, though much smaller . . . this they use for dainty bread buttered with deer suet" (Smith).

(c) PA /*maθo·mina/ 'wild rice, wild water oats' (perhaps originally 'any stiff grass bearing edible grain'), AN in most languages; F /mano·mina/ 'wild rice', pl. /mano·minaki/; C (Swampy Cree only, and evidently a loan from Ojibwa) /mano·min/ 'wild rice, oats', pl. /mano·minak/; M /mano·mεh/ 'wild oats, wild rice' INAN, pl. /mano·menan/; O /mano·min/ 'wild rice, oats'; Mi /malo·mina/ pl. /malo·minaki/ 'rice, oats'; Np /malomin/ 'wheat', also 'rye, oats, barley' (Mathevet *mal8min* "bled" p. 89; Aubery ms. Fr.-Abn. p. 64, *mar8men* "avoine sauvage", "les Loups appellent ainsi le bled"; Aubery ms. Fr.-Abn. p. 412, *mar8men* "orge", "les Loups appellent ainsi les bleds, avoines, segles, &c."); P (and other EA dialects) /ɑpətéləwimin/, pl. /ɑpətələwíminal/ 'rice' (i. e., "laughing berries, grains"), the usual term for 'rice', especially for post-contact *Oryza sativa*; but P (and EA) /málomin/ AN, pl. /malóminak/ 'wild rice, water oats' (*Zizania aquatica* L.), now an obsolescent term; and /málomin/ INAN, pl. /malṓminal/ 'lyme grass' (original meaning), but also used in recent times for introduced wheat, barley, oats, and rye.

The INAN pl. /malṓminal/ refers to _Elymus arenarius_, var. _villosus_ Ernst H. F. Meyer, known variously as 'lyme grass', 'strand wheat', 'wild oats', and 'sea rye', which is found on the beaches and shores of the north Atlantic coast south to Penobscot Bay (sparsely to Cape Cod), along the St. Lawrence Strait and River, and on the shores of many northern inland lakes, especially Lakes Michigan and Superior. The grain is edible, nearly half an inch long, and resembles an oat.

262. STARGRASS (a) /wi·ssaka·n/ 'stargrass, colicroot, unicorn-root' (_Aletris farinosa_ L.). This plant has a very bitter, short, tough, rhizomatous root, the juice of which has medicinal value as an astringent and sudorific. It was used also by the eastern Siouan peoples of the Carolinas and Virginia to treat wounds and snakebites.

(b) _wighsacan_ "a small root which they bruise and apply to the wound . . . so this cureth their hurts" (Smith).

The same term was recorded on Roanoke Island in 1585 by John White. He gives Chowan _wisakon_ "the herb which the savages call Wysauke wherewith they cure their wounds which they receive by the poisoned arrows of their enemies". In Hulton and Quinn ("The American Drawings of John White, 1577-1590", London and Chapel Hill, 1964) this is identified as a species of _Asclepias_ or milkweed. White seems to have had some misunderstanding, since the roots of the milkweeds are toxic and therefore might have been the source of the poison in which the arrowpoints were dipped rather than the antidote.

(c) PA root /*wi·ʔsak-/ 'bitter, painful'; C /wi·sak-/; M /we·ʔsak-/; O /wi·ssak-/; S /wiʔθak-/; P /wəssak-/; Powhatan /wi·ssak- compounded with the abstract noun final PA /*-a·n-/. There are many terms with this root:

PA /*wi·ʔsakanwi/ (II) 'it is bitter'; C /wi·sakan/; M /we·ʔsakan/; S /wiʔθakanwi/.

263. STURGEON (a) /kapa·to·n/ 'Atlantic sturgeon' (Acipenser oxyrhynchus Mitchill).

(b) cuppotoon "sturgeon" (H14), copotone "sturgeon" (Smith).

(c) PEA /*kapa·hše·wa/ 'Atlantic sturgeon'; P (and all EA dialects) /kȁpahse/, pl. /kápahsak/; WA /kapahsá/; Ms and Nr /kapɑhš/, (Cotton kôpposh; Roger Williams kaúposh "sturgeon", pl. kaúposhaûog); Chowan /kapa·hse·w/, (John White, Roanoke Island 1585, coppáuseo with drawing of the sturgeon). The PEA term is a compound of the PA extended root /*kapa·-/ 'away from, out of the water'; C, M, and O /kapa·-/; P /kapɑ-/; and the PA medial /*-ehš-/ 'ear' (for which see DEAF, entry 66).

Powhatan has replaced medial /*-ehš-/ 'ear' with /*-eto·n-/ 'mouth' (see MOUTH, entry 134).

Compare the morphophonemics of Penobscot /kȁpahse/ 'sturgeon', |kapɑ-əhs-ay| with laxing of the penultimate syllable, and /kápɑsse/ 'he disembarks, walks out of a boat or other conveyance', |kapɑ-ohse| with retention of the penultimate tense vowel followed by fortis consonantal gemination.

SYNCOPE

Some Algonquian languages show syncope of short vowels, and each language that exhibits this phonological feature has its own set of rules governing the process. In general, syncope is of a more limited application in Powhatan than in Shawnee, Delaware, Mahican, Western Abenaki, and Eastern Abenaki.

In Powhatan, the low or open short vowels /e/ and /a/ are weak in that they alone are subject to syncope in certain phonological environments, and all other vowels are strong and never syncopated. Within any word, alternating syllables are heavy and light. Syllabic weights are determined by a simple rule. If the first vowel of a word is weak vowel /e/, even-numbered syllables are heavy and odd-numbered syllables are light, but in all other cases odd-numbered syllables are heavy and even-numbered syllables are light.

Two independent types of syncope occur in Powhatan, major syncope and minor syncope.

A. Major syncope never occurs in basic morphemes or themes of less than three syllables, and does not affect initial or final syllables of words. The weak vowels /e/ and /a/ are regularly subject to syncope in light checked or closed syllables which end in a spirant, that is, light syllables closing in /s/ or /h/, except those between identical spirants.

(1) In the following underlying forms syncope occurs in even-numbered light syllables:

|e·mehko·n| → /e·mko·n/ 'spoon'
|pakahkanw| → /pakkan/ 'puccoon, red dye'
|wi·kahkway| → /wi·kkway/ '(his) thigh'
|či·kehkahikan| → /či·kkahikan/ 'broom'

(2) Syncope also occurs in odd-numbered light syllables:

|metemwessiss| → /metemsiss/ 'old woman'

(3) Odd-numbered heavy syllables are not syncopated:

/kake·pehte·w/ 'he is deaf' /ami·nehka·n/ 'seed'

(4) Even-numbered heavy syllables are not affected by syncope:

/nečehča·k/ 'my soul'
/metahkem/ 'louse'

(5) Word initial and final syllables are not subject to major syncope:

/kehtasko·k/ 'large snake'

/wehtawak/ 'his ear'

/očapahk/ 'root'

(6) Words whose base form or theme comprises less than three syllables remain unaffected by major syncope:

/mahkahkos/ 'pumpkins'

/ahkehkok/ 'water-drums, pots'

/ahkehkwins/ 'small pot'

(7) Syncope in even-numbered light syllables does not occur between identical spirants.

/ossaskwe·ss/ 'muskrat' (dialect A)

/mossaskwe·ss/ 'muskrat' (Dialect B)

B. Minor syncope is unrelated to major syncope except that both affect the weak vowels /e/ and /a/. In Powhatan minor syncope is apparently optional or dialectic. It functions independently of the phonological feature of syllabic weight, does not occur in words of less than three syllables, and is limited to word final closed syllables beginning in the sonorants /m/ and /n/ and ending in word final spirant /s/ or a cluster the first member of which is /s/.

(1) Minor syncope does not take place in words of two syllables:

/nenesk/ 'my arm'

/me·nesk/ 'earthwork'

(2) Some examples of optional minor syncope are:

|pare·neskw| → /pare·nesk/ or /pare·nsk/ 'five'

/mahkesenas/ or /mahkesens/ 'shoes'

/apo·nas/ or /apo·ns/ 'loaves of bread'

/akwimess/ or /akwims/ 'loon'

SOME GRAMMATICAL FEATURES OF POWHATAN

A. The noun inflections are:

	ANIMATE		INANIMATE
	Proximate	Obviative	
Singular	(zero)	/-ah/	(zero)
Plural	/-ak/	/-ah/	/-as/

Powhatan does not distinguish the singular and plural obviative of animate nouns, and has generalized the obviative plural inflection /-ah/ from PA /*-ahi/. This is illustrated by such forms as /wi·wah/ 'his wife or wives' and /otessiwah/ 'his testicle(s)'.

The languages which preserve the Proto-Algonquian situation and distinguish number in the obviative are Fox, Kickapoo, Shawnee, Northern Ojibwa, Arapaho, Malecite-Passamaquoddy, and Eastern Abenaki (including Penobscot). Among those which do not distinguish number in the obviative, Menomini, Central and Eastern Ojibwa, Mahican, and Delaware have generalized the original obviative singular inflection PA /*-ali/. On the other hand, Cree, Western Abenaki, all the SNE languages (Massachusee, Narragansett, Mohegan-Pequot, and Nipmuck-Pocumtuck), and Powhatan have generalized the inflection of the obviative plural PA /*-ahi/.

Powhatan is found to be in accord with the SNE group of languages of Eastern Algonquian with regard to both the inanimate noun plural inflection /-as/ and the animate noun obviative inflection /-ah/ which is indifferent to number.

B. Only a few of the pronominal affixes of the Powhatan verb in the independent indicative mode are attested:

(1) The animate intransitive (AI) inflections are:

1 sg. /ne—/ (or with AI themes ending in /-a·/) /ne—m/
2 sg. /ke—/ (or with AI themes ending in /-a·/) /ke—m/
3 sg. /—w/
1 pl. /ne—men/ ('we' exclusive)
12 pl. /ke—men/ ('we' inclusive)
2 pl. /ke—mo·w/ [not attested]
3 pl. /—wak/

Some examples are: /nepensen/ 'I have a mote in my eye'
/pe·w/ 'he comes', /nepya·m/ 'I come'
/nenepa·m/ 'I am asleep'
/kewi·hpe·ntomen/ 'we sleep together'

(2) The transitive inanimate forms (TI) attested have only singular subjects, and fall into the usual three TI classes:

Class 1		Class 2		Class 3	
	pl.		pl.		pl.
1 /ne—amen/	—amena/	/ne—a·n/	—a·na/	/ne—en/	—ena/
2 /ke—amen/	—amena/	/ke—a·n/	—a·na/	/ke—en/	—ena/
3 o—amen/	—amena/	/—o·w/	(?)	/o—en/	—ena/

Negative (Class 1):

{ /ne, /ke, /o } —amo·wen/

Negative (Class 3):

{ /ne, /ke, /o } —o·wen/

Examples of Class 1 are:

/ota·hte·hamen/ 'he extinguishes it (fire, flame)'

/neno·ntamen/ 'I hear it'

/mata neno·ntamo·wen/ 'I do not hear it' (wrongly recorded by Strachey)

/nepo·ta·tamen/ 'I blow (on) it'

/nekontamen/ 'I swallow it'

Examples of Class 2 are:

/nemera·nta·n/ 'I smell it'

/pe·to·w/ 'he brings' (this is probably an objectless-TI)

Examples of Class 3 are:

/nemi·či·n/ 'I eat it'

/netayi·n/ 'I have it'

/netayi·na/ 'I have them' (INAN)

/onamen/ 'he sees it'

/mata onamo·wen/ 'he does not see it'

(3) The transitive animate (TA) verb forms attested are confined to three forms, one of them also represented by a negative. No inverse forms are found in Strachey's materials.

1 sg.—3 sg.	('I—him')	/ne—a·w/
2 sg.—3 sg.	('thou—him')	/ke—a·w/
1 sg.—2 sg.	('I—thee')	/ke—es/
Negative 1 sg.—2 sg.		/ke—ero·w/

Examples are: /newi·skwe·pita·w/ 'I wrap him up with cords'

/nemera·ma·w/ 'I perceive his odor, smell him'

/nepakama·w/ 'I strike him'

/nemo·nsa·w/ 'I cut his hair'

/kemo·nsa·w/ 'you (sg.) cut his hair'

/neki·skama·w/ 'I bite him through'

/ketassames/ 'I feed thee, I give thee food'

/ko·wama·nes/ 'I love thee'

/kenenohto·s/ 'I understand thee (what you say)', |ke-nenohtaw-es| with PA contraction of /*-awe-/ to /*-o·-/ in suffixed inflections before /*θ/, /*š/ and /*l/.

/mata kenenohto·ro·w/ 'I do not understand thee', with the same contraction.

C. The conjunct order is scarcely attested at all in Strachey's materials.

(1) The injunctive mode is involved in a single form: /pya·č/ 'let him come'.

(2) The inanimate intransitive conjunct (II) is given in one participle form:

/o·sa·wa·k/ 'yellow thing, that which is yellow', the suffixed inflection being /-k/ from PA /*-ki/.

(3) One type of initial change found in the conjunct order is noted in which initial /o-/ is replaced by /o·-/. This occurs in the II indicative /osa·we·w/ 'it is yellow' and the conjunct participle /o·sa·wa·k/ 'yellow thing'.

Presumably word initial /a/ and /e/ were changed to /e·/ in conjunct forms also, but no attestations are observed in Strachey's materials.

D. Imperative order forms are found frequently in Strachey's recordings but a complete paradigm is not possible. Bloomfield's presentation of the imperative order of Proto-Algonquian (B146, Section 43, p. 100) calls for some revisions and additions when the evidence provided by other Algonquian languages is considered. No TA imperatives are given by Strachey and these are omitted in the present discussion. The AI and TI verb imperative inflections of selected languages are summarized in the following table:

	PA	F	C	O	S	PEA		PEA-A		
						mD	P	Np	Ms	Pw
(AI):										
2sg.	*-lwe	-no	-y	-n	-lo	-l	-	-s	-š	-s
2pl.	*-ekwa	-eko	-ik	-ik	-eko	-əkw	-əkw	-əkwa	-ək	-ek
(TI): Class 1										
2sg.	*-anlwe	-ano	-ah	-an	-ano	-ah	-a	-as	-ah -aš	-ass
2pl.	*-amwekwa	-amoko	-amok	-amok	-amoko	-amo·kw	-amok	-amokwa	-amok	(?)
(TI): Class 3										
2sg.	*-lwe	-no	-y	-n	-lo	-l	-	-s	-š	-s
2pl.	*-ekwa	-eko	-ik	-ik	-eko	-əkw	-əkw	-əkwa	-ək	-ek

Note: PA *-anlwe = [*-am(w)-lwe] > PEA-A *-anθwe

(1) The transitive inanimate imperative is indifferent as to the number of inanimate objects, distinguishing only the number of the addressee.

(2) Examples of the Powhatan imperative verb are:

(AI) sg.: /pasekwi·s/ 'arise thou!', /pi·ntike·s/ 'enter thou!', /nahapis/ 'sit down!', /či·me·s/ 'paddle thou!'

(AI) pl.: /pya·k/ 'come ye!'

(TI, class 1) sg.: /ontenass/ 'take thou it from there!', /a·htawe·hass/ 'extinguish thou it (fire, flame)!'
The TI plural addressee form is not attested by Strachey, but presumably would be /-amok/ as in /ontenamok/ 'take ye it from there!'

(TI, class 3) sg.: /mi·či·s/ 'eat thou it!'
The TI plural addressee form is not attested, but presumably would be /mi·či·k/ 'eat ye it!'

(3) Examples of Massachusee and Nipmuck-Pocumtuck imperatives are:

(AI) sg.: Np /ləwas/ 'speak thou!' (Mathevet 18as "parle!" pp. 26, 5 /kawis/ 'sleep thou!' (Mathevet ka8is "dors!" pp. 25, 40)

Ms /pəyaš/ 'come thou!' (Eliot peyaush, Mayhew peyosh John 11:34)

Nr /čimaš/ 'paddle thou!' (Roger Williams chémosh)

(AI) pl.: Np /ləwakwa/ 'speak ye!' (Mathevet 18ak8̆a "parlez!" p. 2

/nohpawossakwa/ (Mathevet n8pa8ssak8a "allez en guerre!" p. 9)

Nr /čimak/ 'paddle ye!' (Roger Williams chémeck)

(TI, class 1) sg.: Ms (compare Ms /notam/ 'he hears' (objectless TI), Eliot and Mayhew nootam Psalm 55:17)

Ms /notah/ and /notaš/ 'hear thou!', perhaps representing different dialects, one perhaps distinguishing objectless and objectful TI forms (Eliot nootah "hearken thou!", Mayhew nootash Psalm 45:10)

Np (compare Np /wawαtam/ 'he is knowing, prudent, sober' (objectless TI), (Mathevet 8a8antam "il est sage" p. 42)

Np /wawαtas/ 'be thou wise, prudent, sober!' (Mathevet 8a8antas "sois sage!" p. 42)

(TI, class 1) pl.:

Ms /notamok/ 'hear ye!' (Eliot and Mayhew nootamook "hearken ye!, hear ye!" Psalm 49:1)

Np /wawαtamokwa/ 'be ye wise, prudent, sober!' (Mathevet 8a8antam8g8a "soyez sage!" p. 42)

(4) The delayed or future imperative is attested in a single form by Strachey in his mechecusk which could be read mechocusk, and is evidently to be taken as a writing error for /mi·či·hkas/ 'eat thou it then, by and by, later!' The unattested plural addressee form would be expected /mi·či·hke·k/ 'eat ye it later!' Many Algonquian languages have lost the delayed imperative and it is archaic or obsolescent in others. The prefinal ending or marker of the future imperative is PA /*-ehke·-/, with /*e·/ replaced by /*a/ before certain suffixes by the rules of internal sandhi. Reconstructions of the delayed imperative inflections follow, the Powhatan forms in parentheses being unattested hypothetical constructs:

		PA	C	O	Powhatan
(AI) and (TI, class 3):	2 sg.	*-ehkalwe	-ihkan	-ikkan	-ehkas
	2 pl.	*-ehke·kwa	-ihke·k	-ikke·k	(-ehke·k)
(TI, class 1):	2 sg.	*-amwehkalwe	-amohkan	-amokkan	(-amohkas)
	2 pl.	*-amwehke·kwa	-amohke·k	-amokke·k	(-amohke·k)

E. The diminutives of nouns in Powhatan fall into the following six classe The rules of internal sandhi give occlusive dominance to vowels terminating prior morphemes.

(1) /-ins/:

/ahkehkwins/ 'small pot'

/meno·te·ns/ 'small basket'

/mehtekwins/ 'little stick'

(2) /-e·ns/:

/ato·ns/ 'arrow' (with /-we·-/ replaced by /-o·-/)

/pi·menahkwa·ne·ns/ 'small cord, twine'

Pre-Powhatan /*metenče·ns/ 'mitten' > /metenče·ss/ by progressive dissimilation, reinforced by analogy to the more commo diminutives of classes 5 and 6.

(3) /-es/ and /-is/:

/mahkate·s/ 'small coal, ember'

(4) /-iss/:

/metemsiss/ 'old woman'

(5) /-e·ss/:

/ossaskwe·ss/, /mossaskwe·ss/ 'muskrat'

(6) /-ess/: This is the most common class of diminutive, and is the reflex of both PA /*-ehš-/ and /*-ehs-/.

/wi·ya·ss/ 'meat, flesh'	/ata·nkwess/ 'star'
/e·rikwess/ 'ant'	/atemoss/ 'dog'
/penkwess/ 'gnat'	/kaya·hkwess/ 'gull'
/akwimess/ 'loon'	/a·pikwess/ 'mouse'

/a·po·sse·ss/ 'slowworm, lizard'

/otani·ss/ 'his small (bird's) tail'

/oska·pe·ss/ 'boy attending a chief'

HISTORICAL PHONOLOGY OF POWHATAN

A. The syllabic phonemes of Proto-Eastern-Algonquian (PEA) are preserved unaltered in Powhatan, and the vowel sounds of Proto-Algonquian are maintained in both except that word initial PA /*e-/ appears as PEA /*a-/ and Powhatan /a-/.

PA /*eθkwe·ˀθemwa/ 'bitch' > /askwe·ssem/

PA /*ešpe·wi/ 'it is high' > /aspe·w/

B. The postconsonantal word final short vowels of Proto-Algonquian have been dropped.

PA /*mye·neθki/ 'earthwork' > /me·nesk/

PA /*no·hθa/ 'my father' > /no·ss/

PA /*neni·čya·na/ 'my child' > /neni·ča·n/

C. Proto-Algonquian /*s/ and /*š/ have completely coalesced or fallen together in Powhatan as the indifferent hissing or hushing spirant phoneme /s/. Except when neutralized in word final position in particle and inflectional morphemes, PA /*l/ becomes Powhatan /r/, and except in the same environment when there is an analogically fixed alternation to /*š/, PA /*θ/ becomes Powhatan /t/, falling together with /*t/.

PA /*weθakešyali/ 'his bowels' > /otakesi·s/

PA /*aθemwehša/ 'little dog' > /atemoss/

PA /*le·kawi/ 'sand' > /re·kaw/

PEA /*ta·pawa·ši/ 'seven' > /ta·pawa·s/

PEA /*to·lepye·wa/ 'loggerhead' > /to·repe·w/

PEA /*a·škalaškwi/ 'seaweed' > /a·skarask/

PA /*ši·ˀši·pa/ 'fowl, duck' > /si·ssi·p/

PA /*kweθapeška·wa/ 'he capsizes' > /kotapeska·w/

D. The Proto-Algonquian consonant clusters and their Powhatan reflexes, with reference to examples and the entry number of each are tabulated below. Only the Powhatan equivalents of the PA clusters /*hl/ and /*čp/ remain undetermined. PA cluster /*xk/ is troublesome and is discussed below.

PA	Powhatan	Examples
*nk >	nk	BIG (24), CHINQUAPIN (48), DUST (70), GNAT (95), TASTE GOOD (218), WASH FACE (235)
*hk >	hk	LOUSE (121), POT (158), PUMPKIN (161), ROE (168) ROOT (170), ROPE (171), SEED (179), SHORT (186), SPIT (200), SPOON (201)
*xk >	sk	ARROW (16), LEG (115), MAT (125), NOSE (142), WATER RECEDES (237), WRAP UP (249)
	hk	BLACK (27), CLOUD (51), COAL (52), MEAL, SOFT (126), MORNING (130), NOSE (142), POT (158), PUCCOON (160), SHOE (184), COB (253), NIGHT (255)

*θk > sk	ABOVE (11), FIVE (5), ARM (15), BITCH (26), BONE (3 COAT (53), EARTHWORK (73), SEED (180), SNAKE (196
*šk > sk	BOY (37), CAPSIZE (45), CLAY (50), CUT (63), EYE (79), FLOUNDER (86), FROST (91), GULL (101), LIP (116), MUSKRAT (136), NEW (141), REED (160), RAW (165), STRAWBERRY (206), SEAWEED (238), WHISTLE (240), WAVE (259)
*çk > sk	BLOOD (28), GILL (94), VAGINA (?) (232), BUTTOCKS (252), BLOODROOT (260)
*čk > hk	FISH-HOOK (?) (85), RACCOON (?) (162)
*nl > n	MOTE IN EYE (131), SHARP (182)
*hl (?)	
*ʔl > ss	BEARD (22), FLY (87), LOST (120), NET (139), FLYING SQUIRREL (203)
*nθ > ss	COPPER (57), TAKE FROM THERE (2 sg. TI imper.) (217) EXTINGUISH FIRE (2 sg. TI imper.) (78)
*hθ > ss	COUGH (59), COVER (60), FATHER (80), LIZARD (117), SKIN (188), WORM (248)
*ʔθ > ss	THREE (3), ARROW, FLETCHED (16), BITCH (26), BOAT (31), COUGH (59), FUR (93), NEST (138), OPOSSUM (145), PEANUT (150), REED (167), SQUIRREL (202), SUN (209)
*nš > ns	BRIAR (40), CUT HAIR (64), DOE (67), EYE (79), VINE (233)
*hš > ss	BREAST (39), DOG (68), FEED (82), GNAT (95), PAWPAW (149), PERSIMMON (153), SNAKE, SPECIES (1 TAIL OF BIRD (214), WHISTLE (240), WOOD (247)
*ʔš > ss	EIGHT (8), BIRD (25), HAIR (103), HERON (107), MUSKRAT (136), TESTICLE (220)
*ns > ns	MOTE IN EYE (131), NAME (137), PAROQUET (147), POT, LITTLE (158), WATER RECEDES (237)
*hs > ss	AWL (18), BOY (37), MEAT (127), MIRE (128), WOMAN, OLD (245)
*ʔs > ss	FISH (84), COPPER (58), STARGRASS (262)
*nč > nč	SIX (6), HAND (104), MITTEN (129), THUMB (224), WASH HANDS (235)
*hč > hč	see *ht
*ʔč > hč	CHINQUAPIN (48), SOUL (199)

*nt > nt — CANOE (44), DANCE (65), ENTER (77), HEAR (106), PEANUT (150), SMELL (195), SWALLOW (211), TAKE FROM THERE (217), THROAT (223)

*ht > ht — DEAF (66), EAR (72), UNDERSTAND (230)

*ʔt > ht — BOW (33), FOAM (88), EXTINGUISH (78), SNAKE, LARGE (196), THUMB (224), TREE (226)

---

*mp > mp — MARROW (124)

*hp > hp — PLAY (156), SLEEP WITH (192)

*xp > { hp — GROUNDNUT (100), PIPE (154), SCRAPE (177)

*xp > { sp — BLOODROOT (260)

---

*θp > sp — MORNING (130)

*šp > sp — FULL OF FOOD (92), HIGH (108)

*čp > (?)

The double Powhatan reflexes of PA /*xk/ call for some discussion. A reasonable explanation would be that one dialect of Powhatan had the reflex /sk/ and the other /hk/ for PA /*xk/, and this view finds some support from the fact that it has been demonstrated that at least two dialects are represented in Strachey's recordings and in one gloss, the dependent noun PA /*-xkiwani/ 'nose', Strachey evidently has recorded the variants /mehkiwan/ and /meskiwan/ 'someone's nose'. On the other hand, there is some justification to support a contrary view since Strachey did make some copying or writing errors. Furthermore, it should be pointed out that some Proto-Algonquian reconstructions positing /*xk/ are shaky since they depend for the most part on a single diachronic phonological development that resulted in the comparative contrast of Cree /sk/ with /hk/ in most other languages. The consonant clusters in Algonquian are more volatile than has hitherto been assumed, and in some languages they seem to be more plastic than in others, among them Shawnee, Menomini, and Cree. In most cases discrepant clusters are to be explained as the result of the operations of analogy and assimilative and dissimilative changes within a given language, or as a result of borrowing from a neighboring language during a period of prolonged contact. The phenomenon of cluster plasticity in Algonquian points out the chief weakness in the application of the comparative method of reconstruction, despite unquestionable soundness and obvious virtues, in language stocks in which there are no inherited written records from antiquity that will often provide indisputable solutions to otherwise problematical phonological inductions.

Bloomfield's coded /*xk/ perhaps represents an actual PA /*tk/, and his coded /*çk/ probably is in origin either an actual PA /*lk/ or /*sk/ or both. Arapaho and the Eastern Algonquian languages except Powhatan clearly reflect separate correspondences for PA /*xk/ and /*θk/, Arapaho having /ʔ/ for the former and /x/ alternating with /s/ for the latter. However, Arapaho is not unequivocally contrastive, for in Arapaho PA /*šk/ has the same reflex as /*θk/, and /*nk/ and /*çk/ the same reflex as /*xk/, and PA /*hk/ has the Arapaho reflex /ʔ/ alternating with /zero/.

The reflexes of PA /*hk/ and /*xk/ are kept apart only in Cree, Arapaho, Delaware, Mahican, and Powhatan, but apparently in none of these languages without minor perturbation from borrowing, or from the operations of analogy and assimilation and dissimilation. PA /*hk/ is reflected in Cree and Powhatan as /hk/ and in Delaware and Mahican as /h/, and PA /*xk/ as /sk/ in Cree, and /hk/ in Delaware and Mahican. For example, Delaware /mákahkw/ 'pumpkin' from PA /*mahkahkwi/ 'tub, cask' is certainly a borrowing from languages to the south as is shown by Powhatan /mahkahk/ 'pumpkin' with the same semantic specialization. There are clear examples of glosses which appear to posit PA /*xk/ appearing in Powhatan with both /sk/ and /hk/:

Powhatan /sk/: (1) PA /*mexka·či/ 'leg', Powhatan /meska·t/, Arapaho /wóʔooθ/

(2) PA /*ana·xkani/ 'mat, rug', Powhatan /ana·ska·n/

(3) PA /*newyi·xkwe·piθa·wa/ 'I tie him up, wrap him up with cords', Powhatan /newi·skwe·pita·w/

Powhatan /sk/ and /hk/:

(4) PA /*mexkiwani/ 'nose', Powhatan /meskiwan/ and /mehkiwan/, Arapaho /béʔis/

Powhatan /hk/: (5) PA /*maxkeseni/ 'shoe', Powhatan /mahkesen/, Arapaho /woʔóh/

(6) PA /*tepexkatwi/ 'it is night', Powhatan /tepahkat/, Arapaho /téčeʔ/

(7) PA /*lo·xk-/ 'soft', Powhatan /ro·hk-/

Although a resolution of this difficulty by positing two diverging Powhatan dialects with different reflexes of /*xk/ has much in its favor, it should be recognized that this solution may be all too facile and disguise the fact that some of the reflexes of attributed /*xk/ in Cree, Delaware, Mahican, and Arapaho are subject to perturbation and may be unoriginal in specific cases, and that these languages do not always agree among themselves. If the postulation of two major Powhatan dialects is correct, which seems likely, then dialect A recorded largely by Smith and partly by Strachey and probably the one spoken in the immediate vicinity of Jamestown is the dialect with the reflex /hk/ for /*xk/, and dialect B had /sk/. Unfortunately we lack sufficient information to explicate the details of Virginia Algonquian and its dialects.

The cluster /*xp/ seems to be reflected regularly in Powhatan as /hp/ with the single exception /meskwaspen/ 'bloodroot' recorded by Smith with reflex /sp/. If correct, it tends to confirm that the variant reflexes of /*xk/ and /*xp/ are due to dialect differences within Powhatan.

E. The ancient Proto-Algonquian alternation /*ya·/ : /*yi·/ before /*w/ is faithfully retained in Powhatan.

PA /*netayi·wa·wa/ 'I have him'	>	/netayi·wa·w/
PA /*ma·čyi·wa/ 'he goes off, starts away'	>	/ma·či·w/
PA /*ki·nlyi·wi/ 'it is sharp'	>	/ki·ni·w/
PA /*aškanyi·wi/ (?) 'it is raw'	>	/askani·w/

Powhatan has stabilized both facets of the alternation, on the one hand analogically extending alternant /*yi·/ before other sonorants besides /*w/, and on the other hand analogically retaining primary /*ya·/ in word final.

PA /*netaya·ni/ 'I have it'	>	/netayi·n/
PA /*nema·čya/ 'I go off, start away'	>	/nema·ča·/

F. The ancient Proto-Algonquian alternation /*a·/ : /*e·/ before /*w/ is faithfully preserved in Powhatan.

PA /*ešpe·wi/ 'it is high'	>	/aspe·w/
PA /*wa·pe·wi/ 'it is white'	>	/a·pe·w/ or /wa·pe·w/
PA /*wesa·wye·wi/ 'it is yellow'	>	/osa·we·w/
PA /*kenwe·wi/ 'it is long'	>	/kene·w/
PA /*nepe·wa/ 'he sleeps'	>	/nepe·w/
Compare: PA /*nenepa/ 'I sleep'	>	/nenepa·m/

PA /*pye·wa/ 'he comes' > /pe·w/

Compare: PA /*nepya/ 'I come' > /nepya·m/

PA /*pya·kwa/ 'come ye!' > /pya·k/

PA /*pya·čye/ 'let him come' > /pya·č/

The primary member /*a·/ of the alternation has been stabilized in Powhatan by the innovative suffix /-m/ in first and second person singular AI verbs exhibiting this alternation. The new suffix has been segmented out and analogically transferred from the AI pluralizing suffixes /-men/ and /-mo·w/. The stabilization of the alternation /*a·/ : /*e·/ in this respect differs from that observed in the alternation /*ya·/ : /*yi·/.

G. Contractions of double vowel sequences between nonsyllabics in Powhatan are as follows:

(1) PA /*-iwa-/ > /-i·-/ before /*l/, /*θ/, and /*š/

PA /*mehšiwali/ 'pieces of firewood' > /messi·s/

(2) PA /*-e·we-/ > /-e·/

PA /*weška·pe·wehsa/ 'boy attending a chief' > /oska·pe·ss/

PA /*maxkate·wesi/ 'small coal, ember' (dimin.) > /mahkate·s/

(3) PA /*-ewe-/ > /-o·-/

PA /*newehθaʔθwemwi/ 'I cough' > /no·ssassom/

PEA /*ko·wama·neθe/ 'I love thee' > /ko·wama·nes/

(as if pseudo-PA /*kewewama·neθe/)

(4) PA /*-aya-/ > /-a-/

PA /*neθeʔšiwayaki/ 'my testicles' > /netessiwak/

PEA /*wi·kahkwayali/ 'his thighs' > /wi·kkwas/

PA /*meθkoθayali/ 'coats, robes of fur' > /meskotas/

However, the contraction does not occur between identical or near identical Powhatan nonsyllabics:

PA /*wešaθkwayaki/ 'freshwater mussels > /osaskwayak/

PA /*ahθayaki/ (AN) 'skins, pelts' > /assayas/ (INAN)

PA /*walahakayaki/ 'scales of fish' > /warahakayak/

(5) Between nonsyllabics PA /*-awe-/ contracts irregularly in two patterns both of which date back to Proto-Algonquian times, namely to /-a·-/ or to /-o·-/. In the various surviving languages the treatment varies to some degree in detail.

In Powhatan PA /*-awe-/ contracts to /-a·-/ before /*k/, /*t/,

/*m/, /*n/, and /*h/.

PA /nowawemwa/ 'he comes from there > /nowa·m/

PA /*nemela·ntaweni/ 'I smell it' > /nemera·nta·n/

PA /*wi·yawehsi/ 'meat' > /wi·ya·ss/

In Powhatan PA /*-awe-/ contracts to /-o·-/ regularly only when the /*e/ begins an inflection before PA /*θ/, /*š/, and /*l/.

PA /*kenenohtaweθe/ 'I understand thee' > /kenenohto·s/

PEA (negative) /*kenenohtaweθo·wi/ 'I do not understand thee' > /mata kenenohto·ro·w/, with PA /*θ/ and its alternant analogically restored as late PEA /*l/.

H. The reflexes and contractions of the twelve glide-vowel sequences between nonsyllabics are as follows in Powhatan:

(1) PA /*-wi-/ > { /-i-/ after nonsyllabics except /*k/ ; /-wi-/ after /*k/ }

PA /*pi·ntwike·wa/ 'he enters a dwelling' > /pi·ntike·w/

PA /*amamwilwe/ 'wake thou up!' > /amamis/

PA /*axkehkwinsa/ 'pot' (dimin.) > /ahkehkwins/

PEA /*akwintenwi/ 'canoe' > /akwinten/

PEA /*akwimehša/ 'loon' (dimin.) > /akwimess/

PEA /*ma·nkwipakwi/ 'compound leaf' > /ma·nkwipak/

(2) PA /*wi·/ > /-wi·-/ at least after /*k/

PA /*pasekwi·lwe/ 'arise thou from your seat!' > /pasekwi·s/

(3) PA /*-we-/ > /-o-/ after all nonsyllabics except /*k/ and /*p/

PA /*aθemwehša/ 'dog' (dimin.) > /atemoss/

PA /*wehθaʔθwemwiwa/ 'he coughs' > /ossassomo·w/

Pseudo-PA /*natwemwa/ 'wolf' > /nantom/

However, after /*k/ interconsonantal PA /*-we-/ receives varying treatment in Powhatan. Also, according to Strachey's record, which in this case may show a dialectic difference, /*-we-/ after /*k/ and before /*n/ exhibits a variation.

After /*k/ PA /*-we-/ {
> /-o-/ before /*t/ and /*θ/
> /-we-/ or /-o-/ before /*n/
> /-e-/ before /*p/ and /*m/
> /-we-/ before /*s/ and /*h/ }

PA /*nekwetwi/ 'one' > /nekot/

PA /*kweθapeška·wa/ 'he capsizes' > /kotapeska·w/
PEA /*kwentamwiwa/ 'he swallows' > /kwentamo·w/
PEA /*nekwentameni/ 'I swallow it' > /nekontamen/
PA /*wekwenta·kani/ 'his throat' > /okwenta·kan/
PA /*netehkwema/ 'my louse' > /netahkem/
PA /*wi·kwepyi/ 'bast, wicopy' > /wi·kepi/
PA /*tahkwesiwa/ 'he is short' > /tahkwesiw/
PA /*mekwehsi/ 'awl' > /mekwess/
PA /*e·likwehša/ 'ant' (dimin.) > /e·rikwess/
PA /*a·pikwehša/ 'mouse' (dimin.) > /a·pikwess/
PA /*kwi·škwehšwiwa/ 'he whistles' > /kwi·skwesso·w/

Finally, PA /*-we-/ > /-e-/ after /*p/.

PA /*apwete·wi/ 'it is hot, warm' > /apete·w/

(4) PA /*-we·/ { > /-e·-/ after all nonsyllabics except /*k/
> /-we·-/ after /*k/ }

PA /*kenwe·wi/ 'it is long' > /kene·w/
PA /*kesi·nkwe·wa/ 'he washes his face' > /kesi·nkwe·w/
PA /*eθkwe·ˀθemwa/ 'bitch' > /askwe·ssem/
PA /*newyi·xkwe·piθa·wa/ 'I wrap him up with cords, tie him up in knots' > /newi·skwe·pita·w/

(5) The PA interconsonantal sequence /*-wa-/ in Powhatan, as in many Algonquian languages, receives several contractions, and is often analogically restored.

PA /*-wa-/ { > /-a-/ after /*t/ and /*θ/
> /-o-/ after /*p/ and /*m/
> /-wa-/ or /-o-/ after /*k/ }

PA /*a·laxkwatwali/ 'clouds' > /a·rahkwatas/
Pseudo-PA /*matwahθaya/ 'dressed leather' > /matassay/
PEA /*aθwaškwi/ 'reed, water weed' > /atask/
PEA /*matwakaškwi/ 'prickly pear, balsam-apple' > /matakask/
Pseudo-PEA /*apwahwemina/ (AN) 'grain of parched maize' > /apohomin/ (INAN)

After /*k/ there is often some vacillation between /-wa-/ and /-o-/ due to the operations of analogy, but apparently before /*n/, /*t/, and any cluster Powhatan maintains an invariable /-wa-/, and before /*m/ and

/*k/ a regular contraction to /-o-/ occurs.

PEA /*pahsakwani/ 'mire' > /passakwan/

PA /*mi·kwana/ 'quill, long feather' > /mi·kwan/

PA /*wešekwani/ 'his (fish's) tail' > /wesekwan/ or /osekwan/

PA /*myeškwana/ 'someone's elbow' > /mi·skwan/

PA /*a·laxkwatwi/ 'cloud' > /a·rahkwat/

PA /*takwaškwatwi/ 'there is glazed frost or a crust of ice on the ground or snow' > /takwaskwat/

Pseudo-PA /*axkehkwaʔsenya/ 'stone or metal pot' > /ahkehkwassen/

Pseudo-PA /*weθa·kwame·kwa/ 'codfish' > /ota·kome·k/

PA /*meʔtekwaki/ 'trees' > /mehtekok/

PA /*axkehkwaki/ 'pots' > /ahkehkok/

After /*k/ and before /*h/, /*l/, /*θ/, and /*š/, /-wa-/ seems to be more common, but there is often contraction to /-o-/.

PA /*meʔtekwali/ 'sticks' > /mehtekos/

PEA /*a·škalaškwali/ 'seaweeds' > /a·skaraskwas/

PEA /*aθwaškwali/ 'reeds, water weeds' > /ataskwas/

PEA /*menenakwali/ 'islands' > /menenakos/

PEA /*ma·nkwipakwali/ 'compound leaves' > /ma·nkwipakos/

Pseudo-PEA /*takwahahkwi/ 'green arum, tuckahoe' > /takwahahk/

PEA /*wešekwahameni/ 'he crushes it by tool' { > /osekwahamen/ and > /osekohamen/ }

(6) PA /*-wa·-/ { > /-o·-/ after /*p/, /*t/, and /*k/; > /-wa·-/ after /*θ/, /*š/, and /*s/; > /-a·-/ after /*nš/ and /*ns/ }

PA /*pyi·menahkwa·ni/ 'rope, cord' > /pi·menahko·n/

PA /*wexpwa·kana/ 'pipe' > /ohpo·kan/

PA /*apwa·na/ 'cornbread' (AN) > /apo·n/ (INAN)

PA /*e·mehkwa·na/ 'spoon, ladle' > /e·mko·n/

PA /*wepwa·mi/ 'his thigh' > /opo·m/

{ Late-PA /*neʔšwa·šyeka/; Early-PA /*neʔθwa·šyeka/ } 'eight' > /nasswa·s/

PA /*nemo·nšwa·wa/ 'I cut his hair' > /nemo·nsa·w/

However, if correct, Strachey seems to have recorded an exception in the diminutive form:

PA /*pyi·menahkwa·ne·nsi/ 'small cord' > /pi·menahkwa·ne·ns/

(7) PA /*-yi-/ > /-i·-/ after all nonsyllabics.

PA /*meʔθanyikwa/ 'gray squirrel' > /messani·k/
Pseudo-PA /*aʔlapanyikwa/ 'flying squirrel' > /assapani·k/
PA /*mi·čyilwe/ 'eat thou it!' > /mi·či·s/
PEA /*maškyihkyiwimina/ 'strawberry' > /maski·hki·wimin/

(8) PA /*-yi·-/ > /-i·/ after all nonsyllabics.

PA /*ki·nlyi·wi/ 'it is sharp' > /ki·ni·w/
PA /*aškanyi·wi/ (?) 'it is raw' > /askani·w/
PA /*pyi·menahkwa·ni/ 'rope, cord' > /pi·menahko·n/

(9) PA /*-ye-/ > /-i·-/ after all nonsyllabics.

PA /*ašyeškiwi/ 'clay, mud' > /asi·skiw/
PA /*nyeškwana/ 'my elbow' > /ni·skwan/
PA /*waθanyehši/ 'his (bird's) tail' (dimin.) > /otani·ss/
PA /*mi·čyehkalwe/ 'eat thou it by and by, later!' > /mi·či·hkas/
{ PA /*wasyeʔθanwi/ | PEA /*wasyehθe·wi/ } 'nest' > { /wasi·sse·w/ or | /wači·sse·w/ }
PEA /*ka·škyekwi/ 'ten' > /ka·ski·k/
PEA /*wešyeka·na/ 'roe' > /osi·ka·n/

(10) PA /*-ye·-/ > /-e·-/ after all nonsyllabics except word initial /*n-/.

PA /*no·nšye·swa/ 'doe, matron' > /no·nse·s/
PA /*kakye·pehte·wa/ 'he is deaf' > /kake·pehte·w/
PA /*mye·neθki/ 'earthwork' > /me·nesk/
PA /*mye·wi/ 'path' > /me·w/
PA /*kesi·θenčye·wa/ 'he washes his hands' > /kesi·tenče·w/
PA /*wa·paθanye·wa/ 'adult bald eagle' > /a·patane·w/
PA /*wesa·wye·wi/ 'it is yellow' > /osa·we·w/
PA /*pye·wa/ 'he comes' > /pe·w/
Pseudo-PA /*wa·pa·pye·minšyi/ 'white vine' > /wa·pa·pe·mins/
PA /*pye·ta·wa/ 'he brings it' > /pe·to·w/ 'he bri
PEA /*to·lepye·wa/ 'loggerhead turtle' > /to·repe·w/

However, after word initial /*n-/ the /*n/ is dropped and /*-ye·-/ is retained:

PA /*nye·wwi/ 'four' > /ye·w/

(11) PA /*-ya-/ { > /-i·-/ after all nonsyllabics except /*n/, /*nš/, and /*ns/
> /-a-/ after /*n/, /*nš/, and *ns/ }

PA /*wi·kwepyali/ 'pieces of bast' > /wi·kepi·s/
PA /*weθakešyali/ 'his bowels' > /otakesi·s/
PA /*a?ča·pyali/ 'bowstrings' > /a·pi·s/
PA /*a?lapyaki/ 'nets, seines' > /assapi·k/
PA /*mekyali/ 'scabs' > /meki·s/
PA /*wexkičyali/ 'cobs, plant spikes' > /ohkiči·s/
PEA /*nexkašyaki/ 'my nails, claws' > /nehkasi·k/
PA /*weθenčyali/ 'his hands' > /otenči·s/
PA /*wexpenyaki/ 'groundnuts' > /ohpenak/
PA /*ka·winšyali/ 'briars, brambles' > /ka·winsas/
Pseudo-PA /*wa·pa·pye·minšyali/ 'white vines' > /wa·pa·pe·minsas/

(12) PA /*-ya·-/ { > /-a·-/ after nonsyllabics except /*p/
> /-ya·-/ after /*p/ }

Pseudo-PEA /*ke·kya·ta·ši/ 'nine' > /ke·ka·ta·s/
PA /*neni·čya·na/ 'my child' > /neni·ča·n/
PA /*nete?čya·kwa/ 'my soul' > /nečehča·k/
PA /*we·sa·wya·ki/ 'yellow thing' > /o·sa·wa·k/
PA /*nepya/ 'I come' > /nepya·m/
PA /*pya·čye/ 'let him come' > /pya·č/
PA /*pya·kwa/ 'come ye!' > /pya·k/

I. The treatment of word final glide-vowel sequences varies in different Algonquian languages and in some analogical reshaping and paradigmatic regularization occur. In Powhatan the changes, with a few exceptions, appear to follow regular patterns. Each of these is discussed below:

(1) Single postconsonantal word final glide-vowel sequences of the pattern /*-yV/ and /*-wV/ are entirely dropped, with certain patterned exceptions and irregularities.

PA /*neki·špwi/ 'I have my fill of food' > /neki·sp/
PA /*weθenčyi/ 'his hand' > /otenč/

PA /*nekya/ 'my mother' > /nek/
PA /*aθetwi/ 'it stinks, is rotten' > /atet/
PA /*meçkwi/ 'blood' > /mesk/
PA /*wa·hkwa/ 'fish or frog egg' > /wa·hk/
PA /*aʔta·pya/ 'bow' > /ahta·p/
PA /*aʔlapya/ 'net, seine' > /assap/
PA /*wexpenya/ 'groundnut' > /ohpen/
PA /*nekwetwi/ 'one' > /nekot/
PA /*neʔθwi/ 'three' > /nass/
PA /*mo·wi·čyi/ 'dung' > /mo·wi·č/
PA /*weçkečyi/ 'his buttocks' > /osket/
PA /*weθakešyi/ 'his bowel, entrail' > /otakes/
PA /*ka·winšyi/ 'briar, bramble' > /ka·wins/
PA /*no·nšye·swa/ 'doe, matron' > /no·nse·s/
PA /*eθkwe·ʔθemwa/ 'bitch' > /askwe·ssem/
PA /*mahkahkwi/ 'tub, cask' > /mahkahk/ 'pumpkin'
PA /*meʔtekwa/ 'tree' > /mehtek/ (AN)
PA /*meʔtekwi/ 'stick' > /mehtek/ (INAN)
PEA /*nexkašya/ 'my nail, claw' > /nehkas/
PEA /*akwintenwi/ 'canoe' > /akwinten/

The following exceptions and irregularities are noted:

(1a) Word final /*-wV/ does not invariably disappear without a trace when it is immediately preceded by the weak vowel /*-e-/ in a light syllable followed by certain clusters (which vary with the individual language) and make the /*-e-/ syllable theoretically subject to syncope (in languages having this feature), in which case the /*-e-/ is assimilated to /-o·-/.

PA /*ki·seʔθwa/ 'sun' > /ki·so·ss/

(1b) When a nonidentical glide has been dropped in the penultimate syllable the final syllable nonidentical glide is also dropped, but word rhythm is maintained and the short final vowel is retained.

PA /*wi·kwepyi/ 'bast, wicopy' > /wi·kepi/

This does not occur when the glides are identical.

PA /*nekwetwi/ 'one' > /nekot/

(1c) In bisyllabic words final /*-yi/ > /-i/ when it follows a single nonsyllabic which is preceded by the short weak vowel /*-e-/. This does not occur with final /*-ya/.

PA /*nepyi/ 'water' > /nepi/

PA /*mekyi/ 'scab' > /meki/

But compare: PA /*nekya/ 'my mother' > /nek/

(1d) In bisyllabic words final /*-wi/ is retained following a sonorant-cluster preceded by the short weak vowel /*-e-/.

PA /*penkwi/ 'dust, ashes, dirt' > /penkwi/

(1e) Word final /*-wa/ > /-w/ following /*-k-/ preceded by short vowel /*-i-/ but not long vowels or glide-vowel sequences.

PA /*makikwa/ 'nasal mucus, catarrh' > /makikw/

However, compare:

PA /*meʔθanyikwa/ 'gray squirrel' > /messani·k/

(2) Word final sequences of two short vowels in which the first member is a back vowel, /*-VwV/, following a single nonsyllabic drop only the final vowel.

PA /*atowa/ 'ball, mushroom' > /atow/

PA /*le·kawi/ 'sand' > /re·kaw/

However, following a sonorant-cluster, the whole sequence is dropped.

Pseudo-PA /*maθkawinsowa/ 'paroquet' > /maskawins/

(3) In words of four or more syllables word final syllables of two short vowels in which the first member is the back vowel /*-a-/ in the sequence pattern /*-VyV/ when following a nonsyllabic are reduced to /-e·/.

PA /*meθkoθayi/ 'coat, mantle, robe of fur' > /meskote·/

PA /*wepi·waya/ 'plume, down feather' > /opi·we·/

PA /*neškešayi/ 'my lip' > /neskese·/

{ Early-PA /*memo·tayi/ | Late-PA /*meno·tayi/ } 'bag, basket, sack' > /meno·te·/

PA /*neθeʔšiwaya/ 'my testicle' > /netessiwe·/

PA /*meθa·çkaya/ (?) 'vagina' > /meta·ske·/

PA /*walahakaya/ 'scale of fish or reptile' > /warahake·/

The plurals of these nouns are: /meskotas/ 'coats', /opi·wak/ 'plumes', /neskesayas/ 'my lips', /meno·tas/ 'bags', /netessiwak/ 'my testicles', /warahakayak/ 'scales'.

However, in words of less than four syllables the same sequences /*-VyV/ following a nonsyllabic drop the final short vowel.

PA /*ahθaya/ 'skin, pelt, hide' > /assay/, pl. /assayas/ (INA

PEA /*aθakayi/ 'penis' > /atakay/

(4) Word final PA /*-wayV/ following a nonsyllabic drops the final short vowel.

PEA /*wi·kahkwayi/ 'his thigh' > /wi·kkway/, pl. /wi·kkwas/

PA /*wešaθkwaya/ 'freshwater pearl mussel' > /osaskway/, pl. /osaskwayak/

(5) Word final sequences of two short vowels in which the first member is a short front vowel following a cluster or nonsyllabic preceded by a short front vowel drop the final short vowel, so that /*-iwV/ > /-iw/.

PA /*pekiwa/ 'gum, pitch, resin' > /pekiw/

PA /*mehšiwi/ 'faggot, piece of firewood' > /messiw/, pl. /messi·s/

PA /*ašyeškiwi/ 'clay, mud' > /asi·skiw/

PA /*šekiwa/ 'he urinates' > /sekiw/

However, when this sequence follows a cluster or nonsyllabic preceded by a back vowel or a long vowel the entire sequence is dropped so that /*-iwV/ > /(zero)/, except in words of three syllables.

PA /*ta·waθetone·wiwa/ 'he yawns' > /ta·watetone·w/

PA /*ša?šakiwa/ 'heron' > /assak/

PA /*wa·pa?šakiwa/ 'white heron' > /wa·passak/

PEA /*waθpa·sa·xkiwi/ 'it is morning' > /waspa·sa·hk/

This does not occur in words of three syllables, for example:

PA /*wi·wiwa/ 'he has a wife' > /wi·wiw/

(6) Word final sequences after a nonsyllabic which are composed of a glide followed by two short vowels, the first member of which is a short front vowel, are contracted so that /*-wiwV/ > /-o·w/.

PA /*sehkwiwa/ 'he spits' > /sehko·w/

PA /*kemo·twiwa/ 'he steals (something)' > /kemo·to·w/

PA /*ki·špwiwa/ 'he is full of food' > /ki·spo·w/

PA /*amamwiwa/ 'he awakes' > /amamo·w/

PA /*kwi·škwehšwiwa/ 'he whistles' > /kwi·skwesso·w/

PA /*sanikwiwa/ 'he blows his nose' > /saniko·w/

(7) After a nonsyllabic word final sequences in which the penultimate vowel is long drop only the short final vowel.

PA /*mo·hθe·wa/ 'worm' > /mo·sse·w/

PA /*ketate·wa/ 'otter' > /ketate·w/

PA /*pi·ʔte·wi/ 'foam, froth' > /pi·hte·w/

PA /*kweθapeška·wa/ 'he capsizes' > /kotapeska·w/

PA /*či·me·wa/ 'he paddles, rows' > /či·me·w/

PEA /*kenteke·wa/ 'he dances' > /kenteke·w/

PEA /*po·kete·wi/ 'fire' > /po·kete·w/

(7a) Isolated or solitary preceding glides function in the same fashion as any other preceding nonsyllabic.

PA /*po·yawe·wa/ 'kit beaver' > /po·yawe·w/

PEA /*kawi·wa/ 'he is asleep' > /kawi·w/

PEA /*atowetowe·wa/ 'cymbling, summer squash' > /atowetowe·w/

(7b) Two vowel word final sequences with a penultimate long vowel which follow glides preceded by a nonsyllabic follow the same pattern of dropping the final short vowel, but are modified by the interconsontal glide-vowel sequence rules described in Section H in which the final glide functions as a nonsyllabic.

As in Section H (2):

PA /*pasekwi·wa/ 'he gets up from sitting' > /pasekwi·w/

As in Section H (4):

PA /*kenwe·wi/ 'it is long' > /kene·w/

PA /*kesi·nkwe·wa/ 'he washes his face' > /kesi·nkwe·w/

As in Section H (6):

PA /*nemo·nšwa·wa/ 'I cut his hair' > /nemo·nsa·w/

As in Section H (8):

PA /*ma·čyi·wa/ 'he starts off, goes away' > /ma·či·w/

PA /*ki·nlyi·wi/ 'it is sharp' > /ki·ni·w/

PA /*aškanyi·wi/ (?) 'it is raw' > /askani·w/

As in Section H (10):

PA /*wa·paθanye·wa/ 'adult bald eagle' > /a·patane·w/

PA /*pye·wa/ 'he comes' > /pe·w/

PA /*mye·wi/ 'path' > /me·w/

PA /*kesi·θenčye·wa/ 'he washes his hands' > /kesi·tenče·w/

PA /*wesa·wye·wi/ 'it is yellow' > /osa·we·w/

PEA /*to·lepye·wa/ 'loggerhead turtle' > /to·repe·w/

CONCLUSION

This completes an attempt to render reliable interpretations of the recording of the Powhatan language of Virginia made by Captain John Smith and William Strachey in the first decade of the seventeenth century. Their notations are the oldest known written records of any Algonquian language except for a few terms for birds and fishes recorded by the artist John White about 1585-1587 on the North Carolina coast and a brief vocabulary taken down by James Rosie in June 1605 on the coast of Maine.

The ancient language spoken by Don Luis de Velasco, Powhatan, and Pocahontas has rightly fascinated many people, for aside from purely curious and sentimental interest, its historical and scientific considerations are significant, and Virginia Algonquian probably has provided more loans that were adopted into English than any other single American Indian language.

It is indisputable that there were at least two major Powhatan dialects and probably several minor ones. Besides considerable lexical differences, one dialect preserved initial PA /*we-/ as /we-/ and PA /*wa·-/ as /wa·-/ before nonfinal /*p/, which in the other dialect became /o-/ and /a·-/ respectively. It is unfortunate that inadequate data forbid accurate identification of these dialects and a more detailed presentation of their features. It is perhaps a forlorn hope, but not an impossible one, that further manuscript material may turn up in English or Spanish archives.

Linguistic evidence suggests the following general conclusions:

1. Proto-Eastern-Algonquian (PEA) forms a marginal subdivision within general Algonquian and separated at a very ancient date from Proto-Algonquian (PA). The chief phonological innovations of general PEA were the lenition of preglottalized consonant clusters, the change of PA word initial /*e-/ to PEA /*a-/, and the loss of postconsonantal word final /*-wa/ after all nonsyllabics except /*k/. The chief morphological innovation of PEA which has been ably described by Goddard was a thorough rebuilding of the transitive inanimate verb (TI) so that the PA absolute third person singular ending /*-amwa/ was generalized throughout both the PEA absolute and objective TI paradigms as the PEA theme-sign /*-am-/ of the TI verb.
2. Proto-Eastern-Algonquian after an early separation from Proto-Algonquian

maintained a separate existence for a considerable time and underwent a period of common development. Somewhat later one group situated along the immediate Atlantic coast from the Merrimac River south to Cape Hatteras deviated from the rest of Eastern Algonquian and can be called the archaic coastal type of Proto-Eastern-Algonquian (PEA-A).

The chief innovational developments characterizing the archaic coastal or PEA-A division were the loss of the obviative singular and plural distinctions in nouns which took the form of a generalization of the obviative plural suffix (PA and PEA /*-ahi/), and a unique morphologically conditioned neutralization (environmental phonemic change without loss of contrast) of syllable final PEA /*l/ to PEA /*θ/ in suffixed inflections and particles but not in derivational morphemes, followed by the older and regular alternation of /*θ/ to /*š/ before /*i/, /*i·/ and /*y/, with later analogical extension of this alternation so that alternate /*š/ invariably appeared in PEA-A rather than /*l/ and /*θ/ before all short final vowels in inflections and particles.

As Eastern Algonquian speakers dispersed over a large geographical area during a long period of time, divergence of speech occurred, and each language went its separate way. Later the geographical and linguistic continuity of the PEA-A division was interrupted by the intrusion of other Proto-Eastern Algonquian groups into the middle coastal region. The new arrivals on the coast evidently comprised a more inland group of Eastern Algonquians and were represented by the modern Delawares and Mahicans, whose ancestors would seem to have once occupied central and western New York and Pennsylvania and to have moved eastward and replaced the original PEA-A peoples along the coast from the Hudson Valley southward perhaps as far as Cape Henlopen.

The Powhatan dialects of Virginia, and some other southeastern groups, then remained as the southern representatives of the PEA-A division and the Southern New England (SNE) languages as its northern enclave. Powhatan remained relatively conservative and retained the PEA contrast of long and short vowel phonemes in unaltered form, and shifted PA and PEA /*θ/ to /t/ and PA and PEA /*l/ to /r/.

The dialects of Powhatan form a distinct language group in their own right. Powhatan seems to have retained some of the lexicon of the "central" Algonquian languages not found elsewhere in Eastern Algonquian, for example in such glosses as /ketate·w/ 'otter' and /masa·n/ 'nettle'. Many of the lexical archaisms or innovations of PEA were retained also and show interesting patterns of correspondence with the northern languages of PEA. These include Powhatan /po·kete·w/ 'fire' (with Micmac, Western Abenaki, and Delaware), /akwinten/ 'canoe' (with Eastern Abenaki and Malecite-Passamaquoddy), /ni·mate·w/ 'man' (with Mahican), /wi·kkway/ 'his thigh' (with general Abenaki), /nepass/ 'sun' (with Massachusee), and many others. Some glosses, for example Powhatan /to·repe·w/ 'loggerhead or sea turtle' (PEA /*to·lepye·wa/) and /ta·pawa·s/ 'seven', occur throughout most Eastern Algonquian languages but are not found elsewhere.

5. The SNE languages, representing the northern enclave of the PEA-A division, form a distinct group within Eastern Algonquian and all hold certain traits in common. At the time of discovery, they occupied southern New England and nearly all of Long Island in a region south of the Ipswich and Millers Rivers and westward to the course of the Westfield River, and approximately southwestward to western Long Island Sound and probably at one point to the east bank of the lower Hudson River. Unlike the southern division of PEA-A the SNE languages were decidedly less conservative and underwent a series of phonological changes. The SNE languages have in common a loss of long and short vowel contrasts and have the same vowel phonemes /i, o, ə, a, ɑ/. In all of them PA and PEA /*e·/ and /*a/ have fallen together to /a/, PA and PEA /*e/ became /ə/, and /*a·/ became /ɑ/, a tense back vowel, perhaps in some languages and only in certain environments with a nondistinctive or secondary feature of nasalization which did not appreciably alter the major contrast of lax /a/ with tense /ɑ/. In general all the SNE languages in nouns of two or more syllables irregularly drop final noninflectional syllables ending in /-n/ and /-w/ when preceded by /a, i, ə/, but with some variation of treatment in the different languages and dialects. Thus in the eastern SNE languages /-an/ drops in /ahpih-an/ 'snare' and /wɑw-an/ 'egg' but not in /otan/ 'village'. Also, all SNE languages, with some irregularities, show one of two types of so-called

palatalization of PA and PEA /*k/ before /*i/, /*y/, and /*e·/. The SNE languages in common with all PEA-A languages have /sk/ as the reflex of PA /*çk/ as opposed to /hk/ found in the rest of Eastern Algonquian.

The entire division of SNE languages are conveniently classified into eastern and western groups. The eastern SNE dialects were spoken approximately to the east of the Blackstone River, and southwestwardly a little beyond to Greenwich Bay and the course of the Pawtuxet River. The remainder of the ill-defined area to the west and southwest, including Conanicut Island, Block Island, Fishers Island, nearly all of Long Island, the course of the Connecticut River north to Millers River, and the course of the Housatonic River north to the mountain chain crossing just below Cornwall Bridge, was the province of the western SNE languages.

In eastern SNE dialects PA and PEA /*k/ was fronted to /t/ before /*i/, /*e·/, and /*y/, the local or locative suffix is /-ət/, and PA /*l/, /*θ/, and /*n/ coalesced to /n/.

In the western SNE languages PA and PEA /*k/ was fronted and affricated to /č/ before PA /*i/, /*e·/, and /*y/, but the locative suffix has been analogically (?) restored as /-ək/ (from PA /*-enki/). PA /*l/ and /*θ/ have coalesced in all languages of the western group, however, in three differing mergers. In one subgroup they have coalesced to /l/, in a second they have fallen together with intervocalic /*y/ to give /y/, and in the third subgroup they merged to /r/. The western SNE languages show other minor phonological innovations. For example, by dissimilation /m/ replaced /*w/ in western SNE /wɑm/ 'egg', pl. /wɑmanas/ or /wɑmanš/, from PA /*wa·wani/ 'egg', pl. /*wa·wanali/.

The Eastern Algonquian languages or those which are descendents of PEA can be classified approximately as follows, although some portions of this classification are less certain than others because of the poverty of data. In every case, however, there are reasons of greater or less merit to support the proposed system although explication is too involved to describe here. Major languages are numbered serially in Arabic numerals, and dialects and subdialects of a lower order are mutually intelligible to speakers of all without adaptive familiarity. Intelligibility becomes more facile and general among speakers of more closely related but originally unintelligible Algonquian languages after some period of exposure to such an unintelligible language or with adaptive familiarity. This phenomenon of adaptive multilingualism is quite common among many speakers in the larger Algonquian speech areas. For example, Penobscot and Malecite-Passamaquoddy are unintelligible to naive speakers of both, but during the past century at least and probably to a less degree originally, the majority but by no means all Penobscot speakers either understand or are able to speak both languages with relative ease after some degree of acquaintance. Similar situations exist among various Delaware dialects, between Sauk and Fox, and among northern Ojibwa dialects and Cree.

CLASSIFICATION OF EASTERN ALGONQUIAN:

I. BOREAL DIVISION

1. Micmac

II. SUBBOREAL DIVISION

A. Etchemin

2. Malecite-Passamaquoddy

(a) Malecite
(b) Passamaquoddy

B. Abenaki

3. Eastern Abenaki (Note: Of these, Penobscot and Caniba, at least, have coastal and inland subdialects with partly differing rules of syncope.)

(a) Penobscot
(b) Caniba
(c) Aroosaguntícook
(d) Sokoki-Pequaket (or Pigwacket)

4. Western Abenaki (modern aggregate, St. Francis Abenaki)

(a) Pennacook
(b) Pentucket

III. MEDIAL DIVISION

A. Taconic

5. Mahican (modern aggregate, Stockbridge)

(a) Eastern Mahican
(b) Western Mahican

B. Delaware

6. Munsee (Minsi)
    (a) Northern Munsee
    (b) Eastern Munsee
    (c) Western Munsee

7. Unami
    (a) Northern Unami
    (b) Eastern Unami
    (c) Southern Unami

8. Unalachtigo (?)

IV. ARCHAIC COASTAL DIVISION (PEA-A descendents)

A. Southern New England (SNE)

(I) Eastern SNE (n-languages)

9. Massachusee
    (a) Northern Massachusee (Saugus and Ipswich Rivers)
    (b) Central Massachusee (Natick) (Charles and Neponset Rivers)
    (c) Southern Massachusee (Martha's Vineyard)
    (d) Nauset (Cape Cod and Nantucket)

10. Wampanoag

11. Cowesit (Northern Narragansett)

(II) Western SNE (modern aggregate, Brotherton, for groups [A] and [B])

(A) y-languages

12. Narragansett
    (a) Southern Narragansett
    (b) Niantic

13. Mohegan-Pequot
    (a) Pequot
    (b) Mohegan

14. Montauk (or Eastern Long Island)
    (a) Montauk
    (b) Shinnecock

(B) r-languages

15. Wampano (modern aggregate, Scaticook)
    (a) Quinnipiac
    (b) Mattabesec
    (c) Tunxis
    (d) Siwanoy

16. Insular Wampano
    - (a) Unquachog (Poosepatuck)
    - (b) Setauket
    - (c) Matinecoc
    - (d) Massapequa

(C) l-languages

17. Nipmuck-Pocumtuck (Loup of French missionaries)
    - (a) Nipmuck
    - (b) Nashua
    - (c) Pocumtuck

B. Chesapeake

18. Nanticoke

19. Conoy (Kanawha)

C. Powhatan

20. Chickahominy
    - (a) Chickahominy
    - (b) Appomattox

21. Pamunkey
    - (a) Pamunkey
    - (b) Mattapony

23. Nansemond

D. Windgandcon

24. Chowan

25. Pamlico (Pampticough)

NOTES

1. It is a pleasure to acknowledge that part of this paper was written during 1969-70 when I was holding a John Simon Guggenheim Fellowship.

2. Some references dealing with the Spanish in Virginia are:

Barcia, Andres González de. 1723. Ensayo cronológico para la historia de la Florida. Madrid. Pp. 142-46.

Florencia, Francisco de. 1694. Historia de la provincia de la Compañia de Iesus de Nveva-España. Mexico. (Chapters 2 to 6 and 9 to 14 give accounts of the Jesuit Fathers Martinez, Juan Rogel and Juan Baptista Segura from St. Augustine north to Axacán from 1566 to 1572.)

Lanning, John T. 1935. The Spanish missions of Georgia. Chapel Hill, N. C. Pp. 41-54.

Lewis, Clifford M., and Loomie, Albert J. 1953. The Spanish Jesuit mission in Virginia, 1570-1572. Chapel Hill, N. C.

Lowery, Woodbury. 1911. The Spanish settlements within the present limits of the United States. New York. Pp. 359-66, 458-64.

Zubillaga, Felix. 1941. La Florida. La Misión Jesuítica, 1566-1572, Bibliotheca Instituti Historici Societatis Iesu, Vol. I. Rome.

3. Hamor, Raphe. 1615. A trve Discourse of the present Estate of Virginia, and the successe of the affaires there till the 18 of Iune 1614. London. P. 13.

4. Hilton, William. 1664. A Relation of a discovery lately made on the coast of Florida. London.

5. Stevens, Captain John. 1706. A New Spanish and English dictionary. London: Printed for George Sawbridge. (No pagination.)

Captain John Stevens was familiar with the history of the Spanish language in America, since he was the translator of Antonio de Herrera's "The General History of the Vast Continent and Islands of America", which first appeared in English in six volumes, published at London in 1725-26. It is not likely that Stevens would have incorporated this Algonquian loan in his dictionary if it had not been used by some Spanish speakers in the New World. The first printing of Herrera is: Historia General de los hechos de los Castellanos en las Islas i tierra firme de Mar oceano, 8 vols., 14 maps, Madrid, 1601.

Herrera was the leading authority on Spanish America, having been employed as historiographer to Philip II and III of Spain.

6. Pineda, Pedro. 1740. Nuevo dicionario, Español e Ingles e Ingles y Español. London. (No pagination.)
7. Gatford, Lionel. 1657. Publick Good without Private Interest: or, A Compendious Remonstrance of the present sad State and Condition of the English Colonie in Virginea. London: Printed for Henry Marsh.
8. Smith, John. 1612. A Map of Virginia, with a description of the Covntrey. Oxford: Joseph Barnes.

   Smith, John. 1624. The Generall Historie of Virginia, New-England, and the Summer Isles. London: Printed by I. D. and I. H. for Michael Sparkes.
9. Strachey, William. 1849. The Historie of travaile into Virginia Britannia, ed. Richard Henry Major. London: Hakluyt Society.
10. Harrington, John P. 1955. The Original Strachey vocabulary of the Virginia Indian language. Anthropological Papers, no. 46, Bureau of American Ethnology Bulletin 157. Pp. 189-202.
11. Because of his retiring nature and modesty less real information is known of Bloomfield's methods and manner of thinking than should be the case. Two of his greatest virtues were his perceptiveness and his ability to say things straight in a humble, direct style.
12. Bloomfield, Leonard. 1925. On the sound system of Central Algonquia Language 1:130-56.
13. Lacombe, Albert. 1874. Dictionnaire et grammaire de la langue des Cris. Montreal.
14. Jones, William. 1907. Fox texts. Publications of American Ethnologic Society, Vol. 1. Leyden.
15. Michelson, Truman. 1921. The Owl sacred pack of the Fox Indians. Bureau of American Ethnology Bulletin 72.
16. Jones, William. 1917, 1919. Ojibwa texts. Publications of the American Ethnological Society, Vol. 7. 2 pts. New York.
17. Baraga, Frederic. 1853. Dictionary of the Otchipwe language. Cincinnati. 2nd edition, Montreal, 1878.
18. Cuoq, J. A. 1886. Lexique de la langue algonquine. Montreal.
19. In his 1925 paper in Language 1:134, 136, 138, and 144.

20. Michelson, Truman. 1935. Phonetic shifts in Algonquian languages. IJAL 8:131-71.

21. Bloomfield, Leonard. 1939. Menomini morphophonemics. *In* Trauvaux du Cercle linguistique de Prague 8:105-15. (Reprinted in 1964 by the University of Alabama Press.)

Bloomfield, L. 1941. Proto-Algonquian -iit 'Fellow'. Language 17: 292-97.

22. Siebert, Frank T., Jr. 1941. Certain Proto-Algonquian consonant clusters. Language 17:298-303.

23. Bloomfield, Leonard. 1946. Algonquian. *In* Harry Hoijer, Linguistic Structures of Native America, Viking Fund Publications in Anthropology, No. 6. Pp. 85-129. New York.

24. Abbreviations and coding used in this paper are as follows: an asterisk (*) marks a reconstructed form; > "became or is derived from"; < "coming from"; virgules /.../ indicate a phonemic record; bars |...| indicate morphophonemic constructs; obv. is "obviative", sg. "singular"; pl. "plural"; dimin. "diminutive"; AN animate gender: INAN inanimate gender; AI an animate intransitive verb; II an inanimate intransitive verb; TA a transitive animate verb; and TI a transitive inanimate verb.

PA stands for Proto-Algonquian; PEA Proto-Eastern Algonquian; PEA-A Archaic Coastal group of Proto-Eastern Algonquian; SNE group includes all the closely related dialects of southern New England and Long Island; EA group includes all the Eastern Abenaki dialects, Caniba, Penobscot, Sokoki, and others; F for Fox; C for Cree; M for Menomini; O for Ojibwa; S for Shawnee; P for Penobscot (most divergent member of EA); WA for Western Abenaki (Pennacook or modern St. Francis Abenaki); D for Delaware (mD for Munsee dialect, uD for Unami dialect); Mh for Mahican (not an SNE language); Mi for Miami; Mt for Montagnais (here Lake St. John dialect only); Mc for Micmac; Ml for Malecite; Ms for Massachusee (one dialect often is called Natick); Nr for Narragansett (actually a composite of two dialects); Np for Nipmuck-Pocumtuck (Loup of some French writers); Pq for Mohegan-Pequot; and Ps for Passamaquoddy (closely related to Malecite).

Forms cited here for F, P, mD, uD, Mh, Mt, Mc, Ml, and Ps are from my own field notes. The chief sources for other languages are:

Cree:

Bloomfield, Leonard. 1930. Sacred stories of the Sweet Grass Cree. National Museum of Canada, Bulletin 60. Otawa.

Bloomfield, Leonard. 1934. Plains Cree texts. Publications of the American Ethnological Society, Vol. 16. New York.

Lacombe, Albert. 1874. Dictionnaire et grammaire de la langue des Cris. Montreal.

Watkins, E. A. 1865. A dictionary of the Cree Language. London. 2nd ed. by R. Faries, Toronto, 1938.

(The second edition has additions and some corrections, but introduces some errors which are correctly given in the first edition, so both should be used together.)

Ellis, C. Douglas. 1971. Cree verb paradigms. IJAL 37:76-95.

Menomini:

Bloomfield, Leonard. 1928. Menomini texts. Publications of the American Ethnological Society, Vol. 12. New York.

Bloomfield, Leonard. 1962. The Menomini language. New Haven: Yale University Press.

Bloomfield, Leonard. n. d. Unpublished Menomini dictionary. (Xerox copy kindly supplied by Prof. Charles F. Hockett.)

Ojibwa:

Baraga, Frederic. 1853. Dictionary of the Otchipwe language. Cincinnati. (1st edition.)

Bloomfield, Leonard. 1957. Eastern Ojibwa. Ann Arbor: University of Michigan Press.

Rogers, Jean H. 1963. Survey of Round Lake Ojibwa phonology and morphology, National Museum of Canada Bulletin 194, Paper 4. Ottawa.

Miami and Shawnee:

Voegelin, Charles F. 1939-40. Shawnee stems and the Jacob P. Dunn Miami dictionary. Prehistory Research Series, Indiana Historical Society, Vol. 1. Indianapolis.

Selected unpublished notes on Shawnee (from Voegelin and three early 19th-century sources) and Miami-Illinois (from Volney, Gatschet, Kerr, Gravier, Le Boulanger, etc.).

Southern New England Group (SNE):

Eliot, John. 1663. (Indian Bible) Mamusse Wunneetupanatamwe Up-Biblum God. Cambridge, Mass. (1st edition.) (Charles River).

Williams, Roger. 1643. A key into the language of America. London. (Mixes several dialects, only sometimes indicating them.)

Trumbull, James H. 1903. Natick dictionary. Bureau of American Ethnology Bulletin 25.

Cotton, Josiah. 1829. Vocabulary of the Massachusetts Indian language. Cambridge, Mass. (Largely the dialect about Plymouth and Cape Cod, or Nauset.)

Mayhew, Experience. 1709. Massachusee Psalter. Boston. (In the dialect of Martha's Vineyard.)

Mathevet, Jean-Claude. ca. 1750. Mots loups. (Manuscript; now being edited for publication by Gordon M. Day. It is in the Nipmuck-Pocumtuck language of central Massachusetts and of the middle Connecticut River Valley, and is an l-dialect of the SNE group.)

Speck, Frank G. 1928. Native tribes and dialects of Connecticut: A Mohegan-Pequot diary. In 43rd Annual Report of Bureau of American Ethnology. Pp. 199-287. (This is the SNE dialect of eastern Connecticut, properly Pequot linguistically, rescued by Speck from the last speaker in the first decade of this century.)

25. Goddard, Ives. 1967. The Algonquian independent indicative. National Museum of Canada Bulletin 214. Pp. 66-106. Ottawa. Reference is to Section 4. 5, pp. 78-80.

26. Bloomfield (1946) cited in note 23. Bloomfield, in Section 6, p. 87, says PA /*θ/ was "an unvoiced interdental or lateral" with a query. If my interpretation of PEA phonology is correct, then PEA shows that /*θ/ was not an interdental but a voiceless lateral and the unmarked member of the contrast /*l/ : /*θ/, based only on the privative opposition of voiced/unvoiced. Thus, Bloomfield's second surmise is the preferred solution.

Here neutralization is conceived to apply only to a privative and unidimensional opposition that contrasts two phonemes which differ by the presence or absence of one distinctive feature, and which share a set of other identical features not manifest as an aggregate in any other phonemes in the language. See N. S. Trubetzkoy, Grundzüge der phonologie, Trauvaux du Cercle linguistique de Prague 7:218, (1939): "Aufgehoben können ja nur eindimensionale Oppositionen werden, und diese sind ja bekanntlich in jedem System immer weniger Zahlreich als die mehrdimensionalen."

Contrasts run the gamut from optimal to minimal and therefore may delineate a variety of oppositions. Some oppositions are binary in that they involve two opposing positive but not phonetically coördinate distinctive features, such as interrupted/continuant, strident/mellow, voiced/voiceless, nasal/oral, and tense/lax. Other oppositions are privative and reflect either the presence of a distinctive feature, in which case they distinguish the marked member of a contrast, or the absence of the identical distinctive feature, specifying the unmarked member of the contrast. Some privative oppositions are: voiced/unvoiced (nonvoiced), nasal/non-nasal, and tense/nontense.

Neutralization is the suspension of a privative and unidimensional opposition in certain positions in which the number of phonemes that may occur is smaller than in other positions, or in other words, where there is a phonotactic or sequential constraint. Thus, it is fictional to postulate, as did Trubetzkoy, an archiphoneme for a nonunique phonological representation in lieu of what seemed like arbitrarily assigning one of two ostensibly intersecting phonemes to specify a neutralized segment. On the contrary, a correct recognition of the distinctive features of a language, the types of oppositions it employs, the phonotactic distributional constraints, and a correct analysis of the underlying base units or morphophonemes, allow for unique phonological representations in neutralized environments and non-arbitrarily assign them to the unmarked phoneme in accord with phonetic reality. Sometimes however, as a result of the less sharply defined nature of privative oppositions, a neutralized segment may not be phonetically identical with either of the non-neutralized members or contrasting phonemes but be an intermediate entity. In such cases the unmarked phoneme is recast by assimilation and dissimilation rules which can be defined within the phonotactics of the language, and these often operate so that unmarked feature values usually assimilate to adjacent marked features.

27. Bloomfield (1946), cited in note 23. See Section 20, p. 92.

28. Michelson, Truman. 1933. The linguistic classification of Powhatan. American Anthropologist 35:549.

29. Siebert, F. T. (1941), cited in note 22. Language 17:302.

30. Lawson, John. 1709. A new voyage to Carolina. London. Lawson gives the Pampticough (Pamlico) numeral 'one' as weembot, recorded about 1701; p. 225.

31. In June 1938 Nicodemus Peters, a Munsee Delaware speaker of Smoothtown, Six Nations Reserve near Hagersville, Ontario, gave me some Nanticoke terms which he had learned from a Nanticoke boy he played with when both were between the ages of 8 to 10 years (circa 1870). The numerals for the most part appear to be Algonquian, but do not agree with the known Nanticoke terms or the Powhatan of Smith and Strachey. They may be representative of one of the arcane stray number systems (see Floyd G. Lounsbury, "Stray number systems among certain Indian tribes", American Anthropologist 48:672-675, (1946)), or perhaps the forms of a counting out rhyme, or of the esoteric children's speech reported among some Algonquian peoples, among them the Penobscot and Shawnee. They are, from one to five: /nátta/, /ní·šaw/, /xá·ši/, /né·wiši/, /čínkši/. Among a few other "Nanticoke" terms he recalled is /ní·mataw/ man, which is not Nanticoke but apparently Powhatan, although the alteration of the third vowel is questionable and may be due to faulty memory. This appears to be a linguistic survival, and suggests that a few Powhatan descendents, perhaps from the eastern shore (Northampton and Accomack Counties, Virginia), were incorporated with the Nanticoke, and eventually migrated north to be finally absorbed by various Delaware communities.

Peters also remembered, among others, the corresponding Mahican term, /ní·manaw/ man, formerly current at Smoothtown in the speech of several Mahican families incorporated with the Munsee there.

One of Lounsbury's stray numbers for ten, /wínbet/, which he found in use among the Oneida of Wisconsin, is undoubtedly Munsee /wí·mpat/ with replacement of /n/ for /m/ since labial /m/ does not occur in Oneida or other Iroquoian languages except Cherokee. A group of Munsee who once lived on the White River, Indiana, had migrated to Wisconsin with the Oneida and Stockbridge (Mahican) in the period 1822-1829.